Linguistic Change in French

Linguistic Change in French

REBECCA POSNER

CLARENDON PRESS · OXFORD
1997

Oxford University Press, Great Clarendon Street, Oxford OX2 6DP

Oxford   New York
Athens   Auckland   Bangkok   Bogota   Bombay
Buenos Aires   Calcutta   Cape Town   Dar es Salaam
Delhi   Florence   Hong Kong   Istanbul   Karachi
Kuala Lumpur   Madras   Madrid   Melbourne
Mexico City   Nairobi   Paris   Singapore
Taipei   Tokyo   Toronto
and associated companies in
Berlin   Ibadan

Oxford is a trade mark of Oxford University Press

Published in the United States
by Oxford University Press Inc., New York

British Library Cataloguing in Publication Data
Data available

Library of Congress Cataloguing in Publication Data
Linguistic change in French / Rebecca Posner.
Includes bibliographical references.
1. French language—History.   2. French language—Variation.
3. Linguistic change.   I. Title.
PC2075.P64   1997   440'.9—dc21   97-2027
ISBN 0-19-824036-8

1 3 5 7 9 10 8 6 4 2

Typeset by Joshua Associates Ltd., Oxford
Printed in Great Britain on acid-free paper by
Biddles Ltd., Guildford and King's Lynn

To Yakov Malkiel and to André Martinet,
in gratitude

Preface

The present work is not meant as an introduction either to the history of French, or to general historical linguistics. There is already an abundance of admirable works of this sort. I hope nevertheless it will fill a gap in the present provision of works on such topics. To be honest, my main motivation for writing the book is to help me work out my own ideas about the relationship of language change and linguistic change, between history and language. Although I have been studying the history of the French language for nearly fifty years, and teaching it for nearly as long, I have never found satisfactory answers, in the traditional works, to some of the most puzzling questions.

I believe that the considerable advances in linguistic and in historical methodology have not yet been sufficiently exploited in what should be an interdisciplinary study. I hope that I can contribute in a small way to developing such a study. The present book may inspire others to continue along the same lines.

It is therefore addressed principally to two groups of serious readers: those whose expertise is mainly in linguistics, and those whose particular interest is in the French language, and how it got the way it is. For both I try to give an explanatory account of some well-known, and some less familiar, phenomena in the history of French, showing how they are related to more general principles. I hope that it will also be of use to 'straight' French historians, who only too often neglect the linguistic aspect of social and cultural history, as being too technical and therefore irrelevant.

As a linguist, I concentrate most on linguistic change, rather than on the more accessible aspects of language history. Much of the work may therefore seem abstruse to the general reader. Linguistics tends to be split into factions, each of which communicate little with the others. Linguistic studies in French, in particular, are divided between what may be termed the 'Continental European' and the

'Anglo-Saxon' traditions. I have deliberately abstained from aligning myself with either, but seek, in all approaches, insights that can illuminate the problems of linguistic change. I give guidance on terminology, but have to rely largely on reference to other more general works, of which there is no shortage.

My knowledge of history and sociology is, alas, even less expert than my skill in linguistics, but I have been bold enough to draw on the works of specialists in those subjects. I hope that some more knowledgeable than myself may draw from this book an interest in the relationship between change in language and society.

I wish to make acknowledgement to all those, too numerous to mention, from whom I have learned about the subject-matter of this book, through the written and the spoken word, and especially to my teachers, colleagues, and pupils over the years. The mistakes and misconceptions are, alas, all my own. I find it hard to distinguish precisely from which quarters I have derived my ideas, but have tried in my bibliography to give a representative sample. Cutting the vast bibliography, on which I have drawn, down to something like a reasonable size was difficult. There is no comprehensive and up-to-date bibliography of French linguistic studies, and most textbooks on the History of French cite comparatively few works (perhaps because more extensive bibliographies would be too daunting for the beginner). In order to make this book more useful to advanced students, I have been more copious in my provision. To a large extent references are relegated to the end of each chapter, with suggestions for Further Reading. Here I have tried to confine references to more general linguistic works to the most recent, but I could not refrain from citing older works on French, which I have used extensively for examples. In the chapters on morphology and syntax, in particular, it has not always been possible to separate synchronically from diachronically oriented studies. Indeed one of the points I wish to drive home is that descriptive and historical linguistics have very much in common, and that there is a close-knit relationship between synchronic variation and diachronic change.

For illustrations from texts, most of which figure in works cited in the bibliography, I have given only cursory reference to sources, as my purpose is linguistic, not philological. Where relevant, I mention the approximate date of the text, and the Names index contains a little more information about authors (and about medieval texts whose author is uncertain). I am, on the whole, more concerned with changes in more modern times and therefore cite commentators on language from the sixteenth century on. When one gets to the nineteenth century, it is not easy to distinguish the 'scholarly works' that should figure in the bibliography and the 'sources' that receive summary mention in the Names index: the distinctions I have made are rather arbitrary. Although I assume most readers will be proficient in French, I have provided English translations for examples where appropriate.

I have, as far as possible, summarized data in Tables and Figures and tabulated some chronological material. I have eschewed footnotes, but some parts of the running text appear in small print: these can be skipped by the more cursory reader, but add additional information and comment. I have provided no maps, as there is now available (Rossillon 1995) an elegantly produced handy atlas of French linguistic maps in full colour, which illustrate admirably many of my comments.

My thanks are due to Frances Morphy and Leonie Hayler at the Press for their advice and encouragement, to Christopher Posner for invaluable help with the indexes, with statistical calculations, and with the bibliography, to Mary Worthington for valiant copy-editing, and to Michael Posner for his patience during many tedious months of word-processing.

To me what I have to say often seems rather obvious and banal: it is rather a surprise then to find that even learned colleagues sometimes express puzzlement about it—my ideas may even seem 'above their heads', rather than, as I would have thought, 'beneath their notice'! I hope that this book will at least make the ideas more comprehensible.

REBECCA POSNER

Oxford

Contents

List of Tables		xvi
List of Figures		xviii
Conventions and Abbreviations		xix

Introduction   1

0.1.	Why Another History of French?	1
0.2.	Reconstruction	3
0.3.	History and Language	6

PART I: LANGUAGE CHANGE   9

1. Defining the Domain   11

1.1.	What is French?	11
1.2.	When was France?	14
1.3.	Periodization	16
1.4.	So What has Changed?	20
1.5.	Linguistic Features of Modern French	23
1.6.	When did these Features Arise?	26
1.7.	What has Changed during the Modern French Period?	27
1.8.	Are the French Creoles a Sort of Modern French?	28
1.9.	When did the Creoles Come into Being?	32
1.10.	Standardization: Language Planning and Language Policy	33
1.11.	What is a Standard Language?	34
1.12.	What has to be Done to Standardize?	36
	Selection	36
	Elaboration: Normalization or Status Planning	39
	Codification: Normativization or Corpus Planning	40
1.13.	Was French Standardization Planned?	46

1.14. Why Have a Standard? 46
1.15. Orthographical Reform 50
      Further Reading 55

2. Sociolinguistic History of French 57

2.1. Social History and Language, or Sociolinguistic
     History? 57
2.2. Popular Culture and Language 58
2.3. Urbanization and (De)Proletarianization 59
2.4. Mass Literacy 60
2.5. Schooling 60
2.6. Sociolinguistic Variation 63
2.7. Evidence for Variation at Past Periods 64
2.8. Social Change and Linguistic Change 70
2.9. Causes of Social Change 71
2.10. Socioeconomic Class and Language Change 72
2.11. Popular French 73
2.12. The Role of the Sexes in Language Change 78
2.13. Age and Language Change 79
2.14. Regional Variation and Language Change 80
2.15. The Spread of French in France 83
2.16. Resistance to the Spread of French within France 86
2.17. Beyond the Frontiers of France 89
2.18. Success Story? 90
2.19. Spread of French Overseas 91
2.20. Dialect and Creole 95
      Further Reading 99

PART II: LINGUISTIC CHANGE 103

3. Processes of Linguistic Change 105

3.1. Language History and Historical Linguistics 105
3.2. Language Change and Linguistic Change 106
3.3. Synchronic and Diachronic Linguistics 107
3.4. *Langue*, *parole*, and Norm 109
3.5. Community or Individual Language? 109
3.6. The Role of Language Acquisition 112
3.7. Differences between Languages 112
3.8. Principles and Parameters 113
3.9 Abductive Change 115

3.10. Time's Arrow 118
3.11. Cycles 120
3.12. Drift 120
3.13. Is Change Gradual? 123
3.14. Creolization 127
3.15. Is Change Inevitable? 131
3.16. Interaction between Changes in Subsystems 137
3.17. Evidence 139
Further Reading 142

4. Lexical Change 143

4.1. Lexical Change 143
4.2. Can the Lexicon of a Language Change? 145
4.3. Etymology 148
4.4. Lexical Loss 152
4.5. Lexical Inflation 155
4.6. Borrowing 156
4.7. Word-Formation 165
4.8. Dictionaries and the Evolution of the Lexicon 171
4.9. Synonymy 172
4.10. *Lexicologie* 181
Further Reading 183

5. Semantic Change 185

5.1. Semantic Change 185
5.2. Semantic Change in Individual Lexical Items 187
5.3. Causes of Lexical Semantic Change 190
5.4. Semantic Fields 193
5.5. Utterance Meaning 195
5.6. Tense, Aspect, Mood (TAM) 198
5.7. The Past Imperfect 200
5.8. Other Past Tenses 203
5.9. Periphrastic Verb-Forms 206
5.10. Subjunctive 208
5.11. Definiteness 211
Further Reading 214

6. Phonological Change 216

6.1. Phonological Change—General 216
6.2. Chronology 223

6.3.	Is There a Phonetic Basis for Changes in the History of French?	225
6.4.	Nasal Vowels	230
6.5.	Palatals	242
6.6.	The Simplification of *l mouillé*	249
6.7.	'Palatal' *u*	250
6.8.	Diphthongization and Diphthong Levelling	252
6.9.	Word-Final Consonants and *liaison*	262
6.10.	*E muet, e instable, e caduc, e féminin*	266
6.11.	*Loi de position*	273
6.12.	Vowel Length	282
6.13.	French *r*	288
6.14.	Spelling Pronunciation	290
	Further Reading	292
7.	**Morphological Change**	**294**
7.1.	Morphology	294
7.2.	Morphologization	297
7.3.	Grammaticalization	298
	A. Verb Morphology	**300**
7.4.	Irregular Verbs: Suppletion	300
7.5.	Verb-Person Markers	302
7.6.	Plural versus Singular	304
7.7.	First and Second Person Plural	305
7.8.	Apophony and Analogy in the Present Indicative Paradigms	306
7.9.	Coda Consonant Deletion in Verb-Roots	312
7.10.	Long and Short Roots	313
7.11.	Imperfect Endings	316
7.12.	The *passé simple*	317
7.13.	The Future and Conditional	319
7.14.	The Subjunctive Forms	324
	B. Nominal and Pronominal Morphology	**325**
7.15.	Gender Markers	325
7.16.	Morphological Case	331
7.17.	Old French Nominal Case	332
7.18.	The Possessives	335
7.19.	Demonstratives	340
	Further Reading	343

8. Syntactic Change   344

  8.1. Syntax   344
  8.2. What Counts as a Syntactic Change in the
        History of French?   347
  8.3. Word-Order   349
  8.4. Changes in Word-Order Typology in French   356
  8.5. Adjective Placement   360
  8.6. Interrogation   363
  8.7. Negation   369
  8.8. 'Pro-Drop' and the Extension of the Use of
        Pronoun Subjects   377
  8.9. *Qui/que*   380
  8.10 The Creation of the Definite Article   381
  8.11. Partitive Determiners   390
  8.12. Object Clitics   394
  8.13. Proclisis or Preposing?   400
  8.14. Clitic Climbing   401
  8.15. Clitic Arrays (or Clusters)   404
  8.16. Adverbial Clitics   407
  8.17. Agreement   410
        Further Reading   416

In Place of a Conclusion   419

Bibliography   425
Name Index   489
Subject Index   499

List of Tables

1.1. So what has changed? 22
1.2. Some characteristic features of French creoles 30

2.1. Syntactic socially related variables in modern French—early attestations 76
2.2. Some phonological variables in modern French 77
2.3. French dialect: an illustrative sentence 82

4.1. Some common modern French words that differ from those of other Romance languages 149
4.2. Some Old French words lost or restricted in function during the sixteenth and seventeenth centuries 153
4.3. Some common words and expressions which have begun to be used frequently since the sixteenth century 157
4.4. Modern common lexical items that entered the French language in the seventeenth century 159
4.5. Some core lexical items that have entered French since the seventeenth century 161
4.6. Some examples of loanwords in French, with date of entry 164
4.7. Word-formation: examples 170

6.1. History of vowel nasalization in French (summary) 241
6.2. Palatalization of consonants in French (summary) 248
6.3. Diphthongization of tonic free vowels 253
6.4. Old French sources of modern French *oi* 259
6.5. Sources of modern French [wa] (some examples) 260
6.6. Chronological sequence of rules (some examples of words in *oi*) 261
6.7. *Loi de position* 275

7.1. Verb-person markers 303
7.2. Apophony in the Old French present indicative paradigm 307

7.3.	Verb Roots (Allomorphy)	315
7.4.	Adjectival gender in early Old French	327
7.5.	Adjectival inflection in modern spoken French	329
7.6.	Modern French adjectival gender—a possible account	330
7.7.	Modern French adjectival gender—a generative account	330
7.8.	Nominal case in Old French	333
7.9.	The history of French possessives	336
7.10.	Changes in the singular possessive forms	338
7.11.	History of French demonstratives	341
8.1.	Constituent order	351

List of Figures

3.1.   (Change in acquisition)   116
3.2.   (Aduction)   117
6.1–6.4. (Nasalization)   231–4
6.5–6.6. (Dipthongization)   256
7.1   Imperfect indicative markers   316
7.2.   Analogy in the singular possessives   337

Conventions and Abbreviations

CONVENTIONS

Phonetic transcriptions are in square brackets in the IPA alphabet: thus [lãg]; phonemic transcription appear between slants: thus /lãg/; morphemic or underlying forms are in braces {langue}.

Foreign words in traditional orthography appear in italics: thus *langue*.

Latin words, as is traditional, appear in small capitals: thus LINGUA.

Key-words (which figure in the Subject index) are in bold: thus **linguistics**.

< 'derived from'; > 'develops to'
= 'is equivalent to'
? 'doubtful'
* with etymological forms = 'unattested'; in syntactic illustrations = 'ungrammatical'

In some figures, a simplified set of generative rule conventions is used:

→ 'rewrite as';
/_ (slash-dash) 'in the environment of';
( ) 'optionally', { } 'alternatively';
square brackets [ ] are used for features

In others a simplified version of multilinear phonology conventions is used, with X marking a slot on the 'skeletal' tier, and μ a slot on the 'moraic' tier. σ = 'syllable'. Representation on the 'melodic' tier appears in IPA characters.

In translations parentheses ( ) are used for elements added in the English, and square brackets [ ], for elements present in the French and not in the English.

Cross-references are to Sections.

ABBREVIATIONS

The following standard abbreviations may be used, especially in Tables and Figures:

c.	century
1, 2, 3	first, second and third person
sg.	singular
pl.	plural
m.	masculine
f.	feminine
p.s.	*passé simple*
p.c.	*passé composé*
imp.	*imparfait*
fut.	future
subj.	subjunctive
indic.	indicative
nom.	nominative
acc.	accusative
obl.	oblique
dat.	dative
gen.	genitive
v	any vowel
ṽ	any nasalized vowel
c	any consonant
N	any nasal consonant
O	onset
N	nucleus
R	rhyme
C	coda
TAM	Tense, Aspect, Mood
FUT	Future **TAM** marker
PST	Past **TAM** marker
PFT	Perfective **TAM** marker
PROG	Progressive **TAM** marker
S	Subject; **s** Pronominal subject
O	Object; **o** Pronominal object
V	Verb
V2	Verb second ordering

WH-	WH- (or QU-) constituent, e.g relative and interrogative *qui*, *que* etc.
X	any sentence constituent
COMP	'Complementizer' slot
INFL	'Inflectional' slot
NEG	Negation
N, NP	Noun, Noun Phrase
V, VP	Verb, Verb Phrase
A, AP	Adjective, Adjectival Phrase
P, PP	Preposition, Prepositional Phrase

Introduction

0.1. WHY ANOTHER HISTORY OF FRENCH?

There is an ample supply of books, new and old, on the history of the French language, in all the major languages of the world. The basic facts are common currency, and introductory textbooks, detailed manuals, and research monographs abound. Along with English, which shares with French a good part of its history, French is probably one of the best documented languages in the world. Its history seems to hold few secrets: modern theorists seeking examples of phenomena to illustrate their theories usually turn to works that are fifty, a hundred, years old for their data. Usually they are not disappointed in the accuracy and exhaustiveness of older research, even though they seek to supplement the data in the public domain with new examination of textual evidence.

I can try to justify myself by referring to my title *Linguistic Change* . . ., rather than *History*. The title was chosen because I do not seek primarily to perform one of the tasks of the historian—the reconstruction of the past. This is the philologists' goal. The interpretation of texts and the reconstitution of the language in which they were written is a necessary adjunct to the charting of linguistic change, just as philology is an empty, if beguiling, pursuit without the input of a rigorous linguistic methodology. But, at the extreme, the philologist recreates the language of a single text, or the **idiolect** of an individual writer, and may have little to say about how that language can change over time, except by contrasting it with the language of a later or an earlier text. This is a theme to which I shall return again and again.

Most twentieth-century histories of the French language are in the tradition of the admirable tomes by Ferdinand Brunot (who lived from 1860 to 1938), who from 1901 was the first professor of the French Language at the Université de Paris. His approach has been called *philologie sociologique* (cf. the tributes in the periodical *Français Moderne* 1981), which followed the language through century by century and tried to characterize the language of each epoch, rather than to describe individual idiolects: '*Faute de pouvoir tout exposer, il importe, pour chaque siècle, de mettre en relief ce qui fait son originalité*' (Preface to Brunot 1905–59 vol. 6.1 (1930)). But he confessed to *crainte*, even *angoisse*, as he approached the modern period, because of the wealth of documentation, and he died before his nineteenth-century volumes were published. The sequel was by his professorial successor Charles Bruneau (updating and editing the work until 1972), who fell squarely into the trap Brunot had sought to avoid. The best overall description of nineteenth-century French remains, therefore, Brunot (1899), which was written as a synchronic, not a historical, work.

See Antoine and Martin 1985 for the collective volume covering the period 1880–1914. Other volumes are in preparation, as well as a revision of the whole work.

This brings me to another justification for the present work. Most histories of the French language concentrate on the earlier periods, whereas here I shall be paying as much, or more, attention to more modern times. As has often been remarked, the more remote an object or event in time and space, and the less sound information we have, the freer we feel to speculate: it is usually assumed that change was occurring with great rapidity in Late Latin and in Old French, but that the pace of change has slowed to almost a halt since the seventeenth century. But if we are interested in the mechanisms of change, rather than in reconstruction of the past, it is in the present that we may find answers (in conformity with the **uniformitarian** principle, that things in the past do not differ essentially from the way things are now).

I shall be paying relatively little attention to the very early history—from Latin to early Old French—partly because French shares that history with other Romance languages, on which I have recently written (see Posner 1996).

Apart from those in the Brunot *philologie sociologique* tradition, some of which cover only a limited period of French linguistic history, there are works in this domain which can be classed as 'historical grammars' in the nineteenth-century German mould. These often confine themselves to phonology and/or morphology:

Pope (1934) is an outstanding example, which remains invaluable. Nyrop (1899–1930) is the classic six-volume example of this genre. These works are consultation manuals, that aim to give atomistic coverage of virtually every feature of the language in its diachronic aspects. Most more modern treatises on historical linguistics still draw heavily on this material, though often putting a new spin on it. The present work is more of this ilk, concerned with explanation rather than with exposition of data (which, where appropriate will be presented in tabular form). Unlike traditional comprehensive historical grammars, I select topics for discussion from each level of the language, concentrating on how far, when, and why features have changed.

Needless to say, other general works on the history of French should be consulted by those who wish to satisfy their curiosity further: see the Further Reading sections at the end of each chapter. I should mention here three of the most recent general works: Lodge 1993, Marchello-Nizia 1995, Ayres-Bennett 1996. These are all highly recommended, each of them different from each other and also from the present work. Lodge concentrates on sociolinguistic history and especially the relationship between dialect and standard, covering in more detail some of the material in Chapters 1 and 2 here. Marchello-Nizia concentrates on the evolution of demonstratives and word-order in the transition from Old to Modern French, with a brief glance at phonology. Ayres-Bennett presents a well-chosen set of illustrative texts, with commentaries, for the history of French from the Strasburg Oaths to the present day, a work which admirably complements the present one.

0.2. RECONSTRUCTION

The distinction between the history of a language and historical linguistics (cf. Malkiel 1953–4) is parallel to, but not identical with, another distinction—that between **language change** and **linguistic change** (cf. Antoine 1981, Posner 1994*a*). I shall return, in Chapters 1 and 2, to the idea that the language of a community, as an entity, can change and, in Chapter 3, to the claim that languages are dynamic systems which have their own mechanisms of change. This distinction seems to reflect that made by Saussure between **external** and **internal** history (cf. Droixhe and Dutilleul 1990), where the former is concerned with social and political influences on the language—contact, conquest, control, etc.—and the latter with the **natural** attrition of a language system, by virtue of its use in discourse, and the **adaptive** processes by which the language reforms its system, once disrupted. The former can look like any other sort of history—of events, of technology or of ideas—while the latter is the true domain of the linguist, requiring a specialist interest in what language is, and how it functions. Part II of this book will be concerned with discussion of the latter aspect.

However, here we should look briefly at a type of reconstruction that is not purely **philological** in the sense that we have already used this word, although it is the hallmark of **comparative philology**, which, successfully using methods similar to those of comparative anatomy, seeks to reconstruct the features of prehistoric languages (cf. Hoenigswald and Weiner 1987, Polomé and Winter 1992, Fox 1995).

I shall not be referring to **internal reconstruction**, which plays little part in discussion of the history of French.

By comparing the **family** of obviously related modern Romance languages, we are able to reconstruct the features of a **mother**, a **proto-language**, which resembles the Latin of our texts. We therefore assume that French, like Italian, Spanish, continues, in unbroken tradition, the use of a Latin-like language, which has split into several languages. This squares well with external history, as we know that the present-day Romance area was once part of the Latin-speaking Western Roman Empire. The differences between Classical Latin and our reconstructed proto-language led to the postulation of an intermediate stage, often called **Vulgar Latin** (cf. 1.3).

The Latin of our classical texts is a **dead language**, but, it is assumed, in the Romance languages one (comparatively unattested) Latin variety has survived and diversified over time and space. French, in this scenario, was at one time a single variety of Vulgar Latin, but then could have in its turn diversified into a number of related varieties. These varieties, all found in a circumscribed geographical area, can thus all be called **French**. One of these regional varieties, with some input from others, was codified as the standard language (cf. 1.10–14).

In this scenario, the study of linguistic change must be similar to that of divergence, or **speciation**, to use the Darwinian term. In the evolutionary model, a new species, a variety significantly different from its relatives, with which it can no longer interbreed, will over time, if it is isolated in space from those relatives, become further and further differentiated from them. For living things, the differentiation can be accounted for in genetic terms; for language, it assumes that language usage alters (in more ideologically tinged terminology 'degenerates') constantly where no disciplinary check is applied, for instance by schooling and tradition. Contact with unrelated languages and the like may enter into the differentiation process but are not a necessary part of the classic view. What is central to the view is that communities drift apart physically or spiritually, and cease to communicate with each other in a common tongue.

Reconstruction of an earlier language is possible only when we have evidence of later **daughter** languages; it is clearly easier when we have texts from the stage which we seek to reconstruct. For earlier periods of French the task of reconstruction is fairly straightforward. But this is mainly because of our assumption that most features of the language have *not* changed over time. Thus we can concentrate, as historians of change, on only those that have. In our texts we look for features that would be excluded from similar texts today, even if they occur only rarely and sporadically.

But in assuming continuous transmission and minimal change, we implicitly favour, as the earlier stage of our clearly defined modern French, the textual evidence that is least different from modern usage: other evidence may be ignored (see van Reenen 1992), or excluded from our study of change on the grounds that it stems from 'a different dialect'.

In spite, therefore, of the accepted wisdom, implicit in the methods of comparative philology, that 'language is constantly changing', much of our methodology as linguistic historians depends on the assumption that it does not change all that much. A base of language 'stuff'—arbitrary lexical material—has to persist for us to recognize that a language remains the 'same' through change. When faced by what seems to have been a change in the language, we scan earlier texts for evidence that matches the new usage, assuming that some strategies have survived and been reinforced, whereas rival strategies have been abandoned. Even in the face of global discontinuity, we need to assume continuity: James Milroy (1992) calls this process 'backward projection', with 'canonization' of the variants that have survived in the modern language.

To take one example of lexical semantic change (cf. Rothwell 1993), we assume that modern *jument* in the sense of 'mare' continues uninterruptedly, into French Latin JUMENTUM 'a beast of burden', even though, in the same contexts, Old French texts use *ive* (< EQUA), and modern rural varieties use *cavale* (< CABALLA), forms, which, though reflexes of Latin words for 'mare', are not acceptable in current norms.

We shall be looking in Part II at the apparent paradox in saying that linguistic change over time is inevitable and that we rely on a certain element of stability in language over time in order to reconstruct the linguistic past. We shall also consider how it is that language change (or **shift**?) sometimes appears to be abrupt and conspicuous, whereas traditional wisdom tells us that linguistic change is gradual and imperceptible. Part of the answer may lie in the discontinuity of speakers of the language, who are born and die, contrasting with the more durable continuity of a linguistic community.

0.3. HISTORY AND LANGUAGE

Historical linguistics, in an effort to preserve its identity as a sort of 'linguistics', has tended to scorn 'external history', as outside the scope of the autonomous science of linguistics. Perhaps it is now time to 'put history back into historical linguistics' or, rather, to attempt a reconciliation between sciences that attempt to make sense of the way in which things change over time. History is an important part of our consciousness of our identity, and the perception of change is something which disturbs, or stimulates, us all in our everyday life, and brings home to us the passage of time.

Fashions change in historical scholarship, no less than in linguistics (cf. e.g. Bloch 1954, Gildea 1994, Le Goff and Nora (eds.) 1974, Ricœur 1980). But most external histories of the French language are based firmly, via Brunot, on the history of *arrière-grand-papa* (specifically Michelet 1833–46, which continued to be used in the French education system until the 1960s). The positivist tradition—*histoire événementielle*—of the Third Republic, which also informed much French historical linguistic work, saw history rather as progress towards the present. It was allegedly objective and certainly erudite, based on meticulous study of documental evidence, just like the philological work of the same period.

Some historians see changes as coming from above—the action of the élite; others from below—pressure from the masses. These views can be linked, though they are not coterminous with, the antinomy of change as alternatively progress or decay.

Other views discount political events ('one damned thing after another') and concentrate more on broad sweeps—*la longue durée* (Braudel 1969) and geohistory—and especially on the effects of social and economic changes (e.g. demography, literacy, economic growth, or recession). These historians tend not to rely on documentary evidence (as collected in the Archives, which usually prejudge the question of value of the documents), but to use other resources, like parish registers, account books, etc.

Lodge (1993), a sociolinguistically oriented account of the triumph of the French standard language over the dialects of French, is in this tradition. Using a social networks model, he sees greater social mobility as fostering destruction of traditional linguistic communities. Certainly social and economic factors seem to have favoured language shift—from local varieties to the national language—in the modern period. This is something we shall look more closely at in Chapter 2.

The opposite tendency, of micro-history, attempting to give an account of the way individuals act in the past, is more akin to a philological approach (linguistic and literary history, with emphasis on the close study of texts, cf. Caput (1972, 1975), Rickard (1974, 1989[2]), Ayres-Bennett (1996)).

One current mode in history shifts its emphasis to putting more emphasis on ideology—not only as a major factor in change, but as influencing our view of the past. Myths, fabricated collective memories (cf. Halbwachs 1992), are what shape our view of what happened in the past, and are fuelled by commemorative ceremonies: the French Revolution centenary celebrations in 1989 for instance highlighted new interpretations of that momentous series of events, including the linguistic consequences. In the history of the language *l'imaginaire* is particularly important: a language becomes in the modern period, and nowhere more than in France, a symbol and emblem, first of sovereignty, then of identity and nationality.

After all, 'a language' is not ever a tangible reality, yet it is a shared communal heritage, a manifestation of collective memory. Whereas in the seventeenth century literary French was, like culture, manners, and honour, a prerogative of the élite, a means of establishing and reinforcing authority, at the end of the eighteenth century it came to be regarded as a manifestation of the spirit of the people. What could be more *imaginaire* than that?

So the history of a language is a kind of history, not so much of events but of representations and of myths. Not that there are not relevant events—Villers Cotterêts 1539, the founding of the Académie Française 1635, the edicts of the Revolutionary assemblies, etc.—but these legislative acts reflect a desire to influence reality, rather than being imposed by reality: *l'imaginaire* precedes *le réel*.

FURTHER READING

On the history of French basic works include: Allières 1982, Ayres-Bennett 1996, Berschin *et al.* 1978, Brunot 1905–79, Caput 1972–5, Cerquiglini 1991, Chaurand 1977[2], Cohen 1972[3], Ewert 1933, A. François 1959, Holtus *et al.* (eds.) 1988– , vol. 5.1 (1990), Kukenheim 1967–8, Lodge 1993, Marchello-Nizia 1995, Nyrop 1899–1930, Picoche and Marchello-Nizia 1989, Pope 1934, Price 1971, Regula 1955–66, Rickard 1989[2], Togeby 1974, Walter 1988, Wartburg 1970[10]. For bibliography, see especially Wagner 1955*a, b*, R. Martin 1973, and Bal *et al.* 1991, and the yearly reports in *The Year's Work in Modern Languages*, and the topical reading lists in *La Langue Française*. Relevant studies are to be found in most linguistic journals and especially in those devoted to historical linguistics, like *Diachronica* and *Folia Linguistica Historica*. Journals specializing in Romance languages, in particular, like *Journal of French Language Studies*, *Le Français Moderne*, *La Langue Française*, *Revue des langues romanes*, *Revue de linguistique romane*, *Revue romane*, *Romanische Forschungen*, *Romance Philology*, *Vox Romanica*, and *Zeitschrift für romanische Philologie* carry articles on French linguistic history. Further contributions appear in the *Actes* of the triennial international congress of the *Société de Linguistique Romane*, and in the published papers from the annual American linguistic symposium on the Romance languages.

On the Romance languages, consult especially Harris and Vincent 1988, Holtus *et al.* (eds.) 1988– , Iordan *et al.* 1970, Posner 1966*a*, 1996, Posner and Green (eds.) 1980–93. A new giant collaborative series on the History of the Romance Languages was announced in 1995 by Mouton-De Gruyter, Berlin.

Part I: Language Change

1

Defining the Domain

1.1. WHAT IS FRENCH?

The topic of this book is *Linguistic change in French*. Most of us think we know what French is: it is the language of French grammar books and/or the language in which French texts are written. We cannot properly, as we shall see later, apply the name to a geographical entity, like 'the language spoken in France'. We do know, too, that '*Ce n'est pas français*' is frequently said of familiar expressions, that are certainly used by French-speakers, and are not part of languages other than French. But let us look at the notion that the 'French' we are concerned with is a language identical with **Standard French**.

The first definition offered above seems pretty unambiguous, though a lot will depend on the grammar book—the influential *Bon Usage* (Grevisse 1936[1], 1994[13]), for instance, allows for quite considerable variation in details, precisely because the usage of the authoritative texts on which it is based is not uniform, either on the contemporary level or over time.

The standard language is viewed in the French tradition as a *trésor*, a *patrimoine*—an institution, which has been elaborated and perfected over time. Its history, then, is about its conception, refinement, and imposition. The standard, admittedly based initially on a natural language spoken by the best people in the sixteenth and seventeenth centuries, was codified, embellished, and spread through the population through education and emulation (cf. 1.12–14, 2.15–19). This can be conceived of as a long drawn-out process, as ordinary speakers are induced to shift to more prestigious usage, without losing the illusion of continuity. But it is doubtful whether the standard itself was originally a 'natural language' in the linguist's sense—that is a system built up by the individual child language learner using innate language capacities but drawing on the usage to which the learner is exposed.

Clearly in modern times the standard language has become a natural language for those speakers whose early language experience is limited mainly to input from standard usage. But not for all speakers who think they use French. The standard at its most severe rejects their deviant usage—not just as a different sort of French, but categorically as 'not French'.

However, on rulings about *francité* and correctness, even standard speakers do not always rely on their own linguistic intuition, but tend to resort to authority, in modern times dictionaries or guides to *bon usage*. Where (as often) the guidance is not unequivocal, then they are advised to *tourner autrement*—that is to avoid constructions or items that are dubious.

This is a long-standing habit, inherited from a less libertarian era. In Counter-Reformation France a top person would consult, not his conscience, but a religious mentor, on ethical and doctrinal matters (how he should act and what he should believe). In the same way he would seek expert advice from a language mentor to evaluate performance in speaking and writing French, rather than consulting his own native-speaker intuition. The overall principles applied in the Classical era were based on clarity, elegance, and sobriety, just as social etiquette required decency, decorum, and delicacy—*honnêteté*.

French top people still pay the same homage to good taste, or to fashion, in linguistic as in aesthetic matters, even if no longer on political and religious issues. The **linguistic insecurity** so widespread among ordinary French speakers is born of their conviction that the French language is a cultural *trésor*, which brings into play, not mere everyday native-speaker intuition, but a keen sensibility to linguistic nuances and rhythms, evidenced in the 'best' usage, and a profound knowledge of grammatical niceties, expounded by language arbiters. Appreciation of the language is akin to capacity to assess fine wines or cuisine: it demands assiduous apprenticeship as well as natural endowment. Creativity in language, as in art or cooking, involves stretching the rules sometimes to the limit, without breaking them.

But isn't there another way of looking at language?—as a 'natural' human attribute, to which, miraculously, all human beings have access without any special training, but which they acquire in early infancy merely by dint of absorbing the linguistic input of their environment, and exercising their innate language faculty (cf. 3.6). A child exposed to 'French' input at the acquisition stage will, in this scenario, become a native 'French' speaker. The input can vary, depending on the regional and social environment, and so can, correspondingly, the 'French' acquired. Many 'French' speakers today are conscious of a lack of alignment between their own 'natural' language and the national *trésor*; for some speakers the distance between the two seems unscalable. But they all have an **internal grammar**—approximating to Saussure's *langue* or Chomsky's **competence**—which they bring into play in the linguistic '**performance**' (or *parole*).

But can a 'natural' language have a history? Whereas it is simple enough to envisage a history of the institution of standard French, the idea of a history of a natural language raises conceptual and procedural difficulties. Should we be looking at the (fairly random?) changes in the individual's use during the course of his life? Or do we look for patterned innovations in the internal grammars of children newly acquiring the language of their community? To claim that a community language changes over time implies a directional shift in a substantial proportion of these individual internal grammars. Such a shift must surely be linked to change in input to the acquisition process—that is, the usage of adults must have changed non-randomly over time, so that new learners are exposed to data that differ significantly and non-randomly from those their elders experienced during their own acquisition process. This idea will be discussed at more length in Chapter 3.

The seeming contradiction between the idea of language as a system and the clear evidence of change in languages is a puzzle. As Valéry said '*un système est un arrêt*'—a still snipped out of a moving picture. In language history the solution to the paradox can be sought in the familiar phenomenon of variation within a language community. A historical language is less a structure than an architecture—to borrow a metaphor from Coseriu. It can encompass different varieties, covering perhaps a host of individual internal grammars and endowed perhaps with different social values, which permit normal intercommunication and mutual accommodation between members of the community. Directional change will then entail, over the course of time, the loss of some variant, so that it no longer feeds into the language acquisition process of new learners. One of the tasks of the language historian then will be to trace, not only inevitable innovations in language usage, but also the ways variants drop out of use, and to ask why this should happen.

Part II will examine changes in French from this perspective.

But let us return to our question—what is French? As a 'natural language' it would be what is common to all those individuals who think they speak French as their mother tongue. What limits can we place on this? For instance, is Mauritian creole, French? This is a question we shall return to later in this chapter.

At present let us take a simplistic view and say it is the language of France. Very simplistic, because of course other languages are spoken in France—territorial languages like Occitan, Breton, Alsatian, Basque, as well as immigrant languages of all ilks. But even then we must ask ourselves 'What is France?' or more relevantly, for our historical purposes, 'When was France?', and consequently 'When was French?'

1.2. WHEN WAS FRANCE?

This is a question which has much exercised historians and geographers, who talk of '*l'invention de la France*' (Beaune 1985, Braudel 1985, Chaunu 1982, Le Bras and Todd 1981, Planhol 1988) and the 'myth' of France, which became linked towards the beginning of the modern period with the idea of the French language.

We know of course what France—the hexagon—is today. But it only got roughly to that shape, rather than that of a lozenge, with Henri IV, at the end of the sixteenth century, and swelled to fill more or less its present territory at the end of the seventeenth century. Richelieu had already declared his wish to extend France to the cover the territory of Roman Gaul: Louis XIV more or less attained this goal.

Incidentally, though sixteenth-century apologists connected the myth of the Trojan-Greek origins of the French with the Gauls, the identification of the French with the Gauls was more a Revolutionary idea, which hardly surfaced under the *ancien régime*, when the Franks were more admired. However a subversive undercurrent of thought, especially among sixteenth-century Protestants, linked the Gaulish heritage to the ideas of liberty and resistance to Roman conquerors (shades of Asterix!). The 'Gaulish' and the 'Aryan' myths also tend to fuse (as in Asterix), so that Honoré d'Urfé, for instance, claimed '*Francs se vantent d'être issus des anciens Gaulois*', 'Franks are proud of being descended from the ancient Gauls'. (Cf. C.-G. Dubois 1972, Poliakov 1974.)

Textbooks talk about modern French being based on *francien*, the dialect of the *Île de France*, but most point out that this term was a nineteenth-century invention. Indeed the regional name Île de France was officially used only in the fifteenth century. What *France* really meant before then is disputed.

Franceis began to be used in reference to speech late in the twelfth century, though it was not unambiguously the language name 'French' until somewhat later; it is associated with the idea of France as an entity, however *imaginaire*. *Lingua gallica* was the usual Latin name for the Romance variety, whereas *francisca* was used first for a Germanic language (*francique* is a seventeenth-century coinage). The place name *France* (FRANCIA), of course, preceded the name for the language, though Frankish kings originally ruled over a people, the Franks (REX FRANCORUM), rather than a named territory. Their tongue was presumably Germanic, rather than Romance: only with the Capetians (Hugues Capet 987) did Romance become the only native language of royalty, though it had presumably remained so for most of the population of erstwhile Roman Gaul. It took a long time for French territory to attain the sort of cohesion it was supposed to have had at the Partage de Verdun 843, between Charlemagne's grandsons, when, following the famous Strasburg Oaths, the youngest half-brother Charles le Chauve ('the Bald') received Carolingia or Regnum Francorum as his lot.

The extreme diversity of what is now France is deep-rooted: the difference, especially between north and south—the Occitan-speaking area—is not only linguistic but profoundly cultural. The Albigensian crusade (1209-44) which destroyed the flourishing troubadour culture of the south, and incorporated the Toulouse area into the French kingdom, did little to eradicate the differences: I shall come back to the spread of French in 2.15.

One commentator likens the French feudal kings to a vacuum cleaner sucking up scraps of land over the centuries, but there was

little real direction to this process, or any degre of cohesion until the
show-down under the Valois (from 1328), who challenged English
claims to much of the continental territory, culminating in the so-
called Hundred Years War (1338–1453)—the name is of sixteenth-
century coinage (by Étienne Pasquier). This period had disastrous
effect on France (while England prospered). It nurtured the myth of
France as an entity (Jeanne d'Arc was burned at the stake in 1431),
and a yearning for stability, which opened the way for consolidation
of royal power.

Modern France can be dated back to the end of the fifteenth, or
of the sixteenth, seventeenth, or eighteenth centuries, depending on
the criteria applied. Does this apply also to the **Modern French**
language? Here is the place to discuss the periodization that figures
in most of the textbooks (cf. also G. Eckert 1990).

I.3. PERIODIZATION

Discussion of the history of French normally distinguishes the
successive period languages under the names **Vulgar Latin**, **Old
French**, **Middle French**, **Modern French**. The antinomy here is
between the presumed gradualness and imperceptibility of linguistic
change and the fact that we give different names to sections of the
continuum. This is not quite the same as, but it is related to, the
antinomy **system** versus **change** (cf. 3.3).

The way the dilemma is usually overcome is by ruling that a
language is defined non-linguistically—by its status, regional or
political, but especially psychological. A language has to be
recognized as an entity by the community which uses it. This of
course does not resolve the differentiation between a language and a
dialect—unless we accept Max Weinreich's notorious jokey definition 'a language is a dialect with an army and a navy'. The state
apparatus gives a dialect language status, but not any intrinsic
linguistic or cultural worth.

Everyone agrees that French is now different from Latin, and
indeed from Italian or Spanish. But, if indeed French, Italian, and
Spanish are modern continuators of Latin, when did the differences
arise? Some date them to the time the Roman legions strode into
each new province; others to when the Germanic hordes swept
down on the unprotected Romance speakers of Gaul, Italia, and

Hispania; others to when Christianity imposed a spiritual, but not a political, unity on the Western world, others when the feudal system established loose ties between a host of diverse units, and texts in the vernaculars began to appear. What is certain is that, from a linguistic point of view, the Latin of the best Golden Age authors cannot be the direct predecessor of the Romance vernaculars. So, as we saw above, we invent ('reconstruct') an intermediate *langue romane*, or **Vulgar Latin**, that was either a post-classical continuator of Latin, or a regional or social variant of literary Latin. In reality, it is more a construct based on the features common to all the Romance languages. It certainly was not the language of any attested community (cf. Lloyd 1979).

Emerging from this Vulgar Latin or **Proto-Romance**, seamlessly some would claim, came **Old French** (though interposing an 'immature' **Early Old French** between Latin and the classic texts of the twelfth and thirteenth centuries). Most authorities believe that the textual evidence points to a sudden recognition, round about the turn of the tenth century, that the vernacular which had thus evolved was not 'Latin' (or even 'Romance', understood as a spoken form of Latin). Some would claim that this recognition was due to the revival of learning under Charlemagne, and the influence of non-Romance Latinists (like Alcuin of York); others that close contact with Germanic speakers brought home the fact that languages differ; others that there was a conscious effort to make religious truths accessible to the non-learned. The much-quoted resolution of the 813 Council of Tours, advocating the use of rustic Romance or Germanic in church homilies, is usually advanced as the clinching argument. The ninth-century dating of the birth of French is supported by Nithard's near contemporary account, in his Latin history of Louis le Pieux, of the swearing in 842, before Strasburg, of oaths that are cited (in the late tenth- or eleventh-century manuscript) in both 'Romance' and 'Germanic'.

But the Old French, in which a rich body of texts—hagiographic, epic, romance, historical, theatrical, and administrative—survives, did not really show its distinctive face until well into the eleventh century, and then initially in England, where the Dukes of Normandy had established what has been called the first European *État territorial*.

It is tempting to associate the language we call Old French with feudal society (cf. Bloch 1949). How far this type of social system represented radical 'revolution' or 'mutation', as distinct from a gradual evolution from Carolingian society, is disputed among French historians (for a recent review cf. Bisson 1994). Certainly around about the year 1000, the switch to feudal organization was marked by terminological changes in Latin documents (like CABALLARIUS replacing MILES; SENIOR, DOMINUS; and FEUDUM, BENEFICIUM; and new use of VILLANUS). With new attitudes, only to be expected would be the development of a literary vernacular which would express, or indeed promote, them.

The status and distinctive features of Old French, first called *roman* and then only later *franceis*, differentiate it from the modern language and from Latin. It was closer to Old Italian and Old Spanish than to the modern versions, and perhaps it was at the time considered, like them, as a spoken variant of Latin. Moreover it was always used alongside Latin, in a **diglossic** situation—with Latin as the grammatical, written fixed **High** language, and the vernacular as a variable 'fun' **Low** language, with features associated with orality, even when it is written down. Quite when speakers actually realized that their own idiom was not just 'street' Latin is not wholly certain: the records suggest that there may have been bilingual exchange and **code-switching** at some levels right until the sixteenth century. However, by the thirteenth century it seems clear that there were reasonably cultured people who found Latin inaccessible. We know, moreover, that translations from Latin into French were being commissioned—notably for royal libraries in the fourteenth century. That translation, rather than mere commentary, was practised, indicates a consciousness that the vernacular is not merely a spoken corruption of Latin. Moreover it may be evidence of a desire to 'illustrate' (i.e. lend illustrious status to) the vernacular (cf. 1.12).

Old French (*ancien français*) is usually associated with *le Moyen Age*, a label invented by late fifteenth-century Humanists for the gap between classical glory and its Rebirth (*Rinascimento, Renaissance*). The spoken language of the people of the time is not easy to reconstruct. One problem here is that our earlier records are written exclusively by people who were versed in writing Latin: *l'autre Moyen Age*, the alternative medieval culture, as Le Goff (cf. Le Goff and Nora 1974) calls it, remains pretty silent. Everyone agrees that the twelfth century—the time when the idea of France was being fashioned—is the heyday of Old French. In the thirteenth century

French, with its dialectal variants, was used in charters, alongside Latin.

Some place the beginning of so-called **Middle French** at this period: remember that French was still the prestige language in England at the time (cf. Kibbee 1991), though it was diverging more and more from continental Norman French. Middle French is the most disputed of the period languages (cf. e.g. R. A. Hall 1972): most see it as a 'transition'—when the innovations of modern French had not yet ousted the older varieties. Its time-span is elastic: some would have it stretch from the fourteenth through the sixteenth century, others would confine it to the fourteenth and fifteenth centuries. What is certain is that it cannot have been a 'psychological' entity for speakers. It was probably the disasters of the fourteenth century (wars, plagues), with massive reduction in population—differentially, it would seem, affecting the clerical educated élite—that hastened the loss of the more archaic variants in ordinary speech. Some, though, continued to survive marginally in learned use into the sixteenth century, especially when they were bolstered by parallels from Latin, which was enjoying a rebirth of popularity and prestige. By the fifteenth century, though, errors by writers like François Villon in imitating the 'old language' reveal that it was no longer currently used.

So **modern French** could have been gaining ground, as a spoken idiom in the thirteenth century, with the fourteenth century as its real take-off point. Where I would place the beginning of modern French, as a widely used natural language, is in the late fifteenth century, with its regeneration of the severely depleted population, with consequent greater geographical and social mobility, and in the early sixteenth century, with the return of prosperity and a growing cultural awareness, and especially a born-again keenness to slough off the medieval heritage.

But before the seventeenth century modern French was not yet the sole chosen language of the élite. For one thing it was not yet clear which section of the population was to be dominant. In the second half of the sixteenth century the country was torn by the savagery of the Wars of Religion, in the first half of the seventeenth century by the more frivolous, but still disruptive, *Frondes*.

Only under Louis XIV was linguistic prestige unambiguously bestowed on a small section of the population—the royal courtiers. Their claim sprang not from intellectual distinction, military prowess, administrative flair, or wealth-creating enterprise, but simply from noble rank, whether acquired by breeding or inherited riches, and from the idleness imposed on them.

The spread of their élite language through the whole of the French population was paradoxically a goal of Republican ideals—in principle during the Revolutionary period, but in practice mainly in the Third Republic, when education became universal. If we seek to relate our linguistic periods with turning-points in the development of French society, we must wonder how it is that the Revolution did not bring with it a linguistic change. In some respects it did—in that bit by bit more demotic speech habits penetrated into legitimate usage. But the Romantic linguistic revolt was largely confined to the lexicon and there was little loosening of the grip of classical grammatical attitudes. We shall look later, in this chapter and in the next, at the sociolinguistic history of the last two centuries.

1.4. So What has Changed?

I have divided the domain of the historical study of French into three distinct languages (leaving aside the equivocal **Vulgar Latin** and **Middle French**), of which two are standardized literary languages—**Latin** and **modern French**—and one is represented by a canon of texts in a less unified, but still readily demarcated, language—classical **Old French**. Within each of these language 'states' there is evidence of considerable variation, and overlap with preceding and following 'states'. But it is possible to maintain that each represents a prototype, actively manipulated, perhaps, only by an élite, but which in some sense is accessible to the community from which it springs.

But do these states represent staging posts along the historical linguistic highway? Or are they more like cul-de-sacs, cultural hidy-holes tunnelled out to avoid the bustle of everyday traffic? A more usual image is to suggest that they may represent a surface stability, associated with a settled and ordered cultural vision, which is constantly being undermined by the forces of destruction and degeneration—the workaday discourse requirements of the unciv-ilized common herd. These were the undertones of the label **Vulgar Latin**, as of modern **français populaire** and, for some, of **creole**. For the Old French period we have less evidence of the underdog's language, but we usually assume that the regional variants that leak out into our texts are evidence of an underground flood, of which we can have no knowledge.

Change, it can also be maintained, originates underground and emerges to the surface of the written text only sporadically, until an upheaval turns the whole linguistic set-up topsy-turvy. This sort of thinking seemed to imbue the Prussian-dominated scholarly world of nineteenth-century historical linguistics. It can be contrasted with a French Enlightenment attitude that can view the innovations of the masses as vivacious and expressive, casting off redundancies and looking to the future rather than the past: *français populaire* is seen by some as *français avancé* (cf. 2.11).

Whatever the social status of the historical language states we have described, they may indeed not form a continuum, one imperceptibly changing into the other. Rather they may each represent a crystallization that reflects the *imaginaire* of the period, but which can later become more like a fossilization, which is overturned by a language more appropriate to a new culture. Yet even though there have been changes, there remain certain stable elements that allow us to recognize each stage as the 'same language'. This is more true of Old and Modern French, than of either of these and Latin: but even here, as we shall see in Part II, morphological and lexical similarity persists. That French is a Romance language no one now denies.

I have already controversially maintained that study of language change depends on the assumption that some things have not changed: we would not dream, for instance, of trying to describe change from, say, Old French to Modern Chinese. In Part II, we shall look at linguistic changes, but also point out absence of change. Here I shall merely present in tabular form (Table 1.1) a summary of what I regard as the main phonological, morphological, and syntactic differences between our three language states.

Discussion of most of the changes will be found in Chapters 5, 6, and 7: references are given in brackets to the relevant section. Semantic and lexical changes cannot be so readily tabulated: changes in these spheres will be discussed in Chapters 4 and 5.

TABLE 1.1. So what has changed?

Latin	Old French	Modern French
PHONOLOGY (Chapter 6)		
(6.3) predictable (?tonal) accent	functional stress word accent	predictable rhythmic group accent
(6.4) no nasal vowels (?)	phonetically conditioned vowel nasality	phonological vowel nasality
(6.5) prevocalic ĭ > palatal [j]	palatalization resulting in:	
	?palatal and palatoalveolar affricates	> palato-alveolar fricatives
	[ʦ'], [ʣ'],	> [s], [z]
	[ʧ], [ʤ]	> [ʃ], [ʒ]
	palatal [r'] > [jr]	> [ʁ] ([j] absorbed into preceding nuclear vowel)
	palatal [ɲ]	(> in some varieties [nj])
	palatal [ʎ] (6.6)	> [j]
(6.7) velar [u]	> palatal [y] (or [ju]?)	[y]
(6.8) diphthong levelling	diphthongization,	diphthong levelling
AE > [ɛ], AU > [ɔ]	ŏ > uo > ue	> /ø/ ([œ]) (*loi de position*)
OE > [e]	ō > ou > eu,	> /ø/ ([œ]) (*loi de position*)
	ĕ > ie	> [jɛ]
	ē > ei > oi,	> [wɛ] > [wa]
(6.9) word-final consonants often inflectional	word-final consonants devoiced	*liaison*
(6.10) no schwa	schwa [ə] as allophone of /e/?	schwa lost sporadically
	'feminine e' elided prevocalically	(*e instable*): allophone of /ø/?
(6.10) [h] > ∅	Germanic [h]	> ∅: *h aspiré* blocks elision and *liaison*
(6.12) phonological vowel quantity	Latin vowel quantity lost; compensatory lengthening	loss of phonological vowel length
(6.13) apical [r]	[r] > [z] (?); [rː] > uvular [ʀ]	> [ʁ] in all positions
MORPHOLOGY (Chapter 7)		
Verbal (Chapter 7.A)		
(7.4) 4 conjugations	2 conjugations	1 regular conjugation
(5.7–8; 7.11–12) perfect/ imperfect stem	past punctual/imperfect/ compound perfect	(*passé simple*)/*imparfait*/ *passé composé*

Latin	Old French	Modern French
(7.13) synthetic future and future perfect	'periphrastic' future and 'future in the past'	synthetic future/*GO* future and synthetic conditional
(5.9) synthetic passive	periphrastic passive	periphrastic passive
(5.10) subjunctive	subjunctive	subjunctive non-functional?
(7.5) 6 person inflections	6 person inflections	persons marked by clitic
Nominal (Chapter 7.B)		
(7.15) 3 genders	2 genders	2 genders
(7.16–19) 6 cases	2 cases	caseless
Pronominal		
(8.12–15) stressed personal pronouns	stressed/unstressed personal pronouns	clitic/free personal pronouns
(7.19) 3 grade demonstrative	2 grade demonstrative	one grade demonstrative
(7.19) stressed demonstrative	stressed/unstressed	pronoun/determiner
(7.18) stressed possessive	stressed/unstressed	pronoun/determiner
SYNTAX (Chapter 8, also Chapter 5)		
(8.3–4) **SOV** word-order	**TVO?, V2?,** word-order	**SVO, (SoV)** word-order
(5.11, 8.10–11) no articles	deictic article, specific (definite), indefinite? partitive	noun determiners
(8.8) emphatic subject pronoun (**pro-drop**)	unstressed subject pronoun in certain positions	obligatory subject (**non-pro-drop**)
(5.10) accusative + infinitive in indirect speech	*que* + finite verb	*que* + finite verb
(8.6) -NE, NONNE, NUM interrogative	interrogative inversion ([ti], [ɛsk])	[intonation only]
(8.7) NON etc. negative	*ne . . . (pas)* etc. negative	*(ne) . . . pas* negative

1.5. LINGUISTIC FEATURES OF MODERN FRENCH

Table 1.1 shows that phonological change occurred between all three periods, without any clear sense of direction. Thus Latin **vowel length** (and **syllable quantity**) was lost in Old French, which nevertheless developed towards the end of the period new distinctions of vowel length, as a consequence of **compensatory lengthening**. The Latin **diphthongs** were levelled to monophthongs, but new diphthongs were created in Old French, which in turn were levelled by the modern French period. Some changes seem to follow a pattern: Latin [h] was silent before French came into being, but a new Germanic [h] entered Old French as *h aspiré*, in Germanic loanwords, only to become silent in its turn (though blocking **liaison** in the standard language). The creation of a whole series of palatal consonants in Old French was followed by a simplification which left a much smaller inventory in modern French. These and other changes will be discussed in Chapter 6. All can be paralleled by similar changes in other languages.

In morphology and syntax, the changes that have taken place do appear to show some sort of direction—usually described in terms of **simplification** of the grammar, of a movement to greater **iconicity** (cf. Haiman 1985) or as a move from **synthetic** to **analytic** coding strategies (cf. Schwegler 1990). Whether this constitutes 'progress' or 'decay' depends on one's point of view.

We shall be concentrating more on change from older to modern French than on the changes between Latin and Old French. This means that we have to attempt some sort of description, however perfunctory, of **modern French**. But what should we compare modern French with? The defining limit of **creoles** we shall look briefly at in 1.8. The other comparison that I choose as useful, is with Old French. I have already said that in some ways this resembles Old Italian and Old Spanish almost as closely as modern French. French is a Romance language, as defined by its basic lexical stock (like the creoles) and its morphological structure (unlike the creoles). Modern French differs from Old French and other Romance languages, however, in certain crucial ways. The written standard preserves many of the features of Old French that are not reflected in the spoken language. The following attempts to summarize the defining characteristics of what I wish, provisionally, to call **modern French**: they recapitulate to some extent what appears in the third column of Table 1.1.

Phonology

Modern French has:

no word-stress but a **rhythmic group** stress. This has important effects in such areas as *liaison* and *e instable*, and on the **phonotactic** structure;
no **diphthongs** and no **affricates**;
a series of nasal vowel phonemes.

Morphology

Modern French has:

no **nominal case-system** (contra Old French and Old Occitan); **pronominal case** only in the **clitic** system (if there), and not in the full (**disjunctive**) pronouns;
in the spoken language no consistent morphological means of marking **noun gender** or number;
a well-defined noun **determiner** system, differentiated from corresponding pronouns;
verb person marking principally by **proclitic pronouns**, rather than by **inflectional endings**;
periphrastic or **compound** forms for past and future reference, but no morphological distinction between progressive and habitual **aspect** in the present **tense**.

Syntax

Modern French has:

basically **SVO word-order** (contra **V2** in Old French), but **object pronouns** are usually **proclitic** to the verb that governs them;
rigidly fixed **functional word-order** within the core sentence;
interrogation marking not by **inversion** of the noun-subject, but, in the standard, by pronoun inversion, including **complex inversion** (*but* **intonation** is the main interrogative device in the spoken language);
bipartite negation in the standard, with post-verbal *pas* as the main verb-phrase negator.

Discourse

In Modern French:

spoken style makes great use of **dislocation** and **clefting** to secure *mise en relief*;
tense forms are more linked to chronometrics than in Old French;
written style makes more use, than in Old French, of **hypotaxis**, and **nominalization**.

Lexicon

Modern French:

has drawn heavily on **Latinisms,** rather than preserving inherited words (though the **basic vocabulary** remains relatively unchanged);

changes 'peripheral' vocabulary at a rapid rate, being quick to abandon especially **archaisms** and recent **neologisms;**

tends to eschew lexical **derivatives,** preferring to fill lexical gaps by dint of **change of category** or of **borrowing.**

1.6. WHEN DID THESE FEATURES ARISE?

The features of modern French that I have chosen as diagnostic were almost certainly all in place in the seventeenth century in élite usage. Some of them are almost certainly linked: for instance, loss of inflectional noun case-marking, and verb person marking can be connected with loss of word-stress. Fixing of word-order, restriction of interrogative inversion, strengthening of negation, and the development of new strategies for *mise en relief* can also ultimately be linked to changes in the rhythm of the language, as can levelling of diphthongs, resolution of affricates, and nasalization of vowels. These are matters we shall look in Chapter 6.

It is probable that a form of modern French, as defined by these criteria, was already fast gaining ground in the course of the fourteenth century. But there was no pressure for reduction of variation at a time when an invariable Latin remained the prestige language.

It has recently been suggested (cf. Dorian 1994) that fairly random variation is tolerated as long as the variants carry no social marking. Polarization (and hence reduction) of variants may result from the perception of them as indicative of status within a community.

Standardization (cf. 1.10) eventually proscribed unprestigious variants and opted mainly for modern fashions, rejecting outmoded 'gothic' habits. But there was still abeyance to the past—but only to the far-distant past. Resplendent classical heritage was respected more than dusty medieval ways, and the language was refashioned along the principles, if not the practice, of Latinity.

1.7. What has Changed during the Modern French Period?

Not much since the seventeenth century, it would seem, if we are to measure change by loss of variants. The Classical language reads as quaint but not un-French: it is a variant that remains alive, if stylistically marked, in some sorts of discourse.

Some things have changed though. Attitudes towards the language, for instance. During the sixteenth century, the tone-setting élite absorbed linguistic, as well as cultural, ideas from Italy, where the *questione della lingua*—on the relation between the vernacular and Latin—was at the forefront. Most of the champions of French were adept Latinists, using the 'reborn' classical language that owes much to Erasmus (1466–1536). They often even translated their own works from one to the other language, but serious works were also written initially in French.

They also tended to be attracted early to the Lutheran ideas newly emanating from Germany, which laid emphasis on the use of the vernacular in religious discourse, and they were swayed later towards the Calvinism diffused in French from Geneva. They saw no harm in dialectal diversity (most of them were themselves of provincial origin) and they encouraged 'richness' of choice in language use.

After the religious conflicts of the second half of the century, Latin lost most of its social functions, though it continued as the language of the Roman Church until the 1960s. Under Henri IV who, though Bearnese, was thoroughly versed in French, the influence of Malherbe worked towards 'purification' and unification of a Parisian-based French, which now came to be identified as the language of the realm. This attitude persisted and strengthened through the seventeenth and through the eighteenth century, when codification took on a more deliberately universalist and 'logical' tinge, and French began to supplant Latin as a pan-European language of communication and diplomacy.

The Revolution wholeheartedly adopted the principle of linguistic unity, on the grounds that citizens must have the linguistic means freely to participate in the affairs of the nation. Diversity of language would, on the contrary, perpetuate social divisions. Purity of language would likewise reflect the noble ideals to which all would subscribe.

In the nineteenth and twentieth centuries stances with regard to language have dogged aesthetic and social attitudes, with some loosening of the stranglehold of Academic French. So successively, we have had, for instance, Romantic colourful vocabulary, Parnassian linguistic precision, Symbolist linguistic obscurity, modern attempts to fashion a specifically 'arty', belletristic language or, alternatively, to incorporate popular idiom into literary style.

Less marked have been internal linguistic changes. Once the language was codified and standardized the possible parameters of change were limited. Pronunciation still varies in different areas, and it is possible to discern directional change. The rate of vocabulary innovation and loss is striking. The grammar is less open to mutation, as codification has tended to block social acceptance of innovation. Morphology was more or less fixed in the seventeenth and eighteenth centuries for the written language, though spoken usage can be said to escape from the constraints. Syntax changes have been comparatively few, and can usually be associated with lexical, phonological, or morphological changes. What has apparently changed most have been discourse features, though how far this is an artefact of the changes in the type of the written evidence available over the period is hard to say. Similarly the apparent emergence of a non-regional **popular French** may not be due to change in language reality but an effect of the availability today of evidence for forms of speech that remained underground in the past. These are all questions discussed later.

I.8. ARE THE FRENCH CREOLES A SORT OF MODERN FRENCH?

I said earlier that we would consider French creoles (or more properly, perhaps **French-lexifier creoles**) as a limiting case in our definition of French. I include in my purview those languages, spoken in the New World and on some Indian Ocean islands, which date from the time of the slave-trade (*la traite des Noirs*), but not some other more recent so-called creoles or **pidgins** that have developed in some Francophone African countries and in some Pacific islands. These languages are today spoken in Haiti and in the **DOM**s (*Départements d'Outre-Mer*) that are politically part of the French State (*Guadeloupe, Guyane française, Martinique, Réunion*), in a number of other independent countries that are today officially English-speaking, like Mauritius and the Seychelles in the Indian Ocean, and some Caribbean islands, like Dominica and St Lucia, as well as in Louisiana. In some Caribbean islands where a French creole is no longer currently spoken there are records of use of the language earlier this century—this is true of Trinidad and Tobago, and of Grenada. In all of these areas, the use of creole can be linked with the presence of a black slave population from the seventeenth century (for the New World), and from the eighteenth (for the Indian Ocean). Some of these areas were unpopulated before the colonial era, and in others the native population was more or less exterminated.

To be more accurate, part of the Seychelles population originated mainly from liberated slaves landed there from ships intercepted by British anti-slave-trade missions in the early nineteenth century, but there were also immigrants from Mauritius from the eighteenth century.

Some of these languages are locally known as *patois*: the relationship between overseas dialects and the creoles is discussed in 2.20. The name *creole* was originally used, during the age of colonial expansion, for locally-born inhabitants of French origin, in overseas territories, but it has come mainly to designate a specific black culture, associated with the history of slavery. In French territories, however, creole is today spoken by white inhabitants as well as black, alongside a more standardized French.

The process of creolization will be discussed in 3.14. Today the term 'creole' has been extended by linguists to cover languages that have been 'nativized' from earlier pidgins—like Tokpisin in Papua New Guinea.

The French creoles have lexicons that are overwhelmingly and obviously French, and can be linked closely with popular language in the seventeenth and eighteenth centuries. Some of the common words—like *mirer* 'to see', *bailler* 'to give', *gagner* 'to get', *tenir* 'have', *monde* 'people'—were presumably in common use, though not favoured by the standard. However, in modern times, the grammatical organization of the creoles is acknowledged to be quite different from that of French. Salient differences include the total absence of inherited inflections, of noun gender, and of the definite article. Grammatical marking is effected by the juxtaposing of separable elements: thus the creoles can be said to have carried to its limit the drift already detected in the history of French away from

synthetic and towards **analytic** constructions (cf. Schwegler 1990). Most remarkable is the way in which the creoles use a series of preverbal **tense**, **aspect**, and **mood** (**TAM**) markers, usually derived from French forms. This strongly resembles procedures used in West African languages. The following table gives some idea of the differences between French and the creoles, but also of the resemblances between the creoles from different areas. It is on the basis of such differences that we can claim that the creoles are as different from modern French, as modern French is different from Latin.

Indeed it has been suggested that the change from Latin to Romance was a sort of creolization (cf. Schlieben-Lange 1976).

TABLE 1.2.   Some characteristic features of French creoles

---

1. Most words are invariable, and grammatical functions are shown by separable morphemes.
2. There is no **grammatical gender**. Sex differences can be shown lexically e.g.:
     [papa / mamã bɛf] (*papa / maman boeuf*) = *taureau /vache*.
3. Nouns can be marked as plural by a postposed plural pronoun (< *eux*). A postposed **personal pronoun** is usually used to show possession, e.g.:
     [ʃapo mwɛ̃] *(chapeau moi)* = *mon chapeau*.
4. Lexical verbs usually occur in the infinitive form (*manger, vendre*, etc.), which implies **habitual** or **punctual aspect**, but is unmarked for **tense**. Tense, modality, and other aspects are shown by markers preposed to the verb, e.g.
     [ti] /[te] < *était* = **past tense** or **perfect aspect** (PST, PFT), [ap]/[pe] < *aprés* = **progressive aspect** (PROG), [a] / [va] < *va* = **future tense** (FUT) etc.
5. There is usually no copula in the New World creoles, e.g.:
                 Bougre bon 'The man is good'.
   In the Indian Ocean creoles [se] < *c'est* is used as a copula.
6. There are no **clitic pronouns**, only invariable **disjunctive** forms,
                 e.g. [mwɛ̃ emɛ̃ u] (*Moi aimer vous*) = *Je vous aime*).
   The **reflexive** and **reciprocal** is expressed by *corps* rather than by the reflexive pronoun or *même*:
     [nu te ka ãtãn kɔ-nu] (*Nous était* (PST) *qu'a* (PROG) *entendre corps nous*) = 'We were hearing each other'.
7. There is no **definite article**. A postposed *là* is often used as specifier and noun phrase marker, e.g.:
   Chat blanc là = 'The white cat' / *Chat là blanc* = 'The cat is white'.

The French article is sometimes incorporated into the lexical item: *latab* 'table', [djo] 'water' < *de l'eau*, [zozo] 'bird' < *les oiseaux*.

8. There are few **conjunctions** or **prepositions**. Some Caribbean creoles use **serial constructions**, with a succession of verbs, in contexts in which French would use particles e.g.:

   [pɔte vini mo rob a] (*Porter venir moi robe là*) = 'Bring me the dress!'; [li pov pase m] (*Lui pauvre passer moi*) = 'He is poorer than me'.

   Subordination etc. is often effected by juxtaposition:

   [I di i ke vini] (*Lui dire lui ke* (FUT) *venir*) = 'He said he would be coming'; [fɑ̃m peji-la] (*femme(s) pays là*) = 'woman (women) of the country', [ba mun lisõ] (*bailler monde leçon*) = 'to give a lesson to people'.

9. **Constituent ordering** is almost exclusively Subject-Verb-Object (**SVO**)

10. **Negation** is expressed by by preposed *pa*, e.g.:

    [mwɛ̃ pa kwɛ pɛsõn ap vĩni] (*Moi pas croire personne après* (PROG) *venir*) = 'I don't think anyone is coming'.

11. The sound-system is usually 'simplified' in comparison with standard French, e.g.:

    [y] > [i], [ø] > [e], [ʁ] > [w] or lost, [ʒ] > [z]).

    Assimilation (e.g. **palatalization**, **nasalization**) is frequent.

Here are some examples to illustrate these features:

(1) (*a*) Mauritius

[mo	ti	pu	pe	zue]	*Moi était pour après jouer*
me	PST	FUT	PROG	play	'I would be playing.'

(*b*) Haiti

[lo	w	a	desɑ̃n	l	av	ap	mɑ̃ze]

Lors vous va descendre lui va après manger

Then you FUT descend him FUT PROG eat

'When you come down he will be eating.'

(*c*) Dominica

[jõ	le	kõ	sa	demɛ̃	mwɛ̃	ke	ka

En? l'heure comme ça demain moi (qu'est capable?)

in hour like that tomorrow me FUT PROG

travaj ɑ̃ jadɛ̃ mwɛ̃]

travailler en jardin moi

work in garden me

'At this time tomorrow I shall be working in my garden'.

1.9. WHEN DID THE CREOLES COME INTO BEING?

The first evidence we have of the existence of creole dates mainly from the eighteenth century, with a number of literary and folkloric texts from the nineteenth century.

There is, however, one seventeenth-century text which, if authentic, shows that in the Caribbean, a creole was already in being, and recognizably different from French. In 1671 a small boatful of Frenchmen, with their male slaves, were fishing just off the coast of Martinique, and were surprised to see a merman (presumably some sort of sea-lion). The Jesuit priest, to whom they told their story, had their reports taken down verbatim by a notary. He recorded the slaves' accounts as best he could. Their language, in contrast to that of their masters, looks very much like the modern creole. Here are some examples from two of the witnesses:

(2)   *moi mirer un homme enmer du Diamant, moi voir li trois fois, li tini assés bon visage et Zyeux comme monde* 'Me see a man in sea of the Diamond (Bay); Me see him three times; him have fairly good face and eyes like people'.
      moi n'a pas miré bas li parce li té dans diau, li sembe pourtant poisson. Moi té tini peur bete là manger monde 'Me not look down him because him PST in water, him seem however fish. Me PST have fear beast there eat people'.

In the Indian Ocean, the first evidence we have is from the defence made by a female runaway slave, who was tried round about 1720. According to the Réunion (pre-Revolutionary *Île de Bourbon*) court records she said:

(3)   *Moin la parti marron parce qu'Alexis, l'homme de jardin l'était qui fait à moin trop l'amour* 'Me PST went maroon because Alexis the garden-man PST PROG. make too much to me love'.

For *L'Île de France* (now Mauritius) it was said in 1749 that a 'corrupted French' was used, and the example was cited:

(4)   *Ça blanc là li beaucoup malin; li couri beaucoup dans la mer là-haut* 'That white man there him much cunning; him run much in sea out there'.

Bernardin de St Pierre wrote in his *Voyage à l'Île de France* (1768–70), referring to a sailor:

(5) *Le Patron me dit dans son mauvais patois: 'Ça n'a pas bon Monsié'. Je lui demandai s'il y avoit quelque danger, il me répondit: 'Si nous n'a pas gagné malheur, ça bon.'* The ship's master told me in his execrable dialect: 'That PST not good, sir.' I asked him if there were any danger, he replied to me: 'If we PST not have bad luck, that good.'

By the mid-eighteenth century, white colonists were apparently even writing in creole. The following is a snatch from a song, allegedly composed in Port-au-Prince, Saint-Domingue (now Haiti), by a royal official:

(6) *Mon perdí bonheur à moué | Gié moin semblé fontaine | Dipi mon pas miré toué* 'Me lose happiness to me, Eye me seem fountain, Since me not see you'.

Although used by white colonists (*békés*) the creole was often designated as *petit nègre* or 'Negro-French': in Louisiana it is also called *gumbo* (from the Bambara word for 'okra'). Thus it was seen as associated with the usage of the slaves, and as a simplified form of French, but it also came to be recognized as the first language of children born into slavery.

It is thought that the creoles were created early in the history of French colonization in the seventeenth century, when slaves were imported into the Caribbean islands. They subsequently developed in a different direction from French, which was undergoing standardization, differentiating itself from the popular usage that presumably had informed the creoles.

The process of standardization, which I discuss next, cut off the creoles from other French varieties, so that they developed independently, although with some degree of decreolization in those regions where creole and standard remained in contact.

1.10. STANDARDIZATION: LANGUAGE PLANNING AND LANGUAGE POLICY

Language policy (*glottopolitique*, political linguistics) is associated with action by authority in any sphere involving language.

For instance, whether to encourage minority languages or to impose a uniform state language; whether to promote language studies in the school system; whether to favour some varieties of the mother tongue rather than others; whether to give precedence to some foreign languages rather than others; how to evaluate regional and social variants in language use when assessing the suitability of a speaker for educational qualification or for employment, etc. etc.

No language policy just means the default of conservatism—going on doing what has always been done, however irrational or unjust.

Language planning (or **engineering**) is usually used for a language policy with a positive aim of manipulating language as means of tackling social problems. These may be concerned with the status of disadvantaged minority languages within a political unit, and will often be designed to improve the prestige of such languages, through the process of **standardization**.

I.II. WHAT IS A STANDARD LANGUAGE?

Here it is convenient to distinguish a standard from a **koine**, and a **norm**. 'Norm' (cf. Bartsch 1987) is used for any accepted social institution that does not have the force of law. You are not going to be put in prison for not using your knife and fork properly, or for wearing the wrong clothes for an interview, but you may be ostracized or mocked for making this sort of mistake. Similarly conforming to a language norm usually involves knowing how to speak in a certain situation, recognizing the various degrees of prestige associated with different language use. Familiarity with language norms is part of what Dell Hymes called **communicative competence**, which involves more than just knowledge of the language. The association of language with cultural norms is obvious if we consider the notion of **politeness** in discourse: the way in which you use language, and body language, is regulated by the same sorts of implicit constraint that affect other social acts. Though there are some universal characteristics, acceptable discourse strategies vary between cultures, over space and over time. As with other social norms, language norms can be seen as restrictive, and violations are tolerated in exceptional circumstances. For instance a talented writer may stretch the bounds of normative use, and language games are the very stuff of comedy.

The term 'koine' refers originally to the common written language used in Hellenistic times as an umbrella for several Greek spoken dialects. Earlier written documents would reproduce local dialects, which were in any case interintelligible, but in the later period, perhaps owing to a sense of Greek cultural unity, there was a tendency to reduce the distinctive dialect characteristics in written texts, to produce a more homogeneous code that overlaid the different spoken codes. It was this tradition that was probably passed on to the Romans.

Language planners sometimes seek similar accommodation between related language varieties, in an attempt to weld together different, sometimes antagonistic, groups into one larger community. A sadly unsuccessful example is that of Serbo-Croat, based on the fusion of the closest of the Serbian and Croatian dialects, which would give a common language to the unified Yugoslav nation. A rather different type of accommodation goes under the name of **pidgin** or *sabir*—a spoken jargon of limited functional use that combines, in a more or less structured way, characteristics of two or more natural languages. The *lingua franca*—'Frankish language'—of the Crusaders was a special type of pidgin, which resulted from the accommodation of different Romance languages one to the other, based mainly on Italian, or Latin, but incorporating common features from French, Occitan, Catalan.

A modern standard language has often similarities to a Greek koine, but is usually associated with the monolingual Nation-State. Until recently it was regarded as axiomatic that to be successful a modern State had to reach a certain threshold size and had to have some internal cultural and linguistic cohesion. European standard languages—like Spanish, French, English—were originally established at the same time as the growth of state power.

In the wake of the French Revolution, nationalist ideology associated common language with independent political status. Italian and German were already established written languages; territorial unification should follow, even though there was substantial variation in the spoken dialects. More recently, national groups, like the Catalans, Galicians, or Occitans, seeking political autonomy, have seen standardization as an important part of their ideological struggle.

I.I2. WHAT HAS TO BE DONE TO STANDARDIZE?

The planning of a standard language involves the processes of: (i) **selection**, (ii) **elaboration** and (iii) **codification**. Let us look at each of these in turn and see how far the French standard can be said to have been planned, and to what effect (cf. Lodge 1993).

Selection

What variety should form the basis of the standard? Should it be an archaic rural variety? This is usually associated with some idea of a Golden Age, when the language was uncorrupted by extraneous elements. It also tends to be purist and xenophobic, associated with racism or, at any rate, Romantic ideas about ethnicity and national identity.

This is the choice made by for instance the new Slavonic Nation-States of the Wilsonian era at the end of the First World War: a problem here is that rural parish-pump varieties may differ from the normal usage of the targeted population. The selection of such varieties is also in conflict with doctrine of threshold size of a viable Nation-State. The European countries whose borders were drawn after the defeat of the Austro-Hungarian and Ottoman empires, like Yugoslavia, Czechoslovakia, or Romania, had to cover the territory of more than one language group, and the subordinated communities came to resent the hegemony of the dominant ones.

Should it be, rather, a modern idiom of an urban centre? This would be seen as progressive and populist, cutting ties with an abhorred past, and so associated with radical ideologies.

This is one of the solutions adopted by Catalan standardizers, who take as a basis the usage of thriving and prosperous Barcelona. The Catalan speakers of Valencia or the Balearics may well resent the choice, even when it is tempered by a degree of tolerance of varieties and a respect for the language of older texts.

More often selection of a variety already used for literature and for administration, however far in the past, is frequent, especially when it has international prestige.

Standard Arabic is an example, as was the *katharevousa* Greek standard, which was only fairly recently abandoned in favour of the more modern demotic.

Of course a single dialect does not have to be selected for standardization. In modern times preference is shown for a koine-ization, or what is called a **polynomic standard** like that adopted for modern Occitan. This tolerates regional variants as equally prestigious and abjures rigid purism.

In sixteenth-century France, in practice, the variety selected for generalization throughout the legal system, to replace Latin, was the King's French. This was a koine based on the language of the educated and independent-minded élite of Paris, at that time the largest town in Europe, with an illustrious university, and a powerful legal sector. I shall discuss the much-quoted 1539 Edict of Villers-Cotterêts in Chapter 2. By the time of the Edict a uniform language variety (a koine) had been used for a century in documents in the relatively highly populated and prosperous northerly regions of France, where spoken varieties were almost certainly interintelligible. In the south, where Occitan was still widely spoken, Latin was most often used in documents, at the beginning of the century. But by the end of the century, French had penetrated to most of the south as a legal language.

What exercised the minds of sixteenth-century theorists was however not so much the language of legal documents but the use of the vernacular for more noble and serious purposes—literature, scholarship, religion. The aim was to displace Latin, which became less commonly used as the century went on, though in 1599 the Sorbonne still insisted that only Latin should be spoken or written within its precincts.

The rule was broken by some royal appointees—like Ramus—at the *Collège des lecteurs royaux*, which eventually, in the nineteenth century, became the *Collège de France*.

The advantage of Latin, in the eyes of the scholars, was that it was not only beautiful, logical, and expressive, but also, in its Humanist pristine, uncorrupted form, unchanging and admitting little variation. It was disciplined and therefore eminently teachable, but, alas, it seemed to be beyond the reach of most, who had neither the inclination nor the stamina required to master it. Printing meant that enlightenment could spread to a wider public, who would operate with French rather than Latin. If French could acquire a degree of fixity then it could rival Latin as an illustrious language.

The sixteenth century was perturbed by the shifting nature of the mother tongue: the increase in availability of written texts, past and present, had heightened consciousness of language change. There was, too, already full awareness of the degree of variation, social and regional, within the spoken language. Charles de Bovelles, a conservative churchman from Picardy, in 1533 so despaired of the possibility of a grammatical and uniform French, that he maintained that only Latin could provide the cohering force required to codify the vernacular. Even those who disagreed would often prefer a Latinizing variant of a colloquial one.

For instance, where personal pronoun subjects were obligatorily used in speech, in writing the older Latin-like non-use persisted, or in negation, the *pas* or *point* which had become mandatory in speech could still be omitted in writing, relying on *ne*, the reflex of Latin NON to convey negative force.

There was inevitably disagreement about the regional variety of French to be promoted. Of the forty-eight writers on language during the century only eight were Parisian, though many were educated in Paris (cf. Demaizières 1983). Sylvius (Dubois) and Ramus (de la Ramée) were Picards (as indeed was Calvin); Tory was from Bourges and Meigret, from Lyons. Some of the most illustrious authors, like Ronsard, sought to incorporate regional features, mainly lexical, into their writings. And the more scholarly eloquence of the Paris lawcourts (the Third Estate *noblesse de robe* or *robins*) was preferred to whimsies of the royal courtiers—the Second Estate *noblesse d'épée*—who usually spurned intellectual and cultural pleasures for more robust entertainment.

It was only, as we have seen, under Louis XIV that the definitive selection of the variety for standardization was made. It was to be exclusively the language of the royal court, a tiny leisured circle, qualified only by noble rank, and no longer exercising any real power or filling any function in society, and now deliberately distancing itself from popular culture. This variety laid claim to purity—absence of vulgarity and pedantism—clarity, sobriety, and distinction. It was this variety that was aped by the prosperous middle classes and was adopted with acclaim by the Revolution as the language of the Nation, and imposed on all by the modern education system.

Was this all planned? Not specifically as far as language itself was concerned, but the shaping of the role of the courtier, with prestige but no power, was part of royal policy to establish centralized rule.

It was also the policy of the Revolution and its aftermath to spread élite culture to the masses, and to promote cultural cohesion within the Nation. What was originally meant to exclude the people, was eventually, with universal education, imposed on the people. Throughout, Rome and its language provided the model for policy.

Elaboration: Normalization or Status Planning

The aim of **normalization** or **status planning** is to fit the language for a wider variety of functions. Usually this involves especially vocabulary enrichment, to increase the 'word power' of the language. But where should neologisms be sought? Should one use older forms, endowing them with new meanings? Should one resort to borrowing from other languages or should one coin new derivations from native sources?

Chapter 4 covers in more detail French lexical changes, including the effects of standardization.

The sixteenth-century writers were particularly keen on extending the range of the vernacular to encompass the whole field of learning and feeling. Borrowings from the older language, from dialects, from foreign languages, especially Italian, and most of all from the classical languages were welcomed. There were admittedly satirical gibes at over-prolific borrowing, but word-play and verbal pyrotechnics and exuberance were the order of the day and a rich vocabulary was seen as essential for French to acquire the status of a high-culture language. So derivation and borrowing were rampant.

Enfin Malherbe vint . . . Fashions changed and the salons and royal court sought to restrict vocabulary, to avoid technicalities, pedantic explicitness, or anything smacking of the vulgarity of sons of toil or of the inkhorn. Archaisms were out, as were new derivatives. The search for the *mot juste* often yielded only vague abstractions and vapid paradoxes. Soon a need was felt for clear definition of, and differentiation between, **synonyms** (cf. 4.8): the impoverishment of the vocabulary acceptable in polite society required an effort to make the most of what was left.

The fashion for slimming down the lexicon could not last through the eighteenth century with new technological and scientific advances, new ideas and opinions, so that neologisms again flooded in. As derivational procedures had withered away through want of use, borrowings from other languages formed the bulk of the new words: only in the twentieth century did purism (cf. Jernudd and Shapiro 1989, Sampson 1993, Thomas 1991) step in to try and stem the tide. Here though the motivation was less linguistic than political, as the French élite dreaded the onslaught of American cultural influence. Romanticism brought a nostalgia for the colourful vocabulary of the pre-Classical period, and again the standard turned to dialects, regional and social, to replenish its word-stock. What has survived from the Classical era is a readiness to cast aside words that have outlived their shelf-life, so that French vocabulary, outside the central core, changes quite rapidly.

How much of this is planned? The deliberations of the Académie on the status of neologisms through the centuries, and the more recent anti-English governmental measures can of course be called 'language planning'. But largely the changes in attitudes towards the language have merely tagged along behind other cultural trends.

Codification: Normativization or Corpus Planning

The aims of **normativization** or **corpus planning** are to provide a theoretical base for understanding of the language, a vocabulary (**metalanguage**) for discourse about language and a yardstick for 'correctness' in language use, to enable efficient teaching of language. A comparison is often made with codification of the law: recall that northern French customary law was codified by the end of the sixteenth century, with the goal of eliminating ambiguities and uncertainties. A comparison can be also made with the contemporary regulation of weights and measures and with coinage, which in the centralized State needed to be standardized.

Language is however not quite in the same category. In this case there are different requirements for mother tongue speakers and for foreigners. The latter require an assimilable set of procedures for understanding and reproducing the variety of language which they will most encounter—in travel, commerce, or scholarship, for instance. The former, on the other hand, acquire their mother tongue without tuition. They require a framework, terminological and theoretical, into which they can fit their own experience of the language, as well as guidance in expanding their own linguistic repertoire beyond their own narrow experience.

Central to this latter aim is the initiation of native speakers to the written code: orthography is thus an important preoccupation of language codifiers in the sixteenth century. This is something to which I devote a separate section (1.14). The dictionary also became an essential tool in codification of vocabulary, often consulted even by native speakers for a ruling on whether an item is properly part of the language and what it signifies. In the seventeenth century began the flow of monolingual dictionaries that was later to become a flood (cf. 4.7). Here I shall concentrate on more purely grammatical works, that attempt to codify morphology and syntax.

The early modern theorists were unfamiliar with the problems of mother tongue teaching, which was always informally acquired by direct contact. French was not normally taught in France until quite late in the period, and then initially often only as an introduction to Latin. It is no surprise that the earliest French grammars were designed for non-native speakers, most especially in England (cf. Kibbee 1991), where French remained a language of high prestige. Even after, in the fourteenth century, it ceased to be used as a normal means of communication within England, it was still much in demand for commercial purposes: the wool trade required familiarity with Picard French varieties, and the wine trade with Gascon. The successes of the Hundred Years War brought a boom in French teaching, as there were rich pickings in the newly conquered territories.

The first grammar written for French consumption was that of Jacques Dubois or Sylvius, who wrote in Latin in 1531.

He was a Picard, son of a weaver, who studied medecine in Montpellier, alongside Rabelais. When he wrote his *Isagωge* in 1531 he was lecturing on medicine at the College de Tricquet in Paris—fantastically successfully it seems, as he had 500 students at his lectures and sold 900 copies of his textbook in a single day.

Sylvius approaches French from the standpoint of Latin, but his grammar is descriptive not prescriptive, taking into account variation. One example, discussed in nearly all the grammars, was the morphology of the *passé simple*, within which -*i* endings could interchange with the -*a*, irrespective of conjugation. Though some writers condemned this as inconsistent, Sylvius recognized it as common usage. Sylvius also claimed superiority for Picard, which he regarded as nearer than central French varieties to Latin.

After 1531 Sylvius did not write again on grammar: he took appointment at the College Royal in 1550, and died aged 77 in 1555.

The Grammar of Louis Meigret in 1545 is more radical than that of Sylvius and is written in French. It provides invaluable evidence about the usage, and especially the pronunciation of mid-sixteenth-century French.

About the author we know little except that he was from Lyons and a professional translator from Latin, and that in his mid-thirties he probably composed his grammar, in French with an innovative spelling system, at the invitation of a publisher.

Meigret's account is descriptive of educated Parisian use, though he was criticized for his Lyonese phonetics. He is forthright about many points disputed by other grammarians: *ne* alone is not used in negation without the addition of *pas* and other like particles; there is no agreement of the past participle with *avoir*; personal pronoun subjects are normally used with the finite verb. He is also reasonably permissive about variants within the language.

Apart from grammars designed for teaching Latin and French conjointly, like those of Robert Estienne, which drew heavily on Meigret, the other important grammar for mother tongue speakers are the two versions by Ramus (Pierre de la Ramée) in 1562 and 1572.

Ramus was the son of a Picard charcoal-burner, who walked to Paris at the age of 8 in search of education. He was driven back home by hunger, but eventually at the age of 12 realized his dream, by becoming the servant of the student Sieur de la Brosse. At 21, in 1536, he gained his Mastership of Arts with an attack on Aristotle that rallied crowds of supporters and opponents to his twenty-four-hour-long viva examination. In 1545 (when there was a plague in Paris and Étienne Dolet was burnt at the stake) he began teaching philosophy and mathematics at the Collège de Presles. He was appointed to the Collège Royal by Henri II in 1551 (2,000 people attended his inaugural lecture), and produced on request a project for reforming the Sorbonne. His iconoclasm did not endear him to the university authorities, brilliant though he was, and matters were not improved by his conversion to Protestantism in 1561. It was round about then that he wrote his three grammars of Latin, Greek, and French—the last of these used a new orthography. Though protected by Catherine de

Medici, he was from time to time on the run from anti-Protestant attacks, though he was denied a teaching post at Geneva because of his views on Aristotle, and also perhaps because he was not an orthodox Calvinist. The second version of his Grammar, mainly in traditional orthography, appeared early in 1572, but in the August St Bartholomew's Massacre, he was ambushed and assaulted at his lodgings in Paris, dragged through the streets, mutilated, beheaded, and thrown in the Seine. His bust today stands in the courtyard of the Collège de France.

Ramus's first Grammar was short and apparently largely copied from Meigret. The second was more original and seems to have been written at the request of the King and the Queen Mother. For him *'le peuple est souverain seigneur de sa langue'*, and the best models of French are to be found not among university scholars, but at the Louvre, the Palais de Justice, the Halles, on the Grève, and the Place Maubert: he makes no mention of his mother tongue, Picard. His grammar is descriptive, not prescriptive—for instance he tolerates the common forms *je dirons* etc., which some condemned as vulgar, and, unlike Meigret, advocates agreement of the past participle with *avoir*, according to the rules drawn up by Marot, because it had entered usage.

I have dwelled on the sixteenth-century grammars, to stress that they were more in the nature of descriptive linguistic works than prescriptive grammars (cf. Trudeau 1992). At the time there was more emphasis in literate circles on eloquence than on correctness. It was in the seventeenth century that prescriptive grammars were composed—though again at first mainly for foreigners. The fashionable language arbiters—like Malherbe, Vaugelas, Bouhours—preferred informal remarks about language, criticizing inelegant or archaic usage, but not laying down the law. Language was treated like etiquette—Vaugelas's 1645 *Remarques* can be likened to a courtesy book, guiding the unskilled to imitation of the behaviour of the best people. The *noblesse d'épée*, their swords now laid aside for the silk handkerchief, were allegedly the models for this behaviour—but some of them also presumably needed lessons in polished behaviour and speech, when they first came to Paris from their country estates. Not only the *noblesse de robe*, but also the prosperous unschooled merchant classes, like Molière's *Bourgeois Gentilhomme*, were customers for the services provided by tone-setting writers on language. But this was hardly the sort of codification that modern language planners have in mind. Like other fashions, modish language changed to stay ahead of the mob, and constant vigilance—being 'where it's all happening'—was necessary to keep up with the smart set (from whose company most of the population was excluded). Even though Vaugelas and Bouhours claimed only to record *bon usage,* they sometimes cheated and introduced extraneous criteria.

For instance Vaugelas, while admitting that noble ladies can reply '*Je la suis*', to the question *Êtes-vous contente?*, advises that it is wiser not to imitate them, as the pronoun in this context substitutes for an adjective, not a noun, and should therefore have the 'neuter' form *le* (cf. Ayres-Bennett 1987).

Codification of French really gets going in the eighteenth century, with the 1660 *Grammaire de Port-Royal* providing the first model of 'rational' General Grammar, rather than the 'reasonable' tradition of 'Language as Polite Behaviour', which was most prevalent in the seventeenth century. Ideas about Language Universals and General Grammar had of course been around for a long time, but only in the eighteenth century did they cut free from the biblical traditions of Adamic language and the Tower of Babel.

Many of the grammatical rules which we learn at school today were first fully formulated in the eighteenth century, when some already felt that French, having reached its peak in the Sun King's reign, must now be preserved from decline. But in formulating rules, attention was always paid to the role of reason and logic, and not only to capricious usage. The important contributions in linguistics were to theory, and such issues as language origins and the relationship between language and thought.

The Revolution embraced the codified language wholeheartedly, associating correct language with morality, good citizenship, and law-abiding behaviour: an *Arreté de Police* in 1799 during the Consulate, regulating signs, billboards, and public notices, exhorts Parisians to reform and correct anything '*contraire aux lois, aux mœurs et aux règles de la langue française*'.

The school textbook chosen, in a competition during the Revolutionary period, for use in all communes, was the French part of Llomond's 1780 pedestrian Latin and French grammar, written in the General Grammar style, but concentrating on morphological paradigms. The tradition followed in the nineteenth century with Noël and Chapsal's 1823 school grammar. Even though the

Romantics complained about the straitjacket of codified language, their protests related to vocabulary and not to grammar: revolt against syntax came later and culminated in Roland Barthes's accusation of Fascism levelled against the legitimate language.

During the nineteenth and twentieth centuries, what had been an élite language in its written form was taught to every Tom, Dick, and Harry in the school system: we shall discuss schooling as acculturation, and the pre-eminent role of French language in schooling in 2.4. It was after the introduction of compulsory schooling that the rigid codification that we are familiar with now really took over: the prime role of orthography will be discussed below.

The demands of national examinations required rulings on what was to be regarded as correct. The Education Ministry issued in 1901, and reaffirmed in 1910, a circular decreeing that in examination scripts certain common variants were to be 'tolerated', although still viewed as 'mistakes'. But alas examiners remained intolerant. In the early twentieth century school grammar moved away from the General Grammar tradition to a more positivist part-of-speech grammar: there was comparatively little attempt to explain French constructions in terms of universal semantics, and more description of the mechanisms of grammar, formulated as arbitrary rules. Grammatical terminology was officially unified in 1910 (and revised in 1949 and 1975). It is based mainly on formal criteria, compared with the more semantic bias of General Grammar. The rather rigid part-of-speech codification presents some difficulties in explaining actual usage.

An example—for purists *orange* is classified as a noun, and therefore not subject to agreement when it qualifies another noun, even though it acts like an adjective. They advise avoidance of the quandary of whether or not to add an *s* in a commonplace construction like *les robes orange(s)* by substituting the less natural *les robes couleur orange*.

Distinction (cf. Bourdieu 1977) in modern language use is often associated with pedantic attention to grammatical niceties of this sort or with manipulation of the language as an art-form, rather than as a means of communication of thought. 'Alternative' languages have also made their appearance in modern spoken and written use: we shall discuss popular forms in 2.11.

1.13. WAS FRENCH STANDARDIZATION PLANNED?

Standardization in France was not properly speaking **planned**, although the spread of the standard language (cf. 2.15–19) was originally part of the Revolutionary 'One Nation' ideology. The unification of administrative language was part of a general policy of centralization that began in the sixteenth century, reaching its peak under Louis XIV, and taken over by Republican and Imperial regimes. Codification was originally more a result of the intellectual conviction that language should be 'rational' and preserved from the decadence brought about by unbridled change. Universal education, with its emphasis on the primacy of the written language and of acculturation, brought the imposition of the legitimate code, but sparked off the protest of alternative codes.

But let us return to a fundamental question that we have addressed only obliquely, first in general terms and then specifically in relation to modern French.

1.14. WHY HAVE A STANDARD?

I summarize the possible answers to this question.

1. A standard language enables intercommunication within a population larger than usual linguistic community. Usually it serves as an umbrella for a number of communities with common aspirations, usually related languages.

2. It also serves the needs of popular education, in teaching the written language. In order to facilitate learning, the written code should be approximated to mother tongue usage. Codification of orthography is a linchpin.

3. It is an emblem of ethnic identity, strengthening the bonds between communities that share a common language.

4. The standard can be a means of control. Legitimate language is used in legislation and administration. It can serve an authoritarian regime, by distancing the prestige code from the language of the populace. It can also have a democratic purpose—by encouraging the populace to adopt the same code, in which opinions can be cogently expressed in free discussion, or by tolerating variation

within the code, without stigmatizing some variants as socially unprestigious.

5. A standard language can facilitate trade and mobility within bounds of the linguistic community (in preference to interstate exchange).

6. It can serve as a prestige symbol, for instance, in literature or diplomacy. It can also ensure a wider audience for language-based products (books, newspapers, and, in modern times, broadcasting).

How far did these considerations carry weight in the standardization of French? Let us first of all put aside answer (5), which did not really have significant effect in France before the nineteenth century. Even through the eighteenth century internal customs barriers persisted within France.

In the sixteenth century it would take a month to travel from the north to the south of what became France: even in 1780, with improved roads and transport, it took eight days (contrast the TGV or the aeroplane today). East to west took nearly as long. Trade across the borders still remained more important, and *France Profonde* remained buried in isolation.

Certainly answer (4) points to an important factor in French standardization. Under the *ancien régime*, the written code became a major means of bureaucratic authoritarian domination, with increase in the need for documentation: under François I, great strides were made in this direction, until under Louis XIV very little escaped governmental control. There was also awareness of the role of the press and of the written and spoken discourse in forming opinion and raising consciousness.

Revolutionary ideology, although preaching tolerance in other spheres, was illiberal in its approach to language. It made great play of the power of the Word, and saw unification of the language as a means of instilling loyalty and encouraging participation in the affairs of State.

It was the Revolutionary ideology that pursued aims (1) and (2), which under the *ancien régime* would have been counter-productive, as damaging the distinctions of rank and privilege on which the social fabric depended.

One of the disastrous mistakes made by the Bourbons was to bar the prosperous and educated middle-classes—especially the *noblesse de robe*—from prestigious society and to reinforce their identity with the under-privileged Third Estate.

A major motivation for standardization in modern times has, however, been that mentioned in (3)—as an emblem of ethnic identity. It was French ideology, first enunciated by Herder but developed by Rousseau, that promoted the idea of identity of language and nation (cf. B. Andersen 1991, Balibar and Laporte 1974, Dann and Dinwiddy 1988, Gellner 1983, Gordon 1978, Guilhaumou 1989, Hobsbawn 1990, Siccardo 1984). Nineteenth-century xenophobic nationalism, still, alas, rampant today, became associated with language purism (cf. Jernudd and Shapiro 1989, O. Smith 1984, Thomas 1991).

To its credit, modern France has never officially espoused this illiberal ideology, although the strictures against *franglais* have tended that way. France has however always insisted that Frenchness is not a question of genetics, but of cultural allegiance—hence the promotion of modern *Francophonie*. The French language is seen as a kingpin in French culture, with its emphasis on eloquence and articulate lucidity.

But it was aim (6)—language as a prestige symbol—that was, from the sixteenth and seventeenth centuries, the main motivation for seeking a standardized vernacular. Given that French already had international prestige for literary and diplomatic purposes, why were there moves to 'illustrate' it in the seventeenth century, so as to extend its range to serious, philosophical discourse? Why not continue to use the now purged Latin for such purposes, rather than seek to refine the vernacular?

Remember that the very 'Defenders and Illustrators' were themselves skilled Latinists: Du Bellay said that French was like a spouse, but Latin was like a mistress to him (presumably the former comfortable and everyday, but the latter exciting and inspiring).

Perhaps a parallel with modern standardization will help to explain: usually linguistic nationalists fear extinction of their mother tongue, owing to shift to, or incursion from, a rival and dominant language. Standardization is seen as a way of resisting language death: in this perspective **diglossia**—where the mother tongue is used only as a Low language, with a dominant idiom acting as a High language—is particular anathema. Early sixteenth-century France was still diglossic, though moves were being made to limit the role of Latin in administration. But it was not Latin, more and more the domain of the élite, that posed a threat to French.

Humanism had, in any case, revived also Greek, regarded as superior even to Latin.

It was not surprising that French apologists emphasized the 'conformity' of French with Greek, and the Trojan-Greek origins of the Gauls.

More of a threat, though, was Italian: the *questione della lingua* exercised the minds of Italian Renaissance writers, and in 1525 Cardinal Bembo's influential treatise on Italian *Prosa dalla volgar lingua* appeared. Du Bellay's 1549 *Defense et illustration . . .* was little more that a confused and self-contradictory imitation of Sperone Speroni's 1542 imaginary dialogue, on the same theme in Italian, between Bembo and one Lazaro, a defender of Latin. The French court, especially during the time of Catherine de Medici, was thoroughly Italianized, much to the disgust of the middle classes, especially the Protestants. The whole ethic of court behaviour was modelled on the advice of Castiglione (1478–1529), just as Machiavelli (1469–1527) influenced political behaviour. The 1582 Florentine Accademia della Crusca was the model for the 1635 Académie Française.

French had to get its act together if it was to resist the growing prestige of Italian: even in England, where French was traditionally the prestige language and was still the language of law, Italian began to be popular as a second language in the sixteenth century.

Note that Huguenot refugees from France, and Italians fleeing the Inquisition formed the bulk of language teachers in the later sixteenth century.

There is one more reason that the sixteenth-century scholarly élite wished to promote French, rather than their beloved Latin—a reason which did not find an echo in seventeenth-century apologists. It was to spread the truth and the benefits of learning to a wider range of the populace, who now could be reached via the printed word. The Evangelicals, and especially the Protestants, saw the use of French as a means to bring enlightenment to all. Even the strongly Catholic, but Gallican, Parlement de Paris promoted the art of eloquence in the vernacular. The Jesuits, of whom the French were initially suspicious, eventually also saw their opportunity to gain influence in powerful circles, by using French rather than Latin, and the Jansenists were among the first to introduce the study of French into their schools (note that the tone-setting Port-

Royal Grammar was Jansenist). The use of language in persuasion, not to say propaganda, was fully appreciated, and pamphlets, and chapbooks, were used by the élite to influence the thoughts of the growing literate public, for whom Latin remained an alien language.

1.15. ORTHOGRAPHICAL REFORM

The propagandist uses of language and the promotion of literacy especially favour the standardization of spelling practice, though it was only with the establishment of popular education through schooling that 'good' spelling took on the almost moral overtones that it has today. In this section we shall look principally at the efforts made to reform French orthography in the modern period, and at their outcome.

French spelling, like Topsy, 'just growed'. Traditional accounts of the history of French spelling (e.g. Beaulieux 1927) claim that initially scribes made creative use of Latin letters to represent the phonetic (or phonemic?) shape of the word. Therefore it is assumed that in about the twelfth century there was some sort of regular correspondence between graphy and sound. However, there is some doubt about how far the representation of the so-called Old French dialects merely reflects the tradition of different scriptoria, rather than differences of pronunciation.

All goes awry in the fourteenth century when the growing bureaucratic requirement for written documents spawned numbers of practitioners, who learned to write in Latin, but whose knowledge of that language was limited. Latin and French continued to be used; spoken French proceedings were transcribed as well as may be into Latin, which often was little more than a transliteration of the French. When French was written, its spelling was heavily Latinized.

The Renaissance purification of Latin, including its spelling and pronunciation, was mirrored by similar attempts to tidy up written French and bring it more closely into line with the spoken language. In the sixteenth century the new needs of printing necessitated some serious consideration of standardization of written form: though compositors' practice differed little from that of scribes, even in the liberal use of abbreviations, the printers were often Humanist scholars who sought a rational and aesthetic system of representation.

They were however hampered by technological constraints—having laboriously to fashion fonts by hand with artisanal metalwork methods.

It is often said that the chance for substantial reform in the sixteenth century was scuttled by compositors and copy-editors, but in fact many of the reforms that did catch on were initiated by printers. The conservativism of the Académie is said to have held back even pusillanimous reforms, but we should remember that the august body has always regarded itself as a mere vehicle for *bon usage*, and opinions within it were usually as divided as among the public at large.

There has never been a time in modern France when there have not been movements for spelling reform: these have been particularly vociferous in the last hundred years, when linguists and educationalists have fulminated against the irrationalities of the spelling system. In modern times spelling reform usually aims at simplifying the process of learning to read and write. It is taken for granted that it is easier for mother tongue speakers to cope with some transparent iconic and coherent system of transcribing speech sounds into corresponding alphabetic signs: once the general principles are grasped, then the pupil can compose and construe without having to master a host of exceptional and anomalous forms. Nowadays no one doubts that universal literacy is a desirable and indeed an essential aim, so one would expect all to be in favour of a rational spelling system.

Those traditionalists who shrink from reform of orthography will usually insist on the need for uniformity and continuity, and even sometimes on the requirement of discipline in the learning process, which can be enhanced by having to memorize arbitrary spellings. They may maintain that the written code does not directly map on to the spoken and that, for instance, the orthographical word can represent a morphophonological unit rather than a sequence of phonological units. For instance, *peau* and *pot*, *selle* and *cèle* are distinguished in writing but not in pronunciation, easing the task of the reader, at the expense of the writer.

Opponents of reform may also stress the importance of having an orthographical system that is not directly linked to pronunciation subject to individual, social, and regional variation. Uniform spelling is regarded as a crucial part of language planning, making possible economic provision of printed material for speakers of related language varieties.

This latter consideration was of some importance in sixteenth-century France, but since the acceptance of a standard form of French, it has played, until recently, no part in discussion. Some of the spelling changes accepted by authority since the early sixteenth century are linked to standard pronunciation. The use of diacritical accents, for instance, distinguishes, though not wholly consistently, *é* [e], *è* [ɛ] and *e* [ə]: in word-final position *é* was usual from the sixteenth century, but *è* did not gain admission to the Académie dictionary until 1762 (when *mére* is shown as different from *père*). In the same edition the circumflex replaced *s* as a marker of vowel length (e.g. *même* for *mesme*). The use of the cedilla (*ç* for [s])—a compromise between etymological and phonetic spelling—is one of the earliest diacritics used: its availability as a font for Spanish texts allowed the printer Geoffroy Tory to introduce it into French in 1529.

Other changes aim at a degree of consistency—like the partial abandonment of anomalous spellings with *y*, *z*, and *x*, simplification of double consonants and omission of silent etymological letters. However there has been resistance to such changes, especially when they mask the links of French with Latin. Indeed the 1835 Académie dictionary, just when spelling began to play a key role in primary education, actually retreated from some previous reforms, and laid emphasis on historical linguistic legacy.

Nowadays discouragement of use of diacritics and out-of-the-way typographical features may ensue from considerations of economy and efficiency. Thus, for instance, the timid 1990 recommendations of the *Conseil Supérieur de la langue française*, approved by the Académie Française, advocated the non-use of circumflex accents on *i* and *u*, except to distinguish homonyms, the non-use of hyphens in some compound words, as well as some regularization in the use of diacritic accents. The diacritics seem to be an arbitrary pitfall in the acquisition of the writing skills, and in examinations. Helpful though it may be to foreigners learning to read French that [e], [ɛ], and *e instable* be distinguished graphically, there is little gain for those native speakers for whom they are mainly positional variants. Conversely few speakers today distinguish long from short vowels, so that the graphical distinction between *pâte* and *patte*, or *bête* and *bette* is not reflected in pronunciation.

But the modern French schooling system places great emphasis on the acquisition of spelling, especially as it plays a role in marking grammatical relationships, like agreement, often unmarked in the spoken code. The mismatch between spelling and pronunciation appears more important as the use of 'correct grammatical' French depends largely on spelling: for instance *aimé, aimées, aimer, aimez* ([ɛme]) or *aime, aimes, aiment* ([ɛm]) are distinguished today only in writing and not in speech. Radical educationalists believe that setting so much store in schooling on the grammar of the written code unnecessarily burdens pupils and hampers their linguistic creativity. One way of lessening the strain would be by reducing the degree of arbitrariness in spelling, by comparison with spoken usage.

We should be careful not to ascribe to earlier periods these modern preoccupations. Spelling reformers in the French Renaissance period, when only about 20 per cent of the population was literate, were not concerned with the problems of universal education. Recall that even a (later) progressive like Voltaire thought that the majority of children should not be taught to read and write. In so far as the highly educated élite wished to spread literacy, it was to facilitate reading, rather than writing, which they saw as their own prerogative. Of course, the expansion in the reading public, following the introduction of printing, increased their own influence. This was particularly significant in the religious sphere: many of the sixteenth-century reformers were Protestants who sought to spread the truth, whose pamphleteering activities were quickly countered by their opponents. By the middle of the seventeenth century, with a huge increase in literacy among the urban population, the subversive political pamphlets called *mazarinades* were produced at an astounding rate (some 5,000 different ones were sold in the streets for about the same price as a quarter of a pound of bread). Something approaching modern newspapers came on the scene, in the later seventeenth century, though state censorship limited their scope. The power of the press to mould public opinion was already appreciated at the time: but it was the élite who did the writing, while the public did the reading. Even then those who could read were often familiar with only one sort of notation: for instance, there is evidence that some could read print, but not handwriting, and it seems that Gothic print was for long more popular than other fonts.

How far pressures for uniformity and tradition in spelling came from the commercial requirements of printers is not wholly clear: they seem to have been fairly tolerant in this respect and the early compositors were as flexible as their predecessors, the manuscript copyists (though of course the end-product of their work would be about 1,000 copies, compared with the copyist's single manuscript, and so would exert greater influence). It has, however, been shown that early printed versions do not always mirror the spelling of the original manuscript on which they are based.

More important, perhaps, for sixteenth-century reformers, was the model of Latin. Erasmus advocated changes in the pronunciation of Latin that would make it match more exactly the sequence of letters: it was assumed that this was the way Latin was originally pronounced, and that there had been over time a falling away from Golden Age practice. In a similar way, it was thought that French spelling should iconically represent pronunciation. The distinction between sound and letter was not consistently made until the later nineteenth century, and the concept of **phonemic** spelling did not arrive until the twentieth century.

Remember that in the sixteenth century, and indeed still the seventeenth century, France still had very much an oral culture, and there was very little sense that the written code should be divorced from the oral. Only in the sixteenth century did the habit of silent reading grow up. In Peletier's *Dialogue*, he ascribes to de Bèze the statement: '*Ie puis lire un Liure tout antier, sans an prononcer un seul mot*', 'I can read a whole book without pronouncing a single word of it': but it was probably still true that reading aloud was the usual custom, and so the idea of spelling for the eye, rather than for the ear, was not current, as it is today in the era of rapid-reading techniques.

However the sixteenth century recognized the disadvantages of **phonetic** spelling at a time when pronunciation was so variable: the 'broad transcription', or **phonemic**, method was not yet discovered. Another problem was that at the time the sense-unit, the **word**, received no individual accentuation and had variable pronunciation according to its position within the **rhythmic group**. Thus, following the phonetic principle, it should be spelt differently: for instance *six*, still today pronounced [si], [siz] or [sis], would have three different spellings.

Nevertheless, what animated the Renaissance reformers, more than practical considerations, was an ideological preoccupation with 'truth': writing should be in Pasquier's words '*la vraye image du parler*'. Here, as elsewhere, humans should aim at the exercise of virtue and reason, and seek to extirpate falsity. Accurate spelling was a moral question.

Still, until the nineteenth century, people continued to write much as they liked, without it apparently causing much confusion. The insistence on 'correct spelling' is usually thought to spring from Guizot's education legislation under Louis-Philippe. Then the primary-school education system laid emphasis on the teaching of French and on writing as well as on reading. But, although *dictées* became a central part of teaching methodology, there is no specific reference in any of the official acts to spelling. Yet when state examinations were established, correct spelling was one of the most important criteria for success. So it was the *maître d'école* and not the *Académicien* who called the odds.

A powerful movement for reform had some limited success at the outset of the twentieth century, but distinguished French linguists between the wars achieved little advance. In the 1970s and 1980s governmental support was forthcoming for reforms adumbrated by leading academic figures. Some minor reforms were eventually approved, but by the close of the latest debate in 1991, the right-wing press had succeeded in putting a virtual stop to the proposals. Thus French spelling has changed comparatively little in the last two hundred years.

FURTHER READING

On France: Beaune 1985, Braudel 1985, Chaunu 1982, Le Bras and Todd 1981, Planhol 1988; an excellent collection of linguistic maps for all the French-speaking areas is provided by Rossillon 1995.

On history and language: Burke 1978, 1993, Burke and Porter 1987, Corfield 1991, Lönne 1995, Wolff 1982[2].

On periodization: G. Eckert 1990.

On Vulgar Latin: Grandgent 1908, Herman 1975, Lloyd 1979, Posner 1996, Väänänen 1981, Wright 1982, 1991.

On Old French: Allières 1982, Batany 1982, Cerquiglini 1981, 1991, Hilty 1968, 1973, Kibbee 1991, Lusignan 1987, Moignet 1973, Pfister 1973, Skårup 1975, Zink 1987.

On Middle French: Marchello-Nizia 1979, R. Martin 1978, Martin and Wilmet 1980, Rickard 1976, Zink 1990.

On Renaissance French: Cator and Cave 1984, Fumaroli 1980, Gougenheim 1974, Huchon 1988, Kesselring 1981, Kibbee (1990), Matoré 1988, S.-G. Neumann 1981, Rickard 1968, Rosset 1911, Swiggers and van Hoecke 1989, Waswo 1987.

On seventeenth-century French: (for a commented bibliography of grammatical works) Swiggers 1984; also Ayres-Bennett 1987, Boysen 1973, Dumonceaux 1975, Haase 1888, Radtke 1994, Rickard 1992, Sancier-Chateau 1993, Spillebout 1985.

On eighteenth-century French: A. François 1905, Lodge 1995, Rickard 1981, Séguin 1972.

On nineteenth-century French: Antoine and Martin 1985, Brunot 1899, Saint-Gérand 1993.

On twentieth-century French: Battye and Hintze 1992, Dauzat 1935, Désirat and Hordé 1983, Gadet 1989, Lodge *et al.* 1997, Martinet 1969*a*, Müller 1985, Spence 1996.

On French creoles: for bibliography, M.-C. Hazaël-Massieux 1991; also Arends *et al.* 1995, Bollée 1977*a*, *b*, Carayol 1977, Chaudenson 1979, Dalphinis 1985, D'Ans 1968, 1987, Green 1988, Gueunier 1985, G. Hazaël-Massieux and Robillard 1993, Kreigel 1996, Ludwig 1996, 1989, Manessy 1988, Morgan 1959, 1960, 1976, Valdman 1978*b*, 1992.

On standardization: Balibar 1985, Balibar and Laporte 1974, Bartsch 1987, Baum 1987, Bédard and Maurais 1983, Cooper 1990, Fodor and Hagège 1983–4, Gordon 1978, Grillo 1989, Gruenais 1986, Jernudd and Shapiro 1989, Joseph 1987, Joseph and Taylor 1990, Knecht and Marzys 1993, Lodge 1993, Marcellesi 1986, Maurais 1987, Milroy and Milroy 1985, Posner and Green 1980–93 (vol. 5 1993), Sampson 1993, Scaglione 1984, Thomas 1991, L. Wolf 1983.

On orthography: Baddeley 1993, Beaulieux 1927, Blanche-Benveniste and Chervel 1978, Branca-Rosoff *et al.* 1989, Catach 1968, 1988*a*, 1988*b*, 1989, 1993, Catach *et al.* 1976– , Citton and Wyss 1989, M. Keller 1991, Laparra 1991, Leconte and Cibois 1989, *Le Français Moderne* 44, 1976 (*L'orthographe et l'histoire*), Martinet 1969*b*, Meisenburg 1996, *Rapport général . . .* 1965.

2

Sociolinguistic History of French

2.1. SOCIAL HISTORY AND LANGUAGE, OR SOCIOLINGUISTIC HISTORY?

Language must play an important role in social history: many historical works introduce linguistic evidence, especially concerning lexicon, to illustrate changes in social attitudes and institutions. The other side of the coin is that cultural changes can be more or less directly reflected in language change. Indeed it can be claimed that all language change, as distinct perhaps from linguistic change, must be triggered by changes in the community in which the language is spoken.

Most often, accepted wisdom associates language change with **language contact**—the impact of an alien language, whether that of the conqueror or the trader. Thus, the conquest of Gaul imposed a form of Latin on the vanquished people, but it is claimed that the Celtic **substratum** then so distorted the Latin spoken in Gaul that a new language, Gallo-Roman, emerged. Similarly it is postulated that the Frankish conquerors, in adopting Gallo-Roman, brought to it features from their native tongue and so created French. Such contact usually however induces **language shift** rather than change: this is a question I shall return to below.

First, however, I should like to look at some of the ways in which language and social change have interacted in the modern period, for which our knowledge of the social set-up is much more profound than for the early period of French language history. I shall then return to a consideration of the relationship of socio-linguistic variation and language change, and to the way French spread through France and to overseas territories, changing as it went. But we should bear in mind that even amidst change there was a degree of stability and continuity in both the language and culture.

2.2. POPULAR CULTURE AND LANGUAGE

One change at the beginning of the modern period appears to have been related to participation in popular culture. It is a commonplace that in the Middle Ages cultural and linguistic division tended to be vertical rather than horizontal—for instance, different social classes would use the same regional language varieties and differentiation in their usage would be stylistic rather than linguistic. Burke (1978) maintains that until the sixteenth century the upper classes were bicultural, participating in the popular culture of folk dance and music, riotous carnival, fantastic tales of magic, witchcraft and fabulous beasts, filthy farce, mystery plays and so on— what he calls 'little culture', as well as the more prestigious and less accessible 'big culture' which was the prerogative of the privileged classes. A linguistic parallel can be drawn with **diglossia**, with a universal High language (Latin) actively available only to the privileged, but a localized Low language (the vernacular) used by all. By the seventeenth century popular culture was stigmatized, associated with pagan, uncivilized behaviour: the upper classes sought to distinguish themselves from the vulgar in language as well as in their deportment. *La nostalgie de la boue* certainly continued in practice, but surfaced in theory only in the nineteenth century. With the final disappearance of feudal authority and of the functional differentiation of the Three Estates, *distinction* (Bourdieu 1977) was sought by the forsaking of 'little culture' and of popular language by the upper classes and those who sought to emulate them.

Thus language variants came to be associated with social class rather than with regional origin. In the early seventeenth century the upsurge of literacy enhanced the already considerable class antagonism of the urban population. The rural population was burdened more and more by the taxation that fuelled military adventures and the luxurious life-style of the upper classes: peasant revolts were frequent but brutally repressed.

A consequence for language development was the differentiation between standard and non-standard French. It is usually assumed that the latter evolved rapidly, whereas the former, when codified, remained more or less fixed. However, there is some evidence that so-called 'popular French' (cf. below) probably came into being in the seventeenth century, and that the last three centuries have witnessed fairly stable variation.

Though it was the élite language that was promoted by the Revolution, there were attempts to alter some 'flagship' usages associated with social distinction. One good example is the use of titles and of *tu* and *vous*. During the Reign of Terror the use of *vous* in the singular was viewed as illogical and divisive and *tu* was made obligatory, in tune with the use of *citoyen* as a form of address. Clearly this directive did not outlive the age, but note that even today the use of *tu* is still associated with democratic politics and has increased substantially in modern times (cf. also 3.16).

2.3. URBANIZATION AND (DE)PROLETARIANIZATION

One social change that has certainly had an effect on language in France has been the reduction of the agricultural sector over the centuries, but particularly rapidly since the Second World War, so that only about 5 per cent of the active population is engaged in agricultural activity, whereas in the sixteenth century it was probably about 80 per cent.

The turning-point came in the 1880s when industrial workers slightly outnumbered agricultural labourers.

The decline of agriculture, combined with slow demographic increase over most of the modern period (which was particularly acute in some rural areas), can help to account for the demise of regional dialects (cf. 2.15).

With regard to so-called 'popular French', once seen as the domain of the industrial working class, we should note that the industrial sector was never overwhelmingly large in France and that it has always employed a good proportion of recent immigrants. The northern industrial areas were also badly hit by the First World War devastation and never fully recovered. In the last two decades the 'blue-collar' working-class population, as in other Western countries, is little more than a quarter of the total population, whereas 'white-collar' employees of various sorts are by far the most numerous. The embourgeoisification or deproletarianization of the work-force has, however, been paradoxically accompanied by an expansion in the use of 'popular' streetwise idiom through a wider range of the population (cf. 2.10).

2.4. MASS LITERACY

Literacy among the mass of the population clearly has linguistic consequences, especially in unifying usage. Its role as an instrument of the state was emphasized by Revolutionary ideology. In 1790 (4 November) the newspaper *Feuille villageoise* wrote: '*Pourquoi les droits de l'Homme ont-ils été si tard connus? Parce que le peuple ne savait pas lire, il ne pouvait pas s'instruire par lui-même et il se laissait séduire par les autres.*' However, literacy was quite general in the north and in towns before the Revolution (though there was a significant difference between men and women until the turn of the twentieth century). One might indeed ask whether the Revolution would have been possible without widespread literacy. But research into the history of the spread of literacy (cf. Furet and Ouzof 1977) reveals a wide discrepancy between the north and the south, with a wider gulf between the social classes in the latter. The illiteracy of conscripts gave cause for concern and in the 1830s *écoles régimentaires* were set up to remedy this. Yet in 1848 when universal male suffrage was instituted, 37 per cent of the electorate still declared themselves as illiterate. By the 1850s illiteracy was a source of shame: education was now more clearly seen as a means of social advancement and of proletarian power.

All the same, the spread of French to the south probably owed more to the diffusion in the sixteenth century of the printed word from Lyons among southern notables and to the use of French in the Protestant religion, than to the Villers-Cotterêts decree (cf. 2.15). In some Catholic regions, like Brittany, reading, but not writing, was encouraged under the *ancien régime*: *curés* wanted parishioners to read missals, but feared that writing might be used as a tool for social independence.

2.5. SCHOOLING

The importance of schooling—a potent means of social control—was paramount in the imposition of a language standard. Compulsory schooling in French very nearly hammered the nail in the coffin of regional languages. Radical educationalists today fulminate against the role of language in French education. The fostering of what Balibar (1974) calls *les français fictifs*, with emphasis on written language and especially on spelling, is seen as a prime cause of the linguistic insecurity that besets so many Frenchmen (cf. Gueunier *et al.* 1978).

Under the *ancien régime* schools were almost wholly under religious jurisdiction. The Jesuits established prestigious Colleges, and the Jansenists had their *Petites Écoles*. In 1714 the decree that parents must send children to (fee-paying) schools was directed principally against the Protestants, who had always encouraged literacy; in Strasburg, for instance, Catholics were forbidden to send children to Lutheran schools.

The following gives a summary of the important events in the development of schooling from the mid-eighteenth century to the fall of France in 1940.

1747	*Concours général* initiated.
1766	*Agrégation* initiated.
1792	Condorcet's proposals for state education.
1794	*Grandes Écoles* established.
1800	(Year VIII) secularization of education.
1802	(Year X) Law on education—restoration of Latin. *Lycées* from 12 yrs (with military training).
1808	Establishment of the *Université*. *Baccalauréat, licence, doctorat. École normale.* Primary and women's education mainly in hands of Church.
1816	Decree—school in every commune, free for those who could not pay. By 1820 24,000 (/ 44.000) communes with schools.
1824	Primary-school teachers appointed by episcopate.
1833	Guizot's education laws. *Écoles normales primaires* in each department. Secondary schools in all towns above 6,000 inhabitants. Reading and writing to be taught simultaneously.
1844	Concessions to the Church on education.
1847	Science teaching in *lycées*.
1850	*Loi Falloux* on education. Prefects given right to appoint and dismiss primary teachers. Religious orders could open secondary schools without qualifications.
1862	First woman to take *baccalauréat*.
1865	Education reforms of Duruy. Increased number of state schools, reduced fees. Changes in syllabus. Secular education for girls.
1872	Jules Simon's attempts at modernization of education, frustrated by Church.
1879–82	Education reforms of Ferry. Secularization of *Conseil Supérieur de l'Instruction Publique*. Only state schools could award diplomas etc. *Lycées* for girls. *Écoles normales* for women.

Religious instruction excluded from state schools. Primary education (6–13) obligatory and free.

1883   *Alliance française* founded.
1905   Separation of Church and State.
1940   Vichy government under Pétain. *Écoles normales* abolished. Religious instruction restored.

It was only from 1816 that schools, for boys only, were established in every commune, without fees for the poor. Until 1850 early tuition in reading was of Latin (as many Frenchmen at the time were not mother tongue French speakers, that may not be so bad as it appears). Rote learning was the rule (recall Julien Sorel's feats of memory in Stendhal's *Le Rouge et le noir*). Some pupils were taught to read, but not to write, which in any case consisted mainly in copying out the Bible and legal documents.

Slates were introduced only after Restoration—before that letters were traced in sand trays—and paper was still expensive. Besides, writing was done with quills, with all their attendant disadvantages, until 1830, when metal pens came into use.

Primary-school classes covered all ages (in rural areas especially in the winter, when less labour was required in the fields)—even in 1850 there were up to 100 pupils in a class. At first the often peripatetic teachers, under the control of the local *curé*, were lowly paid, without qualifications. In 1816 a *Brevet de capacité* was initiated and in 1833, with the Guizot reforms, a minimum pay-rate was established. (Note that in 1846 75 per cent of primary teachers were the sons of peasants.)

In spite of the Guizot laws, in 1865, Duruy, minister under Napoleon III, found that 16.4 per cent of children leaving school could not read or write (only 1.2 per cent in Bas Rhin, but 41.2 per cent in the Landes): it was at this stage that girls were admitted to school.

It was only after the Third Republic Ferry reforms in 1879–82 that compulsory universal schooling came into being, with imposition of a uniform French language on all. Use of regional dialects, even in the playground, was harshly punished, but sociolinguistic variation was not eliminated by the efforts of the schools.

2.6. Sociolinguistic Variation

Sociolinguistics is concerned with linguistic variation that is associated with the social rating of speakers: age, sex, socioeconomic rank, educational status, and geographical origin are the variables that are taken into account. Also to be considered are less overtly social criteria like register and style, which relate more to textual characteristics than to speaker status. Historical sociolinguistics, in its turn, can be said to be concerned with the relationship of variation and linguistic change (cf. Romaine 1982).

No one has ever denied that, in actual use of language, there is great variation among different speakers and among groups of speakers. In the past, however, and, by some, even now, it has been questioned whether the variants form part of the same language, or even of **language**, as such. The variants would be labelled as 'mistakes', as 'vulgarisms', as 'barbarisms'. Where there was a cluster of variants, shared by an identifiable group of speakers, there would be talk of *jargon* or patois. How great the differences would have to be for classification as 'another language' is rarely specified. **Language** is, as we have seen, a name often reserved only for the standard or a norm, usually written, that is recognized as a community emblem by a discrete group usually geographically, or ethnically, defined.

How **variation** relates to **change** is not wholly clear, although there is little doubt about how it relates to **shift**—that is, the switch that an individual or community can make in choice of language. The spread of French through France in the modern period involved shift from local varieties to a centralized standard. This started with **koineization** of the northern varieties: the closer the two languages, or varieties, the more likely and probably the less conscious the shift. Koineization is a form of **long-term accommodation**—where **accommodation** refers to the way interlocutors will adjust to each other's usage, in a co-operative or courteous spirit. Where such accommodation is normalized, the result may be an **interlect**—a new language is created, which has features of both its predecessors. An extreme example of this process may be **creolization** (cf. 3.14).

The shift can also mean the abandonment of one language, usually the less prestigious, and the adoption, lock, stock, and barrel, of the dominant language by speakers of the subordinate language. It may be, however, that these speakers' command of the adopted language is insecure, and that they retain some features of their original language. When such speakers are an indigenous population dominated by an incoming people, this is known as the **substratum** effect. This is most obvious in phonology: the pronunciation of French by southern speakers clearly owes much to Occitan, even though in the mouths of those who are no longer Occitan speakers.

We shall look at some alleged similar effects of Celtic on Gallo-Roman in Chapter 6.

Change, as distinct from shift, is usually thought of as gradual and imperceptible, so that speakers do not think to give a different name to the language they use this year from that they used last year, and grandchildren do not experience inordinate difficulty in communicating with their grandparents. In this sense, then, some change must imply variation—the grandchildren's variants co-existing with the grandparents'—followed by the loss of the older variant, with the death of its speakers.

For discussion about the gradual nature of change cf. 3.13.

2.7. Evidence for Variation at Past Periods

Evidence about variation at the present time is abundant—even overabundant, so much so that many linguists prefer to exclude it from their purview, by concentrating on the **idiolect** of a single speaker, or on an idealized **langue** or **competence** compared with **parole** or **performance**.

Our knowledge of past states of the language is however indirect, relying mainly on the evidence of texts. The process of reducing spoken usage to writing must lead to phonetic simplification: it is usually assumed that alphabetic orthography is roughly **phonemic** in character, depending on the writer's perception of the distinctive phonetic features. Thus many of the variants are flattened out in the texts and those variants that are recorded may be more a reflection of the scribe's training and intuitions (or, sometimes of his carelessness) than of actual usage. Intonation and accentuation are rarely marked in texts.

In morphology, syntax, and lexicon, there is more chance that the texts will reflect real variation—but we must remember that the very fact that the text is thought worth writing must mean, at the earlier periods, that it is representative of a particular **register**—often literary or legal. Latin continued to be used for most serious writing, and there was little or no commentary on vernacular usage before the sixteenth century, when direct evidence for linguistic variation began to appear.

The invention of printing and the religious reformation were two of the factors that widened the market for texts, and, consequently, encouraged their production in the vernacular rather than Latin. The growth of centralized political power, and the consequent administrative requirements also favoured the elaboration of the vernacular as a replacement for Latin.

The consequences, for our purposes, of these moves, should be obvious. Printed texts, for one thing, will not show the variation that is characteristic of handwritten texts. On the other hand, as more people learn to write, there will be more informal texts— personal correspondence and the like—and these will show more variety of both register and of social provenance. There will also be printed texts destined for a wider audience than hitherto.

Even more important, the discussion of the choice of a linguistic **norm** will mean that different variants will be passed under review. As we have seen, sixteenth-century France was uncertain whether the norm should be that of the educated Parisian, or whether regional variants should be permitted. Commentators on the language question frequently directly or indirectly refer to variation. The fashionable interest in language fosters the production of texts that lampoon unprestigious usage—so comic reproductions of peasant patois form part of our evidence, to be treated, of course, with great caution, as probably grossly overstated (as e.g. in Molière's comedies). Some of the pamphlets circulated during the Fronde seem to reproduce lower-class usage, probably to make their message more palatable to sympathizers, but less readily accessible to censors: but remember that they were written by educated propagandists, who reproduce comic stereotypes, not a serious representation of actual speech. The following snippet from a Mazarinade of 1649–51 (cf. Deloffre 1961) can give the flavour of such writings. These peasants are discussing in dialect abuses of the administration:

(1)   *Hé ya propou que di nan en vou quarquié? Ce quieble de soudar*
      avanty tou ravagé cheu vou queme dans nout vilage? = *Hé à*
      propos, que dit-on dans vos quartiers? Ces diables de soldats ont-
      ils tout ravagé chez vous comme dans notre village?, 'Hey, by the
      by, what are they saying round your way? Those damned
      soldiers, have they wrecked everything like in our village?'

It is only in the mid-seventeenth century, as we have seen, that
the language of the royal court was prescribed as the norm.
Description of actual usage becomes less important than well-
groomed presentation. However, in recommending *bon usage*
writers will cite examples of less good usage. We may assume
that in most, though not all, cases this provides evidence of
variation in actual speech.

Sometimes, admittedly, the 'mistakes' noted may be merely the product of
invention or inaccurate observation.

These 'mistakes' are often labelled as 'vulgar'—an indication of
social variation—or 'archaic'—of age variation—or 'patois'—of
regional variation. In the seventeenth century, as we shall see,
there is some evidence of sex variation: Vaugelas often commends
the speech of women as preferable usage.

In early seventeenth-century France we have one remarkable
piece of evidence that some of the variants labelled as 'popular'
were in fact current in the highest ranks of society, at least among
children, who spent their early years in the company of wet-nurses
and servants. Louis XIII, until the age of 10, when his father, Henri
IV, was assassinated, was under the care of a doctor, Héroard, who
noted his every action, and recorded most of his utterances, in an
attempt at phonetic rendering. Some of the records show that
variants banned from *bon usage* even today were in fact acquired
by the royal child, even if they were later discarded by him. Here are
some examples from Héroard's notes (Ernst 1985):

(2)   (18 Feb. 1607) *scay pa* = '*je ne sais pas*'; (22 July 1605) *j'ay pa*
      mangé depui je sui pati = '*je n'ai pas mangé depuis que je suis*
      parti'; (12 Sept. 1606) *fau coupé cela* = '*il faut couper cela*'; (20
      May 1606) *ja poin de dangé* = '*il n'y a pas de danger*'; (9 Jan.
      1605) *qu'e qui di?* '*qu'est-ce qu'il dit?*'; (14 Aug. 1605) *pouquoy*
      papa fai cela? = '*pourquoi papa fait-il cela?*'; (29 Apr. 1607) *le*
      Pape est-j pu riche que papa? = '*le pape est-il plus riche que*

papa?'; (26 Oct. 1606) *si vous eussiez venu* = 'si vous étiez venu';
(15 Dec. 1607) *je me coupi* = 'je me coupai'; (10 Jan. 1606) *C'e
guilaume qu'e tombé* = 'C'est Guillaume qui est tombé'; (16
June 1605) *j va faire touné le robiné* = 'je vais faire tourner le
robinet'; (17 Feb. 1606) *j'y veu allé moy a la guere* = 'j'y veux
aller moi à la guerre'; (25 Feb. 1606) *c'e moy qui sui le maite* =
'c'est moi qui suis le maitre'.

In the eighteenth century, more evidence of informal writing and
of commentary on habits of speech becomes available. Apart from
le genre burlesque (cf. e.g. Valli 1984), one source is in advertising
handsheets. A valuable source of evidence is provided by the
Cahiers de Doléances that were produced for the recall of the
États Généraux in 1789. Some of the communes produced documents, written by less highly educated recorders, that may reveal
popular or regional variation. Here are some examples of popular
constructions in the *Cahiers*:

(3)   *c'est les vœux* (for *ce sont les vœux*); *les vœux du peuple sont
général* (for *généraux*); *un chevau* (for *cheval*); *des grands abus*
for *de grands abus*; *à les, de les* for *aux, des*; *avoir* for *être* in the
passé composé; *il y en a-t-il?* for *y en a-t-il?; pas* negation
without *ne*.

Another source, not yet well exploited, are transcripts of evidence,
especially in legal cases, involving for instance slander, where the
exact wording of statements is important. Personal letters also
reveal the existence of variation among the literate population.

Evidence about popular varieties may be deduced also from an examination
of modern overseas varieties that have eluded to some extent the normative
influence exercised in France. Thus Canadian French and creole languages
may reflect some features of seventeenth- or eighteenth-century popular
usage.

In the nineteenth century, with the relaxation of some prejudices
about correctness in language, we begin to find evidence in literary
works of linguistic variants. Honoré de Balzac makes gestures
towards the depiction of different speech styles:

(4)   *Il paraît que ça chauffe dur en Afrique; . . . le plus brave homme,
le plus honnête homme, le roi des hommes, quoi! Est-ce vous
qu'êtes Pierrotin? (Un début dans la vie, 1842); Il prononce*

'ormoire' à la manière du menu peuple; Quoi qui n'y a donc? dit-elle (*Père Goriot* 1834–5); *C'était un ben doux, un ben parfait monsieur, quasiment joli, moutonne comme une fille* (*César Birotteau*, 1837).

George Sand attempts to represent the speech of peasants from Berry:

(5) *Je sais bien qu'il y en a une autre avec qui qu'il voudrait bien s'entendre* (for . . . *avec qui il voudrait*. . .); *Elle a mouru* (for *elle est morte*); *J'y suis naissue* (for . . . *née*); *A présent ça me semble que j'aurais été contente de revoir son lit* (for . . .*il me semble que* . . .): (*Jeanne*, 1844); *A quoi que ça peut servir?* (for *à quoi cela peut-il servir?*); *Il a monté jusqu'au gros chêne* (for *il est monté* . . .); *il avait tombé* (for *il était tombé*): (*Les Maîtres Sonneurs*, 1853); *Il faut que tu n'aies pas de cœur pour venir agacer un quelqu'un qui est dans la peine comme j'y suis* (for . . . *je le suis*): (*La Petite Fadette*, 1848); *N'ayez crainte Brulette que je lui dis* (for . . . *je le lui dis*), *un sien confrère* (for *un de ses confrères*) (*François le Champi*, 1850).

Later Zola claims fleetingly to capture the flavour of working-class speech: '*Mon crime est d'avoir eu la curiosité littéraire de ramasser et de couler dans un moule très travaillé la langue du peuple*' (*L'Assommoir*, 1877). He was not however himself a speaker of popular urban French (in any case his early years were spent in Aix, and he always retained something of his southern accent, especially the 'rolled [r]'). Here are some illustrative examples of his rendering of popular discourse:

(6) *Les deux femmes achevaient de se soulager sur le compte de la Pierronne, une coquette pas plus belle qu'une autre, mais toujours occupée à se visiter les trous de la peau, à se laver, à se mettre de la pommade. Enfin ça regardait le mari, s'il aimait ce pain-là. Il y avait des hommes si ambitieux qu'ils auraient torché les chefs, pour les entendre seulement dire merci. Et elles ne furent interrompues que par l'arrivée d'une voisine qui rapportait une mioche de neuf mois* (*Germinal*, 1885); *Quand je pense qu'on tapait sur l'autre, la vieille, qui était si docile . . . Cette gourgandine-ci ça ne vaut pas un coup de pied au cul* (*La Bête Humaine*, 1890)

Meanwhile, however, the education system was striving to impose on all a single standard, a national language. The effect of this was to widen the reading public, so that folk literature—ballads and pamphlets etc.—became more abundant, while increasing the linguistic insecurity of Frenchmen whose command of the standard is imperfect.

As a wider section of the population attains literacy, more written evidence of popular varieties becomes available. Henri Frei's (1929) work on *La Grammaire des fautes*, which introduced the term *français avancé*, was based on material culled from letters written from the front by *poilus*, 'Tommies', during the First World War, to which Frei had access as an army censor. His contention was that the 'mistakes' made by less-educated speakers, reflected in their letters, cast light on the evolutionary trends of the language.

The representation of uneducated, or 'popular' (cf. 2.11) varieties in literary works appeared at first only reporting direct speech, as in the works of Henri Barbusse, writing during the First World War:

(7) *Et l'pitaine fait un rapport au commandant. Mais v'la que l'commandant, furieux, i's'aboule, en s'couant le rapport dans sa patte: 'De quoi, qu'i'dit, où elle est c'te soupe qui fait cette révolte, que j'y goûte?' On y en apporte dans une gamelle propre. I' r'nifle. 'Ben quoi, qu'i'dit, ça sent bon! On vous en foutra, d'la soupe riche comme ça!'* (*Le Feu: journal d'une escouade*, 1916).

The use of non-standard language as a narrative technique, as in Céline, was an innovation of the inter-war period:

(8) *Y a eu d'abord la dictée, ensuite des problèmes. C'etait pas très difficile, je me souviens, y avait qu'à copier . . . A l'oral je suis tombé très bien, sur un bonhomme tout corpulent qu'avait des verrues plein son nez . . . Vrai il était pas exigeant . . . Mais non mon petit! qu'il me fait . . . J'avais pissé dans ma culotte et recaqué énormément.* (*Mort à crédit*, 1936)

By this period, these representations are not required as evidence of usage, as we have more direct evidence. They can be seen rather as a literary device that may aim at demolition of establishmentarian conceptions of the function of language in the social set-up (cf. Gaitet 1992). Queneau became one of the leaders in this fashion, which sometimes also affected a sort of phonetic transcription, as in the opening phrase of *Zazie dans le Métro* (1959):

(9)   *Doukipudonktan se demanda Gabriel excédé. Pas possible il se nettoient jamais. Dans le journal, on dit qu'il y a pas onze pour cent des appartements à Paris qui ont des salles de bains, ça m'étonne pas, mais on peut se laver sans.*

At present pulp fiction (e.g. by San Antonio) makes ample use of non-standard expressions, which have acquired, for some, a *cachet* of street-wise sophistication and wit.

2.8. Social Change and Linguistic Change

From a plain man's point of view, it seems obvious that social change must entail linguistic change, given that a language is defined by the community that uses it. One problem however is to determine what we mean by social change. Is, for instance, the swing from mini-skirts to maxi-skirts, or from flares to skin-fit jeans, an instance of social change? In examples like this, there is always synchronic variation, with some members of the society refusing to follow the fashion. Besides we know that the change is ephemeral, even if there is sometimes a discernible drift in a certain direction—think of the way it has gradually become normal, in Western society, for women to wear trousers over a fifty-year period.

A change like this is of course linked with a much more important social change, by which women have come to fill more functional roles in the society. We can adduce here evidence of institutional changes, and changes in social values, for which we can seek economic, historical, and ideological causes. We can see this as a part of a structural social change, in which (in Dahrendorf's (1959) terms) the personnel of those in authority has broadened to include women, previously excluded from certain spheres of activity.

Is there any parallel in linguistic change? We have already talked about synchronic variation, in which the whims of fashion may well play a part, especially where a specialized vocabulary or affected pronunciation is concerned.

The question of **drift** will be discussed in 3.12.

But on the relationship of structural social change to linguistic change, we have to be careful about our terminology. Where there is shift of authority from one group of people to another, there is likely to be a shift in the prestigious dialect. But authority is not always the same as prestige: Dahrendorf (1959) cites the examples of medical doctors in Britain and university professors in Germany, as people with prestige but little authority. The parallel in France would probably be with writers, *les intellectuels*. If the prestigious language were that of the most respected, and not the most power-ful, group, it would be quite likely that it would be conservative, pedantic, and mannered. This is to some extent the case in France.

Linguistic change is more likely to occur outside the prestigious language, and to be adopted only reluctantly in it, as the prestigious groups adjust to social change. Thus it is usually assumed that many changes originate in the lower social strata—as **vulgarisms**—and have been adopted into prestigious language only with the devel-opment of democratic government.

Changes that originate in the more prestigious groups are usually termed **innovations**—now nearly all lexical, but in sixteenth- and seventeenth-century France also at other levels (cf. the examples in Part II, like the pronunciation of *oi*, **gender**, the **agreement** of past participles, verb **morphology**). Another source of change may be the upwardly mobile, responsible for **hypercorrections**, as a reaction against vulgarisms (cf., for **spelling pronunciations**, 6.14).

2.9. CAUSES OF SOCIAL CHANGE

What causes social change is much debated. Durkheim saw it as resulting from technological innovation—the Industrial Revolution is the supreme example. Others believe that ideology is of supreme importance, and cite the French Revolution. Both of these examples involve radical and sudden power shifts. They were not reflected by similar linguistic shifts. In France the new power élite fostered the language of the old: the only notable changes at the Revolution were the adoption of [wa] for [wɛ], of [j] for [ʎ] and [ʀ] for [r]. The Romantics advocated a more liberal attitude to vocabulary, but, with Hugo, left syntax 'in peace'. It was not till much later that popular features were admitted to the literary language.

It is difficult to apply to linguistic change the Marxian idea that conflict between social classes is what engenders **endogenous** social change—which in Marx's own terms must be violent, though Dahrendorf (1959), redefining **class** and **conflict**, is able to incorporate into the theory more gradual change.

Indeed Stalin himself made his (fleeting) mark on linguistics by pointing out that language does not change fundamentally—by which he meant **morphologically**—with changes in society. For him 'language is not a superstructure on the economic base', but has it own independent development—a view which we recognize as stemming from nineteenth-century German linguistics.

Obviously, there is, as we have seen, a relationship between **exogenous** social change and language shift. The shift from Old to modern French is bound up with important social changes—the Renaissance, the Reformation, the invention of printing and of gunpowder, the emergence of capitalism, the growth of state power. But none of these things tells us about **endogenous** linguistic change—how the case-system declined, how vowels diphthongized, how ways of expressing negation or interrogation developed. This sort of change will be discussed in Part II. Here we shall look briefly at the way that language change is bound up with socioeconomic variation. We also consider the contention that lower-class usage (*français populaire*) is the locus of change in French, and represents the vanguard (*français avancé*) of future changes in the French language.

2.10. SOCIOECONOMIC CLASS AND LANGUAGE CHANGE

Sociolinguistic study in the English-speaking world is usually associated with the name of William Labov and his school, which seeks to correlate linguistic variants with social factors and which is particularly concerned with change in progress. In many cases it is found that change is more likely to occur in what Labov calls the 'middle classes'—more like *la classe ouvrière* or *artisanale* in French terms, than *la bourgeoisie*. The abundant French Canadian work in this tradition (cf. e.g. D. Sankoff 1986) prefers to work less with socioeconomic class divisions than with *le marché linguistique*—which measures the extent to which speakers are committed, socially and economically, to legitimate language. Clearly those whose livelihood depends on use of the standard will indulge less readily in less prestigious speech habits.

Another sociolinguistic school, associated with James and Lesley Milroy (cf. 1985*b*, 1992), will place more emphasis on social networks, where members are more or less tightly bound by social and family ties. Change will usually be initiated by those on the periphery of such networks, who have contacts outside a cohesive group and can therefore bring into their own network elements borrowed from elsewhere. Lodge (1993) draws substantially on the ideas of this school of thought.

In these and other sociolinguistic models that consider processes of change, the emphasis is usually on variation in relation to a social norm, often a standard language, and more on what I have called **shift**, than on **change**. Changes observed in progress are frequently more like substitutions of inherited elements by those borrowed from another community or style, than organic evolution of inherited stock. More emphasis is placed on processes of diffusion of such elements through a community, than on the origin of innovations as such.

The French linguistic tradition has always prided itself on its attention to social factors, but European French speakers have not on the whole adopted the 'Anglo-Saxon', 'variationist' methodologies (cf. Gadet 1995). This is perhaps to be linked with the different sociological tradition, that puts more emphasis on the effects of social conflicts than on social consensus. It is also perhaps to do with the perception that in Europe standard languages were superimposed on a host of different language varieties, usually territorially based. Hence, most French sociolinguistic research has been devoted to the recording of doomed rural dialects, seen as part of the national heritage, rather than to the study of urban sociolects. We return to the status of the dialects below.

2.11. POPULAR FRENCH

But part of the French tradition in the modern period has also been the recognition of difference between the language of the *peuple*, and that of the *élite*. We have already suggested that in the Middle Ages, the nobility still shared in popular culture, but that divergence became obvious in the seventeenth century, with the prosperous bourgeoisie tending to ape their social superiors in manners and language, even when they could not aspire to the same privileged status. Revolutionary ideology traded on the 'two nations' conception, but sought to make the benefits of High culture open to all.

What appears to have emerged in the nineteenth and twentieth centuries in France, alongside the national standard language, is a nationwide, non-regional non-standard *francais populaire*—a somewhat subversive shadow of the standard, which has gained ground to the extent that it is now part of virtually every Frenchman's linguistic repertoire, to be deployed in certain contexts, including, as we saw above, in some literary texts.

The origin of *français populaire* is usually thought to be in Parisian lower-class usage, with shades of the *argot* of the underworld, of which we have evidence from the fifteenth century. The spread of the variant throughout France was helped by the Revolutionary and the Napoleonic campaigns, when young men from all regions fought together, and by the compulsory military service which has been a feature of French life for the last two hundred years. A more important factor may have been the deliberate suppression of dialect that began during the Revolutionary period, but which really began to bite at the end of the nineteenth century, with compulsory schooling. Doubtless the substantial immigration, linked with the slow demographic growth in France during the nineteenth and twentieth centuries, and high mortality rates during the First World War, also accounts for the establishment of a non-regional working-class idiom, as did internal migration, from south to north, and from country to town.

Precisely what is meant by *français populaire* is not always clear (cf. Valdman 1982). Many writers on French will talk of different levels of language, spoken and written, with *bon usage* divided between high flown *français soutenu*, neutral *français courant*, and everyday *français familier*. Below this last on the scale of formality appears *français populaire* (or even *vulgaire*) with connotations of raciness (or even coarseness). Most commentators will speak of it as *langage*, rather than as a *langue*. Usually its use is associated with lack of education and discipline, but it is also recognized as amusing and creative. Bauche (1920) even claims that it is in some sense superior to the standard:

'. . . *l'idiome parlé couramment et naturellement dans le peuple, idiome que l'homme du peuple tient de ses père et mère et qu'il entend chaque jour sur la lèvre de ses semblables . . . le vrai français, c'est le français populaire. Et le français littéraire ne serait plus aujourd'hui qu'une langue artificielle une langue de mandarins—une sorte d'argot.*

Most Frenchmen will readily produce a long list of words that they regard as *populaire*—many of which they use daily, but would not write in a formal compositions:

(10) *mec, fric, flic, bosser, bouffer, moche, frousse, toupet, engueuler, marrant* etc. etc.

The Larousse series of dictionaries publishes a regularly updated *Dictionnaire du français argotique et populaire*, distinguishing the latter, '*la langue parlée de tous les Français*', from the former, '*un idiome artificiel, dont les mots sont faits pour n'être pas compris par les non-initiés*'. The distinction cannot however be clearly drawn, as *argot* terms enter into more general vocabulary, prompting the coining of new argot terms by the relevant in-groups.

Certainly what at one time were regarded as almost unfit for polite company now forms part of the everyday vocabulary of even respectable matrons. On the grammatical level, such features as omission of *ne* in negatives, or non-use of inversion in interrogatives, or of abundant use of *ça*, have become part of most people's repertoire, though other features like use of *avoir* for *être* in the *passé composé*, or of *que* as a universal relative, are stigmatized as incorrect. What is remarkable about such features is that many of them have been around for a long time. They do not necessarily represent innovations but sometimes are more like archaisms, leftovers from the days before standardization.

The impression is left, not so much of change emanating from the lower-class usage, but of a stable variation between standard and non-standard, possibly throughout the modern period. The diffusion of the popular variety may therefore be more a case of shift, than of change, with language democratization proceeding in step with its social counterpart. Table 2.1 gives a summary of the main areas of variation in modern syntax, with the 'popular' contrasting with the 'standard' construction, together with an estimate of when the 'popular' form was first attested. It is sometimes difficult to be sure about how far a construction dates back, because of the lack of

TABLE 2.1. Syntactic socially related variables in modern French
—early attestations[1]

1. Omission of **negative** *ne* (8.7): in questions, 16th–17th c. In statements, 17th c. (?), 18th c. especially central France, Canada.

2. Absence of **interrogative inversion** (8.6): found in Old French (echoic?); frequent (with *ti*) from 16th c. (modern: Canada *tu*).

3. **Subjunctive, hesitation with negative antecedents** (5.10): *Ce n'est pas vrai qu'elle est arrivée* / *Il n'est pas vrai qu'elle soit arrivée* etc., 17th c. (?).

4. Use of **compound past** as equivalent of **simple past** (5.8): *je suis allé = j'allai*, 17th c. (?), 18th c.

5. Omission of **impersonal** *il* in e.g. *il y a, il faut, il paraît* (8.8): regular in Old French; controversial in 17th c. 'Familier' in 19th–20th c.

6. Use of *ça* for *cela* (7.21): found in Molière (1665) .

7. **Left dislocation** of subject **NP** (8.3): found in Old French (e.g. *Li quens Rollant il est mult irascut* 'The count Roland, he is very angry').

8. Use of **on** for **nous** (7.7): 19th c. (?).

9. Use of *tu* for *on* (7.7): modern? especially in Canada.

10. GO-**future** (5.9): *tu vas venir = tu viendras*, from 16th c.

11. **Conditional** in *si* clause: *Si j'aurais fait cela, j'aurais réussi* for *Si j'avais* . . . Found occasionally in Old French. Especially northern (?).

12. Use of *avoir* for *être* in the **compound past** (5.8): *j'ai tombé* etc. With *aller, venir*, **reflexives** in Old French. Found in 16th c. 'Populaire' in 18th c.

13. *Que* as universal **relative** marker (8.9): *l'homme qu'est venu* for *l'homme qui est venu* (Middle French?); *La chose que j'ai besoin* for *La chose dont j'ai besoin, l'homme que je lui ai donné le livre* for *l'homme qui j'ai donné le livre* (19th c.?)

14. Omission of **complementizer** *que*: *C'est la chose j'ai fait* for . . . *que j'ai fait*; *Il a dit j'ai triché* for *Il a dit que* . . . Found in Middle French. Today mainly in Canada.

15. Non-**agreement** of *c'est*: *c'est eux*. 18th c.

16. Omission of *le* in **clitic cluster** *le lui* (8.15): *Où est le livre? Je lui ai déjà donné*. 'Where is the book, I've already given it to him.' Middle French.

17. Use of **adverbial clitic** *y* for *lui* (8.16): *Je l'y ai donné* 'I gave it to him'. 16th c., west and centre. (NB. *y* as **neuter** object in eastern French: *ça j'y aime* 'That, I like it').

18. Use of **infinitive** with **pronoun subject**: *J'apporte ça pour lui manger* = . . . *pour qu'il le mange* 'I brought that for him to eat'. Not Old French (*lui* would be a **tonic object pronoun** in this context = . . . *pour le manger*). Found today in Northern French, especially in Belgium.

19. **Dislocated word order** (8.3): *Ma sœur y a son fourneau quand tu veux allumer, tu as rien à faire, y a un truc prévu pour* 'My sister, there's her oven when you want to light up, there's nothing to be done, there's a gadget for [that]'. Attested from 19th c.

---

[1] For further discussion cf. Part II: references in brackets to relevant sections.

TABLE 2.2. Some phonological variables in Modern French[1]

CONSONANTS

R-sounds (regional differences)
  apical [r] / uvular [ʀ]/ [ʁ] (6.13)
Consonant clusters (simplification)
  [ɛskyz] / [ɛkskyz] *excuse*, [kɛkʃoz] / [kɛlkʃoz] *quelquechose*, [kat] / [katʁ]
  quatre, [ifɛ] / [ilfɛ] *il fait*
  [lj] > [j] [suje] for [sulje] *soulier* / [suje] *souiller* (6.6)
Palatalization (assimilation: 6.5)
  [kʲi] [ts'i] / [ki] *qui*, [kʲy] [tsʲy] / [ky] *cul*
Liaison (6.9)
(loss of *liaison* consonant)
  [lətʁɛ̃ʔaʁiv] / [lətʁɛ̃naʁiv] *le train arrive*; [pɑ̃dɑ̃ʔynsəmɛn] /
  [pɑ̃dɑ̃tynsəmɛn] *pendant une semaine*.
(*fausse liaison*)
  [sɑ̃vatɑ̃gɛʁ] / [sɑ̃vaʔɑ̃gɛʁ] *s'en va en guerre*.

VOWELS

Loi de position (6.11)
  [e] / [ɛ]   [me] / [mɛ] *mais*, [ʁezõ] / [ʁɛzõ] *raison*, [ʒale] / [ʒalɛ] *j'allais*
        (/ [ʒale] *j'allai*)
  [ø] / [œ]   [ʒœn] / [ʒøn] *jeûne* (/ [ʒœn] *jeune*)
  [a] / [ɑ]   [gato] / [gɑto] *gâteau* / [pat] / [pɑt] *pâte* (/ [pat] *patte*)
  [ɔ] / [o]   [ɔt] / [otʁ] *autre*, [oʃɔd] / [oʃod] *eau chaude*
Vowel length (simplification, 6.12)
  [mɛtʁ] / [mɛːtʁ]/ *maître* (/ [mɛtʁ] *mettre*), [pol] / [poːl] *pôle* (/ [pol] *Paul*)
Nasals (reduction of nasal vowel inventory, 6.4)
  [ɛ̃] for [œ̃] *brun* [bʁœ̃] / [bʁœ̃] / *brin* [bʁɛ̃]
  [ɑ̃] for [ɛ̃] *sain* [sɑ̃] / [sɛ̃]/ *sang* [sɑ̃]
  nasal hardening [saŋk] for [sɛ̃k] *cinq*.

E INSTABLE ([ə], 6.10)
  [aple] /[apəle] *appeler*, [fze] / [fəzɛ] *faisait*,
  [aʁkəttʁijõf] / [aʁkdətʁijõf] *Arc de Triomphe*

---

[1] For further discussion cf. Chapter 6: references in brackets to relevant sections.

evidence of spoken usage, but research often confirms our intuition that 'popular' syntactic usage may have remained fairly stable for some considerable time, but that it came out into the open only recently.

Certain pronunciations are also often associated with popular speech in France today. Table 2.2 gives a summary of some of the variants in modern French. Only in a few cases—like that of pronunciation of *r*, or of *o* in words like *chose, chaude*—can the differences be readily linked with region. Usually the popular variants represent some sort of simplification in contrast to the standard, and very often they have been gaining ground in the modern language.

2.12. THE ROLE OF THE SEXES IN LANGUAGE CHANGE

It is not only social strata and territorial groupings that play a role in language change. Variation in language can also be linked to sex and age. As far as sex is concerned, most investigations have found that women's language more closely approximates to the prestigious norm than men's. In a less-developed society, where their freedom of movement is restricted, this means that women preserve local speech better, just as they are the repository of traditional cultural values. In a modern society, on the other hand, with greater social and geographical mobility, women will emulate the speech models imposed by the powers that be and are quicker to reject non-standard forms. Men will tend to cleave, for in-group use, to non-standard or local varieties which acquire **covert prestige** as a mark of machoism and male bonding, especially among younger speakers.

It is frequently claimed that women's usage had a strong influence on the development of the standard French language in the seventeenth century: certainly language arbiters, like Vaugelas, would use women as informants (cf. Ayres-Bennett 1990*a*, 1994*b*), as their language is naturally more eloquent and less likely to be distorted by book learning. We recall the prestige of the *précieuses* and of the *salons* earlier in the century, and the admiration accorded to Madame de La Fayette and Madame de Sévigné as stylists. The role of women under the *ancien régime* was similar to that in many pre-modern societies—'despised and powerful', as Olympe de Gouges put it in 1791. Excluded from overt political power, they none the less exerted strong social influence.

Revolutionary thought saw this as corrupt, depending heavily on 'pillow talk', and upheld the imposition of '*le langage mâle de la vertu*' (Outram 1987). Although women played an active part during the Revolutionary period, they were, if we are to believe Mme Roland's *Mémoires*, enjoined to stay silent during political discussion, as they were believed to be inclined to frivolity and indiscretion.

It was not until the twentieth century that women assumed a major role in literary matters in France, unlike England, where nineteenth-century novelists like Jane Austen, the Brontës, and George Eliot achieved notable success. Mme de Staël and George Sand may be cited as counter-examples, but they do not figure as major writers, like Balzac, Flaubert, or Stendhal, and they had little influence on mainstream stylistic currents.

In modern times, there is less general support in French-speaking countries for the contention that women's speech differs substantively from men's, though some tone-setting feminist writers do suggest that male control of the language reduce the female to silence (cf. Sellers 1991). Most controversy, however, concerns such issues as the *féminisation* of names of professions—whether one should say, for instance, *Madame le Président* or *La Présidente* (cf. Gervais 1993).

2.13. AGE AND LANGUAGE CHANGE

Age is one of the social variables that is seen as affecting use of language. Young people are perceived as using different pronunciations, vocabulary, and constructions from their elders. It can therefore plausibly be postulated that younger generations are the locus of change in language. Clearly this would be a case of synchronic variation that turns into change as older varieties die with their speakers. One way in which change in progress can be studied is by comparing the usage of older speakers with that of younger speakers—such studies talk about **apparent time** compared with **real time** studies which would trace changes in the usage of the same speakers over time (a more difficult and more long-term type of study).

There are some problems with this way of looking at things:

1. There is some evidence to suggest that young speakers change their manner of speech as they get older, and assume more responsible social roles;

2. Generations are not insulated from each other: people are born and die all the time;

3. It is only in some cultures that young people form a cohesive social grouping—for instance, in modern society when they are schooled in age groups, and even then, unless they are confined to boarding schools or the like, they are in constant contact with people of other ages.

Certainly in modern French-speaking communities, young people are viewed as having 'their own way of speaking'. They are today more inclined to adopt in their speech 'popular' idioms, and ephemeral slang expressions, as well as distortions of the standard language, like *verlan*, 'back-slang'. Fashion, being 'with it' (*branché*, *câblé* etc. 'plugged in') are all-important in French youth culture, so that older speakers often express bewilderment about their children's language. However, there is no evidence that these innovations persist over time, though it is certainly true that popular expressions are now acceptable in a wider range of situations than fifty years ago.

The mechanisms by which language can be said to change between generations will be discussed in 3.6.

2.14. REGIONAL VARIATION AND LANGUAGE CHANGE

That separate communities develop different patterns of language use, even if they were once the same, is a commonplace of language history. Sometimes the differentiation is accidental, as each community randomly chooses different variants in the original unified language; sometimes the differences become emblematic of different territorial loyalties, and can be closely associated with cultural differences.

A classic way of looking at change from Latin to French is through the metaphor of the family tree: Latin splits into several branches of which one is Western Romance, which then again splits to yield a separate Gallo-Roman branch, which then separates again into French and Occitan (and, perhaps, a third member, Francoprovençal). There is no reason to think that the process would stop there, so, in this model, French would then divide into different regional varieties.

At each stage we can speak of the distinct languages as **dialects** of the language higher on the tree: thus French is a dialect of Gallo-

Roman, which in its turn is a dialect of Western Romance. Similarly the languages into which French splits up would be dialects of French. In common parlance, though, the name dialect is usually reserved for a non-standard regional variety, a patois in less learned terminology, implying cultural inferiority and rustic boorishness. The name **language** is, as we have seen, usually reserved for a standardized form, that may be the vehicle for administration or literature.

Our knowledge of dialects during the Old French period is limited. Certainly texts do show regional differentiation, especially in spelling, and it is plausibly assumed that the written variation is linked to differences in the spoken idiom. But it is also possible that this is evidence only of different regional writing traditions, at a time in which there were no uniform conventions. As time went on, the regional differences in continental texts became fewer and tended to occur more and more sporadically in the texts. Texts written in England however preserved their individuality, though we can only guess how far this was just an effect of different spelling, or of mistakes by non-mother tongue speakers.

Here we shall be concerned with the varieties of northern French, and not with Occitan, which was recognized as a different language, representing a different culture, in the Middle Ages. More problematic is so-called Francoprovençal, a name given to a number of varieties spoken in eastern France, Switzerland, and part of Italy, and now confined to Alpine regions, when it survives at all. This never had a separate identity in a corpus of texts, and some regard it as representing a mainly archaic group of northern French dialects, with some links also to the southern Occitan varieties.

In the modern period the 'French dialects' have virtually disappeared. The **death** of these languages has occurred mainly during the twentieth century, and especially since the Second World War: the **shift** to 'French', that is the standard, by most of the nation is chronicled later. However, northern speakers have probably seen themselves as speaking 'French' during the whole of the modern period, if not earlier. Their own dialect was a social or a territorial variant of the language eventually accepted as that of the state, which itself was probably a koineized version of the language current in Paris, for a long time the largest city in Europe, and centre of culture and administration. Today where evidence for dialect usage can still be garnered, mainly among elderly speakers, it

TABLE 2.3. French dialect: an illustrative sentence

	Mon	pauvre	petit	chat	il	est	tombé	de la	chaise
Standard	[mɔ̃	pov(R)	pti	ʃa	il	e	tõbe	dla	ʃɛz]
Orléanais	mõ	po	pti	ʃa	il	a	ʃy	dla	ʃɛːz
Saintonge	ku	pɔv	pti	ʃa	il	a	tõbeɛj	dkal	ʃeɛz
Bourbonnais	mo	poːr	pti	ʃɑ	il	e	tõbe	dla	ʃɛːz
Bourguignon	mo	pur	ptjø	ʃɛː	al	ɛ	ʃy	dlɛ	ʃɛr
Champenois	mo	pov	ti	ʃa	il	e	tõbe	dla	ʃɛːz
Franc-Comtois	mõ	pov	pøti	ʃɛ	ɛl	ɛ	ʃy	dl	ʃɛir
Gallo	mɔ	por	pøti	ʃa	il	ɑ	ʃay	døla	ʃez
Lorrain	mɔ	poːR	ʃatõ/œ̃			lɔ	ʃø	dlɛ	χaːjœR
Normand	mɑ̃	puR	peti	ka	il	a	tœ̃bo	dla	kɛː
Picard									
Lille	mɛ̃	pɔf	pti	kɑ̥	la		y	dəl	kajeχ
Amiens	mɛ̃	pɔf	tjo	kɑ̥	la		y	dal	kajeχ

Source: from A. Lefebvre in Vermes 1988.

is clear that the differences between them are peripheral, concerning mainly a few lexical items and pronunciation. Given some time to adjust, different dialect speakers should experience little difficulty in comprehension. Usually however they prefer to resort to the standard rather than attempting interdialect communication: this is probably because they regard their dialect as a local emblem, to be preserved for in-group interaction. Younger speakers use 'popular' varieties for similar social purposes, as we have seen.

Table 2.3 gives some hint of how close the different modern dialects are. The only substantive way, besides pronunciation, in which this simple sentence differs between the dialects is by the use in some of the archaism *chu* instead of *tombé*. Undoubtedly there has been convergence since the Middle Ages, but it is quite likely that even then the barriers to communication between the different French varieties were not unscalable. When Latin began to lose its position as the interlanguage for the whole of the Western world, accommodation and koineization between the vernaculars in northern France must have got under way.

2.15. THE SPREAD OF FRENCH IN FRANCE

We have seen in Chapter 1 that codification of the French standard was not originally planned, but that the legitimate language was adopted by the Revolution as an emblem of the People. Its imposition on the whole of France and its spread to overseas territories was an aim of the education system. By the mid-twentieth century that aim had virtually been attained, though bilingualism has not been eradicated and today is even tolerated. We may ask, however, whether the suppression of non-French idioms was an aim also of the *ancien régime*.

As evidence that it was, the *Ordonnances de Villers-Cotterêts* (15 August 1539) are usually quoted. Article 111 has taken its place in the *Archives Nationales* to represent the beginning of the destruction of the dialects. Brunot is probably responsible for the textbook acceptance of this interpretation. What the Article actually said was that to avoid ambiguity in edicts, in which Latin words could be misinterpreted, all sorts of legal instruments should henceforth be '*prononcez, enregistrez et delivrez aux parties en langaige maternel françois et non autrement*'.

However there was for a long time dispute about what *langaige maternel françois* meant. Tory (who was from Bourges) had a few years earlier claimed that French was, like Greek, a koine of five dialects: that of the court and Paris, Picard, Lyonnais, Limousine, and 'Provensalle'. Still in 1599 Pierre Rebuffe was insisting '*il y a pluralité de langages françois*' and that other varieties of French could be used: '*car le texte dit "maternel françois", non pas seulement "françois" parce que dans toute la France que ce soit en Auvergne, en Gascogne ou dans tout autre pays de langue d'Oc, le langage qui y est parlé est françois maternel*' (cf. Peyre 1933).

An anecdote in Ramus's 1572 *Grammaire* claims that François I had the deliberate aim of making everyone use French in the lawcourts, and cunningly kept some Provençal protesters hanging round in Paris for so long that they were obliged to learn French. Apparently the story had no basis in fact, and may have been made up to please Ramus's royal patrons at the time.

It is worth placing the *Article* in the context of the long *Ordonnances* document, which was signed in Villers-Cotterêts in

Aisne, 30 kilometres from Soissons, north-east of Paris in Valois country.

The thirteenth-century château had been supplemented by a new one built by François I in 1532. As there was good hunting in the forest, one assumes that the King was residing there that summer.

The *Ordonnances* were the work of Chancellor Poyet, mainly on legal questions, for instance, on criminal procedures, including the institution of torture. They also forbade artisans and *compagnons* the right of coalition; they made *curés* keep baptismal registers; they instituted the use of surnames; and they separated questions of religious faith from state procedures. On the whole, then, they tidied up administration and put more control into the hands of central authority. The language section repeated more forcefully what had previously been decreed—that Latin should not be used in legal proceedings.

We can make comparison with the 1326 Statute of Pleading in England, which said that pleas should be made in English, but that proceedings should be recorded in Latin—apparently excluding French, although law was practised in French until the eighteenth century.

It is possible that the Article was meant as a slap in the face for the learned academic legal fraternity and the *Parlement de Paris*, who still used Latin (although little more than thinly disguised French in pronunciation and syntax). It is pretty certain that the *Ordonnances* were meant to reinforce the power of the throne, but *Article* 111 may also have supported the view of good Humanists that frank use of the vernacular was preferable to corrupt Latin. There is, however, no sure evidence that it was aimed against non-francien vernaculars.

Whatever its intention, however, the effect of the Article was that eventually those scriveners who up to then had written in Latin, especially in the south, were before long recording court proceedings in the vernacular, and especially in the King's French. By the sixteenth century most of northern France had a koine which matched the French written code. This King's French was to spread to educated people in the whole of the kingdom: it is to be assumed that speakers were bilingual in a local variety and French, which replaced Latin as the language of culture.

Education, as we have seen, did not reach remote rural areas until the nineteenth century: the corollary was that a good proportion of the

populace was essentially monolingual in a local variety. What this proportion was is difficult to estimate: at the end of the eighteenth century it was
put at some 31 per cent, and in the mid-nineteenth century at some 25 per
cent; by 1914 virtually everyone knew French, though even today it is not
the first language of all Frenchmen.

We have seen (1.13) that the imposition of a common language,
like a common currency, can be a means of administrative control.
There was no reason why the *ancien régime* authorities should
encourage the command of an élite language by the masses.
Indeed, it was seen as presumptuous for the labouring classes to
seek to acquire education. The spread of French, as of education, to
the underprivileged was always a subversive aim, encouraging their
participation in decision-making processes, and one which the
Protestants, and then the Enlightenment, espoused. The identification of language with nationhood is part of the legacy of the
Revolution, which was officially furthered most strongly after the
French humiliation by the Prussians in 1870.

The first legislative steps in this direction were part of the
educational policy of Revolutionary regimes. A major actor in
this scene was Grégoire, a liberal-minded parish priest from
Lorraine who was a representative of the First Estate in the 1789
États Généraux, and who threw in his lot with the Third Estate at
the showdown in the Versailles *Jeu de Paume*. Already before the
Revolution he had been concerned by the diversity of language
within France:

*En Europe, et nulle part que je sache sur le globe, aucune langue
nationale n'est universellement usitée par la nation. La France a dans
son sein peut-être 8 millions de sujets* [out of *c*.26m] *dont les uns
peuvent à peine balbutier quelques mots estropiés ou quelques phrases
disloquées de notre idiome; les autres l'ignorent complètement . . .*
(*Sur la régénération physique, morale et politique des juifs*: Société
Royale des Sciences, Metz, 1788)

One problem faced by a democratic government is how to inform a
public with no common language: the task of translating all
proclamations proved to be too expensive. Grégoire in 1790
circulated to communes all over France a questionnaire designed
to collect information on the linguistic and moral habits of all
citizens. By the time he reported on it, Louis XVI had been
guillotined (Grégoire voted against this) and the Terror had been

launched. He concluded, from his investigations, that there should be a common language for the Nation—and thought that French should be reformed to make it more logical and more readily assimilable by the People: '*Laisser les citoyens dans l'ignorance de la langue nationale c'est trahir la patrie . . . Je crois avoir établi que l'unité de l'idiome est une partie intégrante de la Révolution . . .*' (16 prairial, An III [June, 1794] *Rapport—Instruction publique: Sur la nécessité et les moyens d'anéantir les patois et d'universaliser l'usage de la langue française*).

More effective in spreading a common language, however, than the recommendations of Jacobin theorists was, as we have seen, the expansion of military service, and increase in geographical mobility among the population. Yet in 1867 Charles Robert (*Secrétaire Général du Ministère de l'Instruction Publique*) reported:

Monsieur le Ministre de la Guerre a fait vérifier, il y a deux ans, au moment du tirage, pour chaque jeune soldat inscrit sur les tableaux de recensement, s'il sait ou non parler français. Il a été constaté que, sur 331.981 conscrits, 220.522 seulement [c.67 per cent] *s'expriment habituellement en français; 32.658* [c.10 per cent] *ne parlent pas du tout le français; 65.879* [c.20 per cent] *ne parlent que très imparfaitement le français, parce qu'ils s'expriment le plus souvent en patois; pour les 12.922 conscrits* [c.4 per cent] *restants, les renseignements ont manqué.*

It was however the educational policy of the Third Republic that most destroyed linguistic diversity within France, aided by shrinking of the rural population and sizeable immigration from abroad, during the twentieth century. Only in the post-Second-World-War period have there been official moves to protect local varieties from extinction, even though folkloric revivals date from the mid-nineteenth century.

2.16. Resistance to the Spread of French within France

Resistance to assimilation to French was strongest in those areas where the local variety was sharply differentiated from French—Germanic Flemish and Alsatian, and Celtic Breton (though Basque has survived less well)—or where it is emblematic of a rival culture, as in Corsica and the Occitan or Catalan areas.

In 1863 Duruy (the minister of Education under Napoleon III) noted that schoolteachers used both French and patois especially in Corsica, Bas-Rhin, Finistère (where 6 per cent of schools used only Breton), Haut-Rhin, Côtes du Nord, Moselle, and Morbihan, whereas in the Pyrénées Orientales only Catalan was used. Moreover he estimated that 11 per cent of school-children aged 7 to 13 (out of a total of about four million) spoke no French and that another 37 per cent could not write French.

The borderline between Romance and Germanic remained fairly stable after the breakup of the Romance Empire, with Germanic making some early territorial gains in the north and the east. Between French and Germanic there has been a stand-off for centuries, with French-speakers sturdily resisting bilingualism and language shift, but not gaining much ground either, except at the expense of Flemish in the north-west.

The comparative willingness of Flemish speakers to shift to French in the medieval and early modern period may be something to do with the prosperous wool trade.

The incursion of French varieties into Flemish territory began early, as attested by the Flemish place-names that remain in French-speaking Picardy. By the end of the seventeenth century the present-day northern frontier of France was more or less established. In an 1861 Flemish poetry contest all the titles submitted were in French and French has today ousted almost completely Flemish within the French frontier.

So unfamiliar to Frenchmen was the use of Flemish within their borders, that in 1916 a Flemish-speaking French soldier was executed as a spy, as it was assumed that he was an enemy infiltrator.

In Alsace the Allemanic dialect has proved more resistant. To secure the co-operation of the population, Louis XIV made con-cessions both on religion (a majority of Alsatians were Lutheran, not Calvinist like the dreaded Huguenots), and on language, when Alsace was incorporated into the French kingdom, bringing with it its trade on the Rhine and its famed vineyards. During the Revolution, in spite of the rhetoric, few practical steps were taken to suppress the *alsacien* dialect. The annexation of Alsace-Lorraine by the Prussians in 1870 imposed German-language administration and education on the province, but the return to France in 1918 boosted bilingualism, with French as the culture language imposed in education and regarded as *chic* in Strasburg society (though pockets of dialect French on the east slopes of the Vosges retreated before *alsacien*). Hitler was careful initially to woo the inhabitants by bestowing special status on Alsace when the Germans reclaimed it in 1940, but in 1944 liberation was warmly welcomed by most. Today *alsacien* is still the preferred language of more than half of the population, though younger generations show signs of deserting it, and official policy supports educational promotion of standard German rather than of the local variety.

Brittany was peacefully incorporated into the French kingdom in 1532, but in the eastern part a northern French variety, Gallo, had been spoken since the ninth century. The French–Breton linguistic frontier has purportedly remained fairly static since then. Although in 1882 Maupassant claimed that one could go a week in Brittany finding no one who spoke French, in 1891 the army authorities were able to cancel all leave for the eleventh Army corps because they were heard speaking Breton in barracks. Today even among Breton-speakers areas everyone is bilingual, and Breton, hampered by the support given to it by the Germans during the Occupation, has had fewer champions than some of the other minority languages. The territorial stability masks a social reality of threatened language death, as younger speakers shift from Breton to French as their preferred language (cf. M. C. Jones 1996).

From early times the south of France was culturally demarcated from the north: not only was Roman civilization more firmly rooted there, and Frankish incursion absent, but also much of the west was long allegiant to the English, rather than the French, crown. Legal traditions were different, as were agricultural and house-building practices. Even more striking perhaps was the existence of a flourishing and prestigious medieval literary culture, represented by troubadour poetry. The northern crusade (1209–44), which aimed to eradicate the so-called Albigensian heresy prevalent in the Languedoc area, effectively destroyed southern power and incorporated the Languedoc region into the French kingdom. But it was not until the seventeenth century that the whole of the south became French, and not until the present century that, with schooling, all its inhabitants had a command of the French language. Even then, for the majority of the rural population it was a second language to a Occitan dialect.

Note that in 1858 the Virgin Mary was alleged to have spoken to Bernadette partly in Gascon (compare this with Jeanne d'Arc's visions when Saint Catherine spoke to her in 'French'). As late as 1890, in an Ariège homicide case a witness gave evidence in patois.

Here resistance to linguistic assimilation stemmed from two different sources: one, the lack of education facilities among much of the impoverished rural population, and the other, a resentment by the regional intelligentsia of the hegemony of the north, coupled with a pride in the regional cultural heritage. These two factors operated through the nineteenth century, even though there was no lack of support for French national ideals. By the late twentieth century the former factor was no longer so operative, owing no doubt to the growing prosperity of the region, as subsistence farming gave way to lucrative tourism and wine production, and to the exceptionally rapid progress of educational advance.

This in its turn tended to strengthen more positive support for the protection of southern culture and language, so that among the younger urban population there are signs of a halt to the decline in use of Occitan, now standardized and accorded some official recognition. Nevertheless, geographical and social mobility has meant that French is the preferred language for most transactions: it is in the Pyrenees region that local dialects most flourish (especially in Roussillon where the Catalan variety is buttressed by the robust standardized form over the Spanish border, and gained particular strength from the influx of refugees during the Franco era).

2.17. BEYOND THE FRONTIERS OF FRANCE

Standard French is the official language in *Suisse Romande*, where it has today virtually ousted the Francoprovençal varieties. The influence of Calvin in Geneva was possibly decisive in the switch to French from Savoyard there. Perhaps too the adoption of an internationally prestigious language, in the modern Helvetian Federation, is meant to raise a barrier against Swiss German. In Italian Val d'Aosta, too, standard French rather than local

Francoprovençal varieties has official status, though Italian here makes substantial inroads.

In Belgium, too, it is the official standard French that is gaining ground at the expense of local Romance varieties—Picard, Walloon, and *gaumais* (a Lorraine dialect)—but the twentieth century has seen a violent kickback of Flemish (in its Dutch standard form) against the incursion of French into its territory.

In these areas educated speakers are barely distinguishable from their French counterparts. A few items—like *septante* for *soixante-dix*, once fairly widespread also in France—are all that mark off their usage. None the less they not infrequently show a certain diffidence about their usage and pronunciation: the Swiss speak more slowly, and the Belgians more nasally than is usual in France. The lack of confidence of Belgians, in particular, about the purity of their usage may be judged by the grammatical guides that are best-sellers there.

Note that Grevisse's invaluable *Le Bon Usage* is a Belgian production.

2.18. Success Story?

Usually the triumph of standard French over other language varieties in France is depicted as an effect of deliberate policy dating back to the sixteenth century. However any such policy was singularly ineffective before the advent of universal education and compulsory military service. Another factor that must have operated, as we have already mentioned, was the relative demographic decline in France, coupled with urban growth, which meant that internal mobility and foreign immigration was significant and so locally based linguistic features tended to be lost. Possibly most important, however, is *l'imaginaire*—an image of national pre-eminence fostered by successive French regimes, and especially the Republican ideals of liberty, equality, and fraternity, according to which a common language accessible to all is an integral element of civil society. The other side of the same coin is, as we have seen, the modern diffusion of a nationwide non-standard French that likewise replaces older local varieties, and eventually is seen as a threat to the dominance of the élitist standard.

However, the triumph of French has led to **language death**, through **shift** from dialect to standard, and from regional to national language (sometimes called **language suicide**). For some speakers it was tantamount to murder by the authorities, especially when it was accompanied by virtual destruction of local cultures. This was felt most strongly in the south, where Occitan speakers had no moral support from a prestige language outside France, but identified with the (eventually successful) militancy of Catalan nationalists in Spain. Already in the mid-nineteenth century, the *Félibrige* led a literary revival, based on the dialects of Provence, but in modern times a **polynomic** standard Occitan, intended to cater for dialect differences, has achieved some official recognition, halting to some small extent the decline of the language. In Corsica (where what historically can be called a Tuscan dialect is spoken) the resentment has flared occasionally into violent action, but has aroused little response from the authorities.

In modern times ecological opinion ('Greenspeak') defends threatened languages, as it does whales and the like, and even in governmental circles there has, since the 1950s, been some recognition of the desirability of preserving regional differences. The generally recognized **linguistic insecurity** (cf. Gueunier *et al.* 1978) of many French speakers can be linked with the perception that their own usage does not carry the prestige of the standard language. Bourdieu has seen this as reducing the underprivileged to silence: '*la seule forme d'expression qui soit laissée bien souvent aux dominés*'.

2.19. SPREAD OF FRENCH OVERSEAS

Here I shall not discuss the promotion of the French standard by those overseas countries that fall within the sphere of French cultural influence—collectively known as *la Francophonie*. Although rigid enforcement of metropolitan educated usage was for long the policy of officialdom, more recently, as the status of French as an international language comes under threat, a more tolerant attitude is taken to local variation, so that, for instance, Canadian variants are no longer viewed as barbarous and even in literary works acquire a certain prestige status.

What I want to look at is the kind of French that early colonizers took overseas, and to relate it to what must have been spoken in

France at the time. The period in question here is mainly the seventeenth century and the early eighteenth century. Before that time France took little active part in overseas colonization: its navy was comparatively insignificant, and indeed for some time French ships sailed under the Dutch flag. In the post-revolutionary period, the French that was exported was the national codified standard and development of local variants was severely discouraged by the education system. In the earlier period however emigrants were usually less privileged: in Canada and Louisiana, for instance, many were indentured to large estates bestowed by royalty to nobles, though there were, in *Acadie* (now Nova Scotia and parts of New Brunswick), for instance, small peasant farmers. The Caribbean islands also attracted small farmers (e.g. in *Saint Barth*) as well as slave-owning plantation owners (e.g.in *Saint Domingue*, later Haiti). In the Indian Ocean the *Île de Bourbon* (Réunion) was peopled originally by small-holders, while a little later the *Île de France* (Mauritius) was settled mainly as a slave-worked plantation culture.

Let us look first at Canada. The following summary gives some dates:

1534   Jacques Cartier entered the St Lawrence, thinking he had found the North-West passage to the Far East. *Nouvelle France* was proclaimed

1637   Richelieu founded a company, with a monopoly in fur-trading, and encouraged immigration. By 1660 there were 2,300 European inhabitants, rising to 55,000 by 1754

1755   The British, who had taken *Acadie*, expelled the French population there (*Le grand dérangement*)

1759   Wolfe captured Quebec, and the British gained sovereignty over the French possessions in what became Canada

So for a hundred years there was a French presence in Canada: today nearly all Quebec citizens have French as their mother tongue, many monolingual, while in some other provinces there is a substantial minority of French speakers.

Who were the immigrants and what did they speak? Although the popular myth of the Norman provenance of French Canadians is fostered (a shopping mall in Quebec has a rustic-looking half-timbered snack-bar, called *Le Trou Normand*), in fact this is true only of the earliest immigrants. Later they came from various parts of north-central France. Recall, too, that womenfolk (*filles du roi*) were more or less forcibly imported from Parisian brothels and orphanages, as partners for lone immigrants. So it is likely that even if they spoke dialect in France, they quite soon developed a koine, which was centred on the Parisian norm: in the eighteenth century French visitors comment on the 'purity' of their language, perhaps referring to its non-dialectal character. This phenomenon of **colonial levelling** is familiar from other languages—English in America and Australia, for instance.

However, the *habitants* were mainly uneducated people, who lost contact with France before the Revolutionary fervour for codified standard, and who in any case had little sympathy with godless Republican France. So it is not surprising that their untutored language owed little to the standardization that so profoundly influenced French usage. What is, perhaps, surprising is that many of the features of Canadian French are paralleled in 'alternative' popular metropolitan French. This suggests that such features were already present in popular language in the seventeenth and eighteenth centuries, even though we have little textual evidence for them.

Québécois pronunciation, especially in Montreal, differs quite substantially from that of Parisian French, particularly in **palatalization** of consonants, **diphthongization** of accented vowels, reduction of unaccented vowels and **nasalization**: some of these developments can be seen as continuing trends already present in France at the time of colonization (cf. Chapter 6). The lexicon is in some ways more conservative than that of standard French, but has also incorporated English loanwords. In syntax and morphology, in particular, most of the distinctive features of *québécois* are mirrored in popular metropolitan varieties, but allowed freer rein in Canada. Other Canadian varieties, like *acadien*, appear more archaic (for instance *h aspiré* is still often pronounced [h]) and reflect more dialectal forms of French (cf. discussion of Louisiana *cajun* below). It is to be noted that Canadian French has recently acquired some degree of prestige in literary circles in France.

Other colonial Frenches of the period show similar non-standard features, with variants. For instance, Réunion has a range of French varieties, which can be linked to seventeenth-century popular French, brought to the island by immigrants, the descendants of whom appear to have survived in isolated interior communities. Usually overseas varieties, including those of isolates in the United States (cf. Valdman 1974), as in Old Mines, Missouri (settled in

1720 from Canada, enhanced by migrants from Louisiana) and in Frenchville, Pennsylvania (settled in 1830 from eastern France), show a degree of simplification, often associated with **creolization**. Indeed it has even been suggested that *joual*—the name jocularly given to Montreal French, because of the local pronunciation of *cheval*—can be called a **creole** (cf. Wittman 1973).

Features shared by these varieties include: reduction of verb inflections; generalization of *avoir* (at the expense of *être*) as the compound past auxiliary; reduction of agreement, though noun gender is retained; simplification of pronoun system (*ça* generalized for both genders); elision of *que*; *qui* elided to *qu'*.

In this context it is worth looking at those localities in which two types of French are used: one seen as a French **dialect** and the other a **creole**. The tiny island of St Barth, in the DOM of Guadeloupe, is a particularly striking example of this, as the small population is nearly wholly white, yet, it is claimed, the two halves of the island remained for two hundred years socially apart, with the westerners, mainly farmers, using a 'Norman' dialect, and the eastern inhabitants, who engaged more in fishing, having developed a creole similar to that of Guadeloupe. The two varieties were exported in the early twentieth century with settlers to neighbouring St Thomas (in the US Virgin Islands), where they persist in the communities of Northside (creole) and Frenchtown (dialect).

St Barth is now an expensive resort for the international jet-set: this has hampered research on the obsolescent language varieties.

The following examples give some taste of the differences between them:

(11) (creole) *Papa mwen mo* 'my father died'; *Ki moun ki di ou sa?* 'Who told you that?'; *Pa ba mwen sa la!* 'Don't give me that!'; *Mwen té ka travay pou mwem té avwer plus de lerjan* 'I was working so I could have more money'; (dialect) *Lé gens, falé ke lé gens resté dans leur kas ou ioy k sonté. Lé batimen k'a pas été perdu, eu sékrazé par morso kom sa.* 'The people had to stay in their houses where they were. The boats that were not lost they were crushed to pieces like that.'

Of particular interest in this respect is the history of some of the Acadians expelled by the British who eventually found their way to

Louisiana, where the modern Francophone *cajuns* claim (somewhat apocryphally) linear descendance from them. Evidence suggests that emigrants to *Acadie* originated mainly in the south-west of the north French area, and their dialects show more rural features than the *Nouvelle France* population. The *cajun* varieties retain some of these features but also have resemblances to metropolitan popular French. We shall briefly look at the historical relationship of this language with the Louisiana **creole**, sometimes called *gumbo* or *mo gain* (= 'I have'), usually associated with the black slave population.

The so-called Louisianan *créoles*—originally adventurers and noble plantation owners—kept abreast with élitist French until the Revolution and Napoleon's sale of the province to the USA, but often also became first-language speakers of the Negro-French variety, having learned it from their black nannies. They eventually shifted to English, especially after the Civil War, so that New Orleans is no longer a French-speaking city.

2.20. DIALECT AND CREOLE

'Cajun' and 'gumbo' are terms with which we are most familiar in culinary or popular music contexts. The former is an Anglo-American corruption of *acadien*, and designated originally the people who were bundled onto boats and deported along the American East Coast in 1755.

Longfellow's poem *Evangéline* gives a romanticized version of this story. Those Acadians who eventually got to France were a thorn in the flesh of the *ancien régime* authorities, who did all they could to get rid of them (including sending some to settle in the Falkland Isles). Later a large contingent was encouraged to settle as independent farmers in the swampy *bayou* region west of the Mississippi in Louisiana, at that time under Spanish rule, where some of their number had already immigrated after their cold welcome from the English-speaking American colonists.

Only a small proportion of Louisianans who call themselves cajuns are descendants of these migrants: the community also embraces other European immigrants—especially from Germany, Hungary, Slovenia—and peoples of Amerindian stock. After Louisiana was sold to the United States by Napoleon, those who remained loyal to their *cajun* identity and language were lowly regarded by English-speaking Americans.

There had since the 1770s been animosity between (mainly cotton and tobacco) *créole* plantation owners, of more direct French stock, and the cajuns. The former, with a reputed lavish and leisurely life-style, retained until the Civil War some of their prestige. When Louisiana sugar production boomed, after slave emancipation in Jamaica in 1838, however, some plantation owners of cajun origin joined the planters' aristocracy, while the poorer *créoles* tended to identify with the cajuns, so that the '*créole*/cajun' distinction became more one of social status than of historical origin. It is probable that many smaller creole and cajun farmers were then driven out from the Mississippi area to more remote prairie-lands of south-western Louisiana.

The sugar plantations devoured slave labour, no longer legally obtainable from Africa, so that quantities of American-born English-speaking slaves were imported from further north to what has been described as the 'most terrifying of hells in the deep South'.

Alongside cajun French and the standard French of the creoles, a 'Negro-French' was identified, now called in scholarly circles 'Louisiana creole'. It is clearly similar to the other French-based creole languages of the Caribbean, especially that of the Lesser Antilles. A picture is painted in earlier linguistic descriptions of three distinct French codes: one used by elegant society, one by the poor and hard-working cajuns, and one by feckless slaves (and in intimate situations by the masters, though less often by the mistresses). Here is a short extract from texts quoted by Alcée Fortier (1884–5, 1891) to illustrate the putative difference between the latter two:

(12) 'Negro French': *Compair Lapin qui té apé couté dit Compair Bouki: mo pas fini avec yé, rété ein pé ta oua comment mo va rangé yé.* 'Brer Rabbit who was listening says to Brer Buck: "I've not finished with them, stay a bit you will see how I fix them".'

'Cajun': *D'abord l'public s'a intéressé a connaite notre histoire mouan j'va dire tout ça j'connais . . . les premiers Cadiens qu'a venu icite étions arrivés du Nord par le Mississippi.* 'First the public has been interested to know our history, me I am going to say all that I know . . . the first Acadians that came here arrived from the north by the Mississippi.'

Cajun, in this description, can be characterized as a French dialect, and gumbo as a French creole. Traditionally the latter is associated with black slaves, and the former with white farmers and fishermen, as well as with Amerindians (cf. Griolet 1986*a, b*). The modern picture is rather different. Francophone Louisiana is now confined to a triangle of twenty-two parishes, south and west of the Mississippi. In some of these, especially within the 'sugar' zone, like St Martin, more creolized French varieties are used, by whites and blacks alike. In others, especially in the prairie areas further west and north, everyone uses more cajun varieties.

It has been suggested that influx into the more central area, of masters, with their slaves, from Haiti, after the slave rebellions there, fuelled the creolized varieties. The Louisianan varieties, however, are much less radical than those of Haiti: some attribute this to more recent decreolization, but it could just as well be linked to conservative speech habits from the beginning, when there was more intimate contact between creole masters and their slaves than was usual in Haiti.

Some Louisiana Francophone communities—even some that fall within the 'sugar' zone—have today few or no black members. Since the Civil War the black population of the deep South has been much depleted by emigration to the north. Whereas in 1737 there were in Louisiana twice as many blacks as whites, and, at the start of the Civil War, roughly the same number of blacks and whites, today less than a third of the population of Louisiana is black.

The French varieties of Louisiana may, by black speakers, have been identified with slavery, so that they were keen to switch to more marketable English. By 1940 white French-speakers in the State outnumbered black French-speakers by two to one, and in 1970 only some 15 per cent of the French-speakers were black.

Detailed up-to-date sociolinguistic data for Louisiana are still unavailable, and the French varieties are fast dying out. At present a survey of cajun usage, financed by the National Science Foundation, under the auspices of the Universities of Michigan and South-West Louisiana, is under way.

Some claim that black and white francophone speakers can be differentiated linguistically, but the evidence we have at present suggests that any differentiation is mainly geographical—but also social or even individual, with shifting between more 'cajun' and more 'gumbo' usage, within the same discourse context, and without speakers being conscious of significant code changes. Even if they were once clearly differentiated varieties, cajun and gumbo have tended to merge into one another, often labelled as **decreolization** of gumbo, alongside **creolization** of cajun.

Modern cajun apologists tend to explain this in terms of the solidarity in protest of the francophone blacks and whites, in face of the anglophone dominant classes. A somewhat romanticized picture is painted of poor cajuns working like slaves alongside slaves, and sharing a sense of injustice. It is not easy to reconcile this picture with the historical facts. One of the bones of contention between the cajuns and the *créoles* at the early period was resentment by the former of forced contact with the latter's slaves, whom they saw as a health hazard and a source of danger. This was especially true in the late eighteenth century, when fear of slave revolt gave rise to a siege mentality among the white communities. However, the cajuns, though poor, were not averse to using slaves themselves. Those who had originally been deported to Maryland from Acadie had worked alongside slaves in the tobacco plantations, and so had become familiar with the 'peculiar institution', which they were not slow to exploit.

The first slaves recorded as purchased by a cajun were bought from a New Orleans trader in 1765, for the purpose of clearing forest. Soon most cajuns had one, two, or three slaves (African and native American), mainly employed in the household as nurse-maids and cooks (cajun cuisine is clearly African in origin). Slaves in eighteenth-century Louisiana, unlike the Caribbean, lived in tightly-knit nuclear family units, and enjoyed a high birth-rate, which suggests a relative degree of well-being. However, there are records of exceptionally inhuman treatment of slaves by Francophone owners, so we should be wary of painting a rosy picture of domestic bliss and racial harmony.

After the Louisiana Purchase there was a dramatic rise in the number of slaves—but, as we have seen, there was probably then a social redistribution, with the go-ahead cajuns identifying with the planter aristocracy, and traditional cajun culture being branded as backward, simple-minded, and contemptible.

Perhaps it was at this period that cajuns, previously reported as dour, abstemious, and hard-working, acquired the easy-going, fun-loving reputation that now adorns the tourist brochures, matching earlier stories about jolly, kindly Uncle Toms singing and dancing the nights away. Cajuns certainly seem to have shown reluctance to fight in the Civil War, and did not identify with the Confederate side.

The historical background may explain two related subordinate languages banding together against the more alien English that has dominated them for the past two hundred years. This would be an excellent example of the sort of long-term accommodation that can be a major source of linguistic change. On the other hand, it could be that the French cajun dialect and the French gumbo creole have never been as sharply differentiated as some creolists would maintain, and that the present state of affairs is merely a continuation of a situation for which past evidence is lacking. I shall return to this question in discussion of **creolization** (3.14).

In any case, by 1970 only some 16 per cent of the inhabitants of Louisiana spoke a French variety: inevitably **asymmetrical bilingualism** has ensued, with French-speakers having to operate in English, but not vice versa. The French varieties are ceasing to be languages of serious discourse, ranking as a leisure language, used mainly for bawdy jokes and country music.

Louisiana 'zydeco' is a anglicization of the cajun pronunciation of *z'aricots* 'beans'.

Yet even those cajuns who speak no French today appear to retain a certain loyalty to their culture. Like the 'creole heritage', cajun folklore has *cachet*, which is marketable in the tourist industry. Only time will tell whether this culture can survive once it loses the support of a living language.

FURTHER READING

On contact: C.-G. Dubois 1972, Fisiak 1995, Guinet 1982, James 1988, Joris 1966, R. E. Keller 1964, Kontzi 1982, Maniet 1963, Musset 1965, Posner and Green 1980–93, vol. 5, Posner 1995*b*, Thomason and Kaufman 1988.
On popular culture: Bourdieu 1977, 1991, Burke 1978, Corfield 1991, D. Roche 1981.
On literacy: Barton 1994, Furet and Ozouf 1977, Graff 1981, 1992, McKitterick 1989, 1990, Nelson 1990, Ong 1982, Stock 1983.
On schooling: R. D. Anderson 1975, Balibar 1974, 1985, Balibar and Laporte 1974, Chervel 1977, Delesalle and Chevalier 1986, Léon 1993.

On sociolinguistics and variation: Achard 1993, Ager 1990, Baddeley 1989, Ball 1997, Baylon 1991, Blanche-Benveniste and Jeanjean 1987, Branca 1983, Brown and Gilman 1960, Calvet 1994, Dees 1989, Durand 1993, Ernst 1985, Gadet 1995, *Grammaire des fautes* . . . 1992, Green and Ayres-Bennett 1990, Gueunier *et al.* 1978, Laberge and Sankoff 1979, Labov 1973, Lambert and Tucker 1976, Marcellesi and Gardin 1974, J. Milroy 1992, L. Milroy 1987, Offord 1990, 1996, Pasques and Baddeley 1989, van Reenen and van Reenen-Stein 1989, Romaine 1982, Sanders 1993, D. Sankoff 1986, G. Sankoff 1980, Stéfanini 1983, Stimm 1980, Swiggers 1985, Thibault 1980, Tousignant 1987, Valli 1983, Walter 1977, 1988, Wheeler 1994.

On social change: Cooper 1990, Dahrendorf 1959.

On popular French: Bauche 1920, Bourdieu 1983, Cohen 1970, Eloy 1985, Fauquenoy-St. Jacques 1985, D. François 1985, Frei 1929, Gadet 1992, Gaitet 1992, Gougenheim 1929*a*, Guiraud 1956, 1965, Langenbacher 1981, Lodge 1994, Nisard 1872, C. Schmitt 1986, Stéfanini 1983, Steinmeyer 1979, Stimm 1980, Valdman 1982, Valli 1983, N. Wolf 1990.

On women's language: Aebischer 1985, Aebischer and Forel 1983, Ayres-Bennett 1990*a*, 1994*a*, Beauchemin 1984, Bierbach and Ellrich 1990, Dahmen *et al.* 1996, Gervais 1993, Houdebine 1979, Irigaray 1987, Sellers 1991, Straka 1952*b*, Yaguello 1978*a,b*.

On regional variation: Benincà 1989, Chaurand 1972, Dees 1980*b*, 1985, 1987, Fisiak 1988, Fouché 1936*a*, Francard and Latin 1995, Gilliéron and Edmont 1903–10, Goosse *et al.* 1996, Guiraud 1968*a*, R. Hawkins 1993, Pohl 1979, Pooley 1994, van Reenen 1989, van Reenen and van Reenen-Stein 1988, Salmon 1991, Schouten and van Reenen 1989, Straka 1972, Straka and Gardette 1973, Tabouret-Keller 1981, Taverdet and Straka 1977, Vermes and Boutet 1987, Vermes 1988, Walter 1976.

On Villers-Cotterêts: Brun 1951, Fiorelli 1950, Peyre 1933, Trudeau 1983.

On Revolutionary language and linguistic policy: Acton 1959, Cellard 1989, Certeau *et al.* 1975, Dann and Dinwiddy 1988, Frey 1925, Guilhaumou 1989, Renzi 1981, Siccardo 1984, Staes 1979–83.

On the spread of French: Lodge 1993, Weber 1977.

On Francophonie: Bostock 1988, Deniau 1995[3], Francard 1994, Robillard and Beniamino 1993, Snyder and Valdman 1976, Valdman 1969, 1979, Walter 1989*a*.

On Canadian French: Asselin and McLaughlin 1981, Barbaud 1984, Blanc 1993, Corbeil and Guilbert 1976, N. L. Corbett 1990, Dumas 1987, Lemieux and Cedergren 1985, Monnier 1986, Morgan 1975, Morin 1994*a*, Mougeon and Beniak 1989, 1994, Niederehe 1996, Niederehe and Wolf 1987, Péronnet 1989, D. Sankoff 1986, Walker 1984, Wittmann 1973.

On St Barth and St Thomas: Benoist 1972, Highfield 1979, G. R. Lefebvre 1976, J. Maher 1988.

On Louisiana: Brasseux 1987, 1992, Broussard 1942, R. A. Brown 1990, Byers 1988, Conrad 1978, Conwell and Juilland 1963, Ditchy 1932, Fortier 1884–5, 1891, 1895, Griolet 1986*a*, 1986*b*, G. M. Hall 1992, Harrison 1882, Hazaël-Massieux and de Robillard 1993, Lane 1934, 1935, Marshall 1982, McDonald 1993, Morgan 1959, 1960, 1970, 1976, I. Neumann 1981, 1985, Phillips 1936, 1979, Posner 1993*b*, Sesto and Gibson 1975, Tentchoff 1975, Tinker 1932, 1935, Valdman 1992.

Part II: Linguistic Change

3
Processes of Linguistic Change

3.1. LANGUAGE HISTORY AND HISTORICAL LINGUISTICS

I have distinguished between **language change** and **linguistic change**, as between the **history of a language** and **historical linguistics**. In Part I, I have concentrated on language change—when a community changes its language. This I would maintain is virtually always a type of language **shift**. That is, the community has shifted its **norm**, so that a previously unprestigious, or even foreign, set of variants becomes accepted by the tone-setting section of the community. At the extreme, other variants, that were previously acceptable, fall into disuse. Such loss would constitute complete change: in fact, total loss of a variant is quite rare when the community retains a consciousness of its past, either through folk-memory or in the shape of texts. In order for such loss to occur, we must assume some social upheaval, which leads to a break with tradition.

Language loss, at its most extreme, is **language death**—which may be consequent on the physical death of the whole community. More often, though, it is 'suicide', when the community shifts first to bilingualism, and then, with generation change, abandons its original language. This change could be seen as irreversible, but it is possible that the original language has not completely disappeared, but merely gone underground (not used in texts), and so can be revived. This approximates to the situation with Catalan and Occitan.

A seeming counter-example is the revival of a thoroughly dead language like that of Hebrew. The peculiar conditions of this revival cannot however be discussed here.

3.2. LANGUAGE CHANGE AND LINGUISTIC CHANGE

In my definition, **language change** must always be social in origin and to some extent willed, or at any rate recognized, by the community in which it occurs. Change in this sense may not affect isolated communities which can remain virtually stable for long periods, but which may then suffer upheaval with the influx of new inhabitants and influences: this can be true of their language, as of their life-style, epidemiology, or ideology. But if in such communities language change is not usual, it is traditionally claimed that nevertheless there will inevitably be **linguistic change**. Since the nineteenth century, it has been taken for granted that the very nature of language implies change, outside the control of the speakers. Each speech act is a new creation, soon to be lost and forgotten. Though, in some sorts of phatic speech, stereotyped formulae can abound, and reducing speech act to writing creates an illusion of stasis, language is more an activity than a thing—an *energeia* not an *ergon*, as Humboldt put it.

Moreover, in many circumstances the speaker is more concerned with getting his message across than with the form of communication: if a grunt or a gesture will do, then why bother with more complex mechanisms? One traditional view of linguistic change is that it represents 'decay', due to slovenly speech, mishearing, misinterpretation, assimilation, and so on: change will primarily originate in the phonetics of speech, when speakers are conserving effort and maximizing efficiency. Counter to this may work the desire to be understood, adequately to express oneself, to persuade, to arouse emotional response: efforts in this direction often can lead to reaction to change, either by restoring the status quo, or by remedial devices, like analogical reformation, which can have knock-on effects throughout the language.

In this view a contrast is drawn between chance, the blind operation of physical laws maximizing efficiency, and choice, the human intervention that militates against such forces. One might therefore conclude that it is choice that triggers change, as the 'natural' propensity would surely be for languages to remain in a maximally efficient state. Human choices can change over time, but the physical laws would remain the same. However, traditional historical linguistics treats the 'choice' element as tending to preserve or reconstruct grammatical structures, while 'change' as such is occasioned by destructive physical forces, at the phonetic level. We return to these questions in 3.15.

Here I cannot discuss at length the question of linguistic change in general. Most of the books devoted to this question prefer to approach it obliquely, by discussing separately phonological, morphological, syntactic, and lexical change. Indeed it can be argued that, by its very nature, linguistic change affects only subsystems of the language and that general principles of global change are not discernible. In the remaining chapters of Part II of this book, I shall look at these different types of change, as they relate to French. I shall break with tradition by starting not with **phonology** (the sound-system), but with **lexicon** and **semantics**, which are more accessible to the non-specialist, and in which the changes are more readily perceptible by language users. However, I discuss change in phonology before **morphology** and **syntax**, because I agree that changes in these latter linguistic levels are to a very great degree dependent on phonological changes.

In this chapter, I shall merely introduce some of the concepts that will be covered in more detail in the following chapters. I refer especially to Roger Lass's 1997 book on *Historical Linguistics and Language Change*, which expands on his earlier (1980) *Explaining Language Change*. Although I am less pessimistic than he about the possibility of explanation, I broadly agree with him about the processes of linguistic change, seeing language not as a static, but as a dynamic system, in the sense of an evolving ensemble where variation of a parameter produces a change of state, as in a meteorological or population system. In such systems, the number of variables is so large that accurate fine-tuned prediction is virtually impossible, although it is feasible to model the systems in such a way that some useful results can be obtained.

3.3. SYNCHRONIC AND DIACHRONIC LINGUISTICS

I shall not here discuss the historiography of linguistic study—most works on historical linguistics provide accounts of such things as Grimm's Law and Neogrammarian methodology. But we should note that whereas the great advances of nineteenth-century histor-

ical linguistics were based on the assumption that individual
linguistic features are always in flux, Saussure initiated the twentieth-century return to synchronic linguistic study by emphasizing
that language is systematic, **structured**, and in some sense unchanging, even though its manifestations are discontinuous and volatile.
Indeed it was held that the only way in which language could
function adequately for communication within a linguistic community is by it being a fixed convention, shared by all members of the
community.

The contradiction between the perception of language as a
semiotic system (with its signs defined in terms of their interrelation-
ship), and the observation of variation and change in language use,
was in part resolved by distinguishing the stable system, *langue*,
from its actuation, *parole*. Innovations can occur in the latter, but
incorporation of these innovations into the former can cause
disruption, and eventually replacement of one *état de langue* by
another. Thus one cannot speak of 'change' of *langue*, but only of
substitution of one *langue* for another. Saussure himself saw the
task of linguistics as the synchronic description of the *langue*, while
diachronic study was concerned only with *parole*.

Successors of Saussure, especially the 'functionalists' of the
Prague School and, in French linguistics, of André Martinet and
his disciples, sought to show how, for instance, a phonetic innovation in *parole*, however triggered, could lead to a restructuring of the
phonological system which seeks a new equilibrium. The sort of
phonological **chain shifts** that can ensue will be discussed in Chapter
6. Language systems, in this perspective, can be seen as always
tending towards stability, but never quite attaining it, as new
stresses again put it under strain. A truly stable language will be a
dead language, no longer used by speakers as a first language.
Indeed, it can be maintained there is no contradiction between
synchronic and diachronic data, and that both are required for
adequate and explanatory linguistic description (cf. Posner 1976*a*).

The workings of **analogy**, which Saussure himself saw as indicative that language structure is a reality for language users, received
particular attention from Prague School theorists, as a way in which
structure is strengthened or renewed in the face of disruptive
accidents. This will be discussed in Chapter 7.

3.4. *Langue*, *parole*, and Norm

Other European Saussurean schools, working with the dichotomy between *langue* and *parole* (or *discours*, for those who wished specifically to include written realizations of *langue*), interposed, between the two, another level, the **norm**. A community norm may not be identical with any individual system, but can represent a compromise between different individual usages, serving communicative purposes. When we talk of language change, we usually mean the change of a norm, not of the system: some **innovations** in usage can be incorporated into the norm which is unlikely to be wholly systematic, including as it does all sorts of anomalies, relics, peculiarities, that have social, but not necessarily linguistic, significance. Other innovations may not catch on and so merely fade away. The process of acceptance into the norm and diffusion through the community is connected mainly with sociocultural factors, though it must be true that truly useful (**adaptive**) innovations, that aptly and economically express things that the society wishes to express, will have more chance of success than others. This is most noticeable with lexical innovation (cf. Chapter 4). However, the whims of fashion can also make their mark on the norm.

It is also recognized that a community frequently has more than one norm. Not only is there individual variation, but different groups within a complex society will also have their own socially marked norms, emblematic of their status. Individuals will frequently have as part of their repertoire more than one norm: their **communicative competence**, a component of their battery of social skills, will guide them as to how and when to make use of each norm. The more skilful language users can manipulate norms, and successfully introduce innovations: traditionally **rhetoric** studies and teaches the tricks of this trade, which can be used more or less consciously by poets, preachers, propagandists, or advertisers. These are questions we have already discussed in Chapter 2.

3.5. Community or Individual Language?

But how does all this relate to the language system? For most Europeans, schooled in the Saussurean tradition and Durkheimian or Marxian sociology, the *langue* is a social entity—an abstract patrimony shared by members of the society. The identification of language with nationality is, as we have seen, a fairly modern idea, but it is today rooted in popular consciousness. Each language is seen as having its own characteristics, at once epitomizing the aspirations of the society (the **Humboldt hypothesis**) and influencing the picture that the society has of the world (the **Sapir–Whorf hypothesis**). In this view the language imposes a pattern on outside reality (cf. Lucy 1992, Gumperz and Levinson 1996): this is most clearly illustrated in the idea of **lexical** and **semantic fields** (Chapters 4 and 5). More controversial is the contention that the morphology of a language imposes constraints on expression—so that, for instance, some languages obligatorily express a notional time-setting (**tense**) for an event, while others have to express the manner (**aspect**) in which the event occurs, whereas yet others merely present the event in a bare unvarnished way. In some languages, similarly, speakers obligatorily indicate their own commitment to a statement (**modality**), whereas in others they can find a form of words which allows a degree of deceit.

As Amerindians are said to have put it: 'White men speak with forked tongue.' All who have had to communicate with people from other cultures, even those which are quite similar to their own, will be aware of the gulfs in comprehension that can open up. We also know that word-spinners even in our own culture can deceive us into believing the incredible.

This is not to say that any language is not capable of clear, unambiguous expression of the truth, but that in some languages the morphological make-up of the language can do this more economically than others. Languages differ not only phonologically and lexically, but also in their **morphology**, traditionally considered to be the most idiosyncratic part of a language. Usually **syntax**, in this view, is not considered separately from morphology, in that both are seen to fulfil similar functions and are complementary. For most historical linguists, morphological (or rather **morphosyntactic**) change is fundamental in the transformation of one language into another. The phonological shape of meaningful units (**morphemes**) can moreover be distorted by phonetic accidents: morphological change will result from therapeutic measures to restore the language to efficient functioning.

American structural linguistics, which developed more or less independently of European structuralism, tends to concentrate less on the social character of language than on the **idiolect** of the individual. There are good observational reasons for this—the individual's system can be constructed from his language use, while the 'language of a society' would tend to be identified with the standardized norm in modern societies, and hard to define in more traditional societies.

There may be also ideological motives for language to be seen as located in the mind of the individual user rather than in the society of which he is a member: the tough 'Lone Ranger' myth can be contrasted with that of cosy 'social solidarity'.

Certainly the Chomskyan view is that language is not primarily a functional tool, developed for communicational purposes, but rather a species-specific human property, located in the mind of each individual. In this view, the 'computational' aspect of language, its **syntax**, not its status as a **sign-system**, is what most characterizes human language. The syntax is bewilderingly complex and endlessly creative, and not transparently functional in all its aspects; it may indeed be dysfunctional. What is to be studied is the **competence** of the speaker-hearer—who can, using his native-speaker intuition, make a judgement on whether a new utterance is part of his language or not. Thus more emphasis is put on the constraints imposed on the language—what cannot be said—than on observational evidence. The locus of the **grammar** is the individual speaker. Communities thus have 'a language' only in the sense that members of that community have developed similar, but not necessarily identical, grammars, which to all intents and purposes can be treated as the same (hence the notorious references to the imagined 'ideal speaker-hearer'). The aim of linguistics is to study **language** not **languages**, in an attempt to discern what is common to all languages. Language, by definition, cannot change and still remain language. But we can compare two time-related version of the 'same language' (a historical language like French) in the same way that we can compare two quite different languages. We shall return to this question below.

3.6. THE ROLE OF LANGUAGE ACQUISITION

Within this sort of model it is usually assumed that the individual's grammar, once formed, does not change, though his **performance** may do so, usually in rather peripheral ways, as by alteration of pronunciation and vocabulary, analogies, contaminations, and incorporation of odd anomalies picked up from contact with other speakers. This may mean that there are add-ons to the grammar but no reorganization within it. It is further assumed that the grammar as such is formed during the first years of life, during the language acquisition stage. The child, using his innate sense of what a language is like, will make use of the language material that he hears around him to construct a grammar which probably approximates to that of his elders, and certainly comprises the same physical items, but which may **reanalyse** in a more economical way some of the anomalies that have accumulated in older people's usage.

The actuation of the new grammar by the youngster may produce performance data that differ little from those of his elders—indeed the young learner will probably learn to accommodate his usage to them. Thus evidence for change in grammar may not be evident in micro-time: only after several generations may we be able to detect, from perceptible data, a displacement in the grammars of most members of a community. Only when utterances which were clearly accepted as part of the language of 'French speakers' at one time are rejected outright by later 'French-speakers' can we really talk of a definitive shift: the speakers may all call their language 'French', but they are actually using different languages.

3.7. DIFFERENCES BETWEEN LANGUAGES

Even if we accept that each individual has his own grammar, or language system, we must still recognize that some of these grammars are more alike than others, and indeed that the realizations, in performance, of different grammars are sometimes virtually identical. On the other hand, though we may agree that language is common to all human beings, we know that different, mutually incomprehensible, languages exist. Abstract universals are useless in getting a message across in a telephone conversation with a monolingual foreigner.

What differs most between languages is their lexicon, morphology, and phonology—what goes to make up what Saussureans call *langue*, the system of signs that represent the interface between meaning and sound. Syntax is less variable between languages, and differences can often be linked to morphological factors. It can however be maintained that semantics is truly universal, reflecting the structure of human thought.

In learning a language—'how to mean'—a child must draw on his *faculté de langage*, but also has handed down to him by tradition a **lexico-phonetic** input, and especially the morphological structures used in the community in which he is living. How does he create from this a 'grammar' different enough from that of his elders for us to talk about 'change'? To address this question we have to have some conception of how grammars can vary, and yet still reflect Universal Grammar.

3.8. PRINCIPLES AND PARAMETERS

An attractive proposal is that the **principles** underlying language are common to all, but allow some limited choices between possibilities (**parameters**): cf. e.g. Cook and Newson 1995[2]. As Chomsky (1981) put it: 'Ideally we hope to find that complexes of properties differentiating otherwise similar languages are reducible to a single parameter, fixed in one or another way.'

An example of a **principle** would be that of **structural dependency**, which states that the rules of language take into account the structural relationship between words and not merely their linear order. Thus the sentence:

(1) *On a élu Chirac Président*
    can be **passivized**, with **movement** of the object noun phrase (NP), as

(2) *Chirac a été élu Président*,
    but not of another NP, as in:

(3) **Président a ete élu Chirac.*

An example of a **parameter** is that of the choice of linear position of the **head** of a phrase (first or last) within that phrase. French is **head-first**—the verb precedes the object; the noun, the adjective; and the determiner, the noun— whereas Latin was probably **head-last**.

The relevance of the Principles-and-Parameters distinction to language acquisition is that the child, in listening to what goes on around him, will, of course, register material items, and apply his innate knowledge of language principles to the analysis of the structures, but he will also make a judgement about the setting of the parameters. The learner would judge, from the data presented to him, whether the language to which he is exposed has or has not a certain feature, and he would construct his grammar in accordance with this judgement. The metaphor usually used here is of an on-off switch: one can also think of the off position as a default, which will operate when the learner is uncertain about which parameter to choose.

Lightfoot (1991) argues convincingly that the only input in the language acquisition process that is 'robust' enough to trigger off 'radical reanalysis' in grammar will be found in fairly basic sentence structures.

In the case of the **head parameter**, at some stage in the passage from Latin to modern French, older speakers may indeed have a head-last setting in their own grammars, based on what they themselves had heard in their infancy, but, for pragmatic reasons, they may have to come to use, in performance, **marked** construc- tions which, to the casual observer, look like head-first. If these occurred in a large proportion of the utterances which the new learner experienced, then he might not discern their marked char- acter, and conclude that the appropriate head parameter setting should be head-first. He would be particularly apt to do so if this were the default parameter setting. His actual use of language would probably differ little from that of his elders, but a stylistic difference between their use of marked and unmarked constituent order could conceivably be discernible. For further discussion cf. Chapter 8.

The Principles-and-Parameters model of linguistic change is plausible enough. But precisely what constitutes a parameter in this model is not clear, and Chomskyan disciples have tended to find new ones to match every postulated syntactic change, without necessarily adducing evidence of the 'cluster' of simultaneous feature changes, or the rapidity of change, that theoretically would ensue from a switch in parametric setting.

The **pro-drop** parameter, which links non-overt expression of the subject with 'morphologically uniform inflectional paradigms' (Jaeggli and Safir 1989) is the one which has provoked most discussion among French linguistic historians, but this controversy seems now to have run its course: cf. Chapter 8.

The more recent **Minimalist Programme** (Chomsky 1993, Webel-huth 1995), extending further the **Principle of Economy**, slashes back some of the undergrowth of earlier models, but it does not seem to have abandoned the Principles and Parameters idea. As far as linguistic change is concerned, the main thrust seems to be that syntactic change is not to be divorced from morphology (thus returning apparently to the older concept of **morphosyntactic** change). Languages can be seen to differ one from the other by the **strength** of their morphological features. This idea looks very much as if it could embrace the much-contested view that syntactic changes from Old French to modern French are related to the impoverishment of inflection in the latter (traditionally seen as occasioned by phonetic attrition). However this cannot be precisely what is meant, as we are told that one difference between English and French (which affects **verb-raising**) is that English has 'weak' verbal features (which are 'invisible' at the level of **Phonetic Form**) whereas French has 'stronger' features (which have to be 'checked' by moving the verb to a higher node at any earlier stage). It is hard, however, to see in what transparent ways modern spoken French verb morphology is very much 'stronger' than that of English, if this term implies more consistent inflectional marking (cf. Chapter 7). A comparison of the older and more modern stages of French could perhaps yield some further conclusions about changes in verb-raising procedures, but what they might be are far from obvious to the sceptic.

Radical *typological* switches that create new languages (like the French creoles) out of inherited language material may be illuminated by the 'parameter setting' hypothesis: cf. 3.14.

3.9. ABDUCTIVE CHANGE

A similar model of change at the stage of language acquisition is associated with neo-Saussurean and functionalist approaches, and has been most clearly developed by Henning Andersen (1973), who does not confine the relevant changes to syntax, and who also addresses the question of the ways the input to the language learning process can alter. The dictum that 'Languages are changing all the time' is not sufficient to explain why there should be alterations, and we should seek to establish what are the constraints on **innovations**. For H. Andersen (1989) these can occur when they are:

1. pragmatically motivated (**adaptive**, as with contact **accommodation**, or a striving for expressiveness, precision, effectiveness, aptness);
2. evolutive (involving the transmission between generations, cf. below for **drift** and **direction**);

or, most frequently,

3. spontaneous, because either they have social value (e.g. are in fashion), or are due to 'low level' phonetic factors (as when 'economy of effort' leads to negligent pronunciation).

Innovation however does not necessarily imply acceptance into the norm, which, we have claimed above, is dependent on social factors. Clearly, however, adaptive and spontaneous innovations with social value have a good chance of diffusion through the community, though phonetic innovations may meet with resistance.

The 'classic' generativist view (cf. e.g. R. D. King 1969*a*) is that the new learner deduces, from the language data that he experiences, a new grammar.

In Fig. 3.1 one must assume that Output 1 and Output 2 (the surface manifestation) are very similar but that some general principles (like the requirements for adequacy, simplicity, and exhaustiveness) must lead to the deduction by the learner of Grammar 2, which is substantially different from the older Grammar 1.

H. Andersen argues that deduction alone would not necessarily lead to the formation of a new grammar and appeals to the Peircean

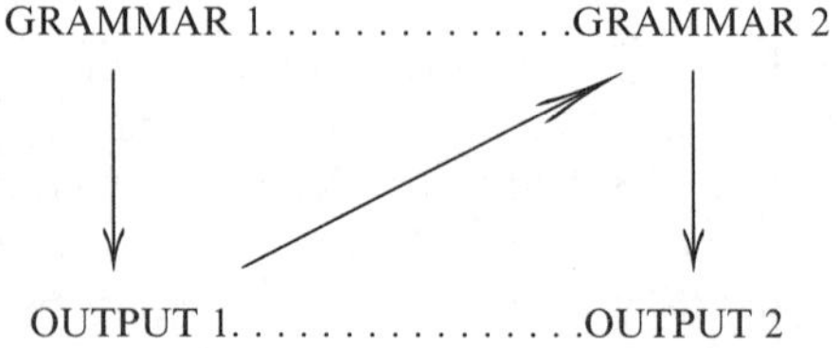

GRAMMAR 1. . . . . .GRAMMAR 2

OUTPUT 1. . . . . .OUTPUT 2

Fig 3.1.

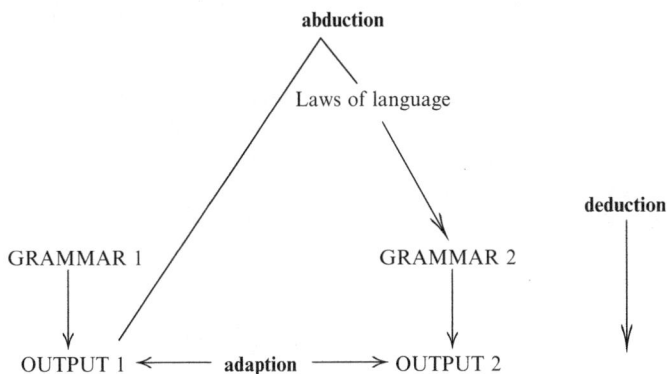

Fig 3.2.

notion of **abduction** (which proceeds from an observed result, invokes a law and infers that something may be the case), compared with **deduction** (which applies a law to a case and predicts a result) or **induction** (which matches a hypothesis to the data).

For instance, in **abduction,** a surprising fact A may be observed; if B were true, then A would not be surprising; hence we suspect (abduce) that B is true.

This, more speculative, procedure is quite likely to result in change. Fig. 3.2 illustrates.

Again Grammar 1 and Grammar 2 are not directly related, but Output 1 and Output 2 adapt, or **accommodate** to each other (i.e. children can talk to their grandparents). From Output 1, the learner, applying the laws of language, will **abduce** a new grammar, but will also deduce, from the laws of language and the new grammar, a new realization of this grammar (Output 2). Thus the learner does not merely apply mechanically his knowledge of the laws of language to his observation of language data, but also introduces into the equation his judgement of what is most likely to be correct. Hence there will be some degree of variation, and unpredictability, in the outcome.

3.10. TIME'S ARROW

The history of a language may be concerned with a series of still pictures, minimally different one from the other, arranged in chronological sequence. The same sort of distribution of stills could well be spread out across space rather than time: contemporary grammars A and B could differ in the same way as successive grammars C and D. Only in the first case, however, would we usually want to talk about change from A to B (but see below for the **wave** theory).

As historians, we are interested in irreversible changes over time: an item or feature once lost cannot be revived. Change implies direction, not only the creation of new, but also the loss of old elements. Yet, historical linguistics rarely makes mention of the oriented and non-reversible character of historical time. As Ardener (1971) so cogently argued, traditional comparative philology derives its 'historicity' from its 'chronologically marked material', and not from its essentially timeless model. What is compared are corresponding items from different related languages, which could be contemporaneous or consecutive—it is only from non-linguistic evidence (like the provenance, character, and date of the textual material used) that we can judge whether they are spatially, socially, or chronologically related. A bonus of 'surplus historicity' does come from the requirement, in Neogrammarian methodology, for successive ordering of phonological rules (cf. 6.2), though even here the ordering could very well be synchronic (part of a speaker's grammar), rather than representative of real time.

Note that the neo-Saussurean linguistic model of Gustave Guillaume's *psychosystématique* or *psychomécanique*, which has had enormous influence on the thinking of French linguists, postulates that the realization of *langue* as *discours* requires a real *temps opératif*, so that even in 'synchrony' operations can occur before or after each other.

Usually, in describing change in language (especially phonological change), we are able to argue, with some conviction, that process A must occur before process B, because the output of A '**feeds**' into B, or '**bleeds**' B of some of its input. We are rarely, however, able to specify exactly, in real time, when either A or B occurred, nor even to guess how much time each of the processes took or whether there was any significant time lapse between them.

Change in real time, I repeat, must involve loss of a linguistic feature or process (or, at the extreme, the death of a language). Loss must be irreversible: modern French cannot reconstitute the Old French nominal case-system; French creoles cannot recreate French grammatical gender. Yet our evidence suggests that some processes are reversed, suggesting that they were not wholly completed and have left traces that survived as variants.

For instance, the fall of word-final consonants in the French early modern period was frequently followed by their restoration, in spelling pronunciation, a little later (cf. 6.14). The phonological rule that deleted all word-final consonants (**truncation**) seems to have operated across the board, so that there was no input left for the rule by the end of the seventeenth century. The rule therefore ceased to operate. But traces of the predeletion situation survived in the graphy, encouraging literate speakers sporadically to pronounce some words as they were written. The obsolete word-final deletion rule could not now apply to these new word-final consonants, so that the new pronunciation was sometimes accepted as the normal lexical form. The results of this process may look like cases of restoration of a former state, but in fact the processes involved are quite different. What was irreversibly lost was not the word-final consonants, so much as the word-final consonantal deletion rule.

In other cases, however, phonological rules that have faded away seem to revive. These usually represent **natural** phonetic processes, like **nasalization** (6.4) or **palatalization** (6.5).

The assimilatory nasalization of a vowel by a following nasal consonant resulted in French in the creation of a nasal vowel phoneme series, when the triggering environment (the nasal consonant) was lost, as a result of the equivalent of the **truncation** rule. But the nasalization rule was also lost, so that modern standard French has oral vowel + nasal consonant sequences. However, in some varieties, especially overseas, the vowel in such sequences is nasalized, and so the rule looks as though it has reappeared and now affects new relevant sequences.

Such recurrences of the same (usually low-level phonetic) rules are sometimes described in terms of **meta-rules**, which can pop up all over the place, but usually with rather different conditioning at different times and in different places.

The notion of irreversibility of linguistic change must apply only to those processes that operate on the system, and without the conscious intervention of the speaker. However, it is also possible that a process operates only in one variety of a language, but that, later, that variety may borrow, from another variety, items that have not succumbed to the process: the incorporation of **Latinisms** into French, often replacing inherited popular cognate forms, is an example (cf. Chapter 4).

3.11. CYCLES

I have been insisting that linguistic change is linear and irreversible. However, it is often maintained that there is no decided direction in language change, but rather a cyclic movement, with features disappearing and then later reappearing.

Here the metaphor is of the succession of the seasons, rather than the other familiar one of progression from birth to death.

If we consider more abstract aspects of language, rather than substantive elements, this view does certainly seem to be valid. Typologically, for instance, it can be claimed that French has moved from a **synthetic** type, with sentence roles coded by internal changes (**inflections**) in the word, to an **analytic** type, in which words are more autonomous and sentence roles are coded by means of ordering and of special particles. However, it looks as if some of these particles, like pronoun subjects or prepositions, are becoming part of the word, and so begin to look like **inflections** (cf. Schwegler 1990). This and similar questions will be discussed in Chapter 8.

A favourite concrete example of cyclicity (cf. Fleischman 1982) in French is the **synthetic future**, like *chanterai* 'I shall sing', which originated as a **periphrastic** (or **analytic**) CANTĀRE HABĒO ' I have to sing', and is being replaced by another periphrastic form *je vais chanter* 'I am going to sing' (cf. 5.9, 7.13).

3.12. DRIFT

In saying that linguistic change is irreversible, do we imply also that it has a goal? Here a parallel with evolution of living beings can be drawn. Do languages change so that they become more adapted to their functions, and better aligned with certain principles of discourse? Do they aim at being simpler, more economical, more expressive, more transparent? This is the view of some linguists who, in the liberal tradition, see language change as progress towards Utopia, whereas more conservative thinkers bewail the lack of stability and discipline which spells decadence from a Golden Age.

Metaphorically language can be viewed not as following a linear path, but rather as suffering the fate of any living organism, to be born, reach maturity, fall into senility, and then die. Hence, Latin, after its decline and fall, was replaced by its off-shoot Old French, which decayed in the Middle French period, to be reborn in a different form as modern French, which in its turn is on the way out, threatened by, horror of horrors, *franglais*, or perhaps *français populaire*. This view implies transitional periods in which speakers are struggling along with a senile or infantile, inefficient and inconsistent language.

Today most linguists would shrink from judging any one language state as superior to any other: each is equally well adapted to its purpose, so change will neither enhance nor impair language. The 'transitional' states represent, not so much decay as uncertainty in the community about the status of different varieties, with one previously unprestigious variety beginning to oust another socially marked variety, usually with a more general change in social attitudes (cf. Chapter 2).

What often strikes observers is that individual and apparently unrelated linguistic changes seem to conspire to lead, or push, a particular language in a certain direction. For instance, in French there has been a tendency over macro-time for inflectional marking to be transferred from the end of the word to the beginning. All sorts of different processes have contributed to this trend: phonological attrition, analogical reformation, cliticization of particles, formation of auxiliary verbs. It all looks more like 'a conspiracy' than a 'cock-up'. Yet who has conspired? Certainly not the speakers, who are usually not conscious of what has been happening. One has the feeling that the language has some dark purpose of its own. The metaphor of **drift** was explicitly introduced by Sapir (1921) to give expression to this feeling: 'Language moves down a current of its own making. It has drift.' Such a directional movement must derive from the unconscious selection by speakers of those variants in language that have a cumulative effect (cf. Malkiel 1981).

The metaphor of the **invisible hand** has been borrowed from

Adam Smith in an attempt to explain such overall directional changes in language (cf. Keller 1990): in this view intentional micro-agency—the achievement of personal satisfaction by the individual—can be seen as achieving macro-causality—social progress.

Market forces, with every individual selfishly maximizing his own profit, will in this scenario yield a successful economy ('the best of possible worlds'). Adam Smith, imbued with the optimism of the liberal Enlightenment, and still retaining remnants of trust in a benevolent deity, saw this as necessarily producing a socially desirable outcome; the general idea today commands fervent support among radical conservatives, for whom prosperity takes precedence over social cohesion. But we recall the comment of the Keynesian economist Joan Robinson: 'The invisible hand acts only by strangulation.' Certainly in language change terms, the pursuit by individuals of social success does frequently induce language **shift** and consequent **death** of subordinated languages and language varieties.

It is hard to see what precisely the invisible hand metaphor adds to the explanation of directionality in linguistic change. Even without a hand operating, we can assume that tone-setting speakers at one time select similar variants and consequently displace the social norm, so that the upwardly mobile will imitate them in their pursuit of social success. We still have to explain why those variants were selected, and how they have a cumulative directional effect: the 'invisible hand' gives a label to these phenomena, but does little to explain them.

I have already mentioned some of the ways in which language is likely to change. There can be assumed to be a natural tendency to move:

1. towards greater **simplification** (rules extend their domain, lexical exceptions are lost);
2. towards greater **transparency** (so that '**underlying**' structures, in the system, become closer to '**surface**' structures, in realization);
3. towards more universality (so that **marked**, language-specific, features will tend to give way to unmarked, more widespread, features).

This should, however, mean that languages get more like each other over time: we know that this is not necessarily so. **Accommodation** between languages in contact does lead to **convergence**, but it must be true that the languages in the world today (some put the number of recognizably different community languages at 5,000 or so) must have differentiated from a smaller number in the past, just as the modern human population has grown by leaps and bounds over the centuries.

This brings us back to our earlier consideration of what constitutes differences between languages, but also forward to a question we shall consider later: Is change inevitable? First however I shall ask: Is change gradual? and consider the 'special case' of **creolization**.

3.13. Is Change Gradual?

Historical linguistics as a scientific endeavour dates from the nineteenth-century recognition that sound-change in language is regular, and the assumption that change originates in variation in pronunciation (cf. Chapter 6). The formulation of a rigorous methodology by the Leipzig-based **Neogrammarians** (*Junggrammatiker*) in the 1870s (including the notorious 'Sound-laws know no exception' dictum) marked a decided step forward. Among their tenets are the assumptions that sound-change is 'blind', and that it is 'gradual'. The former metaphor refers to the observation that sounds change irrespective of the meaning of the utterance, and that the conditioning of the change is purely phonological, mechanical, and physiologically motivated. Thus changes occur in spite of the speakers' intentions. The gradualness of sound-change follows from this: at each step the phonetic (articulatory and perceptual) adjustment must be so minute as to be imperceptible. It is only when a number of shifts have occurred in the same direction that speakers may perceive that a change has occurred.

How the change could be directional and uniform within a community was beyond the ken of most practitioners, who were more excited about working out the implications of their theories, than in philosophical speculation. Hermann Paul (1880) suggested, implausibly, that there was a simultaneous shift in the psychological representation of a sound among all members of the community.

Linguistics took another step forward when there was made a clear distinction between phonetics and phonology, between the sound and the **phoneme** (an abstract segmental unit of phonological structure, which can distinguish one word from another, and which can comprise a number of more concrete sounds or **allophones**). For historical linguists the question then arose of whether it is the sound or the phoneme that changes, or, rather, how imperceptible (low-level) shifts in sounds can feed into change in phonemes, which, because they make a difference of meaning, must be recognized by the speaker as distinct. I shall return to this question in Chapter 6.

Here our concern is with gradualness (cf. Hoenigswald 1964, Desmet and van Hoeke 1992): split or merger in phonemes must imply some sort of quantum leap, even if preceded by allophonic gradient shifts. A firm dividing-line could no longer, therefore, be drawn between gradual and mechanical sound-change and the more disjunctive changes of meaningful elements that must involve the speaker's consciousness. Moreover it was recognized that the random variation of pronunciation does not ordinarily result in a directional displacement of the sort that phonemic change implies. One way of taking account of these considerations is by allowing that changes in one level of linguistic organization can effect changes in other levels, and that phonological change is not exempt from influences from morphology, syntax, or lexicon. Thus we can see change at one level as like the inexorable slide of a glacier, but at another level like a sudden, unpredictable, and catastrophic avalanche.

But gradualness in linguistic change need not be viewed only in terms of innovations arising from imperceptible slippage in articulation or of cases of slight mishearing. More usually it is seen as connected with the way an innovation, of whatever origin, spreads from speaker to speaker through the community, or from element to element within the language. The hypothesis of **lexical diffusion** (Wang 1969) is an example of the latter process. Here the suggestion is that regular sound-change does not affect all words in the language at one and the same time, but diffuses though the lexicon, until it has exhausted all the available input material. An exposition of this theory *avant la lettre* can be found in Posner (1961), where I show that so-called 'sporadic' changes (including 'unnatural' ones like **dissimilation**) may be unsuccessful potentially regular changes, which attack more vulnerable items first, but may, for a variety of reasons, be blocked from extending to the whole of the lexicon. In cases such as these, the 'change'—a new rule—may start off gingerly, with a limited domain, then it may gather speed as it engulfs more and more susceptible elements, before tailing off as fodder runs out, often leaving a residue of unaffected items (cf. the S-curve in Chen 1972). It is only at this last stage, having run its course, that we can talk of a 'regular' sound-change, when the domain of application is exhausted, so that the rule ceases to operate. Analogical reformation of inflectional paradigms on the pattern of certain preferred templates (cf. 7.8) can be another example of the way a change spreads though the language, as can the extension of syntactic rules by elimination of lexically determined exceptions: in these cases, however, the domain of the change remains limited, the course of the change is less predictable and the process is rarely exceptionless (even in the special sense that sound-laws are without exception, cf. 6.1).

Most often, however, linguistic change is seen as gradual in its operation, in the sense that it spreads bit by bit though the community. It can start as the 'thin end of a wedge' in just a few speakers' usage, and gradually gain more ground in social space until it becomes dominant, relegating relics of older usage to a few stereotyped formulae.

Marchello-Nizia (1995), for instance, sees the passage of Old to Middle French as involving a number of processes of this sort, with the Middle French period representing something of a stand-off between rival usages.

In the scenario I have sketched, this would represent the phenomenon not of **change** but of **shift**, with, for instance, the producers of 'Middle French' texts poised on the brink of a choice about which variety is most appropriate for their produce. That an older variety had ceased to enjoy unchallenged prestige can be connected with social change. How the two varieties arose in the first place is a much more difficult, and perhaps more specifically linguistic, question to answer.

The **wave-model** of linguistic spread over geographical space paints a similar picture as that of diffusion through social space. A successful innovation will, in this story, start at a central spot and then, given the right conditions, lap out over neighbouring areas until either it is dammed or it runs out of momentum. This model can allow for complex patterns of changes, as the 'waves' can flood over linguistically unrelated, as well as related languages, and as different innovatory centres can compete, so that intervening areas may show overlapping of different innovatory features, with their languages looking like a haphazard hotchpotch of neighbouring languages on all sides.

The attentive reader might already have guessed my own answer to the question: Is linguistic change gradual? I have previously distinguished between innovation, change, and shift, and have wished to identify change with the completion of an innovatory process, involving loss of older variants. My own taste, as what Lass (1997) calls a 'late-preference' historian, is to see things as happening later, when a macro-story has come to its end, rather than earlier, at an early stage in a micro-story, when directionality is hard to discern, and threatened changes can still be reversed. Alas, in linguistic history we seem to be able to predict only with hindsight; the variables are so complex that we can never be sure what is going to happen next.

Definitive loss of a linguistic feature must be abrupt, though decline in frequency of use and range of domain may be detected over a long time period. Thus, in my terms, the dictum that linguistic change is gradual and imperceptible is misleading. Both innovation and loss must occur at a point of time, but the innovation may spread gradually through the community, and through the lexicon. Definitive loss may have to wait for the last conservative speaker to die, and the final resistant lexical item to fall out of use. This is a very strong requirement that may rarely be attainable in real life. However, we can often write off aberrant items as lexical relics, and assert that a change has been completed as an earlier process is no longer productive.

In modern French, for instance, vowel length distinctions have disappeared from most speakers' repertoires, and hardly anyone audibly distinguishes feminine *aimée* from masculine *aimé*, though some do differentiate *bête* from *bette* (cf. 6.2). We may not wish to conclude that those speakers who still do make occasional vowel length distinctions are not using the French norm, any more than we would exclude from the French-speaking community someone who uses the imperfect subjunctive in conversational style. However we may plausibly assert that the **compensatory lengthening** process that gave rise to vowel length distinctions no longer operates in contemporary French: the rule has been lost, even if there remain some of the items affected by the rule in the past.

Yet it is usually not possible to locate in time a definitive loss until long after the event: the story cannot be coherently told until it has reached its conclusion, and an overall pattern can be discerned.

3.14. CREOLIZATION

The **parameter setting** hypothesis implies sudden change, although it does not exclude the possibility of co-existence of different systems within the same community. In Chomskyan theory, all linguistic change must be grammar change—implying the creation by a child learner of a new system different from that of his elders. But as we have seen it is maintained that such change may be imperceptible in its surface manifestations, in that it does not ordinarily impede communication, nor interrupt continuity.

Creolization is on the other hand seen as a special and sudden case of linguistic change, usually associated with contact between typologically quite different languages, and often believed to be the result of the adoption of a **pidgin**, or simplified, restricted trade jargon, as the first language of a community (**nativization**). In the case of the French creoles, we have little evidence of a French pidgin being used in the creole areas. However, the *lingua franca* (or *sabir*) of the Mediterranean seems to provide a model.

The 'initiation' scene in Molière's *Bourgeois Gentilhomme* exemplifies a Frenchified version of this pidgin.

We have copious evidence, from the sixteenth century on, of Portuguese *lingua do preto* ('black's language'), which we know to have been used by Portuguese and Dutch slavers, in their unsavoury trade. It is claimed by some that this was the language learned by slaves in their sojourns at slave forts on the Guinea Coast and entrepôts on each side of the Atlantic in Cape Verde and Curaçao, and on the long voyage between them. The similarity between English and French New World creoles is sometimes explained in terms of a **relexification** of this Portuguese pidgin, with English and French lexical items, bar a few relics, replacing the Portuguese.

Another hypothesis is that the creoles are 'mixed languages', representing accommodation between European and African languages, or even that they are basically African languages, with European lexical items slotted into West African sentence structures. One of the difficulties with these last suggestions is that we cannot determine which of the host of West African languages could have plausibly provided the basic structure, and we cannot convincingly demonstrate detailed substantive links between creole and African features.

It is sometimes claimed that creoles 'have no grammar' or are like early child language—apparently consisting merely of the haphazard collocation of lexical items. Examination of the complexity of creole structures reveal this view to be untenable, as we have seen: the creoles, unlike pidgins, are true languages, capable of fulfilling all the functions of language, and conforming to the universal principles of language.

If creoles have developed from pidgins, the suggestion that they could have been transformed from a para-language to a fully-fledged language requires some justification. An attractive hypothesis, associated with Bickerton (1981, 1984), derives from the generative model, and eschews the idea of language contact (which Bickerton calls, after Schuchardt, 'substratomane'). Here the story is that children, exposed only to degenerate language material, such as the unstable jargons used in communities with no natural language in common (as for instance in Caribbean slavery conditions), will rely completely on their innate grammar—the **bioprogramme**—to formulate rules for a new language. This will draw for its lexicon on the data presented, but will have a grammatical structure which reflects the universal features of the innate grammar. Bickerton claims that all creoles, of whatever origin, share these basic grammatical features, as a result of a similar genesis. Thus, French creoles are stripped of many of the traditional trappings of French—gender, prepositions, or verb morphology, for instance—but are able to express, with French lexical material, certain basic distinctions, like the difference between specific and non-specific objects, or between anterior and non-anterior events. However, some creoles are more bioprogrammatic than others, depending, for instance, on the degree of contact with a traditional language, or the presence of a stable pidgin.

How far creolization is indeed a different process from other linguistic change, as distinct from being merely a more rapid and radical process, associated with the special social conditions of slavery, is hotly debated. In following chapters we shall compare some French creole developments with parallel changes in metropolitan French. Although in several cases the general **drift** we can discern in popular French is similar to that in the creoles, this similarity can often be ascribed to the strong possibility that the creoles are derived from an early form of popular French, as distinct from the standard language. We have already seen that overseas French dialects, while resembling creoles in many ways, can usually be seen as having different structures.

We have suggested that in Louisiana the *cajun* dialect and the *gumbo* creole have tended to converge, in mutual conflict with English. In those creole areas, however, where both creole and French sit comfortably side by side (as in the DOMs), there is little trace of the **creole continuum** which is held to characterize Caribbean English creoles (where the **basilect** broad creole is regarded as 'bad talk' and speakers, according to social status and register, range through a creole repertoire, via the mixed **mesolect**, to an **acrolect** that approximates to standard English). In the DOMs, on the other hand, the two varieties are regarded as distinct, and used in different circumstances: **code-switching**, with speakers alternating between the two for expressive purposes, rather then indiscriminate **mixing**, is usual. In other areas, there is little interaction between creole and French: in Haiti, for instance, most speakers are monolingual, while in Mauritius, the creole, spoken by all, contrasts with the official language, English.

How then did French 'change into' creole? Or rather, we might ask, how was creole created from French material? It is difficult to deny that there was a West African input into the process. Although there is much linguistic diversity in the area, the languages along the Guinea Coast share certain typological features, including grammaticalized word-order, invariable lexical forms, non-differentiation between lexical categories ('parts of speech'), and the use of arrays of lexical elements to signal tense, aspect, and mood (TAM markers). These can be paralleled in the New World creoles.

On the other hand the African languages in question share characteristics which are not usually present in the creoles—like distinctive tonal systems.

It can be maintained that the difference between French and the creoles is one of type, rather than of system, and that it is a West African type, rather than any substantive elements or individual features, that has been inherited by the creoles. Precisely how this kind of new language could have been created is still disputed.

Given that the newly imported slaves probably rarely shared a mother tongue, perhaps they had to communicate with each other by utilizing their intuition of 'what a language is like'—that is, their typological experience—and furnishing it as best they might with lexical items from the master's language. The new language would be created from this make-shift pidgin, when the first generation of locally born children used the lexical data to fashion their own grammars, setting their **parameters** as for an African language.

This would necessarily be a sudden, one-off occurrence, although thereafter the language could evolve in the same ways as any other language. What is most interesting is that this newly created language did not quickly die out, to be replaced by a variety that was nearer the master's language (**decreolization**), but that it was passed on to newly imported slaves, and to the masters themselves. Possibly the creole came rapidly to be seen as an emblem of identity, and a mark of resistance to domination. It is in maroon (escaped slave) communities, that creoles seem to have been most resilient, and, among French creoles, it is that of Haiti, independent since 1804, and ravaged before then by slave revolts, which has the most evolved and distinctive creole.

The social and linguistic conditions of creolization have not yet been fully clarified. The suggestion that it is not a one-off process, associated with the slave-trade and colonization of the New World, prompts us to ask whether it could explain seemingly abrupt, catastrophic, linguistic changes in the past. Was, for instance, the switch from Latin to French the result of a creolization process? *Mutatis mutandis*, some of the social conditions that prevailed in the Caribbean may have obtained in the Dark Ages: Frankish invaders found, as they settled down, that they had to communicate as well as they could in a foreign tongue—spoken Latin—even with their Gallo-Roman womenfolk. During the language acquisition period, their children may have had experience only of a pidginized and impoverished Latin, and so may have created out of this material a new language. That French is not so radically different from Latin, as the creoles are from French, can be accounted for by the comparatively close relationship between Germanic and Latin varieties, both of which are Western Indo-European, sharing many common features.

However, the comparison can be pushed too far, especially as we know so little about the social and linguistic situation in the Dark

Ages. In particular we have no firm evidence for the dating of the creation of French, nor of an early conscious identification of the language with a community. Besides, we are in danger of so diluting the scope of the term **creolization** that it designates nothing more than a rapid period of linguistic change in which language contact plays a part.

3.15. IS CHANGE INEVITABLE?

It is commonplace, I repeat, to say that 'Languages are constantly changing': I rephrase this as 'Innovations are continually being introduced into usage'. But I insist that such innovations may be ephemeral, and that 'change' can properly be said to occur only when an innovation ousts an earlier feature or process from the language system. However adaptive or natural innovations may be, they may not always gain acceptance in the norm, and be incorporated into the system. We may be able to explain why an innovation succeeded in the past, but cannot predict what will happen in the future.

We are unable to foresee precisely how and when linguistic change will occur, nor what form it will take, although we can confidently predict that, given a long enough run of time, there will be some change. Even though we have a good idea of what sort of changes are likely to take place, we are unable to explain why they should happen in a particular language at a given time, but not in another language or in the same language at another time.

A theory of linguistic change cannot aim, I believe, fully to explain why a particular change takes place, though it can formulate constraints, and predict which changes are likely and make a bet on what changes will not occur. Usually we will presume that where change does occur it will represent a move towards greater simplification, eliminating those language-specific features that are comparatively infrequent among the world's languages. For instance, the unmarked (default) partner in a phonological dichotomy will be retained, at the expense of the less frequent marked partner. Thus, if vowel length distinctions are to be lost, it will be by reduction, by various means, of the long vowels (cf. 6.12): however, such distinctions can persist over very long periods, and new vowel length distinctions can be created by such processes as compensatory lengthening. Similarly one expects vowel nasality, as a marked complexity in the vowel system, to be under threat of elimination (for instance, by simply deleting the nasality element or by hardening it into a consonantal segment). In this case it may be a psychological, rather than a physical, phenomenon: in most languages the assimilatory phonetic nasality that affects vowels in the environment of a nasal consonant is discounted by hearers who often do not perceive it, or dismiss it as an unimportant variant. Yet in most modern French varieties vowel nasality is stable enough, even if there is a tendency to reduce the number of vowels in the nasal series (cf. 6.4). Here one assumes that the existence of a distinctive phonemic nasal vowel series in the language increases the speaker-hearer's awareness and helps to retain the marked feature.

To explain why change should take place at all is difficult enough, if we assume that in order to function efficiently a language has to be structured: when that structure is disrupted by change, how do speakers manage to go on communicating? We have to assume that the speakers have a command of heterogeneous structures that are current in their community, and so are able to switch from one to another, if there is a threat to communication. I have suggested that abandonment of any of these structures over time is more akin to language shift than to linguistic change, and should be explained in sociolinguistic terms. But the proliferation of structures in the first place presumably was a consequence of linguistic changes (unless we implausibly assume that the different structures existed since the beginning of time). However, as I have already suggested, there may be over long periods of time, within a community, stable variation, with comparatively little sign of change or shift.

When a question is impossible to answer, we suspect that it may be misformulated. We can try turning the question of the how, when, and why of linguistic change inside out, and ask rather 'How, why, and when is there no linguistic change?' The fact of linguistic change will be taken for granted, and what we need to explain are the apparent periods of stasis when a language remains fairly stable, in spite of the pressures for change that are exerted through daily use by diverse speakers, and by the hazards of the acquisition process (which, especially if it involves **abduction**, must give latitude for considerable individual variation). True, **Universal Grammar**, the constraints placed on language in general, may account for restrictions on possible change, and phonetic factors, articulatory, acoustic, and perceptual, can place a limit on what phonological changes can succeed. In other words, a language cannot become a non-language, through linguistic change (in spite of the protestations of purists and educationalists, who deplore 'communication by grunt and shrug'), though of course it can die, usually through language shift.

Nevertheless, within these limits there is no reason why linguistic change should not have free rein: again it is probably social factors that operate to block certain changes, presumably at the stage of language acquisition, when the learner deduces, from the reactions of those around him, that some linguistic behaviour is not tolerated in the cultural environment he inhabits.

But this still does not explain why a linguistic change should occur in one language and not in another, or at one time rather than another, nor why some languages, or some stages of the same language, should experience rapid and radical change, whereas others enjoy prolonged stability. The easy answer is that the widespread use of a written version of the language will slow down the processes of change. Clearly, it must hinder loss, as readers will have experience of earlier stages of the language through the texts written in them. This retardation will have more effect in lexicon and morphosyntax, but may even affect phonology, if the graphical form influences pronunciation. But it may be, too, that apparent periods of stability are illusory, merely an effect of textual conservatism. Many of the texts on which we base our knowledge of language in the past are carefully crafted, concealing, rather than revealing, linguistic reality. We know all too well that the language we read today, in newspapers as in literary works, is not always the language of real spoken discourse.

But we are often conscious too that word-spinners, like radio presenters or professional lecturers, may 'talk like books', with few hesitations, repetitions, irrelevancies, ill–chosen words, or incomplete sentences. Illiterate societies have their orators and persuaders quite as often as literate ones, and usually such spokesmen or storytellers are highly respected. Those who set out to instruct, to cajole, or to bamboozle, will usually not introduce the sort of simplifying structural innovations that are most likely to result in linguistic change (though they may very well have an influence in spreading lexical innovations).

Entertainment involving skilled manipulation of language varieties, by stand-up comedians, for instance, can, on the other hand, form a conduit for diffusion of innovations. Non-legitimate language usage is often more fun.

It is usually assumed that under the protective superstructure of a stable legitimate language, written or not, underground forces are mining away at its foundations, and a transformed 'real-life' speech emerges triumphant only when there is a switch of prestige or perception. Thus, in the history of French, the texts of the first millennium of our era were written in Latin, but traditionally it is believed that what was spoken in northern Gaul was much more like the French we know. The first appearance of French texts may have been connected with the Carolingian reform of written Latin, or with social changes that occurred round about the tenth century. Similarly, in modern times, the comparative stability of the modern literary language is thought to hide the changes in the spoken language, which is, however, permitted to show its face today, as a result of greater social democratization and relaxation of perceptions of correctness. Thus apparent linguistic stability is assumed to be merely a false impression conveyed by texts in periods when linguistic control is exercised by a conservative literate élite, and the majority is condemned to silence.

However, it is implausible that the texts, however limited their distribution, can have no relationship to the languages current in the community at the time of their production. Some would claim that the apparently conservative texts could have been conventional representations of a more evolved spoken language, and that account should be taken of the lag between linguistic changes in speech and changes in graphical practice.

True, it is perfectly conceivable that an eighth-century Latin text could have been pronounced as if the words were French: the graphy is merely a convention which can mask the spoken form. But it is hard to believe that the morphological forms of the Latin texts could have been read as corresponding French forms: for instance, CANTĀBŌ could hardly be read as *chanterai*. In such a case, we can, surely, assume a diglossic situation, in which Latin, of a sort, was written and spoken for certain purposes, with a different language, French, being spoken in other circumstances. Again, the redundant Old French case-system (7.17–18) of twelfth-century texts may have had little echo in the spoken language of some users, but it probably remained part of the grammar of others, among whom figured authors like Chrétien de Troyes. Linguistic variation within a community is to be expected, but, I repeat, such variation can remain stable over quite long periods.

So how do we explain the stages of comparative inertia that allow the sort of periodization discussed earlier—with Latin, Old French, and modern French able to be treated as discrete language states, each lasting several hundreds of years? Let us discount pronunciation shifts, lexical innovations, and pragmatic tricks that can alter surface realizations without necessarily affecting structure. Within each of these successive states, the linguistic system seems to have experienced a period of calm with apparent frantic activity between. Here we appeal again to the idea of language being a dynamic system, in which a swirling movement tends to gravitate towards 'attractors' or 'sinks', there to settle until a jolt starts off the movement again. The 'sink' metaphor is similar to that of gutters, storm-drains, or conduits used by Kuroywicz (1949) in describing analogical change: *'Il en est comme l'eau de pluie qui doit prendre un chemin prévu (gouttières, égouts, conduits) une fois qu'il pleut. Mais la pluie n'est pas une nécessité.'*

In language, such settling points seem to be provided by **grammaticalization**, or incorporation of discourse features into the grammar, usually by a unidirectional change in status of linguistic items over time, so that they become more firmly embedded in the system. Traditionally, the term grammaticalization is used when lexical items become functional items. Meillet (1912), who speaks of *'l'attribution du caractère grammatical à un mot jadis autonome'*, gives the example of the verb 'to be' being bleached of its full lexical value ('to exist') to become an **auxiliary** in the **compound perfect**, by a series of steps:

(4) *Je suis celui qui suis* (essence: 'I am the person I am') > *Je suis chez moi* (temporary location: 'I am at home') > *Je suis malade* (temporary state: 'I am ill') > *Je suis parti* (auxiliary: 'I am [have] gone').

Other classic examples in French (cf. Chapters 7 and 8) include lexical nouns *pas* and *personne* becoming **negative** markers, free-standing personal pronouns *je, tu, il*, etc. becoming **clitic** person markers and the noun in ablative case MENTE 'with a mind' becoming the adverbial suffix -*ment*. This latter case, in particular, can also be called one of **morphologization**, when an autonomous **(free-form)** word become a **bound-form** suffix (that is, part of a word).

The term morphologization can also be used when a phonological rule ceases to operate automatically in phonological contexts, but is retained in certain morphological contexts. The example of vowel **nasalization** will be discussed in 6.4.

I use grammaticalization as a cover term to indicate the crystallization into a new formal representation of the expression of meaning or grammatical function. I include under the heading of grammaticalization, the sort of **syntacticization**, by which, for instance, a discourse-based **topic** can become a syntactic **subject** and pragmatic word-order can become fixed and carry grammatical meaning (cf. 8.3). Another type of grammaticalization is called **lexicalization** by which a syntagma becomes fixed as a single lexical item, whose meaning cannot be automatically deduced from the component parts, as in *pomme de terre* 'potato' not 'earth apple'.

As evidence of the cohesiveness of the item, we can point to constructions like *pommes de terre rouges*/**pommes rouges de terre*.

A slightly different case is when a derivative like *laitier* 'milk-person, dairyman' loses its transparency to become a simplex lexical item as in *épicier* 'spice-person' > 'grocer', or even more radically in *boucher* 'buck-person' > 'butcher', or *boulanger* 'bread-ball-person' > 'baker'. Yet another type of lexicalization can be exemplified by the incorporation of the **reflexive** pronoun into an inherent pronominal, like *s'évanouir* 'to faint', where the *se* has morphological and syntactic status, but no lexical meaning (cf. *se laver* 'to wash (oneself)' where the *se* still has reflexive meaning).

Phonologization of **allophones** to become separate **phonemes**, following **phonemic split**, can be seen as another type of grammaticalization, to be discussed in Chapter 6.

A grammaticalized item, like the **morpheme**, **word**, **phoneme**, or grammaticalized construction, like **Subject-Verb-Object (SVO)** word-order, allows economical packaging of information. It is readily acquired, requiring no further analysis. Thus the reinterpretation and imperfect reproduction that makes for change in the language acquisition process may be less frequent with efficiently grammaticalized items and constructions, than with less constrained elements. In a social environment that favours smooth transmission of knowledge from one generation to the next, morphological conventions in particular can resist the attrition and distortion occasioned by phonetic slippage.

Once a language has settled into a steady state, it may take a catastrophe to shake it up again. Some languages, like Icelandic, Lithuanian, or Eskimo, are recognized as having preserved for very long periods complex morphological systems that may have been disrupted in related languages. They often tend to be used in isolated, stable communities: disturbing factors are usually thought to be social in origin—invasions, and the like. Anything which would seriously hamper the language acquisition process—like a physical or psychological rupture of the bond between children and their elders—is however likely to upset the fragile equilibrium and set off a series of interconnected changes that can transform the whole language.

3.16. INTERACTION BETWEEN CHANGES IN SUBSYSTEMS

I have suggested that there may be no such thing as global linguistic change, which affects, rather, individual subsystems of the language. This is not to say that in each subsystem the same sort of principles do not apply: in the absence of special factors, there will be a default movement towards simplification, to unmarkedness and to **transparency** (or **iconicity**). However, as I have pointed out, some aspects of language will change more readily than others. Pronunciation is particularly subject to variation, for reasons associated with differences in individual articulatory habits and social identification. Lexical items come and go, according to the whims of fashion. But frequently these changes have scant impact on any part of the system: this is particularly true of lexical change, which may have little in the way of patterning (except where changes of cultural attitude are signalled lexico-semantically, cf. Chapters 4 and 5).

Morphology, on the other hand, is by its nature systematic and tightly organized: it tends to get stuck in a rut of its own making, requiring some sort of heave from outside to start it moving. Comparatively little leeway for change is available within the syntactic system, though pragmatic requirements can alter the superficial appearance of sentences, and then feed into the system. It can be claimed that semantics is universal, in the sense that all human beings can, if they wish, mean the same things. Yet every sentence uttered is a new creation and has a different meaning. Thus it is hard to know what sense we can attach to the concept of semantic change. I shall be looking at the different subsystems separately in the following chapters, and distinguishing as appropriate between superficial and systemic 'changes'.

Nevertheless, a change in one subsystem can have a knock-on effect in the others, like cannoning billiard balls. Traditionally, it is assumed that phonological change is the prime mover in the process. Grammatical cohesion can be disrupted when an overt marker becomes unrecognizable, or disappears, as a consequence of uncontrollable phonetic distortion, so that speakers have to find fresh means to make their meaning clearer. This can lead to a general upheaval in the system, as the new learner seeks to restore some sort of order to the apparently chaotic signals he receives.

But it can work the other way round too: the borrowing of a foreign lexical item can introduce a disparate phonetic element, which the new learner may then seek to incorporate into the phonological system.

For instance, in modern French the velar nasal [ŋ] of *camping*, *dancing*, *parking*, etc. is sometimes associated with the palatal nasal /ɲ/ phoneme, and sometimes with the dental nasal /n/ phoneme, and sometimes has established itself as a separate phonological item.

Syntactic change can render morphological distinctions redundant, so that they risk the operation of Occam's razor: the modern French fixing of word-order can be said to have permitted the loss of the Old French case-system, and to make noun–adjective gender agreement vulnerable. Similarly morphological change can trigger syntactic change: the levelling of verb person marking can contribute to transforming French into a **non-pro-drop** language. Loss of a lexical item can leave a phonological distinction bereft of exemplars: *jeûne* 'fast' is almost the only safeguard of the obsolescent /œ/–/ø/ contrast, so that its non-use will mean that the contrast will be lost. Furthermore, change of meaning in a word can mean that it ceases to occur in certain constructions, so that syntactic contrasts may be weakened: *espérer* now means only 'to hope' and not 'to wait', so that it is no longer necessary to disambiguate it by the differential use of a dependent indicative or subjunctive.

Examples like these will be discussed in the following chapters. Here I merely wish to stress that no linguistic change can be considered totally in isolation: a single move in the chess-game changes the relationship of all the pieces on the board.

One recent introduction into the terminology of historical linguistics call for special comment. This is **exaptation**, borrowed by Roger Lass (1990) from evolutionary theory, for the use of residue items, washed up on the shore by the waves of change, which, beachcomber-like, the *bricoleur* (DIY enthusiast) language-builder can recycle and cobble for the construction of a new systematic contrast. A simple French example, with some similarities to an English one cited by Lass, might be the *tu/vous* distinction. This quite early in French lost total identification with the singular/ plural distinction (but cf. 2.2), so that *vous* became the default second person pronoun (accompanied usually, when *vous* is the subject, by the distinctive inflectional ending *-ez* [e]). This left *tu* adrift, and able to acquire emotive and social colouring, expressing, at first, the subordinate status of the addressee, whether by age or social standing, but also solidarity among interlocutors of the same status. A further development, found especially in Canadian French, is to refer to an indeterminate human participant in an event (as *on* has tended to move towards the designation of an inclusive plural, replacing *nous* in many contexts, cf. Chapter 8). This has left, in some varieties, many verb paradigms marked by an inflectional ending only in the form which directly addresses one or more interlocutors:

(5) *je* / *tu* / *il* / *on* / *ils* [sot] (*saute, sautes, sautent*), [sote] (*sautais, sautait, sautaient*); but *vous* [sote] (*sautez*), [sotje] (*sautiez*).

Other examples of exaptation will be discussed in Chapter 8.

3.17. EVIDENCE

The traces of the linguistic past that, as historians, we rely on most to reconstruct earlier stages of the language are, as we have already seen, mostly textual. In the earliest periods of French, we seldom know precisely why, or by whom, the texts were compiled. We are not even always sure that they are quite what they seem, and do not represent some sort of hoax, or deliberate deceit. Most of all we cannot be certain how far they are a genuine attempt to capture the reality of the language of their time, nor to what extent, and in what ways, there was variation in this language (cf. Chapter 2).

The 'first French text'—the Strasburg Oaths, 842—presents a good example of the ambiguous nature of this sort of evidence: cf. Cerquiglini 1991, Posner 1993*a*.

However, we are helped in our reconstruction of the past by appeal to the **uniformitarian** principle, which allows us to assume that past languages were examples of language, as we know it now, and that compilers of texts had the same sort of intentions, and made the same sort of errors, as their fellows do today. In studying past French texts, we also assume that not everything has changed, and that any changes will have followed some well-understood pathways.

Some historical linguists, in an attempt to understand the complex social factors that influence change, prefer to concentrate on the present, about which we have more abundant, more reliable, and more manipulable evidence, and to study 'change in progress', rather than in an unfathomable past. I have suggested that, valuable though such study undoubtedly is, it leaves the 'history' out of historical linguistics. History has a tale to tell, and the story-line is stronger if we know how the tale ends. When a linguistic feature has not yet been lost, its fortunes may be reversed (or it may be **exapted** and turn up in another guise). Once it is lost, on the other hand, an irreversible change has occurred, and that part of the story is at an end.

So, for me, a long run of time is required for the study of linguistic change. Yet in the long run we are all dead: real time comparisons on a grand scale cannot be conducted by mere mortals. Thus we do rely very much on textual evidence. This is copious and trustworthy in modern French, so there is much to be said for studying linguistic change over the last five hundred years, rather than over the five centuries before that. Yet linguistic historians often privilege earlier material, perhaps because it is more exotic, but also because it allows greater scope for speculation. The common perception also is that linguistic change was more rampant, and thus more exciting, between the years 1000 and 1500, than between 1500 and 2000.

On the face of it, this seems unlikely, given that in other aspects of life the rate of change has gathered momentum over the centuries. However, it is true that there is less conspicuous variation in the language of published texts in the modern period: since printing and standardization, the legitimate written code barely tolerates variation and experimentation. On the other hand there is, with the spread of literacy, a plethora of unpublished informal writings that can be exploited for their linguistic information. Moreover in the last hundred years we have had, first, phonetic transcriptions, and, later, electronic recordings of actual speech. The sort of corpora of spoken language that have been collected in the last few decades for sociolinguistic study and pedagogical purposes will provide invaluable evidence for students of linguistic change in the centuries to come.

The linguistic interpretation of texts is not however straightforward. In the following chapters we shall adduce evidence from texts to support arguments about the direction and dating of changes in lexicon, phonology, and morphosyntax: sometimes the evidence is ambiguous, and has to be accredited from other sources. Luckily in the modern period we have also more direct evidence, in the shape of comments on usage by contemporaries. We can also attempt to reconstruct chronological variation, by examining modern geographical variation, assuming that some, usually outpost, areas retain more archaic usage, that may have been outstripped in the go-ahead, innovative cultural centres.

But the problem remains that texts, of whatever form, provide evidence only of performance, *parole*, and not of underlying systems. By examining the relative frequency of occurrences of features in our texts, we can guess which of them were widespread and vigorous and which were at a low ebb and circumscribed, and we can reconstruct the systems that may underlie the usage. But we cannot know whether a feature unattested in the texts was merely accidentally absent, or totally ungrammatical. When we cannot consult (long-since-dead) native speakers, there will remain insoluble enigmas.

Further Reading

On linguistic change and historical linguistics: Ahlqvist 1982, Aitchison 1992, H. Andersen 1973, 1975, 1989, 1995, H. Andersen and Koerner 1990, J. M. Anderson 1973, J. M. Anderson and Jones 1974, Anttila 1989[2], Boltanski 1995, Breivik and Jahr 1989, Bynon 1977, Christie 1976, Clark and Roberts 1993, Coseriu 1958, G. W. Davis and Iverson 1992, Gerritsen and Stein 1992, Helgorsky 1981, Hock 1992, Hoenigswald 1960, Jeffers and Lehiste 1979, Joly 1988, C. Jones 1993, J. E. Joseph 1989, Koerner 1983, R. D. King 1969*a*, Koopman *et al.* 1987, Kroch 1989, Labov 1994, Lass 1980*a*, 1990, 1997, Lehmann 1992[3], Lehmann and Malkiel 1968, 1982, Li 1977, McMahon 1994, J. P. Maher *et al.* 1982, van Marle 1993, Paul 1880, Posner 1988*b*, 1990*b*, 1993*a*, 1994*a*, Ramat *et al.* 1987, Trask 1996, Traugott *et al.* 1980, Weinreich *et al.* 1968.

On the role of language acquisition: H. Andersen 1973, Chomsky 1981, Lightfoot 1991, Slobin 1977, Traugott and Smith 1993.

On time in language: Ardener 1971, Chen 1972, Shapiro 1991.

On drift: Lass 1980*b*, Malkiel 1981, Sapir 1921, Vennemann 1974.

On creolization: Arends 1996, Bickerton 1981, 1984, Chaudenson 1988, Holm 1988–9, Manessy 1988, Posner 1980*b*, 1986, 1987, 1993*b*, Schlieben-Lange 1976, Versteegh 1991.

On grammaticalization: Hopper and Traugott 1993, Meillet 1912.

On evidence: Fisiak 1990, Posner 1990*a*, van Reenen and Schøsler 1990.

4

Lexical Change

For most speakers of a language the most obvious linguistic changes
are of words and their meanings. The **word**—in the sense of **lexical
free form**—is the linguistic unit of which the speaker is most
conscious. It is usually seen as a discrete entity, representing a
concept, a distinct meaning. Thus the entry or exit of a word from
contemporary usage, or a shift in lexical meaning, is salient for the
language user. Yet these are the changes which usually occupy least
space in general works about the theory of linguistic change.
Admittedly quite a deal of attention is paid to **borrowing**, in the
context of **language contact**. But, on the whole, discussion of change
in the **lexicon** soon descends to citation of individual examples and a
general picture of how a lexicon changes rarely emerges.

This is partly because it is rather difficult to delimit the **lexicon** of
a language. Can we, for instance, distinguish the individual's
vocabulary from the word-stock available for the whole community?
Is this latter merely the sum of all vocabularies? We all know that
every day we hear previously unknown words, and we may find it
hard to judge whether they are indeed part of our own language.
Nowadays we rush to the dictionary to confirm our intuitions:
word-games like *Scrabble* or crosswords require recourse to a
dictionary to establish an authoritative verdict.

If we are unsure about the scope of the lexicon at any one time,
how can we trace its change over time? Even when we pass
judgement on a word in an old text as 'no longer in use' we risk
revealing our ignorance, for it may well be that indeed the word
figures in a dialectal or technical vocabulary with which we are not
conversant. Similarly we cannot be sure that because we have not
encountered a word in an old text, that that word was not in use at
the time the text was written. Indeed, computer scanning of old texts

has been pushing the 'first appearance' date of many words further and further back into the past.

One way we can get round some of these difficulties is by the use of statistics. We can decide that the modern **lexicon** that concerns us comprises those words that are indubitably known by all speakers of the language, the relatively most frequently used words (arbitrarily drawing the line at, say, one or five thousand, instead of upward of 100,000). Then at least we can make a start on an account of how this limited lexicon came into being over time. The use of lexical statistics seems a far cry from more traditional 'word life-histories' which often concentrate on the 'hard' words and recount amusing anecdotes about the way words are adopted or discarded.

French historical **lexicology** has in more recent time made fruitful use of statistical methods, and I shall not shrink from drawing on this tradition. Another favourite field of research in the French lexicon has been the linking of lexical change to social factors—**la lexicologie**, as initiated by Georges Matoré (1953*a*), caught the imagination of a host of young scholars in the fifties and has continued as a powerful tradition to the present day. Within this school, **neologism** can be seen as a symbol of change of social attitudes. Likewise the growth of specialist languages—of politics, art, technology, and so on—with their own technical lexicons mirrors the history of a nation.

Another, related, approach looks at the **lexical field**: the near-**synonymic** words that interact and shift semantically over time. Sometimes one word will drive out others, or perhaps a number of differentiated words will come to express what was earlier covered by a single word. **Onomasiology**—the study of the way one concept can be expressed by a number of words—links in with the lexical field idea. These methods are well represented in studies of French lexical history.

The most traditional aspect of lexical history is the tracing back of a word to its origins: the term **etymology** implies that the earlier form conforms better to the 'truth', as far as meaning is concerned. I shall discuss the methods and findings of etymological investigation.

One thing that is striking about the history of modern French attitudes to their language has been the intense interest in the lexicon and in defining and delimiting the use of words. The most important instrument for this task is the dictionary. From the sixteenth century **lexicography** was seen as a valuable endeavour, and from the seventeenth century monolingual French dictionaries began to appear. The Académie Française's principal task, recall, was to establish an authoritative dictionary of the language to enhance its prestige. The string of French dictionaries that have appeared to the present day have not usually limited themselves to 'hard words', but give guidance on all aspects of the use of the legitimate language (including advice on what should be avoided), and how to increase the 'word-power' of their users. Of particular interest are the influential **synonym** dictionaries, which, since the seventeenth century, have sought subtly to differentiate words expressing similar things.

The financial support given by the French state to the computerized *Trésor de la langue française* project, with vast and growing data base of French-language texts, shows how interest in the language has not abated today. The information supplied by this enterprise continues to fuel research especially into the history of the French lexicon, and to help to provide a firm scientific base for the study of lexical change that threatens sometimes to be merely a jolly pastime, providing anecdotal amusement—'butterfly collecting' as some sneeringly call it.

4.2. CAN THE LEXICON OF A LANGUAGE CHANGE?

This seems a silly question, especially as I have just claimed that speakers are acutely conscious of lexical changes. However the crucial term here is 'a language'. We have already seen that what precisely is designated by a language name like 'French' is debatable. It can be claimed that the most salient difference between two languages is their lexical items, which are **arbitrary** in the Saussurean sense, and which place the greatest burden on the memory for learners of a foreign language. Traditional **comparative philology** groups languages into families on the basis of their lexico-phonetic similarities (i.e. the way similar concepts are regularly represented by similar sound-sequences). Admittedly additional weight is accorded to **bound** forms (**affixes**), rather than **free forms** (**words**), but this is mainly because the latter are more easily borrowed between languages, and therefore are not quite so diagnostic of common ancestry.

For the purpose of defining a language family, and within that an individual language, we can fix on the criterion of **basic lexicon**—that part of the individual's vocabulary which is learned early in life and which is less likely to yield to language contact pressures. In this case, clearly any major changes in the basic lexicon entails by definition a change of language.

Note that by this criterion the French creoles, whose basic lexicons are comprised, as to more than 95 per cent, of identifiable French words, are indisputably varieties of French, even though they are grammatically distinct.

As an illustration let us look at a sample taken from the *français fondamental* dictionary of the most basic 3,500 words, which make up all but a tiny proportion of the words in any modern French text, and with which it is possible to communicate in French on most everyday topics. I choose, at random, to look at the letter *l*, with some 100 words listed, including essential function words like *le, la, les*. Of these nearly half probably were handed down in uninterrupted succession from Latin, and most have cognates in other Romance languages. They include:

(1) *langue* (LINGUA), *laver* (LAVARE), *lent* (LENTUM), *lieu* (LOCUM), *lit* (LECTUM), *loi* (LĒGEM), *long* (LONGUM), *lune* (LŪNA).

A few have forms that look slightly irregular phonologically, like:

(2) *loup* (LŬPUM) for attested *leu*; *linge* (LINEUM) alongside *ligne* (LINEA),

and some show a shift of meaning from Latin, like:

(3) *lourd* 'heavy' (LŪRIDUM 'lurid'), *loyal* 'loyal' (LĒGALEM 'lawful').

For some, too, the postulated Latin etymon is not classical, like:

(4) *lâcher* 'to let go, slacken'

which seems to derive from a distortion of LAXUM 'loose', with [ks] (x) reversed to [sk], or perhaps from a derivative LAXICARE, compared with:

(5) *laisser*,

the regular development of LAXARE (cf. Italian *lascare* 'to slacken a rope'/ *lasciare* 'to let, leave'). Another example is:

(6) *lessive* 'washing'

from a derivative of LIX 'ash, soda' (used to clean clothing).

Another 20-odd per cent of this basic word-stock also derives from Latin, but has not undergone regular phonological development. Some items have replaced earlier 'popular' words:

(7) *lac* (12th c.) 'lake', earlier *lai* (LACUM); *légume* (15th c.) 'vegetable', earlier *leum* (LĔGŪMEN 'bean').

Others are etymologically related to popular words, but presumably entered the language later:

(8) *leçon* (11th c.), *lecture, lecteur* (14th c.), *lectrice* (17th c.) / *lire* (LĔGĔRE 'to pick out, to read'); *libre, liberté, libération* (14th c.), *libérer* (15th c.), / *livrer* 'to deliver' (LĪBĔR etc. 'free'); *local* (14th c.), *locataire* (16th c.) / *lieu* (LOCUM 'place'); *libraire* (14th c.) / *livre* (LIBRUM 'bark of a tree, book'); *littérature* (15th c.) / *lettre* (LITTĔRA 'letter').

Some of the Latinisms were coined quite late in the history of French:

(9) *laboratoire* (17th c.), *litre* (18th c.), *luxe* (17th c.), *lycée* (19th c.).

This high proportion of basic words of Latin origin establishes French as a Romance language. To these should be added about another 20 per cent of native formations, based on simple words of Latin origin, like:

(10) *laitier* 'dairyman' (14th c. cf. *lait* < LACTEM); *largeur* (13th c. cf. *large* < LARGUM); *lendemain* (< *IN-DE-MANE 'in the morning'); *lieutenant* (13th c. LOCUM-TENENS 'place-holder'); *libre-service* (20th c. LIBRUM + SERVITIUM 'free service')

There are also one or two common *l*-words that appear to be borrowed from other Romance languages. One is:

(11) *lapin* 'rabbit', which replaces (15th c.) *connil/connin* (CŬNĪCŬLUM),

perhaps because of the latter's association with obscene *con* (CŬNĔUS 'wedge'). The modern word seems to be an adaptation of Portuguese *lapão* derived from LĔPOREM 'hare' (*lièvre*). The other is

(12) *liste*

in its modern sense which seems to have been borrowed from Italian in the sixteenth century, though it was originally of Germanic origin.

There are only three other Germanic words in our sample:

(13) *laid* 'ugly', *loger* 'to lodge',

which are found in early texts, and:

(14) *loupe* 'magnifying glass',

found from the fourteenth century for 'precious stone'.

The conclusion we draw from this sample is that, leaving aside phonological alterations and some semantic shifts, the most basic French lexicon is still recognizably Latin, and changes have not been radical.

4.3. ETYMOLOGY

The most traditional way to study history of a word is to search for its **etymology**: that is, for its ancestors in past languages. For the Romance languages we rarely go further back into history than Latin, from which the majority of modern French words are derived. Most of the most common French words have cognates in one or other of the Romance languages. Even where French differs from them (cf. Table 4.1), the modern word has often replaced a more familiar Romance word in comparatively recent times, and, in any case, usually derives from a variant form that can itself be traced back to Latin.

The term 'etymology' itself is composed of Greek elements literally meaning 'talking about the truth': it was originally assumed that if we could go back to the origins of language then we would discover the 'true' meaning of a word, which has since been corrupted. Etymologizing, therefore, long preceded other types of historical linguistic endeavour and was for a long time viewed as part of philosophical semantics.

Before the nineteenth century any fantastical etymology could be

TABLE 4.1. Some common modern French words that differ
from those of other Romance languages

---

assez 'enough' < AD-SATIS(= 'much', cf. Italian *assai*, until 17th c.),
   replaced *trop* 'enough, too much' < Frankish.

beaucoup (1272) compound; replaced *moult* < MULTUS 16th c. and *prou* <
   PRODIS, cf. *peu ou prou* 'more or less'.

cracher 'spit' 12th c. Perhaps onomatopoeic; replaced *espuer* < SPŪTARE.

entendre < INTENDERE, replaced *ouir* < AUDIRE 17th c.

gauche 'left hand' (< Germanic 'to wobble' > 'clumsy'), replaced *senestre*
   < SINISTRA 16th c.

il faut < FALLIT, replaced *estuet* < OPUS EST (15th c.)

joli < *jolif* < Scandinavian? 'gay, merry, jolly' till 17th c.; from 13th c.
   'elegant' > 'pretty'.

lourd 'heavy' from 16th c. < LŪRIDUS 'lurid' > 'stupid'; replaced *grevos* <
   GRAV(EM)-OSUS.

maison < MANSIONE 'place to stay' / *chez* < CASA (also in toponyms e.g.
   Chaise-Dieu).

mauvais 'bad' < MALEFATIUS 'ill-fated'.

méchant 'wicked' < MAL-CADENTE 'falling out badly'.

poule 'hen' < PULLA 'young animal', replaced *geline* < GALLINA.

rien 'nothing' < REM replaced *nient* < NE-GENTEM by 17th c.

sale 'dirty' < Germanic, replaces *put* (cf. *putain* 'whore') < PŪTIDUS
   'stinking'.

songer 'to dream' > 'to think' 18th c. < SOMNIARE / *rêver* 'to wander' till
   17th c. > 'to dream' (of uncertain origin).

toujours (cf. Occitan *totjorn* 'all day, always') compound; replaced *sempre*
   < SEMPER.

viande 'meat' < VIVENDA 'things necessary for life, food' (or perhaps
   derived from VIA 'road, way'), in 16th c. replaced in the culinary sense
   chair < CARNE (> 'flesh', but cf. *charcutier*, 13th–18th c. *chaircutier*).

ville 'town' < VILLA 'country house', while *cité* < CIVITĀTEM > 'citadel'
   from the 14th c. In Old French they could be used interchangeably for an
   urban agglomeration, but *ville* came to have connotations of a more
   modern town, while *cité* was used for a fortified town.

---

accepted as plausible. Usually a vague phonological resemblance
between words at different chronological points sufficed in the
postulation of an etymological relationship, but it was the semantic
connection between two allegedly related words that was regarded
as of prime importance.

A classic comic example is the derivation of the Latin word for 'bee' APES, from AB + PES 'without leg', from which it was deduced that bees originally had no legs. A rather less comic seventeenth-century French example is the derivation of *haricot* 'a kind of bean' from Latin FABA 'a broad bean' (which regularly gives *fève*), on the grounds of similarity of meaning, and some imagined remote phonological similarity (whereas the word was actually borrowed, with the vegetable itself, from Amerindian sources).

Etymology was revolutionized by the realization that sound-change is regular, in the sense that the historical development of sound-segments in given environments is predictable to a significant extent. Now etymological speculation had to be legitimized by reference to regular sound-change: haphazard matching of phonetic similarities would no longer do. Phonological correspondence was paramount in the recognition of derivation. Etymological speculation could then concentrate particularly on semantic questions.

Thus etymology is rarely concerned with transparent etyma, where sound-change has been regular and meaning has changed little, as in:

(15) *faire* < FACERE 'to do'; *dire* < DICERE 'to say'; *voir* < VIDERE 'to see'.

Such forms provide the basic data for the formulation of sound-laws, and pose no problems for the etymologist.

Sometimes, however, words at different chronological stages in a language are clearly closely related semantically, but pose phonological problems, in that they do not conform to the sound-laws formulated on the basis of unproblematic cases. The phonological anomalies are often explained away, by appeal to perturbing factors, like learned development, or by relegating the irregularity to an earlier stage by postulating a variant, unattested (*) etymon as in:

(16) *agir* < AGERE 'to act',

with anomalous phonological form (**aire* is expected) which is explained as a Latinism attested first in the fifteenth century. Another example is:

(17) *tout* 'all' < TŌTUS 'complete',

which would regularly have resulted in *[tø], not [tu], and so it is assumed to derive from *TOTTUS, where the geminate [tt] provides the environment for blocked syllable development of the [o] > [u] (cf. Chapter 6). Similarly:

(18) *pouvoir* (older *poeir*) 'to be able',

is assumed to derive from *POTĒRE, an analogically remodelled form, rather than classical Latin POSSE.

In some cases we are left questioning what precisely the regular sound-change would be, because the evidence is too scant, or ambiguous, as in:

(19) *écrire* / older *escrivre* < SCRĪBERE 'to write'.

More often etymology takes for granted the regular phonological correspondence between chronologically consecutive forms, and concentrates on the semantic shifts that they exemplify:

(20) *on* ' one' < HOMO 'human being'; *savoir* 'to know' < SAPERE 'to taste'; *très* 'very' < TRANS 'across'; *penser* 'to think' < PENSARE 'to weigh' (cf. *peser*); *rien* 'nothing' < REM 'thing'; *mettre* 'to put' < MITTERE 'to send'; *poser* 'to pose, put' < PAUSARE 'to pause'; *chercher* 'to seek' < CIRCARE 'to go around'; *forêt* 'forest < (SILVA) FORESTIS 'wood outside the town'; *rue* 'street' < RUGA 'rut, furrow'; *argent* 'money' < ARGENTUM 'silver'; *souvenir* 'remember' < SUBVENIRE 'to come under'; *mener* 'to lead' < MINARI 'to threaten'; *papier* 'paper' < PAPYRUS.

It is on the basis of such examples that hypotheses about semantic change are formulated.

Etymologists, however, often focus most of their attention on words whose origin is not obvious, either phonologically or semantically. Rigorous procedure demands that they avoid postulating etyma that do not fit into phonological patterns, but they may venture far in postulating non-Latin origins, perhaps onomatopoeic:

(21) *petit* 'small',

or literary:

(22) *manger* 'to eat' < MANDUCARE (from the name of a glutton in comic writing),

or Germanic:

(23) *regarder* 'to look' < *wardon 'to guard'; *bois* 'wood' < *busk 'bush'; *choisir* 'to choose' < *kausjan 'to pick out'.

Sometimes an eccentric semantic development is extrapolated:

(24) *trouver* 'to find' < ?TURBARE 'to disturb'; *tuer* 'to kill'
      < ?*TŪTARE 'to look after'.

How the meaning of a word can change will be discussed in
Chapter 5.

4.4. LEXICAL LOSS

As we shall see (4.5), the lexicons of most literate languages seem to
increase over time, as older words are preserved in texts and so do
not completely lose currency. Archaisms in formal registers can
carry prestige, especially in societies which place high value on
education and tradition, even though old-fashioned speech habits
can attract mockery in the modern environment. French is unusual
in that there seems to have been a definite break in lexical tradition
in the seventeenth century, when élite groups turned their backs on
folk-culture.

Already Renaissance and Reformation France had rejected medieval
attitudes, but then the search was for lexical richness and variety, as
reflecting the diversity of the human condition. Seventeenth-century fashionable society sought, rather, elegance and good taste, with a lexicon that
avoided vulgarity and exuberance, seeking concision and lucidity with the
careful choice of the *mot juste*.

Table 4.2 gives some examples of Old French common words that
were definitively lost from the language during this period. In
discussing **synonymy** (4.9) we shall look at other examples of loss.

Many more words were confined to specialist or dialect usage, as
standardization took hold. Some lexical loss is bound to occur over
time, even in the basic vocabulary, but it is surprising that 38 per
cent of the words in the oldest texts have not survived the thousand
years into modern French. It is even more remarkable that 28 per
cent of them were lost in the seventeenth century, which suggests a
sharp break in continuity.

The explanations often given for loss of words usually point to
the phonological developments of the early modern period, and in
particular to reduction of diphthongs and to final vowel and
consonant truncation, which left the language with many mono-

TABLE 4.2. Some Old French words lost or restricted in function
during the sixteenth and seventeenth centuries

Old French	Modern French
douloir < DOLĒRE (cf. *douleur*)	*souffrir* (< SUBFERRE 'support') > 'suffer'
eissir < EXIRE	*sortir* (< SORTIRI 'throw lots') > 'escape' > 'go out'
faillir < FALLERE 'to trick' > 'to be lacking', 'to err' > (16th c.) 'to be on the point of'	*manquer* < Ital. *mancare* 'to be lacking' (< MANCUS 'maimed, defective')
guerpir < Germanic **werpjan* 'to throw' 'to give in', 'to leave'	*laisser* < LAXARE 'loosen' > 'to let, allow'
	quitter (< QUIETUS 'quiet') > 'to let be', 'to leave'
lé < LATUS 'wide'	*large* < LARGUS 'abundant' > 'wide'
main < MANE 'morning' (cf. *demain*)	*matin* < MATUTINUS 'early in the morning'
noise < NAUSEA 'sea-sickness' > 'row'	*bruit* (< *BRŪGERE 'to roar') > 'noise'
moudre < MULGĒRE, *MULGERE 'to milk'	*traire* < TRAHERE 'to pull' > 'to milk'
muer < MUTARE 'to change' > 'to moult'	*changer* < CAMBIARE (from Celtic) 'to alter, to exchange, to change'
nombre < NŬMERUS 'number, digit' > 'quantity'	*numéro* < Ital. *numero* 'number'; *chiffre* < Ital. *cifra* < Arabic *sifr* 'zero' > 'digit'
od < APUD 'near, with'	*avec* < APUD HOC 'with that' > 'with'
ost < HOSTIS 'stranger, enemy' > 'army'	*armée* (< ARMA 'arms' > 'armed band' > 'army'
quanz < QUANTUS 'how big' > 'how much'	*combien* (< QUŌMODO BENE 'how well') > 'how much, how many'
souloir < SOLĒRE 'to be used to'	*avoir l'habitude* (cf. Latinism *habitude*, also *avoir (à) coutume* (CONSUETUDINE 'condition' > 'appearance' > 'habit' 'custom')

syllabic homonyms. Thus *ost* 'army' would have become identical with *os* 'bone', *eau* 'water', *au* 'to the', while *lé* 'wide' would be indistinguishable from *lait* 'milk', *lez* 'side', *les* 'the'. But other homonymic clashes were not avoided: *saut, seau, sot, sceau* survive, for instance. And if *noif* 'snow' < NIVEM is lost, following a clash with *noix* 'walnut' < NUCEM, *chef* survives homonymy with *chez*, by dint of reintroducing its final consonant, just as does *dot* 'dowry', which clashed with *dos*. Homonymic clashes are perfectly tolerable when there are differences of syntagmatic, paradigmatic, or semantic distribution between the rivals, and French has made ample use of strategies like **spelling pronunciation** (cf. 6.14) to avoid ambiguity.

Another traditional explanation for the loss of words at this period appeals to the search for more substantial lexical forms, when phonological change had reduced words to their minimum syllabic structure. Where a longer version was available, it is true that it did sometimes replace the shorter version: thus *main* 'morning', homophonous with the word for 'hand', gave way to *matin*, *hui* < HODIE was eliminated by the compounded *aujourd'hui*, and *heur* 'luck', homophonous with *heure*, survived only in *bonheur*, *malheur*, and *heureux*. But, again, the French basic lexicon has many very short words: in a wider vocabulary, true, Latinisms have frequently replaced the abbreviated popular forms, but this was probably more a matter of relative prestige, than of word-length.

Indeed, the not infrequent abandonment, in the seventeenth century, of the derivative forms so beloved by the sixteenth, points in that direction. Diminutives, especially, came to be regarded as rather 'twee', and so monosyllabic *gras* 'fat' or *arc* 'bow, arch' were preferred to *grasselet* (but cf. modern colloquial *grassouillet* 'podgy') and *archet* (specialized as a 'bow' for string instruments).

Perhaps a more convincing traditional explanation for word-loss in the early modern period is that morphologically irregular words often gave way to regular rivals: thus *gésir* 'to lie', *quérir* 'to seek', *clore* 'to shut', *ouir* 'to hear', virtually disappeared, leaving only a few set phrases (like *ci-gît* . . . 'here lies . . .', *huis clos* 'in camera'). But even in these examples, although *coucher*, *chercher*, and *fermer* are regular enough, the same is not true of *entendre*. The disfavouring of the older words was a gradual process, though it was usually only in the seventeenth century that a clean break was made, when fashionable attitudes hardened against all that was timeworn and reminiscent of the feudal era.

To some extent the desire to keep up with the fashion, in speech as in other spheres, has remained characteristic of French *civilisation*, so that it has been estimated that about 20 per cent of the current lexicon (taking this as at about 60,000 words) changes within ten years. But here it is mainly the peripheral vocabulary that swirls around: neologisms appear and disappear with the whims of fashion.

This is particularly true, as elsewhere, of the slangy items of street-wise talk, but in France it also affects more intellectual discourse. Attempts by the Académie Française to regulate neologisms, especially loanwords, are only partly successful, so *télécopie* struggles against *fax*, and *logiciel* against *software* (though *but* seems to have overcome *goal* which now = 'goalie').

4.5. LEXICAL INFLATION

Although many words were lost from the French language during the seventeenth century, the overall picture is one of lexical inflation over time. Most words that have outlived their time are not consigned to the dustbin, but to the attic, whence they can be taken out, dusted down, and brought back into use for special occasions. Certainly since 1789 (cf. Brunet 1981) the number of different words (**types**) occurring in texts has not ceased to grow, even though for some individual words the number of instances (**tokens**) has regressed.

Where do all these words come from? And when did they enter the language? Statistical counts, of whatever form—all, of course, based on textual evidence— point to the fact that the modern basic vocabulary was more or less in place by the time of the Old French texts: so that an article in *Le Monde* today will consist mainly of words that were attested by the twelfth century, nearly all of them of Latin origin. If we confine ourselves to a lexicon of the thousand or so most frequent words (cf. Stefenelli 1981), new entries into the lexicon have stayed around the level of about fifty per century, with a jump to eighty in the fourteenth century (mainly Latinisms), and a slight dip in the seventeenth to eighteenth centuries. If however we look at a larger sample (like the 13,481 words of Messner 1975), the ups and downs look more dramatic. The early odd centuries were lean years for durable neologisms, whereas the even ones were fat years. The fourteenth and the sixteenth centuries each yielded some 15 per cent of the modern lexicon: to Latinisms were added Renaissance Italianisms. The eighteenth century did not perform so well, but steady lexical inflation could already be detected, and the nineteenth and twentieth centuries continued the trend, with a greater proportion of loanwords, from regional dialect and from older stages of the language, as well as from foreign languages, especially English.

One may well ask whether what these statistics show is not so much something significant about the contemporary language—the way people spoke at the time—but rather what was thought suitable for the written text. We cannot really believe that seventeenth-century speakers were short of words for everyday objects; the cultural ambience of the time merely precluded serious writers from talking about such mundane things. The sixteenth- and nineteenth-century writers, on the other hand, delighted in such topics, and as time has gone on a greater range of registers are represented in the texts.

Tables 4.3–5 give examples of new words introduced into French in the last four hundred years.

4.6. BORROWING

Purists make a great song and dance about the 'corruption' of the language caused by excessive borrowing from other languages. This is a feature of modern attitudes to language, which is seen as reflecting ethnicity and national culture, and therefore more narrow-minded patriots are resentful of any linguistic incursion by the 'outsider'. However, as we have seen, borrowing from other languages has had no significant effect on the composition of the basic lexicon of French over the centuries.

Quantitatively, the most important type of borrowing that French has known is from Latin, which does not incur such disapproval from the purists, perhaps because they view Latin as an uncorrupted form of French, commemorating all that is holy in the national tradition. In French, Latinisms are fairly easily spotted,

TABLE 4.3. Some common words and expressions which have
begun to be used frequently since the sixteenth century

Lexicalized expressions

bonjour (from 15th c.); *là-dessus, là-haut* (= 'down/up there'); *pourtant*
(1160 = 'because of that' > 'nevertheless' in 16th c., from use in negative
phrases); *en particulier* (= 'singly' > 'especially', rivals *surtout* 'above all'
15th c., replacing Old French *ensoretot, ensorquetot, sor tote rien*); *c'est-à-
dire* (earlier *c'est à savoir*); *après-midi*; *pardon!* (as interjection 16th c., as
noun from early 12th c.); *d'ailleurs* (Old *alliors*, comparative of *alius* >
'elsewhere'); *se tromper* (for older *enganer, decevoir* 'to deceive' >
'disappoint', replacing *desappointer* 14th c. originally 'to destitute',
reborrowed from English 18th c.); *lorsque* as lexicalized conjunction, <
ILLĀ HORĀ 'at that time' + *que*, alongside *quand* (older *quant*) < QUANDO)

Substitutes for older forms

escalier (16th c.) < SCALARIA, after the Occitan form, replacing Old French
degré < DEGRADUS 'from the step' (> 'degree'); *affirmer* Latinism (from
1276) 'to make firm, to affirm', for *afermer*; *promener* Latinism (16th c.) 'to
lead forth', for *pourmener* (13th c.); *culture* Latinism (from 14th c.
'growing', 15th c. used figuratively), for *couture* (/*cousture* < CONSUTURA
'sewing'); *loger* (= 'to lodge, reside', for *manoir* < MANĒRE 'to remain', also
demeurer < DEMORARI 'to tarry'), cf. *loge* 1139 'shelter' < Frankish 'grove',
16th c. 'box (at theatre)', 18th c. 'room' and *logis* 14th–15th c. 'dwelling,
abode')

Change and extension of meaning

avenue (12th c.) 'arrival', (16th c.) 'access road', > 'tree-lined avenue'; *rôle*
< ROTULA 'little wheel' > 'scroll' > (16th c.) 'script' (in theatre) > 'role';
scène < SCAENA 'stage' > (16th c.) 'theatrical production' > also figurative
uses 'part played'; *classe* < CLASSIS 'social class' > (16th c.) also 'school
class' > 'classification'; *avouer* < ADVOCARE 'to call to' > 'to recognize as
master' > (16th c.) 'to confess'; *intérêt* 16th c. 'money interest' < 'what is
suitable' (15th c.) < 'damage(s)' (1290), cf. *intéresser* 14th c. formed on
INTEREST 'it is relevant', *intéressant* beg. 18th c. 'interesting', 1913
'financially advantageous'; *meuble* < MOBILIS 'movable' > (16th c.)
'furniture', cf. Latinism *mobile* 1301; *(s')engager* ('to commit, oblige' < 'to
pay wages, pledge', cf. *gage* Frankish); *repas* < RE-PASTUM 're-fed' > 'food'
> (16th c.) 'meal'; *goût* < GŪSTUS 'tasting' > (16th c.) also 'taste, liking';
impression 'imprint' > (15th c.) 'print' > (16th c.) 'impression'; *collège*
'confederation' > (16th c.) 'educational establishment'; *installer* 'to put in a

Tᴀʙʟᴇ 4.3. (*cont.*)

stall' > (16th c.) 'to install'; *billet* < *bulla* 'seal, blob of wax' > (15th c.)
'short note, letter' > (17th c.) 'entrance ticket' > (18th c.) 'bank note' >
(19th c.) 'travel ticket'.

Borrowings

Italian: *appartement* (16th c.) 'division into parts' > 'flat, part of a house,
apartment'; *campagne* (16th c.) 'campaign' > 'plain' > (17th c.)
'countryside' (cf. *champagne* 'fertile land in a plain' > region of eastern
France > (17th–18th c.) *Champagne*, the fine wine produced in that
region); *réussir* (16th c. from Ital. *riuscire* 'to go out again') 'to result' >
(17th c.) 'to succeed' (cf. *succès* (16th c. Latinism) > 'succession' >
'happening' (mid-16th c.) 'success', rivalled later by *réussite*); *risque* (16th c.
from Ital. *risco*, but used as feminine until 17th c., cf. 18th c. *à toute risque*).

Spanish: *brave* (or < Italian?) < ʙᴀʀʙᴀʀᴜs 'barbarian' > 'courageous' >
(16th c.) 'excellent'; *camarade* < ᴄᴀᴍᴇʀᴀᴛᴀ (16th c.) 'barrack-room',
chambrée) > 'companion at arms' > 'comrade, mate' (cf. *compagnon* (11th
c.), *copain* (18th c.) < ᴄᴜᴍᴘᴀɴɪᴏ(ɴᴇᴍ), (calqued on Germanic *ga-hlaiba*
'with-bread') 'companion, mate').

Latin: (mostly attested first in 16th c.): *attention; contact; initiative; intérieur*
(first attested in 15th c.); *national* (*nation* from 12th c./ *naissance* formed
from *naître*); *patrie; plan* 'flat, plane' (replacing *plain*), 'map' (also spelt
plant, calque from Italian *pianta*?) > (17th c.) 'plan, project' (cf. 16th c.
projet (15th c. *pourjet*) formed from *jeter*); *sérieux* (first attested in 14th c.);
social (little used before mid-18th c.)

Greek *machine* (modern sense 16th c.); *électrique* (1600 for static electricity
< *elektron* 'amber').

New derivatives

début from *but* 'target' (< Frankish?), rivals *commencement*; *départ* (older
departement, departence); *surveiller* (from *veiller* 'to be awake, to keep
vigil'), infrequent before 19th c.; *ensuite* 'following, after', rivalling *puis* <
ᴘᴏsᴛᴇᴀ 'afterwards'.

because the phonological developments that affected inherited
Latin words had transformed their shape so much that they often
had become almost unrecognizable to the inexpert observer. Concomitantly, their meaning often drifted way from the classical one,
so that translators from Latin into French, most frequently in the

TABLE 4.4. Modern common lexical items that entered the
French language in the seventeenth century

Lexicalized expressions

---

avoir l'air . . . (replacing *sembler*); *bien entendu* (= 'of course'); *bon marché*
(= 'cheap, good value'); *d'abord* (= '(at) first', rivalling *premièrement*
'firstly'); *en effet* (= 'in fact' > (19th c.) 'indeed'); *enfin* (= 'to sum up'); *il
arrive* (= 'it happens'); *n'importe* (= 'it doesn't matter'); *parce que*
(= 'because', attested since 13th c. but less frequent than *que, pour ce que,
por o que* etc.); *par exemple* (= 'for example', used as an exclamation from
18th c.); *point de vue* (= 'viewpoint' > 'point of view', (20th c.) 'personal
opinion'); *pas du tout, rien du tout* (= 'not at all, nothing at all'); *s'amuser*
(= 'to enjoy onself', from 'to be bemused', rivalling *se divertir* 'to be
diverted, taken out of oneself', cf. *amusant* 1694); *se rappeler* (= 'to recall to
oneself, to remind oneself', 'to remember' rivalling *se souvenir*); *tout de suite*
(= 'immediately', while *tantôt / aussitôt* 'so/as quickly' > 'immediately,
shortly' are restricted in use, and *maintenant* 'ready at hand' >
'immediately', came (14th c.) to mean 'now'); *tout à l'heure* (= 'shortly', >
(19th c.) 'in a jiff', ousting *tantôt*); *tout d'un coup, tout à coup* (= 'suddenly',
rivalling *soudain*).

Changes and extensions of meaning or function

---

adresse (= 'skill', 'address on letter' < *adresser* 'to direct towards'); *bête*
(= 'stupid' < 'beast' / *animal* = 'animal'); *chance* (= 'chance' < 'fall of
dice'); *concours* (= 'competition' 1660 < 1572 'reunion' < early 14th c.
'recourse'); *content* (= 'happy, content' < 'satisfied' < 'contained');
conversation 'conversation' < 'frequentation', replaces *parlement*; *fumer*
= 'to smoke tobacco'; *étonner* (= 'to astonish' < 'to strike with thunder'/
ébahir 'to amaze, leave open-mouthed, gob-smack' , cf. *bailler* 'to yawn');
gêner (= 'to incommode' < 'to torture'); *guide* = 'guide book', used until
17th c. in either gender for persons; *hôtel* (= 'hotel, hostelry' < 'private
house' < 'alms-house, guest-house'); *opérer* (= 1694 *'exécuter'* < 'to
operate, perform a surgical operation' < 'produce an effect' < 'act, work');
journal 'newspaper' < *papier journal* 1553 < 'daybook', replaces (in 18th c.)
Italianism *gazette*, cf. 1631 *Gazette de France*; *pièce* 'room' < 'piece',
rivalling *salle* < Frankish; *militaire* as a noun, replacing *guerrier* 'warrior',
soldat (16th c. Italianism for *soudard*) 'mercenary, soldier'; *police* 1606 in its
modern meaning, previously = 'administration, polity'; *provincial* in its
modern sense 1671, previously ecclesiastical from 12th c.; *retraite*
'retirement' < 'retreat', also for '(army) pension' 1752; *roman* 'novel' (<
romanz < 'romance' < 'work written in vernacular'); *se produire* 'to occur,

Table 4.4. (*cont.*)

---

happen', previously 'to appear in court', rivalling *survenir, avoir lieu*, cf. also *endroit* < IN-DIRECTUM 'towards' replacing *lieu* < LOCUS from 16th c.; *supérieur* (= 'better' 17th c., earlier 'higher'); *vacance* (= 'school vacation (> (20th c.) holiday') < 'vacancy' < (16th c.) 'lacuna, omission (in text)'); *vite* (adverb, < adjective).

Borrowings

Italian: *café* (1610 for beverage, then first café in Marseilles 1654, entered Italian from Arabic); *groupe*, term originally used in pictorial art 'ensemble', replacing *tourbe* 'crowd, group of people' < TURBA 'tumult, mob', which was pejorative in the 16th c. (cf. also *foule* from *fouler* 'to stamp, to full cloth'); *élève* 'apprentice'.

Latin: *résultat*.

Greek: *gaz* (< *chaos*); *époque* (/ *période* 14th c.)

fourteenth century, felt justified in reintroducing a more recognizable Latin form. Thus:

(25) COMMŪNICARE > *communier* 'to take communion' / *communiquer* 'to communicate'; FRAGILIS > *frêle* 'frail' / *fragile* 'fragile'; NATĪVUS > *naif* 'innocent' / *natif* 'native'; NAVIGARE > *nager* 'to swim' / *naviguer* 'navigate'; PRAEPOSITUM > *prévôt* 'provost' / *préposé* 'employee, official'.

Moreover, new formations based on the Latin form often were preferred to purely native derivatives, especially with a more figurative meaning:

(26) *populaire* (12th c.) *population* (14th c.)/ *peuple* (cf. *peuplade* 'tribe', *peuplement* 'populating, stocking, planting'); *digitale* 'foxglove' (16th c.), *digital* (1732) / *doigt* (cf. *doigtier* 'fingerstall'); *maturation* (14th c.), *maturité* (15th c.) / *mûr* (cf. *mûrissage* 'ripening', etc.); *vital* (late 13th c.) / *vie* (cf. *viager* 'life annuity'); *nasal* (17th c.) / *nez*; *oculaire* (15th c.) / *oeil* (cf. *oeillade* 'wink', *oeillère* 'blinkers', *oeillet* 'carnation').

Latinisms were frequent from the earliest times, usually in theological or scientific contexts, as one would expect from the

TABLE 4.5. Some core lexical items that have entered
French since the seventeenth century

Words for new techniques

automobile (1864 as adjective, *c*.1890 as noun, constructed from Greek
autos 'self' + *mobile*) > *auto* (frequent 1926–37, but largely replaced by
voiture < VĒCTŪRA 'transport'); *avion* (1890, constructed from AVIS 'bird',
replaced *aéroplane* 1855); *car* (1873, from English, > 'long-distance bus,
coach', by abbreviation from *autocar* 1910, cp. *bus* 1907 < *autobus*,
abbreviated from *omnibus*, Latin dative-ablative plural 'for all'); *chemin de
fer* (calque on English *railway* 1823, cf. *train*, < *traîner* 'to drag', calqued on
English 1827); *cinéma* (1900 from Greek *kinema* 'movement'); *disque* (=
'gramophone record' early 20th c. cf. *discothèque* 1932, formed on
bibliothèque); *film* (1889 from English, but *pellicule* 'little skin' used in
photography from 1900); *moteur* (= 'machine' from early 18th c. > 'motor
engine' 20th c.); *émission* (= 'radio signal' from *c*.1900); *photograph(i)e*
(1839 from English, constructed from Greek *photos* 'light' + *graphein* 'to
write', abbreviated to *photo* 1874); *radio* (1930 abbreviated from
radiophon(i)e 1888, ousting *TSF* (*télégraphe sans fils* 'wireless') post Second
World War); *speaker* (borrowed from English = 'radio announcer' 1930);
technique (1721 from Greek *tekhnike* 'art'); *usine* (1732 from Picard <
OFFICINA 'workshop' > 'factory' 19th c., cf. *fabrique* 'place where things are
made, fabricated' 18th c.).

Words for new social phenomena

bonne (= 'servant' 1708, in the 17th c. *ma chère bonne* was a term of
affection, then used by children to their nanny); *client* (= 'lawyer's client'
1437 > 'customer' 1832, cf. *clientèle* end 17th c., 'customers', replacing
chaland < *chaloir* 'friend' > 'customer', cf. 14th c. *achalandé* 'having
customers' > end 19th c. 'well-stocked'); *colonie* (14th c. > 'settlement
abroad' 1842, *colonie pénitentiaire* 1863, *colonie d' enfants* 1879, *colonie de
vacances* 1907); *commune* (= 1789 'territorial circumscription' (< medieval
'free town') > 1793 Revolutionary commune > Paris commune 1871, cf.
communard); *déjeuner* 'lunch' / *dîner* 'dinner' (rivalling *souper* 'supper') <
*DISJEJUNARE 'to break fast' (specialized in 18th–19th c. cf. *petit déjeuner*
'breakfast' 19th c.); *équipe* (1456 'ship's crew', Picard form from Germanic
skip 'ship' > 'team' 1864); *excursion* (16th c. = 'attack on enemy'. Rare till
18th c. > 'outing' 1849); *hôpital* (= 'hospital' from 17th c., frequent from
19th c. replacing *hôtel-Dieu* 13th c. cf. *clinique* 17th c.); *instituteur* (1495 'one
who institutes' > 1734 'a teacher' > end 18th c. replaces *maître d'école* 13th
c. = 'primary school teacher'); *lycée* (16th c. 'Lyceum' > 'high school'

TABLE 4.5. (*cont.*)

1807); *musée* (13th c. 'home of the Muses' > 'museum' 1762); *patron* (= 'patron, protector' > 'head of household' 17th c. > 'boss' 1832); *prévenir* (= 'warn', from early 18th c. < mid 15th c. 'to be, come, ahead of' cf. *avertir* 13th c.); *programme* (= 1680 'notice, billboard' > 19th c. 'syllabus, political programme etc.'); *restaurant* (= 16th c. 'restorative food' > 1666 'bouillon' > 1765 modern sense, with opening of first restaurant in Paris); *syndicat* 1807 'trade union' < 14th c. 'function of the syndic (legal)'.

Generalization of technical or specialized Latinisms

---

accident (12th c. 'fortuitous event or property' > 18th c. 'event with harmful consequences, accident'); *actuel* 'real, actual' > 1750 'contemporary, current'; *appareil* (till 17th c. 'pomp' / 'instrument', generalized in physical sense 19th c.); *formidable* (15th c. 'fearful' > 1831 'huge, extraordinary' > 20th c. (slang) 'very fine, super, great)'; *normal* (15th c. 'regular, conforming to a rule' > 1803 'prescribing a norm, model' > 1845 'ordinary, expected'); *organiser* (14th c. 'to arrange for the organ (musical)', 'to make organic' > 1796 'to assign a permanent structure (political)', > 1801 ' to prepare, put into order, organize').

Generalization of slang words

---

blague ('tobacco pouch' < Dutch early 18th c. > 1809 'joke'); *bonhomme* (1831 'rough drawing , model, of man' > 20th c., 'bloke, guy'); *canard* (a nickname > 13th c. 'duck', replacing *ane* < ANAS, also 18th c. 'cackling, quacking, chattering, gossip' > 1842 'satirical journal, slander'); *se débrouiller* (16th c. 'to clean oneself up' > 1822 ' to get out of trouble, to get sorted'); *(se) foutre* 'to fuck', and 17th c. euphemism *(se) ficher* 'to fix' (> 18th, 19th c. expletive uses, like *foutez/fichez le camp* 'piss off!', '*se foutre/ ficher de* 'to make fun of, not to care a damn for' > 20th c. generalized *foutre/ficher* 'to do'); *gosse* (1796 'kid, youngster' perhaps from Italian, cf. *gonze, gonzesse*); *machin* (*machine* + *engin*? = 'gadget' 1808); *truc* (c. 1800 < Occitan? 'trick' > 'thingummy, whatsit').

New common expressions

---

en principe ('in principle, as a rule' 19th c.); *en train de* ('in the process of' 1735); *quand même, tout de même* ('all the same, nevertheless' mid-19th c.); *merci* ('thank you', frequent from 19th c.)

---

diglossia of the Middle Ages, but it was from the fourteenth century that they flooded in. From the sixteenth century, however, Greek loanwords became more numerous, especially in scientific discourse. Today, it has been estimated that 6 per cent of the most frequently used 1,374 words of *français élémentaire* are *mots savants*, rising to some 25 per cent of the 3,700 words of *français fondamental*. As the size of the sample lexicon increases, so does the proportion of learned borrowings, by leaps and bounds. In technical vocabularies, such words are preponderant: for instance, a modern dictionary of philosophical terms was found to comprise 60 per cent of Latinisms and 30 per cent of Greekisms, with only 8 per cent of inherited French words being considered worthy of inclusion.

Borrowing from other languages has always been fairly insignificant in the standard language, though with inflationary pressures in the modern period the actual number of words entering the language evokes comment among speakers. But quite a few of the words are ephemeral, and whereas the basic lexicon of the language remains fairly stable, neologisms are often quickly replaced by other neologisms. Mainly the number of words, even in a sample of some 60,000 words (the size of a reasonably useful modern dictionary) is quite small: thus it has been estimated that only a thousand or so have been borrowed from Italian (of which almost half in the sixteenth century) and about seventy-five from Dutch (with a shallow peak in the seventeenth century). English loanwords, which cause consternation to modern defenders of French purity, started to encroach in the eighteenth century, but became a deluge from the mid-nineteenth century. However, it is a gross exaggeration to suggest that they present anything of a linguistic menace: that many of them are connected with an American way of life can, however, be seen as a symptom of cultural threat.

Borrowing is a perfectly legitimate way in which the lexicon of a language can fit itself to cope with new phenomena, and French has always responded in a healthy way to the challenge. Perhaps the modern borrowing from English can be seen as a way a balancing the massive incursion of French words into that language during the Norman period. Some early borrowing from Celtic and then from Germanic, in any case, have marked off French from its Romance neighbours: *mouton*, for instance, and *berceau* are of Gaulish, and *besoin* and *choisir*, of Germanic origin. Basically however the

French lexicon remains Latin, even when other Romance languages have opted for other Latin forms (cf. Table 4.1).

Further examples of borrowing are listed in Table 4.6.

TABLE 4.6. Some examples of loanwords in French, with date of entry

---

From Latin (*c*.30% of a normal lexicon, borrowed especially in 14th–15th c.)
actuel (13th c.), *admirer* (14th c.), *agile* (15th c.), *bombe* (17th c.), *bulbe* (15th c.), *caduc* (14th c.), *coaguler* (13th c.), *domestique* (14th c.), *duplicité* (13th c.), *éliminer* (15th c.), *emblème* (16th c.), *équité* (13th c.), *fatal* (14th c.), *fécond* (13th c.), *gangrène* (15th c.), *gladiateur* (13th c.), *hebdomadaire* (15th c.), *illustre* (15th c.), *impérial* (12th c.), *juvénile* (15th c.), *liberté* (14th c.), *locataire* (16th c.), *méridional* (14th c.), *morbide* (15th c.), *neutre* (14th c.), *nostalgie* (18th c.), *opiniâtre* (15th c.), *ostentation* (14th c.), *palper* (15th c.), *pension* (13th c.), *qualifier* (15th c.), *ratifier* (13th c.), *réfuter* (14th c.), *secret* (12th c.), *sincère* (14th c.), *somptueux* (14th c.), *testament* (12th c.), *toxique* (12th c.), *urbain* (14th c.), *véhicule* (16th c.), *vocal* (13th c.), *zodiaque* (13th c.).

From other languages (*c*.3–4% of normal lexicon)

  From other Romance languages (*c*.5% of all borrowings)
    Italian (*c*.3% of all borrowings: mainly 16th c.): *artisan, banque, bulletin, cabinet, caresse, concert, douche, façade, passager; cartouche, escorte, forçat, risque, soldat.*
    Occitan: *abeille, barque, brume, casserole, langouste, salade.*
    Spanish: *anchois, bizarre, camarade, nègre.*
    French dialects (mainly 16th and especially 19th c.)
      Norman: *bouquet, crevette, flâner, marécage, ricaner.*
      Picard-Walloon: *boulanger, cauchemar, cingler, écaille, hagard.*
      Lorraine: *beurre, poêle.*
      Savoyard: *crétin, se fâcher.*

  From Celtic
    Gaulish: *alouette, balai, briser, changer, chemin, cloche, jarret, quai, sapin, suie, valet, vassal.*
    Breton: *bijou, darne.*

  From Germanic
    English (especially in modern period: 8–9% of all borrowings)
      18th c.: *sinécure, pickpocket, bébé, magazine, bifteck, confortable, jungle.*
      19th c.: *sandwich, chemin de fer, cake, clown, reporter, torpédo, tennis, pijama, terminus, express, snob, bar, détective, croquet, interview, pullman.*

20th c.: *weekend, excentrique, paragon, camping, standing, dancing, pullover*.

Frankish (early loanwords, *c.*2% of all borrowings)

Social and military terms: *bande, baron, flèche, garçon, guerre, honte, orgueil, rang; choisir, éblouir, garder, gagner, haïr, souiller.*

Agricultural terms: *blé, bois, framboise, hêtre, jardin.*

Animals, birds: *crapaud, mésange.*

Artisanal terms: *feutre, maçon, tuyau; bâtir, déchirer, gratter.*

Nautical terms: *écume, falaise.*

Colour terms: *blanc, bleu, blond, brun, gris.*

Miscellaneous: *banc, bille, crèche, écharpe, fauteuil, poche, soupe, hanche; frais, gai, laid, long; danser, guérir, rôtir, trépigner.*

Dutch: *bière* (15th c.), *drogue* (14th c.), *frelater* (16th c.) *vase* 'mud, slime' (14th–15th c.).

German: *espiègle* (16th c.), *trinquer* (16th c.).

Norse and Old English (mainly 9th–10th c. nautical terms): *bateau, cingler, nord, sud, est, ouest, vague.*

From Arabic (mainly via Spanish or Italian)

amiral (early), *azimut* (16th c.), *chiffre* (16th c.), *coton* (12th c.), *épinard* (13th c.), *gilet* (16th c.), *hasard* (12th c.), *jupe* (12th c.), *nacre* (16th c.), *orange* (13th c.), *sucre* (12th c.), *tasse* (12th c.), *zénith* (14th c.), *zéro* (15th c.).

4.7. WORD-FORMATION

Perhaps the huge increase in the number of words in modern times is an inevitable effect of the increase in the number of texts, and in the range and variety of their subject-matter and readership. But in formal texts, there is possibly another factor that has to be considered: **lexicalization**—the freezing of a combination of mor-phemes into a single lexical item—can be linked to the modern standard French stylistic predilection for brevity and concision. Thus, for instance, a verbal noun like *arrivée* or *évasion* will be preferred to a wordier construction with a finite verb.

Admittedly there is some resistance in French high style to the lexical monstrosities that Giraudoux called *éponges*, because they swell by taking on extra connotations, and which often make official communications ambiguous and enigmatic. But it does seem that use of lexical derivation takes, in some French styles, the place of syntactic formulation. It is only since the turn of the sixteenth and seventeenth centuries that new native formations began to outnumber inherited Latin words (taking as a sample a lexicon of some 14,000 words in contemporary texts, cf. Messner 1975). But today some 70 to 80 per cent would be words formed from native sources (compared with the 20 per cent or so of the 'basic vocabulary' of 3,500 words).

Let us look at the way French has expanded its vocabulary by means of 'word-formation' processes, and how, over time, different strategies have been preferred. Now no longer productive is that of **back formation** (*dérivation régressive*) by which what looks like a derived form is 'decomposed', to give a new 'simple' form. For instance, *chaque* (15th c.) was 'back'-derived from *chacun*, on the model of *quelque* which had, in the fourteenth century, given rise to *quelqu'un*. In a different sphere, *aristocrate* (16th c.) was formed from *aristocratie* (14th c.), using the same template as that by which later *acrobate* (18th c.) yielded *acrobatie* (1853). In the earliest period, formation of nouns from the lexical root component of verbs was common:

(27) *aide* < *aider*, *cri* < *crier*, *oubli* < *oublier*, *trouble* < *troubler*, *vol* < *voler*

patterned like *chant* / *chanter*. This was still a possibility in the sixteenth and seventeenth century as in:

(28) *visite* < *visiter*, *écart* < *écarter* (from Italian *scartare* 'to put aside a card').

The modern fondness for abbreviations and acronyms, especially in slangy style, is rather different. Most usually only nouns are involved and there is no change of category.

Similarly, masculine nouns could be derived from feminine forms:

(29) *médecin* (14th c. replacing *mire* < MEDICUS 'physician') < *médecine* 'medicine'; *violet* (colour) < *violette* (flower) diminutive of *viole* 'viola'.

Very productive in French has always been the expansion of the lexicon by simple change of category (*dérivation impropre*): thus earlier verb infinitives could become nouns, and even now adjectives and nouns are virtually interchangeable. Any syntagma can be nominalized merely by use of a determiner:

(30) *un je ne sais pas*; *la (sainte) nitouche* (< *n'y touche (pas)*.

Compounding, by simple juxtaposition of two lexical forms, is found less often in the older language, but became frequent in the modern period:

(31) *vinaigre, hôtel-Dieu* (13th c.); *portefeuille* (16th c.) *chou-fleur, perce-neige* (17th c.); modern *belle-fille* (replacing *bru*), *gratte-ciel, bateau-mouche*, etc.

Linking of the two items by means of a preposition is also frequent, though there is some inconsistency in graphical signalling of the lexical status of the combination:

(32) *pomme de terre*; *arc-en-ciel, chef d'œuvre*.

The most usual way of forming new words in French is, however, by **affixation**—the incorporation of a bound morpheme into the body of the word. Normally only relatively frequent simplex words provide the basis for this type of lexical creativity. A distinction is usually made between **productive** affixes, which can be used synchronically to create acceptable new words, and those which have over time ceased to be synchronically analysed as separate elements. Thus:

(33) *apercevoir, ébattre, volaille, châtelain*

can be said to be **lexicalized** as distinct semantic units and no longer to comprise a lexical stem with, respectively, prefixes *a-*, *é-*, and suffixes *-aille* and *-ain*.

Prefixes are usually originally cognate with prepositions:

(34) *sur*(*veiller*); *contre*(*dire*); *par*(*venir*); *pour*(*chasser*),

but often have lost semantic links with their origins. Learned prefixes, like *semi-*, *anti-*, *hyper-*, *ex-*, *quasi-*, *pseudo-*, or semantically transparently prefixes, like *non-*, *demi-*, are today frequent. The most productive of the prefixes is the iterative *re-*, which although lexicalized in many forms (like *recevoir*), retains its identity enough even to allow reduplication:

(35) *Il boit, il reboit, il rereboit* 'He drinks, he drinks again, he drinks yet again'.

It is, however, by **suffixation** that new words are preferentially formed. The most obvious and productive device is the formation of a new verb by the addition of an *-er* infinitive marker: thus *faxer* 'to fax', or *toaster* 'to toast' today cause no more difficulties than *fêter* or *jalouser* (though they may arouse the wrath of purists). New verbs like *chuter*, or *solutionner*, formed on nouns, have even tended to replace the verbs that originally gave rise to the nouns, like *choir* or (*ré*)*soudre*. Some suffixes, though readily recognized as such, are hardly productive at all, and are virtually lexicalized. This could be said of *-at*, which had a particular vogue in the sixteenth and seventeenth centuries:

(36) *assassinat, baccalauréat*; cf. older Latinisms like *avocat, candidat,*

and of earlier *-ie*:

(37) *bourgeoisie, courtoisie, folie, jalousie, maladie,*

which has to some extent been supplanted by *-erie* or *-ise*:

(38) *diablerie, marchandise*

though this latter tends to have taken on pejorative connotations, especially in conjunction with the *-ard* suffix:

(39) *bavardise, faiblardise, débrouillardise.*

Verbal noun formation with *-ement* remains productive (and indeed is favoured by the Académie, as in *flottement* 'floating (in the money market)' compared with *fluctuation* or *flottation*). But such words tend to specialize in abstract meanings, especially in the realm of sentiment:

(40) *attendrissement* (1561); *contentement* (1468); *emportement, recueillement* ('anger', 'meditation', since 17th c.).

They may also tend to be edged out by other forms:

(41) *pleurnichement | pleurnicherie, abolissement | abolition.*

In some cases they have become virtually lexicalized:

(42) *logement, vêtement.*

Many of the most productive suffixes today are of learned origin, like *-tion, -able*, which were rarely attached to popular lexical forms, but often originally formed part of a lexical Latinism:

(43) *certitude* (15th c.); *conception*, which was attested 300 years
before *concept*; *capitalisation* (1829) < *capitaliser* (1820) <
capitaliste (1755); *véritable* (12th c. from the Latinism *vérité* /
vrai < VERACEM); modern *détaillable* < *détailler* 'to retail'
(12th. c. 'to cut into small pieces' < *tailler*).

Learned suffixes like *-iste* and *-isme* are particularly productive
today; though known in the Middle Ages, mainly as part of
Latinisms, they gained ground especially from the Renaissance on:

(44) *barbarisme* (13th c.), *évangéliste* (1190) / modern *wagnérisme*,
aujourd'huiste.

Nouns in *-age*, which are numerous in the lexicon and were very
productive in the Middle Ages, have tended in modern times to
lexicalize or specialize in distribution:

(45) *visage* / older *vis*, *esclavage* (1577) < *esclave* (but modern
boycottage, *reportage* etc. mainly from verbs),

and in meaning, often in reference to agricultural or artisanal
activities:

(46) *abattage* 'animal slaughtering, tree felling' (13th c.) / *abatte-
ment* used figuratively since 17th c. 'depression'; *blanchissage*
(1539) 'laundry' / *blanchissement* (1600) 'whitening'; *finissage*
(18th c.) / *finition* ; *filtrage* (19th c.) / *filtration*.

Thus, although it has been claimed that the seventeenth-century
purist reaction against Renaissance excessive neological derivation
impoverished the standard French language and encouraged the
strategy of borrowing as a means of expanding the lexicon, it seems
that any avoidance of derivation was short-lived. True, earlier
derivatives were often lexicalized and specialized in meaning, but
affixation remained a popular strategy, though learned affixes
flourished more than inherited ones. Moreover compounding
increased its scope, perhaps on the model of Germanic languages,
especially English, in the modern period.

For further examples see Table 4.7.

TABLE 4.7. Word-formation: examples

Derivation

Back formation (*déverbal*):
accord 12th c., *achat* 12th c., *aveu* 13th c., *lâche* 13th c., *retour* 12th c., *relief* 11th c.

Lexicalization of morphological alternant:
poilu 19th–20th c., *accidenté* (16th)–19th c.

Prefixation:
re-; *dé-*: *dérober, détacher, détailler* 12th c., *détaler, désarroi* 13th c., *désintoxiquer* 20th c.

Suffixation:
-able: *pardonnable* 12th c., *faisable, guérissable* 14th c., *effroyable* 14th c., *mettable* 12th c., *serviable* 12th c., *cyclable* 20th c.;
-ible: *corruptible* 13th c., *nuisible* 14th c., *admissible, lisible, audible* 15th c., *conductible* 19th c.;
-aison: *liaison* 13th c., *inclinaison, pendaison,* 17th c., *crevaison* 19th c.
-ation: *inclination* 12th c., *réclamation, approbation* 13th c., *fabulation* 19th c.
-té: *beauté* 11th c.; *bonté, gaieté* 12th c.
-ité: *probabilité* 14th c., *compatibilité* 16th c., *responsabilité* 18th c., *historicité, adiposité* 19th c.
-aire: *humanitaire, protestataire* 19th c., *spectaculaire, déficitaire* 20th c.
-el: *regiel* 10th c. *essentiel, personnel, perpétuel* 12th c., *artificiel* 14th c., *officiel* 18th c., *culturel, structurel* 20th c.
-al: *real (royal), official, journal* 12th c., *verbal* 14th c., *cultural, structural* 19th c.
-eux: *heureux* 12th c., *verbeux, artificieux* 13th c., *officieux* 16th c.
-eur: *chanteur, vendeur* 12th c., *moissonneur* 13th c., *éclaireur, chauffeur* 16th c.
-ier: *régulier* 12th c., *journalier* 16th c., *routinier* 18th c.
-age: *passage* 11th c., *pelage* 15th c., *montage* 17th c., *essuyage* 19th c., *primage* 20th c.
-iste: *royaliste* 16th c. *journaliste, communiste* 18th c.
-ard: *vantard* 16th c., *débrouillard, communard* 19th c., *chauffard, motard* 20th c.
-ment: *dressement, lavement* 12th c., *étonnement, abreuvement, abandonnement* 13th c.; *raisonnement* 14th c., *embarquement, écroulement* 16th c., *débrouillement, bombardement* 17th c.

Compounding

mardi, aujourd'hui, lendemain (12th c.), *grand'mère, sous-bois, arc-en-ciel* (13th c.), *timbre-poste, libre-service, amour-propre, cure-dent, aigre-doux* (modern).

4.8. Dictionaries and the Evolution of the Lexicon

The composition of a dictionary was the prime target of language standardizers in the early modern period. The Italian Accademia della Crusca set the pattern for Richelieu's 1635 Académie française, established first and foremost to make precise the limits of prestigious linguistic usage, especially in the realm of lexicon. To begin with, glosses, collected into glossaries, were compiled to help in the interpretation of those texts that had ceased to be transparent semantically to their readers. In the sixteenth century, with the advent of printing, bilingual dictionaries carried on this tradition in a more systematic way. But it was only in the seventeenth century that the need for monolingual dictionaries was recognized in France.

But what was this need? A native speaker does not require guidance in what items are part of his language and what those items signify. For him the purpose of a dictionary would be to widen his lexical experience, to help him with discourse about unfamiliar topics, and to give him guidance about the most prestigious usage: the need is social, not linguistic. Furetière in 1690 was forthright about this social role and its conservative purpose: '*Il apprendra aux François à parler correctement sa langue . . . [il est] nécessaire pour conserver la langue tout entière à la postérité.*' Consciousness of lexical change and variation caused contemporaries much disquiet: a dictionary would teach how to reduce variation and halt change, in pronunciation, lexical choice, and semantic purport. As Roubaud put it in 1786: '*L'usage qui varie détruit son propre crédit, c'est l'ignorance ou le caprice qui change.*'

The dictionaries that began to roll off the presses in the seventeenth century became more abundant in the eighteenth century, when, in the guise of encyclopedias, they aimed to be the repository of all knowledge, the Open University of the time. The vernacular was no longer viewed as an inheritance shared by all, but something to be studied and refined, almost as inaccessible as Latin had become. The dictionary was to provide the benchmark for legitimate usage, given the fallibility of unschooled native intuition. By the nineteenth century it was an important educational weapon, which would seek to ensure uniformity and regulation of lexical usage.

In the eighteenth century, however, there also began to appear 'hard word' dictionaries, often with specialist coverage—like commerce, music, or the sciences—and also guides to aberrant, neologist, and slangy usage. Some compared non-prestigious with legitimate usage, usually allegedly for the sake of edification, but perhaps also for titillation. Desgrouais's 1766 *Les Gasconismes corrigés* is an early example of the *Dites ... Ne dites pas ...* formula which was to be become familiar later.

How far did the empire of the dictionary succeed in controlling lexical change? It is hard to say: certainly the expansion of the lexicon and the growth of the dictionary industry went hand in hand, but that was only to be expected. In France, a particular aspect of lexical regulation was attempted by synonym dictionaries, which aimed at subtle discrimination between words with broadly the same field of reference. It was felt that by semantic fine-tuning a leaner and more efficient lexicon could perform better than an undisciplined, profuse verbal cornucopia.

Let us look more closely at the question of **synonymy**, within this perspective.

4.9. SYNONYMY

The 1694 Academy dictionary defined a synonym thus: '*qui a mesme signification qu'un autre mot*'. However its Preface qualified the statement by saying: '*Sur quoy on croit devoir avertir que le Synonyme ne respond pas tousjours exactement à la signification du mot dont il est Synonyme, & qu'ainsi ils ne doivent pas estre employez indifferemment l'un pour l'autre.*'

It is a commonplace in works on lexical semantics that there are few, if any, true synonyms, in the sense that one word can indiscriminately be substituted for another in all contexts and registers (cf. Cruse 1986). However, anyone who has used a Thesaurus knows that it is possible in some contexts to replace one word for another, for variety, without noticeably changing the meaning of a sentence, and we all have the intuition that pairs or groups of lexical items have a special semantic resemblance one to the other. We shall be discussing the concept of a **lexical** or **semantic**

field in 5.4. Here we shall call **synonyms** groups of words that overlap partially in distribution and meaning, especially when they are felt to share some 'central' semantic traits but differ in 'peripheral' ways. We shall exclude 'thingummy' words, that can stand for a whole class of others, like *faire* used to refer to any sort of activity, or *aller* for any sort of movement.

From the historical point of view, we concentrate on changes in the relationship between such words, and especially how some fade into oblivion, while others gain ground. In the modern period, a particular feature of synonymy has been the conscious effort of prestigious language users clearly to differentiate between synonyms.

An obvious difficulty for the historian is that we cannot be sure quite what the connotations of a word in past texts were. One line of approach is to count occurrences in successive texts and compare contexts. Stefenelli (1967), from an **onomasiological** standpoint, examined some hundred 'concepts' and their lexical representation in a sample of Old and Middle French verse texts, and was able to show shifts in frequency over time and subject-matter. However, though valuable, such a study cannot give more than an inkling of the intuitions of speakers about the synonyms, especially as, with verse texts, convention and metrical convenience may be all-important. It can be maintained too that 'concepts' themselves are not independent of the words that express them, and that lexical change induces conceptual changes rather than vice versa. Nevertheless, what we can discover from such material is when some synonyms ceased to be used.

Let us look at three simple examples:

(47) **'wife'**: Apart from PAR 'peer, equal' > *per* > *pair* occasionally used to refer to a marital partner, Old French inherited MŬLIER 'woman, wife' > *moillier*; SPONSA 'betrothed' > *espose* > *épouse* (probably formed on the verb *épouser* as the regular development would be *épeuse); FĒMINA 'female, woman' > *feme* > *femme*; UXOR 'wife' > *oissor*.

The first and the last of these have been lost in modern French. It is not improbable that *oissor* was never a very popular word, and it occurs only occasionally in the older, mainly Norman, texts. *Espose* was probably always marked as formal, although appearing fairly frequently in an early didactic text like the *Vie de St. Alexis*, but had the support of *épouser* and *époux* (cf. *mari* < MARĪTUS 'husband' / *marier*). *Moillier* began, however, by being the normal word, but by the time of the flowering of Old French literature, *feme* was more frequent, though different authors still had their own preferences. The spread of the word for 'woman' to mean 'wife' is, of course, commonplace (cf. modern non-standard *ma dame* for *ma femme* 'my wife'), but the complete demise of *moillier* in the sixteenth century is not easy to explain, except in terms of fashion swing. Straka (1979) points out that the variant forms *mou(i)llie(r)* was frequent from the fourteenth century, and that regular loss of the final [r] meant it became homonymous with *mouillé* 'damp' which derived ultimately from the same root as MŬLIER (cf. MOLLIS 'soft'). He postulates that in modern times the homonymy of 'wife, woman' with the words for 'soppy, drippy' proved unacceptable. The growing use of the more formal *époux* /-*se*, probably avoided the ambiguity caused by the polysemy of *femme* 'woman / wife', especially as concomitantly the honorific *dame* < DOMINA was being extended to embrace all respectable women (cf. Grisay *et al.* 1969).

(48) **'face'**: The inherited words were: VĪSUM 'appearance' > *vis*, and its late derivative VĪSATICUM > *visage*; FACIES 'shape, outward appearance, face' > *face*; Greek *kara* > *chiere* > *chère*; VULTUS, VOLTUS 'expression, face' > *vout*.

Of these *visage* remains as a fairly formal word, which appears most frequently in modern texts, but *figure* < 'figure', originally used for the outline of the face, is regarded as more colloquial. *Vis* remained the most frequent word until the fourteenth century, and still was occasionally used in verse in the sixteenth century (cf. modern *vis-à-vis* 'face to face'). It is usually assumed that its unpopularity was connected with its brevity: by the sixteenth century it was usually pronounced [vi], homonymous with *vis* 'screw' or *vif* 'lively' (now [vis], [vif]) and already homonymy with *vie* was threatening, so that the longer form was preferred. *Chère* continued to be used sporadically until the seventeenth century, but confusion with the homonym 'dear' and the locution *faire bonne chère* 'to eat well' (< 'to put on a good face') contributed to its loss from legitimate language. *Vout* was always a minority form, and by the thirteenth century was already seldom used. It leaves no trace in the modern language. *Face* seems to have increased in popularity through the Middle Ages, and retains its physical sense in English. In modern French, however, it is used only figuratively: it has been alleged that confusion with *fesse* 'buttock' led to its avoidance in the physical sense in the eighteenth century.

(49) **'to burn'**: ARDĒRE 'to burn, be on fire' (also figuratively 'to be in love') gave the normal Old French word *ardeir* (also *ardre*,

apparently from *ARDĔRE); less frequent *brusler* 'to consume
by fire' > *brûler* 'to burn' seems to come from USTŬLARE 'to
scorch, to singe', crossed with Germanic (cf. *brenn, brand* also
Old French *bruïr*); *cuire* 'to cook' (< COQUERE) and *graïller* >
griller 'to grill' (< CRATĪCULA 'a little frame, a grill') were also
occasionally used in a general sense.

Ardre / ardoir was still in frequent use in the sixteenth century, but it was
then often co-ordinated with *brûler* (*ars et bruslé* was almost formulaic). In
the seventeenth century it ceased to be used, though *ardent* as an adjective in
figurative senses survived. It is usually claimed that the conjugational
irregularity of *ardre / ardoir* counted against it.

In the sixteenth century, a wealth of synonyms was treasured, as
enhancing the variety and lusciousness of style. In the seventeenth,
on the other hand, redundancy was eschewed. An analogy with
darts might illustrate the difference: the earlier theorists saw a
peppering of missiles around the target as approximating to the
apt expression of the inexpressible, whereas later the aim was
directly at the bull's eye with a single well-placed dart. For the
theorists of classical French, accurate thought was attainable only
through clear, unambiguous expression: a word had to have an
exact meaning, arrived at by the authority of usage and the
convention agreed by good speakers. True, use of synonyms
could add spice to style, as Vaugelas put it: *'comme un second
coup de pinceau qui achève l'image'*. But over-use of synonyms was
condemned: each word should add something new to the meaning,
and, in any case, pairs of synonyms should round off the sentence
and not interrupt the flow.

Discussion of synonymy was soon to become a growth industry.
All the grammarians, lexicographers and *encyclopédistes* meticu-
lously drew distinctions between words: the first full synonym
dictionary was that of the abbé Girard in 1732 (an earlier version
of 1718 was called *Justesse de la langue*) but by the early nineteenth
century so many diverse judgements had been advanced that a
compendium, *Dictionnaire Universel des synonymes de la langue
française* was drawn up by the statesman François Guizot, as a
young man in 1809, going into numerous later editions. It still serves
as a model, and provides material, for modern synonym dictionaries. For Diderot's *L'Encyclopédie* (1751–65, vol. 14), synonymy
was not merely a linguistic exercise, ensuring exact expression of

sincere thought and feelings, but should go further in placing the words within their social and historical context: '. . . *de manière qu'en expliquant la diversité des acceptions, on exposât en même temps les usages de la nation, ses coutumes, son caractère, ses vices, ses vertus, ses principales transactions, etc. et que la mémoire de ses grands hommes, de ses malheurs et de ses prospérités y fût rappelée*'.

The words that attracted most attention were those referring to sentiments and moral attitudes. Let us look at a couple of examples.

(50) **'fear'**: the inherited words were *peur* (*avoir peur* 'to be frightened') < PAVOR and *crainte* (*criembre* < ? TRĒMERE 'to tremble' perhaps crossed with a Celtic **crem*, then remodelled to *craindre* 'to fear'—*cremeur* was also found until the fifteenth century). *Douter* 'to doubt' was also used for 'to fear' till the seventeenth century, as is the derivative *redouter* 'to dread' today. In older texts, *peur* was by far the most frequent word and implied sudden panic, whereas *crainte* and *doute* implied longer-term and less violent fear. *Appréhender*, a Latinism originally meaning 'to seize hold of', came in the sixteenth century to mean also 'to consider as worthy of fear', hence *appréhension*. Other Old and Middle French words included *frayeur*, *timeur* (associated especially with women?), and *tremeur* (the pair *craintif et plein de tremeur* was quite frequent in Middle French).

In post-Revolution texts the verb *craindre* was at first more frequently used, but *avoir peur* overtook it in the mid-nineteenth century: this may merely be an effect of the register used in the texts, as it is likely that *avoir peur* was always more colloquial.

Deimier (1610 *Académie de l'Art Poétique*) was among the first to comment on a register difference, with *craindre*, *crainte* being seen as more elegant: '*Veu bien que la CRAINTE et la PEUR soient une mesme chose pour le sens, on n'en use pas toujours à semblable phrase. Car on dict: Cela fait que j'ay peur que telle chose n'arrive, Cela me donne crainte etc. Et ainsi encore: Vos discours me donnent crainte. . . . Ainsi pour la diversité de ce terme, on dit elegamment en ces façons: J'ai craincte que la liberalité soit connue du tout esteincte.*' The *Dictionnaire de Trévoux* in 1704 was puzzled by the difference: '*C'est une bizarrerie de toutes les langues que des termes absolument synonymes ne s'emploient pourtant pas indiffér-*

emment: CRAINTE et PEUR signifient la même chose; cependant, on ne dit point "il m'a fait crainte".'

Roubaud in 1796 was however clear that they referred to different emotions: '*La CRAINTE est une émotion fâcheuse qui va jusqu'à troubler l'imagination; c'est l'apparence du mal qui la produit . . . La PEUR est une erreur des sens. Faire peur à quelqu'un, c'est le surprendre, lui causer un mouvement d'inquiétude . . . On craint Dieu et il ne fait pas peur; les formes et les attributs qu'on lui prête excitent plutôt notre admiration.*'

By modern times, it became accepted that the difference lay between anticipated and imminent, physical danger: '*On craint un danger probable; on a peur du danger que l'on croit présent et pressant.*' Yet the same distinction has not been drawn between related derivatives. Thus, in modern synonymy dictionaries we read:

CRAINTE: sentiment du péril, menace du danger; PEUR: se rapporte à une chose comme devant être funeste;
CRAINTIF: celui qui d'instinct voit des dangers partout et en tout; PEUREUX: celui qui est sujet à la peur par caractère et aussi par habitude.
Here *peur* seems to be related to imaginary possibility of harm, rather than real danger, whereas *crainte* is a more worthy sentiment. Thus: '*on craint par réflexion . . . elle est toujours raisonnée, sinon raisonnable . . . La peur ne raisonne pas, elle est instinctive, elle est subite.*'

Redouter, on the other hand, is acknowledged to refer to stronger dread and to be used in more formal registers, but it has no corresponding noun (whereas *redoutable* has no correspondent derived from *crainte* or *peur*).

Here we may ask whether the pronouncements of the lexicographers have led to any change in usage, or whether their perception that *craindre* (which was etymologically more 'physical') had come to designate a more decorous emotion, is merely a consequence of its less colloquial character. It is noteworthy that in modern slang, disparaging terms tend to replace colourless *avoir peur*:

(51) *avoir le trac* (1835), *avoir la frousse* (1858) 'to be scared'; (vulgar) *avoir la pétoche* 'to have the wind up', *avoir la trouille* 'to be in a blue funk' (< Flemish 1808), *les avoir à zéro* 'to be scared stiff'.

In my second example, chosen from less frequently used words, etymologically the 'synonyms', *fier* and *orgueilleux*, had quite different origins, but were frequently co-ordinated in Old French texts, especially in reference to the enemy in battle, when they seem to express admiration for war-like qualities, but without a hint of moral approbation:

(52) **'proud'**: *fier* < FĔRUS 'wild, savage' (a meaning kept till the 17th c., when *sauvage* < SILVATICUS 'of the forest' and *farouche* < FORASTICUS 'foreigner' finally replaced it in these senses); *orgueilleux* is from a Germanic word meaning 'outstanding'. Other quasi-synonyms entered the language later, and retained something of their etymological flavour: *hautain* 'high' > 'haughty'; *arrogant*, a 14th c. Latinism; *altier* 'lofty, haughty', a 16th c. Italianism.

Both *fier* and *orgueilleux* denoted qualities that would be admirable in a medieval warrior, but which in more modern society are less well regarded: nevertheless *fier*, originally the more 'untamed' term, is the word now normally used for honest pride, whereas *orgueilleux* is almost wholly pejorative. This difference is little reflected in the judgement made by, for instance, *L'Encyclopédie* (volume 7): '*Le FIER tient de l'arrogant, du dédaigneux et se communique peu; l'ORGUEILLEUX étale l'excès de la bonne opinion qu'il a de lui-même.*' Yet the contemporary Beauzée (1770) characterized *fier* in terms that differentiate it little from *orgueilleux*: '*Le FIER croit que lui seul est quelque chose et que les autres ne sont rien.*'

In this instance, the rather feeble attempts to differentiate the synonyms have had little effect on ordinary usage, though it is hard to measure how far literary practice has followed the dictates of arbiters.

It is to be noted that in modern texts since 1789 (Brunet 1981), *fier* and *orgueil* appear characteristic of the dialogue and poetic registers, whereas neither *fierté* nor *orgueilleux* are used significantly frequently in any kind of text.

It may be that the statistical information drawn from analysis of texts can tell us something about differentiation of synonyms over time, that the painstaking semantic descriptions of synonymists cannot. Where one item in a synonymic group forges ahead in popularity, others may be relegated to backwaters of formal or poetic language, and as they become less used they are regarded as more and more old-fashioned and eccentric by new generations of language learners. Take, for instance the words for 'to try':

(53) *essayer | tâcher | tenter.*

Essayer originated in the meaning 'to weigh', and hence 'to test'. In 1800 it was marginally more frequent in texts than *tâcher*, originally 'to tax', or *tenter*, originally 'to tempt, to touch'. *Essayer* and *tâcher* were close rivals through most of the nineteenth century, while *tenter* kept a low profile. During the twentieth century, however, *essayer* took off, while *tâcher* went into decline in the inter-war period, and *tenter* made a modest gain in popularity.

In this case *essayer* has become by far the most widely used word, while *tâcher*, popular in texts in the 1870s, is branded as out-of-the-ordinary. A rather different picture emerges with words for 'to break', which are often distinguished by synonymists in terms of the type of breakage involved:

(54) *rompre | briser | casser.*

Rompre the original word (RŬMPERE) implies a clean break, and acquired figurative meanings; in 1800 it was used a little less than *briser*, a Celtic word, with the connotations of 'to shatter', but this latter soared in popularity during the early nineteenth century, only to decline steadily till the present day. Meanwhile *casser*, originally 'to damage, to quash', came from nowhere, surpassing the other two at the turn of the century, but then rapidly declined to end up rather less frequently used than the other two in the post-war period.

In this instance, it is hard to interpret the data, except in terms of fickle fashion. In many contexts the three words are interchangeable, and there is no discernable semantic difference. It is possible that *rompre*, with its figurative connotations, fits better with the subject-matter of modern texts, but all three words remain relatively frequent and in close competition.

It is, on the other hand, fairly easy to interpret the rapid rise in the use of the word *information* since the forties, compared with its synonym *renseignement*, which previously had been consistently, and sometimes signally, more frequent. We need look no further than the radio news, Information Technology, and the influence of English, for what looks like a dramatic switch in the popularity of the two items.

In twentieth-century texts, the relative rise in use of 'learned', more internationally current, variants is particularly notable:

(55)   *accumuler* is preferred to *entasser*; *utiliser*, to *employer*; *limiter*, to *borner*; *opinion*, to *avis*; *urgent*, to *pressant*.

On the other hand in some cases an 'older' variant may come into fashion again and rival, or even overtake, a previous favourite:

(56)   *naguère,* now more used than *récemment*; *haïr*, rivalling *détester*; *jadis*, sometimes catching up with *autrefois*.

Fashion alone, surely, can account for victories in the competition between functional items, like adverbs and connectors, in the past two centuries. Take for instance the words for 'however, nevertheless':

(57)   *toutefois | néanmoins | pourtant | cependant.*

Toutefois and *néanmoins* have kept a steady low profile since 1800, but *pourtant* has rapidly increased in popularity, while the erstwhile front-runner *cependant* has declined, their paths crossing in about 1880.

The pattern for words meaning 'especially' is rather different:

(58)   *principalement | spécialement | particulièrement | notamment.*

The first two have stayed at about the same level of frequency throughout the last couple of centuries, while *particulièrement* was by far the preferred form, until in the post-war period the buzz-word became *notamment*, which had started at the bottom of the ladder.

In a similar way, for 'then':

(59)   *ensuite | puis | alors,*

while *ensuite* has retained its inconspicuous position since 1800, *puis* soared to popularity in the nineteenth century to be overtaken once again by *alors* in the twentieth.

For 'certainly' *certes* has clearly overtaken *certainement*, *sûrement*, and *assurément*, while for 'completely' the popularity of *complètement* and *entièrement* is in the balance, and changes from decade to decade.

What emerges from these examples is that there are indeed changes in the relative frequency of synonyms over time. Some of the changes can perhaps be explained in terms of text conventions, but others must be symptomatic of changes in language usage. How are we to explain shifts in lexical fashions? Further investigation is called for.

4.10. *LEXICOLOGIE*

Lexical history is conspicuously linked to social, political, cultural, technological, and intellectual history. The introduction of new terms must sometimes be motivated by innovations that call for a means of expression. The loss of old terms may also be evidence that objects or concepts have fallen out of use. The study of lexical change is, in this perspective, not primarily a linguistic exercise, but can be used as a measure of other changes in society. Titles like *Les mots, témoins de l'histoire* or *Le vocabulaire et la société* strike a familiar chord in French, where tradition favours a sociohistorical approach to linguistic phenomena.

This is the line of the French school of *lexicologie* under the leadership of Georges Matoré (cf. 1953*a*), which has inspired a succession of monographs on innovations in terminology at different periods in the history of French, as well as ongoing interdisciplinary journals and research units. Fascinating though the anecdotal content of lexical studies can be, they can easily deteriorate into an interminable listing of words, without any meaningful pattern. The Matoré method however is to seek to isolate those words that, at a certain point in the history of a society, were emblematic of the values and preoccupations of that society. The aim is to identify for each epoch **le mot témoin**, which '*concrétise un fait de civilisation*', serving as symbol of change, and **le mot clé**, '*un sentiment, une idée*', which represents the ideology of contemporary society.

The first appearance of a neologism would be an important clue to the social climate. Thus examples of **mots témoins** were:

(60) *coke* (1770), seen as the first sign of industrial capitalism; *responsabilité* (1787), representing a new principle of conduct; *magasin* (1820–5) signalling a new conception of trade.

Mots clés can be exemplified by:

(61) *honnêteté*, the behavioural benchmark for the mid-seventeenth century; *beaux arts* introduced in 1640 to distinguish 'high,

élite', from 'popular, utilitarian' culture (note that *artisan* 'craftsman' 1546 (< Italian) was not clearly distinguished from *artiste* till the late eighteenth century); *bourgeois, prolétaire*, political and cultural buzz-words in the period 1827–34; *individualisme* 1826 (coined on *socialisme*, cf. *individualité* 1760, *individuel* 1551, *individual* 15th c.)

In the *lexicologie* tradition, it is assumed that, in the modern era at least, changes come in waves, that can be usefully systematized in terms of generations—of thirty to thirty-five years—whose fresh attitudes are reflected in words that they invent or begin to use much more frequently. Thus the discovery of Renaissance ideas in the early sixteenth century was symbolized by *éducateur* (1527), and the triumph of Humanism marked by *classique* (1548), *chimie* (1554), *athée* (1547). It can, however, be claimed that the choice, by *lexicologistes*, of which innovations are regarded as socially or culturally significant, is fairly arbitrary, and historians, especially outside France, sometimes dismiss the procedures as intuitive and inconclusive.

Statistical studies based on texts can add more substance to them: for instance, it has been shown (Brunet 1981) that *nation*, overwhelmingly a popular word from 1789 to 1820, then fell out of favour until the Second World War when it again soared to prominence, while *société*, which declined in usage from 1835, then reached a new temporary peak at the turn of the century.

At the head of the list of words that attained exceptional relative frequency in intellectual discourse in 1875 were *science, phénomène, maladie, médecin, observation, élément*, while in 1913 the same position was held by *politique, gouvernement, ministre, opinion, intérêt, état*. This example does little more than confirm what we know from other sources, that texts at a certain time will reflect the overriding concerns of their readers: in 1875, the progress of the natural sciences, in 1913, concern about the impending collapse of the political status quo. It tells us little about linguistic change as such, except by reminding us that, in some respects at least, change in the lexicon is inextricably linked with change in society.

Among the studies of lexical innovations spawned by *lexicologie* were those of feudal, Renaissance and classical vocabulary, and terms used in specialized discourse about the railway, medicine, art, politics. Though comparison of different synchronic states of the language can enter into discussion, very little attention is paid to linguistic change as such, except in terms of semantic change, to which we shall return later.

Here we should mention especially ideas associated with 'post-modernist' thought (cf. especially Rorty 1980, 1989, also Malachowski 1990), which seem to see 'vocabulary change' as effecting, rather than just reflecting, cultural change. In this perspective 'language speaks man', in Heidegger's words, systems of belief are inextricably bound up with the ways they are expressed, and language is a means by which human cope with the external world. Changes in attitude, revolutions in ways of thinking, can be thus seen as basically 'vocabulary' changes, when innovators introduce new metaphors, which then become conventionalized and part of the mental make-up of of members of a linguistic community. The way in which the term 'vocabulary' is used here does not chime well with the more down-to-earth lexical approaches I have delineated. In discussion of semantic change we shall come back to these questions.

FURTHER READING

On lexicon: Aitchison 1987, E. V. Clark 1995, Guilbert 1969.

On lexical change in French: for bibliography see Levy and Poston 1957, Levy and Spence 1961, Posner and Green 1980–93 vol. 1. Also Brunot 1928, Chaurand 1977, Frey 1925, Holtus 1990, Mitterand 1963, Posner 1975, 1980a, 1981, Sauvageot 1964, Schöne 1951, Wise 1997, Wunderli 1989, 1990.

On etymology: Brucker 1988, Craddock *et al.* 1980, Guiraud 1964, 1967, Klaus 1985, Malkiel 1976, 1989, 1993, Roche 1990.

On lexical loss: Huguet 1935, Posner 1973, 1975, 1981, Straka 1979a.

On lexical statistics: Brunet 1978, 1981, 1988, Klöden 1987, Messner 1975, 1977, Ch. Muller 1967, 1977, Stefenelli 1981, 1992.

On borrowing: Gebhardt 1974, Guinet 1982, Guiraud 1965, 1968b, Hope 1972, 1980, MacKenzie 1939, Pfister 1972, Picone 1995, Poplack and Sankoff 1984, Poplack *et al.* 1988.

On word-formation: for bibliography see Lloyd 1963–4. Also Corblin 1987, 1991, Darmesteter 1877, Fisiak 1985, Guilbert 1969, 1974, 1975, 1979, Thiele 1987.

On dictionaries: *Autour de Feraud* 1986, Baldinger 1974, Cayrou 1948, Collignon and Glatigny 1978, Dubois and Dubois 1971, Haussmann 1977, Imbs 1961, 1965, 1971, Journet *et al.* 1966–78, Matoré 1968,

Quemada 1968, 1978, Rey 1982, Rey-Debove 1971, Wagner 1967–70, Wooldridge 1979.

On synonymy: Batchelor and Offord 1993, Buridant 1980, Stefenelli 1967.

On lexical fields: Coseriu 1975, Lutzeier 1993, Marxgut 1989.

On lexicologie: for bibliography see Schmitt 1972. Also Conein 1987, Dumonceaux 1975, Glatigny and Guilhaumou 1981, Gougenheim 1962–75, Klein 1976, Matoré 1953*a*, *b*, 1985, 1988, Picoche 1977, Tamba 1987.

5
Semantic Change

All human language has meaning, in the simple sense that its speakers mean something by what they say. It is usually recognized that whatever language they use they can, if they wish, mean the same thing. The semantic potentialities of language are common to all human beings, though they may be expressed differently in different languages. So how can we talk of 'change of meaning' or **semantic change**? In using this term are we saying that the same linguistic expression means one thing at one time, and another at a different time? Or is it, rather, that different speakers, either contemporaneously or successively, employ the same expression to mean different things? This latter dilemma is something most of us are very familiar with: indeed, in everyday conversational exchanges, we often have the feeling that we are talking at cross-purposes, not getting our meaning across to our interlocutors, nor grasping what they are getting at. How, we wonder, can we understand what others mean when they speak? Perhaps we never do completely. But in general, for practical purposes, we get the message accurately enough, making use, as we do, of reference to shared beliefs, to common culture, to context, and to non-linguistic signals of various sorts.

However, in an alien culture, in the present or in the past, we can feel at sea, uncertain of the implications of the linguistic expression of another, hesitant about how to translate it into our own idiom. The problem is not so serious when what confounds us is a small linguistic unit, like the lexical item. We are accustomed to thinking of the lexical item as a chunk of meaning, associated with a phonological form. That different people use the same word, however, to designate different things is part of our linguistic experience. We are interested, but not shocked, to learn that *bureau* once referred to a piece of cloth laid over a table, then came to mean the table itself, then the room in which the table stood, and then an organization which, in principle, has such rooms. Indeed, the only real change that, in this case, has occurred is that *bureau* has ceased today to refer to any sort of cloth. The other meanings of this word are familiar to us synchronically, and we have no difficulty in reconstructing the diachronic process of extension of reference. But, in a text written between the fourteenth and the seventeenth century, *bureau* can give us pause, because our modern interpretations of this word may just not seem to make sense in the context.

Most discussions of semantic change centre on lexical change of this sort. A *voiture* is, in modern contexts, understood primarily as a 'motor car', but we understand that it can also designate other sorts of carriage. On the other hand a *train*, primarily a railway train, is usually dissociated from the 'same' word used in *ralentir le train* in the sense of 'slow down the pace', or *aller son petit train* 'to jog along'. In the former case, there has been perfectly normal synchronic extension of reference, in the latter there has been a **lexicalization** which has divorced the 'railway train' use from its etymological roots, associated with *traîner*.

More problematic than changes in lexical semantics are changes in sentence meaning. First of all, it is quite difficult to find precisely comparable sentences in old and modern texts, so as to compare their meanings. Worse still, we cannot be certain precisely what the old sentences mean, because we have no 'native speakers' to give us the information about their truth-value or their implications. The best we can do is to say that, in some cases, the sentences would not make sense in their context if they were to mean the same as their modern counterparts. Transparent cases like this are, unfortunately, rare. True, we are not infrequently puzzled by what we read in texts, but that can be true of contemporary, as well as of olden, texts.

Of particular interest to the historical linguist is how there have been changes in the contribution that grammatical features or elements have made to the meaning of sentences. What, for instance, was the semantic import of the use or non-use of the definite article in Old French, compared with modern French, or how have tense, aspect, or mood markers contributed differently to the meaning of sentences in the history of French? These are questions that are usually treated as part of syntactic history, but which I prefer to see as first and foremost concerned with historical semantics.

5.2. SEMANTIC CHANGE IN INDIVIDUAL LEXICAL ITEMS

Most discussion of semantic change concentrates on the word. Yet semanticists experience difficulty in how to define synchronically 'the meaning of a word': if we do not know what it is, how do we know when it has changed? We all know that words are usually polysemous, in the sense that in different contexts they can mean different things, and that it is difficult to draw the line between **polysemy**, when one word-form has several meanings, and **homonymy**, when several words with different meanings have the same form.

Some would say that we can talk about the uses of a word, but not about its meaning, which will depend on its contextual relations. Others will say that the meaning of a word can be described only differentially, that is in terms of its relationship with other words, and how it differs from them or is subsumed under them. Yet others will analyse the meaning of a word in terms of semantic primes or **semes**, some of which may be criterial, but others may be only possible or expected: however, creative use of language can also introduce stylistically marked unexpected semes into the equation. Yet others will say that for any speaker a word will normally have a **prototypical** or central meaning, which then can be extended elastically to take in other uses, but will inevitably exclude contradictory meanings.

It can be held that a word-meaning is naturally learned by the speaker-hearer experimentally assigning a prototype meaning, which then can be tested by extending the context of the use of the word, and experiencing the reactions of other speakers. In modern literate societies, the dictionary can provide a short cut in this process, but, as we all know, it is risky to rely on a dictionary in trying to use appropriately a word that we have never come across in discourse.

Thus it can be claimed that some sort of lexical semantic lability—extension, restriction, metaphor and so on—is an ongoing synchronic phenomenon, and not necessarily part of historical linguistics. It is not surprising then that some classic works on lexical semantics, like Bréal (1897), are almost wholly to do with semantic change, rather than with semantic description. We can draw the line by maintaining that it is when a word loses a criterial semantic feature that history comes into it, even though shifts in meaning are an everyday occurrence, to which we are accustomed. **Polysemy** may be the pathway to semantic change, but for such a change to come about, here must also over time occur some **semantic loss**.

In classifying shifts in meaning, appeal is usually made to the same **tropes** that are familiar from rhetoric and stylistics. **Synecdoche** ('part for the whole') is the label given to the process by which *tableau* 'a wooden board' (< TABULA) becomes in the thirteenth century, 'a painting on wood', as in an altar piece.

Just at the same period, perhaps significantly, *panneau*, originally 'a game pouch', came to be used for a 'carved wooden panel', cf. modern *tableau de chasse* 'tally, bag').

Subsequently *tableau* could designate any painting or pictorial scene. The criterial seme, or prototypical sense, of *tableau* has shifted to 'picture ' from 'piece of wood', which is still, however, covertly retained in certain fossilized contexts, as in *tableau noir* 'blackboard', or *tableau d'affichage* 'notice board' (whence the figurative use of *tableau* for a 'table of figures' etc.).

Another often cited example is *verre* in the sense of a 'drink', as in *Je prendrai volontiers un verre avec vous* 'I shall be glad to have a drink with you'—the word for the glass itself coming to indicate the contents of the glass. But here there has been no real change: *verre* still retains its central meaning of the material from which the glass is made (< VITRUM).

It was used for 'drinking glass' first in the late thirteenth century (just when the Latinism *vitre* began also to be used for the material, later specializing as 'a window pane').

The metonymic extension in *un verre de vin* is such a natural extension of use that it does not properly qualify as a diachronic change.

Similarly in examples of **metonymy** ('attribute for thing'), we can maintain that *grève* 'labour strike' has changed its meaning, and is no longer associated with the gravelly bank of the Seine, used as a hiring market (cf. *Place de la Grève*), and *jalousie* 'Venetian blind' has become a different word from the same form meaning 'jealousy'. On the other hand, *cœur* 'courage' has not lost its link with the primary meaning 'heart', and so there has been, in my book, no diachronic change.

Metaphors are 'what we live by' (Lakoff and Johnson 1980): our language use is shot through and through with metaphoric use. When first heard, a metaphor has the same effect as a gesture or facial expression, not so much conveying a message as provoking a response. But the metaphor can die off into literalness and become part of the bed-rock ('coral reef' is a more telling analogy) of the language. When the metaphor is fossilized, memory of the non-metaphorical import of an expression can be virtually lost, and then we can talk of change of meaning. An example is the word *chef* (< CAPUT < 'head') used, since the sixteenth century, only in the sense of 'chief, chef (*de cuisine*), boss', except in set phrases like *de pied en chef* 'from head to foot'. The loss of the criterial meaning of (anatomical) 'head' dictates that we count this as a semantic change, whereas the parallel development with *tête*, as in *tête d'une entreprise*, is to be seen as a synchronic, though conventionalized, metaphor.

For some speakers, the metaphorical use, though remote from the original one, can still be linked with it. *Bidon* 'hot air, codswallop' (and its *verlan* distortion *domb*) can be connected synchronically with the concrete references 'flask, churn' > 'belly', even though for some speakers they are separate lexical items. Exactly when the 'change' spreads to the whole community is hard to detect until after the event: we must assume that young language learners at some point have acquired the erstwhile metaphorical meaning earlier than, or instead of, the literal meaning.

In cases like these the semantic mechanisms at work are the same whether operating synchronically or diachronically. I repeat, however, that I limit the label of 'semantic change' to those instances when there has been over time a displacement of the central or prototypical meaning of a word, and especially when that meaning has fallen out of use, or when what was originally one word has split into two.

The same distinction can apply to what Bréal called *les prétendues tendances* of semantic change. These include:

Weakening: as in *gêne* 'hell' (GEHENNA) > 'discomfort, bother'; *navrer* 'to wound, injure' (< Germanic) > 'to upset' (as in *Je suis navré* 'I'm very sorry');

Euphemism: as in *fille* 'daughter, girl' (< FILIA), used for 'tart, prostitute';

Deterioration: as in *crétin* 'moron, wally' (a dialect form of *chrétien* 'christian'); *benêt* 'simpleton, ninny' (a popular form of *benoît* (< BENE-DICTUS 'blessed' > 'bland, ingratiating' / *bénit* 'holy');

Amelioration: either social, as in *maréchal* (< Germanic) 'groom' > 'marshal, highest army officer' (but cf. *maréchal ferrant* 'blacksmith, farrier'); or emotive, as in *heureux* (< AUGURIUM 'omen') 'victim of chance' > 'lucky' > 'happy'.

In some of these cases there has been change, in that the original form-meaning relationship of the words has definitively altered (so that *enfer* 'hell' is quite different from *gêne*). In others, however, the shift over time is barely perceptible: *fille* still means 'daughter' and *fillette* and *jeune fille* carry no pejorative connotations; *heureux* can be translated as 'lucky' and as 'happy', even though in real life these do not necessarily apply to the same state.

Such general tendencies, which operate in every language, can have the consequence of narrowing the meaning and contextual distribution of a word: as with *viande*, originally 'food', and then only 'meat food'. Alternatively, the meaning and contextual use can be extended: thus *arriver*, from the meaning of 'coming to the bank, disembarking', applied to any sort of arrival. However, I maintain that, properly speaking, a change takes place at the time at which sight is lost of the original central meaning of the word which then begins to fade away and eventually be totally forgotten, as in these two examples.

5.3. CAUSES OF LEXICAL SEMANTIC CHANGE

If the meaning of a word shifts between the usage of different individuals and of the same individual at different times, then we need look no further for the causes of change. Or, at any rate, we take for granted that there will be change, and wonder why some words retain more or less their original meaning. Usually such words are part of the basic vocabulary with an easily identified core-meaning: *père* and *mère* may have changed in their social and emotive connotations, but they have retained over the centuries a biological identity.

But if we expect semantic change in lexical items, can we predict the direction of such changes, and how do we account for semantic loss, when a word no longer means what it used to? Discussion of causes of change are often classified under heads like the following:

Context: *pas* 'step' has become a negative particle, distinct from the noun, by absorbing the meaning of the negative *ne* with which it regularly appeared as an emphatic *forclusif*;

Economic conditions: *ville* ceased to designate a Roman villa, a large country estate, when these fell into disuse and the Germanic type of settlement, *bourg*, became frequent, but it remained, in competition with *cité*, as the name for a larger urban agglomeration. The word *villa* was reimported from Italy in the eighteenth century for a country house, and was then used for the historical villa.

Social conditions: *chétif*, originally a 'captive', acquired, from an very early period, the subsidiary meanings of 'sickly, puny', descriptive of prisoners at the time. It lost its concrete meaning in the fifteenth century when it was replaced by the less emotive Latinism *captif*.

Ideas: *colère* 'bile', from the Greek came early to mean 'anger', which was assumed to be occasioned by an excess of bile, eliminating less colourful *ire* (IRA). The word *bile* was borrowed from Latin in the sixteenth century, when *choléra* was reintroduced for the name of the disease.

Folk etymology (or **contamination**): *forain*, 'fairground', originally 'stranger, foreigner' (< FORANUS, now *étranger*, derived from *étrange* < EXTRANEUS) was, via *marchand forain* 'pedlar', influenced by *foire* 'market, fair' (< FĒRIA 'feast-day'); *plantureux* 'copious', from the word for 'plenty' (derived from *plein* 'full') > also 'fertile' presumably by association with *plante*.

Ellipsis: *camembert* came to be used in the nineteenth century for the famous cheese, for *fromage de Camembert*, the name of the village (in L'Orne) where it originated; *le vapeur* 'steamboat' for *le bateau à vapeur*.

Other attempts at classification use slightly different headings. For instance, French advocates of Durkheimian sociological ideas use three broad categories, of which the third is considered most interesting, because of the light it casts on social history:

1. Purely linguistic factors operate: *on* (< HOMO) is used as a non-specific human subject pronoun, differentiated from *homme* 'man' (< HOMINEM).
2. Words change as things change (*Wörter und Sachen* theory): *voiture* 'carriage' is used for 'motor-car'.
3. Social divisions lead to differentiation of the words that refer to them. Thus to translate 'pay' we have: *salaire* '(monthly or hourly) wage, income support etc.' (< 'salt-money, army pay'); *appointements*

'(annual) salary (for managerial duties)' from the sixteenth century <
'arrangement, putting in order'; *émoluments* 'remuneration (for administrative tasks)' < (thirteenth century) 'profit'; *traitement* 'stipend (for
civil servants)' in the eighteenth century < 'convention'; *honoraires* 'fees'
(for professionals, doctors, lawyers etc.) < (sixteenth century) 'a mark
of honour'; *gages* (for servant etc., now old fashioned) < 'security,
guarantee, evidence'; *paie*, *paye* '(workman's) wages' < 'soldier's) pay'
< 'appeasement'; *solde* '(soldier's / sailor's) pay' from Italian in the
fourteenth century (cf. *sou*).

Attempts to draw up **semantic laws** on the model of **phonetic laws**
have not been conspicuously successful, but some general tendencies
of semantic change can be discerned:

Image drifts: certain metaphors reoccur, as in *comprendre* 'to seize hold of,
grasp' > 'to understand'.
Loi de répartition (Bréal): synonyms tend to acquire different meanings as in
chef / *tête* (cf. 4.9).
Transfers from one semantic sphere to another (Esnault): space metaphors
are used for time, not vice versa e.g. *longueur* 'length' > 'slowness'; (de
Witte): transfers are made from, not to, the human body: *chef* (BUT *tête* <
'egg-shell'); (Bloomfield): transfers are made from concrete to abstract e.g.
penser, 'to weigh' > 'to think', *savoir* 'to taste' > 'to know'; (Ullmann):
transfers are made from 'lower' senses (e.g. touch, heat) to 'higher' (e.g.
acoustic, visual) e.g. *entendre* 'to stretch towards' > 'to hear', *apercevoir* 'to
catch hold of' > 'to perceive'; (Stern): there is generalization of expressions
from emotively important preoccupations e.g. *tirer*, 'to pull' < 'to torture,
to martyr', *chasser* 'to chase < 'to hunt'.

These schematic attempts at explanation give an account of
figurative uses of language, but do not always address the problem
of why there should have been irreversible change—in that an
earlier central meaning of the word has been lost.

Comprendre, for instance, does now centrally mean 'to understand', but it
also still means 'to include', so that *Je n'ai pas compris les frais de voyage*
could be translated 'I didn't understand the travel expenses' or 'I didn't
include the travel expenses'. *Chasser* can still mean 'to hunt' as well as 'to
chase', and *longueur* is used for 'length' in space and time.

Possibly loss of meaning from a lexical item is conditioned more
often by purely lexical factors than by semantics. Where, with the
'lexical inflation' we have already discussed, new words come into
the language, creating a pool of synonyms, then each of the related

words can specialize in certain acceptations, slewing off other, sometimes older, semantic elements. I have already discussed this question under **synonymy** (4.9). Very closely related to this concept is that of the **semantic field** which I shall discuss in the next section.

5.4. SEMANTIC FIELDS

Approaches to lexical semantics that talk about semantic or lexical fields usually hark back to the Saussurean idea that linguistic signs form systems in which items are in a relationship of solidarity, each identified by its position relative to the others, and that the outside world is viewed through the prism of a language, which splits meaning into discrete units corresponding to its signs. Some also subscribe to the **Humboldtean** vision that each culture has its own view of reality, which is reflected in its structuring of meaning, or to the **Sapir–Whorfian** view that our language conditions the way we look at the world.

We may contrast these views with those that see lexical items as almost accidentally linked with semantic configurations, short-cuts which by convention represent, in an economical way, complex ideas. From one point of view, **lexicalization** can represent the effort of a culture to give a name to a concept which it deems important; from the other, the choice of a lexical form to represent a particular complex of universal semantic primes is little more than a convenience. For the former, changes in the meaning of a sign can signal a shift in cultural attitudes; for the latter, it would be merely a chance occurrence, dictated perhaps by some passing whim, and of very little general interest.

A semantic field can be viewed as a 'word-web', in which related concepts are bonded one to the other, and where the speaker discerns patterns of synonymic overlap, so that in some contexts one word can be substituted one for the other without noticeably changing the meaning of a sentence. With lexical inflation (cf. 4.5), there will be new entries into the field which may nudge aside some of their neighbours, which then become more specialized in meaning. This will especially be so if the newcomers carry prestige, like Latinisms in early modern French or English loanwords today, or if they are striking, amusing, or emotive, like colourful metaphors that catch the imagination. On the other hand, in some contexts, it will be easier to make do with frequently used words that have little specific meaning but which can be substituted for a host of others—the fuzzy thingamebob words that are the currency of everyday discourse.

The interplay between different words in the network can sometimes cast light on how and why meaning shifts occur, and especially on how a word can cease to mean what it once did. Let us take as an example the emotive web of words meaning 'to cheat', 'to deceive'.

Both these English words are of French origin, but with the former, a derivative of *échoir* 'to fall out', the relevant semantic development (at first applied to cheating at dice) was probably confined to England. *Décevoir* (older *décoivre*) (< DECIPERE) meant 'to catch out, to cheat' until the sixteenth century, when it moved into the semantic sphere of *désappointer* 'to depose, to let someone down', which fell out of use in French, though it survived in English. It was possibly the entry into the semantic field of *tromper*, in the fourteenth century, that shuffled *décevoir* across into the less sensational semantic slot. Originally meaning 'to play a trumpet', perhaps from fairground usage, *tromper* was clearly more stirring than the inherited word. *Tricher*, originally 'to trifle', also had entered the same sphere, mainly in the context of gambling, as did other words like fifteenth-century slang *duper* (from the word for 'hoopoe', cf. 'to gull', *pigeonner*, *piper*). The passion for gambling in the early modern period may be responsible for introducing into the language the new slangy words that were to drive out older forms like *engeignier* (derived from INGENIUM) and to restrict the now colourless *décevoir* to its modern comparatively blameless meaning.

A similar striving for more vivid expression can account for how *travailler*, derived from the word for an instrument of torture, should have become the usual word for 'to work', pushing *labourer* and *ouvrer* into more specialized areas of work—ploughing and artisanal activity. In its turn *travail(ler)* has become tame and insipid, so that other 'painful' words like *bosser* and *boulot* take over as the colloquial terms.

Thus in seeking to explain the semantic changes undergone by a word, we may gain insights by looking at its relationship with other words in the same semantic field, and especially at new entries which take over its semantic space, while other older forms drop over the edge into nothingness.

At a more philosophical level (cf. e.g. Rorty 1980, 1989) we can question the assumption that language is a mirror of unvarying nature, that reference and meaning remain constant, and that what changes is our way of describing it (and hence our beliefs about it). Thus in seeking to understand what our ancestors meant by a word, like 'trickery', 'knowledge', or 'work', it is not enough to transcode it into modern equivalents. We have, instead, to set each term within an appropriate cultural and intellectual context. How cultural change is effected is beyond the scope of the present work, but we should note that some thinkers appear to see semantic changes as triggering change in belief, rather than the other way round. To quote Nancy Fraser, in Malachowski 1990: 303–21: 'With vocabulary shifts, urgent questions suddenly lose their point, established practices are drastically modified, entire constellations of culture dissolve, to make room for new, heretofore unimaginable ones. Thus vocabulary shifts are for Rorty the motor of history, the chief vehicles of intellectual and moral progress.' It would then have to be individual innovators (poets—'the unacknowledged legislators of the social world') who initiate the change. 'It is their chance words, coming like bolts from "outside logical space", that determine the shape of subsequent culture and society.' If so, the puzzle then would be to discern why some such semantic changes catch on, whereas others, which may be as apt and colourful, die by the wayside.

5.5. UTTERANCE MEANING

If the question of change of word-meaning is ticklish, how much more precarious must be that of change in utterance meaning. An utterance once made is irrevocable. The speaker's intention does not change, although, feeling that what he uttered did not truly betoken what he meant to say, he may attempt to rephrase it. What can change over time is the interpretation put on the utterance by the hearer. Which is the meaning of the utterance—the speaker's intention or the hearer's interpretation? If the former, we can approach change by asking in what different ways a modern speaker would express the 'same thing' as an older speaker. This is not specifically a semantic change question, but brings in every kind of historical change—phonological, morphological, syntactic, lexical, sociolinguistic, stylistic. If the latter, on the other hand, we can envisage the possibility of isolating change in meaning over time from other linguistic change: a contemporary reader's interpretation of a sentence in a text will sometimes, perhaps always, differ from that of readers at later times.

Most discussion of changes in utterance meaning will therefore concentrate on expressions in older texts that have ceased to be semantically transparent over time, seeking to reconstruct what the utterer might have meant, or, rather, what the contemporary hearer would have understood. This is a more feasible exercise with one-word utterances—lexical free-forms—than with sentences, which, at the extreme, can over time appear meaningless, or even ungrammatical. In the same way longer stretches of discourse can sometimes be seen as incoherent; some medieval texts, for instance, leave us puzzled and bewildered if we seek to interpret them with a modern mind-set.

As an illustration, let us take examples from two of the earliest Old French texts. How are we to interpret the following lines, from the turn of the tenth century, if we code them item by item into modern French?

Buona pulcella fut Eulalia	*Bonne pucelle fut Eulalia*
Bel auret cors, bellezour anima	*Beau avait eu* (?) *corps, plus belle âme.*

The lexical items are not all familiar: but we understand *pucelle* for *jeune fille* from our knowledge of Joan of Arc (*La Pucelle d'Orléans*); we reconstruct a comparative BELLATIOREM and a pluperfect HABUERAT from the obsolete isolated forms *bellezour* and *auret*; and we assume that *anima* is a Latinism. *Buona* is odd, but it is the Italian for *bonne*, so we are not too shocked at its use in French. But the text would be totally ungrammatical in modern French, not merely because of the word-order, which is not unheard of in modern verse, but because of the tense usage and the absence of noun determiners. To these questions we shall return below, in discussing how such grammatical elements contribute to the meaning of a sentence and how changes in such elements can contribute to semantic change.

However, the meaning of our lines seems comprehensible enough, if rather pidginized.

From our cultural standpoint, we may jib at the text as a whole, but we can console ourselves with a symbolic interpretation: at the end of the story the 13-year-old girl saint is not consumed by fire, but ascends to heaven in the shape of a dove. What we probably miss are the semantic connotations of *buona*, which seems to have meant in this context 'devoted to God, godly', rather than 'good' in any modern interpretation.

There is one line in this poem though which leaves us bereft of comprehension and has provoked much discussion:

> *Ell'ent adunet* (or *aduret*) *lo suon element*

We cannot decode this in modern French, though we guess, from the context, that it means something like 'She refused to give in'. Yet this would be a perfectly good sentence, give or take a few phonological modifications, in early modern French:

> *Elle en adune* (/ *adure*) *le sien element.*

What gives us pause are the lexical items *adune* (*adure*, if the smudged letter in the manuscript is *r* not *n*), and *element* (as well as the precise anaphoric reference of *en*, but that is often a puzzle in modern French, cf. 8.16). We can use our ingenuity: *aduner* could mean 'to get together' (cf. *un*), and *adurer*, 'to harden' (cf. *dur*); *element* could mean 'strength', 'God' or the fire that Eulalia was cast into. But speculation will not definitively solve our problem.

Surprisingly perhaps, most Old French sentences are reasonably comprehensible to a modern reader, give or take a few vocabulary items and the unfamiliar spelling: this is one of the things that persuades us that they are, in some sense, 'French'. But, especially in the earliest texts, they are sometimes barely grammatical in modern French. Take as an example the first lines of the eleventh-century hagiographic text, the Life of St Alexis, which introduce a familiar *topos*: 'Fings ain't what they used to be'.

(Manuscript variants are given in square brackets)

> *Bons fut li secles al tens ancienur*
> *Quer feit i ert e justise e amur*
> *S'i ert creance dunt or[e] at nul prut*
> *Tut est muez, perdut [perdue] ad sa colur:*
> *Ja mais n'iert tel cum fut as anceisurs.*

In this case obsolete lexical items are interpretable because they are attested elsewhere:

prut as *preux*; *muez*, replaced today by *changé*; *s(i)* < SIC was a commonplace Old French introductory particle; *or(e)* < HORA regularly meant 'now'. *Secle* (modern *siècle*) had the connotation 'secular world' (as distinct from 'heaven'); *créance* is today used only in financial contexts, replaced by the variant *croyance* in the sense of 'belief'; *colur* (= *couleur*) can readily be interpreted figuratively. *Ancienur* can be interpreted as a comparative

'older', or as a genitive plural 'of the older people'. *Ja mais* 'already more'
used with the future *iert* (= *sera*) later generalized as *jamais* 'never'. The
differences in spelling (*tens* = *temps*, *feit* = *foi*, *tut* = *tout* etc.) can easily be
overlooked; case-markings, in this instance (*li secles*, *muez*), are neither here
nor there, either syntactically or semantically.

What is odd, however, is the use of tense: why the alternation
between *passé simple*, *fut*, and the imperfect, *ert* (= *était*)? What is
the tense or aspectual purport of *est muez* and *perdu[e] ad*? Again,
too, the use and non-use of determiners is not crystal clear to a
speaker of modern French.

A full discussion of the ways sentence meanings could have
changed in the history of French—leaving out of account, here,
Latin, which we treat as a 'different language'—would require
detailed discussion of texts (cf. Fleischman 1990). Moreover, to
draw a line here between semantics, syntax, and stylistics is imprac-
ticable (cf. Dembowski 1980). What I shall seek to do in the rest of
this chapter is to explore how the meaning of non-lexical, or
functional, elements can change, and thus affect the interpretation
of utterance meaning, at the level of the sentence. I shall be looking
only at the **determiners** and especially the **definite article**, and at **tense,
aspect, mood** (**TAM**) markers. Classically discussion of these topics
figures under the heading of **syntax**: I prefer the label **semantico-
syntax**, because meaning is intimately involved in their use.

5.6. TENSE, ASPECT, MOOD (TAM)

Languages have the means, morphological, syntactic, or lexical, to
convey certain features about the processes that are lexicalized as
verbs. These are conventionally labelled as **tense**, **aspect** and **mood**
(**TAM**). In French-based creoles, as we saw in 1.8, these are usually
marked by prefixes to the lexical verb-form, but in French a variety
of markers are used. We precede examination of changes, from
Latin to French, in the meaning of some of the markers by a brief
set of definitions.

Tense (*temps*) can be said to locate an event in time: it pinpoints a privileged
time (**locus**) in relation to time **frame** (which is most often the moment of
speech).
Aspect relates the event to the time interval over which it occurs. It can refer
to:

(i) change, that is whether the predicate can be understood as **static** or **dynamic**; (ii) closure, whether the event is seen completed or not (**perfect / imperfect**); (iii) iterativity, whether an event is **habitual** or **repeated**; (iv) durativity, whether the event occurs instantly (**punctual**), or over a length of time (**progressive**).

Mood can be said to refer to the actuality of an event by comparing the event world(s) with the actual world (taking into account such factors as whether the event is possible, necessary, or desirable). In Latin and Romance a morphological contrast is made between **indicative** and **subjunctive**, which roughly seems to have to do with the speaker's perceptions about the reality of the event. The contrast between **epistemic modality**—which characterizes the actuality of the event in terms of alternative possible situations (necessity, possibility)—and **deontic**—which refers to obligation or permission—is not coded in any obvious grammatical way in French (cf. modal verbs like *devoir*, *pouvoir*). I shall not therefore be taking this into consideration. Some theorists distinguish **mood** (which refers to grammatical status), from **modality** (which signals the attitude of the speaker—for example, doubt or emotion) and **mode** (which refers to the pragmatic status of utterance—interrogative, imperative etc.), and **modulation** (e.g. 'must', 'need', 'may' etc. expressed lexically in French). The French term *mode* covers all of these, but I shall take into account only the first two.

In Latin, tense, aspect, and mood were marked mainly by inflectional endings on the verb. Some of these have survived into French, and convey in some cases similar meanings. However, the Latin system has disintegrated over time, leaving many gaps in modern French. Latin verb morphology distinguished clearly between present (INFECTUM 'unfinished') and perfect ('completed') stem, reflecting, though not totally consistently, **imperfective** (including **habitual** and **iterative**) and **perfective** (including **punctual**) aspect. **Progressive** aspect had no grammatical marker.

The stems each entered into three finite **indicative** tenses—**present** (the timeless unmarked form), **future** and **past**—and in the **subjunctive** two parallel forms, with no future. In French the present survives in both indicative and subjunctive, and the past survives as the **imperfect** (*j'aimais*). The other forms have disappeared.

The Latin perfect-stem forms have had an even more chequered career in their passage into French. The present perfect (AMĀUI > *j'aimai*) survives only marginally, with **preterite** (punctual past) functions, being displaced in the modern colloquial language by **compound** forms (like *j'ai aimé*), which earlier had taken over **present perfective** functions. The reflex of the **pluperfect** (past **locus** within a past time **frame**) subjunctive (AMĀUISSEM) was until quite recently used as a past subjunctive (past locus within a present time frame: *j'aimasse*), but it now has virtually fallen out of use. The pluperfect indicative (AMĀUERAM) is attested in only the earliest texts, and then with an uncertain past meaning reference (cf. Moignet 1959*c*).

Each of the active Latin forms had a passive equivalent. In the present-stem forms all were marked by an -R (possibly originally a nominalizing suffix). All of these were lost in Romance, which favoured the compound perfect forms (AMATUS SUM > *je suis aimé*, with present, not past, reference).

It is usually assumed that the introduction of the new compound perfects and the loss of the Latin future and present-stem passives were effected at the Proto-Romance stage. Other changes are thought to have happened later: we shall be concerned here with the semantic changes in the expressions of past and future **tense**, of **aspect** and of **mood** and **modality**. I shall consider, in particular, interchange between aspect and mood connotations and the introduction and **grammaticalization** of **periphrastic** forms, to supplement the inherited inflectional marks.

5.7. THE 'PAST IMPERFECT'

The Latin 'past imperfect' survives in all the Romance languages (and even in some creoles) as a past tense. The name given to the AMĀBAM forms is something of a mistranslation of the Greek equivalent (*paratatikós*), which implied not unfinished action, but an event on which no time limits are placed by the speaker. In Romance it has unmarked semantic characteristics that allow for a range of discourse interpretations. Most usually it is seen as implying incomplete, iterative, or habitual action in the past, continuing its Latin **imperfective** aspectual functions. Some would even claim that it does not have specifically past time reference, but marks principally the incompleteness of the event. Maupas [1607] characterized it thus: '. . . *l'imparfait s'attache à une durée & flux de temps estendu en l'acte qui se faisoit lors dont on parle, & n'estoit encor parachevé*'. The Port-Royal Grammar [1660] went so far as to call it a *temps composé*, combining the present with the past: '. . . *parce qu'il ne marque pas la chose simplement et* *proprement comme faite, mais comme présente à l'égard d'une chose qui est déjà néanmoins passée'.*

In modern French the *imparfait* is often viewed as a past **progressive**, but it functions mainly as a 'backgrounding', scene-setting tense, used when no precise time limits are set for the past event it describes and allowing contrast with a punctual action:

(1) *Quand il regardait la télé, elle donna | a donné un coup de téléphone.* 'When he was watching (while he watched) the TV, she made a telephone call.'

It is also frequently used, since the mid-nineteenth century (though examples can be found earlier), as a conscious stylistic device to give an impressionistic tinge to narrative description, even when the time locus is precisely specified:

(2) *Gianni revenait au bout d'une heure* 'Gianni came back an hour later' (E. de Goncourt).

This is usually seen as an extension of the use of the imperfect in indirect speech, in which the past event is seen through the eyes of the reporter.

Thus *J'ai dit que Gianni revenait* would transpose my direct speech observation *Gianni revient* from a present time frame to a past frame in which I report my speech.

In *discours indirect libre* the reporter is not overtly mentioned, but a past time frame is extrapolated.

Old French use of the indicative in indirect speech (*oratio obliqua*) contexts, where Latin used an accusative and infinitive or a subjunctive, was rapidly gaining ground in the medieval period. It was perhaps through this channel that the *imparfait*, and the related *conditionnel*, forms have taken on almost modal nuances in modern French, hinting at some distancing of the speaker from the event, which is placed in a past time frame, as in the *imparfait d'attenuation*:

(3) *Je voulais vous demander votre bienveillance* 'I'd like to ask you for your support'

or the *imparfait hypocoristique*:

(4) *Comme il aimait bien sa maman!* 'Doesn't he just love his mummy!'

The conditional is frequently used in journalistic style to dissociate the speaker from responsibility for the truth of the utterance:

(5)   *Il aurait tué sa femme* 'He is alleged to have killed his wife'.

The quasi-modal character of the *imparfait* is most evident in its use in hypothetical conditionals after *si*:

(6)   *Si j'avais de l'argent, je t'en donnerais* 'If I had some money, I'd give you some'.

Here the *si* can be seen as acting like an abstract verb of hypothesis ('supposing that . . .'), which would be followed by an *oratio obliqua* construction. In Latin a subjunctive would be usual in both the **protasis** (*si*-clause) and the **apodosis**, in hypothetical conditional sentences, with the imperfect or pluperfect subjunctive used when the condition is presented as contrary to known facts. The imperfect subjunctive (derived from the Latin pluperfect subjunctive) is still current in many Romance languages and is found in some early Old French texts:

(7)   *Se j'osasse parler, je demandasse de quel terre estes nez* (*Couronnement de Louis*, *c*.1130). 'If I dared speak, I would ask where you were born.'

However, though similar uses, often with a mixture of forms, are well attested in Anglo-Norman texts, by the thirteenth century the modern construction with the imperfect indicative is the most frequent in continental texts.

In modern non-standard French, especially in northern regions, the 'conditional' (or 'future in the past' i.e. a future locus in a past frame—*aimerais*) is found in both protasis and apodosis. This usage is attested in earlier texts, and even in Malherbe, but it was ruled out as non-standard in the seventeenth century. Where no *si* is used, double conditional forms are standard:

(8)   *J'aurais de l'argent, je t'en donnerais.*

Perhaps as an extension of its use in hypothetical conditionals, the imperfect can sometimes be used where we would expect a conditional form:

(9)   *Sans moi, il tombait* 'If I hadn't been there, he would have fallen'.

The *imparfait* is a tense that is comparatively little used in colloquial styles, found more often in subordinate, than in main, clauses, and it was very much less frequent in early texts than it is today. Some see its association with modality as linked to its early use preponderantly with modal verbs, like *devoir, pouvoir, savoir*. This could also help to explain the irregular phonological development of the form, by which formal homogeneity of the tense was reinforced by the analogical spread of a single marker through the conjugation system (cf. 7.11). In the modern spoken language the **compound**, originally **perfective**, form (*j'ai chanté*) is the only other past tense. In contrast to this temporal form, it is the quasi-modal, aspectual, rather than the temporal, flavour of the *imparfait* that today comes to the fore. Its 'fuzzy', passe-partout character may well be reflected in its morphology, which stresses the homogeneity of the tense, rather than the morphological conjugation-class of the lexical verb.

5.8. OTHER PAST TENSES

The history of reference to past time in French is something which has long exercised the minds of linguists. We have already seen that the *imparfait* (*j'aimais*) is indeterminate in its reference to time, though it certainly implies the non-actuality of events with which it is associated. The other French inflectional past tense (i.e. past locus in a present frame)—the *passé simple* (*j'aimai*)—has now ceased to be used in the colloquial language and is associated with certain discourse types, like traditional narrative and high-flown rhetoric. Events in the past are today recorded in the *passé composé* (*j'ai aimé*), though this retains still some of its etymological flavour of 'present perfect'—that is, of an action in the past whose results are still felt in the present.

The *passé composé* is transparently morphologically compounded of present tense forms of the **auxiliaries** (cf. 3.15) *avoir* (*j'ai fini*) and *être* (*je suis venu*), with an adjectival non-finite lexical verb form (**past participle**). *Être* is obligatorily used in the modern standard language with selected intransitive verbs, and with all **pronominal** verbs (even with transitive **reflexives** cf. *elle s'est lavée*). The *être* intransitives typically denote change of state (like *naître, mourir*, and verbs involving motion). Such verbs fall into the category called **unaccusative**: their subject NP is not semantically an actor, but a **theme** or **experiencer**. The morphology reflects the almost stative or passive semantics (cf. *elle est morte / elle est tuée*). In Old French the choice of auxiliary was less rigidly determined, and seemed to be linked more closely with the degree of activity denoted by the verb or exerted by its subject. In modern colloquial varieties *avoir* has been generalized, especially where activity is implied, as in *tomber* or *monter* (cf. Table 2.1).

What we are here primarily interested in is the semantic history of the decline and eventual demise of the *passé simple* and the birth and eventual triumph of the *passé composé*. But we may wonder too about the way in which Old French texts seem to play fast and loose with tense reference, passing freely from past to present tense in the same narrative sequence. Puzzling too is the apparent flouting of the aspectual distinction between the *passé simple* and the *imparfait* exemplified in the *Eulalia* and *Alexis* text excerpts quoted above (5.5), in which **preterite** *fut* is used for on-going states, alternating with the anticipated *imparfait* forms. Here is another example, among many others:

(10)   *La ot une fosse parfunde*
       n'ot plus laide en tot le monde
       granz et large estoit l'entrée (*Énéas, c.*1160)
       'There there was [*passé simple*] a deep ditch, there was no uglier in the whole world, big and wide was [*imparfait*] the entrance.'

A facile answer is that our texts are literary artefacts, designed to evoke audience reaction, rather than accurately to mirror events. Such uses are much more frequent in verse epic than elsewhere, and almost completely absent in dialogue texts. Punctual *fut* or *eut* (by far the most frequent examples) grab the attention, set the scene, whereas the default imperfect form (*ert, était, avait*) would be colourless and commonplace. Moreover, where syllable counts are important—as in verse—it was convenient to have the choice between synonymic monosyllabic and bisyllabic forms. This substitution, which reached its peak in the thirteenth century, probably never caught on in the spoken idiom, and so it did not survive when literary practice changed. In 1582, Henri Estienne condemned such uses of the *passé simple* in round terms, stigmatizing them as Germanisms, but examples persist into the seventeenth century.

Similarly in talking about the past, a switch from past to present tense morphology can convey urgency, immediacy: examples of this in Old French narrative are abundant:

(11) *Et li cevax qui ot senti les esperons*
      l'en porta par mi le presse
      se se lance tres entre mi ses anemis
      et il getent les mains de toutes pars
      si le prendent . . . (*Aucassin et Nicolete*, 13th c.)

> 'And the horse who had felt the spurs, carried him, because of that, into the midst of the fray, so he launches himself right among his enemies and they throw out their hands on all sides and thus capture him . . .'.

Overindulgence in this device—where the present perfect can stand in frequently for the preterite—might very well lead to new learners misinterpreting the present perfect form as a preterite, and thus formulating a grammar which dispenses with the apparently redundant preterite forms, except as a stylistic ornament.

Plausible enough, but what evidence have we for the chronology of the displacement of the *passé simple* by the erstwhile present perfect that has become the *passé composé*?

We shall return later (cf. 8.17) to how the evidence of agreement of the past participle in the compound construction can influence our assessment of the status of the *passé composé*.

When did the *passé simple* cease to be current in French? If we take into account formal registers, the answer is 'Never'. But in colloquial registers, where the *passé simple* is certainly not used today, evidence for non-use in the past is hard to come by. Possibly hesitation about its morphology, voiced in the sixteenth and seventeenth centuries, can be taken to show that it had already loosened its grip in everyday speech, as indeed was the (artificial?) *Diktat* that it could refer only to events that had taken place more than twenty-four hours before the act of speech. By the mid-eighteenth century spoken narrative can be reported exclusively in the *passé composé*, though textual evidence is inconsistent even to the present day. In, for instance, the letters written by young soldiers to their relatives at home in Auvergne, during the Revolutionary campaigns of 1792–5, there is ample evidence of use of the *passé simple*, as of the past subjunctive (Bouscayrol 1987).

However, nearly everyone would agree that by the twentieth century there is, in the colloquial language, no semantic difference between the *passé simple* and the *passé composé*. The former, with its function as a punctual past, continues to be used in formal written registers, while the latter no longer denotes only events completed by the present time, but has been extended to refer to events that occurred wholly at a precise time in the past.

Thus it does look as if here there has been a semantic change: in modern colloquial French punctual events in the past can no longer be distinguished morphologically from events that have been completed by the present. The *passé simple* forms today serve to mark a certain type of narrative discourse—just as in some Amerindian languages a distinct verbal morphology is reserved for the recounting of traditional myths.

Compound forms with auxiliaries in the preterite (*j'eus fini*) or the imperfect tense (*j'avais fini*) early replaced inherited pluperfect forms (of which we have only a few examples in very early texts, cf. 5.5). By the fourteenth century the **past anterior** (*j'eus fini*) had become limited in its use and it was rivalled in colloquial varieties by a *passé surcomposé*, with the auxiliary in the *passé composé* (*j'ai eu fini*). This was condemned as vulgar in the seventeenth century, but survives in some varieties (Ayres-Bennett 1994*c*, Ayres-Bennett and Carruthers 1992, Carruthers 1994).

5.9. PERIPHRASTIC VERB-FORMS

Romanists usually distinguish the **compound** tenses, with **auxiliaries** *avoir* and *être* and the **past participle** (the **passive** and the **compound past** tenses) from other **periphrastic** forms, usually consisting of a finite auxiliary or semi-auxiliary and non-finite form of the lexical verb.

In Latin what are known as the **periphrastic** tenses are those composed of the verb 'to be' and the future participle or the adjectival gerundive:

(12) AMATURUS / AMANDUS EST 'He is about to love / he has to be loved'.

The former disappears altogether in Romance. The form with the gerundive (which in French is identical with the present participle) did however survive to signal progressive or continuous aspect, with active rather than passive import. In Old French the construction could be used with *être*, but was most often used with *al(l)er*, which seems to have been **bleached** of its motion connotations:

(13) *Car chevalchiez! Pur qu'alez arestant?* (*Roland*) 'Ride on! Why are you stopping?'

As an aspectual progressive construction, this ceased to be used in modern French, though there are dubious seventeenth-century examples, like :

(14) *Les fous vont l'emportant* (La Fontaine) 'Madmen are getting the upper hand'.

Modern literary examples like:

(15) *Le mal va croissant* 'The ill is growing',

are possible, but imply futurity rather than describing a present event. The more usual type of construction is exemplified by:

(16) *Les affaires allaient en empirant* 'Business was getting worse and worse'.

In the modern language the infinitive has widened its scope to the detriment of the gerund(ive)/present participle forms, and it provides the base, with a 'semi-auxiliary', for newer periphrastic forms. For instance, the older *va chantant* ('he is singing') progressive type was replaced in the seventeenth century by *il est après chanter*, which survives in Canada and some metropolitan dialects: in the creoles *après* has grammaticalized as a pre-verbal TAM marker *ape*, *ap*, or *pe*, to mark progressive aspect. In the standard the construction was condemned as vulgar by arbiters like Vaugelas. French no longer has a grammatical way of marking **progressive** aspect, though at a pinch the meaning can be conveyed by a periphrasis like *il est en train de chanter*—introduced in the eighteenth century.

In the modern language the infinitive also combines with (semi-)auxiliaries to produce what are virtually new tenses. The *GO*-future, used to indicate the imminence of an event, for instance, today hotly rivals the synthetic future in the colloquial language:

(17) *Il va chanter / il chantera*, 'He is going to sing/ he will sing'.

With future reference this form, which is not yet fully **grammaticalized**, dates from the end of the fifteenth century. In earlier texts it still implied motion and its time reference was ambiguous, possibly being used also for past events (as in Catalan today). The most

usual creole future TAM marker (*va, av, a*) is clearly derived from
the *va* of this construction.

Another more or less grammaticalized periphrastic form with the
infinitive is the 'recent past' with the semi-auxiliary *venir de* (a
COME-past), which can be compared with creole TAM markers
derived from *sortir*.

5.10. SUBJUNCTIVE

The forms of the Latin present subjunctive **mood** survive into
modern French—however not without a good deal of **syncretism**
with the indicative, from which they are differentiated only in
comparatively few forms (cf. 7.14). Other tenses of the Latin
subjunctive were less resistant. In spoken French the past subjunctive (*imparfait du subjonctif*) has today ceased to be used—though
still learned as a written form.

The oldest textual evidence we have of substitution of the present subjunctive for the past dates from the mid-nineteenth century, in George
Sand's representation of the colloquial style of peasants from Berry.

The loss of tense morphology squares with the suggestion that the
subjunctive is essentially timeless, expressing the speaker's lack of
commitment to the reality of the event reported. But the subjunctive
is said also to have emotive import, expressing the attitude of the
speaker to the event he reports, or conveying optative or volitive
nuances. In any case, differences of subjunctive tense form depend
automatically on tense sequence (*concordance de temps*) conventions, and not on the real time setting of the event reported. In the
older language, however, use of the past subjunctive can imply a
greater distancing of the speaker from what is reported, as in:

(18) *Mais il m'est vis . . . que l'uns de vos s'en alast aprester* 'I think
     rather that one of you might go and get ready'.

A famous example is the telling irony in Racine's *Andromaque*'s
lament:

(19) *On craint qu'il n'essuyât les larmes de sa mère* 'It is feared that
     he might comfort his mother in her distress'.

The evidence of Louis XIII's childish speech shows that the past subjunctive was still in colloquial use in the early seventeenth century (cf. Branca-Rosoff 1992). This is an example of his usage at the age of 7:

(20) *Je voudré que vous peussié mangé Madame Ga* 'I would like you to be able to eat Madame de Monglat [Louis's *gouvernante*].'

However minimally, the indicative/subjunctive distinction is still part of the grammar of French, although in the spoken language constructions which require a subjunctive tend to be avoided. Descriptions in traditional grammars, which particularly cherish the distinctions, usually claim that the semantics, **optative**, **volitive**, or **potential**, of the subjunctive has remained virtually unchanged since Latin.

Yet it is scarcely used today in main clauses. It does survive as an optative in third person **imperatives**, but except in a few stereotyped expressions (like *Vive le roi!*) such forms are, since the seventeenth century, preceded by a **complementizer** *que*, in keeping with the intuition that they are governed by an underlying verb of command:

(21) *Qu'il vienne* '[I command] that he come'.

The subjunctive is thus used principally in subordinate clauses, reflecting some Latin uses more faithfully than others. In modern French it usually can be viewed as merely an agreement feature, a *servitude grammaticale*. In this respect it serves to reinforce the semanticism of its governing verb or conjunction, which usually implies volition or the lack of certainty inherent in anticipated events.

In other cases the choice seems one of style, with the subjunctive adding a certain air of elegance to the subordinated postposition. This is particularly so after verbs indicating pleasure, anger, fear, and the like. Sometimes, where the choice of mood is prescribed by standard grammars, the choice of the actual verbs involved may seem arbitrary:

(22) *Je suis heureux qu'il vienne* 'I'm happy that he'll come'/ *J'espère qu'il viendra* 'I hope he'll come'.

In Old French *espérer* could mean 'to wait for', taking the indicative, while expressions that unambiguously expressed 'hope' were followed by the subjunctive:

(23) *Car li adversaires a aucune fois esperance que li os soit tost fenis* (Jehan de Meung) 'For the adversary has sometimes hope that the enemy would be soon finished'.

With verbs of saying and thinking, where Latin used the accusative and infinitive construction, a finite verb clause can be used in all the Romance languages. Choice of the subjunctive in such a clause seems to add a nuance of doubt about the subordinated statement in Old French, but interpretation of the difference is not always straightforward:

(24) *Je los que je m'en voise* (*Pathelin*) 'I think [advise] I should go' / *Je lo qu'avec li en alons* (*Miracles*) 'I think [advise] we go with him'; *Il croient bien qu'il acheveront legierement les autres aventures* / *Et lors croient bien tuit cil de la place que Lancelot die voire* (*Queste*) 'They fully believe that they will complete easily the other adventures' / 'And then all those of the place fully believe that Lancelot would be saying true'.

In Old French the verb *cuidier* (< COGITARE) was most often followed by the subjunctive, while *croire* (< CREDERE) was more often used for religious belief and often took the indicative. Its predilection for the subjunctive may have contributed to the demise of *cuidier*.

Hesitation in usage, even at the time of standardization of the language, may account for the formulation, in prescriptive grammars, of the curious rule that the subjunctive should be used after a negative or an interrogative, but not after a negative interrogative:

(25) *Je crois qu'il viendra* / *Je ne crois pas qu'il vienne* / *Crois-tu qu'il vienne?* / *Ne crois-tu pas qu'il viendra?*

In the colloquial language only the indicative is current in all these contexts.

One construction where the subjunctive still can contrast with the indicative is in **restrictive relatives**. The antecedent is understood as non-referential when a subjunctive follows:

(26) *Je cherche une fille qui sache* / *sait le français* 'I'm looking for a [= any / a particular] girl who knows French'.

In Old French this distinction was not consistently made:

(27) *E Deus! dist il, quer oüsse un serjant quil me gardast! Jo l'en fereie franc* (*Alexis*) 'Oh God, said he, I wish I could have a [any] servant who would look after me! I would make him a freedman for it' / *Cil qui a malvais pere, malvais est s'eritez*

(Guernes de Pont-Sainte-Maxence) 'Anyone who has an evil father, evil is his heritage.'

It is also rarely made in modern colloquial speech.

The subjunctive is automatically used in the spoken language in complement clauses dependent on volition verbs, and when introduced by some complementizers (like *avant que*, *pourvu que*, *pour que*, *sans que*), but otherwise occurs rather erratically in the usage of uneducated speakers. It can be maintained that the sort of context in which the subjunctive is used—principally in elaborated discourse, with subordinate clauses—is in any case rare in unplanned everyday spoken usage. Certainly the subjunctive does carry with it an aura of refinement, and so can induce hypercorrect usages, but whether it today contributes to the semantics of the sentence is open to doubt. If it does not, then this certainly represents a change since Latin, and probably since Old French.

In modern French modality can be expressed lexically, especially by the use of **modal verbs** accompanied by the infinitive of the lexical verb. In the creoles there is no trace of the subjunctive, but modal markers have been grammaticalized probably from French modal verbs. Thus in Indian Ocean creoles modal variants of the future markers include *pu* (< *pouvoir*, or *pour*?) and *vle* (< *vouloir*).

As we have seen, in modern French the *imparfait*, and especially the *conditionnel*, forms have also developed modal nuances similar to those once conveyed by subjunctive morphology.

5.11. DEFINITENESS

A salient change in the transition from Latin to Romance was the creation of the **definite article**, which in modern French is part of a system of **determiners**, providing a device for inserting the bare noun into the sentence, acting as **morphological case** (cf. 7.17–18) did in Latin. Whereas the Latin noun had no phonological form not associated with sentence role, in modern French the morphological noun is less variable in form and conveys only lexical content (though it is sometimes morphologically marked also for gender and plurality). **Syntagmatic** strategies, like ordering of elements within the sentence, are more often used to code their grammatical relationships. These will be discussed under **syntax** (Chapter 8). We shall here be concerned with changes in the semantic contribution made by the article to sentence meaning in the passage from Latin to modern French.

Definiteness is sometimes treated as a unitary pragmatic or semantic feature of the **Noun Phrase** (**NP**). It is associated with the definite article forms used with common nouns in languages like English and French, though many languages (including Latin) have no such marker. Some theorists distinguish the article's pragmatic functions, like signalling accessibility (or familiarity), from the semantic functions, like marking referentiality or specificity. These features can be indicated in other ways, for instance by word-order, in articleless languages. In Latin, in the rare cases where it is necessary to specify the definite status of an NP, a lexical means may be found, but, out of context, we cannot be certain whether to translate, for instance, AGGREDIOR HOMINEM as 'I accost the man' or 'I accost a man'.

It is common knowledge that 'definite articles' in many languages are often etymologically and pragmatically related to **deictics** (**demonstratives**, pointing words), but without their specific locational ('here' **proximal**/'there' **distal**) meaning. The physical deictic purport of the demonstrative is 'weakened' over time to **anaphoric** use (referring back to another item in the discourse or context). The Latin demonstrative which gave rise to the French article was the distal **pronoun** ILLE, which also, reinforced by a preposed ECCE 'behold!', forms the base of the French distal demonstrative (*ce* etc., cf. 7.20).

ILLE also survives as a third person pronoun (*il*, *le* etc.), which is also definite in character. The history of the **morphological** relationship between **determiners** and **pronouns** will be discussed in 8.10.

The use of the definite article has never failed to strike observers as an outstanding difference between Latin and Romance. Latin grammarians frequently remarked on the absence, in their own language, of an equivalent of the Greek article, which signalled the specificity of the NP. It has been suggested that the article came into Christian Latin as a transfer from Greek: however evidence from early Latin translations of the Greek New Testament shows no consistent representation of the Greek article. Late Latin texts do make much greater use of demonstratives than in classical times, but the identifier pronoun IPSE 'himself' was used, presumably emphatically, more often than ILLE, and there is no clear evidence that a definite article was in use before the birth of the Romance languages.

The definite article in French seems to have been used initially less as a **specifier**, picking out the individuality of the object designated by the noun, than as a **topicalizer**, anaphorically picking out a noun that is accessible to the hearer. It can however sometimes be interpreted as a demonstrative in Old French, a usage which survives in some stereotyped expressions like *de la sorte, dans le temps* and can still be detected in some seventeenth-century uses:

(28) *Plusieurs voyages en ont été dérangés, le mien est du nombre* (Madame de Sévigné) 'Some journeys were disrupted because of that, mine was of that number'.

As in other languages, the function of the French definite article widened as time went on, as it came to be used with nouns denoting unique objects (that require no specification) and with abstracts (which are non-referential). Remnants of the older use persisted until the sixteenth, and even the seventeenth, century:

(29) *Nature rien ne fait immortel* (Rabelais) 'Nature makes nothing immortal'; *Et crut gagner paradis* (La Fontaine) 'And he thought to attain Paradise',

where *la nature* and *le paradis* would today be mandatory, except in stereotyped expressions. **Generic** use of the article, to denote type rather than an individual, also became normal in the modern period, when the article came to be seen by grammarians as little more than a gender and number marker for the noun.

In modern Romance the definite article is used with very high frequency: in French, in particular, it is one of a series of virtually obligatory determiners (/ *un, du, ce, mon*) that indicate nouniness and mark gender and number.

The development, mainly from the sixteenth century, of the **partitive** article (composed of *de* + the definite article, cf. 8.11), used with non-count nouns, marks an important change in the structure of the NP, which can no longer normally be used without a determiner. The definite article henceforth acts as the default determiner, rather than as a mark of specificity.

In creoles, the definite article, when it survives, is an integral part of the noun, with no semantic input. To mark specificity or NP status other means, like a postposed locative adverb *là*, are used.

Most Old French sentences with articleless NPs would today be ungrammatical. On the other hand some uses of the article in Old French texts would also be ungrammatical in the modern language:

(30) *C'as enpensé, li fiex au roi Charlon?* (*Aliscans*) 'What have you decided, son of King Charles?'

In other cases, the Old French definite article form, used pronominally, would be uninterpretable in modern French:

(31) *Je ne vi cotes brodees ne les le roi ne les autrui* (Joinville) 'I didn't see embroidered bodices, neither those of the king, nor those of others'.

But in the many examples where there are comparable grammatical sentences in Old and modern French the interpretation of the definite article seems to be identical:

(32) *Et la roine prent le chevalier par la main* (*Lancelot*) 'And the queen takes the knight by the hand'; *Quant li rois englés et ses gens veirent les fumiers des Escos* . . . (Froissart) 'When the English king and his men saw the smoke-screen of the Scots . . .'.

It is difficult therefore to talk of change of sentence meaning without reference to syntactic change. The meaning of the definite article itself has changed, especially as it no longer regularly contrasts with a zero article. But in comparable sentences in Old and modern French the contribution to sentence meaning by the definite article often seems to be the same. Perhaps, though, we are missing some of the semantic nuances!

FURTHER READING

On semantics: Aitchison 1987, Baldinger 1980, Cruse 1986, Greimas 1966, Lakoff and Johnson 1980, J. Lyons 1995, Picoche 1986, Rey 1973–6, Sweetser 1990, Tamba Mecz 1988, Tuţescu 1975, Ullmann 1957, Wilmet 1980.

On lexical semantic change: Bréal 1879, Coseriu 1964, Fisiak 1985, Huguet 1967, Posner 1973, 1975, 1980*a*, Ullmann 1952.

On tense, aspect, mood: Bache *et al.* 1994, Benveniste 1959, Binnick 1991, Bybee *et al.* 1994, Chung and Timberlake 1985, Comrie 1978, 1985, Curat 1991, Dahl 1985, David and Martin 1980, Fleischman 1982, 1983, 1990, Fuchs and Léonard 1979, Garey 1957, Guillaume 1929, M. B. Harris 1982, 1986*a*, *b*, Hornstein 1990, Imbs 1960, Klein 1974, Klum 1961, Marchello-Nizia 1985, R. Martin 1965, 1971, Palmer 1986, Pollack 1988, Posner 1972, Reid 1955, 1970, Schogt 1968*a*, *b*, Sten 1952, Traugott *et al.* 1986, Vet 1985, Waugh 1986, Weinrich 1964.

On the imperfect: Dauses 1981, Ducrot 1979, Larochette 1969, Le Goffic 1986.

On past tenses: Benveniste 1960, Dietrich 1987, Engels 1989, Fleischman 1983, Guenthner *et al.* 1978, Guillaume 1938, Harré 1991, M. B. Harris 1982, Harris and Ramat 1987, Kayne 1993, Labelle 1987, Moignet 1959*c*, Molendijk 1990, Schogt 1964, 1968*b*, van Vliet 1983, Waugh 1976, Waugh and Burston 1986.

On periphrastic verb-forms: Benveniste 1965, Flydal 1943, Gougenheim 1929*b*, Létoublon 1984, Roy 1976.

On the subjunctive: Cohen n.d., Connors 1978, Currie 1971, Imbs 1953, Jensen 1974, Ludwig 1988, Moignet 1959*b*, Wunderli 1970.

On definiteness: Abel 1971, Ariel 1988, Battye 1991, Corblin 1987, Drijko-ningen 1993, Galmiche 1989, Greenberg 1978, Guillaume 1919, M. B. Harris 1977, 1980*a*, *b*, Hawkins 1978, Heinimann 1965, 1967, Heinz 1983, Karmiloff-Smith 1979, Kleiber 1986, Krámský 1972, R. Martin 1983, Maurel 1986, Padley 1988, Picabia 1986, Pinkster 1990, Posner 1988*a*, Postal 1966, Selig 1989, Sommerstein 1972, Spence 1983*a*, Trager 1932, Warnant 1980, Wilmet 1986, Zubizaretta and Vergnaud 1992.

6

Phonological Change

6.1. PHONOLOGICAL CHANGE—GENERAL

Classical historical linguistics started from the assumption that linguistic change originates first and foremost in speech-acts, and most often in unperceived phonetic distortion, which may eventually have cumulative effects. Recognition of regularity in sound-change, only dimly perceived before the late eighteenth century, provided the boost for the take-off of the discipline. The regularity had not been obvious to observers while the word, and its meaning, remained for them the paramount linguistic unit: perceiving a patterned relationship between the more abstract and meaningless sound units within the word allowed the breakthrough towards a principled approach to language change. These sound-units (roughly equivalent to **phonemes**) were identified with the segments represented as letters in alphabetic transcription. It is possible that the discussion in early modern Europe about spelling reform (cf. 1.15), and the attempts to match graphy with pronunciation, made thinkers more conscious of the comparative autonomy of the phonological system from the lexico-semantic system of the language. Linguistics, as we now know it, was launched by the new interest in the perplexing interplay between sound and meaning, just as the study of history got its impetus largely from the new-found perception that institutions, like language, change over time.

However patterns that were discerned in correspondences between languages did not necessarily have chronological consequences for earlier thinkers. Thus one might connect French [ʃɑ̃te], [ʃɑ̃], [ʃɛʁ], [ʃe], with Latin CANTARE, CAMPUS, CARUS, CASA, and know that Latin was spoken earlier than French, yet not recognize a linear time relationship between the two nor discern any obvious way to get from one to the other. The spellings *chanter*, *champ* certainly make the equation between French and Latin more obvious, but how do we account for [ʃɛʁ] spelt as *cher*, *chère*, and *chair* and [ʃe], as *chez*? Older spellings like *carn* for *chair* make clearer the relationship to Italian *carne*, for instance, which is close to Latin accusative CARNEM, but do not necessarily help in reconstructing change over time.

As I have already said, the methods of **comparative philology**, impressive as they are, do not in themselves cast light on linguistic change over time, except in so far as the material used in the comparison is chronologically flagged. Thus a comparison between modern French and Latin makes use of our knowledge that Latin is an older language; older French texts can yield information that fills gaps in our reconstruction of the progress from one to the other. Even more important, comparison of French with other Romance languages allow us to reconstruct an intermediate stage, which we take to approximate to a chronological language which we label **Proto-Romance** or **Vulgar Latin** (cf. 1.3). It is armed with this knowledge that we then seek to formulate rules which will explain the correspondences in terms of phonological change.

In doing so, we must also pay attention to what we know about phonetic variation and shift in general: we assume that some types of change are more **natural**, or at any rate more widespread, and so we are comfortable with evidence of such changes in the past. For instance, **assimilation**, where sounds acquire features of surrounding sounds, and simplification, by which more unusual or complex sounds resolve into more commonplace or simple ones, are changes that are found all over the place. It is usually assumed that there is a tension between the natural laziness and inattentiveness of speakers and hearer and the desire for effective communication, between the requirements of speed and of exactitude in linguistic interchange. It is therefore taken as given that, although phonetic slippage will occur all the time, the variation that results may not have dire results on the system as a whole. What the historical phonologist worries about is how the system is affected over time—how variation turns into change.

Today much of the thinking about historical linguistics is concerned with examining 'change in progress', to see, in circumstances about which we have a wealth of contemporary information, what changes are familiar or even potentially universal, and what constraints are placed on change. Most of this work is sociolinguistic in its orientation and is concerned more with the diffusion

of novelties through a community, rather than with the introduction
of novelties in the first place. In this framework, I repeat, it is
difficult to distinguish between **shift**—where a speaker replaces
features of his own system with those of another—and **change**—
where features of his own individual or socially shared language
system are transformed into others.

Another modern approach is, as we have seen, more concerned
with individual grammars and the restructuring that occurs
between generations. In phonological terms this presupposes that
certain directional phonetic slippages occur in the speech of one
generation and then are interpreted differently in the construction
of new speakers' grammars. Thus probably for early speakers of
French a [c] in the reflex of CANTARE was not systematically
distinguished from the [k] in the reflex of COR: they were merely
contextually determined allophones of a single /k/ unit. A new
learner, however, struggling to systematize what (s)he hears, might
well identify this [k] with the similar [k] in reflexes of QUI, leaving [c]
to form the nucleus of a new systematic unit. This story has its
attractions, but says nothing about how the [c] pronunciation came
to be so general and so salient as to feed into the new learner's
acquisition process.

To account for the slippage we must turn back to phonetics,
which, in its modern scientific guise, tells us that articulatory,
acoustic, and perceptive processes in speech are infinitely more
complex than the early linguists could have imagined. So much so,
that some phonologists choose largely to bypass phonetic reality
and to operate with a simplified (and sometimes rather abstract,
apparently arbitrary) set of phonological features, ranged at a more
fine-tuned, 'primitive' level than the sound segment.

Generative phonology has employed various formalisms, of which
multidimensional models now predominate. In these, which take
many forms, lexical elements are represented by a series of tiers,
with a **skeletal**, or perhaps a **moraic** (timing), one dominating old-
fashioned segments at a low level (placing something resembling
actual pronunciation at a **melodic** tier). For the historical phonologist many of the rules, or processes, in generativist description look
familiar: the borderline between synchronic and diachronic is hard
to draw. Indeed those with more abstract tastes view many
diachronic processes—like vowel **nasalization** (6.4)—as still alive
in the internal grammar of present-day French speakers. The more

concrete-minded **natural generativist phonologists** prefer to stick closer to what is actually spoken and heard ('on the surface'), and so assume more **lexicalization**—by which at a certain historical point lexical elements are rewritten to cater for the outcome of diachronic processes. They also make more appeal to **suppletion**—with lexically related, but phonetically dissimilar, items (e.g. *loi* / *légal*) represented in the speaker's grammar by different *ad hoc* underlying phonological representations, rather than derived by rule one from the other.

We should mention the current (1996) fad for phonological analyses in terms of **Optimality Theory**, which postulates a universal set of constraints hierarchically ranked differently in different languages. In a 'minimalist' way, the theory can account for many data without recourse to an elaborate system of rules and/or underlying features. A historian working in this framework would have to envisage a reranking of constraints over time: how and why this should happen has not been properly investigated. Jacobs 1996 economically restates in Optimality terms his earlier, already minimalist, **underspecification** account (Jacobs and Wetzels 1988) of the Latin to Old French **lenition** processes, by which intervocalic consonants 'weaken' (voice, spirantize, and sometimes disappear, cf. below), but confesses himself unable thereby to capture some of the insights that earlier treatments had glimpsed.

All theorists will distinguish low-level, usually **syntagmatic**, phonetic processes, like the assimilation or atonic vowel reduction found sporadically everywhere, from **paradigmatic** phonological processes. For structuralists phonologization entails a restructuring of the phonological system, with loss or creation, merger or split, of **phonemes**. One phonological accident, resulting perhaps from an external circumstance like language contact, can trigger off a wholesale **chain-shift** in the system—either a **push-chain** with a new phoneme entering the system shoving neighbouring phonemes along to collide with others which cannon off one another like billiard balls, or a **drag-chain**, where an empty slot in the system attracts into its space a nearby phoneme, so that the distance between phonemes is increased.

The classic example of a chain-shift is the Germanic consonant shift known as **Grimm's Law**: the introduction of French [y], from Latin ū, (cf. 6.7) can also be described in these terms. An apparently straightforward example involves the Western Romance simplification of Latin intervocalic obstruents with consequent voicing of simple voiceless obstruents (here illustrated with Spanish examples):

(1)   CUPPA > *copa*; RIPA > *riba*;
      GUTTA > *gota*; VITA > *vida*;
      VACCA > *vaca*; AMICA > *amiga*.

In French, the first series remained voiceless (*coupe, goutte, vache*) but the second subsequently opened further and the dental and velar series fell altogether (*rive, vie,* < [viðə], *amie* < [amijə]): this process is sometimes called **lenition** (cf. below), like a similar process in Celtic languages. Thus eventually the original intervocalic consonants of VITA and AMICA became synchronically irrecoverable, though the Latinisms *vital* and *amical* help to keep their memory alive.

The thinking that lies behind the chain-shift idea is that phonemes must be kept phonetically distinct if they are to serve their function of distinguishing between meaning elements. Phonemic merger is potentially pathological, but it is tolerated more readily if the distinction between two phonemes carries little **functional load**: e.g. in modern French **vowel length** (6.12) distinguishes comparatively few items and so can be neglected without too great loss.

Here the **Principle of Least Effort** comes into play: it is assumed that speakers will tend to reduce unnecessary distinctions. They will also tend to eliminate redundancy, so that, e.g. in Latin, where vowel length distinctions were probably doubled up by vowel quality distinctions, the former (regarded as more vulnerable) could be dropped.

The idea that some sound segments, and some contexts, are more vulnerable to change ('weaker') than others is one shared by most historical phonologists, though the definition of phonological or phonetic strength is contentious. For instance the term **lenition** used for early French **voicing** and **spirantization**, with often eventual loss, of Latin voiceless obstruents, implies a strength hierarchy :
voiceless > voiced; plosive > fricative.

However it could be argued that the devoicing of the same voiced obstruents that had become word-final in Old French was a step towards eventual loss:

(2)   CAPUT > *chef* > [ʃe], restored to [ʃɛf]; CLAVE > *clef* > *clé*.

The devoicing may have been not so much a strengthening, as a sort of assimilation to the following silence, and hence, in a sense, a weakening.

In French the historical outcomes suggest that word-initial consonants and the high front vowel /i/ were particularly resistant to change, whereas coda consonants and mid-vowels succumbed readily. It has been maintained that phonological change in French has been determined by changes in articulatory setting or in accentuation patterns. So apparently independent but concomitant changes can be seen as threads interwoven in the same tapestry.

But whatever the theory adopted, few would deny the evidence of regularity of sound-change: a sound in the same phonological environment changes in the same way at the same time in the same place. Whatever its shortcomings, the **regularist** hypothesis was fantastically successful, enabling us to put into order otherwise recalcitrant philological material, to establish, on a principled basis, etymologies, and to predict forms that may be later attested. The **Neogrammarians** elevated the perceived regularity to the status of **sound-laws**, programmatically declaiming that these were without exception. By this they meant regular sound-change was to be taken for granted, and that apparent exceptions should be relegated elsewhere, as due to **analogy**, **borrowing**, **sporadic sound-substitution**, and the like. How to explain sound-laws themselves though was far from easy. They were regarded as 'mechanical' and 'blind'—i.e. conditioned solely by phonological factors and impervious to semantic or grammatical influence as well as imperceptible to language users. They were also seen as 'gradual'—presumably in that the change proceeded in tiny jerks with minimal articulatory difference between each stage. The end result would however be a perceptible shift which affected one linguistic community at one time, and which then ceased to operate.

But how did the sound-laws become virtually exceptionless? The Prussian thinkers who formulated the laws probably had in mind tightly-knit, disciplined linguistic communities where pressures to conform to a social norm were strong. Other contemporary linguists, in France, Italy, Switzerland, and Austria for instance, were more conscious of exceptions and of communicative creativity, of individual idiosyncrasies and the vagaries of fashion, and so they were sceptical of the Neogrammarian doctrine.

This was especially true of those investigators who worked with living languages, especially with non-standards, and so came face to face with variation within the linguistic community. The Neogrammarian doctrine was more appropriate for written texts, where wrinkles have been smoothed out, and for past periods with comparatively little documentation. Most important, I maintain, is that each sound-law applied to a finite time period and to a story that had ended, with the sound-change having run its term when it had affected all the material that could feed into it. If we intervene before the end of the story the sound-change may look more haphazard in its operation, affecting some items before others, and attacking first the more vulnerable victims.

If one closely examines, in the history of a language, so-called **sporadic** change, the contrast with regular change may not be not so stark as the regularist hypothesis would have it. Some changes may be sporadic only in the sense that they have not swept the board like 'regular' changes— perhaps because they have been blocked during their operation by other factors. Such factors may be connected with social prestige, with communicational efficiency or with grammatical transparency.

Currently fashionable is a compromise between the Neogrammarian hypothesis—according to which regular sound-change occurs mechanically, instantaneously, and without exception—and the **lexical diffusion** hypothesis (cf. 3.13)—which suggests that sound-changes begin tentatively in only a few susceptible lexical items, then gather momentum to affect the majority of items, before petering out, leaving a few residual items. Some changes are of the first sort, we are told, and some of the second: this view looks more like a fudge than a compromise. What seems to be true of the history of French is that in the early period, when our information is scant and partial, all sorts of radical and regular phonological transformations were effected, whereas in more modern times, when we have a plethora of evidence, everything looks more messy, and even static, with stable variation persisting over centuries, and no clear picture of regular phonological change.

Does the difference perhaps reside less in the facts than in our perception of the facts? Has phonological change in French really slowed down, with standardization and literacy, or do we have a distorted view of earlier developments? In describing the history of French we are inclined to look to the past to find direct antecedents of the present state, and to bypass data that do not fit into our view of the linear development of the language. We rely, of course, almost wholly on the patchy evidence of written records, without a reliable measure of how they relate to the spoken language. Most of all we find it difficult to reconstruct the precise social role of the spoken vernacular at periods in which Latin remained the prestige language.

Let us look more closely at some aspects of French phonological history, both ancient and more recent. We shall concentrate not only on aspects that are interesting for their own sake, but also on those that provide a background to problems in synchronic French linguistics, or that may cast a light on the methodology of historical linguistics.

6.2. CHRONOLOGY

The assumption that regular sound-changes have a starting and finishing point in time, and are limited in their spatial coverage, allows some apparent exceptions to be classified as borrowings that have been imported from an area not subject to the regular sound-change, at a time after the sound-change had ceased to operate. This is an important feature of the Neogrammarian model. Another salient methodological feature of the assumption of the time-limited operation of a sound-change is that it permits the ordering of phonological rules, in a way that can be linked chronometrically to real-time events. However, as I have pointed out, the establishment of a correlation with real time depends on the chronologically marked evidence and is not part of the method.

However, the method does allow us to state that the outcome of Rule A **feeds** into successive Rules B or C, by effecting changes to items so that they then fulfil the conditions of B or C, and that, on the other hand, Rule A can **bleed** Rules B or C, by changing the items of their potential input in such a way that they no longer fulfil the conditions for B or C. Examples of this sort will be discussed in following sections. Here I shall present a simple illustration of the way in which chronological sequence is established in classical methodology.

The French word *coupe* [kup] is clearly derived from the Latin word CŬPPA, which is assumed, on the basis of the graphy and metrical evidence, to have had a short ŭ and a geminate PP: in French we have a [u] and a simple [p]. We know that Latin geminate obstruents were simplified in 'Western Romance' (Rule A): this leads us to postulate a real-time chronology by which the simplification occurred after the alleged split between Eastern and Western Romance (though what the date of this could be is uncertain within a few hundred years). We must assume, however, that the simplification must have occurred after another change had ceased to operate: this was the 'Western Romance' voicing (**lenition**) of voiceless obstruents (Rule B), which would turn [p] into [b] (and eventually, in French, into [v]). Thus *coupe* tells us that Rule A did not **feed** into Rule B, and must be ordered after it: this is assuming, on the basis of other evidence, that the [p] was still intervocalic (in [kupe]?) while Rule B was still in operation. Here the output of Rule A appears to have undergone no further change for at least a thousand years.

The vowel [u] in *coupe* also tells us something about chronology. A short Latin ŭ is assumed to have become [o] in 'Italo-Western Romance' (that is before the splitting away of central and southern Italian from 'Western Romance', covering Gaul and Iberia). In French only, this [o], when stressed, became eventually [œ] in **free syllables** (ending in a vowel) and [u] in **blocked syllables** (ending in a consonant): these changes (Rules C and D) must have taken place after French split off from the other Western languages. This seems to establish Rules C and D as subsequent to Rule A. However if Rule A had already operated it would have fed our item into Rule C ([ko-pe]) and bled Rule D (which would require [kop-pe], or [kop]): the modern French outcome would have been [kœp], not [kup]. Clearly Rule D has operated, so we must assume that there was still a geminate at the time of its operation, or, less plausibly, that the former intervocalic [p] had already become word-final at the time of the operation of Rule D.

This leaves us in a dilemma: the comparative 'evidence' suggests that the simplification of geminates (Rule A) was an innovation shared by Western Romance languages, but the French evidence tells us that it must have occurred in French independently of the same change in, for instance, Spanish. One way out of the dilemma is to place more confidence in the rigorous methodology that establishes internal ordering, than in the postulation of the real-life existence of unified **proto-languages** like Western Romance. Another is to assume a number of intermediate rules, for which we may have no concrete evidence: for instance, there may have been a Western Romance vowel-lengthening in stressed free syllables (Rule E) which operated after Rule A, but which affected only [ɛ] and [ɔ] in most of the languages (Rule E(i)), but later generalized, in French only, to [o] and [e] (Rule E(ii)). This lengthening could be said to give rise to **diphthongization**, which will be discussed below (6.8).

Working out the relative ordering of phonological rules can look like little more than an amusing intellectual game, but it is a cornerstone of historical linguistic methodology, placing strict constraints on speculation about how a language has changed. As we shall see in our discussion of **nasalization**, the ordering can also be divorced from real-time considerations, and seen as part of the synchronic grammar of native speakers.

6.3. Is There a Phonetic Basis for Changes in the History of French?

Various conflicting hypotheses have been advanced concerning changes in the mode of articulation and accentuation through the history of French, some of which assume successive stages of lax and tense articulation and others which trace changes back principally to shifts in prosodic characteristics.

It is certain that modern French has different accentual patterns from the other Romance languages, which we assume it resembled in earlier times. French words are regularly accented on the final syllable (**oxytonic** accentuation)—if we leave out of account the written '**feminine** *e*'—whereas in most other Romance languages word accent is distinctive (though **paroxytonic** accent, on the penultimate syllable, is the most usual). In this respect **Proto-Romance** is thought to differ from Latin, in which the accent was predictable and linked to **syllable weight** and **vowel length**. With the apparent loss of Classical Latin vowel-length distinctions, perhaps during the Late Latin period, accent-placement was no longer predictable and could distinguish some lexical forms from others. However already in Old French, where atonic vowels were weakened and lost, stress-placement may have ceased to be distinctive (however, on this, cf. discussion of 'feminine *e*', 6.10).

In French, moreover, words are not individually accented within a rhythmic group (sometimes called a breath group). Thus the accent usually falls only on the last syllable of a group of words. These groups are usually, though not always, syntactically delimited: in most discourse they will consist of three or four syllables, but can in rapid speech be longer. Emphasis on individual words in the rhythmic group can be secured by a special *accent d'insistance* which falls on a non-final syllable: e.g. *ímpossible* or *impóssible*, compared with more normal *impossíble*. This type of accent seems to be of a different phonetic character from the normal accent: in some cases it is more like a stress accent, with increase of intensity and raising of pitch, whereas the modern French oxytonic accent seems to consist more in lengthening of the syllable and not in variation of pitch or intensity.

French rhythmic group accentuation is associated with other salient features of modern French (so-called **linking** or **sandhi** processes like *liaison* and *enchaînement* and **elision** especially of *e instable* (or **mute** *e*)). These processes reflect the word-final vowel and consonant **truncation**, which is amply attested for the early modern period. It is therefore usually assumed that, by the sixteenth century, there had been a change in French accentuation from a more familiar word-stress patterning to a rather unusual rhythmic group accentuation. But how and when the change came about is disputed. The first direct evidence of the modern French pronunciation comes from John Palsgrave's description in 1530: '. . . and that is one great cause why theyr tong semeth to us so brefe and sodayn and so harde to be understãded whan it is spoken especially of theyr paysantes or cõmen people . . . sounde them all under one voyce and tenour and never rest nor pause upon any of them except the cõmyng next unto a poynt be the cause thereof.'

Other phonetic features attributed to standard French (though not found in all modern varieties) include the tense pronunciation that inhibits coarticulation of neighbouring sounds, and hence assimilatory processes. Diphthongization of tonic (accented) vowels and slurring of atonic (unaccented) vowels are likewise disfavoured. The description 'syllable-timed' is used to distinguish French from 'stress-timed' languages like English; it implies isochrony of each syllable within the rhythmic group. However 'syllable-timing' has been shown to be a misnomer, perhaps derived from the syllable-counting metrics of French verse (see below). What is certainly true is that standard French enunciation is more 'level' than that of stress languages: the comparison has been made with a machine-gun. Grimarest in 1712 put it like this: '*A la cour on n'a point d'accent dans la prononciation, notre langue n'étant agréable*

*qu'autant qu'elle n'a point d'inflexion . . . Il faut donc prononcer
toutes nos silabes sur un même ton, si l'on veut parler agréablement.'*

French sounds thus retain their individual identity in all positions
within the word. Fronted articulation predominates and obstruents
are pronounced without aspiration. There is also a preference for
free syllables—in that consonants appear more often in the syllabic
onset than in the **coda**, and an avoidance of consonant clusters (but
modern loss of *e instable* seems to reverse this trend). All these
features contribute to the distinctive bell-like phonetic quality of the
modern standard.

We find it hard to accept that French was always pronounced in
this way. Among the features that early distinguished older varieties
of French from other Romance languages were the more extensive
assimilatory processes—like **palatalization** and **nasalization**—and
the marked **diphthongization** of tonic vowels and reduction and
loss of atonic vowels. These developments seem consistent with less
tense articulation and with marked stress accent. True, it is thought
that French may always have tended to front articulation—the
apparently early fronting of [u] to [y], and of [ɑ] to [a] seems to
testify to this, as does, paradoxically, the later attested back
pronunciation of *r* as [ʀ] or [ʁ] (cf. 6.13).

But most pointers indicate a more uneven accentuation, probably
a stress accent, in the earlier stages of the language, totally at odds
with what we know about the modern language. Particularly
significant in this respect was the well-attested Old French distinction between tonic and atonic pronouns and the tendency of the
latter to attach themselves (**cliticize**) to the end (as **enclitics**), or to
the beginning (as **proclitics**), of tonic head-words. Similarly, verb
morphology shows incontrovertible evidence of **apophony**, with
considerable phonetic differences between tonic and atonic forms
in the same paradigm. Moreover the **devoicing** of word-final
consonants seems to indicate that in Old French the word (or,
perhaps, the **nexus** which would include a lexical head-word and its
clitics) rather than the longer rhythmic group (or **cursus**) was the
domain of accentuation.

One effect of the change in the domain of accentuation was that
new strategies for *mise en relief* (**topicalization** or **focalization)** were
introduced in the early modern period when emphasis on one
element of the rhythmic group was no longer easily assured by
stress marking.

So if Old French was phonetically so radically different from the modern language, when and how did the change occur, and what were the wider consequences of the phonetic differences?

Phonological changes that have to be considered in this equation are particularly those associated with assimilatory and stress changes. Here conventional wisdom has it that early Old French had Germanic-like phonetic features, with marked word-stress that differentiated strongly between tonic and atonic syllables, which favoured coarticulation and spread of phonetic features between juxtaposed segments.

What seems to be particularly salient in Old French is the comparative robustness of syllable-initial (**onset**) consonants, whereas those in syllable-final (**coda**) position fade, open, assimilate, and sometimes disappear: thus by the early modern period the only syllable-final consonant that survived was *r*, and that was very much under threat. There came to be a predominance of free syllables. Word-final (or prepausal?) consonants persisted longer but eventually were to succumb (but could be consciously preserved or restored in spelling pronunciation, and could sometimes resurface in *liaison*).

Apocope and weakening of word-final atonic vowels can be seen as part of the same process. A hypothetical parallel can be drawn with tonic vowels that start off vigorously but tail off as falling diphthongs. This postulated Old French *mode décroissant*, collapsing into general laxity, gave way, we are told, to the modern *mode croissant* with an increase of tension through the syllable, and 'trailer-timing' accent on the end of the rhythmic domain. The attrition of atonic word-final elements, which often continued inherited inflections, is thought to have had radical consequences in French morphosyntax: **case** markers disappear, **gender** and **person** markers weaken, **tense** and **aspect** markers are threatened. Hence the tendency of modern French to supplement morphological deficiencies by syntactic devices, or even to **grammaticalize** prefixed elements, where inherited suffixed elements no longer serve their purpose.

We may endlessly speculate about the articulatory mode of Old French, but is there any hard evidence? One source is conceivably the metrics of versification. Here unfortunately the evidence is ambiguous. Old French, like other Romance languages, seems to have used syllable counting, rather than stress measures, in versification. How far Latin models were paramount is difficult to say: the disappearance in Romance of the syllable weight distinctions that were all-important in Latin verse, and the apparent substitution of stress accent in later Latin for classical pitch accent, must have changed the face of versification. But in this sort of cultural domain, tradition reigns supreme.

Some maintain (e.g. Marchello-Nizia 1995) that Old French verse was measured by stress and not primarily by syllables.

What was the precise role of the word-accent in Old French verse, and indeed in later French verse, is disputed. However it is usually maintained that reliance first on assonance, and later on rhyme, was required in early French verse because of its lack of the firm rhythmic patterns associated with stress.

If the early French language verse texts were composed in a language without significant stress rhythms, how it is that the phonological features of Old French match up with those we associate with stress patterning? One solution to this dilemma is to maintain that the relevant phonological changes had occurred prehistorically (probably before the tenth century), and that by the time of the relevant texts (eleventh to twelfth centuries), French had already lost word-stress. Apparent evidence to the contrary must then be explained in other ways. We can, for instance, suggest that changes already under way in the spoken language were slow to surface in texts, which reflect an inherited oral tradition. In the case, for instance, of evidence for devoicing of word-final consonants, we may assume graphical generalization of prepausal variants, even though, internal to the rhythmic group, voiced variants were pronounced.

The significant differences that we can discern, in the 'transition' period (thirteenth to fifteenth centuries) between Old French and Modern French, cannot in this scenario be directly ascribed to changes in articulatory modes or accentuation. But then we would have difficulty in accounting for such changes anyway: there are, for instance, no obvious language contact influences that could have had significant effect on the pronunciation of French.

One way out might be to postulate that during the Old French period different varieties coexisted, some with word-stress (**nexus**) and some with rhythmic-group (**cursus**) accentuation. We could go so far as to suggest that the word-stress type could have been

associated with the (**superstratum**) Frankish element in the population, whereas rhythmic-group accentuation could be linked to
(**substratum**) Celtic influence.

The well-known **sandhi** alternations in modern Celtic lends some plausi-
bility to the latter hypothesis, but a major snag is that in British Celtic
word-initial consonants are mutated, whereas in early French it was word-
final elements that were vulnerable.

The 'transition' in this scenario would not be a change of one
mode to the other, but a shift in prestige from the word-stress mode
to the cursus-accent mode, with the latter triumphing as the
standard state language, in the sixteenth and seventeenth centuries.
This is a hypothesis to which we shall return in the examination of
individual sound-changes. There is certainly evidence in the early
modern period of considerable variation and disagreement about
the relative prestige of variants, but we cannot always make the link
between these and an over-arching phonetic or prosodic mode.

We should note a variant on the 'phonetic mode' hypothesis that is
associated especially with the late Strasburg phonetician Georges Straka,
whose own experiences in a Nazi concentration camp led him to postulate
that certain types of 'weakening' sound-change are found among harassed,
frightened, weary, and underfed populations. For him the prehistoric
phonetic changes in French were of this type, while later Old French
changes indicated a 'stronger', more vigorous set of articulatory habits.
This hypothesis does not very satisfactorily account for the changes which
we postulate for the Middle French period, though admittedly the fourteenth and fifteenth centuries, with plagues, famines, and the Hundred
Years War, resulting in dramatic demographic decline, constituted a trying
time for the French.

6.4. Nasal Vowels

At first sight, the historical development of nasal vowels in French
is easy to explain in terms of a universal assimilatory process: the
nasality of any syllable-final (**coda**) nasal consonant has spread to
the preceding nuclear vowel. With the loss of consonantal occlusion,
we are left with a long (**two-mora**) nasal vowel. This can be shown
diagrammatically (Fig. 6.1).

In modern standard usage it is only the nasal vowel in a stressed blocked
syllable that is always long: *pain* [pɛ̃] / *peinte* [pɛ̃:t]. But even in free syllables

Syllable (σ)

O(nset)   R(hyme)

N(ucleus)   C(oda) [+nasal]

b   ɔ̃ - - - - - - - - - - - (n)

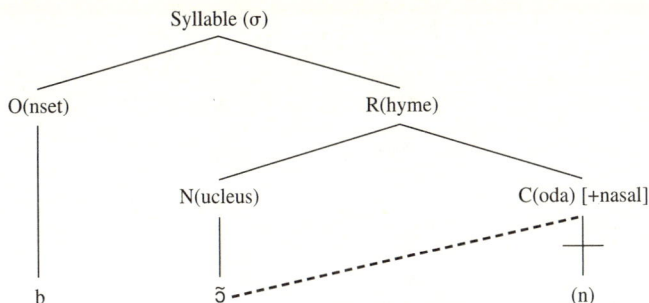

Fig 6.1. (Nasalization)

nasal vowels measure as longer than their oral counterparts, and some phoneticians maintain that French nasals have diphthongal features, even when short: indeed in older graphy, especially before a labial, the nasal vowel was sometimes represented as a diphthong:

(3)   *houme* for *homme*, *chaumbre* for *chambre*.

In some varieties today nasal vowels are discernibly diphthongized. In southern French, where some nasal occlusion tends to be kept, vowel nasality may be confined to the second mora:

(4)   Aix-en-Provence [pɛɛ̃ŋ] *pain*, [paãntø] *pente*.

The standard orthoepic convention is broadly that a graphical nasal consonant is pronounced when it stands between two graphical vowels (VN, as in *bonne*, *humain*, *événement*, *finesse*) whereas when the same consonant stands before another consonant or at the end of a word it is not pronounced as a separate segment, but the preceding vowel is a nasal (ṽ, as in *bonté*, *bon*, *humble*, *un*, *éventuel*, *vent*, *intégral*, *fin*).

Exceptions involve the negative prefix *in-*: *innettoyable* [ɛ̃]: or mainly loanwords: *abdomen*, *weekend* [ɛn]. It was almost certainly the Erasmian reform of spoken Latin that introduced this latter spelling pronunciation into French. Controversy raged throughout the seventeenth century about, for instance, whether *examen* should be pronounced with [ɛn] or [ɛ̃]: in this instance the popular pronunciation prevailed, but this was not always so.

There are further complications. First of all in the standard a graphical *e* in some of the relevant forms is usually not pronounced (*bonne* [bɔn], *événement* [evɛnmã]) so that in terms of the spoken

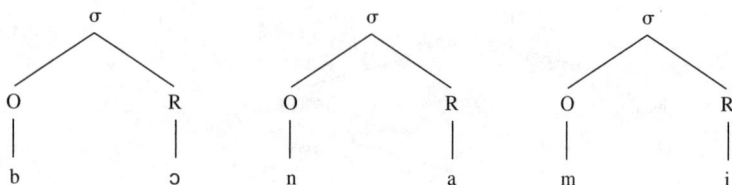

Fig 6.2. (Nasalization)

language the contextual distinction, by which the oral vowel is found in a free syllable and the nasal vowel in a blocked, does not operate. Secondly the normally silent word-final graphical nasal consonant can be articulated in *liaison* contexts—so that at the end of the nasal vowel there is hardening to form a consonantal segment, which is then assumed to act as an onset to the following syllable. Fig. 6.2 illustrates.

In some cases, as the orthoepic convention predicts, the preceding vowel is denasalized, as it is now in a free syllable (usually *bon ami* [ɔ], but, for some speakers, [ɔ̃] is possible). However in some words, it regularly remains nasal (*mon ami* [ɔ̃], *en été* [ɑ̃]). The retention of nasal vowel quality before a *liaison* consonant was regarded as pernickety and purist by some seventeenth-century commentators and variation persists to this day in some cases. But it suggests that for some lexical forms, like *mon* or *en*, most modern standard speakers' underlying representation contains nasal vowels. Thus we must assume that, at least in some cases, nasal vowels are **phonologized**—forming part of the underlying phonological system, rather than being introduced in pronunciation via a phonological rule in the grammar.

Yet there is a well-established (though perhaps not productive) morphological relationship between nasal vowels (ṽ) and oral vowel + nasal consonant (vN) sequences (*bon* / *bonne*, *paysan* / *paysanne*, *flamme* / *flamber*, *vient* / *viennent*), suggesting that they are in some sense alternative realizations of the same underlying form (cf. Table 6.1 for **morphologization**). Yet again, for some vowels the nasal version in these pairs is lower than its oral counterpart (*fin* [ɛ̃] / *fine* [i], *brun* [œ̃] / *brune* [y], *joint* [wɛ̃] / *joignons* [wa]) (cf. Table 6.1 for nasal **laxing** and **lowering**). One consequence is a mismatch between the graphical representation and the pronunciation of nasal vowels in the standard. *Cent* has a nasalized *a* [ɑ̃], rather than *e*, and *cinq* has a nasalized *e* [ɛ̃], rather than *i*. The graphical diphthong *ie* was also threatened with similar lowering but usually retains the [ɛ̃] element: chien [ʃjɛ̃] (but cf. *fiente* [fjɑ̃t]).

Nevertheless, in modern French, nasal vowels contrast with their oral counterparts. Minimal pairs like *bon* / *beau*, *monte* / *motte*, *pente* / *pâte*, *sainte* / *cette* and even *emmener* / *amener* are frequent, confirming for many theorists the separate phonological identity of nasal vowels.

Analyses of nasal vowels in the modern language roughly fall into two camps: more abstract and more concrete. The former envisage the underlying forms in the speakers' grammars as having vn sequences that are subject to nasalization (and consequent lowering) rules. Fig. 6.3 illustrates.

Exceptions to denasalization are explained away in terms of diacritic lexical marking or differences in structural configuration (cf. Tranel 1990). In generative phonological accounts (cf. Schane 1968) the ṽ / vn difference is handled in terms of ordering of rules (cf. 6.2). Fig. 6.4 illustrates. Thus the vn sequence underlyingly is always followed by a vowel and therefore does not feed into Rule 1, where the conditioning environment specifies a following consonant or pause. Rule 2 deletes the nasal consonant when it follows a nasal vowel, and Rule 3 then deletes the word-final vowel [ə] that had blocked operation of Rule 1 in the relevant forms. Cf. Table 6.1 for an account, in a similar notation, of the historical processes, which does not assume retention of word-final [ə].

The 'concrete camp' assumes that nasal vowels are underlyingly present in the speakers' lexicon in contrast to oral vowels. Alternation of the *bon* / *bonne* sort would be a morphological, not a phonological, phenomenon, while the *bon ami* type is one aspect of *liaison*, which involves, in some sense, the **epenthesis** of a consonant within certain vowel + vowel sequences.

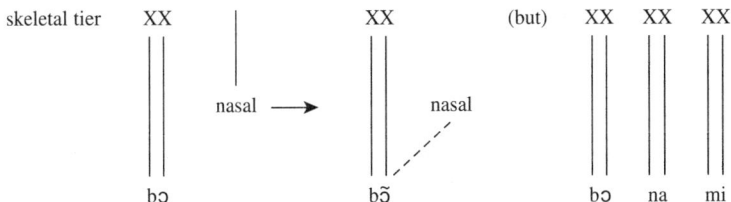

Fig 6.3. (Nasalization)

1. V / __ N $\left.\begin{array}{c} \# \\ \\ \\ C \end{array}\right\}$ ⟶ ṽ   /bon/ > /bõn/

2. N / __ $\left.\begin{array}{c} \# \\ \\ \\ C \end{array}\right\}$ ⟶ ∅   /bõn/ > /bõ/   *bon*

3. V / __   #   ⟶ ∅   /bone/ > /bon/ *bonne*

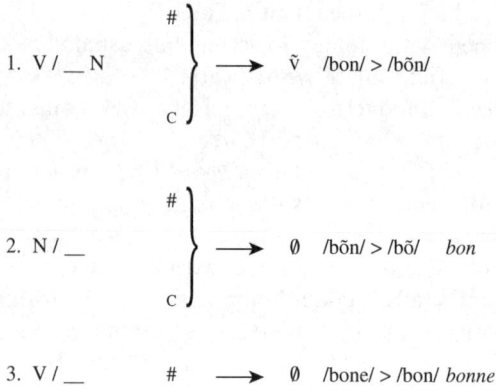

Fig 6.4. (Nasalization)

It has also been suggested that where there is prevocalic ṽ / vɴ alternation, as in *bon*, the forms are **suppletive**, not derived by phonological rule from a single underlying form. With ṽ the *liaison* [n] resyllabifies with the following vowel, whereas with the vɴ sequence the [n] forms the coda of the preceding syllable and inhibits nasalization.

The history of the French nasal vowels has been hotly debated. This is partly because French presents a well-documented example of a fairly rare categorical **phonologization** (either via phonological rules in the grammar or via **lexicalization**) of a low-level phonetic assimilatory process. Spreading of nasal quality from consonants to adjacent vowels is common in many languages, but it often goes unperceived by speakers and hearers. In some modern Canadian French varieties, for instance, contextual nasalization of vɴ is frequent, even though phonological nasal vowels are perceived as less nasal than in the standard. In Haitian creole, where contextual nasalization is also found, ṽ contrasts with ṽɴ, which in turn contrasts with vɴ:

(5)   [pɛ̃] *pain* / [pɛ̃n] *peine*, [ʃam] *charme* / [ʃãm] *chambre*,

so nasal vowels must be considered as lexicalized. It is reported too that in some French varieties, including popular Parisian, there is a contextual progressive spread of nasality from the nuclear vowel to a voiced coda consonant (as in [grɑ̃d] *grande* to [grɑ̃n]), which potentially could result in lexicalized contrasts like [sɔ̃n] *sonde* / [sɔn] *sonne*.

Within Romance, phonological nasalization is unusual—recognized mainly in French and Portuguese—though phonetic nasalization is widespread. The Portuguese nasalization appears to differ both in dating and conditioning from the French: North Italian and Galician dialects appear to have in the past undergone some of the same changes as French and Portuguese respectively, but with subsequent denasalization and sometimes nasal consonant hardening that obscure the processes.

In French nasalization was clearly regressive—that is nasality spread backwards from consonant to vowel (although there is some indication of progressive nasalization in sporadic early graphies like *amin* ?[amĩ]) for *ami*). Modern data suggest that spread of nasality occurred preferentially within the syllable, from the coda nasal to the preceding nasal nuclear vowel and involved attrition or opening of the consonant. Thus the phonologization of nasalization is usually thought to have dated from the same period as the loss in French of syllable-final consonants (cf. Table 6.1). Internal to the word, such loss began early in the history of French and opened the way for **compensatory lengthening**, but at the end of the word **truncation** reached its peak probably in the sixteenth or early seventeenth century. The lowering of the nasal vowels [i], [y] to [ɛ̃], [œ̃] (cf. Table 6.1) and perhaps the reduction of nasal diphthongs [ãĩ], [ẽĩ] (as in *pain*, *éteint*), is thought to have occurred after phonologization, when there was no direct phonological link between ṽ and vN. A reduced subsystem of nasal vowels was thus established, without direct phonetic relationship to oral counterparts: this subsystem has tended to be reduced even further with the course of time so that [œ̃] and [ɛ̃] are today distinguished by comparatively few speakers, and [ɛ̃] tends to be further lowered to [ã] in some varieties, while some speakers even tend to confuse [ã] and [ɔ̃]. Some phoneticians argue that, in the standard, nasalized *a* is any case better transcribed as [ɔ̃], to be distinguished from nasalized *o* which is higher and more rounded ([õ]). Thus there are bound to be problems of perception of the nasal vowels, in interchange between speakers of different varieties.

Note that reduction has not operated in all varieties—especially in northern France and Canada—and that there is a tendency in some varieties to front [ã] to [ã] and to raise [ɛ̃] to [ẽ].

The lowering of nasal vowels in standard French has led some theorists to postulate that there is a universal tendency for nasality to sit better on low vowels. This theory seems to be supported by the apparent earlier nasalization context in French of the low vowel [a] and the tendency to merge [ɛ] with it in nasal environments. The evidence for this early nasalization comes from assonancing verse in which aN and eN sequences often seem to be kept separate from aC and eC sequences. However, it has recently been shown that this evidence is misleading, based on a misunderstanding of statistical probability, and is in any case partially contradicted by later rhyming verse conventions and metalinguistic evidence. Our lack of complete understanding of the conventions governing **assonance** in early verse (in which vowels but not surrounding consonants are matched at the end of a line) means that we cannot rely on this evidence.

Frequent graphical representation of etymological eN sequences as aN suggests that phonetic nasality in these sequences was possibly more salient than place of articulation, but other factors—like the confusion of present participle -*ent* and -*ant* endings as [ã(nt)], and the general tendency to contextual lowering of front vowels in some varieties—are also important. Thus the long-held doctrine of nasalization *par étapes*, with low vowels succumbing earlier than high vowels no longer gets support from the French philological evidence.

The evidence of thirteenth-century charters shows that the graphy *an* was usual, in *temps* [tã], in the north-east. The puzzling [fam] pronunciation of *femme* < FEMINA is usually adduced as evidence of lowering before denasalization: interestingly the charters spell this word as *fame* in the Parisian region and the west, rather less so in the south, but hardly at all in the north-east. This suggests that the lowering under nasalization was independent of the lowering in this word.

Doubt has also been cast on the argument from universals—that there is a **vowel height hierarchy** in nasalization favouring low nasal vowels. In fact it seems that high vowels nasalize more easily, even though nasal quality may be more perceptible in low vowels. The straightforward physiological account of nasality is that it primarily involves lowering of the velum, allowing passage of air though the nose. With vowels that require lower tongue-height, it seems obvious that mechanically the velum can be lower, though experimental evidence does not fully support the hypothesis that this happens universally in the process of vowel nasalization. Recent phonetic research suggests that nasal airflow and sound pressure levels may be more significant factors in the perception and production of nasal vowels: here it is high vowels that should theoretically be 'more nasal' than low vowels.

Be that as it may, standard French today, unlike Portuguese, has phonological nasal vowels only with lower tongue heights; there is however no reason to believe that high vowels [i] and [y] were not nasalized at an earlier period. Whether indeed phonetic nasalization affected some vowels earlier than others is purely speculative— though the alleged data is entrenched in many textbooks. Neo-grammarian doctrine would favour the idea of a once-for-all wave of contextual nasalization: this is linked by some theorists to the putative heavy stress accent and *mode croissant* of early Old French, when there was general attrition of atonic vowels and coda consonants. When nasalization rules became part of the grammar of French speakers, and whether or when nasal vowels were lexicalized, remains a contentious question.

In tune with my own 'late-dating' predilections, I favour the view that contextual vowel nasalization may not have been categorical even in the sixteenth century. Contemporary commentators' description ('sounded in the nose' in Palsgrave's [1530] words, or *épaississement* in Lanoue's [1596]) leave us in no doubt about the existence of vowel nasality but suggests some degree of optionality. It is only by the end of the seventeenth century that we can be sure that **phonologization**, if not **lexicalization**, was completed: already Chifflet [1659] had suggested that there should really be special letters to represent nasal vowels (cf. Table 6.1). Dangeau's [1694] testimony is unambiguous: '*Ces cinq voyèles sourdes s'exprime en Fransois, avec des n, mais il est clair que l'n n'a nule part à leur prononciation, & que le son qui se fait dans ma bouche quand je prononce la prèmière silabe du mot nègoce, la seconde du mot miner, ou la dernière du mot badiner, ne se fait point du tout quand je prononce les mots danser, bien, ingrat, monde, aucun.*'

But what about those vn sequences that are today not nasalized, even though they may be now be (phonetically at least) syllable- or word-final (as in *bonne* [bɔn], *événement* [evɛnmɑ̃])? In the past, it seems, phonetic nasality did spread from a syllable-initial nasal to the preceding nuclear vowel, although in the modern standard this is not so: the graphical trick of doubling the nasal consonant in forms like *bonne* presumably indicates at least sporadic nasalization, and evidence from rhymes seems to bear this out. Descriptions in the sixteenth and seventeenth centuries often refer to the nasal quality of the vowel, though there is dispute about its status. Molière's joke in *Les Femmes Savantes* shows us that some (if only old-fashioned Bélise) pronounced *grammaire* like *grand'mère* (indeed much of the early discussion of this confusion concentrates on the pronunciation of *ai* / *è* as [e] or [ɛ], rather than on the undisputed similarity of the first syllable).

How are we to explain the apparent denasalization? One thing is certain: a vowel quality distinction in *bon* [ɔ̃] / *bonne* [ɔ] or *fin* [ɛ̃] / *fine* [i] must have arisen when the nasal consonant in the feminine form still formed the onset to a final syllable, providing a transparent context for denasalization in free syllables. The final *e* feminine marker is now *muet*—written but not pronounced—so that the relevant syllable is now blocked. But is the *e* still there in the consciousness of the speaker? If so, the 'change' has merely taken place in surface realization of an unchanging underlyng form: /bon/ and /bone/ used to be pronounced [bon] and [bonə] (or probably [bun] and [bunə]), but now come out as [bɔ̃] and [bɔn]—the sort of phonetic variation that is familiar in geographic and social space. But if *e caduc*, or *instable* is no longer part of the French phonological system—merely, rather, a surface lubricant inserted to facilitate surface realization of some underlying clusters—then the alternation between ṽ and vN must be seen as a morphological, not a phonological, phenomenon. There has, in other words, been a substantial change in the organization of the grammar. Much hangs on how we view the history of final vowel and consonant **truncation**.

A particular problem arises with lowering of the high nasal vowels: in order to account for the tongue-height difference of *fin* [ɛ̃] / *fine* [i] and *brun* [œ̃] / *brune* [y], it is usual to assume that the lowering must have taken place only after phonologization of the nasal vowel, with consequent reduction of the nasal vowel inventory.

If, however, the stressed vowels of *fine* and *brune* were still nasalized in the seventeenth century, why were they too not lowered? Here again we meet the contention that the high vowels were never fully nasalized, and in any case readily lost their nasal quality. A parallel is drawn with some inherited eN sequences which denasalized as aN: e.g. *femme* < FEMINA [fam], discussed above.

Here the lowering is assumed to have taken place before denasalization, whereas in *fine* and *brune* denasalization preceded lowering.

However the lowering in *femme* (often written *fame* in older texts cf. above), and other similar forms, can be linked to the frequent contextual lowering of *e* in some varieties.

For [ĩ], we have metalinguistic evidence of lowering in the prestige language by the end of the sixteenth century in words like *fin*, while lowering in e.g. *cousine* was stigmatized as vulgar (forms with [ɛn] in the feminine are still found in some regional varieties). However, it is to be noted that Dangeau [1694] states that the nasal vowels of *bien* and *ingrat* are not the same. Until the mid-seventeenth century evidence for lowering of [y] is even less convincing, especially as there was some confusion about the pronunciation of graphical *eu* as [y] and [œ] (cf. e.g. *(bon)heur* < AUGURIU with [œ], replacing earlier [əy]). In the late seventeenth century, though, we are told that there existed less prestigious pronunciations of e.g. *lune, volume, commune, une* with, apparently, [œ], where [y] is now standard.

Here we must assume social and regional variation with the standard adopting, somewhat sporadically, rather more conservative variants: the distinction between masculine and feminine adjectival forms may have been deliberately exaggerated when the feminine *e* was threatened ([fɛ̃] / [finə], rather than [fɛ̃] / [fɛn].

Another (more remote) possibility is that the final [ə] of the feminine forms provoked lengthening of the preceding syllable (as is found in some modern varieties) and that the tense oral quality of the vowel was thereby reinforced. Neither of these accounts would however explain the high oral vowel in forms like *finesse*: appeal then would have to be made to the analogy of the feminine adjectival form *fine*.

It is highly likely that phonologization affected only those long nasal vowels that resulted from the opening of coda nasal consonants, and not the (shorter?) sporadically nasalized vowels in free syllables. But why should these latter have lost their nasal quality in the modern standard?

Perhaps social pressures favoured spelling pronunciation and tense articulation in which contextual assimilation ('sloppiness') is avoided. The influence of reformed Latin pronunciation no doubt was bound up with this. But also we should note that by the sixteenth century there had developed vːnv sequences, resulting from the loss of coda consonants, or reduction of diphthongs or vowels in hiatus, that seem not to be contextually nasalized, like:

(6) [aːnə] *âne* < ASINU, [abiːmə] *abîme* < ABISMU, [ʃɛːnə] *chaîne* < CATENA; [pɔːmə] (or [paɔmə]) *paume* < PALMA, [ʒɛːnə] *gêne* < GEHENNA.

To these should be added loanwords from the classical languages like:

(7) *digne, âme, flamme,*

which appear not to have been nasalized, though commentators do describe nasal quality in *hymne* and *damne*. Opinion among grammarians was divided especially about the status of nasalization before a graphical double nasal. It seem that a long nasal vowel in this context and similar contexts was not clearly distinguished from the corresponding long oral vowel and that by the seventeenth century the non-nasalized vːnv sequence was well grounded in the language. This may have favoured the denasalization of all nasalized vowels in free syllables.

Later virtual loss of phonological **vowel length** and adjustment of vowel quality in blocked syllables (cf. 6.11) have further complicated the evidence since the seventeenth century. Nasal or non-nasal quality of a vowel preceding liaison [n] seems now to be determined in a way similar to that of blocked syllable adjustment in sequences like *sot avocat*:

(8) [sɔt]-[avoka] / [so]-[tavoka] / [bɔn]-[avoka] / [bɔ̃]-[navoka],

where the first adjectival form in each case is like the feminine form, and the second like the masculine prepausal form (cf. also 7.15).

It seems reasonable to postulate that, while contextual (assimilatory) nasalization dates from the earliest period of French, the phonologization of vowel nasality is a modern phenomenon, which goes hand in hand with other fairly modern developments, like word-final **truncation**, **diphthong levelling**, **compensatory lengthening** and **closed syllable adjustment**, and makes the modern phonological system look very different from that of the Old French period.

TABLE 6.1. History of vowel nasalization in French (summary)

---

1. All vs nasalized by following N (in Old French)?: regressive spreading of nasal feature from consonant to vowel.

   V / _ C [+ nasal]   → [+ nasal]
   e.g. [bõn] *bon* / [bõnə] *bonne*

   Evidence: *nn* graphy; nasal sequences separated from oral sequences in assonance; *en* rhymes with *an* (Chanson de Roland *present : Rollant* etc.); Palsgrave 1530 : '. . sounded . . . somethyng in the noose'.

2. Middle French (?) truncation: word boundaries obliterated. (Nasal consonants are deleted in coda position, as part of general process; word-final and pre-vocalic [ə] is deleted)

   C / _ C ⎫
           ⎬ → ∅   V / _ V ⎫
     #   ⎭   ⎬ → ∅
                             #   ⎭

   e.g. [bõnami] *bon ami*, [bõtɛ̃] *bon temps*, [bõté] *bonté*, [bõ] *bon*
   [bõnami] *bonne amie*, [bõnə tabl] *bonne table*, [bõn] *bonne*.

   Evidence: 16th c. grammarians. e.g. Peletier 1549: *Nous nę prononçons quasi point la lętrę n apres unę voyęle, quand ęlę ét acompagnee d'une tiercę lętrę.*

3. Restructuring in early modern French: introduction of phonemic difference between nasal and oral vowels (loss of phonological conditioning, following loss of coda nasal consonants)

   Evidence: Chiflet 1659: *Les sons de* an, en, in, on, un, *sans prononcer l'*n *seroient de vrayes voyelles si l'on eust inventé quelques lettres particulières pour les signifier.* L'abbé de Dangeau 1694: *Et ainsi voila cinq nouvèles voyèles qui s'écrivent en Fransois avec des n, & qui sont come une classe à part. Je les nomerai voyèles sourdes. . . . On pouroit aussi les nomer voyèles nazales, puisque le nés a quelque part à leur prononciation, & si vous voulés l'examiner soigneusement, vous vêrés que quand vous les prononcés il se fait quelque petit mouvemant dans votre nés.*

4. Denasalization (phonetic rule, probably 17th c.): when followed by a nasal consonant, nasal vowels lose their nasality.

   ṽ / _ N [+ nasal] → [− nasal]
   e.g. *impossible* / *inévitable* [ɛ̃posibl] / [inevitabl]

5. Morphologization: the difference between ṽ and VN acquires morphological status.

   ṽ   →   VN
   [+ masc] [+ fem]
   e.g. [bõ] → [bon] *bon* / *bonne*

TABLE 6.1. (*cont.*)

6. Laxing and lowering of nasal vowels (simplification of the nasal vowel series)

ĩ → ɛ̃	e.g. [fɛ̃] / [fin]	*fin(e)*
ỹ, ø̃, → œ̃	e.g. [brœ̃] / [bryn]	*brun(e)*
õ → ɔ̃	e.g. [nɔ̃]	*nom*
ẽ, ã → ɑ̃	e.g. [pʁɑ̃dʁ]	*prendre*,
	[gʁɑ̃]	*grand*

7. *Loi de position* (mid-vowels in blocked syllables are laxed or lowered cf. below)

v   /_ c#   → [−tense]
[−high]
[−low]

6.5. PALATALS

Palatalization is the process by which non-palatal sounds become palatal. The term is used for the change of Latin high back rounded ū to French high front rounded [y] (cf. 6.7), and for a range of assimilatory processes by which consonantal stricture moves from other places of articulation to the palate. The use of the term in History of French textbooks can be confusing as the end-result of such processes need not involve palatal articulation: for instance, in [fɛ] *fait* < FACTU the CT cluster may indeed have palatalized as a result of fusion of back and front segments, as in Spanish *hecho*, but the French evidence on its own suggests rather an opening of coda [k] to a fricative [χ] and then to a palatal [j] glide which then combined to form a falling diphthong [ai] which subsequently levelled to [ɛ].

Plausibly connected with Gaulish influence (cf. P.-Y. Lambert 1994) is the parallel palatalization of PT and PS:

(9)   CAPTIVUS > *chaitif* > *chétif*; CAPSA > *caisse*

The notion that somewhere along the line from [kt] to [jt] a palatalized cluster (with [c] or [ɟ]?) was pronounced is lent support by the apparent hopping, in French, of palatal glides over intervening consonants:

(10) [ɛr] *aire* [ajrə] < [arja] AREA; [mɛz͂ɔ] *maison* < MA(N)SIONE;
      [pɥi] *puits* < [pyjt̪] < [putju] PUTEU.

In cases like these we assume a stage with a palatalized *r*, *s* and *t*
with later **fission** to yield a palatal glide and a non-palatal consonant.

French loanwords into English provide evidence for a palatalization stage
(cf. Wilkinson 1980):

(11) *urchin* = *hérisson* < *ERICIONE; *sausage* = *saucisse* < SALSICIA, *vetch*
      = *vesce* < VĬCIA (cf. also *finish* = *finiss-*, *cash* = *caisse*).

Whatever the process the end-result in French in such cases is not
usually a palatal consonant:

(12) *fasse* < FACIAT, *force* < FORTIA, *poisson* < PĬSCIONE.

In the case of sequences of *labial consonant + jod* however a **palatal-alveolar**
(or **postalveolar**) consonant [ʃ] / [ʒ] is the regular outcome:

(13) *rage* < RABIE, *sache* < SAPIAT, *singe* < SIMIU.

    In all these examples the initial stage palatalization seems to
involve the **fusion** of a non-palatal consonant with a palatal glide.
In Latin the palatal **glide** or **approximant** (**jod**) was originally a
variant of short ĭ (later joined by short ĕ), which before another
vowel readily lost its syllabic status. Word-initially it must have
early merged with the [dj] and [gj] clusters (and with G before a
front vowel), to give in French a palato-alveolar affricate [dʒ] (>
[ʒ]):

(14) IAM > *ja*, DIURNU > *jour*; GEORGIU > *Georges*, GENTE > *gens*.

In post-consonantal position it palatalized the preceding consonant:
this is most obvious with [lj] and [nj] which remain as [ʎ] and [ɲ] in
most Romance languages:

(15) ALIU > *ail* (for reduction of [ʎ] to [j] in modern French cf. 6.6);
      VINEA > *vigne*.

Coda velar consonants preceding L and N may have opened to jod with the
same consequences:

(16) OC'LU > *oeil*; AGNELLU > *agneau*.

There is graphical evidence for merger between, and probable reduction of, [kj] and [tj] clusters in Late Latin, probably as [ʦ] and [ʣ].

The most interesting palatalization processes in Romance concern however the fronting of Latin back consonants C, G, preceding front vowels (E, I), a familiar type of phonetic assimilation, which is phonologized in all the Romance languages, except Sardinian. It is assumed that the phonetic assimilation must have been a feature of Late Latin.

In Western Romance (as distinct from Romanian) it did not affect the labio-velar QU, which by the time of palatalization could not have merged with C:

(17) QUI > [ki], QUAESTU > *quête* but CIVITATE > *cité* [site], ECCE-ISTA > *cette*.

Cinq [sɛ̃k] must be derived from a dissimilated CĪNQUE and not directly from QUĪNQUE.

Everywhere the outcome of this wave of palatalization is identical with that of *velar consonant + jod*. One assumes therefore that the front articulation of the vowel had the same effect on the preceding consonant as the palatal glide. In French, as in Spanish, the voiceless reflex assibilated to affricate [ʦ], often spelt as *z*. This must have involved a further fronting of the postulated [cj] sequence, and presumably a spreading of the continuant feature from the jod to the obstruent. The central French reflex eventually merged with sibilant [s] < Latin s (whereas some varieties of Spanish still distinguish dental fricative [θ] < [ʦ], from apical sibilant [s] < Latin s):

(18) CĒRA > *cire*, CENTU > *cent*, CINGULU > *cingle*, RADICĪNA > *racine*.

In northern dialects, however, as in Occitan and Italian, a palatal-aveolar affricate [ʧ] (or palatal plosive [c]) was the regular outcome of palatalization of velars before front vowels. It is perhaps worth noting here the (later) Canadian French assibilation of [t] and [d] to [ʦ] and [ʣ] before front vowels and similar processes in Romanian and Brazilian Portuguese.

Where central French palatalization differs most significantly from that of the other Romance languages is in a second wave of fronting of back consonants, this time before reflexes of Latin A.

For this to have happened as an assimilatory process, we must assume a front articulation of *a* as [a], characteristic of this region, (where ū also fronted to [y], but without in this case palatalizing back consonants).

It seems that this palatalization wave was later than the other: for one thing it affects Germanic and Arabic loan words with front vowels, which escaped the first wave.

The results of this fronting, except in the south-east of the region, were different from the earlier one: the Old French reflex of postpause or postconsonantal onset [k] was the **palatoalveolar affricate** [ʧ] (or originally **palatal plosive** [c]), spelt *ch*, in which there was spreading of **coronal** articulation to the preceding consonant:

(19) CANTARE > *chanter*, ARCA > *arche*, Germanic *skina* > *échine*, Arabic *meskin* > Old French *meschin*.

It is assumed that palatalization must have preceded levelling of the Latin AU diphthong, which has the same effect as A on the preceding velar:

(20) GAUDIA > *joie*, CAUSA > *chose*

(but cf. CAUDA > *queue*, where the popular Latin form CODA seems to have survived into Romance).

Phonetic spread of features from palatals to surrounding segments is found all over the place: in some French varieties today *qui*, *cul*, etc. are pronounced with [kʲ] or even [c], and pronunciation of the suffix *-tier* (in e.g. *charcutier*) as [ce] is well attested in the modern period. What is more difficult to explain is how and when the palatal reflexes came to be **phonologized** in the early history of French.

Here one can appeal to the idea of a **push-chain shift** originating in the simplification of Latin labiovelars [kʷ] and [gʷ], possibly already split in classical Latin into two segments [k]/[g] and [w]. In Sardinian, the velar part was lost. Elsewhere in Romance it was the labial element that tended to disappear, first elided before rounded back vowels, and then apparently dissimilated before high and mid-front vowels. With no longer any distinction between the Indo-European inherited velar and labiovelar series, the fronted allophones (?[kʲ] and [gʲ]) of the original /k/ and /g/ phonemes acquired phonological status, distinct from the newly constituted phonemes that grouped some erstwhile allophones of /kʷ/ and /gʷ/ and back allophones of /k/and /g/.

In the other Romance languages the labial element of the original labiovelars was preserved as a [w] glide before A, but in French this too was lost:

(21) *quand* [kɑ̃] / Italian *quando* [kwando].

This levelling is possibly connected with fronting of *a* in French.

Note too that word-initial Germanic [w] seems to have been identified with reflexes of Latin [gʷ] and levelled also to [g], though written *gu*:

(22) *wardon* > *guarder*, *wespa* > *guêpe*, *wisa* > *guise*.

Where Latin QU followed a tonic front vowel, the velar element opened to jod and combined as a diphthong with that vowel, leaving a [w] which merged with [v] from other sources:

(23) EQUA > *ive*, SEQUERE > *suivre*, cf. also Germanic *skiuhan* > Old
      French *eschever*.

This all meant that in central French there arose a phonological contrast between /k/ and the fronted [kʲ] before [a], which was fuelled over the centuries by an influx of loanwords, mainly from Latin and other Romance varieties, beginning in [ka]. The defective distribution of the new voiceless palatalized phoneme might well have discouraged restructuring of the system, but it was soon to be remedied. Redistribution was effected not only by the influx of loanwords which were subject to the second, but not the first, palatalization process, but also by the diphthongization or raising of A in tonic free syllables :

(24) *cher* < CARU, *cheval* < CABALLU,

and of **Bartsch's Law breaking** (in the environment of a palatal consonant) of the resultant *e* to *ie*:

(25) *chien* < CANE, *chie* < *[ʧieje] < CACAT,

as well as by the levelling of [au] from all sources:

(26) *chose* < CAUSA, *chaud* < CALDU.

Thus the voiceless palatalized consonant came to contrast fully in onset position with the voiceless velar. It could therefore take up a position in phonological space between velar /k/ and the assibilated /t͡s/. The (less frequent) voiced palatal (< Gᵃ) merged with the reflexes of Gᵉ,ⁱ:

(27) *jaune* < GALBINU.

The simplification of the medieval affricates:

(28) *chasser* [ʃ] / English *chase* [t͡ʃ], *engager* [ʒ] / English *engage* [d͡ʒ], *fils* [s] / English *Fitz* [ts],

happened in the later Old French period, probably by the late thirteenth century, and can be paralleled by the levelling of diphthongs at a similar period.

The merger of the dental affricates with inherited [s] / [z] is not easy to account for, though we can draw a parallel with the similar merger in modern Spanish varieties, where there has been simplification of the phonological inventory. Perhaps in French we can point to the defective distribution of the dental affricates, which only rarely occurred before back vowels:

(29) *façon* < FACTIONE, Old French *ço* < *ceo* < ECCE HOC (cf. modern *ça* < *cela*).

There was confusion, too, between the affricate [t͡s] and bisegmental [ts] sequences:

(30) 2 pl. verb ending *-ez* < -ATIS,

which were destined for simplification. The merger of /t͡s/ and /s/ led eventually to the creation of homonyms like:

(31) *sire* / *cire*, *saint* / *ceint*, *selle* / *celle*.

But morphological considerations, like the identification of word-final marker as [s], in those post-palatal contexts where it had become [t͡s]:

(32) *filz* < FILIUS, *travailz* < TREPALIOS, *plainz* < PLANGIS,

may have had an effect in the merger.

By the early modern French period palatoalveolar fricatives /ʃ/ and /ʒ/ were established alongside palatal continuants /ʎ/ and /ɲ/.

The phonological status of [j] is less certain as it rarely contrasts with syllabic [i]:

(33) *abbaye* [ei] / *abeille* [ɛj]).

TABLE 6.2. Palatalization of consonants in French (summary)

Jodization

Dj, Gj, $^{V}G^{+i,e}$ (> gj) > [j]   RADIU > *rai*, EXAGIU > *essai*, PAGENSE > *paien*

Hardening of jod

$^{#}$J, $^{#,C}G^{+i,e,a}$, (> j), Bj > [dʒ] > [ʒ]
JAM > *ja*, GENTEM > *gent*, GALBINU > *jaune*, TIBIA > *tige*

Lateral Palatal

Lj, K'L > [ʎ] > [j]   PALEA > *paille*, SOLIC'LU > *soleil*

Nasal Palatal

Nj, GN > [jn] > [ɲ]   MONTANEA > *montagne*, LIGNA > *ligne*

Trill and Sibilants

Rj, KR > [jr] > [r]   PARIA > *paire*, LACRIMA > *lairme* > *larme*

^{V}sj   > [jz] > [z]   RATIONE > *raison*
ssj   > [js] > [s]   MESSIONE > *moisson*

Voiceless Velar and Dental — assibilation

Kj, K$^{+i,e}$ (> [kj]),$^{#,C,#}$Tj, > [tsj] > [s]
FACIAT > *fasse*, CENTU > *cent*, FORTIA > *force*

Voiceless Velar and Labial — coronalization

K^{+a}, Pj > [tʃ] > [ʃ]   FURCA > *fourche*, CANTARE > *chanter*, SAPIAT > *sache*

Table 6.2 summarizes the main palatalizing processes in the history of French.

Assimilatory palatalization of consonants to following front vowels is found in non-standard French (e.g. [kʲi] *qui*, [kʲy] *cul*). In Canada dental plosives undergo assibilation in similar environments (pəʦi] *petit*, [ʦy] *tu*).

6.6. The Simplification of *l mouillé*

In discussion of palatalization, reference was made to the palatal lateral [ʎ], which is no longer part of the modern French phonological system. Usually spelt *il(l)*, as in *oeil* (< OCULU), *fille* (< FILIA), it resulted from early (Proto-Romance?) palatalization of L. Its pronunciation in prestige French is attested well into the nineteenth century.

Littré (1863–72) says: '*La juste prononciation des ll mouillés est souvent manquée . . . à Paris, on le prononce souvent comme un y . . . partout je préviens contre cette prononciation vicieuse.*' Nevertheless Sophie Dupuis in her *Traité de prononciation* (1836) says '. . . *dans la conversation on prononcera bi-ard, bi-et, bi-ot, rou-ier, tâ-ieur etc. pour billard, billet, billot, rouiller, tailleur, sans s'inquiéter des avis contraires ni des réclamations de province.*' By 1871 M. A. Lesaint (*Traité complet de la prononciation française dans la seconde moitié du XIXe siècle*) could say that [j] was '*la prononciation de tout Paris*', and Passy in 1887 and the abbé Rousselot in 1902 were clear that [ʎ] was used nowhere in northern France.

The change of [ʎ] to [j] is easily explained in terms of phonetic simplification (loss of the lateral feature) and is paralleled all over the place (cf. especially Spanish). The question is when the change came about in French. It was first attested in spelling in the thirteenth century, and appears to have been regarded as a popular (especially Parisian) development in the sixteenth and seventeenth centuries. In the eighteenth century commentators ascribe the pronunciation to '*les artisans de Paris*' (1715), '*personnes sans éducation*' (1725), '*le peuple de Paris*' (1754) and, somewhat of a change, '*femmes molles et délicates*' (1785). The 'lower-class' usage fed through to the prestige language after the Revolution.

What is interesting is that the same process affected [lj]—which possibly resolved from an intervocalic cluster to a single segment [ʎ], before simplifying to [j]. This reduction is attested from the late seventeenth century among '*les badauds de Paris*' (Ménage 1675): in the nineteenth century Leconte de Lisle had no compunction about rhyming *souiller* with *soulier*, *piller* with *pilier*, but the simplified pronunciation was not accepted by the modern prestige language.

A comparison can be drawn with palatal *n* [ɲ], as in *agneau*, which some French speakers pronounce as [nj], as in *veniez*.

A different type of simplification, with loss of palatal and not of lateral character, is regular in word-final position in Picard: in the modern standard we note the alternance of:

(34) *péril, gril* [l] / *périlleux, griller* [j].

6.7. 'PALATAL' *u*

Indirectly linked to the palatalizing processes of early French is the development of the 'front' or 'palatal' *u*. French front rounded [y] is the regular reflex of Latin ū: as it is context free, the change is regarded as **spontaneous** and not assimilatory. It is assumed that the Latin sound was a high back rounded vowel [u], like the reflexes in all the other major Romance languages, and the 'palatalization' is often ascribed to Celtic **substratum** influence. The change of [u] to [y] can be seen as 'unnatural', in that the more complex sound, a member of a 'marked' central vowel series, is not found in many languages.

The [y] pronunciation is not confined to central French, but is widespread in Occitan and north Italian dialects, as well as in some Portuguese varieties. It is absent from some northern French varieties, in particular Belgian eastern Walloon and some Francoprovençal dialects, where it is assumed that there was regression to [u] under the influence of neighbouring Germanic dialects. However, the existence of [y] pronunciations in some Germanic varieties has led some to see it as an areal feature and even to postulate a connection with genetic factors.

The connection with Celtic is tenuous, especially as we know little about Gaulish Celtic. The evidence adduced points to Latin loanwords into insular Celtic (e.g. Welsh) in which ū appears as [i]. We have little hard evidence too about the persistence of Gaulish in Roman times, so that the substratum hypothesis is viewed with some scepticism.

Breton is generally thought to have been imported from Britain in the fifth century, although some do believe that it may also have some connection with a Gaulish Celtic that may have survived in the far West.

When [u] fronted to [y] is uncertain. In French the graphy *u* was always used, differentiated from *ou* ([u]) only in the later twelfth century. The [y] and [u] reflexes were also not consistently differentiated in rhyme in medieval northern texts. We know nothing about the pronunciation of [y] before the sixteenth century, when commentators sometimes call it 'Gaulish *u*' and liken it to the Greek, German, and Scottish sounds, commenting on its affinity with [i].

In the sixteenth and seventeenth centuries there was frequent confusion with *eu*, which was still diphthongal in some varieties (e.g. Picard), but levelled to [ø] in the standard.

In English, French loanwords are pronounced with [ju]:

(35) *pure* < *pur*,

and Palsgrave in 1530 still likens French *u* to the sound in *mew*. Contemporary native speaker teachers of French to the English, however, condemned this pronunciation, emphasizing that the lips should be rounded, without movement of the tongue.

It is usually thought that the [ju] always represents an English mispronunciation, with **fission** at **segmental** or **moraic** level, and delinking of the labial element from the palatal. It is possible though that French *u* was originally diphthongal (initially in tonic free syllables but later spreading to pretonic and to blocked tonic syllables?). It would then have levelled to [y] in the same way as [eu] > [ø] in the later Old French period.

The differential development of PŪLICE (> PUL'CE with syncope) 'flea', in French (*puce*) and Old Occitan (*piuce*) suggests that the French, and not the Occitan, fronting may have taken place after the vocalization of preconsonantal [l] to [u]:

(36) [puutse] > ?[puːsə] > [pys], rather than ?[pyutse] > [pjysə],

with loss of syllabic status of [y] and assimilatory raising of [u]. Compare also

(37) [nɥi] < ?[nuijt] < ?[nuejt] < [nɔjt] < NOCTE,

with similar shift of weight and raising.
This would seem to date the fronting to after the twelfth century.

However, if the French graphy *u* did at one time represent [ju] there would be no significant difference from the Occitan form, except that in French it would have levelled to [y]. Besides, in the preconsonantal sequence [il] (in e.g. *fils* <FILIUS), the *l* was lost, so the same could have happened in the sequence [yl]. However, Norse place-names, presumably dating from the

tenth century at the earliest, also show the fronting of [u]. Moreover, [y] did not trigger, at an early period, palatalization of preceding [k].This points to a fairly late date for the fronting.

One postulated effect of the fronting is that it triggered a **drag chain shift** by which Gallo-Roman [o] was raised to the now vacated [u] slot, whenever it was not diphthongized:

(38) ŬRSU > *ours*, *TŌTTU > *tout*.

Another suggestion is that the fronting was conditioned by the existence of four degrees of aperture in the vowel system, after the loss of Latin vowel quantity. Owing to the asymmetry in the articulatory space available at the front and at the back of the mouth, this placed a particular burden on the back series ([u], [o], [ɔ], [ɑ]). The fronting of the high back vowel would in this story be part of a **push chain shift** that originated in the attempt at greater differentiation between [ɔ] and [o], resulting in [o] raising to the [u] slot, and then pushing [u] forward to [y]. The levelling of Latin AU to [ɔ] in French is thought to have accentuated this shift.

French creoles merge [y] with [i]; the other central vowel [ø] is likewise fronted to [e]. Some dialectal French varieties front [y] to [i], though in the east it is sometimes backed to [u]; others tend to confuse [y] and [ø].

6.8. DIPHTHONGIZATION AND DIPHTHONG LEVELLING

Modern standard French does not have **diphthongs** (i.e. two vowels in the same syllable nucleus), if we count the *i* of *pied* and of *abeille* as a **glide** [j], forming part respectively of the syllable **onset** and **coda** rather than of the **nucleus**. What are written as diphthongs may be monophthongs—like *eu* /œ/ (as in *heureux* [œʁø]), or *ou* /u/ (as in *soupe* [sup])—or *onset glide + monophthongal nucleus* sequences— like *oi* [wa] (as in *roi* [ʁwa]).

Besides the 'fixed' sequences of this sort, there are also disyllabic sequences, with two vowels in hiatus, in which the first /u/ or /i/ can be realized phonetically as a glide: *lion* [liɔ̃] / [ljɔ̃], *louer* [lue] / [lwe]. This process is usually blocked by a preceding C*r* cluster: thus *troua* is not homophonous with *trois*. It does not occur over a word boundary: *joua* [ʒwa], but (*il*) *joue à* [ʒua].

Most of the graphical diphthongs are assumed to represent a diphthongal pronunciation at an earlier period: these Old French diphthongs were apparently levelled in the early modern period. The older diphthongs can be a consequence of **vocalization** of consonants:

(39) *chaud* [ʃo] < ?[ʧauð] < CAL'DU, *toit* [twa] < *teit* < TĔCTU,

or of **jodization** in the vicinity of a palatal consonant:

(40) *chien* [ʃjɛ̃] < CANE, *aire* [ɛʁ] < ?[airʲə] < AREA, *poison* [pwazɔ̃] < ?[pɔjzʲõn] POTIONE.

From the point of view of linguistic change the most interesting diphthongs are those that arose prehistorically from **fission** of tonic vowels in a free syllable (though some of the other diphthongs later merged with these). This so-called **spontaneous diphthongization** is exemplified in Table 6.3:

The diphthongization of ō may not have affected all regions: the graphy *u* is found in early texts, and *eu* is characteristic of the Parisian and the Picard region in the thirteenth century. It is to be noted that it is assumed that the dipthongization of Latin ĕ took place also in monosyllabic words with a final consonant, even though in this case the syllable was blocked:

(41) MĔL > *miel*.

It is difficult to explain this in terms of lengthening (cf. 6.12), unless we assume some sort of vocalic off-glide to which the graphical word-final consonant forms a syllabic onset, or that the final consonant is extrametrical.

The traditional story is that all of these diphthongs were originally **falling**, on the basis of evidence of assonancing verse (cf. below), and of the fact that in some dialects the second element

TABLE 6.3. Diphthongization of tonic free vowels

Ĕ (PĔDE)	*ie*	>			[je] / [jɛ]		*pied* [pje]
Ŏ (CŎRE)	*uo*	>	*ue*	>	[œ] / [ø]		*cœur* [kœʁ]
Ē (MĒ)	*ei*	>	*oi*	>	[we] > [wa] / [ɛ]	*moi* [mwa]
Ō (NŌDU)	*ou*	>	*eu*	>	[œ] / [ø]		*nœud* [nø]
A (MARE)	**ae*	>	*e*	>	[e] / [ɛ]		*mer* [mɛr]

of the diphthong is lost. We can however single out the diphthong-ization of the Latin short mid-vowels, on the grounds that this process affected other Romance languages, whereas the others are confined solely to French. Other evidence also suggests that the diphthongization of A, Ē, and ō came later in time.

There seems, for instance, to be a difference between Ē and Ĕ for the relative chronology of diphthongization and of syncope of short Ĭ. In TĔPĬDU, the intertonic Ĭ had not disappeared before diphthongization, which occurred only in free syllables: *tiède*. By contrast, in DĒBĬTA the syncope of the Ĭ seems to have blocked the syllable before diphthongization got going: *dette*. Moreover Old French preconsonantal *l* seems to have inhibited the later diphthongization:

(42) Present subjunctive *ceut* < *celt* < CĒLIT / present indicative *ceile* < CĒLAT; nominative singular *peus* < *pels* / *peil* < PĬLU; but *vueut* < *vuelt* < VŎLIT, *cieux* < *ciels* < CAELOS.

Either the syllable had become blocked by the time of the later diphthongization, or the *l* had already vocalized to [w] which hindered dipthongization. The effect of a following nasal also appears to have been different for tonic free ŏ and ō:

(43) *buon, buen* (but > *bon* by the twelfth century) < BŎNU / *don* < DŌNU.

Another difference may be that the early diphthongization affected mono-syllabic words with a final consonant, whereas in the later wave such words may be treated like blocked syllables: RĔM > *rien* / IAM > *ja*. (The outcome of TRĒS as *trois* is inconclusive, as the final s may not have been pronounced in Latin.)

Diphthongization of Ĕ and ŏ can be seen as Proto-Romance, not only because of some early graphical evidence, but because even today diphthongal reflexes are found in both Spain and Italy, while in other regions it is possible to explain away the monophthongal reflexes in terms of later fusion. There are two major difficulties here: one is that in Spain the diphthongization occurs in both free and blocked tonic syllables (though it is inhibited by a following palatal):

(44) Spanish *fiesta*, French *fête* (< *feste*); Spanish *puerta*, French *porte*.

The other is that, normally, **rising** diphthongs, or *glide + vowel* sequences, result from this diphthongization process, whereas, as we have seen, it is traditionally assumed that in Old French the diphthongs *ie* and *uo* were originally falling.

These paradoxes prompted two radically different hypotheses to account for the Romance diphthongization, both of which originated with the late-nineteenth-century Romanist Schuchardt. The first sees the **fission** of the tonic vowel as due to more intense stress, with consequent lengthening and then a split into two segments, to produce a falling diphthong. It is assumed that this lengthening would be confined to free syllables: Spanish would have subsequently generalized the diphthong to blocked syllables, except before a palatal consonant.

The second hypothesis was that the tonic vowel diphthongization stemmed from **metaphonic** (*umlaut*) raising—a vowel harmony effect triggered by a following high vowel ([i] or [u]). There is ample evidence of this effect in many Romance dialects, where inherited /ɛ/ and /ɔ/ can be replaced by /e/ or /i/ and /o/ or /u/, or alternatively by diphthongal *ie* and *uo, ue*.

In these cases the diphthongs can be rising, or falling. If the latter, the second element is usually a schwa sound.

If we were to assume metaphonic diphthongization in French, Italian, and Spanish we should have to postulate analogical spread of the diphthong to tonic syllables where metaphonic effect is absent.

How does this affect our view of French diphthongization? First, it could help to explain the apparent fluctuating rising/falling character of the *ie, uo* diphthongs. Rising diphthongs could well be **light** (that is, matched up with a single **mora** timing slot, although occupying two slots at the melodic level). Fig. 6.5 illustrates. In phonetically shorter blocked syllables the two segments of a light diphthong could readily fuse to a monophthong and so merge with the reflexes of Latin tonic blocked Ē and Ĕ.

We may contrast these possibly **light** diphthongs with the **heavy (bimoraic)** *ei, ou* falling diphthongs, which are more familiar results of phonetic lengthening in a tonic free syllable. Fig. 6.6 illustrates. If there were also at this stage a lengthening of the light diphthongs in the longer tonic free syllables, we could then envisage that very early in the history of French all tonic free syllables had bimoraic nuclei, which were not phonologically distinct from their counterparts in other positions.

N(ucleus)

|

μ   Moraic (timing) tier

i   ε

u   ɔ

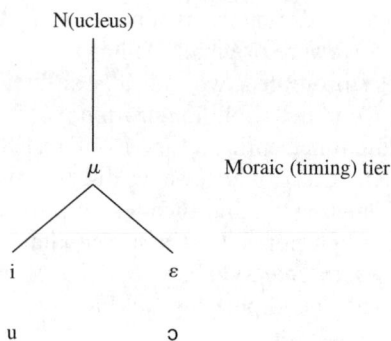

Figure 6.5. (Dipthongization)

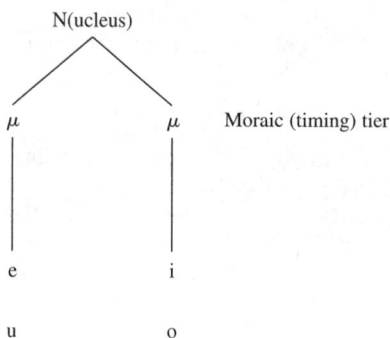

N(ucleus)

μ   μ   Moraic (timing) tier

| |

e   i

u   o

Figure 6.6. (Dipthongization)

Thus the light diphthongs in some varieties might have undergone phonetic lengthening, at the same time as the formation of the heavy diphthongs, with the first element then hardening to a glide which became part of the onset:

(45)   *ciel* [sjɛl] < [ʦʲiɛːlo], *cœur* [kœʁ] < [kwœr] < [kuoːre],

whereas in other varieties it was the first element which lengthened, with the second weakening to schwa. This would account for the different assonating patterns found in early Old French, with the west, and eventually the standard, apparently preferring [jɛ] and [wø] type outcomes, while the east favoured [iə] and [uə] type.

Thus it is possible that a characteristic feature of some varieties of very early French, as distinct from the other Romance languages, was that there was **allophonic** variation in the whole vowel system, with long vowels or diphthongs in inherited tonic free syllables, and shorter counterparts in all other positions.

We have no evidence of diphthongization of Latin ī in central French, but we would not expect to find a special graphy for a diphthong like [ii], would we? It is possible that the [y] from Latin ū was once pronounced as [iu] or [ui], with later fusion: note that in England it was equated with a [iu] diphthong.

However, if this were so, by the time of the first texts it seems clear that one of the conditioning features of this allophonic variation was no longer operative, in that all unstressed Latin final vowels except A had been lost, so that syllables that had been free in Latin were now blocked.

Here, however, we note again that it is possible that word-final consonants may have been treated as extrametrical, and not therefore blocking the final syllable.

In any case, the influx of (mainly learned) loanwords with undiphthongized vowels in tonic free syllables may have upset the balance, and prompted rephonologization of the diphthongs (which in any case were being fuelled from other sources, like jodization and vocalization of [l]). Once the diphthongs were not seen as in complementary distribution to their monophtongal counterparts, then they were free to differentiate—so that *uo* and *ou* fronted to *ue* and *eu*, and *ei* backed to merge with *oi* (as in *noix* < NŬCE).

The reflex of tonic free Latin A, written *e*, but kept separate in medieval rhyme from other *e*s, may have been originally a diphthong like [ai] (cf. the prenasal graphy *main* < MANU), but it eventually merged with other monophthongal *e* sounds.

By the thirteenth century, in most texts, the *ue* and *eu* diphthongs began to be confused in graphy and rhyme: we assume centralization of the front vowel, by assimilation to its back partner with eventual drop of the latter ([wø] / [øw] > [ø:]), or fusion of the two vowels by mutual assimilation.

An interesting example is provided by the word *meute* (< MŎUITA), earlier spelt *muete* which survives in the Parisian district name *la Muette*, in which the levelling did not take place

More unusual is the fate of the *ei* diphthong, and therefore I shall look at this in some detail. An *oi* graphy for *ei* (or *ai*) was infrequent

in the west in the thirteenth century, but *oi, oe, oy* were well attested
in other regions (in the east, it then usually levelled to *o*). *Oi* is still
described by Palsgrave in 1530 as sometimes pronounced as in
English *boy*, but we have evidence for a shift of weight to the second
element which lowered to [e] or [ɛ], while the first element hardened
to a labial glide. In some varieties the glide was lost, a pronunciation
which persists in some forms like *français* [fʁɑ̃sɛ], and which may
continue an old western pronunciation, which was in the sixteenth
century associated with the court. In Parisian the *e* element lowered
further to [a], as in the name *François* [fʁɑ̃swa]. Variation between
[we] and [wa] persisted right through to the nineteenth century, and
indeed still does so in some varieties:

(46) Canada (Beauce County) *moi* [mwe] / *mois* [mwɔ].

A striking bit of anecdotal evidence comes from the Reign of Terror (1794):
accused of saying '*Il faut un roi*' (it would be a capital offence to argue 'We
must have a king'), a lower-class Parisian woman protested that what she
had really said was '*Il faut un rouet*' ('I need a spinning wheel').

The *ei* diphthong was however not the only source of modern *oi*
[wa]. Tables 6.4–6 set out data to illustrate how originally different
sequences converged by the early modern period, then to share
subsequent developments. Table 6.4 gives a summary of the various
sources of the modern *oi*, showing how they came together at the
end of the medieval period.

Table 6.5 gives examples of modern words (with their origins) in
[wa], most of which do reflect an earlier *ei*, but show in the modern
language a degree of homonymy not present in the older language.
Table 6.6 illustrates the possible relative chronology of different
changes in five words that end up with a [wa] pronunciation.

Diphthongization and levelling of diphthongs are processes that
can readily be explained in universal phonetic and phonological
terms. What is more difficult to explain is why in the early history of
French there should have been more extensive diphthongization
than in other Romance languages, and why the diphthongs should
have levelled at a later period. The tonic vowel diphthongization
and subsequent differentiation of the diphthongal elements have
variously been associated with strong and with weak articulation,
which in their turn have been associated with Germanic and Celtic
influence. The phonetic lengthening of vowels in tonic free syllables

TABLE 6.4. Old French sources of modern French *oi*

A. Early Old French *ei*

      (> *oi*[1] [except West and Orléanais] by end 12th c.)

1   < Ē, ĭ tonic and free (or in a monosyllable e.g. TRĒS)

2   < [e] + [j]

        -[kt]-   *teit* < TĒCTU

        -[gr]-   *neir* < NĬGRU

        -[k][E]-   *veiz* < VĬCE

        -[sk][E,O]   *deis* < DĬSCU, *freis* < FRĬSCU

        -[sj], -[rj]; -[trj]-

                      feire < FĒRIA, *cerveise* < CERVĬSIA, *alveire* <
                      ARBĬTRIU

3   < [e] + [jj]

        -[g][E] -   *lei* < LĒGE

        -[k][A]-,-[g][A]- *leie* < LĬGAT, *freie* < FRĬCAT

        -[dj]-,-[gj]-   *enveje* < INVĬDIA, *correie* < CORRĬGIA

B. Early Old French *oi*[2] ([oj])

      < [o] +[j]

             -[rj]-   *dortoir* < DORMITŌRIU

             -[fj]-   *coiffe* < CŌFEA

             -[k][E,I]   *crois* < CRŬCE

             -[stj]-, -[sk][E,I], -[sk][O,U]

                      angoisse < ANGŬSTIA

                      foisne (modern: *fouine*) < FŬSCINA

                      conoistre < COGNOSCERE

C. Later Old French *oi*[3] ([ɔj])

      < AU +[j]

             -[dj]-   *joie*   < GAUDIA

             -[sj]-   *noise* < NAUSEA

      < ŏ + [j]

             [-lj]-, -[nj]-, -[rj]

                      apostoile < *apostolie* < APOSTŎLICU;

                      moine < *monie* < MŎNACU;

                      estoire < *estorie* < HISTŎRIA

(Late 12th c.–early 13th c.) Chrétien de Troyes does not rhyme *oi*[1,2,3] but Gautier
d'Arras rhymes *pot*[(3)] < PAUCU with *mot*[(1)] < ME
In earlier texts: *oi*[3] assonates with [ɔ]; *oi*[2] with [o]. In later texts (12th–13th c.): all
rhyme with *ai* [ɛ].

Source: Data from Fouché (1958: 2. 269–85).

TABLE 6.5. Sources of modern French [wa] (some examples)

Modern French	Early Old French	Latin
oie 'goose'	*oie*	AUCA
bois 'wood'; *boit* 'he drinks'	*bois*; *beit*	(*BUSK); BIBIT
broie	(14th c. *broie*)	(Germanic *BREK)
crois 'I believe'; *croix* 'cross'	*crei*; *croiz*	CRĒDO; CRŬCEM
dois 'I ought', *doigt* 'finger'	*dei*; *deit*	DEBEO; DĬGĬTUM
droit	*dreit*	DIRECTUM
foi 'faith'; *foie* 'liver'; *fois* 'time'	*fei(t)*; *feie*; *feis*	FĬDEM; FICATUM; VĬCEM
froid	*freit*	FRĪGĬDUM
joie	*joie*	GAUDIA
loi 'law'; (*lit* 'bed')	*lei*; (*leit*)	LĒGEM; (LĔCTUM)
moi 'me'; *mois* 'month'	*mei*; *meis*	MĒ; MĒNSUM
noix 'nut'; (*noif* 'snow' replaced by *neige*)	*noiz*; *neis, neif*	NŬCEM; NĬVEM
poids 'weight'; *pois* 'pea'; *poix* 'pitch'	*peis*; *peis*; *peiz*	PENSUM; PĬSUM; PĬCEM
ploie 'he folds'	*pleie*	PLĬCAT
proie 'prey'	*preie*	PRAEDA
quoi 'what'	*quei(t)*	QUĬD
roi 'king'	*rei*	RĔGEM
soi 'oneself'; *sois* 'that I be'	*sei*; *seie*	SĒ; SĬM;
soie 'silk'; (*soif* 'thirst')	*seie*; *sei*	SĒTA; SĬTEM
toi 'you'; *toit* 'roof'	*tei*; *teit*	TĒ; TĔCTUM
trois 'three'; *Troie* 'Troy'	*treis*; *Troie*	TRĒS; TROIA
vois 'I see'; *voix* 'voice'	*vei*; *voiz*	VĪDĒŌ; VŌCEM

is certainly more likely in a language with a stress accent, though it is debatable whether diphthongization betokens more intense stress, or, on the contrary, a fading of muscular tone in articulating a long nucleus.

Perhaps we should be wondering less 'How did diphthongization take place?' and more 'Why were Old French diphthongs salient enough to prompt special graphical representation?' The bewildering complexity of the Old French vocalic system may be a misleading effect of attempts at phonetic, rather than morphophonological, transcription, associated perhaps with the essentially oral character of much of the early material. Later, the weight of tradition was to hinder moves to graphical rationalization.

TABLE 6.6. Chronological sequence of rules (some examples of words in *oi*)

Rules	AUCA	GAU(D)IA	CRŬCEM	FĬCATU	FĪDE
ĭ → e, ŭ → o			kroke	fekato	fede
k$^{+e,i}$ → [-back] → ts^j			krots^{j}e		
^{v}C^v → [+voice]	auga		krodz^{j}e	fegado	
^{v}C^v[+voice] → [-stop]	auja			fejaðo	feðe
g^{+a} [-back] → dʒ		dʒauja			
affricate → fricative		ʒauja	kroz^{j}e		
z^j → jz			krojz		
au → ɔ	ɔja	ʒɔja			
'e[→ ej					fejðe
'_ -a → ə; other V → ∅	ɔjə	ʒɔjə		fejəð	fejð
-ð/ ə_# → ∅ ; -C/ _# → [-voice]			krojs	fejə	fejθ
ej → oj, ɔj → oj		ʒɔjə		fojə	fojθ
V /_# → ∅ ; C /_# → ∅	oj	ʒoj	kroj	fojə	foj
oj → oe → we	we	ʒwe	krwe	fweə	fwe
we → wa ; r → R/ʁ	wa	ʒwaə	kʁwa	fwaə	fwa
	oie	**joie**	**croix**	**foie**	**foi**

Levelling of diphthongs has likewise been associated with the advent of rhythmic group accentuation which is assumed to have replaced Old French word-stress. My exposition has implied rather that quite early in French loss of word-final vowels made opaque the allophonic distribution within vowel phonemes. A change towards rhythmic group, rather than word, accent, would further mean that there was no longer any transparent relationship between stress and diphthongal or monophthongal nuclei. The opacity was intensified by the simplification of some consonant clusters and the creation of others, so that previously allophonic distribution between vowels in free and blocked syllables could be no longer perceived to be phonologically determined. What could be made, for instance of a synchronic distribution like:

(47) *coupe* [ku.pə] (< CŬPPA) / *coup* [kup] (< COL'PU) / *cous* [kus] (< CŎLLOS), *queue* [keu.ə] (< CŌDA) / *cœur* [kuer] < (CŎR) / *cour* [kur] (< COHŌRTE)?

Borrowing further introduced into the lexicon vowel realizations that went counter to the originally allophonic distribution found in inherited words (cf. early undiphthongized forms like *escole, rose, amour*). The result would be that in the grammar of new learners of the language there might be a redistribution of the allophonic variants among existing phonological units, and creation of new ones.

When, in real time, this happened is probably impossible to say. We have no way of discovering what input there was into the language acquisition process of children in the very early period of French: we can probably safely assume that it did not necessarily closely resemble anything we can reconstruct from the texts. By the time textual evidence is copious enough, there was probably already considerable morphologization of originally phonological alternation: these are questions we shall consider under the head of morphology (Chapter 7), especially in consideration of **apophony** in the verb paradigm.

6.9. WORD-FINAL CONSONANTS AND *LIAISON*

Diphthongization and palatalization are examples of phonological changes that occurred mainly in the very early history of French, and for which we rely on reconstruction of a prehistoric stage. I should like to concentrate now on changes that have occurred in the modern period, and for which we have much more evidence. I shall look especially at some noteworthy features of modern French, and try to trace them back in time.

One of these is *liaison*, which is one of the most hotly debated questions in French phonology. For traditional grammarians it is simply a question of when graphical word-final consonants are pronounced within a rhythmic group before a word-initial vowel, and when they remain silent. A distinction is made between 'obligatory liaisons'—usually in close-knit sentence constituents or set phrases—and 'optional liaisons'—defined for the most part as dependent on style and register. There are also some 'forbidden liaisons' which are mainly lexically defined (e.g. the *t* in *et* is never pronounced; no liaison is made before *h aspiré* or after proper names).

It has commonly been observed that liaison is less frequent in modern, colloquial pronunciation than in careful formal speech, and it is postulated that the language is moving towards loss of liaison. On the other hand, in popular speech *fausse liaison*—where an unetymological consonant like [z] (*velours*) or [t] (*cuir*) is inserted between word-final and word-initial vowels—is amply attested, certainly from the nineteenth century, and probably earlier:

(48) *Donnez-moi-z-en; peu-z-à peu; il va-t-et vient; Malbrouk s'en va-t-en guerre.*

Are we to assume that this is an effect of **hypercorrection**, or does it tell us something about the mechanism of liaison? If the latter, then it lends support to the hypothesis that in the modern languages liaison consonants are epenthetically inserted in certain *vowel + vowel* contexts, rather than being present in the underlying form of words and undergoing deletion in most contexts.

A clear-cut distinction is not always made between *enchaînement* and liaison, both of which are **sandhi** or **linking** phenomena, which can be related to **elision**, especially of *e instable* (cf. 6.10). *Enchaînement* is a regular process in modern French: within a rhythmic group, before a word-initial vowel, resyllabification of a word-final consonant occurs so that it forms the onset of the succeeding syllable rather than the coda of the preceding one. Thus a CV(C) syllable structure is favoured.

What do we mean though by 'word-final consonant'? Phonetically most consonants, and some clusters, can occur in this position in modern French, but traditionally most of these are seen as having been 'protected' from attrition by a graphical 'feminine' *e*, which became 'silent' by the seventeenth century (cf. 6.10).

For those who consider 'protective schwa', or 'feminine *e*' to be part of the modern underlying lexical form of the word, the *enchaînement* process involves prevocalic elision of the [ə], with syllabic contraction, rather than resyllabification of the word-final consonant:

(49) [pɔʁtetʁwat] *por-te-é-troi-te*, rather than *por-t'é-troite.*

By contrast, by the sixteenth and seventeenth centuries, a graphical word-final consonant, without the protection of final schwa, was not usually pronounced at all before a word-initial consonant (or a pause?). However, within a rhythmic group, it would form the onset of a syllable with a following word-initial vowel:

(50) *neuf mois* [nø.mwe] / *neuf ans* [nø.vɑ̃] / *j'en ai neuf* [ʒɑ̃nenœf];
  dix mois [di.mwe] / *dix ans* [di.zɑ̃] / *j'en ai dix* [ʒɑ̃nedis].

Today the citation forms *neuf* and *dix* are pronounced [nœf] and [dis], but this is probably due to a restoration of the final consonants in spelling pronuncation (cf. 6.14).

The evidence at this period for regular phonetic loss of graphical word-final consonants is overwhelming: only [l] survived consistently, and [r] sporadically. But in the sixteenth century all could reappear in a liaison form before a word-initial vowel: it seems reasonable to postulate that, where this was regular, the final consonant still formed part of the underlying representation of the word. As time went on, though, fewer of the consonants surfaced in *liaison* contexts, which themselves became fewer. Today [z], [t], and [n] are virtually the only *liaison* consonants productively used. In colloquial usage even these appear relatively infrequently, and then quite often as morphological markers (e.g. [z] as a plural marker: [le.zaᴿbʁ] *les arbres*, [i.zaʃɛt] *ils achètent*; [n] mainly with grammatical elements like *un, en*; and [t] as a verb inflection, as in *c'est-à-dire, vient-il?*).

Theoretical discussion about modern liaison centres round the syllabic, skeletal, or moraic status of the volatile *liaison* consonants compared with fixed consonants. Non-linear phonology allows the formal representation of liaison elements as 'floating'—underlyingly unattached to a syllabic, skeletal, or timing slot, but ready to take on the role of onset to a following nuclear vowel in sentence context. Different theoretical frameworks offer diverse accounts of how this can happen.

But what would be the history of the process? Clearly the 'floating' consonants were at one time 'fixed': most fixed Old French word-final consonants eventually suffered the same fate as medial coda consonants—attrition and elimination. The relationship between survival as *liaison* consonants and resistance to attrition in medial coda position is not obvious: [l] vocalized medially but usually survives as a fixed final; *r* survives medially, and sporadically finally, as a fixed consonant, but is rarely a *liaison* consonant. The medial coda sibilants succumbed slowly, with **compensatory lengthening** of the vowel. Similar interaction between nasals and a preceding vowel dates way back, though when the coda nasal consonant was lost is uncertain. As for [t], this was not an Old

French medial coda consonant: any etymological reflexes had early merged with sibilants:

(51) RETINA > *resne* > *rêne*.

As a word-final, however, [t] served a function in the flexional system, marking the third person: this may have helped to preserve it, if only as a notional entity. -*S* (/-*z*,-*x*) played an even more major role as a flexion, marking nominal plurals and verbal second person.

From a historical point of view, it certainly looks as though liaison processes in the modern colloquial language form an uneasy half-way house between the regular *enchaînement* of the sixteenth century and a foreseeable complete disappearance of Old French word-final consonants. True, in some cohesive groups (like *deter-miner* or *adjective* + *noun*, like *clitic* + *verb*, and like some prepositional phrases) there is still obligatory liaison. They however can be regarded as simple phonological units, as can stereotyped uses like *vis-à-vis* etc. From this point of view, *liaison* consonants may often be more meaningfully treated as medial, rather than as final consonants. In other sequences, *liaison* is so inconsistently used that a formal description of usage eludes us.

What complicates the issue, of course, is the existence, as part of the citation form of some words, of 'fixed' word-final consonants which take part in *enchaînement*, but are never deleted. Some of these result from historically documented restoration of their final consonant—as in *chef, finir* etc.—and indeed some still are supple-tively used in two versions of the same word—like *août* [u] or [ut]. Others were not historically fed into the word-final deletion process, as the consonant had not at the relevant time become final (being followed by -*e* or by another consonant). An easy way synchroni-cally to distinguish fixed consonants from *liaison* consonants is to re-establish after the former a 'silent' abstract final element—an 'empty nucleus' or such—which protects the 'fixed final consonant' from 'floating off'. But this does seem, to the down-to-earth, to be a bit of a cheat, a post-rationalization. Moreover it seems to rely heavily, like traditional grammar, on the evidence of written, rather than of spoken, language (for another account, in Optimality Theory terms cf. Tranel 1996).

Probably, here again, as linguistic historians, we have to say that a consistent story-line cannot be discerned until the plot has run its course. Some French varieties that use very limited liaison only in cohesive **nexus** sequences are possibly reaching the end of the trail, but tradition and morphological convenience maintains, for many speakers and in some styles, a whole lot of anomalies which will go on taxing the ingenuity of the synchronic formalist, and which are not likely to disappear overnight.

6.10. *E MUET, E INSTABLE, E CADUC, E FÉMININ*

The loss of word-final consonants in early modern French seems to be inextricably linked to the similar loss of the word-final vowel (i.e. the 'feminine *e*') and the term **truncation** is sometimes used to cover both processes.

Although elision of feminine *e* and dropping of final consonants are clearly linked historically, difficulties in formulating a coherent synchronic phonological account led to a withdrawal from seeing them as the same process (cf. Schane 1974). Tranel 1996, however, shows that **Optimality Theory** (cf. 6.1) can satisfactorily capture the relationship between the two even at the synchronic level.

Like *liaison*, the question of so-called **mute e** in French excites the interest of the brightest and the best among theoretical phonologists. Mute *e* is not just any old graphical representation without phonetic realization, like the *k* in *knock* or the *b* in *debt*, which can be accounted for by reference to historical change or to misguided attempts to recapture etymological origins. Mute *e* is not always silent: it sometimes has a phonetic representation, hence the designation **e instable**—hovering between absence and presence. The modern term **floating**—extrametrical, unattached to a syllabic, timing, or skeletal slot—does not differ very much in its implication from the traditional one 'unstable'. The designation **e caduc** conveys a more colourful metaphorical flavour, if we understand *caduc* in its etymological sense, implying falling—like the leaves of deciduous trees that according to season are there or not there (the legal sense of *caduc* as 'null and void' is less illuminating). **Feminine e** is a morphologically oriented term: an atonic final *e* (< Latin A) marked feminine gender in many Old French nouns, so that in verse metrics rhymes that include this element are known as feminine rhymes.

For the traditional grammarian, the problem was how to pronounce a graphical *e*. Sixteenth- and seventeenth-century reformers sought to differentiate graphically or diacritically its diverse phonetic realizations—commentators distinguished up to five different pronunciations. The atonic *e* '*son imbecille*', subject to elision, syncope, and apocope, called for special comment. In structuralist phonology, a major preoccupation was how to define the phonemic status of this **schwa** sound—is it a constituent of the phonological system or simply a surface lubricant to aid the enunciation of consonantal clusters? Maurice Grammont's famous *loi des trois consonnes* made a stab at predicting the contextual motivation of the phonetic realization, or epenthesis, of a schwa, by predicting that a [ə] will be inserted to break up a sequence of three consonants. Generativists are, here as elsewhere, divided between the abstract and the concrete camps, as we saw in the discussion of nasalization. The former tend to respect the intuitions represented in traditional orthography and think that the schwa is underlyingly present in lexical representation, but phonetically deleted in some contexts. The latter, by contrast, refuse to admit the existence of a covert phonological element that may never come out into the phonetic open, and so see its fleeting appearances as a surface phenomenon with no lexical status.

The designation of *e instable* as a schwa can be confusing—the term is used in English for an atonic, neutral vowel that relates to different tonic vowels, as reflected in the spelling. In French the spelling is usually *e* (but cf. *monsieur*, *faisons*) and in modern pronunciation overt realization is a rounded central vowel, like that written *eu* ([œ] / [ø]), even though the transcription [ə] is conventionally used for the unstable version. Nevertheless it is hard to find anyone who consistently distinguishes *le rapport* from *leur rapport*, except after a vowel within a rhythmic group, when the 'unstable' *e* of the definite article disappears: *trouvez le rapport* [truvelʁapɔʁ]. Indeed sometimes it seems that a [ø] realization has become lexicalized, especially in initial free syllables, as in *secondaire*, *ceci*.

It appears that in modern Parisian stable [ø] is found more often in formal registers and especially in initial *re-*. It is to be noted, too, that under the *accent d'insistance*, often falling on the initial syllable, [ø] is the usual pronunciation.

Moreover there are two cases in which the postulated Old French schwa bears the accent that falls on the last syllable of a rhythmic group. (I leave aside archaizing *sur ce*, where *ce* continues Old French *ço*, and *parce que* . . . which was not an Old French item.) The first is in the object pronoun *le* (< ILLU, where we assume that a final vowel persisted in forms bearing some degree of stress). When postposed to an imperative, as in *Fermez-le!*, the modern pronunciation is [ø], which is not elided. Until the seventeenth century, however, verse metrics reveal that it could optionally be elided prevocalically, as regularly happened with the vowel of atonic *me*, *te*, *se*. In the later part of the century, language arbiters tell us that the correct pronunciation of *le* here was [lɛ], but lexicalization with [ø] was normal by the nineteenth century (although elision sometimes continues to be found in verse).

We note that in the phonetics lesson in Molière's *Bourgeois Gentilhomme* (1670), the description of pronunciation of the letter *e*, now cited as [ø], seems to refer to [e] or [ɛ], i.e. a vowel somewhere between [a] and [i].

In the other relevant case the modern lexicalization is in [ɛ]: this can represent the final graphical *e* of first person singular forms like *porte*. Here originally the *e* acted as an epenthetic support vowel for a word-final final consonant cluster (**port* < PORTO). By the fourteenth century it had extended analogically to other -*er* verb-forms (*aime* < *aim* < AMO), perhaps as 'protection' against threatened attrition of the word-final consonant. When an enclitic *je* is attached in the interrogative we have *porté-je?* [pɔʁtɛʒ], *aimé-je?* [ɛmɛʒ].

The shift of the accent to the flexional vowel seems to have occurred in the fifteenth century, when it could be spelt *ei* or *é*. Occasionally we find similar forms in other verb conjugations: *perdé-je?*

In the sixteenth century some commentators describe this vowel as an *e féminin*, and in the seventeenth century we have transcriptions like *parl'j'bien?*, but a tonic [e] or [ɛ] seems to have become more frequent.

Today such interrogative forms are seldom used in ordinary discourse, the periphrasis with *Est-ce que (je porte)?* being preferred for the first person singular.

This evidence is supplemented by the hesitation about pronunciation of *e* in word-initial syllables: sometimes it is now lexicalized as [e]—*désir, réforme*—or as [ø] —as in *dehors*—but until the First World War there remained considerable doubt, and even today there is hesitation in words like *cresson* ([ø] or [ɛ]?). Thus doubt is cast on the accepted story that the atonic *e*, whether a default epenthetic vowel or derived from atonic A or protonic E, had a (central) schwa realization in Old French. The evidence is far from conclusive. It is usually assumed that the haphazard spelling of the final atonic vowel in the 842 Strasburg Oaths (e.g. *fradra* < FRATRE) shows phonetic confusion, but even if this were so it would tell us nothing about the phonetic realization of the default vowel.

The much-discussed eleventh-century Cyrillic transcription of *reine* as РБИНА with, it is claimed, the so-called 'hard *jer*' Б representing [ə], proves nothing, though it is unlikely that it is merely a mistake for Latin REGINA (РЕГИНА would have been the usual graphy at the time). The БИ transcription could be read as a monophthong [ɨ], or as a falling diphthong [o̯i] or [ə̯i], rather than as the bisyllabic vowel sequence [əi] postulated for this period of French: *roine, roiene, royenne* spellings are attested only in the thirteenth century. A regular outcome of [rəinə] would have been in French *[ʁi:n], not [ʁɛn]: influence of *roi* (< *rei* < REGE) is assumed (within *roine*, but not *roi*, a sixteenth-century simplification of [wɛ] to [ɛ]). The final A of the Cyrillic graphy is in any case inconsistent with the hypothesis that it represents the French form ending in [ə]. We have to assume Slavization, substituting a feminine marker [a] for French feminine *e*.

There is some indication from Old French rhyming schemes that atonic *e* was not phonologically differentiated from its tonic counterparts, though a shorter, less qualitatively distinct, phonetic realization would be expected, and total elision was frequent. For protonic reflexes of Latin E sounds, an [e] articulation is likely. We are unsure of the pronunciation of the tonic free reflex of Latin A, written *e*, but it was differentiated in rhymes, before the thirteenth century, from popular reflexes of Latin E sounds, and associated rather with the E of Latinisms. The 'feminine *e*' < A of atonic final syllables could well have been a variant of this mystery sound (?[eː] or [ai]). If this were so, there would have been a phonological distinction, based on stress placement rather than primarily on vowel quality, between e.g.:

(52) *porte* < PORTAT and *porté* < PORTATU.

Protonic, as well as tonic blocked, A is normally shown as *a* in graphy:

(53) *lef* / *laver* < LAVO / lavare, but *lief* / *lever* < LEVO / LEVARE.

It is possible that it was pronounced something like [ɐ] in Old French: in some texts there is graphical confusion between *e* and *a*—cf. thirteenth century east Champagne:

(54) *aglise*, *essis* for *église*, *assis*.

After a palatal protonic A was written *e*:

(55) *cheval* < CABALLU; cf. *achever*, *acheter* < *ADCAPERE, *ADCAPTARE, with stem-stressed forms *achief*, *achate*,

where the former shows 'Bartsch's breaking' in a post-palatal free syllable. In the sixteenth century this *e* sometimes did not count as a syllable in verse ([ʃval]). In some northern varieties, though, it had full syllabic status and was raised to [I] or [i].

I am suggesting that the default vowel of Old French may have been more like a front [e] than a central [ə]; some claim that even today /e/ is the 'underspecified' vowel which can surface as [ø] or [œ] in atonic syllables (but as [i] or [y] in some northern dialects). But if so, when did the atonic vowel assume its front-central rounded pronunciation, and how is this related to the /œ/ phoneme? Palsgrave in 1530 tells us that final atonic *e* is 'sounded almost lyke *o* and very moche in the noose': the nasal quality seems to be regional (Norman), and the reported rounded character reminds one of Occitan reflexes of final atonic A. Most other commentators refer to 'weak', 'obscure', 'muffled' pronunciation, and by the late seventeenth century comparison is made with Hebrew *scheva*. The *Grammaire du Port Royal* in 1660 describes '*un son sourd conjoint aux consonnes lorsqu'on les veut prononcer sans voyelle*'—in other words a neutral epenthetic 'floating' segment.

For comparison we note that some early sixteenth-century commentators describe *eu* as a diphthong (possibly a Picard regionalism). Later, however, descriptions do talk in terms of a monophthongal simultaneous enunciation of *e* and *u*, and during the seventeenth century it was likened to German *ö*, Danish *ø* etc. As for the relationship of this sound to 'mute e', we note that Oudin in 1633 writes *deu* for *de*, and Hindret in 1687, *ampakeuter*, *keunouille* for *empaqueter*, *quenouille* (though preferring *anvoyez-lai* to *anvoyez-leu* for *envoyez-le*).

We guess therefore that, in some varieties, the *e instable* was by then seen as a variant of /œ/, rather than of /e/. Today in its 'default' status it appears as the hesitation marker *euh*, especially when this provides a site for *enchaînement*. Thus, a recent transcription of a conversational exchange gives:

(56) . . . *la fatigue euh euh d'une fin de nuit*. . .
    [la.fa.ti.gø.ʔø.dyn.fɛ̃.dnɥi]

More strikingly [œ]/[ø] acts as the support vowel in *verlan* ('back-slang'), which tends to abandon original vowels and to reverse consonants, fleshed out with a [œ] nucleus:

(57) *arabe > beur, femme > meuf.*

It is also used in popular, emphatic speech to provide support for a final consonant: *c'est débil-eu!*. This is almost regular in some southern varieties: *eau Javel* [o.ʒa.vɛ.lø].

What makes it doubly difficult to locate changes of *e instable* in time is not only the considerable regional and social variation, but also the conservative effect of versification, in which the graphical *e*, except when elided prevocalically, is counted as a syllable. The comparative freedom of the sixteenth century, when an apostrophe could replace a silent *e*, was lost in the strict versification rules of the seventeenth century. But even here a verse final atonic *e* (in *rimes féminines*) was always 'extrametrical'—presumably reflecting its 'mute' character in prepausal position.

In older French, a similar phenomenon was found at the mid-verse caesura (the so-called *coupe épique* or *féminine*, which contrasted particularly with the sung *coupe lyrique* where the *e* was syllabic). From the sixteenth century final *e* could occur at the caesura only if it was elided prevocalically, and began never to be counted when preceded by a tonic vowel (e.g. *vie* [vi:]). Even earlier, verb flexions in *e instable* (e.g. *-ent*) tended not to be counted as syllabic (hence 1 p.sg. imperfect *eie* < -EBAM early came to be written as monosyllabic *eis*, then *ois*, *ais*). Anomalies were avoided in classical versification by allowing such inflected forms to be used only at the end of a line (when they were counted as 'masculine' not 'feminine' rhymes).

One question we must ask is whether the atonic final *e* was ever lost, or whether it has remained, to the present day, a 'floating', 'weightless' element. As such, it would protect preceding consonants from, first, devoicing, then elimination, and it would lengthen preceding vowels, but be itself overtly realized only in certain sentence-internal positions.

Old French graphy inconsistently attests to the devoicing of word-final obstruents:

(58) *neuf* < NOVE, *grant* < GRANDE, *larc* < LARGU.

How far this represents canonically a prepausal pronunciation, we do not know: etymological graphy became more usual in later periods. We do have ample evidence by the sixteenth century that there was voicing of word-final voiceless obstruents in sentence prevocalic position, and erosion of all consonants in preconsonantal position. Before a final atonic *e*, however, Old French obstruents (after early voicing and opening) regularly remained intact. Thus, while a final devoicing rule was still operative in the relevant variety, the 'protective' *e* must have remained in place. Cases like *verte* [vɛʁt] < vĭrĭde have to be seen as morphologically conditioned, with 'feminine *e*' added to the Old French masculine form with a devoiced final consonant.

In some regional varieties devoicing does affect word-final consonants after fall of the *e*: Picard [saʃ] *sage*, and even [vãt] *vend(re)*. The [ʒ] > [ʃ] change is attested in the east central varieties, and in Paris, in the thirteenth century (cf. *frommache* for *fromage*). On the whole, though, devoicing may have been a transient stage in the regular loss of word-final consonants, for which we have evidence in graphy and rhyme from the thirteenth century. (From the seventeenth century, note, word-final consonants have frequently been restored, in spelling pronunciation, cf. 6.14.)

In Old French there is not infrequently hesitation about the use of the 'support' *e* after word-final consonant clusters:

(59) *salz* / *salze* 'willow' < SALICE; *home* < HOMINE / *dam* < DOMINU.

Doublets were useful to facilitate levelling out of syllable counts in verse, well into the modern period (cf. e.g. *avec/avecque*). The final atonic *e* also assumed an important morphological role as marker of the feminine, of the subjunctive, and of the *er* conjugation.

It is likely that in early modern French post-tonic *e* had been regularly lost in colloquial speech, but the influence of graphy and versification has kept its memory alive, and it can take on the guise of a paragogic [ø], to permit resyllabification of a word-final coda

consonant, and of a morphological marker: as such, it is in some
varieties rephonologized as a variant of /œ/. In protonic position,
however, the *e* was more robust, and has frequently been lexicalized
as /e/ or /œ/. The description of the results of this complex history
presents a challenge to the synchronic linguist, especially as there is
considerable variation over time, between individuals and between
social and regional groups.

At this point it is appropriate to say a word about so-called *h aspiré*,
which, in the few words in which it occurs, interferes with normal modern
French liaison and elision processes. It originated in Germanic loanwords
into Old French, where it was presumably pronounced as an aspirate,
unlike the purely graphical н of Latin, which had ceased to be pronounced
long before the Romance period. In most modern pronunciations it too is
silent, though it can block liaison and/or elision, with a good deal of
regional and individual variation. Already in the sixteenth century we
learn from commentators that it had fallen out of use for many speakers,
but it persists today in some marginal regional uses—for instance, in
Normandy, Brittany, in east France, and in some Canadian varieties. In
the prestige varieties early in this century it still could be heard as a slight
aspirate (or as a glottal stop or even as [ɥ]) in some words, but today it
would be regarded as un-French by most speakers. It is assumed that its
maintenance was due to the efforts of linguistic arbitrators, who bemoaned
the negligence of those who confused, for instance, *les héros*, with *les zéros*.
Some new loanwords, especially from German and English (cf. *le hard*
'hardware', *le hip* 'the hippy') have been endowed with the *h*, though liaison
and elision is rarely consistently practised in all derivatives. Note, however,
that in *verlan* vocalic word-initials are invariably treated as if they were
preceded by *h aspiré* ([laøk] not *[løk] = '*la queue*', [leuf] , not *[lezuf] = '*les
fous*' cf. Plénat 1995). In modern analyses, *h aspiré* has usually been
described as a consonant which lacks phonetic content, but some see it as
phonologically more closely linked to schwa (cf. *dors/dehors* [dɔʁ] /[dəɔʁ]).
Given the inconsistency of usage, it is probably better (with Tranel 1995*a*, *b*)
to describe *h aspiré* in terms of a lexically determined language-specific
anomaly, a cultural product of history, rather than to seek fruitlessly a
satisfactory analysis in terms of phonological universals.

6.11. *Loi de position*

Two interrelated changes that appear to affect mainly the modern
French period are to do with **compensatory lengthening** and **syllabic**

vowel adjustment. *Loi de position* is the name traditionally given to the latter process, for which we have evidence since the sixteenth century, by which it seems that the timbre of mid-vowels ([ɛ] / [e], [ɔ] / [o], [œ] / [ø]) is somehow dependent on accent and syllabic structure. When they are unaccented the lower (open, lax) vowels tend to raise (close, tense). When they are accented, there is a tendency for the higher vowels to appear in a free syllable, and the lower in a blocked syllable. This is described by structuralists in terms of **neutralization** of the distinction in this series, with the **archiphoneme** (written E, O, Ø) realized with a different timbre in tonic free and blocked syllables.

Neutralization of the mid-vowels is familiar from Spanish where [ɛ] and [ɔ] are found only in blocked syllables and are not phonemically distinct from the [e] and [o] of free syllables (cf. e.g. *perro* [ɛ] / *peso* [e]). In standard Italian on the other hand, the two series are kept distinct, in tune with etymological origin (cf. *pesca* 'peach' [ɛ] < PERSICA / 'fishing' [e] <PĬSC-). However there is a tendency to neutralization in regional Italian varieties.

In tonic free syllables in modern French we find only [o] (not [ɔ]) and in tonic blocked syllables only [ɛ] (not [e]). In other cases the *loi* does not operate without exception, in the standard language. Table 6.7 illustrates.

Note that even where there is apparent regular alternation within the limit of the word, this does not normally extend across word boundaries: thus the vowel of *chez* [ʃe] does not normally lower in *chez Albert*, though some speakers may pronounce *heureux ami* and *sot ami* as [œʁœzami] and [sɔtami].

The fact that there is a number of morphologically related forms which alternate between the use of the tense of lax vowel, according to whether it appears in a free or blocked syllable, strengthens the case for regarding the alternation as phonologically determined:

(60) *premier* [e] / *première* [ɛʁ], *sot* [o] / *sotte* [ɔt]·, *heureux* [ø] / *heureuse* [œz]

The alternation can be related to the **closed syllable adjustment**, discussed by synchronic generativists:

(61) *céder* [e] / *cède* [ɛ]; *lever* [ə] / *lève* [ɛ].

Note that the [e] in this type of alternation is historically of late origin: for the [ə] / [ɛ] / [e] alternation (cf. discussion of **apophony** in 7.8).

TABLE 6.7. *Loi de position*

Free tonic syllable in modern French

[o] *beau* < BELLUS [bo], *gros* < GROSSU [gro], *haut* < ALTU [o], *tôt* <
TOSTUS [to];

[ø] *ceux* < *cels* < ECCE-ĬLLOS [sø], *feu* < *fueu* < FŎCU [fø], *peut* < puet <
*PŎTET [pø], *peu* < PAUCU [pø];

[e] often: *pied* [pje] < PĔDE, *fée* < FATA;
 but, in the standard [ɛ] may be used especially for graphical *ai* (e.g.
 lait), and [e] can be distinguished from [ɛ]:
 dé < DATU [de] / *dais* <DĬSCU [dɛ], *épée* < SPATA [epe] / *épais* < *espeis*
 < SPĬSSUS [epɛ], *gué* < *WAD [ge] / *gai* < *WAHI [gɛ]; *porterai* [e] /
 porterais [ɛ].
 This distinction is not made by many speakers, who pronounce either
 [e] or [ɛ], depending largely on their regional origin.

Blocked tonic syllable in modern French

[ɔ] *corps* < CŎRPU, *or* < AURU, *corde* < CŎRDA; *cogne* < CŬNEAT, *grogne*
 < GRŬNNIT. But [o] before 'lengthening' consonants, [z], [v]:
 chose, cause < CAUSA, *rose* < ROSA, *pauvre* < PAUPER),
 though many speakers, especially from the South, use [ɔ] in these
 words. In the standard, in a number of words the [o] / [ɔ] difference is
 distinctive in blocked syllables:
 saule [sol] < Germanic *sahla* (influenced by *saus* < SALICE?) / *sol* [sɔl]
 < (15th c.) SŎLU; *heaume* [om] < Germanic *helm* / *homme* [ɔm] <
 HŎMĬNE; *rauque* [rok] < (13th c.) RAUCU / *roc* [rɔk] < (16th c.) RŎCCA
 (cf. *roche*); *hôte* [ot] < HŎSPITE / *hotte* [ɔt] < Germanic *hotta*.
 Some of the words with [o] are modern loanwords (cf. for instance the
 names *Paul* [pɔl] and *Paule*, a later introduction, [pol]). Others have an
 [o] regularly derived from [au] < ALᶜ: the graphy *au* whatever its origin
 is often interpreted as [o].

[œ] *neuf* [nœf] < *nuef* < NŎVE, *seul* [sœl] < SOLU, *meuble* < *mueble* <
 MŎBĬLE [mœbl], *club* [clœb];
 but in a few words some speakers distinguish [œ] from [ø] in blocked
 syllables, with the latter apparently derived from an earlier long vowel:
 jeune [ʒœn] < *JŎVENE / *jeûne* [ʒøn] < JĔJŪN-; *veulent* < [vœl] < *vuelent*
 < *VŎLUNT / *veule* [vøl] < *VOLU

[ɛ] *belle* [bɛl] < BĔLLA, *grec* [grɛk] < GRAECU, *mère* [mɛʁ] < MATRE, *maire*
 < MAJORE [mɛʁ], *tête* [tɛt] < TESTA, *dette* [dɛt] < DĒBITA .

Since initiation of discussion on the *loi de position* in the 1930s there has been dispute about the mechanisms involved, and about the role of syllabification, as distinct from that of a following consonant, in the contemporary language. A recent suggestion is that the determining factor is a difference in the structure of the **metrical foot** rather than in the type of syllable.

Bearing in mind these controversies, let us address the following questions about the history of the process:

1. What universal phonetic or phonological principles would account for the *loi*?
2. When did the *loi* start to operate?
3. Why has the *loi* not operated across the board, and why does it operate more completely in some areas than in others?
4. Is there any other way of explaining more satisfactorily, than by the *loi de position*, the same historical data?

The answer given to the first question is usually that vowel allophones in blocked syllables are phonetically shorter than those in free syllables and that shorter vowels tend to be laxer and lower than longer vowels. We therefore anticipate phonetic lowering in blocked syllables. But why should there have been phonological merger, especially in the mid-vowels, in French? Do we make appeal to the principles of economy of effort and to the notion of **functional load**? This term, recall, relates to the relative productivity of the distinction between two phonemes in threatened contexts, and hence to how much depends, in communicational terms, on preserving the distinction. A view, associated with Martinet's functional structuralism, is that where the functional load borne by a distinction is low, that distinction may be under threat, with the possibility of merger when other circumstances permit. Let us examine the relevant data from this point of view.

(*a*) The [œ] / [ø] distinction in blocked syllables affects only a few items (*jeune* / *jeûne*, *veulent* / *veule*) and is acknowledged to be virtually ineffectual. However in Normandy, east, and the centre, as well as in Canada, older speakers may preserve a length difference, and in Brittany, Paris, and the centre a timbre difference; in the south there is more often no distinction.

(*b*) The [ɔ] / [o] distinction in blocked syllables appears more stable: the identity of a fair number of items, usually with a different etymological history, seems to be dependent on it, though it is often lost in southern varieties. For *sotte* / *saute* etc. for most speakers in northern France there is only a difference of timbre, but for some there is a also difference of length. (*c*) The standard [ɛ]/[e] distinction in free syllables is unstable in most informal varieties, even though morphological identification may rely on the distinction. However in some cases (as in the contrast between the first person singular ending in the *passé simple ai* [e] and the imperfect *ais* [ɛ]), the distinction is of little relevance to the modern spoken idiom. In most of France (except perhaps Brittany, and parts of the east and the south-east) no overt phonetic difference is made between e.g. *piquet* / *piquait* / *piqué*, without this occasioning any apparent breakdown of communication. It is to be noted that a few speakers retain an older distinction between word-final *-é* and *-ée*, either as a length or a timbre difference.

Here there is no clear correlation between functional load and tendency to change. As anticipated, the [œ] / [ø] distinction, which seems to serve little function in the modern language, tends to be lost, but it is hard to see why the [ɔ] / [o] distinction is more resistant to change than the [ɛ] / [e] distinction: indeed the assymetry of the buccal cavity is thought to favour a great number of distinctive vowels at the front of the mouth than at the back. However the relationship between the *loi de position* and differences in vowel length does point perhaps to the operation of a general principle: we shall return to this in 6.12.

To the second question about dating, the traditional answer is that the *loi* started in the fifteenth or sixteenth centuries and is continuing to operate today, though it has been blocked by various conservative forces.

Today it seems, even if sporadically, to operate for modern loanwords, and for abbreviations and slang-words:

(62) [pœb] 'public house' (/ [pyb] 'advertising'), [kɔk] 'coke' (/ [kok] 'cocaine, coca-cola'), [agrɛg] from *agrégation*. In *verlan*, *nez* comes out as [zɛn], but *chaud* retains its original vowel, as [oʃ]; *femme* can be either [mœf] or [møf], and *juif* [fœʒ] or [føʒ].

Certainly the evidence for differences in the pronunciation of *e*, which were not correlated directly with etymological origin, is abundant in the commentaries of sixteenth-century writers. By the eighteenth century the distribution was more or less fixed; an earlier Parisian tendency to use [ɛ] in all tonic free syllables seems to have been replaced in the twentieth by the modern tendency to use [e].

The evidence for *o* is less clear, as early discussion (as by Tabourot in 1587) tended to focus on the [u] / [o] alternation, which divided the *ouistes* (originally the royal courtiers) from the *non-ouistes*. The pronunciation of *o* as [o] or [ɔ] in tonic blocked and protonic syllables, regarded as more learned, acquired prestige, though eventual adoption by the standard is rather arbitrarily distributed between items (cf. *poche / bouche, colombe / couleur*). By the eighteenth century the [u] pronunciation had lost favour, but the modern distribution of [o] or [ɔ] was not yet established: for instance Girard (in 1716) describes *sot* as having a 'short' vowel (in contrast to e.g. *hôte*), and Domergue (in 1795), a southerner, seems to suggest that *eau* and *bateau* are pronounced with [ɔ]. In classical loanwords an [oː] pronunciation originally prevailed in blocked syllables (as in *atome*), though in modern times [ɔ] is more frequent (*téléphone*).

For the central vowels [œ] / [ø], which result mainly from resolution of the earlier *eu* and *ue* diphthongs in tonic free syllables, rhyming together and spelt alike from the late twelfth century, we have no evidence of articulatory differences before the late seventeenth century and no reliable description till the nineteenth century. It is quite possible that there were length differences, which would not be reflected in rhyming patterns.

It is tempting to relate the vowel neutralization to the loss of word-final **feminine** *e* which had the effect of blocking tonic syllables in many words. However there is evidence of the merger of inherited [e] and [ɛ] in some phonetic contexts in tonic blocked syllables (i.e. where there had been no diphthongization), as well as in protonic syllables, from a much earlier period, probably starting first in the north. Thus especially before *r* and preconsonantal *s* there seems to have been merger, so that:

(63) *vert* 'green' vĭRĬDE and *ver* 'worm' < VĔRME, *creste* 'crest' < CRĬSTA and *teste* 'head' < TĔSTA,

could, by the thirteenth century, assonance together in some texts. Yet the merger could not have been general, as the two *e*s develop differently in the eastern and the western dialects. It is assumed that lowering of [e] spread to the centre from the northern varieties, so that an inherited [e] in a blocked syllable (e.g. *sec* < SĬCCU) came to be pronounced [ɛ]. In loanwords (like *thème*, or *scène*) [ɛ] was also usual.

The hypothesis that the operation of the *loi* is linked to loss of word-final atonic vowels (and consequent blocking of the tonic syllable) appears also to be countered by the chronological evidence for the central and back vowels: final schwa must have ceased to be pronounced, in some varieties at least, long before the modern distribution was reliably attested. Furthermore, in southern varieties, where final schwa *is* often pronounced, the *loi de position* seems to operate more consistently than in the standard.

We note the evidence for differentiation in Toulouse French at the beginning of the nineteenth century:

(64) [ʃɔdə] *chaude*, [famœzə] *fameuse*, (but [mo] *mot*),

where there was lowering without loss of the word-final vowel.

However, the contention that final schwa, even though it is not normally phonetically realized, can still be present in the lexical make-up of the modern language can be squared, in moraic theory, with some of the facts. We would have to assume a synchronic deletion rule affecting word-final schwa, with transfer of the mora attached to it to the stressed vowel, which could then be protected from shortening and lowering in blocked syllables (cf. 6.12 for vowel lengthening).

In answering the third question posed above (why has the *loi* not operated across the board?) appeal is usually made to the influence of graphy and schooling which has blocked the ongoing process. The implicit assumption behind the question is the Neogrammarian notion that a mechanical phonetic law will operate instantaneously and without exception. However, the exceptionless character of a diachronic sound-law becomes evident only when it has gone its full term, and, it is maintained, the *loi de position* is still active. To the suggestion that the tense high vowels were immune to a laxing tendency, reference is made to Canadian French varieties that have taken a further step, lowering high vowels in blocked syllables:

(65) *vite* / *vie* [vɪt] / [vi], *puce* / *pus* [pʏs] /[py], *coupe* / *cou* [kʊp] / [ku].

The low vowels ([a] / [ɑ]) are admittedly affected nowhere, but if the action of the *loi* is one of lowering (as distinct from laxing) in blocked syllables, then it would operate vacuously on the lowest possible series.

We note that in Haitian creole the mid-vowel distinctions are phonological, as evidenced by the following minimal pairs, in which there has been deletion of consonants that persist in standard French:

(66) [mo] 'word' / [mɔ] 'dead person', [sɔt] 'stupid' / [sot] 'go out', [bebe] 'baby' / [bɛbɛ] 'mute', [paʁetdevãm] 'don't stay in front of me' / [paʁetdevãm] 'appear before me' (Valdman 1978*b*).

Because of the manifest inconsistencies in the synchronic operation of the *loi*, some would reject any attempt at overall explanation of the phenomena described. Others will see the modern standard, not as a consistent rule-governed language, but as a coexistence of different systems: Valdman (1978*a*), for instance, describes the phenomena in terms of the 'levelling of clashing complex systems in flux'. One may very well ask how a child learning the French language can make anything of such apparent chaos: the answer could be that the anomalous forms have to be learned individually or as minor patterns, and that spelling plays a great part in imposing the accepted pronunciation.

This, however, does not provide any sort of answer to the questions about change in the past. It must be true that by the early modern period the mid-vowel system of French had re-arranged itself, compared with the original inherited system. The creation of new long vowels, through **compensatory lengthening**, and through **diphthong levelling**, was a salient feature of the run-up to the modern period: hence [ɛː] [œː] and [oː] could now feature in tonic syllables, both free and blocked. The fall of word-final consonants and atonic vowels, operating over a long period, must have been changing the syllabic structure of words. But what was the precise effect on the tonic vowels?

The suggestion than phonetic vowel length played a part in *loi de position* phenomena is attractive: the shorter vowel of the blocked syllable would, in this scenario, lower. The evidence that the modern homophony of *mer* (< MARE) and *mère* (< MATRE) followed a period in which they were pronounced respectively [mɛr] and [merə], does certainly suggest that the loss of final schwa was a relevant factor. Contemporary commentators certainly thought so: more modern theorists (e.g. Montreuil 1995) suggest that the moraic value of the final vowel, when deleted, is transferred to the preceding stressed vowel, which is thus lengthened. How this could result in lowering of the vowel is not clear.

We assume that the lowering of the tonic vowel in *mère* was independent of the lowering in, for instance, *crête* or *maître*, which occurred at an earlier period. The [ɛ] in *crête* (<CRĬSTA) would have lowered from [e] before compensatory lengthening, and in *maître* (< MAGISTR-) the [ai] sequence presumably levelled directly to an [ɛː], on which the phonological length had no raising effect.

With the back rounded vowels, however, compensatory lengthening did apparently trigger raising:

(67) *côte* [kot] 'coast' < CŎSTA (/ *cote* [kɔt] borrowed from QUOTA) ;
  saute [sot] < SALTA).

It is hard to explain this difference of treatment of back and front vowels in terms of universal processes. We do know however that raising of the back vowels was a feature of Old French, and we may see the possible entry, in the early modern period, of a new member into the back vowel series (with the velarization of [aː] to [ɑː], under the influence of compensatory lengthening) as a trigger for the raising of [ɔː] to [oː].

The tendency in older popular Parisian speech to front [ɔ] to [œ] (*C'est jeuli, le Mareuc!*) can conceivably be associated similarly with a rounding of [ɑ] to [ɒ] which used to be a feature of this variety.

In the front series, historical conditions were different: the *e* that developed from Latin tonic free A was not in the twelfth century associated in assonance and rhyme with the *e* in blocked syllables, but only with *e* sounds in Latin loanwords. How it was pronounced is unknown, but usually it is assumed that it was resolved from an earlier diphthong [ai] as [eː], possibly higher or longer than inherited [e] < Ē / Ĭ. If there was danger of confusion, this might have applied pressure for inherited [e] to shift lower to [ɛ]. In the sixteenth century the reflex of tonic free A eventually merged with the inherited *e*s but was differentiated from the newer long [ɛː].

Certainly what resulted was an overall simplification of the vowel system, though anomalies remain. To maintain that the system continues to progress towards greater simplification is nowadays unfashionable: the complex sociolinguistic state of the modern French language must baffle attempts at prediction for the future.

6. 12. Vowel Length

An unusual feature of the phonological history of French, linked, it would seem, with the *loi de position*, is the fleeting appearance of a phonological vowel length distinction in the late medieval and early modern period. In the sixteenth century commentators were divided on whether indeed there were vowel length differences (leaving aside feminine *e* which all agreed was short). Regional variation, but also, perhaps, a difference of perception, may account for the divergent opinions.

True, there were attempts, as in Italy, to establish a verse metrics on the Latin model distinguishing between heavy and light syllables and without rhyme, but some of its advocates were adamant that this was an art-form and not related to ordinary speech. Examples of this type of verse and the music to which it was set suggest that probably it is rhythmic stress rather than lexical vowel quantity that identifies the 'long' vowels in the metre:

(68)   —   ˅   ˅   —   ˅   —   ˅   —

   Vous   me   tu   ez   *si   douce ment*

   S'il   faut mourir   *mouron   d'amour.*

   Many of the early commentators talk at length about French long vowels, though often their descriptions suggest a timbre rather than, or as well as, a length difference (as in [ɔ] / [oː]). Vowel length seems to have carried some prestige, and classical loanwords were often endowed with a long tonic vowel.

   Although some speakers today do distinguish, rather inconsistently, long and short [ɛ] sounds:

(69)   *belle | bêle, faites | fête, renne | reine,*

there is ample evidence, from the nineteenth century, of levelling in favour of the short vowel. In other cases where a length distinction is attested for earlier times, today this persists mainly as a timbre difference, with erstwhile long mid rounded vowels higher than their short counterparts:

(70)   *pomme | paume*; *jeune | jeûne.*

As for the low vowel, there has been velarization of the long version in some varieties:

(71) *tache* [a] / *tâche* [ɑ],

but this difference has tended to disappear in modern pronunciation.

Phonological length can be distinguished from the phonetic lengthening of tonic vowels before single coda voiced continuants:

(72) *port, porc* [pɔːʁ] / *porte* [pɔʁt]; *prise* / *vite* [priːz] / [vit]; *rage* / *nappe* [raːʒ] / [nap].

Phonological vowel length as a feature of classical Latin, was lost in all the Romance languages. One source of its reappearance in French was from the syllabic contraction of vowels in hiatus:

(73) *câble* < *caable* (Norman) / *chable* (CATABOLA), *mûr* < *meur* (MATURU); *chaîne* < *chaeine* (CATENA), *vis* < *veis* (VĪDISTI), *-îmes* (-ĪUĬMUS), *coule* (CŪCŬLLA, cf. *cagoule*, a south-western form).

The use of the circumflex accent was not generalized until the eighteenth century and it was used as a diacritic to show that an etymological segment (especially 'silent *s*') had been lost. It came to be interpreted as a sign of vowel length and 'spelling pronunciation' (distinguishing, for instance,

(74) *goûte* (< GŪSTA), from *goutte* (< GŬTTA),

which were attested as identical in the eighteenth century) was advocated by some nineteenth-century elocutionists (cf. also 6.14).

Although this type of contraction is attested in spelling and in verse metre from the thirteenth century, there was still considerable variation in the sixteenth century. '*Les rencontres de voyelles . . . qui ne se mangent point*' (in Ronsard's words), may have been eschewed in verse between words, but word-internal bisyllabic vowel sequences (as in *mouettes, cria*, etc.) remained frequent. Vowel length was discounted in syllabic metre, and the syllabic status of vowel sequences remained uncertain: sixteenth-century poets were not averse to using variants to pad out or thin down their lines of verse.

In some cases, threatened contraction was averted and a reinforced hiatus survives to this day:

(75) *péage* < PEDATICU / *âge* < AETATICU.

There is also still fluctuation between bisyllabic and monosyllabic (glide + vowel) realization with some sequences:

(76) *lion* (LEONE), *fuir* (FUGERE), *viande* (VIVANDA), *oui* (HOC-ILLE).

Another source of early modern French vowel length was **compensatory lengthening**, after the vocalization of syllable-final consonants and glides:

(77) *autre* [oː] (< ?[ɔː] < [au] <[al]) *altre*; *feutre* [øː]< *feltre*, *bête* [ɛː] < [ɛs] *beste*; *faire* [ɛː]< [aj] (< FACERE).

The loss of coda nasal consonants also triggered lengthening of the preceding vowel, which nasalized: here it is the nasal quality that is regarded as phonologically distinctive and not the concomitant vowel length.

The result of these lengthening processes is said to have been the creation of phonological **bimoraic** vowels: in **autosegmental** terms these are single segments mapped onto two timing slots (cf. 6.8). In compensatory lengthening, with opening of a **coda** consonant, the nuclear vowel spreads to take over the position in the moraic tier that had previously been occupied by the coda. In syllabic contraction, a protonic nucleus amalgamates with a juxtaposed tonic to form a **heavy diphthong**. Features from the original tonic vowel then spread to the erstwhile protonic, resulting in a long vowel.

In some modern French varieties there is a diphthong where a long vowel appeared in the standard as a consequence of compensation or contraction:

(78) Canada (Beauce) [meit] *maître* (/ [mɛt] *mettre*), [paut] *pâte* (/ [pat] *patte*), [ʒøun] *jeûne* (/ [ʒœn] *jeune*).

It is possible that this is a conservative, not an innovative, feature in varieties that did not adopt the tense articulatory mode that characterizes the modern standard.

If we accept the hypothesis (Chene and Anderson 1979) that phonological compensatory lengthening occurs only when the system already contains phonologically long vowels, we must assume that in French the process was subsequent to that of syllabic contraction.

The simplest example of contraction in French is usually assumed to be in a bisyllabic sequence of protonic and tonic blocked identical vowels: the protonic vowel is said to have lost its syllabic but not its segmental status, forming a single long vowel in a heavy tonic syllable. However, even though the two vowels had the same graphical representation (usually as *a, e, u*), it is unlikely that they were phonetically identical. There is no good reason therefore to see this as a different process from the contraction of other bisyllabic vowel sequences. In the sixteenth century we still find alternative spellings, like *sel / seel* < sĭgĭllu (modern *sceaux* [so] is from the plural form with vocalization of the [l]). Names like *Baal* can still count as two syllables in metre.

The dating of contraction is hard to pinpoint, as we have seen. Compensatory lengthening accompanied, by definition, the loss of coda consonants and glides, about which we have more evidence. We can be certain, from the unanimous comments of contemporaries, that by the early sixteenth century preconsonantal word-medial [s] has been lost in Parisian French, though in some words (e.g. *triste*) it reappeared in spelling pronunciation (cf. 6.14). In word-final, especially pre-pausal, position, however, it continued to be pronounced by some speakers right through the seventeenth century. In spelling it survived into the eighteenth century perhaps as a diacritic marking vowel length.

Usually the loss of coda [s] is dated as far back as the eleventh century in some varieties and in certain contexts (cf. English loanwords *blame* from *blasme*, but *feast* from *feste*). By the twelfth century the *s* before a voiced consonant was ignored in rhyme, to be followed in the thirteenth by *s* before a voiceless consonant: however the effacement was never completed in some northern dialects, where sometimes it is replaced by *r*. In some early texts other graphies are used: *d* is frequent in Anglo-Norman texts and *h* is found in Walloon.

As for preconsonantal and pre-pausal *l*, it probably always had velar colouring in most French varieties, with vocalization to [u] as an expected variant. Certainly, sporadic spelling alternations are found at all periods.

A regional alternation with *r*, suggesting a 'light' rather than a 'dark' *l*, accounts for forms like *caviar* (< Italian *caviale*).

Early assonancing sequences afford no evidence of vocalization of *l*, but by the twelfth century it is attested in rhyme. In the early sixteenth century [ao], [au] are described as preconsonantal pronunciations of *al* (though in a few words, e.g. *calme*, the spelling pronunciation prevailed). Later in the century a monophthongal [oː] pronunciation was judged more prestigious. For *ol*, [ou] /[u] and [oː] seem to have alternated, invoking the *ouiste* dispute. As for *el* ([ɛl]), a complication is that a low vowel is assumed to have been inserted epenthetically between the original nuclear vowel and the vocalized [u]: the *eau* triphthong (as in *beaux* < *bels*) that resulted later levelled to [o] (probably via [oː], with a variant [joː], spelt *iau*, which persists regionally).

Metrical evidence in the thirteenth century suggests monosyllabic status for the similar *eaue* spelling (< AQUA). Here [ewə] (cf. the variant *eve*) apparently also developed an epenthetic vowel. *El* from Latin ĭL and AL was not affected in this way:

(79) *cheveux* < CAPĬLLOS, *pieux* (Picard) < PALOS,

but there is little evidence of vowel lengthening.

As for diphthongs deriving from *vowel + jod* sequences, rhymes attest levelling of *ai* to [ɛ] in the thirteenth century, though [ɛj] was found in some contexts in the standard until the late seventeenth, and in northern dialects [aj] persisted longer.

The upshot is that it is far from clear that syllabic contraction chronologically preceded compensatory lengthening in French; variation persisted over a long period, but, if anything, opening of medial coda consonants happened earlier than contraction of vowels in hiatus. Moreover it is not certain that vowel lengthening regularly resulted from loss of coda consonants.

Another complication is that the Old French diphthongs that derived from tonic stressed vowels did not, when levelled, result in long vowels. Therefore we assume that they were not necessarily, at the time of levelling, **heavy diphthongs**. Here we can contrast *ie* and *oi* which result today in a two segment *glide + vowel* sequence, where the glide forms part of the syllable onset:

(80) *ciel* [sjɛl] (< CAELU), *moi* [mwa] (< MĒ),

and monosegmental *eu* and *ei*, *ai* (before a nasal) in which there is no evidence of lengthening of the vowel:

(81) *peu* (< PAUCU), *pleine* (< PLĒNA), *laine* (< LANA).

Difference in vowel timbre can here be accounted for by the *loi de position*.

Yet some of these diphthongs regularly fell together with the later formed diphthongs originating from *vowel + glide* sequences, and they underwent the same later developments, but without lenghening. Thus the the nucleus of *moi* does not differ from that of *noix* (< NŬCEM), *moite* (< MŬSTEU) or even *moelle* (< MEDŬLLA). Worse still, early modern French *eu* could end up as [œ] or [ø], not only in *cheveu* and *peu*, but also in formerly bisyllabic *heur* (< AUGŪRIU) and *feu* (< FATŪTU), where syllabic contraction should have produced [yː] (as in *sûr* < *seur*).

This latter type of variation was frequent enough in the sixteenth century for [yː] to be used conventionally for any graphical *eu* in *rimes chartraines* (implying that this was a western pronunciation, from Chartres).

To discern a clear line of phonological development in the complex and contradictory information we have about modern French is no easy task, not least because speakers themselves had strong perceptions about what the language *should* be like. There seems to have been interaction of two modern developments— compensatory lengthening and *loi de position*—both of which involved some degree of phonetic duration shifts, which could be transferred into vowel timbre differences. These developments in turn interact with levelling of diphthongs and with final vowel and consonant **truncation**. This last process, which seems to have been completed by the end of the seventeenth century, had particularly important repercussions on the morphological system. Subsequent **morphologization** of phonological features may help explain apparent anomalies.

Note that in varieties where phonological vowel length persists in blocked syllables, as in some Quebec usage (Montreuil 1995), it is most usually associated with vowel quality distinctions.

Whether vowel length distinctions are or have been phonological in modern French is possibly a pseudo-problem. In some varieties there may be a fairly consistent phonological distinction; in others, not. The standard picks and chooses between variants rather at random: the notion of vowel length seems to have been emblematic at the time of standardization (probably because of Latin), and grammarians may have exaggerated its importance in French, elevating a contextual feature to an abstract ideal. In the long run, language users trim off such superfluous decoration, so that today vowel length distinctions as such are not part of most French speakers' internalized system, though earlier contextual lengthening is reflected in differences of vowel quality. Viewed *sub specie aeternatis* the introduction and demise of vowel length was a blip in the history of French which might have been overlooked if it had occurred in a period when documentation was less abundant and interest in language less intense.

6.13. FRENCH *R*

One change in the modern language which attracts attention is that which affected the character of the *r* sound. In the modern French standard *r* is articulated at the back of the mouth. The exact articulatory position varies—hence the different designations **dorsal**, **uvular**, **velar**, **pharyngeal**, or in non-technical usage *grasseyé*. In some varieties it can be **trilled** ([ʀ]), but usually it is a **voiced constrictive** ([ʁ]). In some contexts it can be a **devoiced fricative**: in 'vulgar' Parisian usage there is low voiced pharyngeal constriction without friction.

Back pronunciation of *r* is often cited as an areal feature of a swathe of north-western Europe, which may derive from the articulatory habits of the prehistoric inhabitants, from similar genetic proclivities or from spread from a prestigious centre (like Paris).

Some regional French varieties still use an apical *r* that can be trilled or **flapped**, but this pronunciation is today mainly used by elderly, rural speakers. We assume that in older French the apical *r* was normal, as in most other Romance languages and, presumably, in Latin. The acceptance of the back pronunciation in all positions into the prestige French norm seems to have been completed at the Revolutionary period.

However it may be that the back pronunciation for 'strong' *r*—in initial position and when **geminate**—may be older. Differentiation between 'strong' [rː] and 'weak' [r] is found elsewhere in Romance— in standard Spanish for instance the former is strongly trilled but the latter is a light flap, while in some American Spanish, Portuguese, and Occitan varieties the former is a uvular trill or velar fricative while the latter is **dental**.

In older French there is ample evidence, from rhymes, of the attrition of syllable-final *r*, and by the seventeenth century word-final *r* was regularly lost—though frequently restored in spelling pronunciation (cf. *aimer* [ɛme] / *finir* [finiʀ]). Moreover from the sixteenth century we have anecdotal evidence about the pronunciation of intervocalic *r* as a voiced (dental?) fricative or sibilant (*Pazi* for *Paris* etc.), still found in Central dialects, where [ð] or [z] persists. Remnants of this process in the modern standard are found in forms like:

(82) *chaise* / *chaire* < CATHEDRA, *bésicles* (earlier *bericles* < a derivative of BERYL).

We may speculate that the fricative sounds originally involved some retroflexing of the tongue tip, as is suggested by the sporadic lowering of preceding mid vowels under their influence.

The changes that seem here to have occurred in French are:

1. *phonetic*: the trilled 'strong' *r* 'backed' in regional varieties, which then acquired some prestige in Paris;
2. *phonological*: perhaps as a reaction against the tendency to attrition of intervocalic and syllabic final *r*, there was merger between the 'strong' and the 'weak' *r*, which contrasted only in intervocalic position:

(83) *mari* / *marri, guère* / *guerre*).

Thus the back *r* penetrated to all positions in the word, perhaps aided by spelling pronunciation.

But when did this happen? Commentators from the sixteenth to the mid-eighteenth century leave us in no doubt that the /r/–/rː/ contrast existed at that time, but in some varieties merger was already adumbrated. In central regions the threat of the potentially more significant confusion between intervocalic [r] and [z], as in:

(84) *père* / *pèse, frère* / *fraise*,

may have hastened the merger. From mid- and late seventeenth-century comments we know that Parisians tended to pronounce *père* as *perre* etc., though such habits were stigmatized. The phonetics lesson in Molière's *Bourgeois Gentilhomme* suggests a fully trilled apical [r], but no reference is made to position within the word: '. . . *en portant le bout de la langue jusqu'au haut du palais, de sorte qu'étant frôlée par l'air qui sort avec force, elle lui cède, et revient toujours au même endroit. . .*'

The use of apical *r* in (early colonized) Canadian maritime varieties but of back pronunciation in (later colonized) *québécois* points either to a change in French usage during the seventeenth century, or to a difference of regional provenance of immigrants. In most creoles the *r* sound falls altogether or is realized as [w], suggesting that it was not a rolled apical *r* that entered these languages in the seventeenth century. This type of pronunciation also enjoyed some prestige (among the *inc'oyables*) in France in the early nineteenth century, when the dreaded R-word (Revolution) was shunned in fashionable society.

Our evidence suggests that some Parisian speakers had already in the seventeenth century adopted, at least in some contexts, a back articulation of *r*, often described as lax or effeminate, perhaps by importation of regional usage. But we have no clear description of this type of pronunciation before the nineteenth century, when it acquired prestige and began to oust other varieties. Nor have we any agreed phonetic explanation of how the back pronunciation was introduced. Delattre sees it as related to a general change in articulatory modes in the early modern period: in the '*mode tendu*', anticipation of the tongue position of the following vowel would inhibit the free use of the tip of the tongue required in an apical trilled *r*. Vibration might thus be transferred to the back of the mouth. By contrast, Straka views the change as an effect of weakened articulation, when the speaker fails to produce the characteristic vibration with the tongue tip, but succeeds in producing a similar acoustic effect by vibration of the uvula or the softer dorsal regions.

6. 14. Spelling Pronunciation

In the modern period, since the seventeenth century, the influence of graphy on pronunciation has been marked, as is to be expected in a society where literacy has become widespread. Usually 'spelling pronunciation' is not systematic, and affects only some of the words that are graphically similar. Probably the most frequent phenomenon is in the articulation of 'silent letters'—as with the [p] in *cheptel, prompt, sculpteur.* This is particularly common with word-final voiceless consonants, which were deleted in the spoken language by the seventeenth century, but were retained in the graphical form, and often restored in pronunciation, as in:

(85) *net, sept, cep, cinq, août, marc, porc, tabac, dot, coq, neuf, œuf.*

Another frequent pronunciation, in this case obviously hypercorrect, is to pronounce any vowel marked with a circumflex accent as long, even with vowels that were regularly attested as short in the eighteenth century, like [i], [y] and [u]:

(86) *abîme, dîne, île, brûle, flûte, croûte, goûte.*

Sometimes a regular sound-change appears to be reversed, because it has not been registered by the graphy—as with the intervocalic clusters *cr* [ɡʁ], *cl* [ɡl], now pronounced [kʁ], [kl] in

(87) *secret, reine claude* (but cf. *second* [səɡɔ̃]).

Another not dissimilar case is the restoration of an [ɛ] in place of the [ɑ] that resulted from lowering in the (prevocalic) sequence *en*, in:

(88) *hennir* (< HĬNNĪRE), *ennemi* (< ĬNĬMĪCU), *étrenne* (< STRĒNA),

although *femme* (< FĔMINA) retains the lowered vowel.

Certain graphical conventions have also led to misreadings: thus an *e* following a *g* is seen as indicating the pronunciation [ʒ], not [ɡ], so that a word like *gageure*, originally [ɡaʒœʁ] is now pronounced [ɡaʒyʁ]. On the other hand, before *i*, a *u* following *c* or *g*, signalling that it is pronounced [k] or [ɡ], is assumed to be itself pronounced, as [ɥ], in:

(89) *anguille* [ɑ̃ɡɥij] (< ANGUĬLLA), *linguistique* [lɛ̃ɡɥistik].

Similarly an *i* in the *ign* graphy for [ɲ] is read as attached to the preceding vowel so that for [aɲ], is pronounced [eɲ] in the name *Montaigne* (/ *montagne* < MONTANEA), and for [oɲ] we have [waɲ] in :

(90) *témoigner* (< TESTIMŌNI-ARE), *poignet* (< PŬGN-), but *oignon* [oɲɔ̃] (< *ŬNIONE).

Doubtless in these former two cases, the influence of *témoin* and *poing* was decisive (cf. 6.8).

The *ill* graphy for [ʎ] (> [j]) also caused confusion, so that from the seventeenth century we have evidence of *anguille* pronounced as [ãgiʎ], for [ãgil] and, from the nineteenth, of *vaciller* (< VACILLARE), *scintiller* (< SCINTILLARE) as [vasije], [sẽtije], though *ville* (< VILLA) remains as [vil].

FURTHER READING

On phonology: Goldsmith 1995, Hooper 1976, Kenstowicz, 1994, Trask 1995.

On phonological change in general: Chen and Wang 1975, Eckert 1991, R. D. King 1967*a*, *b*, 1969*b*, Kiparsky 1988, Koerner 1982, Labov 1972, 1994, Martinet 1955, Posner 1961*a*.

On French phonology: Delattre 1966, Durand and Hintze 1995, Durand and Lyche 1994, Fouché 1933, 1936*a*, *b*, Grammont 1914, Klausenburger 1994, Koschwitz 1893, Lyche 1994, Martinet 1945, 1958, Martinon 1913, Passy 1886, 1887, Rousselot and Laclotte 1899–1902, Straka 1952*a*, 1979*b*, 1990, Tranel 1981, 1987, Walter 1977, 1982.

On phonological change in French: Carton 1974, Fouché 1952–69, Haudricourt and Juilland 1949, Herslund 1976, Klausenburger 1974*b*, 1985, La Chaussée 1977, Lesaint 1890[3], Martinet 1985, Millet 1933, Morin 1989, 1993, 1994*a*, Pope 1934, Posner 1974, 1976*b*, Rosset 1911, Straka 1979*b*, 1981, 1985, Thurot 1881–3, Tranel 1981, Walter 1989*b*, Zink 1986.

On chronology: Posner 1979, Straka 1953.

On phonetic modes and prosody: Allen 1973, Burger 1957, Delais 1994, Dell 1984, Elwert 1965, Garde 1968, Grammont 1908, Guiraud 1970, Hannahs 1995, Klausenburger 1970, 1974*a*, 1985, Le Hir 1956, Lote 1949–95, P. Martin 1987, Matte 1982, Montreuil 1994, Pensom 1993, Pulgram 1965, 1970, 1975, Scott 1986, Selkirk 1982, Straka 1964, Suchier 1963[2], Wenk 1983, 1987, Wenk and Wioland 1982, Wexler 1964, 1966, Zwanenburg 1965.

On nasalization: Chen 1972, Hajek 1993, 1997, Maeda 1993, Matte 1984, Y.-C. Morin 1983*a*, 1994*b*, Posner 1971, 1974, van Reenen 1985, 1987, 1988*a*, *b*, Rochet 1976, Schane 1968, Tranel 1981.

On palatalization: A. Burger 1955, Calabrese 1993, Clements 1976, Dauzat 1927–8, Densusianu 1900, Gamillscheg 1940, Meyer-Lübke 1925, 1936, Posner 1979, Ringenson 1922, Straka 1965*b*, Wilkinson 1980.

On l mouillé: Baddeley 1989*a*, Chaurand 1989, Pasques 1989, Straka 1981.

On palatal u: van Deyck 1992, Tuaillon 1972.

On dipthongization and levelling: H. Andersen 1972, Hilty 1969, Leonard 1978, Posner 1966*b*, 1976*b*, Purschinsky 1980, Schürr 1970, Spore 1972.

On liaison: H. Andersen 1986, Ashby 1981*b*, Delattre 1966, Green and Hintze 1990, Klausenburger 1994, Morin 1986*a*, 1987, 1992*b*, Schane 1974, 1978, Tranel 1990, 1995.

On mute e: Azra and Cheneau 1994, Basbøll 1994, Delattre 1966, Klausenburger 1994, Martinet 1969*a*, Martinon 1913, Y.-C. Morin 1979, 1987, 1989, Plénat 1995, Pooley 1994, Sampson 1980, Spence 1982, Tranel 1995*a*, Watbled 1991.

On the loi de position: van der Bussche 1984, Delattre 1959, Fouché 1935, McLaughlin 1983*a*, *b*, Morin 1983*a*, 1986*b*, 1991, Morin *et al.* 1990, Rochet 1982, Spence 1988, Straka 1981, Tranel 1985, 1995, Valdman 1978*a*.

On vowel length: Bichakjian 1986, Chene and Anderson 1979, Clements and Keyser 1983, Hayes 1989, Hock 1986, Hyman 1985, Montreuil 1995, Y.-C. Morin 1985, 1989, 1992*a*, Y.-C. Morin and Dagenais 1989, Y.-C. Morin and Desaulniers 1991, Y.-C. Morin and Ouellet 1991, Seklaoui 1989, Straka 1959, Wetzels and Sezer 1986.

On French r: Delattre 1944, Leonard 1965, Lozachmeur 1976, Martinet 1962, Posner 1976*b*, Reighard 1986, Straka 1965*a*.

On spelling pronunciation: Buben 1935, Straka 1981.

7

Morphological Change

7.1. MORPHOLOGY

It is claimed that the term **morphology** was coined by Goethe for the study of living forms. Its use in linguistics for the form of words dates from the middle of the nineteenth century. **Inflectional** morphology is usually distinguished from **derivational** (word-formation).

In this chapter I shall consider only the former, as the latter was discussed under lexical innovation (4.7).

Inflection (or **flexion**), we recall, is a metaphor that suggests the bending of the end of the word, according to its form-class or **category**, to enable it to hook into the sentence structure.

For most laymen **grammar** (originally to do with written form) is identified with morphology, as distinct from **syntax**, the way words are disposed within a sentence. This perception is a heritage from the Graeco-Latin tradition, which placed most emphasis on inflectional morphology—verb **conjugation** and nominal and pronominal **declension**. This was only to be expected in descriptions of highly **synthetic** Indo-European languages, in which the function of the word within the sentence is signalled largely by changes in the form of the word. A non-inflected language is consequently often regarded as 'without grammar': in the Middle Ages, Latin was regarded as the grammatical language, of which the Romance vernaculars were only pale shadows.

At the birth of comparative philology, with August von Schlegel, a distinction was drawn between **synthetic** languages, with inflections, **agglutinative** languages—where grammatical functions and categories are denoted by separable elements affixed to the word—and **analytic**, or **isolating** languages which use syntactic, rather than morphological, devices to show relationships between free-standing words. This morphological **typology**, further refined, is still useful, and finds its place in the study of language change. The obvious way in which many Indo-European languages have over time simplified their inflections is seen by some as a sign of progress, by others of decay.

Schlegel suggested that the maintenance of a complex inflectional system required effort and discipline and that loosening of social and institutional bonds allowed free rein to natural drift towards simplification. French is the Romance language which has moved furthest along the road to analytic structures, if we except the creoles which have virtually lost all signs of inflections. However, as we shall see, some see a **drift** from analytic to agglutinative to synthetic as part of a **cycle**, that builds morphology over time.

The morphology of a language is traditionally regarded as its scaffolding, its most durable and identifying feature, compared with labile phonology and ever-changing lexicon. Thus traditional comparative philology will place emphasis, in genetic classification, on **bound** forms with grammatical function, rather than on **free** forms (individual words) with lexical meaning. The recognition that this attitude privileges the Indo-European languages led to the structuralist description of the meaningful units of a language in terms of **morphemes**, abstract units of form-meaning, grouping together concrete **(allo)morphs**, just as **phonemes** group together **(allo)phones**.

How the sound level maps on to meaning level was to remain a bone of contention: some established an intermediate **morphophonological** or morphonemic representation, which became, to all intents and purposes, the underlying **systematic phonemic** representation of generative phonology.

Whereas morphology had represented the most important part of grammar in traditional and structuralist models, for generativists it has taken second place to syntax, and indeed for many it has no separate existence as a linguistic level—being merely part of phonology, of syntax, or of lexical representation. Languages like French, which retain some inherited inflections, still can, to some extent, be described adequately in a traditional **Word-and-Paradigm (WP)** way—which lists differently inflected versions of the same word in a **paradigm**. A similar model has been called **a-morphous** (not 'without form', but 'without morphs').

Most recently, morphology has come into its own again, if only as a language-specific trammel on Universal Grammar. Inherited lexical and morphological quirks may affect the workings of Universal Grammar, in that they may induce differences in **parameter-setting**.

The disagreement about what morphology is reflects in discussion of how morphology changes. For the Neogrammarians, change as such stemmed from unconscious phonetic shifts; speakers are of course aware of the meaning level of language and so we expect morphology to be more stable. But the blind workings of sound-change disrupt the morphology, by distortion and erosion of overt morphological marking. Restoration or renewal of phonological cues of grammatical function is achieved by analogical reformation: thus 'irregular' paradigms will be regularized and there will be moves to greater iconicity or transparency in the matching up of grammatical form and function. **Analogy** is thus the countervailing force to sound-change: regularity in one is the source of irregularity in the other.

Apart from analogy, most historical linguistics treatises have little to say specifically about morphological change. Usually it is lumped together with syntactic change (as **morphosyntax**), as similar grammatical functions may be filled in the same language at different times, or in different varieties, by morphological or by syntactic processes. Traditional philological works treat morphology as a corollary of phonology. Structuralists, on the other hand, regard morphology in terms of tightly knit systems, each composed of a closed set of items which can undergo seismic change, once a weak link has been broken. Generativists are ambivalent about morphological change: most seem to view grammatical items as no more than rather idiosyncratic lexical items (dominated by functional categories), whose phonological make-up may be complex. Changes come from the syntax, the lexicon or the phonological component of the grammar, but there is little that can be labelled morphological change as such. It is the Natural Generativists, who pay more attention to surface manifestations of grammatical functions, who have shown most interest in morphology, synchronic and diachronic.

I have suggested (3.15) that morphology is more resistant to change than other levels of language, as it represents a fixed formalized packaging of certain functional features that are obligatorily expressed in a specific language. The learner, in the acquisition process, grasps at quite an early stage the idea of morphological patterning, as is revealed by the commonly observed analogical forms of child language, when it is beginning to approximate to adult language. The acquisition of morphological form thus may be something for which the *faculté de langage* is particularly suited, so that reanalysis is less frequent here, than with syntax or phonology. Analogical levelling is, in this view, an over-learning process which imposes structure where, by accident or inertia, anomalies persist in the inherited language.

In the rest of this chapter I shall look at parts of French morphology that cast light on more general questions of change. On the whole it is true to say that French has conserved more traces of inherited inflection in the verb system than in the nominal system, but even there the marking of **person**, or of **tense**, **aspect**, and **mood (TAM)** has undergone considerable transformation over time. As for the pronominal and determiner systems, French has created in the modern period new structures that look very different from those of past eras.

I shall divide the more detailed discussion into two parts: A. verbal morphology (7.4–14); B. nominal and pronominal morphology (7.15–7.19). First we shall look again at some general questions raised in Chapter 3.

7.2. Morphologization

Sometimes a phonological rule is not conditioned solely by phonological factors (as in Neogrammarian sound-change), but is operative only when some morphological features are present. The term **morphologization** is used when, historically, an erstwhile phonological rule has ceased to operate automatically, but when its effects remain as relics in certain morphological contexts. One oft-quoted example in French concerns nasalization: in the modern language the phonological distinction between nasal and oral vowel becomes a morphological marker of grammatical gender (as in *bon/bonne*).

This is sometimes described in terms of **rule inversion**, where a rule of the type:

$$A \rightarrow B \text{ (with phonological conditioning)},$$

gives way to:

> B → A (with morphological conditioning).

What has happened is that a significant number of lexical items in one morphological class have retained the earlier alternation between vN and ṽ. What was originally an automatic phonological alternation has been lexicalized, but the still discernible patterning allows analysis in terms of a morphological rule, starting from the new underlying lexical form. Thus, we have claimed, the regular Old French assimilatory nasalization process:

(1)   v → [+nasal] / _N (/bon/ → [bõn]),

is not a feature of the modern standard. Nasal vowels are phonologically distinct from their oral counterparts, but are not normally followed by a nasal consonant.

Yet gender alternation between a nasal vowel and an oral vowel + nasal consonant sequence, shows a minor regularity. Some lexically marked feminine forms with an oral vowel followed by an overt nasal consonant can be derived from a masculine base with a nasal vowel, by means of a morphological rule:

(2)   ṽ→[−nasal] / _N [+fem]   (/bõn/ → [bɔn]).
                              [+adj]

Thus, the earlier nasalizing phonological rule has become **morphologized** as a denasalizing rule.

The term **morphologization** is also used to describe a type of **grammaticalization**, by which an independent element becomes a bound affix.

7.3. GRAMMATICALIZATION

Grammaticalization (sometimes **grammaticization**) is a term used for the process by which an autonomous 'lexical' item becomes a (closed set) grammatical item (cf. 3.15). Most strikingly, it can describe the process by which a free word can become a **bound** form, that occurs only as part of an autonomous word (also called **morphologization**). At the extreme it becomes an **inflectional affix** which has no independent existence but which signals the grammatical relationships of its host.

The French example usually cited of extreme grammaticalization is the formation of the synthetic **future** (7.13) from an erstwhile periphrasis:

(3) *je partirai* < PARTIRE + HABEO 'I have to go'.

Here the erstwhile autonomous verb HABERE 'to possess' has been **semantically bleached** so that today it provides merely the inseparable inflection of the future stem. The separate elements of the more recent *GO*-future (cf. 5.9), as in *je vais partir* (attested since the sixteenth century), still retain a degree of syntactic autonomy. But there has evidently been a loss of the notion of movement that is normally associated with *aller*.

Some other examples will be discussed in Chapter 8, under the heading of syntax.

In this chapter I shall refer to the way in which a new grammatical category of **determiner** was created during the history of French (7.18–19), by differentiation from etymological pronouns. The **definite article** has already been discussed under semantics (5.11); it can be argued that its historical relationship to the third person pronouns is a morphological one. However the whole question of the link between the articles and the clitic pronouns will here be treated under syntax (8.10–12).

The dictum 'Today's syntax is tomorrow's morphology' reflects the interaction of the two traditional grammatical levels. The *passe-partout* term **morphosyntax**, now coming back into fashion, is convenient to express the way in which sometimes more morphological and sometimes more syntactic devices are used to convey similar functional and semantic signals. From a historical point of view this is metaphorically described in terms of a never-ending cyclical movement between **synthesis** (word-based morphological marking) and **analysis** (sentence-based syntactic marking). The implication is that there is constant flux: however, it is noteworthy that morphological markers tend to be comparatively stable, and even outlive their functional usefulness. They can even acquire new functions by the process of **exaptation** (3.16).

I would argue that grammaticalization is a means by which communities maintain a certain degree of linguistic stability, threatened by the variations of speech acts and communicative interaction, but always held within the limits prescribed by the nature of language itself.

A. VERB MORPHOLOGY

7.4. IRREGULAR VERBS: SUPPLETION

Most French verbs are morphologically **regular**, by which we mean that any form of the verb can be predicted if we know any one form. Verbs are traditionally classified according to their infinitive form, which in French usually derive by regular sound-change from their Latin etyma:

(4)   *porter* < PORTARE, *devoir* < DEBĒRE, *prendre* < PREHENDĔRE, *dormir* < DORMĪRE.

These forms are usually more differentiated than other parts of the verb and can be misleading as a predictor of other forms: for instance *ir* is used for irregular verbs like *sortir, dormir*, as well as regular verbs like *finir*. In this latter case phonological alternation was avoided diachronically by the incorporation of the so-called **inchoative** -SC- affix into forms of the present verb stem, so that the word-accent never fell on the original root:

(5)   FĪNISCO > *fenis* / FĪNĪRE > *fenir* / FĪNĪVIT > *fenit*.

The spread of [i] to the initial syllable, as in *finir* < *fenir*, where one must assume dissimilation of ī, dates from the fourteenth century: earlier Old French preferred *finer*, formed on the noun *fin*.

The two truly regular conjugations are the -*er* type and the *finir* type, which is today barely productive (but cf. airport-speak *amerrir* 'to splash-down', by analogy with older (seventeenth-century) *aterrir* 'to land'). By far the greatest majority of French verbs belong to the -*er* conjugation, which is fully productive. Even within this regular conjugation, however, there is the minor (ir)regularity of **closed syllable adjustment**, which may be of a phonological, rather than a morphological, order (cf. 6.11).

Most French very common verbs, as well as some obsolescent verbs, are irregular: synchronically forms are **suppletive**, i.e. learned as separate items, rather than formed by rule. This is to be expected when the verbs are encountered early in the acquisition process. In the case of infrequently used verbs, on the other hand, mistakes are frequent in the anomalous forms, which may even be lost, as in **defective** verbs like:

(6)   *choir* < CADĒRE, *clore* < CLAUDĔRE, *traire* < TRAGĔRE.

However sometimes in the more frequent irregular verbs there is still limited patterning—so that, for example, *tenir* (< TĔNĒRE) has come to resemble *venir* (< VĔNĪRE). Generativists attempt to describe alternances in terms of synchronic (morpho)phonological rules (usually lexically determined), but probably these are not part of the acquisition process. However it is not unlikely that at the stage of language learning when analogical remodelling comes into play, young speakers devise their own idiosyncratic rules to account for anomalies. These are usually abandoned when schooling, or mockery, establishes a more conventional set of rules.

An example, recounted to me by Marcel Cohen, is of the young child who analysed the subjunctive form *vienne* / indicative *vient* as determined by a female subject on the pattern of *ancienne* / *ancien*.

Most of the modern suppletion arose originally from the action of sound-changes, but they can result also from analogical remodelling.

We shall be looking at some examples in following sections.

However, some of the suppletive forms are inherited, or come from the amalgamation of different lexical items into the same microsystem. The verb 'to be' offers illustrations of both processes. Thus

(7)   *suis, est, soit, sont, fut*

continue

(8)   SUM, EST, SIT, SUNT, FUIT,

while

(9)   *été, était, étant*

come from forms of STARE 'to stand' (Old French *ester*):

(10)   STATU, STABAT, STANTE.

Être and *serai* are assumed to be formed on an *ESSERE for ESSE, which may be influenced by SEDERE 'to sit', or, in the former case, by STARE.

Note that until the fourteenth century reflexes of the future ĔRO etc. continued to be used, as:

(11) *ier(t), iermes, ierent | er(t), ermes, erent.*

In thirteenth-century charters they were confined to northern texts, and then used relatively rarely.

The verb 'to go' also exhibits merger of three different verbs. ĪRE survives only as a future stem *irai* etc. (though in Old French derivatives like *suralleront* are attested). The present indicative follows a familiar template, with differentiated ending-stressed first and second person plural forms. Here, though, the stem-stressed forms derive from VADĔRE:

(12) Old French *voi | vai, vas | vais, va | vait, vont,*

whereas the ending-stressed:

(13) *allons, allez*

seem to come from an attested form ALARE, which some see as a reduction of AMBULARE. This *-er* conjugation set of forms has taken over most parts of the verb. In Old French the present subjunctive had three alternative forms. Two derived from *ALJAM etc.: surviving *aille* shows **palatalization** of the *l*, the other, assumed to be Norman and lost in the late Middle Ages, shows hardening of the jod (to a palatoalveolar?) in *alge, auge*. The remaining one, *voise*, apparently an analogical formation on *voi* (< *VAO for VADO), was still current at Vaugelas's time among '*le peuple de Paris*', but was condemned in legitimate language.

7.5. VERB-PERSON MARKERS

The history of marking of verb-person in French is the standard illustration of a possible synthetic → analytic → synthetic cycle. In Latin six verb-persons were marked fairly consistently by a final morpheme (though there was some fusion of functions—for instance, the ō of the first singular present indicative can signal ā conjugation class, present tense and indicative mood as well as person). In Old French the distinctions were obscured somewhat by sound-changes, but as Table 7.1 shows, in the present indicative at least there was still in principle a full set of differentiated markers (though where the verb root ended in *s* the first and second person singular (*finis*) were identical).

There was however conflict between the tendency to paradigm levelling and the preservation of person differentiation: devoicing of final consonants and frequent palatalization in the first person singular left this person form out of line. As early as the twelfth century a 'protective schwa' was being added in *er* conjugation forms (*dur* 'I last' > *dure*), allegedly by analogy with those forms where there was an off-glide from a final cluster (*porte*). This

TABLE 7.1. Verb-person markers

Present Indicative			*Present Subjunctive*		
Latin	**Old French**	**Modern French**	**Latin**	**Old French**	**Modern French**
1. -ō	∅	*-e, -s*	-M	∅, *-e*	*-e (sois)*
2. -S	*-es, -s*	*-es, -s*	-S	*-s, -es*	*-es (sois)*
3. -T	*-e, -t*	*-e, -t (va)*	-T	*-t, -e*	*-e (soit)*
4. -MUS	*-om, -ons*	*-ons (sommes)*	-MŬS	*-ons, -iens*	*-ions*
5. -TIS	*-ez, -iez*	*-ez (êtes)*	-TĬS	*-ez, -iez*	*-iez*
6. -NT	*-ent (ont)*		-NT	*-ent*	

EXAMPLES

1. LĔVO: *lief, je lève*; LAVO: *lef, je lave*; VENDO: *vent, je vends*; DĪCO: *di, je dis*; PLANGO: *planc, je plains*; *NASCO: *nais, je nais*; OPERO: *uevre, j'œuvre*; DŌNO: *doins, doing, duins, je donne*; DĒBEO: *dei, je dois*; AUDIO: *oi, [j'ouis]*; PLACEO: *plaz, je plais*; TĔNEO: *tieng, je tiens*; FACEO: *faz, fac, fach, je fais, fois*; *MORIO: *muir, moerc, je meurs*; COGĬTO: *cui(t), cuic, [je cuide]*; SEDEO: *sie, siec, je (m'as)sieds*.
2. PLANGIS: *plainz*; PLANGIAS: *plaignes*; DONES: *doignes, doinses, donges*.
3. VINCIT: *veint, vaint, il vainc*; VĔNIT: *vient*; VENIAT: *viegne*.
4. DĪCĬMUS: *dimes, nous disons*; FACĬMUS: *faimes, nous faisons*; VENIAMUS: *vegniens, que nous venions*; SAPIAMUS: *sachiens, que nous sachions*; SŬMUS: *sons, nous sommes (esmes)*.
5. FACĬTIS: *faites*; -ĒTIS, -ĪTIS > *eiz, -iz* (north); *-eiz* in future and past subjunctive, replaced by *-ez, -iez*.
6. HABENT: *ont*; FACIUNT: *font*. Dialectal forms: east *-et*; *-ient*, especially in imperfect (*estient*), pres. subj. (*pouissient*); *-ont* (as in future) especially in preterite (*trovont*); *-ant* esp. in past subjunctive (*deïssant* rhyming with *enfant*).

graphical *e* sometimes counted as a syllable in verse. In irregular verbs, and sporadically even in *er* verbs, the *s* of the second person singular was, from the twelfth century, being extended to the first person singular.

This was hindered somewhat in the sixteenth century by grammarians who maintained that such extension was improper, but Vaugelas in 1647 clearly thought that a *liaison* [z] could be used after, e.g. *je fais*. Even in 1704 the Académie advocated the use of *scay*, *voy* (for *je sais*, *je vois*), but by now this must have been merely a graphical recommendation, as in *fais*, *dis* the *s* was said to signal the lengthening of the vowel.

With final vowel and consonant **truncation** in the early modern period, the markers were further threatened. Already endings like *-ent* and the *-e* of the first person singular imperfect *-eie* < ĒBAM frequently failed to count as a syllable in verse, and the spelling *-ois* in the imperfect became general.

The result was that in most paradigms the singular forms and the third plural were identical. In the present indicative there was a distinction only where a consonant-final root marked the plural:

(14)   *doit* [dwa] / *doivent* [dwav], *lis* [li] / *lisent* [liz].

However, final *s* and *t* could still be used as *liaison* consonants, and, in any case, the first and second plural endings remained distinctive.

Conventional wisdom has it, however, that the erosion of the person endings accounts for the introduction of the quasi-obligatory use of the personal pronoun subject, and its cliticization to the verb. Moreover, it is maintained by some that in the modern language the clitic is fast becoming a true inflection. This is a question we shall look at under the heading syntax (cf. **pro-drop** 8.8).

We note that in creoles and some other 'advanced' French varieties, there is no morphological person marking, which is effected by the use of subject pronouns.

7.6. PLURAL VERSUS SINGULAR

In some irregular verbs the present indicative plural persons are distinguished from the singular by the use of a consonant-final root (cf. 7.9). There has also been a tendency to make a distinction, in some tenses, by having tonic endings for the plural, compared with the singular tonic roots. The first and second person plural normally are ending-stressed in any case, so it is only the third person plural that is in question. Tonic endings for this person are found in some irregular monosyllables:

(15) *ont, font, vont, sont,*

and in the future tense:

(16) *chanteront,*

where the ending is assumed to derive from the relevant *avoir* form (*AUNT for HABENT). This form (or *-ant* like the present participle ending?) extended in many non-standard varieties to other verbs. Western varieties sometimes level all the plural persons, distinguishing them by use of the singular clitic pronouns: the use of *je dirons* is often commented on by sixteenth-century grammarians, and there is ample evidence of generalized third person plural tonic endings in popular seventeenth-century speech, even in Paris. In the standard however, these tendencies were suppressed.

7.7. FIRST AND SECOND PERSON PLURAL

What is surprising, in view of the alleged analytic drift in the history of French, is the retention of distinctive endings for the first and second plural. More striking is the way in which these persons were standardized, as *-ons* and *-ez*, through most verbs and tenses. Only in the moribund preterite do we find the alternative *-mes*, *-tes* endings. The latter is still found in:

(17) *êtes, faites, dites,*

though the parallel forms to these last two:

(18) *faimes, dimes,*

disappeared during the twelfth century, leaving only *sommes* as a relic. We assume a development which retains some degree of stress on the ŭ of -MŬS:

(19) FACIMUS > ['fajməs], -ĀVIMUS > ['ɑ:məs].

Sommes < SŬMUS remains a puzzle: it appears from the twelfth century as a rival to regular *sons*, and we have to assume some complex analogical reformation.

The generalization of *-ez* is not problematic: as [ets] (> ? [eʦ]) it was the regular development of -ATIS, lexically the most widespread form. Regular *-eiz* and *-iz* (< -ĒTIS, -ĪTIS) are found in eastern varieties.

The origin of *-ons* is, on the other hand, baffling. Some suggest influence of the tonic *-ont* ending, some that of the *sons*, later replaced by *sommes*, and yet others a phonetic development like rounding of [a] by the following labial.

In thirteenth-century charters, the marker in present indicative was *-om*, *-on* etc., rather than *-ons*, in the south-west of the *oïl* territory, while in the imperfect indicative bisyllabic *-(i)iens* was preferred to *-(i)ions* in the east. Joinville, in the early fourteenth century, consistently used the *-iens* ending in the imperfect indicative, though he still often uses *-ons* in the present subjunctive.

What however is interesting is that French picks out these persons for special morphological treatment. This is to some extent paralleled by peculiarities in the function of these persons. The use of *vous* for polite address to single persons developed particularly in the late medieval and early modern period, though it was hotly combatted, as undemocratic and ungrammatical, during the Revolutionary era. It is to be noted that in some *cajun* French varieties of Louisiana, it is only with the polite form that the [e] ending is retained, whereas the familiar second plural is accompanied by a flexionless form, where the whole paradigm has been levelled.

As for the first plural, in the standard *nous* is both inclusive ('me and you') and exclusive ('me and him'): in some varieties the latter is designated by *nous-autres*. But it is also noteworthy that in popular speech the *nous* is very often replaced by *on* accompanied by a third person singular verb form (cf. 3.16).

7.8. APOPHONY AND ANALOGY IN THE PRESENT INDICATIVE PARADIGMS

Table 7.2 illustrates the complex interaction of sound-change and analogy in French present indicative verb-forms. The **diphthongization** of tonic stressed vowels in **free syllables** (cf. 6.8) meant that the root vowel in the present indicative paradigm could have different values, according to whether the accent fell on the ending (as in the

TABLE 7.2. Apophony in the Old French present indicative paradigm

(Representative stem-stressed forms are contrasted with ending-stressed forms. The modern forms are cited in brackets, with orthographical representation where appropriate and phonetic transcription with the clitic subject pronoun).

(a) Verb-roots in front vowels

Ě, AE

CRĚPO -AT	*crief, crieve,* (> *crève* [ʒəkʀɛv])	*crevez* ([vukrəve])
ABRĚVIO	*abriege* (> *abrège* [ʒabʀɛʒ])	*abregiez* (> *abrégez* [vuzabreʒe])
VĚNIO	*vien, vieng, ving* (> *viens* [ʒvjɛ̃])	*venez* ([vuvne])
SĚDEO, SEDET	*sie, siet/ sit* (> *sied(s)* [sje] cf. *asseoi(s/t)*[1]	*seyons* ([nusejɔ̃], cf. *assoyons*)
QUAERO[2]	*quier* (> *acquiers* [ʒakjɛʀ]	*querez* (> *acquérez* [vuzakeʀe])
PRĚCO	*pri, proi* (> *prie* [ʒəpʀi])	*preions* (> *prions* [nupʀijɔ̃])
NĚCAT[3]	*nie, neie, noie, naie* (> *noie* [inwa])	*neions, noions* (> *noyons* [nunwajɔ̃])
NĚGO	*ni, noi* (> *nie* [ʒni])	*neiez, neiiez* (> *niez* [vunije])
*IĚCTAT[4]	*giete, gete* (> *jette* [iʒɛt])	*gitez, getez* (> *jetez* [vuʒte])
APPĚLLO	*apele* (> *appelle* [ʒapɛl])	*apelez* (> *appelez* [vuzaple])
SĚMĬNAT	*seme* (> *sème* [isɛm])	*semez* ([vusme])

Ē, Ĭ, OE

CĒLAT	*çoile* (> *cèle* [isɛl])	*celez* ([vusle] cf. *recélez* [vursele])
SPĒRAT	*espeire, espoire* (> *espère* [ilɛspeʀ])	*esperez* (> *espérez* [vuzɛspere])
*EX-FRĪDAT[5]	*esfreie, esfroie* (> *effraie* [ilefʀɛ])	*esfreez* (> *effrayez* [vuzefʀeje])
DĒBO	*dei, doi* (> *dois* ([ʒdwa])	*devez* ([vudve])
PLĬCO	*plei, ploi* (> *plie* [ʒəpli], *ploie* [ʒəplwa])	*pleiez, ploiez* (> *pliez* [vuplije], *ployez* [vuplwaje])

TABLE 7.2. (cont.)

*MĬNO (for MĬNOR)	mein (mène [ʒmɛn])	menez ([vumne])
POENAT	peine ([ipɛn])	pener (> peiner [pɛne])
VĬGĬLAT	veille ([ivej])	veilliez (> veillez [veje])
DĬGNO	deing (> daigne [ʒdɛɲ])	deignier (> daigner [dɛɲe])

Ī

SCRĪBO	escrif (> écris [ʒekʁi])	escrivons, escrisons (> écrivons [ekʁivɔ̃])
RĪDEO	ri (> ris [ʒʁi])	riez ([rije])
FINĪSCO	fenis (> finis [ʒfini])	fenissez (> finissez [vufinise])

(b) Verb-roots in rounded vowels

Ŏ

ŎPĚRO	uevre (> œuvre [ʒœvʁ])	ovrez (> oeuvrez [vuzœvʁe])
PRŎBAT	prueve (> prouve [ʒəpʁuv])	provez (> prouvez [vupʁuve])
*PŎSSIO[6]	puis (>/ peux (ʒpɥi] / [ʒpø])	poez (> pouvez [vupuve])
PLŎVET[7]	pluet (> iplø])	ploveir (> pleuvoir [plœvwaʁ])
*MŎRIT[8]	muert (> meurt [imœʁ])	morez (> mourez [vumuʁe])
MŎRDIT	mort (> mord [imɔʁ])	mordez ([vumɔʁde])

Ō, Ŭ

PLŌRAT	plore, ploure, plure, (> pleure [iplœʁ])	plorez, plurez (> pleurez [vuplœʁe])
CŬRRIT[9]	cuert, queurt (> court [ikuʁ])	corez (> courez [vukuʁe])
NŌDAT	neue (> noue [inu])	noez (> nouez [vunwe])
TORNO	tor(n) (> tourne [ʒtuʁn])	torner (> tourner [tuʁne])

Ū

FŪMAT	*fume* ([ifym])	*fumez* ([vufyme])
CONDŪCĬT	*conduit* ([ikɔ̃dɥi])	*conduisez*[10] ([vukɔ̃dɥize])
NŪTRĬSCĬT[11]	*norrist* (> *nourrit* [inuʁi])	*norrissez* (> *nourrissez* [vunuʁise])
MANDŪCAT[12]	*manjue, mangue* (> *mange* [imɑ̃ʒ])	*mangiez* (> *mangez* [vumɑ̃ʒe])

(c) Verb-roots in A

LAVO	*lef* (> *lave* [ʒlav])	*lavez* ([vulave])
AMO	*aim* (> *aime* [ʒɛm])	*amez* (> *aimez* [vuzɛme])
*ADCAPTO	*achate* (> *achète* [ʒaʃɛt])	*achetez* ([vuzaʃte])
*ADCAPO	*achief* (> *achève* [ʒaʃɛv])	*achevez* ([vuzaʃve])

[1] *Asseois* etc. appeared in the 17th c., but were not in general use till the 18th. Forms like *assisons* are also found in the 17th.

[2] *Quérir*, a 17th-c. form of *querre*, is defective, but derivatives, like *acquérir*, retain all forms. Forms like *acquerissés* are also attested.

[3] The differentiation between *nier* and *noyer* (= 'to kill' then 'to drown') dates from the late Middle Ages.

[4] For IACTAT, a frequentative from IACĔRE.

[5] From Frankish *frida* cf. German *Friede*.

[6] Replacing classical PŎSSUM.

[7] For classical PLŬERE, some forms of PLOVERE are attested in Late Latin.

[8] For classical deponent MŎRITUR.

[9] *Courir* was used alongside Old French *corre, courre* from the end of the 13th c. till the 17th c. A form without geminate *rr* is assumed to account for the diphthongization in stem-stressed forms: one would expect the spellings *ou, eu*, but *ue* is also attested.

[10] The regular outcome *conduites* is not attested.

[11] Presumably from an inchoative form of NŪTRĪRE, though the outcome of the root vowel suggests a short Ŭ.

[12] The syncope of the vowel in the ending stressed forms suggests a short Ŭ, but the

first and second person plural, and certain infinitives) or on the root. Presumably as long as the difference was **allophonic** this presented little inconvenience to language users, but with the introduction of new loanwords and the interaction of other sound-changes this **apophony** within the paradigm must have

ceased to be transparent, so that the different forms would have to
be learned separately, rather than worked out by a rule of thumb.

With the reflexes of ī and ū, where there was no obvious
diphthongization, there was no graphical problem: the stems of
écrire and *fumer* retain the same vowel throughout the paradigm.
Similarly when the root-vowel was in a blocked syllable at the
relevant period, it did not diphthongize:

(20) *veiller* (< vĭgĭlare), *daigner* (< dĭgnare), *mordre* (< mŏr-
     dĕre), *tourner* (< tornare).

The pattern of paradigms in which there has never been root-vowel
alternation thus provided a template for analogical paradigm
levelling. Sometimes the levelling was effected on the model of the
stem-stressed forms, as in:

(21) *pleurer, peiner, aimer, œuvrer.*

Perhaps the singular persons were more familiar in these verbs: this
is almost certainly true of *pleuvoir* (*il pleut*). More often it was the
ending-stressed forms—perhaps on the model of the infinitive—that
provided the model, as in:

(22) *laver, courir, nouer, prouver.*

Occasionally lexical items are differentiated by the levelling procedure, thus:

(23) *nier / noyer, plier / ployer.*

A new cultural difference between *déjeuner* and *dîner*—the first and the
second main meal of the day—was highlighted in the early modern period by
specializing the stem-stressed form of dis-jejunare 'to break fast' ([de'jeun]
(> [de'ʒœn]) differently from the ending stressed ([diej'ne] > [diːne]).

Analogical paradigm levelling is to be expected if we assume a
tendency to match one lexical form with one meaning. In traditional
terms, sound-change has upset a systematic morphological relationship and analogical change seeks to re-establish one. But in French
today there is vowel alternation even in words in which Latin ĕ or ē
was in a blocked syllable at the time of diphthongization, like:

(24) *appeler* < appĕllare, *semer* < sēmnare < sēminare.

In Old French we have no evidence of alternation in such cases:
however, as we have seen, it is usually maintained that the atonic
graphic vowel *e* was early reduced to a schwa, whereas the tonic

vowel retained its full pronunciation. Alternation between [ɛ] and the *e muet* remains a feature of modern French, and has affected words with other etymological vowels, like:

(25) *acheter* < ADCAPTARE.

It is sometimes called **closed syllable adjustment**, which we have related to the *loi de position* (6.11): in modern French *sème* [sɛm] has a blocked syllable and *semez* [sə-me], a free syllable. This template of alternation is clearly recognizable in the modern language, though it is to some extent lexically determined (cf. *scelle / sceller* < SĬGĬLLARE, with [ɛ] in both types of syllable).

For those who analyse *sème* as still having a final vowel (cf. 6.10), its difference from *semez* is described in terms of the **foot** rather than the syllable, with the combination of *tonic syllable + atonic syllable* ([sɛ-mə]) forming the domain that accounts for the vowel adjustment.

In modern French we have no principled way to account for the fact that sometimes the atonic vowel variant in such alternations is a schwa and sometimes an [e]:

(26) *jeter, crevez / espérez, cédez.*

Historically we know that variation between schwa and [e] in protonic syllables is attested from the early modern period, with the [e] pronunciation being more associated with careful speech and learned items.

Céder, for instance, is a fourteenth-century Latinism, and the retention of the coda *s* in *espérer* testifies to Latinizing pronunciation.

I have already suggested (6.10) that the modern pronunciation of overt schwa as a front central rounded vowel may be fairly recent. Thus, we could see the [e] pronunciation as conservative, which would square with its use in more careful style: the stylistic variation persisted even after standardization.

For instance the nineteenth-century lexicographer Littré recommended an [ə] pronunciation in *receler*, while contemporaneously the Académie preferred [e]: other commentators are tolerant of either.

Remnants of the tonic vowel diphthongization are comparatively rare in modern French verb forms, and indeed even in Old French attestation is somewhat sporadic. The *ie* diphthong from tonic free ĕ, well attested in Old French, had disappeared from most verb forms by the sixteenth century, remaining mainly in verbs that are irregular in other ways—like common *venir* (< VĚNĪRE) or uncommon *acquérir* (< AD-QUAERERE).

The *ei/oi* diphthong (< Ē, Ĭ) alternation, not so well attested in Old French, survives in irregular verbs like *devoir, recevoir, boire*.

The common verb *voir* (< VĬDERE), had already, by the thirteenth century, levelled its paradigm on the model of the stem-stressed forms:

(27)   *veons > voions*.

Usually in the verb-forms, levelling favoured the non-diphthongized vowel: however in, for instance, the lexicalized verbal nouns *espoir* and *effroi* the reflex of the diphthong persisted when it was lost in the verb paradigm.

In some verbs the *eu* reflex of tonic free ō and ŏ was still current in seventeenth-century usage (when still pronounced as a diphthong by some). Alternation (between [u] and [ø] or [œ]) still persists in some common words like

(28)   *vouloir, pouvoir, mourir*.

On the whole it is probably safe to say that where there still is alternation between reflexes of the old diphthong and the simple vowel, either the verb is a moribund relic, or there is **suppletion** in a commonly used verb, with the separate forms learned as individual items.

Normative grammarians have always been particularly concerned to resist reckless analogical levelling. Vaugelas in 1647, for instance, regrets the incursion of analogical *peux* into the realm of *puis*. He accepts *treuve* but admits that *trouve* is now more common, and maintains the legitimacy of archaic *assient*, against *asseient* or *assoient*.

School grammar from the nineteenth century has imposed, as best it could, the arbitrary distribution of analogical and apophonized forms: levelling carries the stigma of childishness or illiteracy and so the morphology remains frozen more or less at the stage it had reached in the eighteenth century.

7.9. CODA CONSONANT DELETION IN VERB-ROOTS

Another source of 'irregularity' (or of the operation of minor rules) in French verb-stems is a result of the historical processes of the vocalization or fall of preconsonantal coda consonants (cf. 6.12). Already in Old French, for instance, *dorm* < DORM(I)O contrasted with *dors* < DORMIS: it was quickly to be levelled to *dor*, in accord with a familiar template by which the singular forms contrasted with the plural: *dormons, dormez, dorment*. Similarly *vif* < VĪVO was reformed on *vis* < VĪVIS, and contrasted with *vivent*, as did *doit* (*dift* in the Strasburg Oaths), with *doivent*. Likewise *valt* < VALET became *vaut* and contrasted with *valent*.

Today, as a result of word-final consonant deletion in the modern period (cf. 6.9), *perd* [pɛʁ] contrasts with *perdent* [pɛʁd], *part* [paʁ] with *partent* [paʁt], *plais* [plɛ] with *plaisent* [plɛz], *prend* [pʁɑ̃] with *prennent* [pʁɛn].

The contrast between singular and plural was sometimes enhanced by the levelling of **palatalized** first person singular forms. Distinctive Old French first person palatalized forms like *vail* < VALEO, *vueil* < *VOLEO for VOLO, *puis* < *POSSEO for POSSO tended over the centuries to be levelled to fit in with the other singular persons. True, *sai* < SAPEO (/ *savons*) may have influenced the other singular forms, but Old French *set* could be a regular phonological development of SAPET, and so it is merely the orthography that has changed, in the modern period when *ai* was identified with [ɛ]. It is fairly certain though that *savent* was a fairly early reformation of regular *sevent* (< *SAPENT) on the analogy of *savons, savez*.

7.10. LONG AND SHORT ROOTS

We have suggested that in irregular verbs there is a present indicative template which distinguishes the singular from the plural roots, with the latter retaining a final consonant which is lost in the former. This difference can be described in terms of allomorphy, with a longer root (iconically) signalling plurality. This is echoed in the regular *ir* conjugation where the singular allomorph (/fini/) is contrasted with the plural (/finis/).

Where there is such an alternation, the longer allomorph (with a final consonant) is used in the present subjunctive and the imperfect. Sometimes the infinitive and future uses the shorter form:

(29) *fini-r(-a)* , *boi-r(e)-a* (but *bevra, buvra*, etc. were used until the sixteenth century), *écri-r(e)-a* (older *écrivra*), *li-r(e)-a*.

This reduction was frequent in northern thirteenth-century charters: *ara* for *avra* etc.

But more regularly it is the longer form that is preferred in these forms:

(30) *dev -oir /ra, viv -r(e)/-a, mord -r(e)/-a, sort-ir-a, mett -r(e)/-a,*
      av -oir /ra (*aura* with vocalization of the *v* triumphed in the
      sixteenth century).

Many irregular futures have an allegedly **epenthetic** consonant between the stem and the *r* future marker. This often represents rather a hardening of a root-final continuant or sibilant:

(31) *pre(n)-d-ra, vie(n)-d-ra, plai(gn)-d-ra, cou(s)-d-ra, connai(ss)-t-ra*
      (the type *-istra* is also attested for some regular *ir* verbs).

This hardening is characteristic of the western, central, and southern French areas in the thirteenth century. It affected also preconsonantal *l*, presumably happening before it vocalized:

(32) *vol-d-ra* > *voudra, val-d-ra* > *vaudra.*

Where the long form ended in a voiced sibilant hardening is often not attested, but analogical forms like *plaisira* or *nuiserai* are found from quite early in Old French.

Table 7.3 gives three examples of how root allomorphy has evolved in three irregular verbs. In spite of the apparent extreme irregularity of *plaindre*, *dire*, and *faire*, there has been quite considerable morphological simplification after the havoc that sound-change wrought in Old French. For *plaindre* six different (phonetically conditioned) root forms resolved in modern French to three suppletive forms. In the sixteenth century there was a tendency to level on the basis of the infinitive. In *faire* six different forms merged into three: note here that the present indicative third person plural *font* has a short root and a tonic person marker (cf. also *vont*, *sont*). The changes in *dire* appear less radical, if we assume that the modern preterite forms have a root in /d/ whereas the present roots are /di/ and /diz/.

With monosyllabic verb forms there is some dispute about where the root ends and the person or tense marker begins: an 'a-morphous' morphology can avoid the difficulty by eschewing segmentation of this sort, preferring the idea of a spell-out of grammatical features. However, from a diachronic perspective there are some interesting things to learn from the development of person and TAM (tense-aspect-mood) markers.

TABLE 7.3. Verb Roots (Allomorphy)

Old French				Modern French
PLANGĚRE (PLANXI)				
	plain(d)re			
PLANG-	[plang-]	PLANGUNT	*planguent*	/plɛɲ/ *plaignent*
		PLANGO	*planc, plaing*	/plɛ̃/ *plains*
	[plaɲ-]	PLANGIMUS	*plagnons*	/plɛɲ-/ *plaignons*
		PLANGITIS	*plagnez, plaigniez*	/plɛɲ-/ *plaignez*
	[plɛɲ-]	PLANGAT	*pleigne*	/plɛɲ-/ *plaigne*
	[plajn-]	PLANCTUM	*plaint*	/plɛ̃/ *plaint*
		PLANGIT	*plaint*	/plɛ̃/ *plaint*
		PLANXI	*plains*	/plɛɲ-/ *plaignis*
	[plajns-]	PLANXISTI	*plainsis*	/plɛɲ-/ *plaignis*
		PLANXISSEM	*plainsisse*	/plɛɲ/ *plaignisse*
	[plajnd-]	PLANGERE	*plaindre*	/plɛ̃d-/ *plaindre*
DĪCĚRE (DĪXĪ)				
	dire			
DĪC-	[di-]	DĪCO	*di*	/di/ *dis*
		DĪCIMUS	*dimes, dions*	/diz-/ *disons*
		DĪCAT	*die*	/diz-/ *dise*
		DĪCITIS	*dites, diez, disez*	/di/ *dites*
		DĪCĚRE	*dire*	/di/ *dire*
	[diz-]	DICĒBAM	*diseie*	/diz-/ *disais*
		DIXI	*dis*	/d-/ *dis*
		DIXERUNT	*distrent*	/d-/ *dirent*
	[dez-]	DIXISTIS	*desistes*	/d-/ *dîtes*
	[de-]		*deistes*	
FACĚRE (FĒCĪ)				
	faire			
FAC- FĒC-	[faj-]	FACIO	*faz (fach), fois* (16th c.)	/fɛ/ *fais*
		FACIMUS	*faimes, faions, (façons)*	/fəz-/ *faisons*
		FACTUM	*fait*	/fɛ/ *fait*
	[f-]	FACIUNT	*font*	/f-/ *font*
		FĒCĪ	*fis*	/f-/ *fis*
	[fe-]	*FACERE-AT	*fera*	/f(ə)/ *fera*
		FĒCISTĪ	*feis*	/f-/ *fis*
	[fajz-]	FACĒBAT	*faiseit*	/fəz-/ *faisait*
	[fez-]	FĒCISTI	*fesis*	/f-/ *fis*
	[fas-]	FACIAM	*face (faise)*	/fas-/ *fasse*
			(Picard *fache*)	

7.11. IMPERFECT ENDINGS

One striking analogical generalization in French concerns the past
imperfect indicative endings, which in all verbs are:

(33) *ais, ais, ait, ions, iez, aient.*

The imperfect marker can be described as having a tonic allomorph
[ɛ] (or [e] in some varieties) and a pretonic allomorph [i]/[j], suffixed
to the long verb root. It is used for all verbs, whether regular or
irregular.

Until the fourteenth century reflexes of Latin ERAT etc. were still in sporadic
use, but the regularized *était* replaced them.

As we have seen, French has only one fully productive conjugation: we should expect that if a tense/aspect marker were to be
generalized to all verbs it would be that of the *er* verbs. However, as

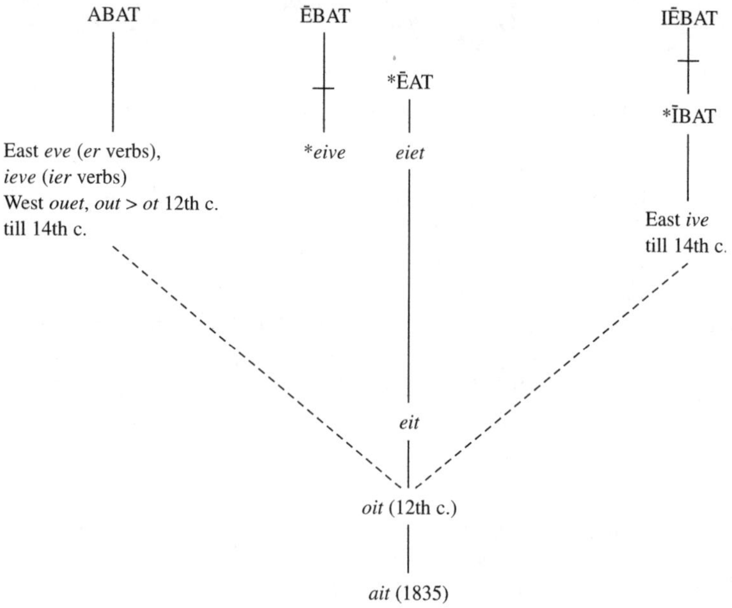

Figure 7.1. Imperfect indicative markers

Fig. 7.1 shows, the ĀBAT endings disappeared in the fourteenth century.

The Latin -B- marker was possibly from a periphrastic form with the verb 'to be' (cf. FUIT 'he was', and the future ending -ĀBIT), combined with the Indo-European imperfect marker A (as in ERAT). The ĪRE conjugation had an -ĪBA- marker that was replaced in the Classical language by the -IĒBA- of the Ĕ conjugation, but which seems to have survived, or to have been reintroduced, in some Romance languages, including eastern French varieties.

Curiously the surviving French marker appears to derive from an irregular development of the -ĒBA- ending, with loss of intervocalic B > *EA (cf. also Spanish *ía*). It may be that the generalization of this contracted ending comes from the **future-in-the-past** or **conditional.**

Unconvincingly, conventional wisdom tells us that the *EA derives from dissimilated forms of HABĒBAT, DEBĒBAT. These forms would have, in this story, retained the B of the root, even though this is frequently lost in other forms (cf. *a* < HABET, *doit* < DEBET). It has also been suggested that modals and auxiliaries are found more frequently than most verbs in the imperfect, and so they could have exerted analogical influence.

Whatever the micro-history of the imperfect ending, the result has been its total regularization. Note that the imperfect is one of the few synthetic verb paradigms that has survived intact into modern French. It was comparatively little used in texts before the modern period, but has come to represent a default past tense, with a range of connotations that are difficult to characterize.

For its semantics and comparison with the *passé composé* and the *passé simple* cf. 5.7.

7.12. THE *PASSÉ SIMPLE*

Whereas the **imperfect indicative** has been regularized, acting as an unmarked past, parallel with the default present indicative, the inherited Latin **preterite** (*passé simple, passé historique, passé défini*) is in modern French morphologically irregular and textually confined to certain types of discourse. Indeed it can be claimed that it does not form part of the active linguistic competence of most French speakers, although its third person forms are recognized by nearly all, even by children, who encounter them in fairy-tales.

The preterite forms are usually, following the Germanic philological tradition, divided into **weak** and **strong** types. The former derive from regular Latin **perfect** stems, in which U ([w]) is suffixed to the present stem: AM-Ă-U-, FIN-Ī-U-. The Ē conjugation type did not survive into French. The person endings of the perfect were in Latin idiosyncratic:

(34) Ī, ISTĪ, IT, IMUS, ISTIS, ĒRUNT.

In Latin already the [w] element vocalized or fell, with apparently **compensatory lengthening** of the preceding vowel or following consonant. In French the result was that the accent fell regularly on the stem vowel:

(35) *ai | i, as | is, a | it, ames | imes, astes | istes, erent | irent.*

Note that in the singular of the *finir* type, the forms are identical with the present indicative.

The first person plural form soon acquired the preconsonantal *s* of the second person plural; lengthening consequent on the opening of the sibilant accounts for the eventual graphy with a circumflex accent.

Also found in the sixteenth century is analogical *arent* for *erent* (where the raising of tonic free A was phonologically regular).

More striking in the early modern period is the tendency to regularize these forms by generalizing one or the other set, usually the *i* forms. Grammarians commented frequently on this type of mistake. There was also some confusion between the *i* type and a newly created late Latin reduplicated **weak** type, modelled on VENDĬD-:

(36) *vendei, -is, -iet, -imes, istes, ierent.*

In some varieties some of these forms came to resemble the imperfect forms, but in the standard they merged with the *i* preterite type.

Very many Latin perfect stems were, however, anomalous, inherited mainly from Indo-European sources. In modern French, where these survive, they are **suppletive**:

(37) *fut* < FUIT; *fis* < FĒCĪ, *vins* < VĒNĪ (with **metaphonic raising** of the stem vowel and analogical addition of *s*), *eut* < HABUIT.

Often, though, they have been remodelled on the *i* type:

(38) *écrivit* for *escrist* < SCRIPSIT; *ceignit* for *ceinst* < CINXIT.

Today most of the irregular *passé simple* forms, although little used, are familiar because they resemble the **past participle**, especially where this is based on a *ŪTU type which spread at the expense of others:

(39) *bu* < *beu* < *BIBŪTU for BIBITU, *couru* < *CŬRRŪTU for CŬRSU.

In some cases, however, where the past participle has an *u* form, the *passé simple* has not followed it:

(40) *lu* / *je lis*, *vécu* / *je vis*

It has sometimes been claimed that a cause of the loss of the *passé simple* in the modern period is its morphological irregularity. Possibly it is truer to say that it has remained irregular because it is so little used in normal discourse. Or rather, that the burden of memorization of the suppletive forms is felt to be heavier in a tense that it so little used in the spoken language. After all, the past participle probably retains as many inherited anomalies as the *passé simple*, but it is in constant use, in the compound forms, and so speakers are less conscious of the morphological irregularities it presents.

7.13. THE FUTURE AND CONDITIONAL

Discussion of the morphology of the so-called **Romance future** is a set-piece of most introductory works on morphological change. To call it 'Romance' is a misnomer, as the *chanterai* type of synthetic future in question is found only in the major Western Romance varieties, and even there it is usually not a preferred colloquial way of referring to future events. What observers sometimes fail to recognize is that the related so-called **conditional**, or future-in-the-past, even more of an innovation in Romance, is rather more widespread and robust than the future form, and may even pre-date it.

The suggestion that the future form was created to fit the requirements of early Christians to express the idea of predestination ('it has to be' > 'it will be') does not hold water.

There are several aspects of the French synthetic future that make it a good presentational topic in historical linguistics treatises.

First, there is the problematic character of future tenses in general. We cannot speak of future events with the same degree of certainty that we can describe past or present events. There is no common inherited Indo-European future tense, and many languages manage very well without one, making do with the default present indicative. Where there is a morphological future it is often related to the subjunctive, implying doubt or subjectivity of judgement. Periphrastic futures are common—in Romance there are transparent structures that bring in the notions of will, desire, obligation, or motion. The French *chanterai* type is said to originate as a periphrastic obligative form: 'I have to sing', but it is no longer separable into its constituent units. It is therefore frequently chosen as a graphic example of how an analytic form has resolved into a new synthetic form, and of the cyclic change from **synthetic** to **analytic** and back again.

But the history of this form has its problems, too. The Latin future forms in -B- were an innovation, but did not spread to all the regular conjugations: AUDIAM, for instance, appears to come from a subjunctive form. We know that phonologically the -B- forms were threatened in the late Latin period when B merged with 'consonantal' U ([w]). Thus regular perfect inflections like -ĀUIT became identical with future inflections like -ĀBIT. However, as we saw in our discussion of the *passé simple*, the perfect tense forms were substantially rejigged, and in French no remnant of the Latin -U- survived.

In spite of their phonological vulnerability, the classical future forms remain intact in Late Latin texts right through to the eighth century. True, there are Late Latin examples of the sequence infinitive + HABĒRE from which the French future is supposed to have derived, but they occur more often with a past tense of HABĒRE, and in any case cannot unambiguously be read as having future reference.

One jokey example in the (seventh century?) pseudo-Fredegar history is often quoted: Justinian was said to have given the name to the place DARAS in a peremptory reply to someone saying NON INQUAM: DABO = 'I do not say: I will give'. It is hard to place much reliance on this evidence, which is possibly Latinization of a vernacular form, in the tenth-century manuscript: even if *daras* were a genuine popular form, it would be just as likely to mean 'you have to give', as a future 'you will give'. (Note too that French uses a reflex of DONARE, not of DARE, for 'to give'.)

Yet the very first French texts, in the ninth or tenth centuries, have clear examples of the French synthetic future and conditional forms. The Strasburg Oaths have *salvarai, prindrai*, which can be read 'I shall save, take', or 'I have to save, take', and the Eulalia poem has the conditional *sostendreiet* 'she would sustain' or 'she will have sustained'. Note that in the latter example, there has already been hardening of continuant *n* to [d] (cf. 7.10), so that there is no transparent link between an infinitive *sostenir* and the future stem.

Other very early examples of the same kind are:

(41) *didrai, estrai, podra, lairai* for modern *dirai, serai, pourra, laisserai.*

Because the other major Western Romance languages have similar future forms, it is assumed that the *chanterai* type must have developed in the course of our first millennium at the Proto-Romance stage. In Spanish, Occitan, Catalan, and Portuguese, however, the two parts of the sequence were separable by an object pronoun (a process known as **tmesis**):

(42) *cantar-lo-he(i)* 'I shall sing it'.

It is assumed that a similar separation may have been possible in early Old French, though we have no examples. The possibility was lost in modern Spanish, Occitan, and Catalan, but persists in standard Portuguese, as a rather precious stylistic device. There seems to have been some degree of reanalysis in early modern Portuguese so that future stems came to be aligned more closely to the infinitive forms.

In Italian, the synthetic future was not attested until fairly late, and tmesis was not usual. What is interesting though about standard Italian is that the conditional form is composed, not with the imperfect of HABERE, but with the perfect form:

(43) *canterebbe* < CANTARE + HABUI / *chanterais* < CANTARE + HABEBAM.

There are also problems about the way the synthetic future forms are derived. One is syntactic: the difference of placement of the auxiliary in the compound perfect (*j'ai chanté*) and the synthetic future (*je chanterai*). This difference can be neatly ascribed to the chronology of changes in word-order typology (cf. 8.4).

There are also however purely morphological problems. One concerns the future stem, which is not identical with the infinitive, and another with the personal endings, which are not identical with the HABĒRE forms, the long root in *av-* never appearing. It must thus be assumed that by the very earliest attested French examples, the derivation of the tense forms was no longer transparent, which suggests that the forms had **grammaticalized** much earlier in French than in Spanish, Occitan, Catalan, and Portuguese.

Yet analogical forms based on the infinitive began to appear especially from the sixteenth century, suggesting a move towards reanalysis, to which grammarians lent their support. Analogical reformation of the infinitive affected especially the *-ir* conjugation:

(44) *courir* replacing *corre courre* (but cf. *courrai*), *bouillir* for
      boudre (cf. *bouillirai*, but also non-standard *bourai*).

There was a tendency also to generalize the infinitive form as the future stem:

(45) *mentirai* for *mentrai*, *sortirai* for *sortrai*.

Moreover the *-r* of the *ir* infinitive was restored in the course of the seventeenth century, so that forms like *finirai* are transparent, whereas the relationship between *mener* [mne] and *mènerai* [mɛnre] is less so.

The Old French future stem, I have suggested, regularly comprises a long lexical root + the future marker *r*. The root frequently shows hardening of a continuant or sibilant (cf. 7.10). As similar hardening occurred before the *r* of the infinitive, and of certain other forms:

(46) *voldrent* < VOLUERANT, *fistra* < FĒCERAT,

we can assume that this was originally a phonologically conditioned alternation, which then was analysed as allomorphic suppletion.

The stressed endings of the future are idiosyncratic, but can be identified, except in the first and second person plural with the *avoir* present indicative paradigm. In the two anomalous persons *passe-partout -ons* and *-ez* (earlier *-eiz* < ĒTIS) endings were eventually introduced.

It would appear however that the future second plural [ɛ] was distinguished from the present form [e], in prestige varieties until the eighteenth century.

In the much more regular conditional, imperfect endings are affixed to the future stem: any connection with the *avais* paradigm appears remote.

The origin of the future *r* marker may very well be from the infinitive, but we note that a similar marker appears also in some early Old French forms etymologically derived from the Latin pluperfect indicative (cf. Moignet 1959*a*):

(47) *auret* < HABUERAT, *duret* < DEBUERAT, *voldret* < VOLUERAT, *vindra* < VĒNERAT.

The tense value of these forms is not wholly clear in the texts: they appear only for the most common verbs and almost exclusively in the third person singular.

Note that attested plurals like *vidrent* could conceivably derive from perfect VĪDĒRUNT, though pluperfect VĪDERANT would give a more regular outcome.

Although the *-ret* forms are usually interpreted as **anteriors**, they seem in the earliest texts to be almost synonymous with the *passé simple*. Similar forms in other Romance languages, however, take on past subjunctive or conditional functions. There is some hint of this in Old French: one manuscript of the eleventh-century Saint Alexis poem has, for instance:

(48) *Se je pousse, si t'oure costumé* 'If I had been able (POTUISSEM) then I would have (HABUERAM) looked after you'.

By the early twelfth century, the *-ret* forms had virtually disappeared, but some manuscripts write, for instance:

(49) *devret* for *devreit* or *voldret* for *voldreit*,

where the verse form suggests that indeed the stress may be on the first, not the second, syllable. So it is possible that the conditional form and the *-ret* form merged as one.

In the regular verbs, it has been suggested that the French future stem may be derived not from the infinitive but from the Latin imperfect subjunctive (e.g. AMĀRET), which may have yielded the so-called **personal infinitive** in Portuguese and Sardinian, where there are stressed plural inflectional endings:

(50) Portuguese *cantarmos, cantardes, cantarem*)

One would have to assume in this case that in French stressed person markers were then extended to the whole future/conditional paradigms.

It is easy to discern a pattern link between the French conditional and imperfect which are distinguished only by the presence of absence of future marker *r*. The future form presents a less regular pattern: although the singular endings are like those of the *er* conjugation *passé simple*, there is no such similarity in the plural.

Whereas the conditional has extended its ground and reaffirmed its solidarity with the imperfect, during the history of French, the future tense has not proved to be so robust. In modern colloquial French, as in other Romance languages, the synthetic form is giving way to newer periphrastic futures, in particular the type *je vais chanter* which came on the scene as a future tense-form in the early modern period (cf. 5.9).

7.14. THE SUBJUNCTIVE FORMS

In modern French only the present subjunctive remains in collo-quial use, and even that is formally identical with the present indicative in the regular -*er* conjugation, except in the first and second person plural, where the forms (*ions*, *iez*) resemble the imperfect indicative. The inherited forms were -*ons*, -*ez* /-*eiz*: -*iens* (later -*ions*), -*iez* were introduced into central texts in the thirteenth century (earlier in the east), allegedly on the analogy of *aiens* / *aiez* , reduced forms of HABEAMUS, HABEATIS.

Where a verb has a long and a short root, however, it is the former that is used in the present subjunctive. There are also some suppletive forms, reflecting regular **palatalization** of *consonant + jod*:

(51) *aille* < *ALIAT, *sache* < SAPIAT, *fasse* < FACIAT, *veuille* < *VOLEAT; *puisse* < *POSSIAT.

The forms *soit* and *ait* seem to continue SĬT and *AJAT (for HABEAT).

It is noteworthy that most of these suppletive forms (not those for *faire* or *aller*) are used in the imperative.

The **imperfect subjunctive** is closely linked morphologically to the *passé simple*, and continues the configuration of the Latin **pluperfect subjunctive**, with an -ss- marker:

(52) AMĀVISSEM > *aimasse*, AMĀVISSET > *amast* > *aimât*.

In the first and second plural, the -*er* conjugation forms were not usually distinguished in Old French from those of the -*ir* conjugation:

(53) *amissons, amisseiz* < AMĀVISSĒMUS, AMĀVISSĒTIS,

presumably by analogy or because of differential contraction of the stem in the Latin ending-stressed forms. Peletier in 1555 suggested that this pronunciation was due to the 'softer' speech of women. In the seventeenth century, however, these forms were seen as anomalous and banned from the standard, even though there had previously been a tendency to level all the -*er* imperfect subjunctive forms in the same direction.

It is to be noted that here, unlike the *passé simple* but like the present subjunctive, there has been introduction, in the early modern period, of the -*ions* and -*iez* endings.

B. NOMINAL AND PRONOMINAL MORPHOLOGY

7.15. GENDER MARKERS

French nouns are distributed between two **gender** classes: **masculine** and **feminine**. The Latin **neuter** has been lost in all the Romance languages, except for a few relics. In French most neuter nouns have become masculine (e.g. *miel* < MEL), but some are feminine (e.g. *mer* < MAR): in Old French more were feminine, but the influence of Latin restored some to masculine gender in the early modern period. Most modern loanwords fall into the masculine, regarded as the unmarked, gender. Although many nouns referring to male and female animate beings are respectively masculine and feminine, there is no overall semantic coherence in the gender category, and inanimates fall haphazardly, it seems, in either category. Mainly the Latin gender is inherited, and has little synchronic function, except in so far as **agreement** (cf. 8.17) ensures textual cohesion.

Grammatical gender is described as being purely morphological by modern French grammarians, although some speak of '*sexe fictif*'. Its arbitrary character was recognized by the Port-Royal grammar of 1660, which saw it as aiding comprehension and as an embellishment:

. . . on a jugé à propos pour rendre le discours moins confus, & aussi pour l'embellir par la variété des terminaisons, d'inuenter dans les adjectifs vne diuersité selon les substantifs ausquels on les appliqueroit . . . comme ces mesmes adjectifs se pouuoient attribuer à d'autres qu'à des hommes ou à des femmes, ils ont esté obligez de leur donner l'vne ou l'autre des terminaisons, qu'ils auoient inuentées pour les hommes & pour les femmes. . . . Quelquesfois par quelque sorte de raison, comme lors que les offices d'hommes, Rex, Iudex *. . . sont du masculin, parce qu'on sous-entend* homo *. . . D'autrefois aussi par vn pur caprice, & vn vsage sans raison; ce qui fait que cela varie selon les Langues, & dans les mots mesme qu'vne Langue a empruntez d'vne autre; comme* arbor *est du feminin en Latin, &* arbre *du masculin en François. . . .*

There is no transparent overt morphological marker of inherent gender in the noun itself, though a good guess can be made at the gender of most nouns, on the basis of their form (cf. Tucker *et al.* 1977). Martinet *et al.* (1979) distinguishes the meaningless formal modifications of gender from the 'sex marker' *-esse*: '*Il y a en français, et c'est tout autre chose, un monème de sexe féminin, manifeste dans le -esse de princesse ou d'anesse, donc avec une forme distincte -esse et un sens, caractérisé et non présent ailleurs, de "sexe féminin".*'

Note, however, that in official statements on '*féminisation*' of professional titles it is firmly stated '*le suffixe féminin "esse" n'est plus employé en français moderne: une poétesse*' (*Journal Officiel*, 16 March, 1986).

Traditionally the **determiners**, particularly the **definite article** forms, are held to be primarily gender markers, but before another vowel, the vowel of, for instance, *le* / *la* is elided. Unsurprisingly, mistakes are sometimes made by native speakers, in the gender of uncommon vowel-initial words. On the whole, however, the gender differences are well entrenched in all French varieties, with the exception of the creoles, where gender differences are totally absent, though a few lexicalized feminine forms survive. In some French varieties gender agreement is infrequent with predicative adjectives.

There is no determiner gender marking in the plural. Moreover, in the singular gender marking is absent before all vowel-initial words (where *l'*, *mon* etc., [sɛt] *cet(te)* are used for both genders). Here it appears that phonological preference for syllabic onsets overrides the gender-marking requirement (cf. Tranel 1996). The **disagreement** of the singular possessives (apparently masculine *mon* etc. with feminine nouns) was first attested in the 'Middle French' period. Earlier the vowel of the feminine (*ma* etc.)

elided prevocalically, as in the definite article. In the demonstrative, prevocalic masculine *cet* reflects older *cest*, compared with modern truncated preconsonantal *ce*. Until quite recently the indefinite article also tended not to mark gender prevocalically, where masculine *un* was pronounced [yn] like the feminine *une*. In the twentieth century the prevocalic pronunciation [œ̃n] has become standard (cf. Posner 1985*c*).

Apart from determiners and referent pronouns, gender is overtly marked mainly in agreeing adjectives. Today well over half of French adjectives remain unmarked for gender, but many commoner ones have distinctive gender-marked forms. Most of these are easy to account for historically: as the graphy still shows, a final *e* continues the A that was characteristic of the Latin first (mainly feminine) declension (cf. Table 7.4). The operation of some phonological rules in early Old French would have eventually made the relationship between masculine and feminine forms somewhat opaque. The Old French *e* marker was extended to adjectives that were previously unmarked for gender like:

(54) *grant* < GRANDE, *vert* < VĬRĬDE, modern feminines *verte*, *grande*.

That *e*, as we have seen, 'protected' the preceding consonant from devoicing and erosion. Thus in modern French the feminine

TABLE 7.4. Adjectival gender in early Old French

Early Old French {feminine} realized as final unstressed /e/ ([ə] ?) < A (Latin first declension). Some adjectives unmarked for gender originally— e.g. *grant* (especially Latin third declension).

Phonological rules (cf. Chapter 6)

---

1. palatalization
   /g/, /k/ → [ʤ], [ʦ]   /_ /e/ (< A) *large, longe, blanche*
2. word-final devoicing
   C   → [-voice]   /_ #   *larc, lonc, vif, vuit, gris*
   [+ voice]
3. ? palatal-sibilant resolution
   [ʃ]   → [js]   /_ #   *fresche | freis*
4. lateral vocalization
   [+lateral] → /u/   /_ C   *bels* → *beus*, *viels* → *vieus*

---

adjective often ends in a consonant, which is lost in the masculine.
The consonant is also often present in derivatives of the adjective:

(55) *petitesse, finesse, longueur, blancheur, franchise.*

Bonté, apparemment are among the exceptions. The longer form can also
appear in *liaison* contexts with certain adjectives (cf. 6.9. *bel ami* etc.).
However, when other adjectives are preposed to vowel-initial masculine
nouns (cf. 8.5) a 'feminine' form is not used: [frãami] *franc ami*, not
*[frãʃami].

The problem in description of the modern French alternation,
which is clearly patterned, although lexically and morphologically
determined, is how to predict the feminine form from the masculine.
A consonant can be appended, but which one? If we start from the
feminine as the basic long form in gender-triggered alternations, we
can often derive the masculine from it, in a partly predictable way,
by deletion of the final consonant (cf. Table 7.5 for a straightforward listing of the morphonological alternations in the modern
spoken language). Table 7.6 presents a possible formalization for
modern French, postulating a morphological rule for the formation
of the masculine, which deletes, in certain adjectives, a final
consonant of the feminine form, and which regularly deletes a
final nasal and nasalizes the preceding vowel (cf. 6.4). However,
the majority of adjectives remain unmarked for gender, and, of
those that are marked, the variants are so diverse that we have to
postulate suppletion. Considering the feminine form to be 'basic',
moreover, seems to be at odds with the perception that the masculine is the unmarked form.

From the historical point of view, it seems that what was in Old
French a relatively transparent and simple morphological mechanism, consisting of the addition to the masculine form of a {feminine}
morpheme, has become over time, in the spoken language, an
opaque and complex one, which is not easily described in terms of
morphemes. Although the written language conceals it, there has
certainly been a change. But can the change be regarded as
morphological in character?

Generativists who maintain that final **mute** *e* is synchronically present treat
it as a gender marker: for them there has been no change. However, this
means that the morphophonology of adjectival gender marking is seen as
also subject to lexically marked phonological rules (cf. Table 7.7 for the

TABLE 7.5. Adjectival inflection in modern spoken French

A. NO CHANGE

1. -v #	*joli(e)*, *bleu(e)*
2. -c #	*rapide*, *sage*

B. CONSONANT DELETION

1. /t/ →	∅	*saint(e)* /sɛ̃(t)/; *petit(e)* /pti(t)/; *vert(e)* /vɛʀ(t)/; *haut(e)* /o(t)/; *sot(te)* /so/ ∼ /sɔt/.
2. /d/ →	∅	*grand(e)* /gʀɑ̃(d)/; *lourd(e)* /luʀ(d)/; *froid(e)* /fʀwa(d)/
3. /z/ →	∅	*mauvais(e)* /movɛ(z)/; *jaloux* ∼ *jalouse* /ʒalu(z)/
4. /s/ →	∅	*doux* ∼ *douce* /du(s)/; *bas(se)* /ba(s)/; *gros(se)* /gʀo(s)/.
5. /ʃ/ →	∅	*blanc(he)* /blɑ̃(ʃ)/; *frais* ∼ *fraiche* /fʀɛ(ʃ)/.
6. /k/ →	∅	*franc* ∼ *franque* /fʀɑ̃(k)/.
7. /g/ →	∅	*long(ue)* /lɔ̃(g)/.
8. /l/ →	∅	*saoul(e)* /su(l)/.
9. /j/ →	∅	*gentil(le)* /ʒɑ̃ti(j)/.
10. /kt/ → ∅		*distinct(e)* /distɛ̃(kt)/.

C. CONSONANT DELETION + VOWEL VARIATION

1. vN → ṽ		*vain(e)* /vɛn/ ∼ /vɛ̃/; *fin(e)* /fin/ ∼ /fɛ̃/; *brun(e)* /bʀyn/ ∼ /bʀœ̃/; *bon(ne)* /bɔn/ ∼ /bɔ̃/; *roman(e)* /ʀoman/ ∼ /ʀomɑ̃/
2. /ɛʀ/ → /e/		*entière* ∼ *entier* /ɑ̃tjɛʀ/ ∼ /ɑ̃tje/
3. /ɛl/ → /o/		*belle* ∼ *beau* /bɛl/ ∼ /bo/
4. /ɔl/ → /u/		*folle* ∼ *fou* /fɔl/ ∼ /fu/
5. /iɲ/ → /ɛ̃/		*maligne* ∼ *malin* /maliɲ/ ∼ /malɛ̃/
6. /ɛj/ → /ø/		*vieille* ∼ *vieux* /vjɛj/ ∼ /vjø/

D. OTHER CHANGES

1. /v/ → /f/		*vive* ∼ *vif* /viv/ ∼ /vif/
2. /z/ → /ʀ/		*moqueuse* ∼ *moqueur* /mɔkøz/ ∼ /mɔkœʀ/

---

formalization of Kiefer 1973). In any case **suppletion** still has to be assumed, to account for way-out alternations like *belle* / *beau*, *vieille* / *vieux*.

The change over time can be seen to have originated in phonology (loss of final vowels, which resulted in the loss of overt realization of

TABLE 7.6. Modern French adjectival gender—a possible account

Morphological rules

C → ∅/_ {−feminine} (lexically marked)
/lɔ̃g/ → /lɔ̃/ *long(ue)*, /griz/ → /gri/ *gris(e)*, /blɑ̃ʃ/ → blɑ̃/ *blanc(he)*
VN → ṽ /_ {−feminine}
plɛn/ → /plɛ̃/ *plein(e)*, /bɔn/ → /bɔ̃/ *bon(ne)*.

BUT most adjectives unmarked for gender
Some suppletion—e.g. /bo/ v. /bɛl/ *beau / belle*, /vjø/ v. /vjɛj/) *vieux / vieille*

TABLE 7.7. Modern French adjectival gender—a generative account

Morphological Rule₁ (gender)

---

0 → ɛ/ {+adjective}
{−masculine}

Phonological Rules

---

1. v [−low] → [+low] /_ C v   *sot ~ sotte* [o] ~ [ɔ], *léger ~ légère* [e] [ɛ]
2. VN → ṽ /_ # }
          C }   *bon* [ɔ̃], *fin, vingt* [ɛ̃])
3. [−voiced] → [voiced] /_ v *vif ~ vive, heureux ~ heureuse*
4. [k] → [ʃ] /_ +v (when marked for this rule e.g. *blanc ~ blanche*)
5. [r] → [z] /_ +v (when marked for this rule e.g. *vendeur ~ vendeuse*)
6. ∅ → [s] /_ +v (*s* doubling e.g. *bas ~ basse*)

Morphological suppletion

[bɛl] *belle* → [bo] *beau*, [nuvɛl] *nouvelle* → [nuvo] *nouveau*, [fɔl] *folle* → [fu]
fou, [mɔl] *molle* → [mu] *mou*, [vjɛj] *vieille* → [vjø] *vieux*.
(Feminine adjective ending in consonant: consonantal deletion and vowel
adjustment—lexically determined.)

Source: Kiefer 1973.

the feature {feminine}, and loss of word-final devoicing and other
marks of word boundaries). But, given the resultant morphophonological chaos, why was such an opaque and inefficient system
retained? Why has French kept gender distinctions, even though
they have little semantic coherence and grammatical function?

Although the morphophonology has changed, and there has been marginal reassignment of some lexical items, the morphological classes seem to have remained stable. All 'core' French varieties retain the masculine/feminine distinction, though it is totally lost in the creoles, in which inherited morphology has disappeared or been completely restructured. This is perhaps an example of the comparative immobility of morphology in normal circumstances. Although the gender distinction is barely functional in modern French, it has resisted loss, perhaps because it was enshrined in the graphical morphophonological system at the time of standardization. Some sound-changes which would have further eroded the distinction have been blocked, so that, for instance, the atonic feminine definite article remains as *la*, though we would have expected weakening to *le* (which actually happens in Picard).

7.16. MORPHOLOGICAL CASE

Modern French can be said to have lost morphological **case** since the Old French period. True, there is still a distinction between subject and object clitics in some persons:

(56) *je* / *me*; *tu* / *te*; *il* / *le*; *elle* / *la*; *ils, elles* / *les*,

but it can be maintained that these are more in the nature of person inflections than of pronouns in colloquial French (cf. 8.8). Some of these forms historically are derived mainly from clearly marked Latin object / accusative forms:

(57) EGO/ MĒ, TU /TĒ.

But note that even in Latin the case-marking on NŌS and VŌS was defective.

In Old French most of the personal pronouns were still case-marked, and could appear in stressed or unstressed position. The modern clitics derive from the old unstressed forms. As for the free-standing, **disjunctive** personal pronouns, in modern French these are caseless, though most derive from stressed Old French oblique forms:

(58) *moi, toi, lui, eux,*

which took over the functions of the stressed nominative pronouns by the fourteenth century.

The Old French stressed first and second person singular forms were often not distinguishable from the unstressed, though a curious *gie* form is found, alongside distinctive, and more regular, *jo*, *jou* (< EGO), which in the thirteenth century was confined to the far north. In much the same area the form *mi* (< *miei*) was preferred to *moi*.

Elle(s) was newly introduced as a disjunctive pronoun at the same period, to replace *li* (< *liei* < *lei* < *ILLAEĪ, FOR ILLAE), perhaps to enhance the gender and number marking.

One feature of modern French is the apparently overt distinction of case between third person accusative and dative clitics:

(59) *la, le / lui; les / leur.*

The *lui, leur* forms may be regarded as **pro-PPs** (i.e. standing in for a **prepositional phrase,** *à* + animate NP), rather than simply case-marked datives. The *lui* form replaced, in the sixteenth century, the etymological dative masculine unstressed *li* < ILLĪ, which was identical with the stressed feminine form. In Anglo-Norman texts *lui* was generalized much earlier, and could be used for females, as in most of the manuscripts of the *Alexis* story:

(60) *N'at mais anfant lui volt mult honorer* 'He had no other child and wanted to honour her greatly' (Another manuscript has *mult la vout honorer*).

For discussion of the sequence *le lui* cf. 8.15.

In thirteenth-century charters from the north, the masculine tonic *lui* was also often reduced to *li* (cf. also the confusion of *cui* and *qui*).

Leur derives from the Latin masculine genitive plural ILLŌRUM, though in some dialects a reflex of dative plural ILLĪS survives in Old French.

7.17. OLD FRENCH NOMINAL CASE

The loss of morphological case is a feature of the early modern period. Old French inherited from Latin a very reduced system, not only in the pronouns but also in nouns. Table 7.8 gives examples of the two-case (**nominative / oblique**) system in classical Old French.

TABLE 7.8. Nominal case in Old French

	Singular		Plural	
nominative	*murs*	MURUS	*mur*	MURI
	pedre(s)	PATER	*pedre*	PATRES
	sire	SENIOR	*seignor*	SENIORES
oblique	*mur*	MURUM	*murs*	MUROS
	pedre	PATREM	*pedres*	PATRES
	seignor	SENIOREM	*seignors*	SENIORES

The nominative form was used for the subject of the verb, and the oblique form was used for other arguments, usually, but not always, with a preposition for indirect objects. Most feminine nouns did not overtly mark case, though there was some analogical extension of the nominative singular marker in words like *maison* or *flor*.

The oblique form could be used very restrictively as a genitive mainly for a singular human possessor (usually male):

(61)   *li fiz le rei* 'the king's son' (cf. the English name Fitzroy).

The more normal way of indicating the possessor NP is to precede it with the *de* preposition, but *à* can be used in contexts similar to those in which a bare oblique form was possible in Old French. The variation seems to have been regional.

We may ask: was the loss of nominal case due to phonological factors? In most masculine nouns the phonological support for the system came from the final *s* marker of nominative singular and oblique plural. Usually by the end of the Middle Ages the oblique form was generalized, and so the *s* came to mark the plural, as it already did in the feminine. Most traditional treatments of the history of loss of case in French see it as indeed triggered by the erosion and ultimate elimination of word-final *s*. Others argue that French rejigged its system to place more weight on the consistent marking of plurality, pointing out that word-final *s* persisted as a liaison consonant. It can also be maintained that the liaison [z] has been reanalysed in some varieties as an initial plural marker:

(62)   *les arbres* [le-zaʁbʁ]; *les œufs* [le-zø].

In French creoles this plural marker has sometimes been lexicalized.

The retention of word-final Latin *s* in the Western Romance languages, where it normally is a nominal and pronominal plural marker, is in itself puzzling, as evidence suggests that already in colloquial Latin it fell quite early. It is usually argued that its persistance in the West was an effect of the influence of prestige usage, which succeeded in fostering reaction against the vulgar habit of dropping the [s]. Similarly it is argued that the retention of a vestigial case system in French and Occitan may be owed to the greater impact of schooling in this part of the Empire.

We may further ask: did the nominal case-system serve a function in Old French? Conventional wisdom maintains that the modern French fixed word-order arose as a consequence of the loss of the case-system. It is observed that, in the older texts, inversion of subject and verb is more usual than it is today, and it is assumed that the overt nominative marking of subject nouns made this possible. However it has been conclusively shown that it is very rare in Old French texts for the subject sentence role to be marked only by the nominative flexion. Where there is more than one lexical argument of the verb, the relative roles of subject and object are usually unambiguously conveyed by other means—like word-order and the **lexical sub-categorization** of the verb. At best the case-marking merely reinforces what is signalled by other means.

It is not surprising then that, from an early period, cases are not consistently and correctly marked in graphy. This is most obvious in western texts; some sophisticated eastern poets, like Chrétien de Troyes (or his scribe Guiot de Provins), are pretty scrupulous in their use of case-forms, though not without some **hypercorrection**. The impression one gets, then, is that case-marking was fairly redundant, and may not have been consistently observed in the spoken language, but was maintained in literary works as a prestige feature. By the fifteenth century, case-markers were scattered round rather haphazardly: Villon's ballad ostensibly written in *vieil langage françoys* is a clear example of this.

However, the nominal (and adjectival) case endings were not the only means of marking case in Old French. More important were the case-marked determiners, the use of which became more and more prevalent with the passage of time (cf. 8.10). The masculine definite article, in particular, clearly distinguished:

(63) *li* nominative singular and plural / *le* oblique singular / *les* oblique plural.

The *li* plural form was a regular development of ILLĪ, but the singular presupposes an unetymological replacement of ILLE by *ILLĪ. The third person singular subject pronoun *il* also seems to be derived from the same form (with **metaphonic** raising of the initial [e] to [i]). The analogical influence of the interrogative pronoun *qui* has been, somewhat implausibly, suggested.

For discussion of the relationship between determiners and pronouns, and between interrogatives and relatives, cf. 8.9–10.

The early modern French changes in the morphology of the determiners go hand in hand with syntactical changes, to give a new look to the language, compared with that of the classical Old French texts. Case was no longer morphologically marked, but more weight was given to **number** (singular versus plural) differences and word-order signalled more clearly the sentence role of lexical arguments. This type of change can be connected with the growth of literacy and with the striving for newer means of expression of the period, which also turned its back on archaisms and outworn manners of speech.

7.18. THE POSSESSIVES

If we look at the history of a tightly knit system like that of the possessives in French, we may have the impression of such a *fouillis d'analogie* that knowledge of sound-laws help only to spot what has not happened when it should have. Clearly the French possessives are related to those of Latin, but hardly any member of the system has followed a totally regular development. Table 7.9 gives a simplified impression of part of the Old French system and the modern system that has replaced it.

As usual, the phonological development in Old French differs according to whether the item is stressed or unstressed. In free syllables a stressed vowel is **diphthongized**: hence, for instance, TŬA > *toue* > *teue*. The inflectional consonantal final of monosyllabic words is treated as **extrametrical**, so that diphthongization also takes place in MĔUM and TŬUM, which should give **mie* and **tou*. Exceptionally, in these forms the final nasal is retained in Old French: *meon*, from MĔUM, is attested in the Strasburg Oaths, but *mien* is the usual form, which supplanted also any potential reflex of

TABLE 7.9. The history of French possessives

Latin

nom.	MĔUS	MĔA	TŬUS	TŬA	SŬUS	SŬA	NŎSTER	*VŎSTER	ILLŌRUM
acc.	MĔUM	MĔAM	TŬUM	TŬAM	SŬUM	SŬAM	NŎSTRUM	*VŎSTRUM	

Old French

atonic

nom.	mes	ma	tos	ta	sos	sa	nostre	vostre
obl.	men	ma	ton	ta	son	sa	nostre	vostre

tonic

	*MĒA(M)	*TŎUM		*SŎUM				
nom.	miens moie	tuens	teue	suens	seue	nostre	vostre	leur
obl.	mien moie	tuen	teue	suen	seue	nostre	vostre	leur

Modern French

determiner

	mon, ma	ton, ta	son, sa	notre	votre	leur

pronoun

le mien	le tien	le sien	le nôtre	le vôtre	le leur
la mienne	la tienne	la sienne	la nôtre	la vôtre	la leur

MEUS (with addition of the nominative marker *s* in *miens*). The TŬUM reflexes suggest a short ŏ (*tuon*, *tuen*) rather than the ŭ of Classical Latin (even though the feminine *toue*, *teue* does seem to derive from TŬA). On the other hand, the *meie*, *moie* of the first person feminine must come from an unattested Latin form with a long vowel Ē (though Picard *miue* probably derives, via *mieue*, from a form with a short ĕ). The VESTER Latin form did not survive and a remodelling on the basis of NOSTER is assumed: the rather rare plurals *nostres* and *vostres* gave way to shortened *noz* and *voz*.

So far so good, perhaps, but the *teue*, *seue* forms were frequently remodelled to *toie*, *soie*, after *moie*, which survived till the fifteenth century. Earlier, in the thirteenth century, the masculine forms became *tien*, *sien*, by analogy with *mien*, and, by the sixteenth century, the feminines had been reformed on the same pattern: *mienne*, *tienne*, *sienne*. Mention should also be made of *leur* <

ILLŌRUM which replaced SUUS as the plural third person possessive, and acquired a plural *s* from the fourteenth century.

The atonic forms are less surprising, if we accept the syllabic reduction, which some relegate to the pre-French era. It is perhaps odd that *ma, ta, sa* retain a feminine *a*, and that *mon* should have replaced etymological *men*. The most unusual development is that by which the prevocalic feminine *m'*, with elision of *a*, was replaced in the fourteenth century by 'masculine' *mon*, an apparent case of **disagreement** (cf. 7.15). Lexicalized *ma mie* 'my lady friend' (not 'my crumb') survives, differentiated from *mon amie* 'my (female) friend'.

Clearly, analogy has been hard and haphazardly at work here. Fig. 7.2 gives a schematic picture to the way this has worked in some forms: dotted lines represent analogical influence.

But the process can also be described in terms of the substitution of morphophonological processes for earlier purely phonological ones, for which the conditioning had disappeared, and which had yielded apparently chaotic results. Table 7.10 contrasts the two sorts of processes. In Old French there is allophonic alternation of the masculine singular forms, conditioned solely by stress, whereas from early modern French the modern singular possessive forms can be derived from the lexical base of *mon, ton, son*, by means of

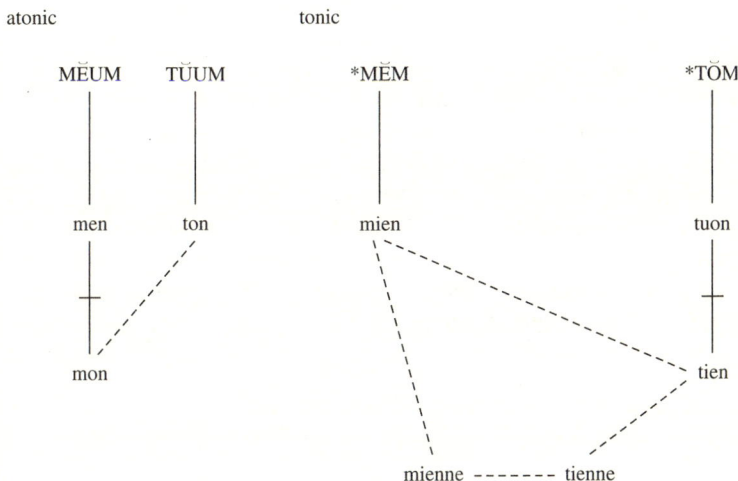

Figure 7.2. Analogy in the singular possessives

TABLE 7.10. Changes in the singular possessive forms

Old French phonological rules:

$[\varepsilon]$ /   [+ stress] → [iɛ]   *mien*
        [− stress] → [ə]   *men*

$[\mathfrak{o}]$/   [+ stress] → [uɔ]   *tuon, suon*
        [− stress] → [o]   *ton, son*

Modern French morphonological rules?

$[\tilde{\mathfrak{o}}]$ → [jɛ̃] /   [+ possessive]
             [+ singular]
             [+ adjective]
    mon, ton, son → *mien, tien, sien*

$[\tilde{\mathfrak{o}}]$ → [a] /   [+ possessive]
             [+ singular]
             [+ determiner]
             [+ feminine]
    mon, ton, son → *ma, ta, sa*

$\tilde{v}$ → vN /   [+ feminine]
             [+ adjective]
    mien, tien, sien → *mienne; tienne; sienne.*

morphologically conditioned rules, which make reference to the morphological features of [adjective] v. [determiner], as well as of gender. This type of reanalysis could very well have occurred in the acquisition process, with new learners trying to make morphophonological sense of alternations, when the phonological distinction between erstwhile tonic and atonic forms was no longer transparent.

But the process can also be viewed as symptomatic of a more fundamental **categorial change**, by which possessive pronouns came to be systematically distinguished from possessive determiners. Thus, in older French:

(64) *Le mien ami, un mien ami, cest mien ami,*

the *mien* was adjectival. This 'strong' form could also be used without a **determiner**, just as the 'weak' form *mon* could occur with a determiner. The difference was possibly one of emphasis or stress: as one might expect, the tonic form was found more naturally with a determiner. The strong adjectival form was also used predicatively:

(65) *L'ami est mien.*

In the pronominal use *le mien*, it was the *le* that filled the pronominal function, accompanied by adjectival *mien* (cf. *le rouge* 'the red one', where it is usually assumed there has been deletion of a noun, but in which it can also be claimed that the *le* 'stands for' a noun: cf. 8.9). Later (in the sixteenth century?) *le mien* was lexicalized as a pronoun and the *le* was identified with the **definite article** (a **determiner**). The adjectival use of *mien* was eventually lost. In modern French we have in predicative position, instead of the earlier type as in (65):

(66) *l'ami est à moi.*

Earlier *le mien ami, un mien ami, c'est mien ami* are today rendered as something like:

(67) *l'ami que j'ai, un de mes amis, celui qui est mon ami.*

The 'weak' form *mon*, on the other hand, has become specialized as a determiner or **possessive article**, and so it can no longer be accompanied by another determiner. It seems to have inherent definite reference, and so can be related functionally to the definite article.

The distinction between the two sets of forms (pronoun and determiner) was not clearly drawn until the seventeenth century, when the determiners *notre* and *votre* were also distinguished, arbitrarily, from the pronominal forms *(le) nôtre* and *(le) vôtre* by the quality of the vowel. But the reorganization of the morphological patterning seems to have been well under way in the fourteenth century.

Here we seem to have an example of morphosyntactic change rather than morphophonological change, with analogy and sound-change conspiring to create new categorial distinctions. However far-fetched it may seem, the notion of a radical upheaval in the system in the early modern period is borne out by parallel changes in the demonstrative system, which I shall examine next.

7.19. Demonstratives

Demonstratives or **deictics** are pointing or indicating functional items. In Latin there were three series, corresponding to the three verb persons: HĬC 'this (here by me)', ĬS(TE) 'that (there by you)', ĬLLE 'that (there by him)'. The third type was recruited in French for both third person pronoun and definite article forms: the relationship between them will be discussed in 8.10.

Modern French does not distinguish morphologically nearby **proximal** ('this') from far-off **distal** demonstratives ('that'): since the fifteenth century the distinction is made lexically by optional adjunction of *ci* (*ici* 'here' < ECCE-HĪC) and *là* 'there'(< ILLĀC).

Today *là* does not unambiguously signal 'over there', so an expanded *là-bas* 'down there' is frequent, while *(i)ci* is comparatively little used.

In Old French, unlike some other Romance languages, there was no second person 'middle-distance' demonstrative ('that near you'). The only survival of the proximal HĬC type was in the neuter singular form HŎC, which persists in *oui* < *oïl* (< HŎC-ĬLLE), in *avec* < *avuec* < *APUD-HŎC 'among this', and in *ce* < *ço, ceo* (< ECCE-HŎC). The prefixing of ECCE 'behold!' to the demonstratives is found in many of the Romance reflexes. As Table 7.11 shows, the Old French forms seem to derive from *ECCE-ĬSTE and *ECCE-ĬLLE types: an initial *i* found sporadically in these forms may be a remnant of the Latin initial vowel, or may represent an on-glide.

It is likely that the difference between the two series was never only one of location (cf. Kleiber 1987). The ĬLLE forms were more likely to be the default (rather as 'that' is in English), and were used in sequences like *cil qui* 'the one that' where no location is implied.

What is striking about the changes in early modern French is not only the loss of locative reference in the demonstratives, but also the clear differentiation between the determiner and pronoun forms.

The case distinctions were lost relatively early, in the thirteenth century. The anomalous vowel of masculine nominatives *cil* and *cist* is explained by **metaphonic** raising of the [e] (< ĭ) by a following ī, that was etymological in the plural but not in the singular (cf. also *il* and *li*). There was very likely to have been influence of the personal pronoun forms *il* etc. on the 'distal'

TABLE 7.11. History of French demonstratives

Old French Pronouns

	Proximal < *ECCE-ISTE		Distal < *ECCE-ILLE	
	Masculine	**Feminine**	**Masculine**	**Feminine**
Singular				
nom.	*cist*	*ceste*	*cil*	*celle*
oblique	*cest*	*ceste*	*cel*	*celle*
dative	*cestui*	*cesti*	*celui*	*celi*

Neuter *ço, ceo, ce* (< *ECCE-HOC)

Plural				
nom.	*cist*	*cestes*	*cil*	*celles*
oblique	*cez*	*cestes*	*cels*	*celles*

Modern French demonstratives (from 15th–16th centuries)

	Determiner		Pronoun	
	Masculine	**Feminine**	**Masculine**	**Feminine**
Singular				
	ce(t)	*cette*	*celui*	*celle*

Neuter
cela (ça)   *ceci*

Plural				
	ces	*ces*	*ceux*	*celles*

(default) series, which survives as pronouns. Marchello-Nizia (1995) sees the *celui* etc. forms as emphatic, as were, for her, the forms with an initial *i-*.

The weak points in the system were the etymological **dative** singular forms, used especially after a preposition, and the **proximal** plurals. Already in Old French the dative forms were frequently used as emphatic pronouns for human referents, and the feminine forms were rare. The *celui* form very likely came to be seen as composed with the *lui*, which, as we have seen (7.16), became a non-case-marked freestanding third person pronoun (cf. also *ceux*, *celle(s)* / *eux*, *elle(s)*). The *ce* element was probably analysed as the demonstrative particle, especially as, by the thirteenth century, there was truncation of the final consonant in the preconsonantal forms of *cest* [set] and *cel* [sel]. Moreover the neuter pronoun *ço*, *ceo* was always written *ce*, *cie*, *cei* in the southern and central dialects.

Ce could rhyme with [e] until the sixteenth century, and also with **feminine e**, which, I have maintained (6.10), may not have been weakened to schwa [ə] until later. Note however that we have ample evidence that the determiner forms *cet* and *cette* were reduced to [st] in the sixteenth century (and in modern non-standard varieties), and that the modern standard pronunciation with [ɛ] represents a hypercorrection. The treatment of *ço* > *ce* incidentally parallels that of *je* < *jo* < EGO. Modern *ça* is an abbreviation of *cela* in which the locative adverb was adjoined to *ce*: it is attested from the seventeenth century.

The masculine and feminine plural proximal forms had by the twelfth century merged as *cez* [sets], except in the west, where *cestes* (?[seːtəs] or [seːtes]) survived until the fourteenth century. *Cels* regularly became *ceus*, with vocalization of [l] to [u], but in unstressed position, as when used adnominally, it reduced to *ces* (like the preposition + article *dels* > *des*): thus, with the simplification of affricates, *cez* and *cels* merged as [ses] (cf. Dees 1971).

Thus, in the plural the locative distinction within the system was seriously threatened. However the radical reorganization of the system (creating a determiner paradigm out of the proximal forms, while specializing the distal forms as pronouns), cannot be ascribed merely to the interplay between sound-change and analogy. If we assume that in Old French, as in Latin, the demonstratives were pronouns, which could be used adnominally (rather than, as conventional wisdom would have it, pronoun-adjectives), then what we see in the early modern period is the creation of a new **determiner** paradigm, contrasting with the pronominal forms. The parallel with the **possessives** is obvious: we can also point to the creation of caseless personal pronouns in the same period.

The model for the creation of a determiner system must have come from the **definite article**, which still in Old French retained some demonstrative force and some pronominal characteristics. Modern French is unusual among the Romance languages in that it does have a full set of determiners distinct from the pronouns: this is a question I shall return to in the discussion of **article and pronoun** in 8.10.

FURTHER READING

On morphology: S. R. Anderson 1988*a*, 1992, Bybee 1985, Dressler 1985, Matthews 1991, Wurzel 1989.

On French morphology: Gertner 1973, Iliescu and Mourin 1991, Kiefer 1973, Pinchon 1986, Pinchon and Couté 1981, Rigault 1971, Schane 1968.

On morphological change: S. R. Anderson 1988*b*, Booij and van Marle 1995, S. Davis and Napoli 1994, Fisiak 1980, Hagège 1993, Malkiel 1963.

On French historical morphology: Andrieux and Baumgartner 1983, Champagne 1993, Herslund 1976, Klausenburger 1974*b*, 1979, 1993, La Chaussée 1977, Lanly 1977, Picoche 1979, Pope 1934, Walker 1981.

On morphologization: Klausenburger 1979.

On grammaticalization: Berchem 1973, Benveniste 1968, Heine *et al.* 1991, Heine 1994, Hopper 1991, Hopper and Traugott 1993, Pagliuca 1994, Traugott and Heine 1991, Vincent 1995.

On suppletion: Aski 1995, Markey 1985, Mel'čuk 1976, Rudes 1980*a*, Tranel 1990.

On verb person markers: N. L. Corbett 1969, Morin and Bonin 1992.

On the 'on' pronoun: Ashby 1992, Blanche-Benveniste 1987, Le Bel 1991, Posner 1994*b*.

On analogy: Anttila 1977, Bybee 1980, Dauses 1991, Kiparsky 1974, Kuryłowicz 1949, Malkiel 1960, 1980, Mańczak 1958, Skousen 1992, Thomason 1986, Vincent 1974, Wahlgren 1920, Walker 1995, Wheeler 1980, 1985, 1993.

On the future and conditional: Baker 1937, Fleischman 1982, Posner 1965.

On the imperfect and passé simple: Dardel 1958, Posner 1961*b*, 1965, Togeby 1964, Wahlgren 1920, Wilkinson 1973–5, 1978–83.

On the subjunctive: Wheeler 1985.

On gender: Corbett 1991, M. Durand 1936, Greenberg 1978, Ibrahim 1973, Keys 1957, Mok 1968, Rigault 1971, H. Séguin 1979, Spence 1980, 1983*b*, Tucker *et al.* 1977.

On case: Blake 1994, Dardel, 1964, Laubscher 1921, Palm 1977, Pensado 1966, Plank 1979, van Reenen and Schøsler 1986, 1988, Schøsler 1984, Spence 1965, 1966, 1971, Woledge 1973, Woledge *et al.* 1967, 1969.

On possessives: Goyens and van Hoeke 1991, Lyons 1986, Manzelli 1990, Mourin 1981, Plank 1984, Posner 1988*a*, 1990*a*, Rickard 1959, Togeby 1968, Wunderli 1978.

On demonstratives: Dees 1971, Kleiber 1983, 1987, Marchello-Nizia 1995, Pohoryles 1966, Price 1968, 1969.

8

Syntactic Change

8.1. SYNTAX

Linguists differ about what phenomena should be treated under the heading of **syntax**. Traditionally, in Romance studies, it is preferred to link morphology and syntax closely together, as **morphosyntax**, which covers the categorial status, syntactic use, and semantic value of morphological forms. For some, syntax is virtually synonymous with the ordering of elements within a **sentence**, the syntactic unit: in the Saussurean tradition, this is largely a matter for *parole*, the surface realization of the underlying system, *langue*, which is seen as the object of linguistics. So much depends on individual choice and on **pragmatic** factors that some deny the validity of the sentence as a unit of linguistic organization, preferring instead to study the **utterance**, a fleeting and spontaneous expression of **discourse**. From a diachronic point of view, it has also been maintained that syntax is frozen discourse, a product of literacy or planned speech— parallel to the view of morphology as fossilized syntax.

It is only in the second half of the twentieth century that syntax became in itself a serious topic of linguistic investigation. There is no consensus, however, on precisely what the status is within the language of the syntactic component, nor what would be the most valid way of studying it. **Generative** syntax sometimes maintains the autonomy, and indeed the primacy, of a syntactic component, which is 'hard-wired' in the human species: hence the importance of investigation of the language acquisition process, which can help us distinguish what is innate in language, from what is culturally assimilated. However different generative schools (and the same ones at different times) have widely divergent views about what sort of underlying knowledge generates the infinite variety of actual speech-acts, and on how much reliance we can place on the evidence of native-speaker intuitions about their language.

One problem that is relevant to the study of syntactic change is how, if there is a universal, species-specific syntactic component, different historical languages can have differing syntax. One way out of this dilemma is to resort once again to the idea of **morphosyntax**: what is apparently different about the syntax is fundamentally dependent on the morphology, which, like the lexicon, must be part of a cultural legacy. Moreover, as we saw in Chapter 3, it is maintained that the principles of **universal grammar** (**UG**) present a (limited) number of choices along **parameters**, which the child learner sets in a certain direction, on the basis of the language data which (s)he experiences during the acquisition process. Different languages will have diverging parameter settings: more important for our purposes, the child may **reanalyse** input data in a different way from a previous generation, with the result that there has been a syntactic change, even though there is not initially a surface manifestation of the change in structure. What parameters precisely are susceptible to this switch of setting, and how this can be detected from past evidence, has exercised the ingenuity of many generativists over the last decade or so. We shall examine some of their ideas later in this chapter.

It can however be denied that the construction of sentences depends solely on a grammar that is acquired very early in life. Speakers are conscious of their syntax, as of their lexicon, and can go on all through life acquiring new habits and skills. More complex sentence structures are characteristic of educated usage and planned discourse, so it is not surprising that different individuals may make diverse judgements about their acceptability or appropriateness. **Reanalysis** need not occur only in childhood: adults too may seek to make sense, in their own terms, of what they hear from others. An important source of syntactic change in adulthood must be generalization or **extension**, by which a syntactic structure associated perhaps with a limited set of lexical items or semantic values can be extended to others: one standard example in French is the **hypercorrect** use of the subjunctive after *après que*, on the model of *avant que*. Syntactic **borrowing** is also frequent, where a speaker tends to translate literally from another language or variety: this was a potent source of syntactic change in the early modern French period, when French was beginning to replace Latin as the vehicle for serious discourse and writers skilled in Latin prose attempted to transpose their thoughts into the vernacular.

In more traditional works on the history of French, syntax plays a minor role. This is partly because textual evidence rarely provides comparable sentences that are chronologically flagged, whereas it is easier to match smaller units, like sound-segments or words. Where the same text recurs at different periods—as with the Lord's Prayer—usually the weight of tradition ensures that the rendering remains fairly constant. One source of evidence is from translations at different periods of the same text (cf. Goyens and van Hoecke 1992, Rickard 1993): even here, however, the range of individual variation can be considerable. It has been maintained that syntactic history presents insoluble problems, in that, for the past, we can make no use of native-speaker grammaticality judgements to tell us what was *not* a possible construction. We rely mainly on assuming that, on the whole, French syntax has remained fairly constant, and we concentrate on the examination of textual examples that are framed in terms not current today. Here we may be faced with a problem of discontinuity, in that the past example may be from a variety, regional, social, or individual, that is not the direct ancestor of the French with which we are today familiar.

This of course most affects the comparison of the modern standard with older non-standardized texts, which may very well represent a usage which died out. The diversity of evidence from the wealth of Old French texts is hard to handle within the framework of theories that presuppose a degree of uniformity: the fact that many of the older texts are available only in later, perhaps corrupt, copies compounds the difficulty. The copious evidence from thirteenth-century charters, so valuable for the historical description of phonology and morphology, is of comparatively little use in syntactical study, as much of the content of the charters is formulaic, conventional, and probably archaizing.

Syntactic history is easier to describe on the macro-level than by the meticulous comparison of near contemporaneous texts. It seems clear, for instance, that Latin sentences are constructed differently from those of modern French: it is not so clear, though, that Old French lies somewhere in between on the same line of progression. One significant step in the study of French syntax was within the framework of **typological** history. Observing a certain tendency to consistency of word-order typology in the languages of the world, it has been assumed that the passage from Latin, as a subject-object-verb (**SOV**) language, to modern French, as a subject-verb-object

(SVO) language, would be accompanied by a number of other changes. This is something we shall return to (8.3–4).

8.2. What Counts as a Syntactic Change in the History of French?

Some modern accounts of historical syntax pay scant attention to chronological succession, treating different periods of the same language in the same way as independent contemporaneous languages. In this view, syntax is seen as structure without lexical or phonological content, a skeleton with no flesh: what is handed down over time is the content, the flesh, but structure is fashioned anew by each new speaker. It can be maintained, moreover, that there is no relevant raw syntactic data independent of interpretation and analysis, and that any account of syntactic history must be firmly rooted in a theory of syntactic structure.

In the present context, we are concerned primarily with examining the available data and trying to make sense of what appear to be changes in French over time. I shall therefore steer clear of too rigid a commitment to any theoretical framework, and stick to accounting for what seems to have happened, rather than illustrating a more general theory. There remains the problem of how to identify what happened as syntactic rather than morphological, lexical or semantic. To some extent the choice is arbitrary, given the way different threads are entwined, with phonology also playing a major role.

Changes in **grammatical meaning**—of use of **tense**, **mood**, or of markers of **definiteness** and the like—are usually counted as syntactic in traditional French historical grammars. I have preferred to treat such topics under **semantic change**. Similarly the development of **compound verb forms**, like the *passé composé* and the **passive** forms, can legitimately be discussed in terms of semantic change, even though the **ordering** and **agreement** phenomena involved fall in more readily with syntax.

Even more problematic are the changes, over time, in ways of **coding** grammatical functions or **sentence roles**, like subject or object. During the history of French, as we have seen in our discussion of **case**, there has often been a switch from morphological to syntactic coding, from **synthetic** to **analytic**, in typological terms. I have chosen to treat some such cases under morphology and others under syntax. The evolution of verb **person markers** falls in with both morphology and syntax. The development of **subject clitics** in the early modern period looms large in recent syntactic accounts, and is linked with word-order changes, whereas the evolution of person **inflections** is mainly a question of **morphophonology**.

The history of other **clitic pronouns**, including their ordering and the evolution of **reflexive** forms, also figures prominently in modern syntactic discussion: I shall also consider concomitantly the history of their relationship to the article forms.

Usually histories of French start as far back as Latin, so that it is regarded as legitimate to regard the differences of Latin and modern French **word-order** as a French syntactic change. We shall see, however, that quite what the nature of this change was is not totally clear. We do know however that the ordering of elements in Old French texts is not always permissible today: often some of the changes have been described as tending towards more 'direct', 'natural', or **iconic** ordering, and were seen by classical French commentators as showing progress in the language towards greater clarity, simplicity, and logic, though the loss of musicality and expressiveness that a more fixed word-order entailed was also sometimes lamented. The rules governing word-order within the sentence were codified in the early modern period, to be violated only in poetic usage. Yet in the modern language **topicalization**, **dislocation**, and **clefting** can move around the elements of the sentence to give them prominence in discourse. These are topics that may conveniently be discussed together.

It is often suggested that the history of French shows a change in complex sentence structure from **parataxis** to **hypotaxis**: this is clearly nonsensical if our starting-point is Latin, which had sophisticated hypotactic constructions. Perhaps the alleged change is illusory, depending on the type of early Old French evidence we have, rather than on the nature of the language. Nevertheless, such topics as **complementation** and **relativization** must fall under the heading of syntax, and changes in these spheres will receive some treatment here. The evolution of new **subordinating conjunctions** however is, I think, better treated as lexical change.

Changes in **negation** strategies in French could, conceivably, also be seen as largely lexical in character, but traditionally are counted as syntactic. So is **interrogation**, which in the history of French wavers uncertainly between syntactic and lexical coding strategies. I shall consider these topics in this chapter.

What is, at a casual glance, noticeable is that the syntactic features that distinguish French from the other Romance languages do not date very far back. Some modish syntacticians see the fundamental changes as initiated as late as the sixteenth century, with a 'knock-on effect' carrying on into the seventeenth century. Thus, we are told (Roberts 1994: 235) that 'a whole series of important syntactic changes . . . provide us with an example of how parametric changes may cascade through a system over a period of time'. This view is based on the hypothesis that a **parametric** change from Old French to modern French syntax is connected with some sort of 'weakening' of verb morphology—a sophisticated elaboration on a familiar story among traditional philologists. These latter however usually prefer to date the innovations earlier—possibly in fourteenth-century colloquial language—and talk of a 'lag' (rather than a 'knock-on effect') before written styles fully admit the changes.

In any case there is a contrast between the late syntactic changes and the phonological changes that differentiated French from its congeners at an early period. The impression one gets is that there was rapid phonological change as Latin transformed into French, that radical morphological reformations occurred during the Middle Ages, but that unalloyed syntactic change dates almost wholly from the early modern period. It is hard to know, though, whether this is, again, merely an illusion, conjured up by our greater knowledge of limits on acceptability in the modern period. Again one may wonder whether these clear-cut limits are not principally an effect of the **normative** attitudes to the language that characterize the post-standardization era. Certainly it seems that once the language was standardized, there was little or no further syntactic change. True, there have been innovations, giving rise to stylistic and register variation, but the syntax of the legitimate language of the end of the seventeenth century remains valid and prestigious today.

8.3. WORD-ORDER

Discussions in the classic works of change in French word-order are mainly concerned with the **grammaticalization** (cf. 7.3) of constituent order from the 'free' ordering of Latin and Old French. The standard story is that loss of case morphology meant that sentence roles had to be shown by ordering, so that so-called **direct order**, with the subject preceding the verb and the object following, became a feature of modern French, which was praised as logical and natural. What then provoked comment was **inversion**—that is verb-subject ordering—which was associated with **interrogation** or with certain stylistic devices.

The establishment of **SVO** ordering in the modern language became a favourite topic in the 1960s following Joseph Greenberg's tone-setting hypothesis about word-order universals (presented originally in 1961 though published in its definitive form in 1966). It was noted that there is a decided correlation among languages in the world between the ordering of the verb and its object and other ordering—so that it was postulated that languages tended towards a consistent type, with ordering of dependent elements either before or after their **head** (or **operator**). A **VO** language (**head-first**) would tend, for instance, to have preposition + noun, noun + adjective, auxiliary + verb ordering, whereas an **OV** (**head-last**) language would have noun + postposition, adjective + noun, verb + auxiliary ordering.

Of course, controversy rages about which element of the sequence is the head and which the dependent element. This is not a hare we can pursue here.

Table 8.1 gives a summary of the possibilities of ordering the main constituents of a basic sentence, with mention of languages which appear to favour each ordering, and some illustrative examples from French. A distinction is usually made primarily between those **OV** languages in which the object follows the verb, and **VO** languages where the object precedes the verb; the position of the subject is seen as secondary, but normally, perhaps for pragmatic reasons, the subject precedes the object.

Latin, like many other inflectional languages, is usually seen as an **OV** language (but cf. 8.4). Modern French, on the other hand, is apparently a **VO** language. The question is then how and when did the change come about and how has this affected the ordering of other elements. Take for instance the auxiliary + verb ordering. In modern French auxiliaries, as expected, precede the lexical verb: *il a chanté*. But we have seen that at the time of the formation of the

TABLE 8.1. Constituent order

VO

SVO	VOS	VSO
(French, English)	(Malgache)	(Celtic)
In the old language frequent but not dominant	Old French: rare **VoS**: Old French esp. in questions, imperatives *Faites le vos?* Do you do it? *Manjue-le tu* You eat it!	Old French questions and subordinates *quant ot li pedre le clamor de sun* *fils* when the father heard his son shouting (**VS** fairly frequent with intransitives *Vait s'en li pople* The people go away) Modern French **VsO** in questions

OV

SOV	OVS	OSV
Most frequent (Latin) Old French infrequent	rare (Hixkaryana) Old French frequent with topicalization of **O**	rare (Apurina) Old French very rare
Li rois Tristan manace The king threatens Tristran	*Trestuz les altres ne pris je mes un guant* All the others I don't give a fig for.	*mult gran duel cil en avrum* Great pain these will have thereby
Si vos le pechié de la roine volez laissier If you want to leave aside the queen's sin. **SoV** modern French	*Mei veit?* Do you see me? *L'altre meitieit avrat Rollanz.* The other half Roland will have. **oVS** in questions from 13th century	

Note: **S, O** are used for full lexical **NP** subject and object, while **s, o** indicate pronominal subject and object.

future tense forms the auxiliary seems to have followed the lexical verb: *il chanter-a*. This seems to be readily explained by a change between times in the word-order typology of the language, dated to the 'prehistoric' period, before the appearance of French texts. Another example could be found in the **grammaticalization** of adjective + noun sequences like DULCE + MENTE ('with a sweet mind'), which became adverbs in which *-ment* is a bound suffix (*doucement* 'sweetly, softly'), perhaps aided by the change of normal ordering to noun + adjective, which left this construction more or less stranded. In a similar way the old ordering **OV** is seen to have left relics in the placement of clitic object pronouns: *Jean aime Marie* but *Jean l'aime*, which is assumed to reflect an earlier type: **Jean Marie aime*. We shall examine some individual cases like these to see how far the hypothesis fits the facts.

We shall also look at the contention that in the history of French there has been a transition from an **SOV** type to a **SVO** type, through a stage in which the basic ordering could be more meaningfully be described as **TVX**, with the topic **T** argument (not necessarily the subject) placed in initial position (before the verb **V**) and residual material **X** bringing up the rear.

The ordering of clitic pronouns, relative to the verb and among themselves, has been subject to change in the history of French and is a fruitful topic of much discussion. The cliticization of the subject clitic has in generative studies been related to word-order and other changes: in the context of the so-called **pro-drop** (8.8) parameter, along which French is distinguished from other Romance languages (in that the subject of a verb has (nearly) always to be overtly expressed), this question deserves special attention.

One difficulty, however, is that different theorists are not at one about quite what they are examining. Word-order typologists, and most traditionalists, look at the actual order of elements in the sentence, as it is written or spoken. For many generativists, however, this ordering may be the result of **movement** from other **base-generated** positions, the nature of which are somewhat controversial, and imply hypotheses about universal structural characteristics.

Sometimes movement is postulated, where more traditional grammarians see none. For instance the normal post-verbal ordering of modern French adverbs (*il chante souvent* compared with English 'he often sings') is by some seen as resulting from movement of the verb leftwise over the adverb which is base-generated in the initial position of the verb-phrase (VP). If this is so, then there has been a change since Old French when adverbs could appear in a variety of positions in the sentence, most frequently pre-verbally or at the end of a clause:

(1)   . . . *le bourc asprement fut gardé longuement* (Philippe de Novare, *Mémoires*) '. . . the town was fiercely defended for a long time'.

It is hard however to define precisely what change has taken place, as in literary style the adverb can still appear in diverse positions, determined by considerations of harmony and rhythm:

(2)   *Mais sa raison sans cesse lutte et souvent l'emporte contre son coeur* (Gide, *Symphonie Pastorale*) ' But his reason ceaselessly struggles against and often triumphs over his emotions'.

However a comparison of translations (by Buridant 1987) from the Latin of a historical text, dating respectively from the late thirteenth and from the end of the fifteenth centuries, suggests that this may have been the crucial time, in this as in other respects, for the fixing of the modern French word-order. Thus the earlier (Burgundian) version has:

(3)   *Il osoit cuidier qu'il legierement vaincroit le roi* 'He ventured to think that he easily would overcome the king',

whereas the later ('*francien*') version postposes the adverb to the verb. The change however may be more to do with the cliticization of the subject pronoun in the later version, than with verb movement.

Most French speakers would judge that the prefixing of the adverb to the verb represents a stylistically motivated transformation, from a basic unmarked order where the adverb immediately follows the finite verb. Longer adverbs, on the other hand, are often transposed to the end of the sentence even in colloquial style:

(4)   *Elle se moque de lui continuellement* 'She makes fun of him continually'.

In the modern language, with infinitives short adverbs normally are preposed and longer ones postposed. In some styles however a distinction is made between, for instance, *vouloir bien* and *bien vouloir*, the former, a more traditional ordering, being seen today as more peremptory, and the latter as more polite. The ordering of adverbs in compound tenses merits particular attention, as elements interposed between the auxiliary and the participle can give a clue to the degree of grammaticalization of the form.

A major problem in discussing the status of **SVO** (or **SVX**) ordering in modern French is that in the spoken idiom the so-called unmarked order hardly ever occurs. Instead of a straightforward formally correct:

(5)   *Le chat est sur le toit* 'The cat is on the roof',

we will hear in colloquial speech:

(6)   *Le chat, il est sur le toit, Il est sur les toit, le chat, C'est le chat qui est sur le toit, Il y a le chat qui est sur le toit* (or even *J'ai mon chat qui est sur le toit*).

with, respectively, **left dislocation**, **right dislocation**, **clefting** or the use of a **presentative**.

Probably right dislocation has always been rather more colloquial than left. In this construction an already known NP is added as an afterthought (**antitopic**):

(7)   *Et l'ot prisse, Yseut la belle* (Béroul) 'And he had taken her, the fair Isolde'.

Even the classic eulogy of so-called **direct** word-order in French (Rivarol's 1784 *Discours sur l'universalité de la langue française*) makes abundant use of such devices as **pseudo-clefting**:

(8)   *Ce qui distingue la langue française des langues anciennes et modernes, c'est l'ordre des mots,*

where constituents of the sentence which 'logically' are subordinate are brought into relief. Indeed the watchword '*Ce qui n'est pas clair, n'est pas français*' is not, as it would claim, a clarion call for **iconic** ordering of grammatical constituents, but an assertion of the **pragmatic** requirement to highlight salient discourse components, which cannot, in the modern language, normally receive distinctive stress.

A strictly syntactic approach to French word-order usually assumes that such *mise en relief* strategies involve **movement** of constituents from their underlying positions to new positions outside the basic sentence structure. Thus left or right dislocation will be described as the movement, into a **topicalized** or **focalized** position, of an NP, which will be copied as a pronoun in the basic sentence:

(9) *Ces Romains sont fous* > *Ces Romains, ils sont fous | Ils sont fous, ces Romains* 'These Romans are crazy'.

However, in some cases the intonation patterns of such utterances do not clearly indicate dislocation. Thus the so-called right-dislocated version with no pause before the focalized constituent (*Ils sont fous ces Romains*) could conceivably be described as representing **VS** ordering, with the pronoun subject construed as an inflectional person marker rather than a syntactic constituent. Similarly:

(10) *Elle le lui a donné, Marie, le livre, à Jean* 'She gave it to him, Mary, the book, to John',

could be construed as representing **VSO** ordering, with the clitic pronouns, integral parts of the verb and marking the grammatical relations of its arguments, allowing the lexical NPs considerable freedom in their ordering, which is dependent on their prominence in the discourse.

The changes that appear to have occurred in the history of French may be less, then, to do with a fixing of the order of constituents than with development of grammatical apparatus, like **pronoun copying** and **clefting**, which legitimizes the 'alogical' constituent ordering. As much of this apparatus, even today, is characteristic only of the spoken idiom, it is hard to discern from textual evidence when it came into use. There are some examples of **dislocation**, especially right dislocation, in Old French texts, but we cannot estimate how prevalent it was in the spoken language. **Clefting** was pretty certainly in common use by the sixteenth century:

(11) *Car c'est moy que je peins* (Montaigne) 'It's myself that I'm depicting',

but we do not know how far it was current earlier.

In some early examples an apparently case-marked relative *cui* appears where the more neutral form *que* would be used today:

(12) *C'est votre amor cui je voil demander* 'It's your love that [to which] I want to ask'.

Perhaps we can date the weakening of the demonstrative *ço* to a pre-sentative by referring to the substitution of examples like *c'est moi* 'it's me', for older forms, with person agreement and morphological case-marking, like *ce sui je* 'that am I'. This switch dates back to the late fourteenth century.

It is tempting to link the development of *mise en relief* devices to loss of word-accent. Emphasis on any particular element of the sentence could no longer be procured simply by intonation and stress changes. This assumption would date the changes to the 'Middle French' period. However, such devices may well have been much earlier part of a variety of the colloquial language. In any case most penetrated into legitimate written style by the seventeenth century.

8.4. CHANGES IN WORD-ORDER TYPOLOGY IN FRENCH

In modern French the neutral order is assumed to be **SVO**, though in practice, as we have seen, the colloquial language uses various highlighting strategies. The most frequent ordering among the world's languages is **SOV**, and it is usually thought that Latin had this basic word-order.

The empirical evidence for this contention is not uncontroversial. In Latin main clauses the ordering of the constituents is fairly free, depending on pragmatic and rhythmic considerations. Familiar as most Latinists are with the down-to-earth style of Caesar, they assume that his rather monotonous **verb-last** structures are close to the spoken idiom, but there is wide variation between authors and periods. It is probably safe to say that there was a trend towards **SVO** ordering in the later period, but it is not as marked as we would wish. Perhaps we should rely less on the evidence of main clauses, in which typically a message is conveyed, and more on subordinate clauses which tend to contain older information and therefore are less influenced by pragmatic considerations. Here the **SOV** structures are more in evidence in the Classical language, whereas **SVO** becomes more frequent later.

In earlier Old French **SVO** ordering, though frequent, was not dominant (cf. Table 8.1), but by the thirteenth century it had gained ground, and was probably **grammaticalized** by the fifteenth century (although other orders survived as relics into the seventeenth century).

SOV ordering is fairly rare in Old French, occurring most in subordinate clauses. However a pronoun object (shown as **o** in Table 8.1) normally precedes the verb in modern French and frequently did so in Old French (cf. 8.12). **Verb-first** structures, which are regarded by some as basic in Celtic, are found in Old French especially in questions and in imperatives.

In some cases however it appears that the verb in topicalized and so placed in initial position:

(13)   *Ot le Guillaumes* 'William *heard* it'.

This is fairly frequent with intransitive verbs.

What is striking in Table 8.1 is that the **OVS** ordering, which is extremely rare, if not completely absent, among the world's languages as a basic order (some say confined to a few Brazilian Amazon languages like Hixkaryana), is well represented in Old French texts, especially in verse. It does not however appear to be a neutral ordering, but usually involves topicalization of the object, with consequential inversion of the subject. The Old French movement into initial position of any topicalized element is frequent:

(14)   *Granz est la joie* 'Great is the joy'; *Ce ne feist pas nus hons* 'That no man did', *Mielz sostendreiet les empedementz* '*Rather* would she suffer torture'.

Dardel 1989 argues that the **OVS** ordering was possibly the unmarked one for **Proto-Romance**, and that it replaced an earlier 'Gaulish' **VSO** ordering in French territory. Here the problem is discerning from textual evidence whether a construction is emphatic or neutral.

Preposing the lexical NP object to the verb ceased to be normal in thirteenth-century texts, but traces remain until the seventeenth century. Perhaps the enigmatic Mallarmé line:

(15)   *Un coup de dés jamais n'abolira l'hasard*

is a later remnant of **OVS** ordering (not 'A throw of the dice never will do away with chance', but 'Chance never will do away with a throw of the dice').

Often in Old French the topicalized element is the subject of the verb, so that the surface construction is indistinguishable from a **SV(O)** ordering. Thus it is assumed that Old French **TV(X)** ordering (where **X** stands for any element) allowed the transition to the

modern ordering. In Old French where the subject pronoun preceded the verb it is assumed to be stressed:

(16) *Il s'en issi entrementiers du palais* '*He* meanwhile went out of
      the palace'.

The process by which unstressed subject pronouns came to precede the verb
will be discussed in 8.8. In early Old French the unstressed pronoun object
never appeared in initial position, though there are examples of the
topicalization of the stressed form:

(17) *Moi prendés com le vostre sierf* (*Courtois d'Arras*, c.1200) 'Take *me* as
      your servant'.

In the thirteenth century, however, we begin to find modern-looking
examples like:

(18) *Me volés vous tuer?* (*Jeu de la Feuillée*, c.1275) 'Do you want to kill
      me?'

In earlier Old French texts the most frequent ordering in main
clauses is obviously similar to that of so-called **Verb-second (V2)**
Germanic languages: in the *Chanson de Roland*, for instance, 77 per
cent of declarative main clauses have the verb in second position.
This type of ordering seemed a little later to become almost an
obsession, in that the introductory particle *si* (< SIC 'thus') came to
be very frequently used, almost without semantic justification,
triggering inversion of the verb and subject:

(19) *Si s'en vint a une fause posterne, si s'en ist il de le vile.* 'Thus
      came he to a false postern, thus *he* got out of the town'.

In this example, note, there is no use of an unstressed subject pronoun after
the verb in the first clause, but in the second it is assumed that the inverted
pronoun is stressed (cf. 8.8).

The alleged **V2** character of Old French is often attributed to
Frankish influence, though there are some doubts about whether
indeed the German varieties themselves were **V2** at the period in
which the influence could have been exerted (by the eighth century).
Similarly the fronting of the verb in **interrogative** constructions is
often seen as Germanic in character.

As it became obligatory in later French to express overtly the
subject, even when it was pronominal, the modern **SVO** ordering
became grammaticalized: this change was probably fairly complete

by the early fifteenth century (cf. 8.8). What happened in the later medieval period looks like de-Germanization, and can be connected with the change in accentuation patterns of the language. Whether this signified a change in a single variety or the result of the substitution of one variety for another, as a result of switch in prestige from a more 'Germanic' type to, say, a more 'Celtic' type, can only be a matter for (idle?) speculation. It is however tempting to link the changes to changes in social attitudes, with the aristocratic, feudal 'Frankish' culture losing out to more modern ways of thinking, and a revival of 'Gaulish' mythologies as part of an assertion of national identity.

V2 ordering in French, as elsewhere, may have developed from an underlying verb-first order, where topicalization fronted other elements, leaving the verb in the second place in the clause. In the early Old French texts, in particular, verb-first ordering is not infrequent, and it survived principally in **polar interrogatives** and **imperatives** (cf. Table 8.1). The suggestion that originally in Germanic the verb in second place was an auxiliary which cliticized to the tonic first underlying element, in accordance with **Wackernagel's Law**, makes little sense for French. If the original French underlying order was indeed verb-first, then of course the postulated contrast between 'Germanic' and 'Celtic' ordering is irrelevant.

In modern French **stylistic inversion**, especially with intransitive verbs, is still a feature of more elevated registers:

(20) *Là dansaient les filles* 'There danced the girls'.

It is found also in subordinate clauses with a **heavy NP** subject:

(21) *Le cadeau qu'a apporté le jeune homme qui est venu* 'The present the young man who came brought (/ brought by the young man . . .)'.

One feature of rather formal style, favoured in official documents, is the use of an impersonal construction with a 'dummy' pronoun subject *il*, which allows inversion of the logical subject (like English presentative 'there'):

(22) *Il en sortit un cri* 'A cry emerged from him; There emerged from him a cry'; *Il lui vient une idée* 'An idea came to him; There came to him an idea'.

Only indefinite subjects are normally permitted in this type of construction:

(23) *Il arrive des invités* (/ *les invités) 'Guests (/ The guests) are arriving; ?There are arriving some (/ ?*the) guests'.

The construction seems to have appeared in the 'Middle French' period.

We may compare similar later Old French examples where the pronoun and the verb agree with the postposed lexical subject in what looks like **right dislocation**:

(24) *Il i vont cil viel prestre* 'They go there, those old priests; There are those decrepit priests who go there'; *Il morront maint chevalier* 'They will die, many knights; There are going to die lots of knights'.

However in Old French, even when the subject pronoun was not used, there was not always verb agreement:

(25) *Parmi Paris en vat trois paire* 'There goes through Paris three peers'.

A modern passive construction, beloved of officialese, seems to be a further development of the presentative impersonal:

(26) *Il a été mangé beaucoup de pizza dans ce bistro* 'Lots of pizza has been eaten in this bar; There's been a lot of pizza eaten in this bar.'

It can even occur with intransitive verbs, rare examples being found from the Middle French period: *Il fut dansé* 'There was dancing' (Commynes).

8.5. ADJECTIVE PLACEMENT

Language typology studies, as we saw (8.3), show that **SVO** languages tend to postpose adjectives to their nouns (and adverbs to their verbs), whereas **SOV** languages prepose them. We also saw (8.4) that it is assumed that Latin was, like other ancient Indo-European languages, a basically **SOV** language, and that modern French is basically **SVO**. It is to be expected then that there would have been a change of adjectival ordering from pre-nominal to post-nominal, in the transition from Latin to French.

Modern French adjectives do normally occur after the noun they modify, though with some noteworthy exceptions, especially in the modern standard language. In Old French adjectives were more frequently preposed than in the modern language. In classical Latin, however, as distinct from earlier Latin, it is far from sure that pre-nominal adjective placement was the rule, although it was common. In the grammar books a distinction is often made between **determining** (or 'emphatic') and **attributive** adjectives, the latter appearing most frequently after the noun and the former before. Marouzeau (1922–49) put it more graphically: '*L'esprit place l'épithète après le substantif et l'âme la place plus volontiers devant.*'

In modern French a similar distinction is made, and it looks as if there may have been no change. In many cases there is still a semantic difference between the postposed and the preposed adjective:

(27) *familles nombreuses*, 'large families' / *nombreuses familles*, 'numerous families'; *un ancien combattant* 'an ex-serviceman' / *un combattant ancien* 'an ancient combattant'; *une curieuse femme* 'an odd woman'/ *une femme curieuse* 'an inquisitive woman'.

In discussion of possessives (7.18) I drew a distinction between the adjectival use found in Old French and in other modern Romance languages and their use as determiners in modern French. Determiners are always preposed to their nouns and can be seen as an integral part of them.

In some literary and pretentious official styles preposed adjectives have become very nearly the norm, though found more in definite NPs than in indefinite. The justification given for the different placement is that the preposed adjective is more subjective and emotive, enhancing the semanticism of the noun (*doux miel*, 'sweet honey') whereas the postposed adjective is contrastive (*vin doux* 'sweet (not dry) wine'). The difference has been variously described in terms of restrictive and non-restrictive qualification, of predicative or attributive status, of intrinsic and extrinsic characterization, of reference and referent modification or of relative emphasis.

A few common, usually monosyllabic, adjectives are normally placed before the noun. They usually indicate common scalar or affective notions—'good-bad', 'young-old', 'small-large', 'fine, beautiful' (*beau*), 'pitiable', 'dear' (*pauvre, cher*):

(28) *le pauvre homme* / *l'homme pauvre* 'the poor (pitiable) man' / 'the poor (poverty-stricken) man'; *la chère maison* / *la maison chère* 'the dear (beloved) house'/ 'the dear (expensive) house'.

The preposed adjective can be thought of as almost incorporated into its noun. Indeed bound suffixes express some of the same scalar and affective notions in other Romance languages: similar suffixes have mainly fallen into disuse in French, since the sixteenth century. In modern French where the accent falls on the final syllable of the rhythmic group the adjective will naturally usually receive more stress when postposed than preposed, and so can be seen as more emphatic. Usually the postposed adjectives can be related more to **predicative** (*attribut*) use:

(29) *L'homme est pauvre* 'The man is poverty stricken' (not 'pitiable'); *La maison est chère* 'The house is expensive' (less likely 'beloved').

Participial adjectives, in keeping with their predicative status, most usually follow their nouns; where they are preposed they have fewer verbal characteristics.

In modern usage lexical slippage can result in a greater range of adjectives being used prenominally:

(30) *Air France vous souhaite un agréable voyage* 'Air France wishes you a pleasant journey',

perhaps influenced by the formulaic '*Bon voyage*'. Television presenters similarly wish you *Excellente soirée!* rather than the usual *Bonne soirée!* Such usage is sometimes stigmatized as an erroneous Anglicism.

In the modern literary language extensive use is made of the stylistic device of preposing adjectives that would normally follow their noun:

(31) *un obstiné silence, sa coutumière méthode, un noir rougoiement.*

It is tempting to see the stylistic habit as a conscious echoing of Latin literary practice, rather than as directly inherited from Latin through Old French. Certainly the early grammarians attempted to draw up rules about the placement of adjectives: in the sixteenth century it became accepted that colour adjectives should follow the noun, and in the seventeenth century there was a consensus about the list of common adjectives that normally precede the noun. But a firm ruling was not forthcoming: it was held that native intuition and good taste should prevail here, as elsewhere.

Some adjectives can only with great manœuvring appear before the noun. This is true in general of past participles and of 'pseudo-adjectives' in phrases like *le discours présidentiel* ('the president's speech', not 'the speech which is a president'), or *un linguiste traditionnel* ('someone who does traditional linguistics', rather than 'a linguist who is traditional'). Colour adjectives are always postposed except in overtly poetic style.

In the history of French there does seem to have been discontinuity in transmission, as Old French texts frequently, indeed probably normally, prepose adjectives to their nouns:

(32) *blances mains* = *des mains blanches*; *curteise dame* = *une dame courtoise*; *l'anglois roy* = *le roi anglais*; *son aisné frère* = *son frère aîné*.

In the earlier texts some 60 per cent of adjectives were preposed (though this figure is skewed by the regular preposing of the most common adjectives). In thirteenth-century prose a tendency towards postposition began to be discernible, though in the 'Middle French' period there was no clear patterning, with variation between authors: however, Latinate adjectives did tend to be postposed, rather than preposed.

The habit of preposing is maintained in northern and eastern varieties for some adjectives, including even colour adjectives: influence from German is usually invoked. A similar influence may have been exerted on literary Old French. Nevertheless the influence of Latin on literary style was felt from the time of the Renaissance and of standardization, and preposing of the adjective became a device for tempering its qualificative characteristics, and especially for signalling figurative or emotive nuances.

8.6. INTERROGATION

Intimately connected with constituent ordering is the expression of interrogation in the history of French. There is, surely, little doubt that there have been changes in the way a question is asked as the **VS** ordering of 'interrogative inversion' has lost ground. This is most obvious with **polar (yes/no) questions**, which in the modern spoken language are usually marked only by intonation, or by the prefixing of *est-ce que*:

(33) *Jean vient? Est-ce que Jean vient?* 'Is John coming?'

The latter form, which dates from the fifteenth century and was accepted as standard in the seventeenth, is sometimes regarded as more emphatic, though it cannot easily be seen as an inversion of:

(34) *C'est que Jean vient* 'It's that John is coming',

which has semantic nuances of causation, contradiction and the like.

The non-inverted question structure is like that of the other Romance languages, and probably of spoken Latin: written Latin usually made use of the interrogative particles -NE, NONNE and NUM.

In modern colloquial French 'interrogative inversion' is hardly used in polar questions, except in the *vous* person. Evidence from child language acquisition suggests that it is learned first at school age. In written French, however, such interrogation is obligatorily marked by the postposing of the subject pronoun to the verb, even where a lexical subject is present:

(35) *Vient-il?, Jean vient-il?*

The former construction is called **simple**, the latter **complex inversion**. The latter cannot readily be seen, in the modern language, as an inversion of left dislocated:

(36) *Jean il vient*,

which is characteristic of a more colloquial register. The earliest examples of the construction do however suggest **left dislocation** (8.4), as in the much-quoted:

(37) *L'aveir Carluns est il appareilliez?* (*Roland*) 'Charles's goods, are they ready?'

This type of interrogation remained rare in texts until the fourteenth century. The following quotation from a popular song does however suggest that perhaps **right dislocation** was already, by the late thirteenth century, current in the colloquial idiom:

(38) *Me siet il bien li hurepiaus?* (*Jeu de la Feuillée*) 'Does it suit me, the cap?'

However, from the fourteenth century **complex inversion** became the usual way of asking a question with a lexical subject. By the early seventeenth century it was the recommended construction in text-books for foreigners:

(39) *Jehan ha til disné?* 'Has John dined?' (Sainliens, 1609).

Earlier, interrogative inversion of the verb and a lexical subject **NP** was possible, though never very frequent, in polar questions and it remained a possibility in the literary language in the sixteenth century, especially with modals:

(40) *Doibt son malheur estre estimé offense?* (Marot) 'Ought his ill-luck be judged offence?'

In the seventeenth century, however, this type of inverted question was regarded as precious, and Malherbe rejected as incorrect Desportes's formulation:

(41) *Viendra jamais le jour qui doit finir ma peine?* 'Will the day that ends my suffering ever come?'

Possibly such inversion had always been stylistically marked: many of the early examples suggest a degree of surprise or emphasis like non-interrogative verb-first examples:

(42) Eve: *Est tel li fruiz?*; The Devil: *Oïl por veir* (*Mystère d'Adam*, *c.*1170) 'Is the fruit really like that?' 'Yes! I assure you!'; *Durrad li fiz Ysaï a vus tuz champs e vignes . . .?* (*Quatre Livres des Rois*, late 12th c.) 'Will the son of Isaiah give to you all the fields and vines . . .? (translating NUMQUID OMNIBUS VOBIS DABIT FILIUS YSAÏ AGROS ET VINEAS. . .?); *Las! est morte m'amie?* (*Chastelaine de Vergi*, *c.*1288) 'Alas! is it true that my lady-friend is dead?'

It is possible that in such contexts we have not **stylistic inversion** (cf. 8.4), but **right dislocation** with a null subject pronoun (cf. 8.8). The lexical subject could be interpreted as a (known) **anti-topic**, with emphasis placed on the verb.

Not infrequently the Old French polar question was headed by an emphatic particle (like *enne* or *dun*) which would, during the **V2** period, regularly trigger inversion of the subject:

(43) *Dun ne jetad une femme sur lui une piece de muele del mur. . . ?* (*Quatre Livres des Rois*) 'Then didn't the woman throw at him a stone from

the wall. . .? (NONNE MULIER MISIT SUPER EUM FRAGMEN MOLAE DE MURO. . .?).

Indeed in Old French texts it is not always easy to judge, out of context, whether an inverted construction is meant as a question.

In modern French inversion of the lexical **NP** is still possible with 'partial' (**WH-** or **QU-**) questions:

(44) *Quand est arrivé Pierre?* / *Quand Pierre est-il arrivé?*

This ordering has been described as residually **V2**, where the **WH-** element (usually inherited from Latin—e.g. QUI 'who', UBI 'where', QUANDO 'when') appears in topic position, triggering inversion. In modern style **complex inversion** is more frequent, and sometimes there are semantic nuances distinguishing the two types of construction. Thus in:

(45) *Quand votre fils est-il mort?* / *Quand est mort votre fils?* 'When did your son die?',

the former would be normal, while the latter could be seen as insensitive, implying more emphasis on the event of the death than on the son.

With *pourquoi* only **complex inversion** is acceptable: perhaps this is something to do with the comparatively late development of this originally compound form ('for what') as a **WH-** interrogative particle. However there are early modern examples of **stylistic inversion** with *pourquoi*, in elevated style:

(46) *Et pourquoi commandent les hommes, si de n'est pour faire que Dieu soit obéi?* (Bossuet) 'And why are men in command, if it is not so that God may be obeyed?'

Other originally compounded **WH-**interrogatives like *comment* and *combien* are not subject to the same restriction in the modern language, though relevant examples are hard to find. Even when *combien* is part of the subject NP we usually find complex inversion:

(47) *Combien de jeunes gens n'ont-ils pas été sauvés?* (Balzac) 'How many young men have not been saved?'

On the other hand, *que* as an object interrogative pronoun ('what?') today requires **stylistic inversion**, though in the classical period complex inversion was possible. However, in all but elevated style the periphrastic *qu'est-ce que?*, without inversion, is preferred (though here too inversion is regarded as more stylish):

(48) *Que fait Marie? | Qu'est-ce que fait Marie? | Qu'est-ce que Marie fait? 'What is Mary doing?'*

In non-standard usage non-inversion after fronted **WH-** particles is frequent, sometimes with the insertion of other morphological material that makes the non-inversion more palatable:

(49) *Quelle heure il est?*; 'What time is it?'; *Où que tu vas?* Where are you going? *Comment est-ce tu fais cela?* 'How do you do that?' *Qu'est-ce que c'est qu'on a vu?* 'What have we seen?'

Also frequent in colloquial use are **WH-in situ** questions:

(50) *Tu as fait quoi?* 'You did what?'; *Tu as acheté combien?* 'You bought how much?'; *Tu es allé où?* 'You went where?'

These are frequently used (not merely, as in English, as **echo-questions**), and they appear to be gaining ground in modern speech. They are learned at an early stage in the acquisition process. They seem however to be unattested before the modern period, though this may be a reflection of their colloquial status, rather than of ungrammaticality in the older language.

Interrogative inversion is usually seen as resulting from Germanic influence in the early stages of French. I have suggested that it is connected with **verb-first** and **verb-second** ordering (8.4). Certainly inversion of the pronoun subject in questions is attested early. As it continues in the standard language today, it could be claimed that there has been little change since the beginning of French.

However, the modern colloquial avoidance of pronoun inversion, and the virtual loss of **stylistic inversion** in questions, suggest that there has in the course of history been some reanalysis. It is noticeable that in Old French the use of subject pronouns in postverbal position was more frequent in questions than in other sorts of inverted structures. This suggests that the pronoun subject was often stressed. In the mid-twelfth-century *Mystère d'Adam*, for instance, we find:

(51) *Forma il tei pour ventre faire?* 'Did *he* create *you* to provide a womb?',

where the *tei* is certainly stressed and follows the subject pronoun, which seems also to be stressed. We can contrast this with the early thirteenth-century *Aucassin et Nicolete* example, where the hero is vehemently accusing his father:

(52) *Avés le me vos tolue në enblee?* 'Have *you* taken and stolen her from me?'

Here the object pronouns appear to be **enclitic** to the finite verb and the *vos* is given prominence immediately after the auxiliary verb (not, as in **stylistic inversion**, after the whole Verb Phrase).

In the fourteenth century, however, the inverted pronoun appears to have lost its emphatic character and to have become reanalysed as a mark of interrogation: hence the increased use of **complex inversion**, which was no longer seen as a type of **dislocation**. In the sixteenth century we have the first overt indications that there had been reanalysis, when a *-t-* began to be inserted in writing before the inverted pronouns *il(s)* and *elle(s)* and when the final *e* of the first person singular ending became stressed in, for instance, *porté-je?* It was not long before there were comments on an interrogative *ti* particle used with all persons in popular speech: the *t* infix was also extended to other contexts like *voilà-t-i(l)*, *c'est-i(l)* and other 'inverted' sequences:

(53) *Peut-être Marie reviendra-t-elle* 'Perhaps Mary will come back'; *Hélas!, cria-t-il, je meurs* 'Alas, he cried, I'm dying'.

The particle [ti] was written in various ways by authors imitating popular speech (e.g. as *t'y*). In post-Second World War France it is now rarely heard, but in Quebec further reanalysis has identified it with the second singular pronoun *tu* (which is also used as an indefinite human pronoun equivalent to standard *on*).

The comparatively frequent use of interrogative pronoun inversion, in modern colloquial French, with *vous* is not surprising, as questions are most frequently addressed to an interlocutor, and the inverted pronoun could be readily reanalysed as a question-marker (especially as the *-ez* inflection on the verb effectively identifies its subject). Why the *vous* person should be treated differently from the *tu* person is more difficult to understand: perhaps the polite use of *vous* for a single interlocutor can account for its being singled out in this way (cf. 7.5).

The other interrogative particle [esk] which made its appearance in texts first in the fifteenth century in **WH-** questions and then, in the sixteenth century, in polar questions, was analysed as an inverted form *est-ce que*. As such, it may have been more prestigious and so it had a less chequered history than the 'popular' [ti] particle. Its convenience is that it effectively allows non-inversion, while preserving the myth beloved to grammarians that inversion is somehow more stylish. However, it still seems to have been fairly infrequent in the seventeenth century.

Non-inverted polar questions are rare in texts before the fifteenth century: one difficulty here is that without agreed punctuation marks (like ?) a written text cannot clearly distinguish a question from a statement, without some syntactic, morphological, or lexical marker. It is not impossible, therefore, that some varieties of spoken French have always used non-inverted questions. However it is only in the seventeenth century that we have overwhelming evidence for their popular use, rivalling the type with inversion (or [ti]).

For the medieval French varieties that had verb-first and verb-second ordering, subject-verb inversion would be quite natural: that such ordering was associated with interrogation may well owe something to Germanic influence at the early period. However, when an inverted subject pronoun could no longer bear stress in clause-internal position, it may have come to be interpreted as a mark of interrogation, to be reduced in some unprestigious varieties to an invariable interrogative particle.

8.7. NEGATION

Less obviously connected with word-order is one syntactic change that has almost undisputedly taken place during the history of French, which concerns negation strategies. However, it has been linked with word-order typological changes, in so far as there appears to be an ongoing switch from pre-verbal to post-verbal marking of verbal negation. Originally *non*, and then *ne(n)*, was used before a verbal expression to negate it. Then this negator came to be reinforced by another element, most often *pas*. This latter could originally appear in various stressed positions within the clause but then, like many adverbials, its position became fixed to that immediately following the finite verb, and it became virtually an obligatory part of the negator. In modern non-standard varieties the *ne* of the bipartite negator is frequently lost and post-verbal *pas* remains the main clausal negator. In French creoles, on the other hand, the [pa] precedes the **TAM** markers prefixed to the verb.

Thus there appears to have been a cyclical change by which a pre-verbal negator is replaced by a post-verbal negator, to be replaced in the most advanced varieties by a pre-verbal negator. Let us look more closely at parts of this process, which is inextricably entangled with other changes in the history of French.

In Latin traditional grammar, clausal negation is seen as effected primarily by the 'negative adverb' NON, which normally precedes its verb and can be regarded as part of the verb phrase (**VP**). This survives as French *non*, used mainly to deny a proposition, or in adversative contexts. Where a reflex of NON is used in clausal negation, it has become a pre-verbal clitic *ne*. In Latin a N(E) prefix also serves to negate other elements such as (N)UMQUAM '(n)ever', (N)ULLUS 'none/some'. The latter form still exists in French as *nul(le)*, today rather literary in tone, but the negative NUMQUAM gave way to NON . . . UMQUAM > *ne . . . onques*: it was replaced in the seventeenth century by *(ja)mais* 'never' (< MAGIS 'more'), originally positive and used only with future reference.

Nunqua in the Strasburg Oaths is probably a Latinism; the Eulalia *nonque* looks more genuine, though it is just possible that it represents a regional form of *non* (cf. Walloon [õŋk], [sõŋk] for *on, son* and [nuk] for *nul*).

NIHIL 'nothing', and NEMO 'nobody', which was already defective in Latin, do not survive: in Old French new morphologically negative pronouns were formed by prefixing the negative element *ni* < NEC:

(54) *niun*, < NEC-UNU; 'nothing': *nient* (modern *néant* now used only as a lexical noun) < NEC-ENTE or NEC-GENTE.

What is striking is that modern French negative items are derived from etymologically positive ones, while most of the inherited negative items have been lost. Originally **polarity** items associated with *ne(n)* in sentence contexts have taken on negative semantism when used alone. Today they can still be used with *ne*, but the effect is of **negative concord**, rather than of double negation. These items, known as *forclusifs*, often derive from nominals and include:

(55) *personne* 'nobody'/ *une personne* 'a person', *rien* 'nothing' < older *une rien*, modern (16th c.) *un rien* 'a nothing' < REM 'thing', *pas, point* 'not' / *un pas, un point* 'a step, a point'.

In the same way *aucun* (< ALCUNUS 'something') and *jamais* (< IAM-MAGIS 'yet more') have become negative. *Plus* remains ambiguous, though its different meanings are sometimes differentiated phonetically:

(56) [plydpɛ̃] *plus de pain* 'no more bread' / (*un peu*) [plysdəpɛ̃] '(a bit) more bread' (*davantage* also replaces *plus* in its positive connotations in modern usage).

Use of such items as indubitable negatives is clearly attested in the seventeenth century, and probably were in use earlier.

Other Old French negative polarity items do not survive as negatives:

(57) older *mie* 'not' / *une mie* (< MICA 'a crumb'); *âme* 'nobody'/ *une âme* (< ANIMA 'a soul'); *goutte* 'nothing' / *une goutte* (< GUTTA 'a drop').

Originally the polarity item would be matched to the meaning of the verb; thus *mot* would be used with *dire*, *goutte* with *boire*, *pas* with *aller*.

The modern restrictive *ne . . . que* 'only, nothing but' is a shortened form of the older *ne . . . mais (que)* 'not more than':

(58) *Li povres n'en out mais une oueille* (*Quatre Livres des Rois*) 'The pauper had only a ewe' / *Sa hanste est fraite, n'en ad que un trunçun* (*Roland*) 'His shaft is broken, there is only a stump of it left'.

It is today rather literary and *seulement* is more commonly used (in Canada, also *juste*). From the nineteenth century an overtly negative *pas* could be inserted before *que*:

(59) *L'homme ne se nourrit pas que de pain* 'Man lives not by bread alone' (cf. *Ce n'est pas rien* 'It's not nothing').

In Middle French the *que* could have exceptive force without *ne*: this usage is still found in the seventeenth century:

(60) *Je veux être pendu si j'ai bu que de l'eau* (Molière) 'I want to be hanged if I have drunk anything but water'.

Acquisition of negative meaning by erstwhile positive items can be seen to result historically from the very frequent use of certain items in post-verbal position, in the scope of a pre-verbal negative. The process is of course well known from other languages, like German or English: nominals originally designating some insignificant item (as in 'not a whit', 'not a jot') are frequently used to reinforce the negative.

In the earliest French texts the negator could well have been tonic:

(61) *Elle colpes non auret* 'She had *no* sins': *Non vueil* 'I do *not* want'.

The use of *non* persisted in stereotyped phrases, with *avoir*, *faire*, and *être*, as late as the eighteenth century.

But very soon the reduction and elision of the vowel suggests cliticization:

(62) *Ja mais n'iert tels* 'Never more will there be such a one'; *Ço ne sai jo* 'That *I* don't know'.

The longer prevocalic form *nen* may have carried some stress, but its use may merely have been a device for metrical purposes, to provide an extra syllable, in verse. It is also possible that there was amalgamation with the 'adverbial' clitic *en*.

The *ne* clitic always occupied the first place in a clitic array, and obligatorily accompanied even etymologically negative reinforcing elements:

(63) *Nulz ne se doit en vous fier* 'Nobody ought [not] to trust in you'; *N'as fait noient* 'You have done nothing'.

In the later Old French texts, negation is not so frequently effected by *ne* alone in main clauses, and by early modern French the use of reinforcers (*forclusifs*) had become virtually obligatory. Palsgrave in 1530, for instance, said: 'For whereas they put *ne* before theyr verbes so often as they express negation, like as we use "nat" in our tong after our verbes, they also put after theyr verbes *pas*, *poynt* or *mye* which of theymselfe signifye nothyng but onely be as signes of negation.' Twenty years later Meigret states that not to use *pas* or *point* would be '*bien froedes*'. By the seventeenth century *pas* had become the main negator, and *point* was described as more emphatic, while *mie* was archaic and dialectal.

In the modern standard a sole *ne* element seems little more than a decorative expletive, mainly in complement clauses dependent on some verbs or introduced by a conjunction with 'negative semantics'. True, in modern literary usage *ne* alone can be used to negate a few verbs—mainly *savoir*, *oser*, *pouvoir*—in stereotyped phrases. By the fifteenth century, apart from formulae and some other special contexts, *ne* was rarely used alone as a negator in main clauses, though in certain specific contexts, and in subordinate clauses, it remained a distinct possibility. Relics remain even today, however, of so-called *ne explétif*, *ne redondant* (or, even, *ne abusif*) which was used in the older language in certain adverbial and complement clauses.

Here the *ne* appears to have acted more as a concord marker than as a true negative. One may, for Old French, highlight the optional use of *ne* used after verbs of fearing, and other verbs with psychologically negative resonances, and after certain temporal conjunctions like *ainz que*, *avant que* 'before'. These seem never to have been used as full negatives with *forclusifs*, and may have had some of the same connotations as the subjunctive, implying a distancing of the speaker from the truth of the proposition expressed in the subordinate clause:

(64) *Li Diex d'Amors ot grant peeur | Que Sa gent n'i fust toute occise* (Jehan de Meung *Roman de la Rose*) 'The God of love was afraid that his people might [not] be all slain'.

. . . *ge cuit bien que vos le verroiz ainçois que ge ne ferai* (*Mort Artu*). '. . . I think truly that you will have seen him before I shall [not]'.

This type of *ne* usage, although officially still allowed, has probably not been part of the colloquial language since the seventeenth century.

The *ne* with a subjunctive could imply 'until, before', as in:

(65) *Non feray que n'ayez pris vostre repas* 'I shall not do it until you eat your meal [while you have not eaten . . .]'.

With *avant que* the use of *ne* was rare before the fifteenth century; curiously in the last hundred years its use in formal registers has become more frequent, perhaps as a marker of formality in discourse.

Slightly different was the negative concord *ne* used after patently negative verbs, like *nier* 'to deny', *défendre* 'to forbid', conjunctions like *sans que*, or, most often, in clauses dependent on comparisons of inequality. In these contexts a *forclusif* could be used in Old French and it seems that the negative force was more strongly felt:

(66) *En cele biauté sans faille m'enorgeuilli un poi plus que je ne deusse* (*Queste*) 'Of this beauty without blemish, I was a bit prouder than I ought [not] to have been'.

In the seventeenth century omission of *ne* in such contexts was regarded as '*peu élégant*' and use of a full negative was not infrequent:

(67) *Vous avez plus faim que vous ne pensez pas* (Molière) 'You are hungrier than you [don't] think'.

This was not unknown earlier:

(68) *Je vous aim plus que vos ne faciés mie* (*Aucassin et Nicolete*) 'I love you more than you do [not]'; . . . *plus hault que ne fut jamais homme* (Commynes) '. . . taller than ever man was [not]'.

Similar uses later came to be stigmatized as popular. Boinvilliers in 1802 spoke of '*les ignorants qui disent "La vertu vaut mieux que non pas les richesses"*'.

It is the use of *ne* with comparatives that has survived best in modern French, though some make a fetish of using it after *craindre*, a word marked, in any case, as literary (cf. 4.9). Grammarians have been ambivalent: an *Arrêté Ministériel* of 30 July 1900 decreed '*on tolérera la suppression de la négation ne*' in the relevant contexts, while in 1965 the Académie advocated non-use after certain conjunctions. There remain a few contexts in which the *ne* can truly negate:

(69) *Il n'y a personne ici que Marie . . . ne connaisse | connaisse* 'There is no one here that Mary . . . doesn't know / knows.

Non-standard French tends to suppress the *ne* in pre-verbal position, leaving the old reinforcer, *forclusif*, as the marker of negation: the loss is categorical in some varieties, in Canada for instance. In most French usage, however, omission of *ne* is variable, depending much on region, register, and socioeconomic factors, but especially on degree of education. Small children seem to learn the use of the negative without *ne*, but they incorporate it into their usage, as a stylistic variant, at a late stage of acquisition.

Usually the loss of *ne* is linked historically with phonetic weakening and cliticization of *ne*, which was squeezed between the subject and the object clitics. This weakening tended to favour obligatory use of the reinforcer in the final stressed position of a rhythmic group. The reinforcer was then **grammaticalized** and there may have been a category change for some items. Thus, *pas* changes from a nominal to an adverbial: this change must have been obvious when the use of an overt determiner with a nominal became virtually obligatory, and *pas*, bereft of a determiner, could be reanalysed as a form distinct from the nominal *le pas*.

Thus an intimate connection with the change in stress-patterning and the cliticization of the subject pronouns is assumed. The weakened pre-verbal negator, which was always shadowed by a *forclusif*, had then become redundant, and so it could be neglected. There is some evidence that in colloquial French seventeenth-century use, the *ne* was already sporadically dropped in negative sentences, though the standard continued to dictate its use. This hypothesis is lent some support by the fact that modern Occitan varieties began, in the sixteenth century, to use post-verbal [pa], clearly borrowed from colloquial French, as the main sentential negator.

There are apparent examples from the fifteenth century of *point* and *jamais* used alone as negators, mainly in subordinate clauses and with infinitives, perhaps to mark more emphatic negation than *ne* alone. Certainly in negative direct and indirect questions *pas* or *point* alone was still normal in the seventeenth century, but it could be claimed that there is no true negation, nor indeed interrogation, in:

(70) *Avais-je pas raison?* (La Fontaine) 'Was I not right?' (i.e. 'Surely you recognize that I was right!'),

where it is reassurance, not information, that is sought, and the *pas* is a polarity item, rather than a true negative. Vaugelas agreed that non-use of *ne* here was acceptable, but judges it '*plus élégant*' to insert it.

Current conventional wisdom among generativists is that negation can be represented as a (universal?) non-lexical functional projection, which is ordered hierarchically above the **Tense projection**. The **head** of this projection would be the negator (*ne*, often called in French the *discordantiel*), but in **specifier** position there would be an 'operator' (the *forclusif*, e.g. *pas*). When the (finite) verb raises to receive (or to 'check') tense and agreement features, the head negator raises with it (and may cliticize to it), whereas the operator remains in post-verbal position. The difference between Old and Modern French negation could therefore be resolved simply by postulating that earlier *ne* could negate on its own, and the operator could be non-overt (i.e. absent in the surface representation), whereas today the *ne* needs the overt presence of an operator (e.g. *pas*) to fulfil its negative function. In non-standard French it is the negative head (*ne*) that is non-overt (or perhaps merely subject to deletion by a low-level phonetic rule, which tends to generalize in some varieties), so that in the surface representation the whole burden of negation falls on the post-verbal operator.

One feature we should consider is the similarity in distribution and history between most of the *forclusifs* and of adverbials. Most important, however, we need to take account of the intuition that it is the 'operator' elements (especially *pas*) that have become the true negators, while the *ne* is little more than a decoration maintained by tradition.

The generative story also leaves us with the old-fashioned problems of explaining how and when the 'head' negator lost overt expression in non-standard usage. Comparison with other Romance languages suggests that loss of the NON reflexes was not necessarily preceded by phonological weakening, but it does appear to be correlated with subject cliticization and changes of accentuation.

Standard French, however, insists on the overt expression of both elements in bipartite negation, whenever the verb is present. This is in tune with its 'hypercharacterizing' tendency and its insistence on clarity and overt expression of semantic elements. Complete loss occurs in those non-standard varieties that have experienced a cultural break with the French tradition: predictions that future French will not preserve bipartite negation strategies are therefore shaky.

Note that whereas older French often used an apparent clitic *ne(n)* with a pronoun as a denying 'no!':

(71) *nen-il* (> *nenni*), *ne-gie* 'not-he, not-I',

the modern language uses only the full stressed form *non* (or even, since the sixteenth century, *non pas*, with simply *pas* as a possibility in modern colloquial usage). Note too that, curiously, in certain fixed formulae in colloquial style the negative can be omitted completely:

(72) *T'occupe!* 'Don't worry!'

8.8. 'Pro-drop' and the Extension of the Use of Pronoun Subjects

Already, as we have seen, in Old French texts by far the most frequent word-order was **SVO**: this was especially so in subordinate clauses, but in main clauses fronting of topicalized elements was usual. Where the pronoun subject occurred in clause-initial position it is assumed that it too was emphatic and tonic (though this is not always evident from the written form). Where another constituent occupied this topic position the subject followed the verb. Most frequently post-verbal subject pronouns were not used; where they do appear a tonic form is usual.

The vowel of the *je* form was elided before another vowel, presumably when the pronoun was not emphatic:

(73) *Se j'ai parenz nen i at si prot* 'If I have relatives, there is none so worthy'.

A weak form could also occur post-verbally, as attested in the rhyme *criemge* 'fear I' / *vienge* 'let him come [present subjunctive]' (*Roman de Troie*).

The so-called 'omission of the pronoun subject' is seen as parallel to the non-use of weak subject pronouns in other Romance languages (and in Latin), where inflections usually adequately signal the person of the verb. Modern French has been viewed as **parametrically** different from Old French in that it is no longer, in Chomskyan terms, a **pro-drop** or **null subject language** (**NSL**)—that is, there now is obligatory overt expression of the subject **pro**(noun), except in the presence of a lexical NP subject. The inherited subject pronouns survive only in their atonic forms as **clitics** attached to the finite verb **host**. They are unstressed and inseparable from the verb.

They can even be viewed as virtually bound person inflections, substituting functionally for the inherited person endings that have been eroded by phonological change. This is particularly true of those varieties that frequently echo the lexical subject with a vestigial pronoun:

(74) *Jean il vient* / *moi je viens, toi tu viens.*

How widespread this **clitic doubling** is can be disputed. Some claim that it always represents **left dislocation**, but others detect no prosodic evidence of this in some types of speech. In any case, in the spoken language a lexical **NP** appears in subject position comparatively infrequently without some sort of extra structure (like dislocation or clefting). It could also be claimed that the third person forms act as a default, with zero person marker, so that *il(s)* etc. is not as functionally important, as a person marker, as *je* or *tu*: thus it is not surprising that the doubling is rarely found with indefinite subjects. Note that in the modern standard a third person disjunctive pronoun can still be used without clitic doubling, mainly in adversative contexts:

(75)   *Lui est venu mais elle non* 'He came but not *her*'.

Note too that, for reference to inanimates, *ça* (/ *c'*) tends to be preferred to third-person clitics; it can even be used as an unmarked form with animates:

(76)   *Les petites filles ça dort toujours bien* 'Little girls always sleep well'.

What interests us is how and when the change(s) took place. The evidence of Old French texts suggests that even at an early period the language was not **pro-drop** in the same way as modern Italian or Spanish, which in this respect are similar to Latin. In literary texts of the later twelfth century a distinct difference is to be discerned between direct speech and narrative, and between main and subordinate clauses. Non-use of a pronoun was frequent mainly in those contexts where there would have been inversion of a lexical subject—that is when there has been topicalization of another element, which is fronted to clause-initial position, with the verb in second place. The loss of this **V2** ordering in the late Middle Ages can readily be connected with the development of **proclitic** subject pronouns in main clauses (in subordinate clauses the process seems to have begun earlier), and with the loss of the word accent. On the morphological level the adoption of the former stressed forms (*moi, toi, lui, elle(s), eux*) as caseless disjunctive pronouns (cf. 7.17), can also be linked to the change. Another pointer can be found in the use of the **expletive** pronoun *il* (earlier also *el*) as a dummy subject with non-argumental verbs and impersonal expressions:

(77)   *Il pleut* 'It's raining'; *Il faut* 'It's necessary'; *Il y a* 'There is'.

In modern colloquial speech *ça* is also used with non-argumental verbs. In Old French *ço* was similarly used. Note that an impersonal verb in Old French often introduced a noun in the oblique case:

(78) *N'i ad paien* (*Roland*) 'There was no pagan',

though the use of object pronouns with impersonals, as in :

(79) *Il le faut* 'It must be',

was current only from the fifteenth century.

These developments are dated mainly to the 'Middle French' period. By the fourteenth century some texts had already taken on a fairly modern look, but there was considerable variation between texts, with in the fifteenth century some recrudescence of non-use of the subject pronoun, perhaps as a conscious 'ye olde' feature (e.g. by Commynes, cf. Wartburg 1941). This happened especially when context made the identification of the subject obvious. Even in the seventeenth century there were still examples of non-imperative finite verbs without overt subjects, but these tended to be in subordinate clauses, particularly with the *vous* person. In conjoined or sequential verb-phrases in the standard, and with some impersonal verbs in non-standard speech omission of the pronoun subject is still possible.

In the imperative the non-use of the subject pronoun is for many verbs the only mark of its modality. In Old French, on the other hand, a pronoun (*tu / vous*) could be used. It is impossible to tell whether these were stressed forms: this use had disappeared by the sixteenth century.

The **pro-drop** change must have taken place in some varieties when it was no longer easy to distinguish a stressed from an unstressed subject pronoun, so that a **TVX** construction was reanalysed as **SVX**, the most frequent sequence. We can assume that the **cliticization** of the pronouns is part and parcel of the change from **word-stress** to **rhythmic group stress**, and was originally phonologically determined. Generativist efforts to demonstrate the change as primarily syntactic and parametric have revived interest and led to re-examination of the already voluminous empirical studies on the theme: more recently it has become once again fashionable to see the change as more morphological than syntactic. Attempts to date the transformation of the language to the sixteenth century, with consequences that spill over into the seventeenth, and to ascribe it to major structural reanalysis consequent on 'weakening' of agreement and inflection, remain unconvincing.

Undoubtedly the attrition and reorganization of the person endings must have encouraged the more frequent use of pronouns, but the relative chronology of the changes suggests that obligatory expression of the subject was not a direct result of such weakening. It seems to be only during the more modern period that non-standard usage has tended to extend the clitics to function more as person inflections. Even so, the *nous* and *vous* persons usually retain their distinctive *-ons* and *-ez* inflectional endings. However, the former is often replaced by a construction with an indefinite *on* subject in colloquial speech. Note also that there are varieties (in Louisiana *cajun*, for instance) that distinguish the polite singular *vous* form, with *-ez*, from the familiar plural, with no distinctive ending.

A contrast can be drawn with the creoles where the erstwhile tonic pronouns have become the only, and obligatory, person markers as part of a set of pre-verbal markers accompanying an invariable verb stem.

8.9. *QUI/QUE*

Pressures of space preclude an extended discussion here of the *qui* / *que* distinction in French relatives, which has been linked to the **pro-drop** question. French, unlike other Romance languages, distinguishes the nominative *qui* from non-case-marked *que*.

Qui is also used as a post-prepositional animate relative pronoun, deriving from the Old French dative form *cui*.

In Middle French texts there is some evidence for a tendency to use a single relative form for both nominative and accusative (manifested in modern colloquial usage by the elision of *qui* to *qu'* before a vowel). However there are also hints that the nominative form *qui* was equated with the sequence *qu'il*, at a time when overt expression of the subject became obligatory (cf. Valli 1984, 1992). This suggestion is given support by the rather odd use of *qui* in constructions like:

(80) *L'homme que j'ai dit qui est venu* 'The man that I said came',

where the *qui* acts like a complementizer *que* + pronoun *il*. The so-called **predicative relative** (or **pseudo-relative**), as in:

(81) *J'ai vu Jean qui est venu* 'I saw John come',

suggests that the *qui* acts a bit like complementizer *que*, as in:

(82) *J'ai vu que Jean est venu* 'I saw that John came'.

It may also cast light on the puzzling use by La Bruyère:

(83) *Depuis plus de sept mille ans qu'il y a des hommes et qui pensent* . . .
    'For the seven thousand years that there have been men and who (/
    that they?) have thought . . .'

The morphological *qui* / *que* distinction in the relatives is complicated by the parallel distinction in the interrogatives, which is
known in the other Romance languages. In this case, though, *qui*
is not case-marked, but implies human status. The two series have
intertwined in the course of history.

8.10. THE CREATION OF THE DEFINITE ARTICLE

We have already discussed (5.11) the way the **definite article**—a
determiner that is etymologically related to Latin **pronouns**—has
developed in the transition from Latin to French, and in particular,
how a **locational demonstrative** becomes **definite**, or a **deictic**
becomes **anaphoric**. The weakening of demonstrative to definite
and thence to **gender** marker or **NP** marker is very generally attested
in the languages of the world (Greenberg 1978).

A question that is comparatively rarely posed is about the
category change—how a third person **pronoun** becomes a **determiner**. This is partly no doubt because the category change is not so
salient as the semantic change, and, more important, because the
question is meaningless in the absence of a clear-cut distinction
between the two categories of pronoun and determiner—which has
been described (Harris 1977, 1980*a*, *b*) as merely an 'over-rigid',
'surface structure' distinction. Structuralists have tended to see the
article in French as a number-gender marker and for some (e.g.
Dubois 1965) the French article and clitic pronoun are merely
distributional variants. Generativists often see the article as a
spell-out of a **definiteness** feature, the semantic status of which we
have discussed (5.11).

Rather than talking about **pronouns,** modern theoreticians often prefer the term 'pronominal', which includes 'null pronouns' (cf. 8.8). Here I am concerned only with overt substitutes for full lexical **NP**s—pronouns as grammatical elements that may be vehicles for certain features, like gender, number case, and which are interpreted as referring to lexical **NP**s that are accessible to the hearer. Where a pronoun is used in discourse, the reference in usually topical and therefore highly accessible: the information conveyed by the pronoun need therefore be only slight.

The functional category **determiner** is not universally recognized: in some grammatical models it is the name given to an overt grammatical adnominal element, which modifies a noun in a way not dissimilar to a lexical adjective, but with a rather different distribution. An overt determiner facilitates identification of referent of the noun which it accompanies, by means of **deixis** (**demonstratives** e.g. *ce*), or by signalling anaphorically its individuality (**definite article** e.g. *le*) or its type (**indefinite article** e.g. *un*). The demonstrative and **possessive** (e.g. *son*) determiners are regarded by some as composed of a definite marker supplemented by an extra semantic element, though this 'reductionist' thesis is disputed by others (cf. Kleiber 1986). Nevertheless, most accept that the definite article is a central element of a determiner system in languages which have such a system.

In terms of function, determiners and pronouns are similar: the relevant functions can be filled in various ways in different languages. Western grammatical tradition recognizes the pronoun as a category, but is uncertain about the status of the definite article, especially as many Indo-European languages do very well without such a morphological category.

In Latin, as we have pointed out (5.11), there is only rarely any substantive ambiguity about whether a noun is 'definite' or not, and other mechanisms can be used for assuring anaphoric reference (Lepschy 1980, Maurel 1986, Pinkster 1990).

In modern French, the semantic contribution of the definite article can be minimal, especially with abstract nouns, or, for instance, in **inalienable possession** constructions:

(84) *J'ai mal à la tête* 'My head hurts',

where it has been characterized as a **non-argumental pronominal** (Guéron 1983, 1985), or as an **expletive** determiner which functions as a pronominal (Zubizaretta and Vergnaud 1992). In Guillaumean *psychosystématique*, the role of the Romance article is to 'anchor' the noun, with its airy virtualities in *langue*, to down-to-earth *discours*, by circumscribing its scope. This is not dissimilar from the generative notion that the **NP** is **bounded** or **saturated** by the article. In this way it would function in a similar way to Latin case endings.

The older Romance tradition (cf. Padley 1988) has treated the **article** primarily as a morphological gender, number- and case-marker. Before the modern period it was not seen as a separate category from the pronoun: this perception may be connected with the way Latin was taught (Heinimann 1965, 1967). French possessive and demonstrative determiners are still treated as pronouns used adjectivally in most standard normative grammars.

Although traditionally the article is viewed as subordinate to the noun, recent theories claim that it is in fact the **head** of the **NP** (Hudson 1984) or, among some generativists, a higher **Determiner Phrase (DP)** projection (cf. Drijkoningen 1993). Thus a pronoun could be underlyingly an article whose lexical noun has been deleted (cf. Postal 1966), or the article would be underlyingly a pronoun to which a noun is predicated: cf. Sommerstein (1972). The article would, as it were, establish nominal status, whereas the noun supplies lexical content.

Similar views have been expressed by Guillaumeans: Larochette (1974) suggests that the Postal position is valid for the Saussurean *signifiant*, while the Sommerstein approach is appropriate for the *signifié*.

In the history of French, what is at issue is how the semantic relationship has come to be reflected in the morphology. The French determiners derive from **weak pronouns**, Old French unstressed variants of full (**strong**) pronouns. The radically divergent phonological development of stressed and unstressed forms has favoured semantic and syntactic differentiation. The syntactic function and distribution of the definite determiner is also different from that of the weak pronoun, even though they are often morphophonologically similar. The relationship of the pronoun to the verb, on the other hand, looks superficially like that of the determiner to the noun.

In modern French pronouns (including **non-argumental expletives** as in *il pleut, il faut*) **cliticize** to their verb. Functionally both definite determiners and clitic pronouns can be viewed as acting like inflections. This represents a change from Latin which had distinctive nominal and verbal bound inflectional suffixes.

But precisely what sort of change has there been? One possibility is that Latin had determiners which sometimes surfaced as pronouns, but rarely in adnominal position. In French, perhaps as a consequence of the collapse of the case-system, the ILLE forms have increasingly been used simply as noun-markers. There would thus have been merely a redistribution of elements that already existed, rather than a structural change. Whereas in Latin a zero determiner was the default marker, the ILLE definite article—a semantically **bleached** demonstrative—is the default marker in French, where it is a necessary adjunct to the noun in the absence of other overt determiners.

The incorporation of the article into the lexical noun itself, as found frequently in French creoles, and occasionally in the standard:

(85) *lierre* 'ivy' < HEDRA,

would be the culmination of this process.

Though this hypothesis conjures away the puzzle of the development of the definite article, it leaves us needing perhaps to account for the development of French third-person **clitic pronouns** from putative Latin determiners. We have to assume that the pronoun is a default determiner with a null noun, and that phonological requirements of the rhythmic group (cf. 6.3) led to its cliticization. Eventually, when language learners misunderstood its status, it would undergo syntactic incorporation into the verb, as an agreement marker.

Another, more interesting, possibility is that a morphological determiner system, which includes as a central member the definite article, has been newly created in French. Determiners would derive from Latin pronouns which, in some conditions, lose their NP status. This is nearer to the traditional story.

The creation of a determiner system, differentiated from the pronominal system, would involve a radical shift in morphological structure. How could such a thing happen? How and why should a nominal determiner system develop? Most interestingly to the linguistic historian: When did the change come about?

Although it is usually assumed that the development of the definite article preceded the split-up of the Romance languages, in fact early medieval French uses are, by and large, compatible with regarding the definite determiner as a weakly deictic or anaphoric pronoun. It is only when, later, it came to be used with abstract nouns and the like—with no anaphoric function—that it could be properly considered to be a default noun-marker. This process, as we have seen, was not complete until the early modern French period, when a 'zero determiner'—or perhaps more properly, just no determiner—could no longer be used with, for instance, non-count nouns.

However, even leaving aside stereotyped uses (as in *j'ai faim*), the definite element of the **partitive** determiner (cf. 8.11) is omitted in some circumstances—for instance with the object of a negative verb:

(86)   *Je n'ai pas de pain* / *J'ai du pain,*

or in the standard, before a preposed adjective:

(87)   *de nouveaux amis* / *des amis.*

Are, nevertheless, **determiners** distinguished from **pronouns** in modern French? Besides the definite article and, perhaps, some **quantifiers**, the determiner class comprises the **indefinite article**, the **possessives** and the **demonstratives**. The latter two are often regarded as spell-outs of a combination of the definite article and a personal genitive and a deictic element respectively. They are consistently distinguished from their pronominal counterparts in modern French—an innovation dating probably from the 'Middle French' period (cf. 7.18–19). The first is identical with the **numeral** 'one' and still can be regarded as a numeral rather than a determiner. Its main pragmatic use remains that of identifying the type, but not the individuality, of a new element in the discourse.

Certainly the French grammatical tradition was slow to recognize the existence of an indefinite article. The use of a plural of *un* would seem to contradict its numerical semantics. It was used mainly to designate a collective, especially a pair:

(88)   *unes grosses levres* 'a [pair of] thick lips', *uns grans dens* 'a [mouthful of] big teeth'.

This usage was still found in the early sixteenth century, but disappeared in modern French.

The view of the definite article as essentially a pronoun is useful in explaining Old French free-standing 'article' forms used as pronominals:

(89) *le Perceval* = 'the [horse] of Perceval'; *Por la Charlon* 'For the [sword] of Charles'.

This usage was fairly rare and died out before the modern French period.

The status of the 'article' remains contentious in modern examples like:

(90) *le manteau vert et le rouge* = 'the green coat and the red one'.

It has been argued (Ronat 1977) that, as *liaison* is allegedly blocked in examples like:

(91) *les robes noires et les oranges* 'the red dresses and the orange ones',

there has been noun deletion leaving a trace.

Given some of the uncertainties surrounding *liaison* phenomena in modern French (cf. 6.9), it may be unwise to rely too much on this evidence. A more convincing case would be:

(92) *la robe noire et la orange*;

however, many native speakers reject this (preferring elided *l'orange*), or at least avoid it as 'precious'. Such a usage may be acceptable in a sequence:

(93) *la noire, la orange, la verte,*

but this may be an effect of the fact that many vowel-initial colour terms are still felt as nouns:

(94) *l'orange* 'orange' [the fruit] , *l'émeraude* 'emerald' [the jewel]).

Normative grammars are curiously silent on this question. The French definite determiner, we recall, can in modern usage receive emphasis—as in the *restaurateur*'s:

(95) *LA bisque de homard* '[Here is] the lobster soup!'

With a vocalic initial

(96) *LE agneau rôti* 'the roast lamb',

this use is more problematic.

On the other hand, it can be argued (Warnant 1980) that in *le rouge* in (90) *le* is a pronoun, whereas in, for instance, *le rouge* 'red, redness' *le* is an article (presumably used with generic purport, modifying the noun *rouge*). The anaphoric reference of 'pronominal *le*', but not of 'article *le*', is in this case regarded as central.

Although, etymologically, the French third person subject pronouns are related to the definite article forms, they are sufficiently different in form not to be seen as paradigmatic variants. *Il* (and the later analogical plural *ils*) derives from form *ILLĪ for ILLE, which also gives the Old French nominative article forms *li*, replaced in modern French by the oblique *le*, *les*. The feminine subject pronouns, too, come from a Latin form that seems to have been accented on the first syllable: *elle(s)* from ILLA(s), whereas *la*, *les* are from forms accented on the second syllable.

It is the object clitic pronouns that are morphologically virtually identical to the definite article. However the phonological development of these has differed somewhat, mainly in the modern period.

For instance, the *l* of pronoun forms is liable to elision: this is most obvious in the masculine subject clitic *i(l)*, but is also found in non-standard usage with the feminine and plural accusative clitics. Elision of *l* seems rarely to affect definite article, as distinct from pronoun, forms in modern French, though in Canada *la*, and then *les*, are especially affected (still rather less than the homonymic pronouns), mainly when the *l* is in intervocalic position (cf. Poplack and Walker 1986). In adolescent conversation in north-eastern France, Armstrong (1996) reports up to 17 per cent deletion in definite article forms, but gives no data for object clitics. The widespread and longstanding non-standard use of *y* for standard *lui* (older *li*) (as well as, in some regions, for *le* when referring to a non-animate) may also be an elision phenomenon.

In modern standard French, moreover, the object pronoun forms *le* / *les* do not, like the article forms, encliticize and fuse with preceding *de*, *à* to give *du* / *des*, *au* / *aux*.

The fusion of the encliticized article with the preposition was phonologically regular for preconsonantal *del* > *deu* > *du*, but the change *dels* > *des* is irregular (cf. *als* > *aus* (*aux*), but also *as*, especially in northern varieties).

This distinct treatment seems to be of modern origin: in Old French the weak pronoun frequently cliticized to a preceding element, but only a tonic (dative?) pronoun would be found immediately after a preposition. With changes in clitic placement in the 'Middle French' period (cf. 8.13), the sequences *de* / *à* + weak object pronoun before an infinitive became possible: it has been claimed (Foulet 1924) that, in this context, the pronouns *le* / *les* were accented, and therefore not encliticized to preceding *de*, *à*. We can suggest, rather, that the *de*, at least, in this position was not a preposition but a complementizer (cf. Huot 1981).

The status of *à* is more problematic, as **clitic climbing** (cf. 8.14) was usual in finite verb + *à* + infinitive sequences. It is possible that *à* in this case was a preposition introducing a nominal infinitive. Compare modern:

(97)   *Il est facile de le faire*,

where the *de le faire* appears to be a complement of *est facile*, with **tough movement**:

(98)   *C'est facile à faire*,

where the infinitival phrase seems to be an adjunct of *facile*, forming an adjectival phrase *facile à faire*.

There are a few examples of the reduced form *du* being used in Middle French for the *de* + pronoun + infinitive sequence: where they are apparently attested, it is assumed that the *le* element is an article used before a substantivized infinitive, and not a pronoun (cf. 8.12). I cite one example that does not readily fit into this pattern:

(99)   *Après ces parolles respondit le cappitaine qu'il avoit bien dit et qu'il ne restoit que du faire* (Jean de Bueil, *Le Jouvencel*, vol. 1, p. 79) 'After these words the captain replied that he had spoken well and that nothing remained but to do it'.

It is conceivable that in the fifteenth century (the date of the manuscripts of this text), pronoun and article were not yet distinguished morphologically as in modern French.

Against those who would maintain that we have here, as elsewhere, a substantivized infinitive with a definite article, note that *de* is here much more like a complementizer rather than a preposition: compare *il ne reste que l'action* / *d'agir*. However, the example is isolated; one with a plural *des* = *de les* would be more convincing, in that the substantivized infinitive has no plural.

Whatever the case in the 'Middle French' period, the different phonological treatment of article and pronoun in modern French suggests that they are regarded as (near) homonyms rather than as members of the same category. But in modern French both the article and the pronoun have become proclitic to its host—respectively the noun and the verb. If both article and pronoun are viewed as **agreement markers**, then the parallel development is unsurprising. In the case of the clitic object pronoun, the 'agreement marker' categorization rests on the assumption that the clitic refers to a definite full lexical noun phrase in object position (normally following the verb), that can be 'understood' or 'deleted', but which may also surface in a **clitic-doubling** (cf. 8.12) construction (usually seen as **left** or **right dislocation**).

Discourse evidence suggests that French full lexical NPs within the sentence occur most often in post-verbal **focus** position, whereas overt pronouns are more frequently found as **topics**, pre-verbally. The clitic-doubling device makes it possible for the object lexical NP not only to be elided, but also to be singled out as a topic (**left dislocation** cf. 8.3), without violating the conventions of fixed order syntax or of discourse strategies. I suggest that here a verb prefix (the clitic pronoun) foreshadows the head of the object noun phrase (the article). Such an assumption would square with the view that demonstrative and possessive determiners can include a definite element, which would surface in the related clitic.

But are these agreement markers cliticized determiners or pronouns? Modern French stands out as possibly the only Romance language which virtually always requires an overt noun determiner, and which has developed a distinctive system of possessive and demonstrative determiners (cf. 7. 18–19). It has also cliticized to the verb both subject and object pronouns, which act like inflectional prefixes, while grammaticalizing the ordering of lexical elements within the sentence. I maintain that the definite article is indeed a member of the determiner system and it is tempting to classify the third person clitic pronouns as determiners too, especially as they usually bear comparatively little morphological relationship to the disjunctive pronouns (*lui, eux, elle(s)*) which behave like full **NP**s.

But the third person clitics also form a paradigm with first and second person clitics and they do not fuse, as articles do, with preceding prepositions. So this suggests that they are distinct from the determiners in the modern standard. The distinction may owe something to influence from grammatical arbiters.

The distinction between determiner and pronoun may not hold for all varieties of French: see the Canadian tendency to elide *l* in article as well as pronoun. Moreover the **partitive article** (cf. 8.11) *des,* which in standard usage can be used only as a determiner, can, in non-standard usage, act more like a pronoun:

(100)   *Y'en a des j'vous jure i'f'raient mieux d's'occuper d'leurs oignons*
'There are those, I swear to you, they'd do better to mind their own business'.

Karmiloff-Smith (1979) also quotes childish use of a possessive determiner as a pronoun:

(101)   *donne-ta,* like *donne-la.*

In Old French the case-marked article acts rather like a Latin nominal inflection. As there was no close morphophonological resemblance between the inflected article and its pronominal counterparts, we should perhaps conclude that, as in Latin, nominal and verbal inflections were distinct. Old French may be seen almost as having partially restored an obsolete declensional system (7.16) with what means came to hand, in spite of the ravages that time, language contact, and phonological attrition had wrought.

A change seems to have taken place, though, with the development, from the same etymological source, of third person clitic pronouns and definite determiners, as differentiated verbal and nominal agreement markers. This seems to have happened between the 'old' and the 'modern' language, but may not, of course, be a chronological phenomenon so much as an artefact of the textual evidence we have. Loss of word-accent and reliance on word-order, rather than inflection, to signal syntactic relationships are certainly factors that could have operated to facilitate the shift.

The French creoles can be said to have made another radical shift in their abandonment of both the definite article and the clitic pronouns, as well as in their reliance on word-order to signal sentence roles.

8.11. PARTITIVE DETERMINERS

Modern French, I have maintained, has developed in the course of its history a distinctive set of determiners and it differs from the other Romance languages in its reluctance to use determiner-less Noun Phrases. We have seen (5.11) that during the course of history originally articleless NPs, like those referring to abstracts or unique objects, came to be used with the definite article. Furthermore, with non-count nouns and indeterminate plurals the so-called **partitive** determiners, or articles, *du, des*, etc. replaced, by the seventeenth century, constructions without an article in examples like:

(102) *Donnez-moi (du) vin* 'Give me (some) wine'; *J'ai vu (des) chevaliers* 'I saw (some) knights'.

Similar uses are found in Italian, but are optional, with the northern varieties favouring them more than central or southern varieties.

These newly fashioned determiners are clearly derived from *de* + definite article sequences (*de le > del > du* originally preconsonantal; *de les > dels > des* cf. 8.10), and are identical morphologically with sequences of the preposition *de*, used genitively or directionally, followed by a definite article, referring to a specific individual:

(103) *Le chien du berger* 'The shepherd's dog, the dog belonging to the shepherd'; *Je viens du cinéma* 'I am coming from the cinema'.

It is not always clear whether indeed a partitive article or a preposition + definite article is being used, and interpretation may depend on the semantics of the noun itself:

(104) *Prenez du gateau!* 'Have some of the cake!' / *Prenez du vin!* 'Have some wine!'

In sequences which call for both prepositional *de* and a partitive, one *de* is deleted (this is attested from the fifteenth century):

(105) *J'ai besoin (*de) du pain* 'I have need of some bread' / 'I need some of the bread'

The French partitive article can be related to the pan-Romance prepositional (*de*) partitive construction with a quantifier:

(106) *Beaucoup des chevaliers* 'Many of the knights',

and to what is sometimes known as the **pseudo-partitive**:

(107) *Beaucoup/Pas de chevaliers* 'Many / No knights',

where a partitive *de*, unaccompanied by the article, may be regarded as a case-marker, recalling the Latin use of genitive case (and later of DE) to refer to a part of a whole.

Constructions like these were quite frequent in French by the twelfth century, even, when a non-count noun was involved, without an overt quantifier:

(108) *Il n'ont le jur de pain mangied* (*Quatre Livres des Rois*) 'They haven't eaten (any) bread all day'.

However, in the 'Middle French' period the usage was not totally regular. In the standard today the bare partitive *de* is used when the noun is preceded by an adjective, or is dependent on a negative:

(109) *manger de bon pain, ne pas manger de pain* (cf. also Exx. 86, 87).

This construction could also be used in Old French with possessives:

(110) *Dont prent li pedre de ses meillours serjanz* (*Alexis*) 'Then takes the father (some) of his best servants'.

In some cases it could also be followed by the definite article:

(111) *Si leur fu bien avis que ch'estoit de le gent l'empereur* (Robert de Clari) 'Thus it was truly their opinion that it was (some) of those (?) followers of the emperor';

as the article here is not enclitic, it may be emphatic and have some demonstrative force.

In phrases like *une table de bois* 'a wooden table' the noun forms part of an adjectival phrase, made up of partitive *de* and a generic NP: a distinction can be made, for instance, between *le chien de berger* 'the sheep-dog' and *le chien du berger* 'the shepherd's dog, the dog belonging to the shepherd'.

Similar adjectivals can be formed with other parts of speech , e.g. *une table de trop* 'a superfluous table'.

Another survival of the *de* partitive may be found in adjectival phrases qualifying an indefinite NP, as in *quelqu'un d'intelligent* 'somebody intelligent', *une table de cassée*, which differs from *une table cassée* 'a broken table' in indicating a non-specific table selected from a (known?) set of broken tables (cf. Tellier and Valois 1996). Similarly examples like *deux de rouges* 'two red ones' suggest the choice of two from a set of red things (but cf. also 8.16).

Use of partitive articles as such was well established by the fourteenth century, especially with words referring to food and drink, but they remained optional until the sixteenth. Maupas (1607) opined: '*Ce seroit baillant, disant "Baillez-moy vin", "J'ai acheté bois"'*, and later seventeenth-century arbiters sought to determine the precise rules that should govern the use of the partitive. Violations of the rules, which still find their place in prescriptive grammars, were often condemned as 'Gasconisms'.

The definite article component of the modern partitive article forms must have generic, rather than specific, meaning: the generic use of the definite article was not found in the early medieval texts, so it is not surprising that the partitive article developed quite late.

It is usual to describe the French singular partitive article, subject to certain lexical and syntactic constraints, as determining non-count nouns. The plural partitive is normally seen, on the other hand, as the plural of the indefinite article which is identical with the numeral 'one' (UNUS).

For an older use cf. Ex. 88 and for the link between the partitive and the adverbial INDE cf. 8.16.

French determinerless noun-phrases, except with proper names and in some stereotyped expressions, were virtually banned from the language at the time of standardization. Verb + noun sequences like:

(112) *J'ai faim* 'I am hungry' ['I have hunger'],

tend to be treated in the modern language as single units. For instance, *faim* in this sentence cannot pronominalize:

(113) **Je l'ai, *J'en ai.*

Note that Malherbe judged *avoir de tort* more acceptable that *avoir tort*, while advocating *avoir foi*, not *avoir de foi*.

Sometime the articleless noun can be interpreted adjectivally:

(114) *Il y a fromage et fromage!* 'There are some things that are more cheese-like than others!'

In the modern language the partitive article has extended to uses like:

(115) *Ça, c'est du confortable!* 'That's what I really call comfortable!'; *Il y a du Louis XV chez cet homme-là* 'That man has something of Louis XV about him',

where the definite article element is clearly generic, introducing an adjectival noun (*le confortable* 'what is comfortable', '*le (style) Louis XV*') and the *de* element is partitive ('a bit of', 'something like').

8.12. OBJECT CLITICS

The syntactic question that has probably provoked more discussion in recent years than any other within Romance is that of object pronouns and their ordering relative to the verb. In French, in particular, **disjunctive** or full forms differ substantially from their **conjunctive** (**weak** or **clitic**) counterparts, reflecting earlier morpho-phonological variants, when stressed and unstressed vowels were differentiated phonetically. In French today, where there is rhythmic group stress (cf. 6.3), the difference in form between the object clitic forms (attached to—'leaning on'—the verb **host**) and their caseless full pronoun counterparts cannot be linked to stress differences, and they have to be seen as **suppletive**:

(116) *me | moi; te | toi; les | eux, elles.*

What is even more striking about the object clitics is not their form, but the fact that they precede the finite verb, whereas full lexical noun objects follow the verb:

(117) *Je le vois | Je vois le garçon* 'I see him | I see the boy'.

As we have seen (8.3), it has been suggested that the clitic ordering represents a fossilized leftover from earlier Latin (and Indo-European) **SOV** ordering, but the historical evidence lends little support to the hypothesis. The differences in form and in positioning between clitics and full pronouns mean that the modern French clitics are classified as **special clitics** (Zwicky 1976). In the early language, on the other hand, there seem to have been **simple clitics**, phonetically reduced forms that, when unstressed, were attached to the beginning (**proclitic**) or the end (**enclitic**) to a stressed host form, but still recognizable as related to the full forms. Thus, in the older language so-called **weak** and **strong** pronouns were variants, depending on difference of emphasis. The unstressed object forms were often postposed to an initial-of-clause element—whether the verb, the subject or another stressed word:

(118) *Delivred me ad de mun enemi* (*Quatre Livres des Rois*) 'He has delivered me from my enemy'; *Jo te livrerai tun enemi* (*Quatre Livres des Rois*) 'I will deliver to you your enemy'; *Si l'amad un des fils le rei* 'So one of the sons of the king loved her'.

This is a pattern familiar in other Indo-European languages, by which an atonic element cannot begin a clause (**Wackernagel's Law** is paralleled in Romance by the **Tobler–Mussafia Law**).

How far the Old French forms were truly enclitic, however, is problematic. *Me* and *te* rarely appear in truncated form, except in the earliest texts:

(119) *Nem fesis mal* (*Roland*) 'Don't harm me!'

They may normally have been treated as full pronominals, even when unaccented. The third person forms on the other hand were abbreviated throughout the medieval period:

(120) *Jel baiserai* (Guillaume le Vinier) 'I'll kiss her'.

This would be in tune with their never acting as full pronominals but only referring anaphorically to an already known lexical element.

Today, I repeat, even the non-anaphoric object clitics differ from the equivalent full forms. Romance philologists, from the beginning of the discipline, have favoured the idea that they represent agreement markers on the verb—echoing the person, and sometimes case and gender of its non-subject **arguments** (cf. 8.10).

Parallels have been drawn with Basque, where the verb morphologically incorporates elements representing all of its arguments.

The term **objective conjugation** is used to encapsulate the idea that erstwhile clitics are today **grammaticalized** as verbal affixes. In this view, the clitics are not properly **pronouns**—particles standing for nouns the lexical content of which is known from other sources— but they are more like morphological bound affixes, showing within the verb form itself what its arguments are.

Proponents of this view point to the widespread occurrence in Romance of **clitic copying** or **doubling**, by which a full lexical object and a clitic can both appear in the same clause. They see the clitic as an agreement particle, reflecting with the lexical argument, rather than as a pronominal reduction of a lexical object. Such **doubling** was condemned as repetitious and pleonastic (**expletive**) by tone-setting arbitrators at the time of standardization of French, and so it is, in the modern language, attested mainly in non-standard and dialectal usage.

The **expletive pronoun** is characteristically used, as we have seen (8.3), with **left dislocation** or **right dislocation**, which are frequent colloquial constructions:

(121)   *Le livre je le lui ai donné, à Jean* ' The book, I gave it to him, John'.

In some varieties there is no intonational indication that similar sequences are indeed dislocations, rather than simple clauses.

Non-pronoun status of clitics is also suggested by the various uses of the **reflexive** clitics, for instance in **inherent pronominals**, where the clitic cannot easily be seen as standing in for arguments of the verb:

(122)   *Il s'évanouit* 'He faints'; *Je m'en souviens* 'I remember it'; *Elle se moque de lui* 'She makes fun of him':

Even more so the reflexive pronoun in **middle** (or **passive**) constructions can hardly be seen to have argumental status:

(123)   *Cela ne se fait pas* 'That's not done'; *La porte s'ouvre* 'The door opens'; *Je me suis vu bouleverser* 'I got knocked over'.

Historically there has been much fluctuation between **pronominal** verb forms and their simple equivalents. On the whole it seems that the various pronominal uses developed historically from true **reflexive** uses where the pronoun did have argumental status (as in *Je me lave* 'I wash myself').

Moreover, the conception of the clitic as a substitute for a noun is undermined by the use popular speech makes of a string of clitics, without any clear relation to arguments of the verb. This is particularly true of the so-called **dative of interest**, where a clitic *me* or *te* (sometimes plural *vous*) can be preposed to the verb to add vividness and relevance to a narrative:

(124)   *Il te me lui a flanqué une de ces gifles* 'He gave him a real clout for me, so there you are'; *Au Mont Saint Michel la mer te vous monte à une de ces vitesses* 'At the Mont St Michel the sea comes up on you really fast'.

The so-called **adverbial clitics** (8.16) are also difficult to square with the equation of clitic with pronoun. Another apparent anomaly lies in the use of a neuter clitic as a substitute for a deleted, or dislocated adjective:

(125) *(Jeune) il l'est* '(Young) he is [it]'.

In non-standard varieties the clitic can mark gender, so that, to a question, a female speaker might reply:

(126) *(Êtes-vous contente?) Je la suis* '(Are you happy?) I am [f.]'.

This usage was noted by Vaugelas in the seventeenth century, but came to be condemned in the standard, on the grounds that the clitic is not a gender-marked pronoun, referring to the feminine noun, but a **pro-adjective**, which should be genderless.

In tune with the received wisdom that all shared Romance features must originate in Latin colloquial usage, it has been maintained that the increase in the frequency of pronoun usage in the later Latin texts indicates that cliticization was already under way. However the textual evidence can also be read as suggesting that the modern state of affairs dates from the late medieval period at the earliest. In Old French it is not always easy to discern, from the textual evidence, whether a pronoun was stressed or unstressed: not only was the spelling inconsistent but there was often no graphical distinction between stressed and unstressed forms for the third person accusative pronouns nor for the first and second person plurals. Doubt persists especially when the pronoun is postposed to the verb: we cannot, for instance, be sure whether the pronouns in the following are enclitic or full forms:

(127) . . . *por conseiller vos de ceste chose* (*Mort Artu*) '. . .to counsel you about this matter'; . . . *car ce seroit folie se je tendoie a avoir la.* (*Queste*) '. . . for it would be folly if I tried to have it'.

The atonic pronoun, frequently used in second position, between the subject and the finite verb, over time came to attach itself proclitically to the verb, and the ('**Tobler–Mussafia**') ban on it appearing in initial of clause position disappeared. Proclisis seems to have been well established in French by the fourteenth century and examples of unstressed pronouns begin to appear in initial position:

(128) *T'a il rien fait?* (*Cent Nouvelles Nouvelles*) 'Has he done nothing to you?'

The traditional explanation for the switch in French was that there was a change of sentence rhythm, in the late medieval period, from descending to ascending, with consequent rightwise cliticization, rather than leftwise: that is, **proclisis** began to be preferred to **enclisis**. The hypothesis seems to square with the resistance to proclisis in positive imperative sentences (which, it is assumed, retained descending rhythm longer, because the stressed verb was clause initial). In medieval French postposition of the pronoun to the imperative verb was regular only when it was in initial-of-clause position:

(129) *Or vos en ales et dites li* . . . (*Roman de Troie*) 'Now go away and tell him.'

By the eighteenth century postposition of the object pronouns became characteristic of the imperative (though literary examples of older ordering can be found):

(130) . . . *me donne un baiser* (Musset) '. . . give me a kiss' (for *donne-moi un baiser*).

In the modern language the pronouns in imperatives cannot properly be described as clitics. True, in the negative imperative we have the usual atonic proclitics, but in the positive the object pronouns can occur in rhythmic-group-final position that requires stress:

(131) *Ne me le donnez pas!* / *Donnez-le-moi!* 'Don't / give it to me!'; *Ne le dis pas!* / *Dis-le!* 'Don't / say it!'

In the former example, conjunctive *me* is replaced by disjunctive *moi*, while in the latter the conjunctive form is not replaced by disjunctive *lui*, but there is stress on the *schwa* that in other contexts can occur only in unstressed syllables (cf. 6.10). Even where the standard language dictates a clitic, non-standard varieties frequently prefer a full form:

(132) Standard *Donnez-m'en* / Non-standard *Donnez moi-z-en* 'Give me some of it'.

The fact that sentence-initial atonic pronouns were first attested in the thirteenth-century texts in polar interrogative sentences (with assumed ascending rhythm) appears to provide additional evidence of the influence of phonetic changes on pronoun placement:

(133) *Le me creantez vos? (Queste)* 'Do you promise me it?'

By the end of the thirteenth century, too, the old tonic object pronoun forms (*moi, toi* etc.) started to be used to replace disjunctive subject pronouns (*jo, tu* etc.) while the atonic subject pronouns cliticized to the verb to become virtual inflections (cf. 8.8). It is assumed, recall, that it was around this time that word-stress gave way to rhythm-group stress in French, so that the inherited tonic / atonic distinctions no longer made phonological sense. What resulted was a wholesale reorganization of much of French morphology.

The other Romance languages regularly postpose atonic object pronouns, not only to positive imperative verbs but also to non-finite verb-forms—most generally to the infinitive. In Old French this was also a (rare) possibility, though more frequently an originally dative tonic pronoun was preposed to the infinitive, especially when the referent of the pronoun was human:

(134) *Pour garder le / pour lui garder* 'to keep it / him'.

Postposition of the strong form to the infinitive was also possible, in **right dislocation**:

(135) *Ja mes n'avrai talent de combatre moi a lui (Queste)* 'Never till *I* wish to fight *him*'.

A preposed atonic third person pronoun would be indistinguishable in most cases from an article introducing a substantivized infinitive (8.10):

(136) *Car ma dame la royne a bien gent pour le deffendre* 'For my lady the queen has plenty of people to defend him/ for the defence'.

Occasionally, though, both article and pronoun are used in the same construction. In :

(137) . . . *au metre le en tere (Mort Artu)* '. . . on burying him [at the putting him in the ground]',

an article has fused with the preposition (cf. 8.10) and a pronoun is postposed (though apparently not enclitic) to the infinitive. Here the infinitive appears to have both nominal and verbal characteristics.

By the fourteenth century use of the preposed tonic pronoun was unusual, but examples are found until the late fifteenth century. In modern French the erstwhile atonic form is always proclitic to the infinitive:

(138) *pour le garder*.

8.13. PROCLISIS OR PREPOSING?

For older stages of the language it is often impossible to tell whether a pronoun is incorporated metrically to a preceding or following word:

(139) *A mangier li dunad* 'Give him something to eat'; *A ocire me manace* 'He threatens to kill me'.

Preposing of the pronoun to the finite verb is usually equated with proclisis, but in the medieval language the pronoun was sometimes enclitic to a preceding word rather than proclitic to the following verb, and there are not always clear indications of which:

(140) *Jol dis* > *Je le dis* 'I say so'; *Jo l'otreie* > *Je l'offrirais* 'I would give it'.

More to the point though is the question of whether indeed the forms in question are, at any point in time, syntactic clitics—that is reduced elements standing in for argumental full forms that have gravitated towards the head of their phrase. Are the modern clitics, rather, **inflexional affixes** that have become an integral part of the verb? It looks as if, over time, there has been a drift towards affixation. In the modern standard, however, the perception of speakers, influenced no doubt by the written language, is that the clitics retain some degree of autonomy, and stand somewhere between full words and bound affixes.

We can consider this question in the context of **clitic climbing**, which I shall next examine. It can be argued that when the pronominal element is attached to a verb phrase **(VP)**, rather than to a verb alone, then it is more like a word then an morphological affix. Thus, in the earlier construction:

(141) *Je le veux faire* 'I want to do it',

the *le* is separated from its governing verb *faire* and is proclitic instead to the whole verbal group. In the modern construction, however:

(142) *Je veux le faire,*

the *le* can more readily seen as an agreement prefix on the infinitival verb form.

Changes in ordering of **clitic arrays** (8.15) may also indicate a tendency of the pronominals to change status over time: this is, as we shall see (8.16), particularly striking in the case of the **adverbial** *en.*

8.14. CLITIC CLIMBING

There has been a documented change in the modern period in French of object clitic placement in a two-verb construction, where the second verb is an infinitive. This type of sequence is more frequent in the modern than in the medieval language, mainly owing to an increase over time in the use of infinitival complementation, rather than of finite clauses introduced by **complementizer** *que*, when the subject of the two verbs is identical:

(143) *Or ai talent ke chant* (*Châtelain de Coucy*, end 12th c.) 'I feel like singing [I have an urge that I should sing]' (= *J'ai envie de chanter*)

In the sixteenth and seventeenth centuries the influence of Latin led to the extended use of infinitival complementation with 'saying' verbs where there is a change of subject between the main verb and the subordinate. This was an imitation of the Latin **accusative and infinitive** indirect speech construction. In some contexts this construction is rather bookish and there is disagreement among speakers about when it is appropriate. In other contexts, however, a prepositional infinitival construction has replaced one with a finite verb, and the subject of the lower verb appears as the cliticized indirect object of the upper verb:

(144) Old French *Comanda lui que s'armast* 'He ordered him to get armed' = Modern *Il lui commanda de s'armer.*

In those finite verb + infinitive sequences where the two verbs share the same subject, a clitic pronoun object of the infinitive is usually in Old French attached proclitically to the finite verb: this process is called **clitic climbing** or **promotion**. It is assumed that this is an effect of the close cohesion (**clause union** or **'mateyness'**) between the two verbs, which are treated syntactically as a single unit.

Clitic climbing is found from the earliest period, and it is, in most other Romance languages, still a more colloquial construction for some sequences. With **causatives** (**factitives**) and in **perception** verbs (where the clitic can refer simultaneously to the object of the finite verb and the subject of the infinitive) climbing is still the rule in French:

(145)   *Je l'ai fait venir* / *Je le vois venir* 'I made him come / I see him come'.

The infinitival construction after perception verbs seems to date from the thirteenth century and increased in popularity later. These verbs also allow a more idiomatic so-called **predicative** (or **attributive**) **relative** (**pseudo-relative** in generativist terminology) construction, where the clitic is preposed to the main verb:

(146)   *Je le vois qui vient* 'I see him coming'.

This is related to presentative forms like:

(147)   *Le voilà qui vient* 'Here he comes [See him there who comes]'.

In Old French a gerundive (*-ant* form) was also frequently used:

(148)   *De toutes pars les veist on fuiant* (*Les Narbonnais*) 'One could see them fleeing on all sides',

but by the seventeenth century it was regarded as rather archaic. Old French occasionally used a gerundive also with **factitives**:

(149)   *Et Lancelos le nos a hui fait entendant* (*Queste*) 'And Lancelot has today made us understand it'.

Sometimes in the modern language the clitic (especially the reflexive) can attach to the infinitive, when there is a close semantic connection between the two:

(150)   *Nous l'avons fait se laver* 'We made him wash (himself)'.

In older French texts, a reflexive pronoun would usually not be used in this context unless it were stressed:

(151)   *Il l'oi soi porofrir* (Chrétien de Troyes) 'He heard him issue a challenge [put *himself* forward]'.

With **modals**, which are normally followed by a bare infinitive, clitic climbing was frequent in French until the seventeenth century, when it was ruled out by grammarians, largely on the grounds that it is more logical to attach the pronoun to the verb which governs it. In the modern language the object pronoun is proclitic to the infinitive:

(152) *Je peux la voir* / older *Je la puis voir*.

In older French texts only a tonic pronoun could appear before the infinitive:

(153) *Le roy veult soy acquitter envers toy* 'The king wishes to acquit himself towards you'.

Encliticization to the infinitive was quite rare (cf. 8.13).

One assumes that in the older language, where climbing was regular, there was considerable cohesion between the modal and the lexical verb, occupying a single verb slot in the clause. Such cohesion seems to have been most strongly felt in the Middle French period, when the infinitive could dictate the choice of auxiliary in compound tenses (as in Italian today):

(154) *Li mareschaux n'estoit voulu venir à lui* (*Livre de la Conqueste*) 'The marshals didn't want to come to him'.

Examples of this kind are very rare and may show Italian influence.

The climbing pattern seems sporadically to have spread by analogy to other finite-verb + infinitive sequences, even where the infinitive is introduced by a preposition:

(155) *Emmeline sa mere la commença a enseignier* (*Miracles*) 'Emmeline her mother began to teach her'.

Climbing was more usual when the infinitive was introduced by *à* than by *de* (cf. 8.10, 8.12). This suggests that *de* was less often a preposition introducing a nominal infinitive, than a complementizer introducing an infinitival clause.

In the modern period, there has been a reaction against climbing, with a tendency to cliticize the object pronoun to the verb to which it most closely relates semantically. In French, climbing with modals is certainly no longer permitted in the standard. The intervention of language arbiters seems to have been decisive, but no doubt the changing status of the infinitive at this period also was a factor. Whereas previously the infinitive was 'nounier' in character, in the modern period it acquired more verbal semantic features. This was perhaps linked to its increased use in complementation. Thus in most cases the finite-verb + infinitive combination came to be viewed as bi-clausal, rather than, as earlier, monoclausal with the infinitive acting as the object of the verb.

In the case of factitives and perception verbs, where the subject of the infinitive is also the object of the finite verb, the infinitive and its subject is, on the other hand, today treated as a **small clause**, dependent on the main verb. With factitives, when the infinitive has an expressed object, its subject is 'demoted' to indirect object status:

(156)	*Je l'ai fait faire à | par lui, Je le lui ai fait faire.* 'I had him do it'.

Another factor that could conceivably have played a minor part in the change was that certain sequences were, by the seventeenth century, ambiguous, as a consequence of phonological change:

(157)	*Je le veux tuer* 'I want to kill him' | *Je le veux tué* 'I want him killed'.

The fixing of word-order also may have played some role. Thus in:

(158)	*Il te vit embrasser la jeune fille* 'He saw you kiss the girl',

the meaning today is unambiguous, whereas earlier it could have meant 'He saw the girl kiss you', with postposition of the lexical subject to its infinitive, and cliticization to the finite verb of the object of the infinitive.

8.15. CLITIC ARRAYS (OR CLUSTERS)

One effect of the abundant use of clitic pronouns in French is that it is possible, theoretically at least, to have a whole sequence of clitics before or after the verb. In practice, it is quite rare to have an array of more than two non-subject clitics, and virtually unknown to have more than three. Even then one of the three must be an **adverbial** clitic (cf. 8.16):

(159)	*Jean me l'en a rapporté* 'John brought me it from there'

As we have seen (8.12), seemingly superfluous clitics may appear in colloquial usage, usually to involve participants in the discourse—typically **datives of interest** (or **ethic datives**), but also with no apparent function.

The modern standard has set rules on how the non-subject clitics should be ordered in an array. These rules do not reflect medieval usage which was more flexible (though it is not always certain from the textual evidence, as we have seen, whether or not the pronouns were clitics and which pronouns received special emphasis). On the whole the modern rules favour an order that, in proclisis, place first, second person and then third person reflexive clitics before other third person clitics, third person 'accusatives' (with reference to the direct object) before 'datives' (with reference to the indirect object), and adverbial clitics (pro-PPs) after all others. A favourite mnemonic device, in football (soccer) playing countries (hockey will do as well), is the team line-up using (rather old-fashioned terminology):

forwards (**personal forms**)	*me te se nous vous*
half-backs (**'accusative' anaphoric forms**)	*le la les*
backs (**'dative' anaphoric forms**)	*lui leur*
goalkeeper (**pro-PP**)	*y*
linesman (**pro-PP**)	*en*

An exception seems to be formed by the (rare) sequential use of *le /la, y* and *lui / leur*:

(160)   *Marie l'y lui soumettra demain* 'Mary will submit it to him there tomorrow'.

After an imperative there is a switch in positions—the half-backs usually appear nearest the verb and either the goalkeeper or linesman at the end of the sequence. The final element in the sequence is stressed, but preceding pronouns can be cliticized to it.

The post-verbal sequence *m'y*, as in:

(161)   *Menez m'y!* 'Take me there!',

was condemned by Vaugelas as '*mauvais et ridicule*', though he accepted *l'y*. Non-standard varieties use:

(162)   *Menez-moi-z-y!*

There has also been hesitation since the seventeenth century about the relative ordering of the personal forms and the accusative anaphoric forms:

(163)   *Dites-le-moi! / Dites-moi-le!* 'Tell it me! / Tell me it!'

The former sequence was normal in Old French and is preferred today.

Ambiguity arises with use of the personal clitics (*me* etc.) in both accusative and dative roles, as they show no overt case distinction. There is, in the standard, a ban on sequences like:

(164) **Il me te confie* 'He trusts me to you / you to me',

where a full **PP** (*à moi, à toi*) must be used to refer to the indirect object. A similar ban operates to prevent the personal clitics from being used in conjunction with the 'dative' anaphoric clitics (*lui, leur*).

In colloquial and older varieties there is a tendency to omit third person accusative reference from the clitic array. The use of both clitics in *le lui* sequences was imposed by the standard, in the interests of clarity, with language arbiters insisting on the overt mention of each argument of the verb. But it was not mandatory till the eighteenth century, after much dispute among grammarians, first being codified in 1640.

Discussion abounds on the ways to account for the ordering, which sometimes are described in terms of surface filters that have no underlying significance, of the case marking on the clitics, or of the degree of activity or prominence of the participants in the activity denoted by the verb. The ordering puzzle most discussed is the third person 'accusative-dative' ordering (*le lui, les leur,* compared with 'dative-accusative' in *me le* etc.). Those who seek some sort of logicality in the ordering argue that the 'accusative' forms are more dependent on the verb and so should appear nearer to it, whereas the 'dative' forms, often referring to animates, can occur at a greater distance from the verb.

However, the ordering of the French third person clitics seems primarily to be a leftover from the medieval regular ordering, when 'accusative' third person pronouns often appeared first in the array, because they were frequently enclitic to the first element in the clause. Such an ordering was normal before the thirteenth century:

(165) *Vous le me dites* 'You tell me it'.

If the personal form was stressed it appeared first:

(166) *Moi le donna* (*Ille et Galeron* c.1180) 'He gave it to *me*'.

The change from *le me* to *me le* ordering seems to be coeval with the change from enclisis to proclisis and the loss of **V2** order (cf. 8.4). The modern ordering is found from the fourteenth century, and was generalized in the sixteenth century. Here again the cliticization of the subject pronouns had a hand in the change. In Old French the sentence could begin with a stressed subject pronoun with an encliticized third person object pronoun (*jol* etc.). This was no longer possible when subject pronouns could no longer stand alone.

It was at the same period that the erstwhile stressed form *lui* began to be substituted for the unstressed dative *li*. In Old French the sequence *le li* was rare, and the dative form *li* probably was reinterpreted as the sequence *l'y*, with the 'adverbial' clitic preceded by the 'accusative' clitic:

(167) *Li empereres li otroia* (Villehardouin) 'The emperor granted it to him'.

The substitution of *lui* for *y* here was part and parcel of an attempt to distinguish the animate **dative**, or 'indirect object' (third argument) form *lui* from the 'adverbial' **pro-PP** *y*, which I shall discuss in the next section.

8.16. Adverbial Clitics

French, like some other modern, and most older, Romance languages, uses clitic pronoun-like forms for **locative** reference. These are derived from Latin ıbı 'there', or perhaps ʜıc 'here', (*y*), and ıɴᴅᴇ 'thence' (*en*):

(168) *Il y va* 'He goes there' (/ *Il va à Paris*); *Il en vient* 'He comes from there' (/ *Il vient de Paris*).

The earliest French occurrences of both ıbı and ıɴᴅᴇ reflexes are found in the Strasburg Oaths:

(169) . . . *nun li iv er* 'I will not be to him in this respect. . .'; *int returnar* '. . .to turn back from it'.

Already the forms seem to act as a stand-in for a prepositional phrase (**pro-PP**) rather than just locational adverbs. *Y* came regularly to stand in for almost any *à* + **NP** sequence while *en* substituted for *de* + **NP**:

(170) *J'y pense* = *Je pense à cela* 'I think of it'; *J'en ai peur* = *J'ai peur de cela* 'I am frightened of that'.

They can also double up a right-dislocated preposition + infinitive sequence:

(171)   *David y est obligé, à payer* 'David is obliged to pay [to (do) it]'; *Jean en a découragé Marie, de partir* 'John discourages Mary from going away [from it]'; *Marie en est heureuse, de partir* 'Mary is happy to go away [to (do) it]'.

In Old French they could refer to human beings:

(172)   *Quatre conteses sempres i at mandedes* (*Roland*) 'Four countesses still he has sent to him' (modern clitic *lui* or **PP** *à lui*); *Pitiet en at* (*Roland*) 'he had pity on him' (modern **PP** *de lui*).

The placement of *y* and *en(t)* relative to the verb was in Old French similar to that of unstressed object pronouns:

(173)   *Tout vous en voliez oster* (*Queste*) 'You want to take all of it away'; *J'avroie le corage de mettre i main* 'I would have the courage to place hands on it'; *Je le vous baille a faire ent chou que vous vaurres* (Robert de Clari) 'I give it to you to do with it what you want'; *Alum nus ent!* (*Quatre Livres des Rois*) 'Let's go off!'

En widened its scope with the development in early Modern French of the **partitive article** (8.11), which by origin was compounded with *de*:

(174)   *J'achète du pain* 'I buy some bread' > *J'en achète* 'I buy some [of it]'; *J'ai beaucoup de cela* 'I've a lot of that > *J'en ai beaucoup* 'I've a lot [of it]'.

An extension of this use is exemplified in:

(175)   *Je veux quatre livres* 'I want four books' > *J'en veux quatre* 'I want four [of them]',

where the pronominal suggests that it substitutes for a full noun phrase with a partitive *de* covertly accompanying the numeral (cf. 8.11).

When the language was standardized it was decreed that *y* and *en* should be confined to reference to inanimates:

(176)   *Je lui réponds* 'I reply to him' / *J'y réponds* 'I reply to it (e.g. *à une lettre*)'; *Je reçois sa réponse* 'I receive his reply' / *J'en reçois la réponse* 'I receive the reply from it (e.g. *de ce bureau*)'.

However this distinction does not hold water in actual usage and there has been much fluctuation since the seventeenth century, especially with *y*:

(177) *J'y rapporte toutes choses* (Madame de Sévigné) 'I link everything to you [to it]'; *Le tiroir devait lui | ? y appartenir, à cette table* 'The drawer should belong to it, to this table'.

En is usually confined to non-animate reference, but possessives are also used in contexts like:

(178) *Je ne vois pas la maison, mais je vois son toit | j'en vois le toit* 'I can't see the house but I see its roof'.

In some varieties (as in east French dialects) *y* can be also be used as a neuter accusative pronoun:

(179) *J'y fais* 'I do it' (= *Je fais ça*). Cf. also colloquial *Ça y est* [saje] 'That's it!'

Y and *en* sometimes seem to have no specific function, as in *en imposer, en vouloir à quelqu'un* or *n'y pouvoir rien, il y a*.

In modern French when both adverbial clitics are present they are ordered *y en*. Effectively this occurs only in phrases like:

(180) *Il y en a . . .* 'There are some . . .',

in which the [jɑ̃ⁿ] is treated as a single element.

In principle it is possible to say:

(181) *J'y en ai mis beaucoup* 'I've put a lot of it there',

but today one of the clitics would be in practice replaced by a full form:

(182) *J'y ai mis beaucoup de cela | J'en ai mis beaucoup là*.

In the seventeenth century we do find:

(183) *Je n'y en ai point vu* (Molière) 'I didn't see anything of it there'; *J'y en vois si peu* (La Bruyère) 'I see so little of it there'.

In medieval French the ordering *en i* was usual (though examples are fairly infrequent):

(184) *La en i ad assez de morz* (Villehardouin) 'There there were a lot of them dead'; *Mult en i ad d'ocis* (*Quatre Livres des Rois*) 'There were a lot of them killed'.

En came, in the early modern period, to be more closely related to its verb. In *s'en aller*, for instance, the clitic retains some separate morphological identity in the standard, but *s'enfuir* and *s'endormir* have gone a step further by incorporating the clitic into the lexical form of the verb. This development is tied in with the idea that the clitic is an inflectional prefix. However, this cannot apply to use with the imperative, where *en* can occur in clause-final position and bear stress.

By the sixteenth century the pre-verbal *y en* order was preponderant (and the modern graphy for *y* had become accepted). This order was then adopted in the seventeenth century as standard.

Vaugelas advised: '*Il faut dire "il y en a" et jamais "il en y a" comme l'on disoit anciennement.*' By 1698 the Académie declared: '*On a peine à croire que l'on l'ait jamais dit.*'

8.17. AGREEMENT

We have argued that the French clitics can be regarded as **agreement markers**. **Agreement**, or **concord**, is an important part of the French morphosyntactic set-up. Usually by this term we mean the morphological way verbs match up with their subjects, adjectives with their nouns, and anaphoric pronouns with their co-referential nouns. Agreement is one way in which textual cohesiveness is reinforced by morphological conventions: the **controlling** element transfers to its satellite certain of its features—like case, gender, person, number. If we see clitics as affixes which signal the relationship of the verb to its arguments, then we are extending somewhat the traditional scope of agreement, but we are not distorting it.

Apart from this extension, agreement strategies have not basically changed in the history of French. What has happened is that the morphological markers of subject–verb and noun–adjective agreement have become less consistent and less clearly marked, partly as a consequence of phonological attrition, but also, as we have seen, by paradigmatic simplification. More reliance is made today on positioning of related elements than on morphological variation. Thus subjects precede their verb: when they follow the verb may not always show appropriate morphological agreement, as in non-standard presentative use:

(185)　*C'est les flics* 'It's the cops'.

Similarly adjectives are juxtaposed to their nouns, but when used predicatively they may, in non-standard usage, not agree in number and gender, especially if they are located at a distance from the controlling noun. With conjoined nouns, too, gender agreement in the adjective is preferentially made with the juxtaposed noun, whereas standard grammar dictates use of a 'neutral' (i.e. masculine) form:

(186) *Les hommes et les femmes élégantes* 'Elegant men and women'.

Speakers are advised in cases like this to '*tourner autrement*' to avoid the conflict and to say:

(187) *Les femmes et les hommes élégants.*

There is also a tendency for pronouns that hark back to animates, to reflect sex, animacy, or plurality in the real world rather than the gender and number of the world of grammar:

(188) *Où est le docteur? Elle est dans le salon* 'Where is the (female) doctor? She is in the drawing-room.'

One way agreement strategies have shifted in the course of the history of French is to do with **past participles**. These originate as passive verbal adjectives which we expect to agree in gender, number (and case where appropriate) with the nouns with which they are linked. When used predicatively, whether as descriptive adjectives, as part of the morphological **passive**, or of the perfect of an **unaccusative** (5.8) or **pronominal** (**reflexive**) verb, they agree with the subject of *être*:

(189) *Elles sont soignées*; *Elles ont été tuées*; *Elles sont arrivées*; *Elles se sont lavées* 'They (f.) are well turned out; they have been killed; they have arrived; they have washed themselves'.

This is no more than we expect. What is new in French is that in the **compound past** (**perfect**) tense with the *avoir* auxiliary the participle can also agree with its direct object of the verb, but only if it linearly precedes the verb:

(190) *Les lettres que j'ai écrites*; *Je les ai écrites* / *J'ai écrit les lettres* 'The letters I have written; I have written them [the letters] / I have written the letters'.

For the majority of past participles, there is today no phonetic mark of this agreement. Thus:

(191) *Je l'ai aimé* 'I loved him' / *Je l'ai aimée* 'I loved her',

are indistinguishable for most modern standard speakers, though, as we have seen (6.12), until fairly recently a vowel length distinction persisted.

In writing many speakers fail to mark the agreement, of which they probably are not aware: hence since 1902 the French education authorities have (in principle) 'tolerated' mistakes in agreement in examination scripts.

The agreement of the past participle with the object of the compound verb is clearly a remnant of an older stage in which the *avoir* was still a full verb, not an **auxiliary** (3.15), in such constructions, and the participle was more adjectival. The modern **compound past** (*passé composé*) has become more cohesive and today it is used in the same way as morphologically simple tenses, to refer to events in the past (5.8). The order auxiliary + participle is now obligatory (as we would expect in a **VO** language), but some adverbs, including negative *pas*, still can intervene between the two. It can therefore be argued that it is not fully **morphologized** to count as a single inflected word. In any case it would be unlike other unitary verb forms in that the person inflections appear internally, not word-finally, and that it can inflect (on the participle) for gender.

However, if we continue to view the participle in the *passé composé* as adjectival in character, why should it agree only with a preceding, and not a following, direct object? It is true, as we have seen, that participial adjectives normally follow their nouns, and so it is more likely that the participle will be seen to have adjectival qualities if it refers to a preceding noun. But it seems ludicrous to imagine that the participle hovers between verbal and adjectival status, to fall into different camps with a slight switch in construction. No wonder, then, that over the centuries past participle agreement of this sort has intrigued linguists, who have tried to make semantic or syntactic sense of it.

One recent suggestion is that the preceding object acts like the subject of the participle to trigger agreement in a **small clause**, which is dependent on the finite *avoir* form.

Until the fourteenth century textual evidence shows that the object of the participle, more often than not, preceded it. Noun objects were frequently topicalized, but did not always trigger agreement:

(192) *Malveise garde t'ai fait sus mun degret* (*Alexis*) 'I gave you inadequate protection under my stairway'.

It is possible that here agreement was not made with a non-specific NP object. In modern French this type of non-agreement has survived with impersonal verbs:

(193) *Les chaleurs tropicales qu'il a fait* 'The tropical heat that has occurred'.

When however the object intervened between the auxiliary and the participle agreement was most frequently, though not invariably, made:

(194) *Vos li avez tuz ses castels toluz* (*Roland*) 'You have taken from him all his castles'.

In cases like these *avoir* can almost be interpreted as a full verb and *tolu* as a passive participle used adjectivally.

Old French poets were quick to make use in rhyme of the possibility of the variation between agreeing and non-agreeing participle, especially to distinguish between masculine and feminine rhyme schemes.

When the participle agreed with a following object, it is possible to view the noun as transposed, from the slot before the participle into final (**anti-topic**) position:

(195) *Et maintenant qu'elle ot dite ceste parole* (*Queste*) 'And now that she had said this word' (< *elle ot ceste parole dite* 'she has this word said').

In other examples, without agreement, the two verbal elements can be seen as more closely associated, with the object postposed:

(196) *J'ai creu vostre parole* (*Chastelaine de Vergi*, *c*.1290) 'I believed your word.'

Again here, though, the addition or subtraction of a syllabic **feminine** *e* was made good use of in versification.

Agreement was particularly frequent (though still not obligatory) when the object pronoun preceded the finite verb:

(197) *Neporquant les a salués* (*Chrétien de Troyes*) 'Nevertheless he greeted them'.

Topicalizing fronting of *avoir* to clause-initial position was rare, suggesting that it already was treated as an unemphatic (auxiliary?) form. Fronting is however found, after an emphatic element, when it is followed by its pronouns. In:

(198) *Sire, ai le ge fait* (Chrétien de Troyes) 'Sire, I have done it',

both pronouns seem to carry some stress. Most examples of this sort are interrogatives. Agreement of the past participle appears to be optional:

(199) . . . *pere, aves les vos obliees?* (*Aucassin et Nicolete*) 'Father, have you forgot them?'; *Nos qatre dex ont les il retenu?* (*Chanson d'Aspremont*) 'Our four gods, have they kept them?'

Possibly the difference here is that the doubled pronoun in the latter example (with **left dislocation**) is atonic and so it does not trigger agreement. Unambiguously unstressed forms in such constructions are rare. In:

(200) *As l oid?* (*Quatre Livres des Rois*) 'Have you heard it?',

the elided pronoun appears to be proclitic to the participle, rather than enclitic to the finite verb.

Agreement could occur even if the past participle was fronted:

(201) *Traveilliez les ot* . . . (*Vair Palefroi*) 'He had hustled them . . .'

This is comparable with the fronting of the participle with a lexical object:

(202) *Ceinte a l'espee* (*Amis et Amile*) 'He has girded the sword'
      (< . . . *a l'espee ceinte*)

What emerges from numerous detailed investigations of earlier French usage is that there was great flexibility, but that, as time went on, the ordering auxiliary + participle + noun object grew more frequent and participial agreement with the object concomitantly decreased. Agreement between a proclitic object pronoun and the participle that governs it remained frequent, though not categorical, in the sixteenth century.

Note that we have suggested that the object clitic can itself be viewed as an agreement marker, so the idea that it might trigger morphological agreement in the participle is not outrageous.

In the sixteenth century the notorious rule about agreement with a preceding direct object was formulated by Marot in a 1538 poem, possibly with his tongue in his cheek, and not without arousing dissent at the time and later. Doubtless sixteenth-century grammatical opinion was influenced by Italian. In modern Italian the participle regularly agrees with a preceding third person object clitic pronoun, but not with a fronted noun object; earlier usage fluctuated, as it did in French.

The rather arbitrarily formulated rule was later accepted by the standard. Vaugelas declared: '*En toute la Grammaire Française, il n'y a rien de plus important ny de plus ignoré.*' The rule was rationalized by appeal to perceptual strategies: where the object has been fronted from its logical (post-verbal) position, its grammatical features of gender and number are echoed in the participle that governs it, in the interests of cohesiveness.

Grammarians from the seventeenth century on, having accepted the rule in principle, have devoted much effort to working out the rationale of ambiguous cases. Thus, for instance, a distinction can be made between (homophonous):

(203)   *Je les ai vu piller* 'I saw them being robbed',

and:

(204)   *Je les ai vus piller* 'I saw them robbing',

or between:

(205)   *Les trois millions qu'a coûté cette maison* 'The three million this house has cost',

and:

(206)   *Les mille efforts qu'a coûtés cette épreuve* 'The thousand efforts that this test has required'.

In most of these discussions the guiding principle is to identify the logical object of the participle which will trigger the agreement. Sometimes, however, phonological considerations have entered into it: for instance, when the participle was followed by other material there was hesitation about the vowel lengthening or consonant insertion that might ensue:

(207) *Elle s'est rendu[e] Catholique* 'She became a Catholic'; *Elles se sont fait[es] rendre* 'They gave themselves up'.

The acceptance of the past participle agreement rule seems to be a clear-cut case of a change in usage, which was induced by a misunderstanding on the part of sixteenth-century grammarians who were confused by the apparent chaos of contemporary usage, and who were influenced by the prestige of Renaissance Italian. Modern speakers of legitimate French have adopted the rule into their own grammars, regarding it as a mark of *bon usage*.

In literary French agreement can even sometimes be made with a preceding *en*, in spite of its status as **pro-PP** rather than **pro-NP**. This is found particularly in the presence of a quantifier:

(208) *Et de ce peu de jours si longtemps attendus | Ah malheureux! combien j'en ay déjà perdus* (Racine) 'And of these few days awaited for so long. Alack a day! how many I have already lost [of them]'; '*Ce sont vos lettres qui m'ont grisées | Ah! songez combien depuis un mois que vous m'en avez écrites* (E. Rostand) 'It is your letters that have intoxicated me. Ah! think how many you have written me [of them] in the last month'.

It has been argued that this happens only when the *en* refers to items in a known set. However this is not true of all examples. In the following (from Stendhal's correspondence) we may have merely (orthographical) hyper-correction:

(209) *Ses ordres, s'il en a donnés, ne me sont parvenus* 'His orders, if he gave any [of them], haven't reached me'.

However, for many speakers, the agreement rule is inoperative, and may be viewed as an arbitrary and unwanted intrusion from school grammar. In the varieties used by these speakers the loss of agreement is to be linked with the reanalysis of the participle in the compound tenses as more verbal than adjectival, and as active rather than passive.

FURTHER READING

On syntax: Belletti and Rizzi 1995, Matthews 1981, Roberts 1996, Trask 1993.
On French syntax: Blanche-Benveniste *et al.* 1984, Harmer 1979, Hollerbach 1994, M. A. Jones 1996, Le Bidois 1971.

On historical syntax: Faarlund 1990, Fisiak 1984, Gerritsen and Stein 1992, Haiman 1974, Harris and Campbell 1995, Joseph 1983, Li 1977, Lightfoot 1979, 1988, 1991, Traugott 1965, 1969.

On the history of French' syntax: Ashby 1982, 1991, Foulet 1928[3], Gamillscheg 1957, Haase 1888, M. B. Harris 1978, Herslund 1980, 1990, Ménard 1973[3], Schwegler 1990, Skårup 1975, Sneyders de Vogel 1927[2].

On word-order and word-order change: J. N. Adams 1977, 1994, M. Adams 1988*b*, Atkinson 1973, Barnes 1985, Battye and Roberts 1995, Bauer 1992, Bichakjian 1987, 1989, Blinkenberg 1928, Buridant 1987, Clifford 1973, Crabb 1955, Dardel 1983, 1989, Dardel and Haadsma 1976, Dees 1980*b*, Dill 1935, G. Eckert 1986, Fleischman 1991, Foulet 1924, Geisler 1982, Greenberg 1963, Haarhoff 1936, M. B. Harris 1984*a*, *b*, J. A. Hawkins 1983, 1994, Herman 1954, Lambrecht 1981, 1987, Le Bidois 1952, Lewinsky 1949, Li 1975, 1976, Lightfoot 1995, Lightfoot and Hornstein 1994, Lindhorst 1978, Mangold 1950, Marchello-Nizia 1995, Marx 1881, Panhuis 1982, 1985, Picard 1992, Pollock 1989, Price 1961*a*, 1973, van Reenen and Schøsler 1992, 1995, Richter 1903, Rickard 1962, Roberts 1994, Schlickum 1882, Thurneysen 1892, Vance 1996, Vennemann 1974, Wall 1980, Williams 1994, Zwanenburg 1978.

On adjective placement: Bartning 1980, Dardel 1987, Delomier 1980, Førsgren 1978, Leischner 1989, Waugh 1977, Wilmet 1981.

On interrogation: Coveney 1995, 1996, Finke 1983, Foulet 1921, Goody 1978, Kaiser 1980, Kayne 1972, 1983, Korzen 1983, 1985, Obenhauer 1976, Posner 1995*b*, Renchon 1967, Rizzi and Roberts 1989, Roberts 1993, 1994, Schulze 1884, 1888, Ultan 1978, de Wind 1994.

On negation: Ashby 1981*a*, 1991, Ayres-Bennett 1994*a*, Bernini *et al.* 1987, von Bremen 1986, Coveney 1990, 1996, Degraff 1993, Gaatone 1971, Haegeman 1995, R. Martin 1966, 1972, Martineau 1994, Massicotte 1986, Milner 1979, Möhren 1980, Moignet 1959*b*, 1965, Cl. Muller 1978, 1991, Offord 1976, Posner 1984, 1995*b*, Price 1962, 1978, Quéffelec 1988, Rowlett 1993, Sankoff and Vincent 1977, Schwegler 1983, 1988, Sturm 1981, Winters 1987.

On pro-drop: M. Adams 1987*a*, 1988*b*, Ashby 1982, 1991, Auger 1993, 1994, 1996, Blanche-Benveniste 1994, Dufresne and Dupuis 1994, Foulet 1935, Franzén 1939, Grad 1964, Haiman 1974, Hirschbühler 1990, Hirschbühler and Junker 1988, Humphreys 1932, Jacob 1990, Offord 1971, Piatt 1898, Posner 1994*c*, Price 1961*b*, 1973, Priestley 1955, Rizzi 1984, Safir 1986, Vance 1988, 1989, Vanelli *et al.* 1985, Wartburg 1941.

On qui / que: Cinque 1995, Deulofeu 1981, Guiraud 1960, Jokinen 1978, Kayne 1976, R. Martin 1967, Moignet 1967, Moreau 1971, Posner 1985*a*, Prebensen 1982, Rothenberg 1979, Schwarze 1974, Wilmet 1978.

On the articles: cf. Chapter 5 on 'definiteness'; also Ashby 1984, Picabia 1986, Posner 1995*a*, Renzi 1979, Schmitt 1987.

On object clitics: Ashby 1977, 1991, Benincà 1995, Borer 1986, Foulet 1935, Herschensohn 1980, Jacobs 1993, Kayne 1991, Klavans 1985, Kok 1985, Labelle 1985, Lerch 1940, C. Lyons 1990, Melander 1928, Meyer-Lübke 1897, J.-Y. Morin 1975, Y.-C. Morin 1979, 1981, Ramsden 1963, Rivero 1986, Uriagereka 1995, Wanner 1974, 1986, 1987, Zwicky 1985.

On clitic climbing: Galet 1972, Kayne 1989*b*, Moignet 1970, Napoli 1981, Pearce 1982, 1990.

On clitic arrays: Baciu 1983, Emonds 1975, Iordanskaja 1982, Laenzlinger 1993, Posner 1980*b*, Seuren 1976, Wanner 1974.

On adverbial clitics: Elliott 1986, Gaatone 1980, Le Flem 1986, Pinchon 1972, Pollock 1986, Ruwet 1990, Wunderli 1982, 1987.

On past participle agreement: Blinkenberg 1950, B. Brown 1988, Høybye 1944, Kayne 1989*a*, 1993, Lefebvre 1988, Levitt 1973, Moravcsik 1978, Moritz and Valois 1994, J. C. Smith 1992, 1995.

In Place of a Conclusion

I cannot hope to summarize what I have said in the course of this book, but I should like to repeat some of the general points I have made and tried to illustrate.

Language change and linguistic change can be distinguished, in much the same way as language history and historical linguistics. The former is a sort of history, with some of the same aims: the reconstruction of the past and the tracing of changes. A 'language', within this perspective, is a social institution, with variation commensurate with the size and complexity of the community which uses it. What most people mean by the 'language' is a prestigious **norm**, which may be only one of a number of competing norms within the community. Native speakers of a language will usually acquire, as one of their social skills, a feeling for the significance of the norms and when and how they should be used. Some speakers remain in a more or less child-like state, in not knowing how to handle any norm other than the one that predominates in their environment. Resistance to other usages may be ideologically motivated—by purism, snobbery, or xenophobia, for instance—or may be a consequence of lack of exposure to, or inability to absorb, the requisite social experiences.

Language change, within this perspective, is usually a kind of language shift, by which speakers abandon one norm and adopt another. This can happen gradually, as the older norm is used in fewer circumstances and by fewer speakers, or it can come about suddenly, when there is some sort of social catastrophe, like the destruction of a large part of the population, or subjugation by an alien authority. One can postulate that the substitution of Latin for Gaulish, as of standard French for dialectal French, was effected in the former way, whereas the adoption by African slaves of a variety of French was a much more catastrophic shift. In both cases the abandoned norm may leave traces in usage of the newly preferred norm, but in the latter case these traces will be more salient, so that the adopted language can be seen as a new creation, rather than a continuation of an older language. When the differences are typological, involving profound differences in the organization of the grammar, then we can talk about **creolization**: this is necessarily an unusual development, as it occurs in unusual circumstances.

However, the question arises of how there were different norms in the community to start with. This is simple to answer when the norms represent unrelated languages—it is to be assumed that the norms were introduced with the people that used them. Thus it is assumed that the Gauls spoke Gaulish (possibly a number of varieties, perhaps also a **koine**), but the Roman invaders spoke Latin (which had a standardized written norm). Similarly the African slaves spoke a variety of West African tongues, and perhaps a koineized version, while their slave-masters spoke French. In each case the shift, from Gaulish to Latin, or from an African language to French, must have been fully recognized by the speakers, though in the former case it was probably voluntary, and in the second imposed.

Where the norms that are in competition are more closely related, as between French and other French or Occitan dialects, however, the shift may not have been so noticeable: probably there was always accommodation between the different norms, with koineized varieties current in the community, and speakers not always aware of which variety is being used. This is where the question—how did a community develop different norms?—becomes difficult to answer. Are we to assume that Picardy had a different norm from Champagne ever since both regions adopted a Romance idiom? This is possible if we imagined a different pattern of Latinization and of contact influences. The processes of linguistic change would operate at this stage, to differentiate still further *picard* and *champenois*, as they each worked through the mechanical consequences of the original differences (by **deductive** or **adaptive** innovation), and, possibly, opted for different variants as emblematic of their own communal identity. The history of French would in this case be largely a matter of the resolution of any conflict between the varieties.

This is the essence of one of the classical accounts, which usually assumes the triumph of one French variety, with some input from others, which nevertheless may retain some vitality as non-standard, unprestigious varieties associated with the less privileged members of the community.

Another classical account—that of comparative philology—assumes a proto-northern French, which embodies the shared distinguishing features of French, as distinct from, say, Occitan, and from which, in the process of time, differentiated into different regional varieties, like *picard* and *champenois*, by much the same processes of linguistic change, but probably with less prominent operation of deductive changes.

Whichever one of these two models we favour, we are assuming that the original differentiation of varieties arose from external events and communal attitudes—language shift, contact influences, isolation of the communities, assertion of identity. Internal linguistic factors can exacerbate the differentiation but not initiate it. In an imaginary world therefore we could envisage a stable, unchanging language, in a protected environment—a pre-Babel Golden Age. Our view of isolated communities as having 'conservative' languages is presumably influenced by such preconceptions: often we latch on to a few features, usually morphological, which confirm the view and ignore others, usually phonological, which would contradict it.

Another view could treat as 'conservative' any koineized community language, which selects the common features of related dialects and avoids the more extreme variants. Usually such varieties are used in wider communities, where social or economic factors require more mutual support and solidarity between their members. In European terms such communities are a feature of the modern era, and are linked with greater administrative complexity and division of labour. We associate them especially with conquest, as in the Roman Empire, and with centralized authority, as in modern France. The model of classical Indo-European philology paints a picture of domination of an invading master-race, with imposition of its language, over the subjugated indigenous population. Another possible model is less warlike, involving more co-operation and less conflict, with spread of new techniques and interdependence and accommodation in both socioeconomic and linguistic behaviour: Renfrew (1987) has developed a model of this sort for the Indo-European languages. If we regard 'language' as a means of achieving social cohesion and bonding, then clearly the more symbiosis there is between neighbouring communities, the more they will seek a common means of communication.

However, a 'language', which changes, can be, in this view, more like French *langage* than *langue*; moreover we may distinguish *une langue*, the tool used by a community, from *la langue*, a mental system possessed by all individual human beings, with surprising universal features in the organization of the system, and considerable constraints on variability. 'Linguistic change' as distinct from 'language change', in my terminology, would affect the system, or more probably its subsystems, and the items that compose them. How the system can change over time and space is the subject-matter of historical linguistics, a subdiscipline of linguistics, just as language history is a subdiscipline of history. The main aim of linguistics is the description and explanation of language as a system: the added adjective 'historical' places an emphasis on change and on the time dimension.

The hypothesis which I have embraced is that a linguistic system is a dynamic one, and that change in one parameter can have consequential effects on the whole system, though these may take some time to work through the whole system, and may be blocked by other factors. The historical linguist will seek to detect the way in which the system changes, by observing differences of usage over time and space. Change in a parameter may very well be occasioned by some external influence, like language contact, but may also sometimes be just a chance occurrence. The operation of linguistic change can work to destroy the social function of language, and so can be resisted by speakers, if they are conscious of it. More often, though, without fully realizing what is going on, they will make repairs, by cobbling together what material is at hand, so that a new system can emerge from the old. The performance data that emerges from the new system may be similar enough initially for speakers to fail to recognize that any linguistic change has taken place: different generations still have the impression that they can communicate with each other. The historical linguist can perhaps discern a change in progress, but properly, like the historian, rather than the sociologist, he should look to the completion of the change, the end of the story, in order to get a bird's-eye view of the whole process.

This brings me to another controversial view I have advanced: that change over time is, by definition, directional and implies irreversible loss, at time $t+n$, of items and processes that were current at time t. At any one point of time, there will be a number of variants, norms comprising slightly different items and processes, current in a community. The variation can remain stable for a considerable length of time, marking different social values or discourse registers. Only when one of the variants has been lost has there been change, or definitive shift. Loss here is most discernible for processes. Items comparatively rarely disappear completely: they hang around as anomalies, leftovers, sometimes in specialist or regional usage, and may even be **exapted**, dragooned into new uses.

In some cases the ultimate cause of the change is social—fashionable desire for novelty, shift of prestige, need to express new concepts or designate new objects, desire for greater expressiveness. In other cases, the change may originate in the system—a move to greater simplicity, economy, elegance, generality, equilibrium, a requirement more sharply to contrast items that risk merger. The latter type of change can occur only at the language acquisition stage, when the child learner is constructing his grammar on the basis of the language data he perceives in his environment. Evidence for such changes will be found in the community at large only after a lapse of time when the older grammars have died, with their speakers. Such evidence is hard to find in a social environment in which there is inter-generational harmony. At times of social upheaval, when children have less careful surveillance from their elders, the effects of 'linguistic change' is more likely to be experienced as 'language change'.

I have tried to illustrate these concepts by reference to the French language and its history. I have maintained that radical language change occurred between Latin and Old French, though there continued to be variation between the two sets of varieties, in a diglossic situation, for many hundreds of years. Latin effectively disappeared as an operational language only in the seventeenth century (and as a special religious language only in the 1960s), although already at the end of the twelfth century there were clear signs of its demise as a spoken idiom.

Between Old French and modern French the change was not so radical, as the varieties were closely related and not so distinctly socially marked. It is only after the twelfth century that the 'modern' variety gained ground in texts, and it only completely ousted the 'older' variety in the seventeenth century.

French is unusual, among languages with a well-documented history, in the way in which the modern language made a fairly clean break with its medieval past, and launched on a new path. A comparison can be made with English, where the change of direction in the language can be attributed to the influence it underwent from the French of the Norman conquerors. In French itself it is difficult to point to a similar external trigger. It does appear, however, that the emergence of national consciousness during the Hundred Years War, the intellectual and spiritual impetus of the Renaissance and the Reformation, and the growth of a centralized state administration all had their effect on linguistic attitudes. The evolution was gradual, in the sense that there must have been coexistence of variants for a considerable time, but eventually older habits were abandoned, and the modern language emerged as distinct from that exemplified in the classic medieval texts.

The change between French and French creoles must have been more sudden than that between Latin and French, and more far-reaching than that between Old French and modern French. The peculiar social conditions that occasioned the creation of the totally new languages were, thankfully, unusual, and barely outlived the seventeenth and eighteenth centuries. The genesis of the creoles, however, can provide us with valuable evidence of how language changes typologically while preserving inherited lexical material, and can give us new insights into the processes of linguistic and language change.

Bibliography

Abel, F. (1971), *L'Adjectif démonstratif dans la langue de la Bible latine. Étude sur la formation des systemes déictiques et de l'article défini des langues romanes* (Tübingen, Niemeyer) (Beiheft 125, *Zeitschrift für romanische Philologie*).

Achard, P. (1993), *La Sociologie du langage* (Paris, PUF) (*Que sais-je?*).

Actes XVIIe Cong. (1984–6), *Actes du XVIIème Congrès International de Linguistique et Philologie Romanes (Aix en Provence 26 aout–3 septembre 1983)*, 9 vols. (Marseilles, Lafitte).

Acton, H. B. (1959), 'The Philosophy of Language in Revolutionary France', *Proceedings of the British Academy*, 1959, 199–220.

Adams, J. N. (1977), 'A Typological Approach to Latin Word-Order', *Indogermanische Forschungen*, 81: 70–99.

—— (1994), 'Wackernagel's Law and the Position of Unstressed Personal Pronouns in Latin', *Transactions of the Philological Society*, 92: 103–78.

Adams, M. (1987), 'Old French and the Theory of Pro-Drop', *Natural Language and Linguistic Theory*, 5: 1–32.

—— (1988*a*), 'Parametric Change: Empty Subjects in Old French', in Birdsong and Montreuil (1988), 1–16.

—— (1988*b*), 'Les Effets du verbe second en ancien et moyen français', *Revue québécoise de linguistique théorique et appliquée*, 7: 13–40.

Aebischer, P. (1948), 'Contribution à la protohistoire des articles ILLE et IPSE dans les langues romanes', *Cultura Neolatina*, 8: 182–203.

Aebischer, V. (1985), *Les Femmes et le langage: répresentations d'une différence* (Paris, PUF).

—— and Forel, C. (eds.) (1983), *Parlers masculins, parlers féminins?* (Paris, Delachaux et Niestlé).

Ager, D. (1990), *Sociolinguistics and Contemporary French* (Cambridge, CUP).

—— (1996), *'Francophonie' in the 1990s: Problems and Opportunities* (Clevedon, Avon, Multilingual Matters).

Ahlqvist, A. (ed.) (1982), *Papers from the Fifth International Conference on Historical Linguistics* (Amsterdam, Benjamins).

Aitchison, J. (1987), *Words in the Mind: An Introduction to the Mental Lexicon* (Oxford, Blackwell).

Aitchison, J. (1992), *Language Change: Progress or Decay?* (Cambridge, CUP).

Allen, W. S. (1973), *Accent and Rhythm. Prosodic Features of Latin and Greek: A Study in Theory and Reconstruction* (Cambridge, CUP).

Allières, J. (1982), *La Formation de la langue française* (Paris, PUF) (*Que sais-je?*)

Andersen, B. (1991) [1983], *Imagined Communities: Reflections on the Origin and Spread of Nationalism* (London, Verso).

Andersen, H. (1972), 'Diphthongization', *Language*, 48: 11–50.

—— (1973), 'Abductive and Deductive Change', *Language*, 49: 567–95.

—— (1974), 'Towards a Typology of Change: Bifurcating Changes and Binary Relations', in J. M. Anderson and Jones (eds.) (1974), 2: 18–62.

—— (1980), 'Morphological Change: Towards a Typology', in Fisiak (1980), 1–50.

—— (ed.) (1986), *Sandhi Phenomena in the Languages of Europe* (Berlin, Mouton-De Gruyter).

—— (1989), 'Understanding Linguistic Innovations', in Breivik and Jahr (1989), 5–28.

—— (ed.) (1995), *Historical Linguistics 1993: Selected Papers from the 11th International Conference on Historical Linguistics, Los Angeles 16–20 August 1993* (Amsterdam, Benjamins).

—— and Koerner, K. (eds.) (1990), *Historical Linguistics 1987* (Amsterdam, Benjamins).

Anderson, J. M. (1973), *Structural Aspects of Language Change* (London, Longman).

—— and Jones, C. (eds.) (1974), *Historical Linguistics: Proceedings of the First International Conference on Historical Linguistics*, 2 vols. (Amsterdam, North Holland).

Anderson, R. D. (1975), *Education in France 1848–1870* (Oxford, OUP).

Anderson, S. R. (1988*a*), 'Morphological Theory', in Newmeyer (1988), 1. 146–91.

—— (1988*b*), 'Morphological Change', in Newmeyer (1988), 1. 324–62.

—— (1992), *Amorphous Morphology* (Cambridge, CUP).

Andrieux, N., and Baumgartner, E. (1983), *Systèmes morphologiques de l'ancien français A. Le Verbe* (Bordeaux, Bière).

Antoine, G. (1981), 'L'Histoire de la langue: problèmes et méthodes', *Le Français Moderne,* 49: 145–60.

—— and Martin, R. (eds.) (1985), *Histoire de la langue française.* Tome 14: (*1880–1914*) (Paris, CNRS).

Anttila, R. (1977), *Analogy* (The Hague, Mouton).

—— (1989^2) *Historical and Comparative Linguistics* (Amsterdam, Benjamins).

Ardener, E. (1971), 'Social Anthropology and the Historicity of Historical

Linguistics', in E. Ardener (ed.), *Social Anthropology and Language* (London, Tavistock Publications), 209–41.

Arends, J. (ed.) (1996), *The Early Stages of Creolization* (Amsterdam, Benjamins).

—— Muysken, P., and Smith, N. (eds.) (1995), *Pidgins and Creoles: An Introduction* (Amsterdam, Benjamins).

Ariel, M. (1988), 'Referring and Accessibility', *Journal of Linguistics*, 24: 65–87.

Armstrong, N. (1996), 'Variable Deletion of French /l/: Linguistic, Social and Stylistic Factors', *Journal of French Language Studies*, 6: 1–21.

Ashby, W. J. (1977), *Clitic Inflection in French: An Historical Perspective* (Amsterdam, Rodopi).

—— (1981*a*), 'The Loss of the Negative Particle *ne* in French: A Syntactic Change in Progress', *Language*, 57: 674–87.

—— (1981*b*), 'French Liaison as a Sociolinguistic Phenomenon', in Cressey and Napoli (1981), 46–57.

—— (1982), 'The Drift of French Syntax', *Lingua*, 57: 29–46.

—— (1984), The Elision of /l/ in French Clitic Pronouns and Articles', in E. Pulgram (ed.) (1984), *Romanitas: Studies in Romance Linguistics* (Ann Arbor, University of Michigan Press), 1–16.

—— (1988), 'The Syntax, Pragmatics and Sociolinguistics of Left- and Right-Dislocations in French', *Lingua*, 75: 203–29.

—— (1991), 'When Does Variation Indicate Linguistic Change in Progress?', in *Journal of French Language Studies*, 1: 1–19.

—— (1992), 'The Variable Use of **on** versus **tu** in Spoken French', *Journal of French Language Studies*, 2: 135–57.

—— Mithun, M., Perisinotto, G., and Raposo, E. (eds.) (1993), *Linguistic Perspectives on the Romance languages: Selected Papers from the 21st Linguistic Symposium on Romance Languages (Santa Barbara, California, 21–24 February 1991)* (Amsterdam, Benjamins).

Aski, J. M. (1995), 'Verbal Suppletion: An Analysis of Italian, French and Spanish "to go"', *Linguistics*, 33: 403–32.

Asselin, C., and McLaughlin, A. (1981), 'Patois ou français?: la langue de la Nouvelle-France au 17ᵉ siècle', *Langage et Société*, 17: 3–57.

Atkinson, J.C. (1973), *The Two Forms of Subject Inversion in Modern French* (The Hague, Mouton).

Atti. XIV Cong. 1976–81, *Atti del XIV Congresso Internazionale di Linguistica e Filologia Romanza, 15–20 aprile 1974*, 5 vols. (Naples, Macchiaroli/Amsterdam, Benjamins).

Auger, J. (1993), 'More Evidence for Verbal Agreement-Marking in Colloquial French', in Ashby *et al.* (1993), 179–98.

—— (1994), 'On the Nature of Subject Clitics in Picard', in Mazzola (1994), 159–79.

Auger, J. (1996), 'Subject-Clitic Inversion in Romance: A Morphological Analysis', in Parodi *et al.* (1996), 23–40.

Autour de Féraud. La lexicographie en France 1762 à 1835 (1986) (Paris, École normale supérieure des jeunes filles).

Ayres-Bennett, W. (1987), *Vaugelas and the Development of the French Language* (London, MHRA).

—— (1990*a*), 'Women and Grammar in Seventeenth Century France', *Seventeenth Century French Studies*, 12: 5–25.

—— (1990*b*), 'Variation and Change in the Pronunciation of Seventeenth-Century French', in Green and Ayres-Bennett (1990), 151–79.

—— (1994*a*), 'Negative Evidence: Or Another Look at the Non-Use of Negative *ne* in seventeenth-century French', *French Studies*, 48: 63–85.

—— (ed.) (1994*b*), *La grammaire de dames* (*Histoire, épistémologie, langage*, 16.2).

—— (1994*c*) 'Quelques considérations sur l'usage des formes surcomposées en français du XVIe au XVIIIe siècle', in *Opérateurs et constructions syntaxiques, Évolution des marques et des distributions du XVe au XXe siècle* (Paris, École Normale Supérieure), 149–75.

—— (1994*d*), 'Elaboration and Codification: Standardization and Attitudes towards the French Language in the Sixteenth and Seventeenth Centuries', in Parry *et al.* (1994), 53–73.

—— (1996), *A History of the French Language through Texts* (London, Routledge).

—— and Carruthers, J. (1992), '*Une regrettable et fort disgracieuse faute de français*'?: The Description and Analysis of the French *surcomposés* from 1530 to the Present Day', *Transactions of the Philological Society*, 90: 219–57.

Azra, J.-L., and Cheneau, V. (1994), 'Jeux de langage et théorie phonologique. Verlan et structure syllabique du français', *Journal of French Language Studies*, 4: 147–70.

Bache, C., Basbøll, H., and Lindberg, C.-E. (eds.) (1994), *Tense, Aspect and Action: Empirical, and Theoretical Contributions to Language Typology* (Wiesbaden, Harrassowitz).

Baciu, I. (1983), 'Constraints sur les séquences de clitiques en français', *Revue roumaine de linguistique* (1983), 67–75.

Baddeley, S. (1989*a*), 'Le Traitement de *l* mouillé au XVIe siècle', in Baddeley (1989*b*), 105–17.

—— (ed.) (1989*b*), *La Variation dans la langue en France du XVIe au XIXe siècle* (Paris, CNRS).

—— (1993), *L'Orthographe Française au temps de la Réforme* (Geneva, Droz).

Baker, A. T. (1937), 'Le Futur des verbes avoir et savoir', *Romania*, 63: 1–30.

Bal, W., Germain, J., Klein, J. and, Swiggers, P. (1991), *Bibliographie sélective de linguistique romane et française* (Brussels, Duculot).

Baldinger, K. (ed.) (1974), *Introduction aux dictionnaires les plus importants pour l'histoire du français* (Paris, Klincksieck).

—— (1980), *Semantic Theory: Towards a Modern Semantics* (Oxford, Blackwell).

Balibar, R. (1974), *Les Français fictifs, le rapport des styles littéraires au français national* (Paris, Hachette).

—— (1985), *L'Institution du français: Essai sur le colinguisme des Carolingiens à la République* (Paris, PUF).

—— and Laporte, D. (1974), *Le Français national: politique de la langue nationale sous la Révolution* (Paris, Hachette).

Ball, R. (1997), *The French-Speaking World: A practical introduction to sociolinguistic issues* (London, Routledge).

Barbaud, P. (1984), *Le Choc des patois en Nouvelle-France* (Quebec, Presses de l'Université).

Barnes, B. (1985), *The Pragmatics of Left Detachment in Spoken Standard French* (Amsterdam, Benjamins).

Bartning, I. (1980), *Syntaxe et sémantique des pseudo-adjectifs français* (Stockholm, Almqvist & Wiksell).

Barton, D. (1994), *Literacy: An Introduction to the Ecology of Written Language* (Oxford, Blackwell).

Bartsch, R. (1987), *Norms of Language* (London, Longman).

Basbøll, H. (1994), 'The Feature Composition of French schwa in its Relation to the "full" Vowels', in Lyche (1994), 61–72.

Batany, J. (1982), 'L'Amère Maternité du français médiéval', *Langue française*, 4: 29–39.

Batchelor, R. E., and Offord, M. H. (1993), *Using French Synonyms* (Cambridge, CUP).

Battey, A. (1991), 'Partitive and Pseudo-Partitive Revisited: Reflections on the Status of *de* in French', *Journal of French Language Studies*, 1: 21–44.

—— and Hintze, M.-A. (1992), *The French Language Today* (London, Routledge).

—— and Roberts, I. (eds.) (1995), *Clause Structure and Language Change* (Oxford, OUP).

Bauche, H. (1920), *Le Langage populaire: Grammaire, syntaxe et dictionnaire du français tel qu'on le parle dans le peuple de Paris* (Paris, Payot).

Bauer, B. L. M. (1992), *Du latin au français: le passage d'une langue SOV à une langue SVO* (The Hague, Gegevens).

Baum, R. (1987), *Hochsprache, Literatursprache, Schriftsprache: Materialien zur Charakteristik von Kultursprache* (Darmstadt, Wissenschaftliche Buchgesselschaft).

Baylon, C. (1991), *Sociolinguistique: société, langue, discours* (Paris, Nathan).

Beauchemin, N. (1984), 'Quelques différences entre le vocabulaire des hommes et celui des femmes, en québécois parlé', *Actes XVIIe Cong.*, 5. 194–205.

Beaulieux, C. (1927), *Histoire de l'orthographe française*, vol. 1: *Formation de l'orthographe, des origines au milieu du XVIe siècle*. vol. 2: *Les Accents et autres signes auxiliaires* (Paris, Champion).

Beaune, C. (1985), *Naissance de la nation française* (Paris, Gallimard).

Bechert, J., Bernini, G., and Buridant, C. (eds.) (1990), *Towards a Typology of European Languages* (Berlin, Mouton de Gruyter).

Bédard, E., and Maurais, J. (eds.) (1983), *La Norme linguistique* (Quebec, Le Robert).

Belletti, A., and Rizzi, L. (eds.) (1995), *Parameters and Functional Heads: Essays in Comparative Syntax* (Oxford, OUP).

Benincà, P. (ed.) (1989), *Dialect Variation and the Theory of Grammar* (Dordrecht, Foris).

Benoist, J. (ed.) (1972), *L'Archipel inachevé. Culture et société aux Antilles françaises* (Montreal, Presses de l'Université de Montréal).

Benveniste, E. (1946), 'Structure des relations de personne dans le verbe', *Bulletin de la Société Linguistique de Paris*, 43.1 no. 126: 1–12.

—— (1959), 'Les Relations de temps dans le verbe français', *Bulletin de la Société Linguistique de Paris*, 54: 237–250; reprinted in Benveniste (1966), 1: 69–82.

—— (1960), 'Être et avoir dans leurs fonctions linguistiques', *Bulletin de la Société Linguistique de Paris*, 55: 113–34, reprinted in Benveniste (1966), 1: 187–207.

—— (1965), 'Structures des relations d'auxiliarité', *Acta linguistics hafnensia*, 9: 1–15.

—— (1966), *Problèmes de linguistique générale* (Paris, Gallimard).

—— (1968), 'Mutations of linguistic categories', in Lehmann and Malkiel (1968), 85–94.

Berchem, T. (1973), *Studien zum Funktionswandel bei Auxiliaren und Semi-Auxiliaren in den romanischen Sprachen* (Tübingen, Niemeyer) (*Zeitschrift für romanische Philologie*, Beiheft 139).

Bernini, G., Molinelli, P., and Ramat, P. (1987), 'La Négation (discontinue) en roman et en germanique', in Buridant (1987), 21–51.

Berschin, H., Felixberger, J., and Goebl, H. (1978), *Französische Sprachgeschichte. Lateinische Basis. Interne und externe Geschichte. Sprachliche Gliederung Frankreichs. Mit einer Einführing in die historische Sprachwissenschaft* (Munich, Hueber).

Bichakjian, B. H. (1986), 'When Do Lengthened Vowels Become Long? Evidence from Latin and French, and a Paedomorphic Explanation', in Wetzels and Sezer (1986), 11–36.

—— (1987), 'The Evolution of Word Order: A Paedomorphic Explanation', in Ramat *et al.* (1987), 87–107.

—— (1989), 'The Current Evolution of French Word-Order: Claims and Caution', in Walsh (1989), 37–52.

Bickerton, D. (1981), *Roots of Language* (Ann Arbor, Karoma).

—— (1984), 'The Language Bioprogram Hypothesis', *The Behavioural and Brain Sciences*, 7: 173–221.

Bierbach, C., and Ellrich, B. (1990), 'Französisch: Sprache und Geschlechter', in Holtus *et al.* (1988–), 5/1: 248–66.

Binnick, R. I. (1991), *Time and the Verb: A Guide to Tense and Aspect* (Oxford, OUP).

Birdsong, D., and Montreuil, J.-P. (eds.) (1988), *Advances in Romance linguistics* (Dordrecht, Foris).

Bisson, T. N. (1994), 'The "Feudal Revolution"', *Past and Present*, 142: 6–42.

Blake, B. (1994), *Case* (Cambridge, CUP).

Blanc, M. (1993), 'French in Canada', in Sanders (1993*b*), 239–56.

Blanche-Benveniste, Claire (1987), 'Le Pronom *on*: propositions pour une analyse', in Jean-Claude Chevalier and M.-F. Deport (1987), *Mélanges offerts a Maurice Molho*, vol. 3 (*Les Cahiers de Fontenay*, 48) (Fontenay: Editions Hispaniques), 15–30.

—— (1994), 'Quelques caractéristiques grammaticales des "sujets" employés dans le français parlé des conversations', in Yaguello (1994), 77–108.

—— and Chervel, A. (1978), *L'Orthographe* (Paris, Maspéro).

—— Deulofeu, J., Stéfanini, J., and Eynde, K. van der (1984), *Pronom et syntaxe: L'approche pronominale et son application au français* (Paris, SELAF-CNRS).

—— and Jeanjean, C. (1987), *Le Français parlé* (Paris, Didier).

Blinkenberg, A. (1928), *L'Ordre des mots en français moderne* (Copenhagen, Munksgaard).

—— (1950), *Le Problème de l'accord en français contemporain: essai d'une typologie* (Copenhagen, Munksgaard).

Bloch, M. (1949), *La Société féodale* (Paris, Albin).

—— (1954), *The Historian's Craft* (Manchester, University Press).

Bollée, A. (1977*a*), *Le Créole français des Seychelles: Esquisse d'une grammaire, textes, vocabulaire* (Tübingen, Niemeyer).

—— (1977*b*), *Zur Entstehung der französischen Kreolendialekte im Indischen Ozean. Kreolisierung ohne Pidginisierung* (Geneva, Droz).

Boltanski, J. (1995), *La Linguistique diachronique* (Paris, PUF) (*Que sais-je?*).

Booij, G., and Marle, J. van (eds.) (1995), *Theme: Mechanisms of Morphological Change* (Dordrecht, Kluwer).

Borer, H. (ed.) (1986), *The Syntax of Pronominal Clitics* (San Diego, Academic Press).

Bostock, W. W. (1988), 'Assessing the Authenticity of a Supra-National

Language-Based Movement: la Francophonie', in C. H. Williams (ed.), *Language in Geographic Context* (Clevedon, Avon, Multilingual Matters), 73–92.

Bourdieu, P. (1977), *La Distinction* (Paris, Minuit).

—— (1983), 'Vous avez dit "populaire"', *Actes de la recherche en sciences sociales*, 46: 98–105.

—— (1991), *Language and Symbolic Power* (Oxford/Cambridge, Blackwell/Polity).

Bourhis, R. Y., and Lepicq, D. (1993), 'Québécois French and Language Issues in Quebec', in Posner and Green (1980–93), 5. 345–3.

Bouscayrol, R. (1987), *Cent lettres de soldats de l'An II* (Paris, Aux Amateurs du Livre).

Bouton, C., Brunet, B., and Calvet, L. J. (eds.), (1985), *Hommage à Pierre Guiraud* (Paris, Les Belles Lettres).

Boysen, G. (1971), *Subjonctif et hiérarchie* (Odense, University Press).

—— (1973), *Précis de syntaxe française du XVIIe siècle* (Odense, University Press).

Branca, S. (1983), 'Les Débats sur la variation au milieu du XIXe siècle', *Recherches sur le français parlé*, 5: 263–90.

Branca-Rosoff, S. (1992), 'Le Subjonctif du roi Louis XIII: Emplois dans les complétives', *Recherches sur le français parlé*, 11: 111–32.

—— , Guirand, Ch., and Schneider, N. (1989), 'Les Archives révolutionnaires de la région de Marseille: état d'une recherche sur l'orthographe des textes', *Recherches sur le français parlé*, 9: 9–37.

Brasseux, C. A. (1987), *The Founding of New Acadia: The Beginnings of Acadian Life in Louisiana, 1765–1803* (Baton Rouge, La., Louisiana State University Press).

—— (1992), *Acadian to Cajun: Transformation of a people, 1803–1877* (Jackson, University Press of Mississippi).

Braudel, F. (1969), *Ecrits sur l'histoire* (Paris, Flammarion), trans. *On History* (London, Weidenfeld and Nicolson, 1980).

—— (1985), *L'Identité de la France* (Paris, Arthaud-Flammarion).

Bréal, M. (1879), *Essai de sémantique, science des significations* (Paris, Hachette).

Breivik, L. E., and Jahr, E. H. (eds.) (1989), *Language Change: Contributions to the Study of Its Causes* (Berlin, Mouton de Gruyter).

Bremen, K. von (1986), 'Le Problème des forclusifs romans', *Lingvisticae Investigationes*, 10: 223–65.

Broussard, J. F. (1942), *Louisiana Creole dialect* (Baton Rouge, La., Louisiana State University Press [reprint New York, Kennikat Press 1972]).

Brown, B. (1988), 'Problems with Past Participle Agreement in French and Italian Dialects', in Birdsong and Montreuil (1988), 51–66.

Brown, R. A. (1990), *Pronominal Equivalence in a Variable Syntax* (Ann Arbor, University Microfilms).

Brown, R., and Gilman, A. (1960), 'The Pronouns of Power and Solidarity', in T. A. Sebeok (ed.) (1960), *Style in Language* (Cambridge, Mass., MIT Press).

Brucker, C. (1988), *L'Étymologie* (Paris, PUF) (*Que sais-je?*).

Brun, A. (1951), 'En langage maternel françois', *Le Français Moderne*, 19: 81–6.

Brunet, E. (1978), *Le Vocabulaire de Jean Giraudoux: Structure et évolution* (Geneva, Slatkine).

—— (1981), *Le Vocabulaire français de 1789 à nos jours d'après les données du 'Trésor de la Langue Française'* (Geneva/Paris, Slatkine/Champion).

—— (1988), *Le Vocabulaire de Victor Hugo* (Geneva/Paris, Slatkine/Champion).

Brunot, F. (1899), 'La Période contemporaine (1850–1900)', in L. Petit de Julleville, (ed.) (1894–1900), *Histoire de la langue et de la littérature française*, Tome VIII (Paris, Colin).

—— (1905–59) [1966–79²], *Histoire de la langue française des origines à nos jours* (Paris, Colin).

—— (1928), *Les Mots témoins de l'histoire* (Paris, Firmin-Didot).

—— and Bruneau, C. (1961²), *Précis de grammaire historique de la langue française* (Paris, Masson).

Buben, V. (1935), *Influence de l'orthographe sur la prononciation du français moderne* (Bratislava, Université Komensky).

Burger, A. (1955), 'Phonématique et diachronie à propos de la palatalisation des consonnes romanes', *Cahiers Ferdinand de Saussure*, 13: 19–22.

Burger, M. (1957), *Recherches sur la structure et l'origine des vers romans* (Geneva, Droz).

Buridant, C. (1980), 'Les Binomes synonymiques: esquisse d'une histoire des couples de synonymes du Moyen Age au XVII⁼ siècle', *Bulletin du Centre d'Analyse du Discours, Université de Lille*, 4: 5–79.

—— (1987), 'L'Ancien Français à la lumière de la typologie des langues: les résidus de l'ordre OV en ancien français et leur effacement en moyen français', *Romania*, 108: 20–65.

—— (ed.) (1987), *Romanistique-Germanistique. Une confrontation. Actes du Colloque de Strasbourg organisé par le Centre de Philologie Romane 23–24 mars 1984* (Strasburg, Association des publications près les Universités de Strasbourg).

Burke, P. (1978), *Popular Culture in Early Modern Europe* (London, Temple Smith).

—— (1993), *The Art of Conversation* (Cambridge, Polity).

—— and Porter, R. (eds.) (1987), *The Social History of Language* (Cambridge, CUP).

Burke, P., and Porter, R. (eds.), (1991), *Language, Self and Society: A Social History of Language* (Cambridge, Polity).

Bussche, H. van der (1984), 'L'Ouverture de la voyelle (*e*) issue de (*e*) roman entravé (Ē,ı latins) en ancien français. Essai de datation et de localisation', *Folia Linguistica Historica*, 5: 41–90.

Bybee, J. (1980), 'Morphophonemic Change from Inside and Outside the Paradigm', *Lingua*, 50: 45–59.

—— (1985), *Morphology: A Study of the Relationship between Meaning and Form* (Amsterdam, Benjamins).

—— (1988), 'The Diachronic Dimension in Explanation', in Hawkins (1988), 350–79.

——, Perkins, R., and Pagliuca, W. (1994), *The Evolution of Grammar: Tense, Aspect and Modality in the Languages of the World* (Chicago, University Press).

—— and Newman, J. E. (1995), 'Are Stem Changes as Natural as Affixes?', *Linguistics*, 33: 633–54.

Byers, B. A. (1988), *Defining Norms for a Non-Standardized Language: A Study of Verb and Pronoun Variation in Cajun French* (Ann Arbor, University Microfilms).

Bynon, T. (1977), *Introduction to Historical and Comparative Linguistics* (Cambridge, CUP).

Calabrese, A. (1993), 'Palatalization Processes in the History of Romance Languages: A Theoretical Study', in Ashby *et al.* (1993), 66–83.

Calvet, L.-J. (1994), *La sociolinguistique* (Paris, PUF) (*Que sais-je?*).

Campbell, R., Goldin, M. G., and Wang, M.C. (eds.) (1974), *Linguistic Studies in the Romance Languages* (Washington: Georgetown University Press).

Caput, J. P. (1972, 1975), *La Langue française; histoire d'une institution* (Paris, Larousse).

Carayol, M. (1977), *Le Français parlé à La Réunion* (Paris, Champion).

Carruthers, J. (1994), 'The *passé surcomposé régional*: Towards a Definition of its Function in Contemporary Spoken French', *Journal of French Language Studies*, 4: 171–90.

Carton, F. (1974), *Introduction à la phonétique du français* (Paris, Bordas).

Casagrande, J., and Saciuk, B. (eds.) (1972), *Generative Studies in Romance Syntax* (Rowley, Mass., Newbury House).

Catach, N. (1968), *L'Orthographe française à l'époque de la Renaissance. (Auteurs-Imprimeurs-Ateliers d'Imprimerie)* (Geneva, Droz).

—— (1984), 'L'*e* moyen: phonème plein titre ou son de passage?', in *Au bonheur des mots. Mélanges en l'honneur de Gérard Antoine* (Nancy, Presses Universitaires), 61–9.

—— (1985), 'La Bataille de l'orthographe aux alentours de 1900', in Antoine and Martin (1985), 237–51.

—— (1988*a*), *L'Orthographe* (Paris, PUF).

—— (ed.) (1988*b*), *Histoire et structure des orthographes et systèmes d'écriture* (Paris, CNRS).

—— (1989), 'Norme et variation autour de l'Académie française, au XVIIe Siècle', in Baddeley (1989*b*), 45–59.

—— (1993), "The Reform of the Writing System', in Sanders (1993*b*), 139–54.

—— Golfand, J., and Pasques, L. (1976–), *Dictionnaire historique de l'orthographe française (RENA)* (Paris, CNRS).

Cator, G., and Cave, T. (eds.) (1984), *Neo-Latin and the Vernacular in Renaissance France* (Oxford, OUP).

Cayroux, G. (1948), *Le Français classique: Lexique de la langue du six-septième siècle* (Paris, Didier).

Cellard, J. (1989), *Ah! ça ira, ça ira . . . Ces mots que nous devons à la Révolution* (Paris, Balland).

Cerquiglini, B. (1981), *La Parole médiévale. Discours, syntaxe, texte* (Paris, Minuit).

—— (1991), *La Naissance du français* (Paris, PUF) (*Que sais-je ?*).

Certeau, M. de, Julia, D., and Revel, J. (1975), *Une politique de la langue: la Révolution française et les patois* (Paris, Gallimard).

Champagne M. (1993), 'From Old French to Modern French: The Evolution of the Inflectional System', in Ashby *et al.* (1993), 259–70.

Chartier, R., Compère, M. M., and Julia, D. (1976), *L'éducation en France du 16e au 18e siècle* (Paris, Société d'édition d'enseignment supérieur).

Chaudenson, R. (1979), *Les Créoles français* (Paris, Nathan).

—— (1988), 'Le Dictonnaire du créole mauricien: où l'on reparle (à nouveau mais pour la dernière fois!) de la génèse des créoles réunionnais et mauricien', *Études créoles*, 21: 73–127.

Chaunu, P. (1982), *La France* (Paris, Laffont).

Chaurand, J. (1972), *Introduction à la dialectologie française* (Paris, Bordas).

—— (1977), *Introduction à l'histoire du vocabulaire français* (Paris, Bordas).

—— (1981), 'Concepts et méthodes de Ferdinand Brunot (1860–1938)', *Le Français Moderne*, 49: 99–118.

—— (1989), '*L mouillé*: quelques aspects des variantes graphiques médié-vales et régionales', in Baddeley *et al.* (1989*b*), 89–103.

Chen, M. (1972), 'The Time Dimension: Contribution towards a Theory of Sound Change', *Foundations of Language*, 8: 457–98.

—— and Wang, W.- S. (1975), 'Sound-Change: Actuation and Implemen-tation', *Language*, 51: 255–81.

Chene, B. de, and Anderson, S. R. (1979), 'Compensatory Lengthening', *Language*, 55: 505–36.

Chervel, A. (1977), *. . . et il fallut apprendre à écrire à tous les petits français: Histoire de la grammaire scolaire* (Paris, Payot).

Chomsky, N.A. (1981), *Lectures on Government and Binding* (Dordrecht, Foris).

—— (1993), 'A Minimalist Program for Linguistic Theory', in K. Hale and S. J. Keyser (eds.) (1993), *The View from Building 20: Essays in Linguistics in Honor of Sylvain Bromberger* (Cambridge, Mass., MIT Press), 1–52.

Christie, W. (ed.) (1976), *Current Progress in Historical Linguistics* (Amsterdam, North Holland).

Chung, S., and Timberlake, A. (1985), 'Tense, Aspect, Mood', in T. Shopen (ed.), *Language Typology and Syntactic Description* (Cambridge, CUP), 3. 202–38.

Cinque, G. (1995), 'The Pseudo-Relative and ACC-ing Constructions after Verbs of Perception', in G. Cinque (1995), *Italian Syntax and Universal Grammar* (Cambridge, CUP), 244–75.

Citton, Y., and Wyss, A. (1989), *Les Doctrines orthographiques du 16ᵉ siècle* (Geneva, Droz).

Clark, E. V. (1995), *The Lexicon in Acquisition* (Cambridge, CUP).

Clark, R., and Roberts, I. (1993), 'A Computational Model of Language Learnability and Language Change', *Linguistic Inquiry*, 24: 299–345.

Clements, G. N. (1976), 'Palatalization: Linking or Assimilation?', *Chicago Linguistic Society*, 12: 96–109.

—— and Keyser, S. J. (1983), *CV Phonology* (Cambridge, Mass: MIT Press).

Clifford, P. (1973), *Inversion of the Subject in French Narrative Prose from 1500 to the present* (Oxford, Blackwell).

Cohen, M. S. R. (n.d. ?1960), *Le Subjonctif en français contemporain* (Paris, Centre de la documentation universitaire).

—— (1972³) *Histoire d'une langue: le français* (Paris, Editions Sociales).

—— (1970), 'C'est rigolo n'est pas "populaire"', *Le Français moderne*, 38: 1–9, reprinted in F.J. Hausmann (ed.) (1983), *Die französische Sprache von Heute* (Darmstadt, Wissenschaftliche Buchgesellschaft), 306–14.

Collignon, L., and Glatigny, M. (1978), *Le Dictionnaire. Initiation à la lexicographie* (Paris, Cedic).

Comrie, B. (1978²) *Aspect* (Cambridge, CUP).

—— (1985), *Tense* (Cambridge, CUP).

—— (1989), *Language Universals and Linguistic Typology* (Chicago, University Press).

Conein, B. (ed.) (1987), *Lexique et faits sociaux* (*Lexique*, 5).

Connors, K. (1978), 'The Meaning of the French Subjunctive', *Linguistics*, 211: 45–56.

Conrad, G. R. (ed.) (1978), *The Cajuns: Essays on their History and Culture* (Lafayette, University of Southwestern Louisiana).

Contreras, H., and Klausenburger, J. (eds.) (1981), *Proceedings of the Tenth*

Anniversary Synmposium on Romance linguistics (Seattle, University of Washington).

Conwell, M., and Juilland, A. (1963), *Louisiana French Grammar*, vol. 1 (The Hague, Mouton).

Cook, V. and Newson, M. (1995²), *Chomsky's Universal Grammar* (Oxford, Blackwell).

Cooper, R. L. (1990), *Language Planning and Social Change* (Cambridge, CUP).

Corbeil, J.-C., and Guilbert, L. (eds.) (1976), *Le français au Québec* (*Langue Française*, 31).

Corbett, G. G. (1991), *Gender* (Cambridge, CUP).

Corbett, N. L. (1969), 'The French Verbal Flexion *-ons* as a Result of Homonymy: A Study in Structure and Analogy', *Romance Philology*, 22: 421–31.

—— (ed.) (1990), *Langage et identité: Le français et les francophones d'Amérique du Nord* (Quebec, Presses de l'Université Laval).

Corbin, D. (1987), *Morphologie dérivationnelle* (Tübingen, Niemeyer).

—— (ed.) (1991), *La Formation des mots: structures et interpretations* (Lille, Presses Universitaires).

Corblin, F. (1987), *Indéfini, défini et démonstratif: Constructions linguistiques de la référence* (Geneva, Droz).

Corfield, P. J. (ed.) (1991), *Language, History and Class* (Oxford, Blackwell).

Coseriu, E. (1958) [1978³], *Sincronía, diacronía y historia. El problema de cambio lingüístico* (Madrid, Gredos).

—— (1964), 'Pour une sémantique diachronique structurale', *Travaux de Linguistique et de Littérature de Strasbourg*, 2: 139–86.

—— (1975), 'Vers une typologie des champs lexicaux', *Cahiers de lexicologie*, 27: 30–51.

Coveney, A. (1990), 'The Omission of *ne* in Spoken French', *Francophonie*, 1: 38–43.

—— (1995), 'The Use of QU-Final Interrogative Structures in Spoken French', *Journal of French Language Studies*, 5: 143–71.

—— (1996), *Variability in Spoken French: A Sociolinguistic Study of Interrogation and Negation* (Exeter, Elm Bank).

Crabb, D. M. (1955), *A Comparative Study of Word-Order in Old Spanish and Old French Prose Works* (Washington, Catholic University Press).

Craddock, J. R., Dworkin, S., and Poghirc, C. (1980), 'Romance Etymology', in Posner and Green (1980–93), 1: 191–240.

Cressey, W. W., and Napoli, D. J. (eds.) (1981), *Linguistic Symposium on the Romance Languages* (Washington, Georgetown University Press).

Cruse, D. A. (1986), *Lexical Semantics* (Cambridge, CUP).

Curat, H. (1991), *Morphologie verbale et référence temporelle en français moderne: essai de sémantique grammaticale* (Geneva, Droz).

Currie, M. (1971), 'La Proposition substantive en tête de phrase dans la langue française. Aperçu historique', *Studia Neophilologica*, 43: 31–71.

Dagenais, L. (1990), 'De la fermeture des [œ] à la finale absolue en français général aux 18ᵉ et 19ᵉ siècles', *Neophilologus*, 74: 330–52.

—— (1991), 'De la phonologie vers 1700: les systèmes vocaliques de Hindret (1687, 1696) et de Vaudelin (1713, 1715)', *La Linguistique*, 27: 75–89.

Dahl, O. (1985), *Tense and Aspect Systems* (Oxford, Blackwell).

Dahmen, W., Holtus, G., Kramer, J., and Metzeltin, M. (eds.) (1987), *Latein und Romanisch* (Tübingen, Narr).

—— Holtus, G., Kramer, J., Metzeltin, M., Schweickard, W., and Winkelmann, O. (eds.) (1996), *Sprache und Geschlecht in der Romania* (Tübingen/Basle, Francke).

Dahrendorf, R. (1959), *Class and Class Conflict in Industrial Society* (London, Routledge & Kegan Paul).

Dalphinis, M. (1985), 'Bases historiques du developpement du patwa a Sainte-Lucie', *Études creoles*, 8: 226–46.

Dann, O., and Dinwiddy, J. R. (eds.) (1988), *Nationalism in the Age of the French Revolution* (London, Hambledon).

D'Ans, A. M. (1968), *Le Créole français d'Haïti* (The Hague and Paris, Mouton).

—— (1987), 'Quelques interrogations sur l'identité créole: Repères théoriques et exemples haïtiens', *Études creoles*, 9: 92–113.

Dardel, R. de (1958), *Le Parfait fort en roman commun* (Geneva, Droz).

—— (1964), 'Considérations sur la déclinaison romane à trois cas', *Cahiers Ferdinand de Saussure*, 21: 7–23.

—— (1983), 'Déclaratives romanes à verbe initial', *Vox Romanica*, 42: 263–9.

—— (1987), 'La Place de l'adjectif épithète en proto-roman', *Vox Romanica*, 46: 1–25.

—— (1989), 'L'Hypothèse d'une base OVS en protoroman', *Probus*, 1: 121–43.

—— and Haadsma, R. A. (1976), 'Le Rejet du verbe dans les subordonnées romanes', *Vox Romanica*, 35: 24–39.

Darmesteter, A. (1877), *De la création actuelle des mots nouveaux dans la langue française et des lois qui la régissent* (Paris, Vieweg).

Dauses, A. (1981), *Das Imperfekt in den romanischen Sprachen: Seine Bedeutung im Verhältnis zum Perfekt* (Wiesbaden, Steiner).

—— (1991), *Sprachwandel dürch Analogie: zu den Gründen des sprachliches Wandel* (Stuttgart, Steiner).

Dauzat, A. (1927–8), 'Essais de géografie linguistique. Deusième série. Troisième Partie. Aires fonétiques. 1. Les sous-produits de *C* (+ *A* latin) dans la Gaule romane', *Revue de philologie française*, 39: 98–127; 40: 31–55.

—— (ed.) (1935–49), *Où en sont les études de français? Manuel général de linguistique française moderne*, with *Supplément (1935–48)* (Paris, D'Artrey).

David, J., and Kleiber, G. (eds.) (1986), *Déterminants: syntaxe et sémantique* (Metz, Centre d'analyse syntaxique, Faculté des Lettres et Sciences Humaines).

David, J., and Martin, R. (eds.) (1980), *La Notion d'aspect* (Paris, Klincksieck).

Davis, G. W., and Iverson, G. K. (eds.) (1992), *Explanation in Historical Linguistics* (Amsterdam, Benjamins).

Davis, S., and Napoli, D. J. (1994), *A Prosodic Template in Historical Change: The Passage of the Latin Second Conjugation into Romance* (Turin, Rosenberg & Seiler).

Dees, A. (1971), *Étude sur l'évolution des démonstratives en ancien et en moyen français* (Groningen, Wolters-Nordhoff).

—— (1980*a*), *Atlas des formes et des constructions des chartes françaises du XIIIe siècle* (Tübingen, Niemeyer) (Beiheft 178, *Zeitschrift für romanische Philologie*).

—— (1980*b*), 'Variations temporelles et spatiales de l'ordre des mots en ancien et moyen français', in Wilmet (1980), 293–303.

—— (1985), 'Dialectes et scriptae à l'époque de l'ancien français', *Revue de linguistique romane*, 49: 87–117.

—— (1987), *Atlas des formes linguistiques des textes littéraires de l'ancien français* (Tübingen, Niemeyer) (Beiheft 212, *Zeitschrift für romanische Philologie*).

—— (1989), 'La Réconstruction de l'ancien français parlé', in Schouten and van Reenen (1989), 125–34.

Degraff, M. (1993), 'A Riddle on Negation in Haitian', *Probus*, 5: 1–2l, 63–93.

Delais, E. (1994), 'Rythme et structure prosodique en français', in Lyche (1994), 131–50.

Delattre, Pierre (1944), 'A Contribution to the History of "*r* grasseyé"', *Modern Language Notes* (December 1944): 562–4, reprinted in Delattre (1966), 206–7.

—— (1959), 'Rapports entre la durée vocalique, le timbre et la structure syllabique en français', *French Review*, 32: 547–52; reprinted in Delattre (1966), 105–10.

—— (1966), *Studies in French and Comparative Phonetics: Selected Papers in French and English* (The Hague, Mouton).

Delesalle, S., and Chevalier, J.-C. (1986), *La Linguistique, la grammaire et l'école 1750–1914* (Paris, Armand Colin).

—— and Gary-Prieur, M.-N. (eds.) (1976), *Lexique et grammaire* (*Langue française*, 30).

Dell, F. (1984), 'L'Accentuation dans les phrases en français', in F. Dell,

D. Hirst, and J.-R. Vergnaud (eds.), *Forme sonore du language: Structure des représentations en phonologie* (Paris, Hermann), 65–122.

Deloffre, F. (ed.) (1961), *Agréables conférences de deux paysans de Saint-Ouen et Montmorency sur les affaires du temps* (Paris, Les Belles Lettres).

Delomier, D. (1980), 'La Place de l'adjectif en français: bilan des points de vue et théories du XXe siècle', *Cahiers de lexicologie* 37: 5–24.

Demaizières, C. (1983), *La Grammaire française au XVIe siècle: les grammaririens picards* (Lille/Paris, Université/Didier).

Dembowski, P. F. (1980), 'Romance Historical Syntax', in Posner and Green (1980–93), 1. 157–72.

Deniau, X. (1985, 1995^3), *La Francophonie* (Paris, PUF) (*Que sais-je?*).

Densusianu, O. (1900), 'Sur l'altération du *c* latin devant *e*, *i* dans les langues romanes', *Romania*, 29: 21–333.

Désirat, C., and Hordé, T. (1983), *La Langue française au 20e siècle* (Paris, Bordas).

Desmet, P., and van Hoecke, W. (1992), 'Le Caractère graduel ou discret du changement phonétique: un faux problème?', in Lorenzo (1992–6), 5: 79–96.

Deulofeu, J. (1981), 'Perspective linguistique et sociolinguistique dans l'étude des relatives en français', *Recherches sur le française parlé*, 3: 135–95.

Deyck, R. van (1992), 'La Palatalisation gallo-romane du /ū/ latin, analysée en corrélation avec le sort des /ō, ŭ/ latins. Diatopie et diachronie', in Lorenzo (1992–6), 5: 115–28.

Dietrich, W. (1987), 'La Grammaticalisation du passé composé dans les langues romanes', in Buridant (1987), 81–96.

Dill, W. (1935), *Die Wortstellung in den Cent Nouvelles Nouvelles* (Münster, Pöppenhaus, Paris, Droz).

Ditchy, J. K. (1932), *Les Acadiens louisianais et leur parler* (Paris, Droz).

Dorian, N. C. (1994), 'Varieties of Grammar in a Very Small Place: Social Homogeneity, Prestige Norms, and Linguistic Variation', *Language*, 70: 631–97.

Dressler, W. U. (1985), *Morphonology: The Dynamics of Derivation* (Ann Arbor, Karoma).

Drijkoningen, F. (1993), 'Movement and the DP-hypothesis', *Linguistics*, 31: 813–54.

Droixhe, D., and Dutilleul, T. (1990), 'Externe Sprachgeschichte', in Holtus *et al.* (1988–), 5/1. 437–70.

Dubois, C.-G. (1972), *Celtes et Gaulois au XVIe siècle: Le développement d'un mythe nationaliste* (Paris, Vrin).

Dubois, J. (1962), *Le Vocabulaire politique et social en France de 1869 à 1872* (Paris, Larousse).

—— (1965), *Grammaire structurale du français: nom et pronom* (Paris, Larousse).

—— and Dubois, C. (1971), *Introduction à la lexicographie: le dictionnaire* (Paris, Larousse).

Ducrot, O. (1979), 'L'Imparfait en français', *Linguistische Berichte*, 60: 1–23.

Dufresne, M., and Dupuis, F. (1994), 'Modularity and the Reanalysis of the French Subject Pronoun', *Probus*, 6: 103–23.

Dumas, D. (1987), *Les prononciations en français québécois* (Quebec, Presses Universitaires).

Dumonceaux, P. (1975), *Langue et sensibilité au XVIIe siècle: L'évolution du vocabulaire affectif* (Geneva, Droz).

Durand, J. (1993), 'Sociolinguistic variation and the linguist', in Sanders (1993*b*), 257–86.

—— and Hintze, M.-A. (eds.) (1995), *French Phonology: Morae, Syllables, Words* (*Lingua* 95).

—— and Lyche, C. (1994), 'Phonologie multidimensionnelle et phonologie du français', in Lyche (1994), 3–32.

Durand, M. (1936), *Le Genre grammatical en français parlé à Paris et dans la région parisienne* (Paris, Bibliothèque du *Français Moderne*).

Eckert, G. (1986), *Sprachtypus und Geschichte. Untersuchungen zum typologischer Wandel des Französischen* (Tübingen, Narr).

—— (1990), 'Periodisierung', in Holtus *et al.* (1988–), 5/1: 816–29.

Eckert, P. (ed.) (1991), *New Ways of Analyzing Sound-Change* (San Diego, Academic Press).

Elliott, W. N. (1986), 'On the derivation of *en*-clitics', in Borer (1986), 97–121.

Eloy, J-M. (1985), 'A la recherche du "français populaire"', *Langage et Société*, 31: 7–38.

Elwert, W. T. (1965), *Traité de versification française des origines à nos jours* (Paris, Klincksieck).

Emonds, J. (1975), 'A Transformational Analysis of French Clitics without Positive Output Constraints', *Linguistic Analysis*, 1: 3–24.

Engels, D. M. (1989), *Tense and Text: A Study of French Past Tenses* (London-New York, Routledge).

Ernst, G. (1985), *Gesprochenes Französisch zu Beginn des 17 Jahrhunderts. Direkte Rede in Jean Héroards 'Histoire particulière de Louis XIII' (1605–1610)* (Tübingen, Niemeyer) (Beiheft 204, *Zeitschrift für romanische Philologie*).

Ewert, A. (1933), *The French Language* (London, Faber).

Faarlund, J. T. (1990), *Syntactic Change: Towards a Theory of Historical Syntax* (Berlin, Mouton de Gruyter).

Fauquenoy-St. Jacques, M. (1985), 'Les structures populaires du Québécois', in Bouton *et al.* 193–204.

Finke, A. (1983), *Untersuchungen zu Formen und Funktionen der Satzfrage im Theater des 17. und 18. Jahrhunderts* (Geneva, Droz).

Fiorelli, P. (1950), 'Pour l'interprétation de l'ordonnance de Villers-Cotterêts', *Le Français Moderne,* 18: 177–88.

Fishman, J. A. (1972), *Language and Nationalism: Two Integrative Essays* (Rowley, Mass., Newbury House).

Fisiak, J. (ed.) (1980), *Historical Morphology* (The Hague, Mouton).

—— (ed.) (1984), *Historical Syntax* (Berlin, Mouton de Gruyter).

—— (ed.) (1985), *Historical Semantics and Historical Word-Formation* (Berlin, Mouton de Gruyter).

—— (ed.) (1988), *Historical Dialectology: Regional and Social Variation* (Berlin, Mouton de Gruyter).

—— (ed.) (1990), *Historical Linguistics and Philology* (Berlin, Mouton de Gruyter).

—— (ed.) (1995), *Linguistic Change under Contact Conditions* (Berlin, Mouton de Gruyter).

Fleischman, S. (1982), *The Future in Thought and Language* (Cambridge, CUP).

—— (1983), 'From Pragmatics to Grammar: Diachronic Reflections on Complex Pasts and Futures in Romance', *Lingua,* 60: 183–214.

—— (1990), *Tense and Narrativity: From Medieval Performance to Modern Fiction* (Austin, Tex., University of Texas Press).

—— (1991), 'Discourse Pragmatics and the Grammar of Old French: A Functional Reinterpretation of *si* and the Personal Pronouns', *Romance Philology,* 44: 251–83.

Flydal, L. (1943), *Aller et venir de suivis de l'infinitif comme expressions de rapports temporels* (Oslo, Kommisjon hos Jacob Dybwad).

Fodor, I. and Hagège, C. (eds.) (1983–4), *Language Reform: History and Future,* 3 vols. (Hamburg, Buske).

Førsgren, M. (1978), *La Place de l'adjectif épithète en français contemporain. Étude quantitative et sémantique* (Stockholm, Almqvist & Wiksell).

Fortier, A. (1884–5), 'The French Language in Louisiana and the Negro Dialect', *Transactions and Publications of the Modern Languages Association of America,* 1: 96–111.

—— (1891), 'The Acadians in Louisiana and their Dialect', *Publications of the Modern Language Association,* 6: 64–94.

—— (1895), *Louisiana Folk-Tales, in French Dialect and English Translation* (New York, G. E. Stechert [reprint New York, Kraus reprints 1972]).

Fouché, P. (1933), 'La Prononciation actuelle du français', *Le Français Moderne,* 1: 43–67.

—— (1935), 'L'évolution phonétique du français du XVIe siècle à nos jours', in Dauzat (1935), 13–54.

—— (1936*a*), 'Les Diverses sortes de français au point de vue phonétique', *Le Français Moderne,* 4: 199–216.

—— (1936*b*), 'L'État actuel du phonétisme français', *Conférences de l'Institut de Linguistique de l'Université de Paris,* 4: 37–67.

—— (1952–69) *Phonétique historique du français*, 3 vols. (Paris, Klincksieck).

Foulet, L. (1921), 'Comment ont évolué les formes de l'interrogation?', *Romania*, 47: 243–348.

—— (1924), 'L'Accent tonique et l'ordre des mots: formes faibles du pronom personnel après le verbe', *Romania*, 50: 54–93.

—— (1928), 'La Difficulté du rélatif en français moderne', *Revue de philologie française et de littérature*, 40: 100–24, 161–81.

—— (1928³), *Petite syntaxe de l'ancien français* (Paris, Champion).

—— (1935), 'L'Extension de la forme oblique du pronom personnel en ancien français', *Romania*, 61: 257–315, 401–63.

Fox, A. (1995), *On Linguistic Reconstruction* (Oxford, OUP).

Francard, M. (ed.) (1994), *L'Insécurité linguistique dans les communautés francophone périphériques* (Louvain, Institut de Linguistique).

—— and Latin, D. (1995), *Le Regionalisme lexical* (Brussels, Duculot).

François, A. (1905), *La grammaire du purisme et l'Académie française au XVIIIe siècle* (Paris, Société nouvelles de librairie et d'édition).

—— (1959), *Histoire de la langue français cultivée des origines à nos jours* (Geneva, Jullien).

François, D. (1985), 'Langue populaire', in Antoine and Martin (1985), 225–324.

Franzén, T. (1939), *Étude sur la syntaxe des pronoms personnels sujets en ancien français* (Uppsala, Almqvist).

Frei, H. (1929), *La grammaire des fautes* (Paris, Geuthner).

Frey, M. (1925), *Les Transformations du vocabulaire français à l'époque de la Révolution (1789–1800)* (Paris, PUF).

Fuchs, C., and Léonard, A. M. (1979), *Vers une théorie des aspects—les systèmes du français et de l'anglais* (The Hague, Mouton).

Fumaroli, M. (1980), *L'Âge de l'éloquence. Rhétorique et "res literaria" de la Renaissance au seuil de l'époque classique* (Geneva, Droz).

Furet, F., and Ozouf, J. (1977), *Lire et écrire: L'alphabétisation des français de Calvin à Jules Ferry* (Paris, Minuit).

Gaatone, D. (1971), *Étude descriptive du système de la négation en français contemporain* (Geneva, Droz).

—— (1980), 'La Syntaxe de *en* et l'obsession de la solution unitaire', *Lingvisticae Investigationes*, 4: 181–201.

Gadet, F. (1989), *Le Français ordinaire* (Paris, Armand Colin).

—— (1992), *Le Français populaire* (Paris, PUF) (*Que sais-je?*).

—— (1995), 'Variabilité, variation, variété: le français d'Europe', *Journal of French Language Studies*, 6: 75–98.

Gaitet, P. (1992), *Political Stylistics: Popular Language as a Literary Artifact* (London, Routledge).

Galet, Y. (1972), *L'Évolution de l'ordre des mots dans la phrase française de*

1600 à 1700: La place du pronom personnel complément d'un infinitif régime (Paris, PUF).

Galmiche, M. (1989), 'A propos de la définitude', *Langages*, 94: 7–37.

Gamillscheg, E. (1936), *Zum romanischen Artikel und Possessivpronomen* (Berlin, Akademie der Wissenschaften).

—— (1940), 'Zur Palatalisierung im Romanischen', in N. M. Caffee and T. A. Kirby (eds.), *Studies for W.A. Read* (Baton Rouge, La., Louisiana State University Press), 183–200.

—— (1957), *Historische französische Syntax* (Tübingen, Niemeyer).

Garde, P. (1968), *L'Accent* (Paris, PUF).

Garey, H. (1957), 'Verbal aspect in French', *Language*, 33: 91–110.

Gebhardt, K. (1974), *Das okzitanische Lehngut im Französischen* (Bern, Lang).

Geisler, H. (1982), *Studien zur typologischen Entwicklung: Lateinisch-Altfranzösisch-Neufranzösisch* (Munich, Fink).

—— (1992), *Akzent und Lautwandel in der Romania* (Tübingen, Narr).

Gellner, E. (1983), *Nations and Nationalism* (Oxford, Blackwell).

Gerritsen, M., and Stein, D. (eds.) (1992), *Internal and External Factors of Syntactic Change* (Berlin, Mouton de Gruyter).

Gertner, M.H. (1973), *The Morphology of the Modern French Verb* (The Hague, Mouton).

Gervais, M.-M. (1993), 'Gender and language in French', in Sanders (1993*b*), 121–38.

Gildea, R. (1994), *The Past in French History* (New Haven, Yale University Press).

Gilliéron, J., and Edmont, E. (1903–10), *Atlas linguistique de la France* (Paris, Champion).

Glatigny, M., and Guilhaumou, J. (1981), *Peuple et pouvoir: Études de lexicologie politique* (Lille, Presses Universitaires).

Goldsmith, J. A. (ed.) (1995), *The Handbook of Phonological Theory* (Oxford, Blackwell).

Goody, E. N. (ed.) (1978), *Questions and Politeness* (Cambridge, CUP).

—— (ed.) (1995), *Social Intelligence and Interaction: Expressions and Implications of the Social Bias in Human Intelligence* (Cambridge, CUP).

Goosse, A., Klinkenberg, J.-M., Blampain, D., and Wilmet, M. (1996), *Le Français en Belgique. Une communauté, une langue* (Brussels, Duculot).

Gordon, D. C. (1978), *The French Language and National Identity* (The Hague, Mouton).

Gorog, R. P. de (1973), 'Bibliographie des études de l'onomasiologie dans le domaine du français', *Revue de linguistique romane*, 37: 419–66.

Gougenheim, G. (1929*a*), *La Langue populaire dans le premier quart du XIXe s. d'après le Petit Dictionnaire du peuple de J.C.L.P. Desgranges* (Paris, Les Belles Lettres).

—— (1929*b*), *Étude sur les périphrases verbales dans la langue française* (Paris, Les Belles Lettres).

—— (1962–75), *Les Mots Français dans l'histoire et dans la vie*, 3 vols. (Paris, Picard).

—— (1974), *Grammaire de la langue française du XVIIe siècle* (Paris, Picard).

Goyens, M. and Hoecke, W. van (1991), 'L'Emploi des possessifs du latin au français moderne', *Katholieke Universiteit Leuven preprint*, 136.

—— (1992), 'La Traduction comme témoin de l'évolution linguistique', in Lorenzo (1992–6), 5: 13–32.

Goyens, M., and Swiggers, P. (1989), 'La Grammaire française au XVIIe siècle. Bibliographie raisonnée', in Swiggers and van Hoecke (1989), 157–73.

Grad, A. (1964), 'Contribution à la syntaxe des pronoms personnels sujets en ancien français', *Linguistics*, 5: 3–20.

Graff, H. J. (ed.) (1981), *Literacy and Social Development in the West: A Reader* (Cambridge, CUP).

Grammaire des fautes et français non conventionnels (1992) (Paris, École normale supérieure).

Grammont, M. (1908), *Petit traité de versification française* (Paris, Armand Colin).

—— (1914), *Traité pratique de prononciation française* (Paris, Delagrave).

Grandgent, C. H. (1988), *An Introduction to Vulgar Latin* (New York, Hafner).

Green, J. N. (1988), 'Romance creoles', in Harris and Vincent (1988), 420–73.

—— and Ayres-Bennett, W. (eds.) (1990), *Variation and Change in French* (London, Routledge).

—— and Hintze, M. A. (1990), 'Variation and Change in French Linking Phenomenon', in Green and Ayres-Bennett (1990), 61–88.

Greenberg, J. H. (ed.) (1963, 1966²), *Universals of Language* (Cambridge, Mass., MIT Press).

—— (1963), [1966²], 'Some Universals of Grammar with Particular Reference to the Order of Meaningful Elements', in Greenberg (1963), 58–90.

—— (1978), 'How Does a Language Acquire Gender Markers?', in Greenberg *et al.* (1978), 2: 47–82.

—— Ferguson, C. A., and Moravcsik, E. (eds.) (1978), *Universals of Human Language* (Stanford, Calif., University Press).

Greimas, A.-J. (1966), *Sémantique structurale* (Paris, Larousse).

Grevisse, M. (and A. Goosse) (1936, 1994¹³), *Le Bon Usage* (Brussels, Duculot).

Grillo, R. D. (1989), *Dominant Languages: Language and Hierarchy in Britain and France* (Cambridge, CUP).

Griolet, P. (1986*a*), *Cadjins et créoles en Louisiane: Histoire et survivance d'une francophonie* (Paris, Payot).

—— (1986*b*), *Mots de Louisiane—Étude lexicale d'une francophonie* (Paris, Gothembourg).

Grisay, A., Lavis, G., and Dubois-Stasse, M. (1969), *Les Dénominations de la femme dans les anciens textes littéraires français* (Gembloux, Duculot).

Gruenais, M.-P. (1986), *États de langue. Peut-on penser une politique linguistique?* (Paris, Fayard/Fondation Diderot).

Gsell, O., and Wandruszka, U. (1986), *Der romanische Konjunktiv* (Tübingen, Niemeyer).

Gueunier, N. (1985), 'Variation individuelle chez des locuteurs du sud reunionnais', *Études creoles*, 8: 161–74.

—— Genouvrier, E., and Khomsi, A. (1978), *Les Français devant la norme: Contribution à une étude du français parlé* (Paris, Champion).

Guenthner, F. J., Hoepelman, J., and Rohrer, C. (1978), 'A Note on the *passé simple*', in C. Rohrer (ed.) (1978), *Papers on Tense, Aspect and Verb Classification* (Tübingen, Narr), 11–36.

Guéron, J. (1983), 'L'Emploi "possessif" de l'article défini en français', *Langue française*, 58: 23–35.

—— (1985), 'Inalienable Possession, PRO-inclusion and Lexical Chains', in Guéron *et al.* (1985), 43–86.

—— Obenauer, H.-G., and Pollock, J.-Y. (eds.) (1985), *Grammatical Representation* (Dordrecht, Foris).

Guilbert, L. (ed.) (1969), *Le Lexique* (*Langue française*, 20).

—— (ed.) (1974), *La néologie lexicale* (*Langages*, 36).

—— (1975), *La Créativité lexicale* (Paris, Larousse)

—— (1979), *Néologie et lexicologie: Hommage à Louis Guilbert* (Paris, Larousse).

Guilhaumou, J. (1989), *La Langue politique et la Révolution française* (Paris, Méridiens-Klincksieck).

Guillaume, G. (1919), *Le Problème de l'article et sa solution dans la langue française* (Paris, Hachette).

—— (1929), *Temps et Verbe* (Paris, Champion).

—— (1938), 'Theorie des auxiliaires et examen des faits connexes', *Bulletin de la Société Linguistique de Paris*, 39: 5–23, reprinted in G. Guillaume (1964), *Langage et science du langage* (Paris/Quebec: Nizet/Laval UP), 73–86.

Guinet, L. (1982), *Les Emprunts gallo-romans au germanique (du Ier à la fin du Ve siècle)* (Paris, Klincksieck).

Guiraud, P. (1956), *L'Argot* (Paris, PUF) (*Que sais-je?*).

—— (1960), 'Le Système du rélatif en français populaire', *Langages*, 3: 40–9.

—— (1964), [1979^4] *L'Étymologie* (Paris, PUF) (*Que sais-je?*).

—— (1965), *Les Mots étrangers* (Paris, PUF) (*Que sais-je?*).

—— (1967), *Structures étymologiques du lexique français* (Paris, Larousse).

—— (1968*a*), *Patois et dialectes français* (Paris, PUF) (*Que sais-je?*).

—— (1968*b*), *Les Mots savants* (Paris, PUF) (*Que sais-je?*).

—— (1970), *La Versification* (Paris, PUF) (*Que sais-je?*).

Guizot, F. (1809), *Dictionnaire universel des synonymes de la langue française* (Paris, Didier).

Gumperz, J. J., and Levinson, S. (eds.) (1996), *Rethinking Linguistic Relativity* (Cambridge, CUP).

Haarhoff, A. (1936), *Die Wortstellung in den 'Quatre Livres des Rois'* (Münster, Pöppinghaus).

Haase, A. (1888), *Französische Syntax des XVII. Jahrhunderts* (Oppeln/Leipzig, Franck); trans. (1969) *Syntaxe française du XVIII*[e] *siècle* (Paris, Delagrave).

Haegeman, L. (1995), *The Syntax of Negation* (Cambridge, CUP).

Hagège, C. (1987), *Le Français et les siècles* (Paris, Odile Jacob).

—— (1993), *The Language Builder: An Essay on the Human Signature in Linguistic Morphogenesis* (Amsterdam, Benjamins).

Haiman, J. (1974), *Targets and Syntactic Change* (The Hague, Mouton).

—— (ed.) (1985), *Iconicity in Syntax* (Amsterdam, Benjamins).

Hajek, J. (1993), 'Old French Nasalization and Universals of Sound-Change', *Journal of French Language Studies*, 3: 145–64.

—— (1997), *Universals of Sound-Change in Nasalization* (Oxford, Blackwell).

Halbwachs, M. (1992), *On Collective Memory* (Chicago, University Press) (translated from *Les Cadres sociaux de la mémoire*).

Hall, R. A., Jr. (1972), 'Is Middle French Necessary?', in Valdman (1972), 217–21.

Hall, G. M. (1992), *Africans in Colonial Louisiana: The Development of Afro-creole Culture in the 18th Century* (Baton Rouge, La., Louisiana State University Press).

Hannahs, S. J. (1995), *Prosodic Structure and French Morphophonology* (Tübingen, Niemeyer).

Harmer, L. (1954), *The French Language Today* (London, Hutchinson).

—— (1979), *Uncertainties in French Grammar* (Cambridge, CUP).

Harré, C. E. (1991), *Tener + Past Participle: A Case Study in Linguistic Description* (London, Routledge).

Harris, A. C., and Campbell, L. (1995), *Historical Syntax in Cross-Linguistic Perspective* (Cambridge, CUP).

Harris, M. B. (1977), 'Demonstratives, Articles and Third Person Pronouns in French', *Zeitschrift für romanische Philologie*, 93: 249–61.

—— (1978), *The Evolution of French Syntax: A Comparative Approach* (London, Longman).

—— (1980*a*), 'The Marking of Definiteness in Romance', in Fisiak (1980), 141–56.

448   *Bibliography*

Harris, M. B. (1980*b*), 'The Marking of Definiteness: A Diachronic Perspective', in Traugott *et al.* (1980), 75–86.
—— (1981), 'On the Conditional as Mood in French', *Folia Linguistica Historica*, 2: 55–69.
—— (1982), 'The "Past Simple" and the "Present Perfect" in Romance', in Vincent and Harris (1982), 42–70.
—— (1984*a*), 'On the Causes of Word Order Change', *Lingua*, 63: 175–204.
—— (1984*b*), 'On the Strengths and Weaknesses of a Typological Approach to Historical Syntax', in Fisiak (1984), 183–97.
—— (1986*a*), 'The Historical Development of si-clauses in Romance', in Traugott *et al.* (1986), 265–84.
—— (1986*b*), 'The Historical Development of Conditional Sentences in Romance', *Romance Philology*, 39: 405–36.
—— and Ramat, P. (eds.) (1987), *Historical Development of Auxiliaries* (Berlin, Mouton de Gruyter).
—— and Vincent, N. (eds.) (1988), *The Romance Languages* (London, Croom Helm).
Harrison, J. A. (1882), 'The Creole Patois of Louisiana', *The American Journal of Philology*, 3: 285–96.
Haudricourt, A., and Juilland, A. (1949), *Essai pour une histoire structurale du phonétisme français* (Paris, Klincksieck).
Haussmann, F. J. (1977), *Einführung in die Benutzung der neufranzösischen Wörterbücher* (Tübingen, Niemeyer).
—— (ed.) (1983), *Die französische Sprache von Heute* (Darmstadt, Wissenschaftliche Buchgesselschaft).
Hawkins, J. A. (1978), *Definiteness and Indefiniteness* (London, Croome Helm).
—— (1983), *Word Order Universals* (New York, Academic Press).
—— (1994), *A Performance Theory of Order and Constituency* (Cambridge, CUP).
Hawkins, R. (1993), 'Regional Variation in France', in Sanders (1993*b*), 55–84.
Hayes, B. (1989), 'Compensatory Lengthening in Moraic Phonology', *Linguistic Inquiry*, 20: 253–306.
—— (1995), *Metrical Stress Theory: Principles and Case Studies* (Chicago, University Press).
Hazaël-Massieux, G., and Robillard, D. de (1993), 'Bilingualism and Linguistic Conflict in (French) Creole-Speaking Societies', in Posner and Green (1980–93), 5: 384–406.
Hazaël-Massieux, M.-C. (1991), *Bibliographie des études créoles* (Montagny, Marquis).
Heine, B. (1994), *Auxiliaries: Cognitive forces and grammaticalization* (Oxford, OUP).

—— Claudi, U., and Hunnemeyer, F. (1991), *Grammaticalization: A Conceptual Framework* (Chicago, University Press).

Heinimann, S. (1965, 1967), 'Die Lehre vom Artikel in den romanischen Sprachen von der mittelalterlichen Grammatik zur modernen Sprachwissenschaft: Ein Beitrag zur Geschichte der grammatischen Begriffsbildung', *Vox Romanica*, 24: 23–43; 26: 180–92.

Heinz, S. (1983), *Determination und Re-präsentation im Altfranzösischen* (Munich, Fink).

Helgorsky, F. (1981), 'Les Méthodes en histoire de la langue. Evolution et stagnation', *Le Français Moderne*, 49: 119–44.

Hensey, F., and Luján, M. (eds.) (1976), *Current Studies in Romance linguistics* (Washington, Georgetown University Press).

Herman, J. (1954), 'Recherches sur l'ordre de mots dans les plus anciens textes français en prose', *Acta Linguistica Academiae Scientiarum Hungaricae*, 4: 69–94, 351–79.

—— (1975), *Le Latin vulgaire* (Paris, PUF) (*Que sais-je?*).

—— (1990), *Du latin aux langues romanes: Études de linguistique historique* (Tübingen, Niemeyer).

Herschensohn, J. (1980), 'On Clitic Placement in French', *Linguistic Analysis*, 6: 187–219.

Herslund, M. (1976), *Structure phonologique de l'ancien français: Morphologie et phonologie du francien classique* (Copenhagen, Akademisk Forlag).

—— (1980), *Problèmes de syntaxe de l'ancien français* (Copenhagen, Akademisk Forlag).

—— (1988), *Le datif en français* (Louvain, Peeters).

Highfield, A.R. (1979), *The French dialect of St. Thomas, U.S. Virgin Islands: A descriptive grammar with texts and glossary* (Ann Arbor, Karoma).

Hilty, G. (1968), 'La Séquence de Sainte Eulalie et les Origines de la langue littéraire française', *Vox Romanica*, 27: 4–18.

—— (1969), 'Zur Diphthongierung im Galloromanischen und Iberoromanischen', in W. D. Lange and H. J. Wolf, (eds.) (1969), *Philologische Studien für Joseph M. Piel* (Heidelberg, Winter), 95–107.

—— (1973), 'Les origines de la langue littéraire française', *Vox Romanica*, 32: 254–71.

—— (ed.) (1993), *XXe Congrès International de Linguistique et Philologie Romanes*, 5 vols. (Tübingen, Francke).

Hirschbühler, P. (1990), 'La Légitimisation de la construction V1 à sujet nul en subordonnée dans la prose et le vers en ancien français', *Revue québécoise de linguistique*, 19: 33–55.

—— and Junker, J. (1988), 'Remarques sur les sujets nuls en subordonnés en ancien et moyen français', *Revue québécoise de linguistique théorique et appliquée*, 7: 63–84.

Hobsbawn, E. J. (1990), *Nations and Nationalism since 1780: Programme, Myth, Reality* (Cambridge, CUP).

Hock, H. H. (1986), 'Compensatory Lengthening: In Defense of the Concept "mora"', *Folia Linguistica*, 20: 431–60.

—— (1991²), *Principles of Historical Linguistics* (Berlin, Mouton de Gruyter).

Hockett, C. F. (1965), 'Sound Change', *Language*, 41: 185–204.

Hoenigswald, H. M. (1960), *Language Change and Linguistic Reconstruction* (Chicago, University Press).

—— (1964), 'Graduality, Sporadicity, and the Minor Sound Change Processes', *Phonetica*, 11: 202–15.

—— and Wiener, L. F. (1987), *Biological Metaphor and Cladistic Classification: An Interdisciplinary Perspective* (London, Pinter).

Höfler, M., Vernay, H., and Wold, L. (eds.) (1979), *Festschrift Kurt Baldinger zum 60 Geburtstag: 17 November 1979* (Tübingen, Niemeyer).

Hollerbach, W. (1994), *The Syntax of Contemporary French: A Pedagogical Handbook and Reference Grammar* (Lanham, Md., University Press of America).

Holm, J. (1988–9), *Pidgins and creoles*, 2 vols. (Cambridge, CUP).

Holtus, G. (1990), 'Geschichte des Wortschatzes', in Holtus *et al.* (1988–), 5/1. 519–29.

—— Metzeltin, M., and Schmitt, C. (eds.) (1988–), *Lexikon der romanistischen Linguistik*, 8 vols. (Tübingen, Niemeyer).

—— and Radtke, E. (eds.) (1986), *Sprachlicher Substandard* (Tübingen, Niemeyer).

Hooper, J. B. (1976), 'Word Frequency in Lexical Diffusion and the Source of Morphophonological Change', in Christie (1976), 95–105.

Hope, T. E. (1972), *Lexical Borrowing in the Romance Languages: A Critical Study of Italianisms in French and Gallicisms in Italian from 1100 to 1900* (Oxford, Blackwell).

—— (1980), 'Interlanguage Influences', in Posner and Green (1980–93), 1. 245–87.

Hopper, P. J. (ed.) (1982), *Tense-Aspect: Between Semantics and Pragmatics* (Amsterdam, Benjamins).

—— (1991), 'On Some Principles of Grammaticization', in Traugott and Heine (1991), 17–35.

—— and Traugott, E. C. (1993), *Grammaticalization* (Cambridge, CUP).

Hornstein, N. (1990), *As Time Goes By: Tense and Universal Grammar* (Cambridge, Mass., MIT Press).

Houdebine, A-M. (1979), 'La Différence sexuelle et la langue', *Langage et société*, 7: 3–30.

Høybye, P. (1944), *L'Accord en français contemporain. Essai de grammaire descriptive* (Copenhagen, Host).

Huchon, M. (1988), *Le Français de la Renaissance* (Paris, PUF) (*Que sais-je?*).

Hudson, R. (1984), *Word Grammar* (Oxford, Blackwell).

—— (1996), *Sociolinguistics* (Cambridge, CUP).

Huguet, E. (1935), *Mots disparus ou vieillis depuis le XVIe siècle* (Geneva, Droz).

—— (1967), *L'Évolution du sens des mots depuis le XVIe siècle* (Geneva, Droz).

Hulk, A. (1993), 'Residual Verb-Second and the Licensing of Functional Features', *Probus*, 5: 127–54.

Hulst, H. van der, and Smith, N. (eds.) (1982), *The Structure of Phonological Representations* (Dordrecht, Foris).

Humphreys, H. L. (1932), *A Study of Dates and Causes of Case Reduction in the Old French pronoun* (New York, Institute of French Studies).

Huot, H. (1981), *Constructions infinitives du français; le subordonnant 'de'* (Geneva, Droz).

Hyman, L. M. (1985), *A Theory of Phonological Weight* (Dordrecht, Foris).

Ibrahim, M. H. (1973), *Grammatical Gender: Its Origins and Development* (The Hague, Mouton).

Iliescu, M. and Mourin, L. (1991), *Typologie de la morphologie verbale romane* (Innsbruck, Amoe).

Imbs, P. (1953), *Le Subjonctif en français moderne* (Baden-Baden, Verlag für Kunst und Wissenschaft).

—— (1960), *L'Emploi des temps verbaux en français moderne* (Paris, Klincksieck).

—— (ed.) (1961), *Lexicologie et lexicologie françaises et romanes: Orientation et exigences actuelles. Strasbourg 12–16 Novembre 1957* (Paris, CNRS).

—— (ed.) (1965), *Les Exigences de la lexicographie moderne: de Littré au Trésor de la langue française* (Paris, Klincksieck).

—— (ed.) (1971), *Trésor de la langue française: Dictionnaire de la langue du XIXe et du XXe siècle* (Paris, Klincksieck).

Iordan, I, Orr, J., and Posner R. (1970), *Introduction to Romance Linguistics: Its Schools and its Scholars* (Oxford, Blackwell).

Iordanskaja, L. (1982), 'Le Placement linéaire des clitiques pronominaux non-sujet en français contemporain', *Lingvisticae Investigationes*, 6: 145–67.

Irigaray, L. (ed.) (1987), 'Le Sexe linguistique' (*Langages*, 85).

Jacob, D. (1990), *Markierung von Aktantenfunktionen und 'Prädetermination' im Französischen* (Tübingen, Niemeyer) (Beiheft 231, *Zeitschrift für romanische Philologie*).

Jacobs, H. (1991), 'A Non-Linear Analysis of the Evolution of Consonant + Yod Sequences in Gallo-Romance', *Canadian Journal of Linguistics*, 36: 27–64.

Jacobs, H. (1993), 'The Phonology of Enclisis and Proclisis in Gallo-Romance and Old French', in Ashby *et al.* (eds.) (1993), 149–64.

—— (1996), 'Lenition and Optimality Theory', in Parodi *et al.* (1996), 253–67.

—— and Wetzels, L. (1988), 'Early French Lenition: A Formal Account of an Integrated Sound Change', in H. van der Hulst and N. Smith (eds.) (1988), *Features, Segmental Structures and Harmony Processes* (Dordrecht, Foris), 105–29.

Jaeggli, O., and Safir, K. (eds.) (1989), *The Null Subject Parameter* (Dordrecht, Kluwer).

—— and Silva-Corvalán, C. (eds.) (1984), *Studies in Romance linguistics* (Dordrecht, Foris).

James, E. (1988), *The Franks* (Oxford, Blackwell).

Jeffers, R. J., and Lehiste, I. (1979), *Principles and Methods for Historical Linguistics* (Cambridge, Mass., MIT Press).

Jensen, F. (1974), *The Syntax of the Old French Subjunctive* (The Hague, Mouton).

Jernudd, B., and Shapiro, M. (eds.) (1989), *The Politics of Language Purism* (Berlin, Mouton-de Gruyter).

Jokinen, U. (1978), *Les Relatifs en moyen français: Formes et functions* (Helsinki, Suomalainen Tiedeakademia).

Joly, A. (ed.) (1988), *La Linguistique génétique. Histoire et théories* (Lille, Presses Universitaires).

Jones, C. (ed.) (1993), *Historical Linguistics: Problems and Perspectives* (London, Longman's).

Jones, M. A. (1996), *Foundations of French Syntax* (Cambridge, CUP).

Jones, M. C. (1996), 'The Role of the Speaker in Language Obsolescence: The Case of Breton in Plougastel-Daoulas, Brittany', *Journal of French Language Studies*, 6: 45–74.

Joris, A. (1966), 'On the Edge of Two Worlds in the Heart of the New Empire of Northern Gaul during the Merovingian Period', *Studies in Renaissance and Medieval History*, 3: 3–52.

Joseph, B. D. (1983), 'Language Universals and Syntactic Change', *Language*, 56: 345–70.

Joseph, J. E. (1987), *Eloquence and Power: The Rise of Language Standards and Standard Language* (London, Frances Pinter).

—— (1989), 'Four Models of Linguistic Change', in Walsh (1989), 147–57.

—— and Taylor, T. J. (1990), *Ideologies of Language* (London, Routledge).

Journet, R., Petit, J., and Robert, G. (1966–78), *Mots et dictionnaires 1798–1878*, 11 vols. (Paris, Les Belles Lettres).

Jullien, B. (1875), *Les Éléments matériels du français, c'est-à-dire les sons de la langue française* (Paris, Hachette).

Kaiser, E. (1980), *Strukturen der Frage im Französischen. Synchronische und diachronische Untersuchungen zur direkten Frage im Französischen des 15. Jahrhunderts (1450–1500)* (Tübingen, Narr).

Karmiloff-Smith, A. (1979), *A Functional Approach to Child Language: A Study of Determiners and Reference* (Cambridge, CUP).

Kayne, R. S. (1972), 'Subject Inversion in French Interrogatives', in Casagrande and Saciuk (1972), 70–126.

—— (1976), 'French Relative *que*', in Hensey and Luján (1976), 255–99.

—— (1983), 'Chains, Categories External to S and French Complex Inversion', *Natural Language and Linguistic Theory*, 1: 107–39.

—— (1985), 'L'Accord du participe passé en français et en italien', *Modèles Linguistiques*, 7: 73–89.

—— (1989*a*), 'Facets of Romance Past Participle Agreement', in Benincà (1989), 85–101.

—— (1989*b*), 'Null Subjects and Clitic Climbing', in Jaeggli and Safir (1989), 239–61.

—— (1991), 'Romance Clitics, Verb Movement and PRO', *Linguistic Inquiry*, 22: 647–86.

—— (1993), 'Towards a Modular Theory of Auxiliary Selection', *Studia Linguistica*, 47: 3–31.

Keller, M. (1991), *Ein Jahrhundert Reformen der französischen Orthographie. Geschichte eines Scheiterns (1886–1991)* (Tübingen, Staffenburg Verlag).

Keller, R. E. (1964), 'The Language of the Franks', *Bulletin of the John Ryland's Library, Manchester*, 47: 101–22.

Keller, R. (1990), *Sprachwandel. Von der unsichtbaren Hand in der Sprache* (Tübingen, Francke) (1994) *On Language Change: The Invisible Hand in Language*, trans. B. Nerlich, with additions, London, Routledge).

Kenstowicz, M. (1994), *Phonology in Generative Grammar* (Oxford, Blackwell).

Kesselring, W. (1981), *Dictionnaire chronologique de vocabulaire français*, vol. 1 (Heidelberg, Winter).

Keys, A. C. (1957), *French Masculine Nouns in -e: The Historical Approach to a Problem of Gender* (Auckland, University College Press).

Kibbee, D. A. (1990), 'Language Variation and Linguistic Description in Sixteenth Century France', *Historical Linguistics*, 17: 49–65.

—— (1991), *For to speke Frenche trewely: The French language in England, 1000–1600: its status, description and instruction* (Amsterdam, Benjamins).

Kiefer, F. (1973), *Generative Morphologie des Neufranzösischen* (Tübingen, Niemeyer).

King, L., and Maley, C. (eds.) (1985), *Selected Papers from the Thirteenth Symposium in Romance Languages* (Amsterdam, Benjamins).

King, R. D. (1967*a*), 'A Measurement of Functional Load', *Studia Linguistica*, 21: 1–14.

454 *Bibliography*

King, R. D. (1967), 'Functional Load and Sound-Change', *Language*, 43: 831–52.

—— (1969*a*), *Historical Linguistics and Generative Grammar* (New Jersey, Prentice Hall).

—— (1969*b*), 'Push Chains and Drag Chains', *Glossa*, 3: 3–21.

Kiparsky, P. (1974), 'Remarks on Analogical Change', in J. M. Anderson and Jones (1974), 257–75.

—— (1988), 'Phonological Change', in Newmeyer (1988), 1. 362–415.

Klaus, G. (1985), *Das etymologische Wörterbuch des Französischen im 19. Jahrhundert. Untersuchungen zu seiner Anlage und seiner Bedeutung für die Etymologie anhand ausgewälter Werke* (Frankfurt-am-Main, Lang).

Klausenburger, J. (1970), *French Prosodics and Phonotactics* (Tübingen, Niemeyer) (Beiheft 124, *Zeitschrift für Romanische Philologie*).

—— (1974*a*), 'A Note on the Evolution of Stress in French', *Semasia*, 1: 65–70.

—— (1974*b*), *Historische französische Phonologie aus generativer Sicht* (Tübingen, Niemeyer).

—— (1979), *Morphologization: Studies in Latin and Romance Morphophonology* (Tübingen, Niemeyer).

—— (1985), 'French Historical Phonetics "demystified" ', *Romance Philology*, 38: 324–30.

—— (1993), 'On the Evolution of Latin Verbal Inflection into Romance: Change in Parameter Setting', in Ashby *et al.* (1993), 165–76.

—— (1994), 'How Abstract is French phonology? A Twenty Five Year Retrospective', in Lyche (1994), 151–67.

Klavans, J. (1985), 'The Independence of Syntax and Phonology in Cliticization', *Language*, 61: 95–120.

Kleiber, G. (1983), 'Les Démonstratifs (dé)montrent-ils? Sur le sens référentiel des adjectifs et pronoms démonstratifs', *Le Français Moderne*, 51: 99–117.

—— (1986), 'A propos de l'analyse "Adjectif démonstratif = article défini + élément déictique", ou sur l'irréductibilité des symboles indexicaux', in *Actes XVIIᵉ Cong.* 1984–6, 4. 193–212.

—— (1987), 'L'Opposition *cist/cil* en ancien français ou comment analyser les démonstratifs', *Revue de linguistique romane*, 51: 5–35.

—— (1994), *Anaphores et pronoms* (Brussels, Duculot).

Klein, H. G. (1974), *Tempus, Aspekt, Aktionsart* (Tübingen, Niemeyer).

Klein, J. R. (1976), *Le Vocabulaire des mœurs de la 'vie parisienne' sous le Second Empire: Introduction à l'étude du langage boulevardier* (Louvain, Nauwelaerts).

Klöden, H. (1987), *Zur lexikalischen Dynamik der französischen Schriftsprache vom 17. bis 20. Jahrhundert* (Passau, Andreas-Haller-Verlag).

Klum, A. (1961), *Verbe et adverbe: Etude sur le système verbal indicatif et sur le système de certains adverbes de temps à la lumière des relations verbo-adverbiales dans la prose du français contemporain* (Uppsala, Almqvist & Wiksell).

Knecht, P., and Marzys, Z. (eds.) (1993), *Écriture, langues communes et normes. Formation spontanée de Koinès et standardisation dans la Galloromania et son voisinage. Actes du colloque tenu à l'Université de Neuchâtel du 21 au 23 septembre 1988* (*Université de Neuchâtel. Travaux publiés par la Faculté des Lettres* 42) (Neuchâtel, Faculté des Lettres, Genève, Droz).

Kock, J. de (1975), 'Pour une nouvelle définition de la notion d'auxiliarité', *La Linguistique*, 11: 81–92.

Koerner, E. F. K. (1982), 'The Neogrammarian Doctrine: Breakthrough or Extension of the Schleicherian Paradigm?', in Maher *et al.* (1982), 129–52.

—— (ed.) (1983), *Linguistics and Evolutionary Theory: Three essays by August Schleicher, Ernst Haechel and Wilhelm Beck* (Amsterdam, Benjamins).

Kok, A. de (1985), *La Place du pronom personnel régime conjoint en français: Une étude diachronique* (Amsterdam, Rodopi).

Kontzi, R. (ed.) (1982), *Substrate und Superstrate in den romanischen Sprachen* (Darmstadt, Wissenschaftliche Buchgesselschaft).

Koopman, W., Leek, F. van der, Fischer, O., and Eaton, R. (eds.) (1987), *Explanation and Linguistic Change* (Amsterdam, Benjamins).

Korzen, H. (1983), 'Réflexions sur l'inversion dans les propositions interrogatives en français', in M. Herslund, O. Mørdrup, and F. Sørensen (eds.) (1983), *Analyses grammaticales du français: Etudes publiées à l'occasion du 50ᵉ anniversaire de Carl Vikner* (*Revue Romane*, supplement 24) (Copenhagen, Akademisk Forlag), 50–85.

—— (1985), *Pourquoi et l'inversion finale en français: Étude sur le statut de l'adverbial de cause et l'anatomie de la construction tripartite* (*Revue Romane*, supplement 30) (Copenhagen, Munksgaard), 24: 50–84.

Koschwitz, E. (1893), *Les Parlers parisiens: anthologie phonétique* (Paris, Welter).

Krámský, J. (1972), *The Article and the Concept of Definiteness in Language* (The Hague, Mouton).

Kriegel, S. (1996), *Diathesen im Mauritius- und Seychellenkreol* (Tübingen, Narr).

Kroch, A. S. (1989), 'Reflexes of Grammar in Patterns of Language Change', *Language variation and change*, 1: 199–244.

Kukenheim, L. (1967–8), *Grammaire historique de la langue française*, 2 vols. (Leiden, Universitaire).

Kuryłowicz, J. (1949), 'La Nature des procès dits "analogiques"', *Acta Linguistica*, 5: 15–37.

Labelle, M. (1985), 'Caractère post-lexical de la cliticisation française', *Lingvisticae Investigationes*, 9: 83–96.

Labelle, M. (1987), 'L'Utilisation des temps du passé dans les narrations françaises: le passé composé, l'imparfait et le présent historique', *Revue romane*, 22: 3–29.

Laberge, S. and Sankoff, G. (1979), 'Anything *you* can do', in T. Givón, (ed.) (1979), *Syntax and Semantics*, 12 (also in G. Sankoff 1980: 239–50).

Labov, W. (1972), 'Resolving the Neogrammarian Controversy', *Language*, 57: 267–308.

—— (1973), *Sociolinguistic Patterns* (Pennsylvania, University Press).

—— (1994), *Principles of Linguistic Change*, vol. 1: *Internal Factors* (Oxford, Blackwell).

La Chaussée, F. de (1977), *Initiation à la morphologie historique de l'ancien français* (Paris, Klincksieck).

Laenzlinger, C. (1993), 'A Syntactic View of Romance Pronominal Sequences', *Probus*, 5: 241–70.

Lakoff, G., and Johnson, M. (1980), *Metaphors We Live By* (Chicago, University Press).

Lambert, P-Y. (1994), *La Langue gauloise: description linguistique, commentaire d'inscriptions choisies* (Paris, Errance).

Lambert, W., and Tucker, G. R. (1976), *Tu, vous, usted: A Socio-Psychological Study of Address Patterns* (Rowley, Mass., Newbury House).

Lambrecht, K. (1981), *Topic, Antitopic and Verb Agreement in Non-Standard French* (Amsterdam, Benjamins).

—— (1987), 'On the Status of SVO Sentences in French Discourse', in R. Tomlin (ed.) (1987), *Coherence and Grounding in Discourse* (Amsterdam, Benjamins), 217–61.

Lane, G. S. (1934), 'Notes on Louisiana French I: Spoken Standard French of St. Martinville', *Language*, 10: 323–33.

—— (1935), 'Notes on Louisiana French II: The Negro French Dialect', *Language*, 11: 5–16.

Langenbacher, J. (1981), *Das néo-français: Raymond Queneaus Sprachkonzeption und kritische Auseinandersetzung mit dem Französischen der Gegenwart* (Frankfurt-am-Main, Lang).

Lanly, A. (1977), *Morphologie historique des verbes français* (Paris, Bordas).

Laparra, M. (1991), 'L'Orthographe: quelle réforme?', in *Le Français et le réforme* (*Pratiques* 71), 113–25.

Larochette, J. (1969), 'Problèmes de grammaire transformationnelle. L'imparfait et le passé simple', *Linguistics Antverpiensia*, 3: 133–94.

—— (1974), 'Syntaxe et sémantique', *Le Français Moderne*, 42: 324–31.

Lass, R. (1980*a*), *On Explaining Language Change* (Cambridge, CUP).

—— (1980*b*), 'Language, Speakers, History and Drift', in Koopman *et al.* (1980), 151–76.

—— (1990), 'How to Do Things with Junk: Exaptation in Language Evolution', *Journal of Linguistics*, 26: 79–102.

—— (1997), *Historical Linguistics and Language Change* (Cambridge, CUP).

Laubscher, G. G. (1921), *The Syntactical Causes of Case Reduction in Old French* (Princeton, University Press).

Lauefer, C., and Morgan, T. E. (eds.) (1991), *Theoretical Analyses in Romance Languages* (Amsterdam, Benjamins).

Léard, J. M. (1982), 'Essai d'explication de quelques faits de morphosyntaxe du québécois: le pronom relatif en diachronie structurale', *Revue Québécoise de Linguistique*, 12: 97–143.

Le Bel, E. (1991), 'Le Statut remarquable d'un pronom inaperçu', *La Linguistique*, 27: 91–109.

Le Bidois, G. and R. (1971), *Syntaxe du français moderne* (Paris, Picard).

Le Bidois, R. (1952), *L'Inversion du sujet dans la prose contemporaine* (Paris, d'Artrey).

Le Bras, H., and Todd, E. (1981), *L'Invention de la France* (Paris, Pluriel).

Leconte, J., and Cibois, P. (1989), *Que vive l'orth[t]ograph[f]e* (Paris, Seuil).

Lefebvre, C. (1988), 'Past Participle Agreement in French: Agreement = Case', in Birdsong and Montreuil (1988), 233–41.

Lefebvre, G. R. (1976), 'Français régional et créole à St. Barthélémy', in Snyder and Valdman (1976), 122–46.

Le Flem, D. C. (1986), 'Un trait archaïque du franco-québécois: les pronoms pléonastiques *en* et *y*', in *Actes XVIIe Cong.* 1984–6, 4: 253–66.

Le Goff, J., and Nora, P. (eds.) (1974), *Faire de l'histoire* (Paris, Gallimard).

Le Goffic, P. (ed.) (1986), *Points de vue sur l'imparfait* (Caen, Université).

Le Hir, Y. (1956), *Esthétique et structure du vers français d'après les théoriciens, du XVIe siècle à nos jours* (Paris, PUF).

Lehmann, W. P. (1992^3), *Historical Linguistics: An Introduction* (London and New York, Routledge).

—— and Malkiel, Y. (eds.) (1968), *Directions for Historical Linguistics* (Austin, Tex., University of Texas Press).

——— (1982), *Perspectives on Historical Linguistics* (Amsterdam, Benjamins).

Leischner, S. (1989), *Die Stellung des attributiven Adjectivs im Französischen. Eine rechnerunterstützte Analyse* (Tübingen, Narr).

Lemieux, M., and Cedergren, H. (1985), *Les Tendances dynamiques du français parlé à Montréal* (Quebec, Office de la langue française).

Léon, A. (1993), *Histoire de l'enseignment en France* (Paris, PUF) (*Que sais-je?*).

Leonard, C. S., Jr. (1965), 'Strong /R/ and weak /r/ in Gallo-Romance', in *Romance Philology*, 18: 296-9.

—— (1978), *Umlaut in Romance: An Essay in Linguistic Archaeology* (Grossen-Linden, Hoffmann).

Lepschy, G. (1980), 'L'Uso dell'articolo: confronti interlinguistici', in J. Bingen, A. Coupez and F. Mauret, *Recherches de Linguistique*.

Hommage à Maurice Leroy (Brussels, Éditions de l'Université de Bruxelles), 119–24.

Lerch, E. (1940), 'Proklise oder Enklise der altfranzösischen Objektpronomina? (Monistische und pluralistische Sprachanschung)', *Zeitschrift für romanische Philologie*, 60: 417–501.

Lesaint, M.-A. (1890³), *Traité complet de la prononciation française dans la seconde moitié du XIXᵉ s* (Vogel, Chr./Halle, Gesenius).

Létoublon, F. (1984), 'Il vient de pleuvoir, il va faire beau: verbes de mouvement et auxiliaires', *Zeitschrift für französische Sprache*, 94: 25–41.

Levitt, J. (1973), 'The Agreement of the Past Participle in Modern French: Orthographic Convention or Linguistic Fact?', *Linguistics*, 114: 25–41.

Lévy, Paul (1933), 'La Langue française en Alsace et en Lorraine de 1648 à 1870', *Le Français Moderne* 1: 144–59.

Levy, R., and Poston, L. (1957), 'A Bibliography of Longer French Word Studies', *Revue de linguistique romane*, 21: 145–82.

—— and Spence, N. C. W. (1961), 'A Supplementary Bibliography of Longer French Word Studies', *Revue de linguistique romane*, 25: 144–60.

Lewinsky, B. (1949), *L'Ordre des mots dans Bérinus: roman en prose du XIVᵉ siècle* (Göteborg, Runqvist).

Li, C. N. (ed.) (1975), *Word Order and Word Order Change* (Austin, Tex., University of Texas Press).

—— (1976), *Subject and Topic* (New York, Academic Press).

—— (1977), *Mechanisms of Linguistic Change* (Austin, Tex., University of Texas Press).

Lightfoot, D. (1979), *Principles of Diachronic Syntax* (Cambridge, CUP).

—— (1988), 'Syntactic Change', in Newmeyer (ed.) (1988), 1. 303–23.

—— (1991), *How to Set Parameters: Arguments from Linguistic Change* (Cambridge, Mass., MIT Press).

—— and Hornstein, N. (eds.) (1994), *Verb Movement* (Cambridge, CUP).

Lindhorst, P. (1978), 'L'Ordre des constituants S, V et C dans les textes en prose en ancien français', in R. E. V. Stuip (ed.) (1978), *Langue et littérature françaises du Moyen Age* (Assen, Van Gorcum), 12–23.

Lloyd, P. M. (1979), 'On the Definition of "Vulgar Latin": The Eternal Return', *Neuphilologische Mitteilungen*, 80: 110–22.

—— (1963–4), 'An Analytic Survey of Studies in Romance Word-Formation', *Romance Philology*, 17: 736–70.

Lodge, R. A. (1991), 'Authority, Prescriptivism and the French Standard Language', *Journal of French Language Studies*, 1: 93–111.

—— (1993), *French: From Dialect to Standard* (London, Routledge).

—— (1994), 'Was There Ever a Parisian Cockney?', in Parry *et al.* (1994), 35–73.

—— (1995), 'Les *Lettres de Montmartre* et l'idéologie normative', *Revue de Linguistique Romane*, 59: 569–73.

—— Armstrong, N. R., Shelton, J. F., and Ellis, Y. M. L. (1996), *Exploring the French Language* (London, Arnold).

Long, M. (1979), 'On Romance Preterites and the Nature of Phonological Change', in F. H. Nuessel, Jr. (ed.) (1979), *Essays in Contemporary Romance Linguistics* (Rowley, Mass., Newbury House), 230–46.

Lönne, K.-E. (ed.) (1995), *Kulturwandel im Spiegel des Sprachwandels* (Tübingen/Basle, Francke).

Lorenzo, R. (ed.) (1992–6), *Actas do XIX Congreso Internacional de Lingüística e Filoloxía Románicas. Universidade de Santiago de Compostela 1989* (Coruña, Fundación Pedro Barrié de la Maza, Conde de Fenosa).

Lote, G. (1949–95), *Histoire du vers français* (Paris/Aix, Boivin/Hatier/ Université de Provence), 8 vols. (published posthumously, one more volume yet to be published).

Lozachmeur, J.-C. (1976), 'Contribution à l'étude de l'évolution de *r*', *Revue de Linguistique Romane*, 40: 311–20.

Lucy, J. A. (1992), *Language Diversity and Thought: A Reformulation of the Linguistic Relativity Hypothesis* (Cambridge, CUP).

Ludwig, R. (1988), *Modalität und Modus im gesprochenen Französich* (Tübingen, Narr).

—— (ed.) (1989), *Les Créoles français entre l'oral et l'écrit* (Tübingen, Narr).

—— (1996), *Kreolsprachen zwischen Mündlichkeit und Schriftlichkeit. Zur Syntax und Pragmatik atlantischer Kreolsprachen auf französischer Basis* (Tübingen, Narr).

Lusignan, Serge (1987), *Parler vulgairement. Les intellectuels et la langue française aux xiii*e *et xiv*e *siècles* (Paris, Vrin; Montreal, Presses Universitaires).

Lutzeier, P. R. (ed.) (1993), *Studien zur Wortfeldtheorie* (Tübingen, Niemeyer).

Lyche, C. (ed.) (1994), *French Generative Phonology: Retrospective and Perspectives* (Salford, AFLS/European Studies Research Institute).

Lyons, C. (1986), 'On the Origin of the Old French Strong–Weak Possessive Distinction', *Transactions of the Philological Society* (1986), 1–41.

—— (1990), 'An Agreement Approach to Clitic Copying', *Transactions of the Philological Society* 88: 1–57.

Lyons, J. (1995), *Linguistic Semantics: An Introduction* (Cambridge, CUP).

McDonald, R. A. (1993), *The Economy and Material Culture of Slaves: Goods and Chattels on the Sugar Plantations of Jamaica and Louisiana* (Baton Rouge, La., Louisiana State University Press).

Mackenzie, F. (1939), *Les Relations de l'Angleterre et de la France d'après le vocabulaire. I. Les infiltrations de la langue et de l'esprit anglais: anglicismes français* (Paris, Droz).

McKitterick, R. (1989), *The Carolingians and the Written Word* (Cambridge, CUP).

—— (ed.) (1990), *The Uses of Literacy in Early Mediaeval Europe* (Cambridge, CUP).

McLaughlin, A. (1983*a*), 'Les Relations entre le timbre du *e* accentué et la chute du cheva final en français', *Revue québécoise de linguistique*, 12: 9–36.

—— (1983*b*), 'L'Ouverture des [e] accentués, mais qui donc voudrait défendre "l'hypothèse syllabique"?', *Revue québécoise de linguistique*, 12: 63–8.

McMahon, A. (1994), *Explaining Language Change* (Cambridge, CUP).

Maeda, S. (1993), 'Acoustics of Vowel Nasalization and Articulatory Shifts in French Nasal Vowels', in M. K. Huffman and R. A. Krakow (eds.) (1993), *Nasals, Nasalization and the Velum* (*Phonetics and Phonology*, 5) (San Diego, Academic Press), 147–67.

Maher, J. (1988), The Creole of St-Barthélemy: A Preliminary Sketch', in *Economies langagières dans quelques créoles des Amériques* (1988) (Paris, Editions l'Harmattan), 77–101.

Maher, J. P., Bombard, A. R., and Koerner, E. F. K. (eds.) (1982), *Papers from the Third International Conference on Historical Linguistics* (Amsterdam, Benjamins).

Maiden, M. (1992), 'Irregularity as a Determinant of Morphological Change', *Journal of Linguistics*, 28: 285–312.

Malachowski, A. (ed.) (1990), *Reading Rorty* (Oxford, Blackwell).

Malkiel, Y. (1953–4), 'Language History and Historical Linguistics', *Romance Philology*, 1: 65–76.

—— (1960), 'Paradigmatic Resistance to Sound-Change', *Language*, 26: 281–346.

—— (1963), 'Tendances générales du développement morphologique', *Lingua*, 12: 19–38.

—— (1976), *Etymological Dictionaries: A Tentative Typology* (Chicago, University Press).

—— (1980), 'Laws of Analogy', in Fisiak (1980), 283–8.

—— (1981), 'Drift, Slope and Slant: Background of, and Variations upon, a Sapirian Theme', *Language*, 57: 535–70.

—— (1989), *Theory and Practice of Romance Etymology: Studies in Language, Culture and History* (London, Variorum).

—— (1992), *Diachronic Studies in Lexicology, Affixation, Phonology: Edita and Inedita, 1979–1988* (Amsterdam, Benjamins).

—— (1993), *Etymology* (Cambridge, CUP).

Mańczak, W. (1958), 'Tendance générales des changements analogiques', *Lingua*, 7: 298–325, 387–420.

Manessy, G. (1988), 'Créolisation et creolité', *Études creoles*, 10: 25–38.

Mangold, M. (1950), *Études sur la mise en relief dans le français de l'époque classique* (Mulhouse, Bahy).

Maniet, A. (1963), 'Le Substrat celtique dans les langues romanes; les problèmes et la méthode', *Travaux de Linguistique et de Littérature de Strasbourg*, 1: 95–200.

Manzelli, G. (1990), 'Possessive Adnominal Modifiers', in Bechert *et al.* (1990), 63–111.

Marcellesi, J-B. (ed.) (1986), 'Glottopolitique' (*Langages*, 61).

—— and Gardin, B. (1974), *Introduction à la sociolinguistique: la linguistique sociale* (Paris, Larousse).

Marchello-Nizia, C. (1979), *Histoire de la langue française aux XIVe et XVe siècles* (Paris, Bordas).

—— (1985), *Les Phrases hypothétiques commençant par 'si' dans la langue française des origines à la fin du XVIe siècle* (Paris, Droz).

—— (1995), *L'Évolution du français: Ordre des mots, démonstratifs, accent tonique* (Paris, Armand Colin).

Markey, T. L. (1985), 'On Suppletion', *Diachronica*, 2: 51–66.

Marle, J. van (ed.) (1993), *Historical Linguistics 1991: Papers from the Tenth International Conference of Historical Lingusitics, Amsterdam, 12–16 August, 1991* (Amsterdam, Benjamins).

Marouzeau, J. (1922–49), *L'Ordre des mots dans la phrase latine*, 3 vols. (Paris, Champion).

Marshall, M. M. (1982), 'Bilingualism in Southern Louisiana: A Sociolinguistic Analysis', *Anthropological Linguistics*, 24: 308–24.

Martin, P. (1987), 'Prosodic and Rhythmic Structures in French', *Linguistics*, 25: 925–49.

Martin, R. (1965), 'Temps et aspect en français moderne', *Travaux de Linguistique et de Littérature de Strasbourg*, 3: 67–79.

—— (1966), *Le Mot RIEN et ses concurrents en français du XIIe au XVIe siècle à l'époque contemporaine.* (Paris, Klincksieck).

—— (1967), 'Quelques réflexions sur le système relatif-interrogatif QUI/CUI/QUE/COI en ancien français', *Travaux de Linguistique et de Littérature de Strasbourg*, 5: 97–122.

—— (1971), *Temps et aspect: Essai sur l'emploi des temps narratifs en moyen français* (Paris, Klincksieck).

—— (1972), 'La "Négation de virtualité" du moyen français', *Romania*, 93: 20–49.

—— (ed.) (1978), *Études de syntaxe du moyen français* (Metz, Centre d'analyse syntaxique).

—— (1983), 'De la double "extensité" du partitif', *Langue française*, 57: 34–42.

—— and Martin, E. (1973), *Guide bibliographique de la linguistique française* (Paris, Klincksieck).

Martin, R. and Wilmet, M. (1980), *Manuel du français du Moyen Âge: syntaxe du moyen français* (Bordeaux, Sobodi).

Martineau, F. (1994), 'Movement of Negative Adverbs in French Infinitival Clauses', *Journal of French Language Studies*, 4: 55–75.

Martinet, A. (1945), [1971²], *La Prononciation du français contemporain: témoignages recueillis en 1941 dans un camp d'officiers prisonniers* (Paris, Droz).

—— (1955), *Économie des changements phonétiques* (Berne, Franck).

—— (1958), 'C'est jeuli, le Mareuc!', *Romance Philology*, 11: 345–55, reprinted in Martinet (1969a), 191–219.

—— (1962), 'R, du latin au français d'aujourd'hui', *Phonetica* 8: 193–202 (reprinted in Martinet 1969a).

—— (1969a), *Le Français sans fard* (Paris, PUF).

—— (1969b), 'La Réforme de l'orthographe française d'un point de vue fonctionnel', in Martinet (1969a), 62–90.

—— (*et al.*) (1979), *Grammaire fonctionnelle du français* (Paris, Crédif).

—— (1985), 'La Prononciation du français entre 1880 et 1914', in Antoine and Martin (eds.) (1985), 25–40.

—— (1990), 'Remarques sur la variété des usages dans la phonie du français', in Green and Ayres-Bennett (1990), 13–26.

Martinon, P. (1913), *Comment on prononce le français* (Paris, Larousse).

Marx, G. (1881), *Ueber die Wortstellung bei Joinville* (*Französische Studien*, 1.3.2) (Heilbronn, Henninger).

Marxgut, W. (1989), *Der französische Sozialwortschaft im 17. Jahrhundert. Ein Beitrag zur paradigmatischen Semantik* (Rainweg, Egert).

Massicotte, F. (1986), 'Les Expressions de la restriction en français de Montréal', in D. Sankoff (1986), 325–33.

Matoré, G. (1953a), *La Méthode en lexicologie* (Paris Didier).

—— (1953b), *Le Vocabulaire et la société sous Louis-Philippe* (Geneva/Lille, Droz).

—— (1968), *Histoire des dictionnaires français* (Paris, Larousse).

—— (1985), *Le Vocabulaire et la société médiévale* (Paris, PUF).

—— (1988), *Le Vocabulaire et la société du XVIIᵉ siècle* (Paris, PUF).

Matte, E. J. (1982), *Histoire des modes phonétiques du français* (Geneva, Droz).

—— (1984), 'Réexamen de la doctrine traditionnelle sur les voyelles nasales du français', *Romance Philology*, 38: 15–31.

Matthews, P. H. (1981), *Syntax* (Cambridge, CUP).

—— (1991), *Morphology* (Cambridge, CUP).

Maurais, J. (ed.) (1985), *La Crise des langues* (Quebec/Paris, Conseil de la langue française/Le Robert).

—— (1987), *Politique et aménagement linguistique* (Quebec/Paris, Conseil de la langue française/Le Robert).

Maurel, J. P. (1986), 'Le Paramètre "absence d'article" en Latin', in David and Kleiber (1986), 203–15.

Mazzola, M. L. (ed.) (1994), *Issues and Theories in Romance Linguistics: Selected Papers from the Linguistic Symposium on Romance Languages XXIII April 1–4, 1993* (Washington, Georgetown University Press).

Meillet, A. (1912), 'L'Évolution des formes grammaticales', *Scientia*, 12 (reprinted in *Linguistique historique et linguistique générale* 1958 (Paris, Champion), 159–74).

Meisenburg, T. (1996), *Romanische Schriftsysteme im Vergleich. Eine diachronische Studie* (Tübingen, Narr).

Melander, J. (1928), *Étude sur l'ancienne abréviation des pronoms personnels régimes dans les langues romanes* (Uppsala, Almqvist & Wiksell).

Mel'čuk, I. A. (1976), 'On Suppletion', *Linguistics*, 170: 45–90.

Ménard, P. (1973³), *Syntaxe de l'ancien français* (Bordeaux, Sobodi).

Messner, D. (1975), *Essai de lexicochronologie française* (Salzburg, Universität).

—— (1977), *Einführung in die Geschichte des französischen Wortschatzes* (Darmstadt, Wissenschaftliche Buchgesselschaft).

Meyer-Lübke, W. (1897), 'Zur Stellung der tonlosen Objektspronomina', *Zeitschrift für romanische Philologie*, 21: 313–34.

—— (1925), 'Beiträge zur romanischen Laut- und Formenlehre 6, Die gruppe *ct*', *Zeitschrift für romanische Philologie*, 45: 641–61.

—— (1936), 'Zur Geschichte von latein *Ge, Gi* und *j* im Romanischen', *Vox Romanica*, 1: 1–31.

Michelet, J. (1833–46) [1879²], *Histoire de France* (Paris, Marpon/Flammarion).

Millet, A. (1933), *Les Grammairiens et la phonétique ou l'enseignement des sons du français depuis le XVIᵉ jusqu'à nos jours* (Paris, Monnier).

Milner, J.-C. (1979), 'Le Système de la négation en français et l'opacité du sujet', *Langue française*, 44: 80–105.

Milroy, J. (1992), *Linguistic Variation and Change* (Oxford, Blackwell).

—— and Milroy, L. 1985a), *Authority in Language: Investigating Language Prescription and Standardisation* (London, Routledge).

—— (1985b), 'Linguistic Change, Social Network and Speaker Innovation', *Journal of Linguistics*, 21: 339–84.

Milroy, L. (1987), *Observing and Analysing Natural Language: A Critical Account of Sociolinguistic Method* (Oxford, Blackwell).

Mitterand, H. (1963), *Les Mots français* (Paris, PUF) (*Que sais-je?*).

Möhren, F. (1980), *Le Renforcement affectif de la négation par l'expression d'une valeur minimale en ancien français* (Tübingen, Niemeyer) (Beiheft 75, *Zeitschrift für romanische Philologie*).

Moignet, G. (1959a), *Essai sur le mode subjonctif en latin postclassique et en ancien français* (Paris, PUF).

Moignet, G. (1959*b*) [1963], *Les signes de l'exception dans l'histoire du français* (Geneva: Droz).

—— (1959*c*), La Forme en re(t) dans le système verbal du plus ancien français', *Revue des langues romanes*, 73: 1–65.

—— (1965), 'L'oppposition NON/NE en ancien français', *Travaux de Linguistique et de Littérature de Strasbourg*, 3: 41–65.

—— (1966), 'Sur le système de la flexion à deux cas de l'ancien français', *Travaux de Linguistique et de Littérature de Strasbourg*, 4: 339–56.

—— (1967), 'Le système du paradigme QUI/QUE/QUOI', *Travaux de Linguistique et de Littérature de Strasbourg*, 5: 75–95.

—— (1970), 'Le Pronom personnel avec l'infinitif dans *La mort le roi Artu*', in *Mélanges de langue et de littérature du Moyen Âge et de la Renaissance offerts à Jean Frappier* (Geneva, Droz), 2: 831–44.

—— (1973), *Grammaire de l'ancien français: Morphologie-syntaxe* (Paris, Klincksieck).

Mok, Q. I. M. (1968), *Contribution à l'étude des catégories morphologiques du genre et du nombre dans le français parlé actuel* (The Hague, Mouton).

Molendijk, A. (1990), *Le Passé simple et l'imparfait: une approche reichenbachienne* (Amsterdam, Rodopi).

Moll, A. (ed.) (1985), *XVI congrés internacional de lingüística i filologia romàniques, Actes* (Palma de Mallorca, Moll).

Monnier, D. (1986), *La Perception de la situation linguistique par les Québécois* (Montreal, Conseil de la langue française).

Montreuil, J.-P. Y. (1994), 'On prosodization', in Lyche (1994), 211–38.

—— (1995), 'Weight and Length in Conservative Regional French', *Lingua*, 95: 77–96.

Monville-Burston, M., and Waugh, L. R. (1985), 'Le Passé simple dans le discours journalistique', *Lingua*, 67: 121–70.

Moravcsik, E. A. (1978), 'Agreement', in Greenberg *et al.* (1978), 4. 331–74.

Moreau, M.-L. (1971), ' "L'Homme que je crois qui est venu"; *qui*, *que*: relatifs et conjonctions', *Langue française*, 11: 77–90.

Morgan, R., Jr. (1959), 'Structural Sketch of Saint Martin Creole', *Anthropological Linguistics*, 1/8: 20-4.

—— (1960), 'The Lexicon', *Anthropological Linguistics*, 2: 7–29.

—— (1970), 'Dialect Levelling in Non-English Speech of Southwest Louisiana', in Gilbert, G. (ed.) (1970), *Texas Studies in Bilingualism: Spanish, French, German, Czech, Polish, Serbian and Norwegian in the Southwest* (Berlin, De Gruyter), 51–62.

—— (1975), *The Regional French of County Beauce, Quebec* (The Hague, Mouton).

—— (1976), 'The Saint Martin Creole Copula in Relation to Verbal Categories', in Snyder and Valdman (1976), 147–65.

Morin, J.-Y. (1975), 'Old French Clitics and the Extended Standard Theory', *Chicago Linguistic Society Papers*, 11: 390–400.

Morin, Y.-C. (1979), 'More Remarks on French Clitic Order', *Linguistic Analysis*, 5: 293–312.

—— (1981), 'Some Myths about Pronominal Clitics in French', *Linguistic Analysis*, 8: 95–108.

—— (1983*a*), 'De la (dé)nasalisation et de la marque du genre en français', *Lingua*, 61: 133–56.

—— (1983*b*), 'De l'ouverture des [e] du moyen français', *Revue québécoise de linguistique*, 12: 37–61.

—— (1985), 'Pour une histoire des voyelles longues en français', *Journal of the Atlantic Provinces Linguistics Association*, 6/7: 1–27.

—— (1986*a*), 'On the Morphologization of Word-Final Consonant Deletion in French', in H. Andersen (1986), 167–210.

—— (1986*b*), 'La Loi de position ou de l'explication en phonologie historique', *Revue québécoise de linguistique*, 15: 199–232.

—— (1987), 'French Data and Phonological Theory', *Linguistics*, 25: 815–43.

—— (1989), 'Changes in the French Vocalic System in the 19th Century', in Schouten and van Reenen (1989), 185–94.

—— (1991), 'Old French Stress Patterns and Closed Syllable Adjustment', in Wanner and Kibbee (1991), 49–76.

—— (1992*a*), 'Phonological Interpretation of Historical Lengthening', MS.

—— (1992*b*), 'Compensatory Lengthening in the History of French: The Evolution of the Diphthongs *ai*, ou, and *eu*', MS.

—— (1993), 'La Rime d'après le *Dictionnaire des rimes* de Lanoue 1596', *Langue française*, 99: 107–23.

—— (1994*a*), 'Les Origines historiques de la prononciation du français du Québec', in Mougeon and Beniak (1994), 205–36.

—— (1994*b*), 'Quelques réflexions sur la formation des voyelles nasales en français', *Communication and Cognition*, 27: 27–110.

—— and Bonin, M. (1992), 'Les -*s* analogiques des 1 sg. au XVIe siècle. Les témoignages de Meigret et Lanoue', *Revue Québécoise de Linguistique*, 21: 33–63.

—— and Dagenais, L. (1988), 'Les Normes subjectives du français et les français régionaux: la longueur vocalique depuis le 16e siècle', in van Reenen and van Reenen-Stein (1988), 153–62.

—— and Desaulniers, G. (1991), 'La Longeur vocalique dans la morphologie du pluriel dans le français de la fin du 16e siècle d'après le témoignage de Lanoue', in D. Kremer (ed.) (1991), *Actes du XVIIIe Congrès International de Linguistique et de Philologie Romanes* (Tübingen, Niemeyer), 3. 211–21.

—— Langlois, M.-C., and Varin, M. E. (1990), 'Tensing of Word Final [ɔ] to [o] in French: The Phonologization of a Morphophonological Rule', *Romance Philology*, 43: 507–28.

Langlois, M.-C., and Ouellet, M. (1991), 'Les [ɛ] longs devant [s] en français: sources historiques et évolution', *Revue québécoise de linguistique*, 20: 11–33.

Moritz, L. and Valois, D. (1994), 'Pied-Piping and Specifier Head Agreement', *Linguistic Inquiry*, 2: 667–707.

Mougeon, R., and Beniak, E. (eds.) (1989), *Le Français canadien parlé hors Québec: aperçu sociolinguistique* (Quebec, Presses de l'Université Laval).

—— (eds.) (1994), *Les Origines du français québécois* (Quebec, Presses de l'Université Laval).

Mourin, L. (1981), 'Possessifs romans', *Revue roumaine de linguistique*, 26: 341–66.

Müller, B. (1982), 'Geostatistik der gallischen/keltischen Substratwörter in der Galloromania', in O. Winkelmann and M. Braisch (eds.), *Festschrift für Johannes Hubschmid zum 65. Geburtstag* (Bern/Munich, Francke), 603–20.

—— (1985), *Le Français d'aujourd'hui* (Paris, Klincksieck).

Muller, Ch. (1967), *Étude de statistique lexicale: le vocabulaire du théatre de Corneille* (Geneva, Slatkine).

—— (1977), *Initiation à la statistique lexicale* (Paris, Hachette).

Muller, Cl. (1978), 'La Négation explétive dans les constructions complétives', *Langue Française*, 39: 76–103.

—— (1991), *La négation en français: syntaxe, sémantique et élements de comparaison avec les autres langues romanes* (Geneva, Droz).

Musset, L. (1965), *Les Invasions: Les Vagues germaniques* (Paris, PUF) (trans. 1975 *The Germanic Invasions: The Making of Europe AD 400–600*, London, Elek).

Napoli, D. J. (1981), 'Semantic Interpretation vs. Lexical Governance', *Language*, 57: 841–87.

Nelson, J. L. (1990), 'Literacy in Carolingian government', in McKitterick (1990), 258–96.

Nespor, M., and Scoretti, M. (1985), 'Empty Elements and Phonological Form', in Guéron *et al.* (1985), 203–35.

Neumann, I. (1981), 'Quelques observations sur la situation actuelle du créole en Louisiane', *Te Reo*, 24: 37–54.

—— (1985), *Le Créole de Breaux Bridge, Louisiane: étude morphosyntaxique—textes—vocabulaire* (Hamburg, Buske).

Neumann, S.-G. (1959), *Recherches sur le français des XVe et XVIe siècles et sur sa codification par les théoriciens de l'époque* (Lund, Gleerup/Copenhagen, Munksgaard).

Newmeyer, F. J. (ed.) (1988), *Linguistics: The Cambridge Survey*, 4 vols. (Cambridge, CUP).

Niederehe, H.-J. (ed.) (1996), *Études québécoises: bilan et perspectives. Actes du Colloque scientifique à l'occasion du Centre d'Études Québécoises à l'Université de Trêves, 2–5 décembre 1993* (Tübingen, Niemeyer).

—— and Wolf, L. (eds.) (1987), *Français du Canada, Français de France: Actes du Colloque de Trèves du 26 au 28 septembre 1985* (Tübingen, Niemeyer).

Nisard, C. (1872), *Étude sur le langage populaire ou patois de Paris et de sa banlieue* (Paris, Francke).

Nyrop, K. (1899–1930), *Grammaire historique de la langue française*, 6 vols. (Copenhagen, Gyldenhal).

Obenhauer, H.-G. (1976), *Études de syntaxe interrogative du français. Qui, combien et le complémenteur* (Tübingen, Niemeyer).

Offord, M. H. (1971), 'The Use of Personal Pronoun Subjects in Post-Position in Fourteenth Century French', *Romania*, 92: 37–64, 200–45.

—— (1976), 'Negation in Bérinus: A Contribution to the Study of Negation in Fourteenth Century French', *Zeitschrift für romanische Philologie*, 92: 313–85.

—— (1990), *Varieties of Contemporary French* (Basingstoke, Macmillan).

—— (1996), *A Reader in French Sociolinguistics* (Cleveland, Avon, Multilingual Matters).

Ong, W. J. S. J. (1982), *Orality and Literacy* (London, Methuen).

—— (1992), 'Writing is a Technology that Restructures Thought', in P. Downing, S. D. Lima, and M. Norman (eds.) (1992), *The Linguistics of Literacy* (Amsterdam, Benjamins), 293–319.

Outram, D. (1987), '*Le Langage mâle de la vertu*: Women and the Discourse of the French Revolution', in Burke and Porter (1987), 120–35.

Padley, G. A. (1988), *Grammatical Theory in Western Europe 1500–1700*. vol. 2. *Trends in Vernacular Grammar* (Cambridge, CUP).

Pagliuca, W. (ed.) (1994), *Perspectives on Grammaticalization* (Amsterdam, Benjamins).

Palm, L. (1977), *La Construction* **li filz le rei** *et les constructions concurrentes avec* **a** *et* **de** *dans des œuvres littéraires de la seconde moitié du XIIe siècle et du premier quart du XIIIe siècle* (Uppsala, Almqvist & Wiksell).

Palmer, F. R. (1986), *Mood and Modality* (Cambridge, CUP).

—— (1994), *Grammatical Roles and Relations* (Cambridge, CUP).

Panhuis, D. G. J. (1982), *The Communicative Perspective in the Sentence: A Study of Latin Word-Order* (Amsterdam, Benjamins).

—— (1985), 'Is Latin an SOV Language?: A Diachronic Perspective', *Indogermanische Forschungen*, 89: 140–59.

Parodi, C., Quicoli, C., Saltarelli, M., and Zubizarreta, M. L. (eds.) (1996), *Aspects of Romance Linguistics: Selected Papers from the Linguistic Symposium in the Romance Languages XXIV, March 10–13, 1994* (Washington, Georgetown University Press).

Parry, M. M., Davies, W. V., and Temple, R. A. M. (eds.) (1994), *The Changing Voices of Europe: Social and Political Changes and their*

Repercussions, Past, Present and Future (Cardiff, University of Wales Press).

Pasques, L. (1989), 'Le Traitment de *l* mouillé d'après les grammairiens et l'usage au XVIIe siècle', in Baddeley (1989), 123–36.

—— and Baddeley, S. (1989), 'Alternances vocaliques de type sociolinguistique au XVIe et XVIIe siècles', in Baddeley (1989*b*), 63-8.

Passy, P. (1886), *Le Français parlé* (Heilbronn, Henninger).

—— (1887) [1932[14]] *Les Sons du français: Leur formation, leurs combinaisons, leur représentations* (Paris, Firmin-Didot/Didier).

Paul, H. (1880), *Prinzipien der Sprachgeschichte* (Halle, Niemeyer).

Pearce, E. (1982), 'Infinitival Complements in Old French and Diachronic Change', *Studies in the Linguistic Sciences*, 12: 117–45.

—— (1990), *Parameters in Old French Syntax: Infinitival Complements* (Dordrecht, Kluwer).

Pensado, C. (1966), 'Inversion de marquage et perte su système casuel en ancien français', *Zeitschrift für romanische Philologie*, 102: 272–96.

Pensom, R. (1993), 'Accent and Metre in French', *Journal of French Language Studies*, 3: 19–37.

Péronnet, L. (1989), *Le Parler acadien* (New York, Peter Lang).

Peyre, H. (1933), *La Royauté et les langues provinciales* (Paris, Presses modernes).

Pfister, M. (1972), 'La Répartition géographique des éléments franciques en galloroman', *Revue de linguistique romane*, 37: 123–45.

—— (1973), 'Die sprachliche Bedeutung von Paris und der Île-de-France vor dem 13. Jahrhundert', *Vox Romanica*, 32: 217–53.

Phillips, H. (1936), *Étude du parler de la paroisse Evangeline, Louisiane* (Paris, Droz).

—— (1979), 'Le Français de la Louisiane', in Valdman (ed.) (1979), 95–110.

Piatt, H. (1898), *Neuter il in Old French* (Strasburg, Goeller).

Picabia, L. (ed.) (1986), 'Déterminants et détermination' (*Langue française*, 72).

Picard, M. (1992), 'Aspects synchroniques et diachroniques du *tu* interrogatif en québécois', in *Revue québécoise de linguistique*, 21: 65–74.

Picoche, J. (1977), *Précis de lexicologie française: L'Étude et l'enseignment du vocabulaire* (Paris, Nathan).

—— (1979), *Précis de morphologie historique du français* (Paris, Nathan).

—— (1986), *Structures sémantiques du lexique français* (Paris, Nathan).

—— and Marchello-Nizia, C. (1989), *Histoire de la langue française* (Paris, Nathan).

Picone, M. D. (1995), *Anglicisms, Neologisms and Dynamic French* (Amsterdam, Benjamins).

Pinchon, J. (1972), *Les Pronoms adverbiaux en et y: Problèmes généraux de la représentation pronominale* (Geneva, Droz).

—— (1986), *Morphosyntaxe du français. Étude de cas* (Paris, Hachette).

—— and Couté, B. (1981), *Le Système verbal du français* (Paris, Nathan).

Pinkster, H. (1990), *Latin Syntax and Semantics* (London, Routledge).

Planhol, X. de (1988), *Géographie historique de la France* (Paris, Fayard).

Plank, F. (1979), 'The Functional Basis of Case Systems and Declension Classes: From Latin to Old French', *Linguistics*, 17: 611–40.

—— (1984), 'Romance Disagreements: Phonology Interfering with Syntax', *Journal of Linguistics*, 20: 329–49.

Plénat, M. (1995), 'Une approche prosodique de la morphologie du verlan', *Lingua*, 95: 97–129.

Pohl, J. (1979), *Les Variétés régionales du français* (Brussels, Éditions Universitaires).

Pohoryles, B. M. (1966), *Demonstrative Pronouns and Adjectives in Garin le Loheren and Gerbert de Metz* (New York, Pace College).

Poliakov, L. (1974), *The Aryan Myth* (London, Chatto-Heinemann, for Sussex University Press).

Pollack, W. (1988), *Studien zum Verbalaspekt mit besonderer Berücksichtigung des Französichen* (Bern/Frankfurt-am-Main/New York/Paris, Lang).

Pollock, J.-Y. (1986), 'Sur la syntaxe de *en* et le paramètre du sujet nul', in M. Ronat and D. Couquaux (eds.) (1986), *La Grammaire modulaire* (Paris, Minuit).

—— (1989), 'Verb-Movement, UG and the Structure of IP', *Linguistic Inquiry*, 20: 365–424.

Polomé, E. C., and Winter, W. (eds.) (1992), *Reconstructing Languages and Culture* (Berlin, Mouton-de Gruyter).

Pooley, T. (1994), 'Word-Final Devoicing in a Variety of Working-Class French: A Case of Language Contact?', *Journal of French Language Studies*, 4: 215–33.

Pope, M. K. (1934) [1956], *From Latin to Modern French with Especial Consideration of Anglo-Norman. Phonology and Morphology* (Manchester, University Press).

Poplack, S., and Sankoff, D. (1984), 'Borrowing: The Synchrony of Integration', *Linguistics*, 22: 99–135.

—— and Miller, C. (1988), 'The Social Correlates and Linguistic Processes of Lexical Borrowing and Assimilation', *Linguistics*, 26: 47–104.

—— and Walker, D. (1986), 'Going through /L/ in Canadian French', in D. Sankoff (1986), 173–97.

Posner, R. (1961*a*), *Consonantal Dissimilation in the Romance Languages* (Publications of the Philological Society 19) (Oxford, Blackwell).

—— (1961*b*), 'The Imperfect Endings in Romance', *Transactions of the Philological Society* (1961), 17–55.

—— (1961*c*), 'Phonology and Analogy in the Formation of the Romance Perfect', *Romance Philology*, 17: 419–31.

Posner, R. (1965), 'Romance Imperfect and Conditional Endings: A Further Contribution', *Studia Neophilologica*, 37: 3–10.

—— (1966*a*), *The Romance Languages: A Linguistic Introduction* (New York, Doubleday).

—— (1966*b*), 'Rumanian and Romance Phonology', *Romance Philology*, 19: 450–9.

—— (1971), 'On Synchronic and Diachronic Rules: French Nasalisation', *Lingua*, 27: 184–97.

—— (1972), 'Aspects of Aspect and Tense in French', *Romance Philology*, 26: 94–111.

—— (1973), 'Homonymy, Polysemy and Semantic Change', *Language Sciences*, 27: 1–8.

—— (1974), 'Ordering of Historical Phonological Rules in Romance', *Transactions of the Philological Society* (1974), 98–127.

—— (1975), 'Semantic Change or Lexical Change?', in M. Saltarelli and D. Wanner (eds.), *Diachronic Studies in Romance Linguistics* (The Hague, Mouton), 177–82.

—— (1976*a*), 'The Relevance of Comparative and Historical Data for the Description and Definition of a Language', *York Papers in Linguistics*, 6: 75–87.

—— (1976*b*), 'Phonemic Overlapping and Repulsion Revisited', in *Linguistic and Literary Studies in Honor of Archibald A. Hill* (Lisse, de Ridder), 1: 235–43.

—— (1979), 'Chronologie de la palatalisation romane', in *Atti XIV Cong.* 1976–81, 3. 35–52.

—— (1980*a*), 'Historical Romance Lexicology and Semantics', in Posner and Green (1980–93), 1. 175–90.

—— (1980*b*), 'Romance History—Creolization and Decreolization? or Diffusion and Focussing?' *York Papers in Linguistics*, 10: 173–92.

—— (1981), 'Lexical Gaps and How to Plug Them', in T. E. Hope, R. Harris, and G. Price (eds.), *Language, Meaning and Style: Essays in memory of Stephen Ullmann* (Leeds, University Press), 117–35.

—— (1984), 'Double Negatives, Negative Polarity and Negative Incorporation in Romance: A Historical View', *Transactions of the Philological Society* (1984), 1–26.

—— (1985*a*), 'Diachronic Syntax: Free Relatives in Romance', *Journal of Linguistics*, 21: 181–9.

—— (1985*b*), 'Histoire de la négation et la typologie romane, *Actes XVIIe Cong.* 1984–6, 2. 263–71.

—— (1985*c*), 'Non-Agreement on Romance Disagreements', *Journal of Linguistics*, 21: 437–51.

—— (1985*c*), 'Post-Verbal Negation in Non-Standard French: A Historical and Comparative View', *Romance Philology*, 39: 170–97.

—— (1986), 'La Créolization—altération typologique?', *Études créoles*, 9: 127–34.

—— (1987), 'Creolization and Syntactic Change in Romance', in Ramat *et al.* (1987), 473–81.

—— (1988*a*), 'Definiteness and the History of French Possessives', *French Studies*, 42: 385–97.

—— (1988*b*), 'Language Variation, Change and Typology in Romance', in J. Albrecht, J. Lüdtke, and H. Thun (eds.) (1988), *Energeia und Ergon. Sprachliche Variation—Sprachgeschichte—Sprachtypologie. Studia in honorem E. Coseriu* (Tübingen, Narr), 3. 161–6.

—— (1990*a*), 'Linguistics and Philology, Parametric Change and Romance Possessives', in Fisiak (1990), 337–51.

—— (1990*b*), 'Romance Comparative Grammar and Linguistic Change', in H. Andersen and Koerner (1990), 399–409.

—— (1993*a*), 'Latin to Romance (Again!): Change or Genesis?', in van Marle (1993), 265–79.

—— (1993*b*), 'La Romanité des langues créoles à base lexicale romane', in Hilty (1993), 5: 253–63.

—— (1994*a*), 'Historical Linguistics, Language Change and the History of French', *Journal of French Language Studies*, 4: 75–97.

—— (1994*b*), 'Non-Topical Human Agents in Romance: A Historical and Pragmatic Approach', in C. Lupu and G. Price (eds.) (1994), *Hommages offerts à Maria Manoliu-Manea* (Bucharest, Pluralia), 100–21.

—— (1994*c*), 'Third-Person Subjects in French: A Historical View', in Yaguello (1994), 109–24.

—— (1995*a*), 'Article and Pronoun in Romance: A Historical View', in J. Veny (ed.), *Estudis de lingüística i filologia oferts a Antoni M. Badia Margarit* (Barcelona, Abbadia de Monserrat), 2. 93–102.

—— (1995*b*), 'Contact, Social Variants, Parameter Setting and Pragmatic Function: An Example from the History of French Syntax', in Fisiak (1995).

—— (1996), *The Romance Languages* (Cambridge, CUP).

—— and Green, J. N. (eds.) (1980–93), *Trends in Romance Linguistics and Philology*, 5 vols. (Berlin, Mouton de Gruyter).

Postal, P. (1966), 'On the So-Called "Pronouns" in English', in F. Dineen (ed.) (1996), *Monograph on Languages and Linguistics*, 19 (Washington, Georgetown University Press) (reprinted in D. A. Reibel and S. A. Schane (eds.) (1969), *Modern Studies in English, Readings in transformational Grammar* (Englewood Cliffs, NJ, Prentice-Hall), 201–24).

Prebensen, H. (1982), 'La Proposition relative dite attributive', *Revue Romane*, 17: 98–117.

Price, G. (1961*a*), 'Aspects de l'ordre des mots dans les *Chroniques* de Froissart', *Zeitschrift für romanische Philologie*, 77: 15–48.

Price, G. (1961*b*), 'Contribution à l'étude de la syntaxe des pronoms personnels sujets en ancien français', *Romania*, 87: 476–504.

—— (1962), 'The Negative Particles "pas", "mie" and "point" in French', *Archivum Linguisticum*, 14: 14–34.

—— (1966), 'Contribution à l'étude de la syntaxe des pronoms personnels sujets en ancien français', *Romania*, 87: 476–504.

—— (1968), 'Quel est le rôle de l'opposition CIST/CIL en ancien français?' *Romania*, 89: 240–53.

—— (1969), 'La Transformation du système français des demonstratifs', *Zeitschrift für romanische Philologie*, 85: 489–505.

—— (1971), *The French Language: Present and Past* (London, Arnold).

—— (1973), 'Sur le pronom personnel sujet postposé en ancien français', *Revue Romane*, 8: 226–36.

—— (1978), 'L'Interrogation négative sans *ne*', *Studii şi Cercetări Lingvistice*, 5: 599–606.

Priestley, L. (1955), 'Reprise constructions in French', *Archivum Linguisticum*, 7: 1–28.

Pulgram, E. (1965), 'Prosodic Systems: French', *Lingua*, 13: 125–44 (reprinted in Pulgram (1988), 2. 167–84).

—— (1970), *Syllable, Word, Nexus, Cursus* (The Hague, Mouton).

—— (1975), *Latin-Romance Phonology: Prosodics and Metrics* (Munich, Fink).

—— (1979), 'The Accent in Spoken Latin', in Höfler *et al.* (eds.) (1979), 139–44 (reprinted in Pulgram (1988), 2. 118–22).

—— (1988), *Practicing Linguist: Essays on Language and Languages, 1950–1985* (Heidelberg, Winter).

Purschinsky, J. (1980), 'Romance Historical Phonology', in Posner and Green (1980–93), 1. 77–103.

Queffélec, A. (1988), 'La Négation "explétif" en ancien français: une approche psycho-mécanique', in A. Joly (ed.) (1988), *La Linguistique génétique. Histoire et théories* (Lille: Presses Universitaires), 419–43.

Quemada, B. (1968), *Les Dictionnaires du français moderne (1539–1863): Étude sur leur histoire, leurs types et leurs méthodes*, 2 vols. (Paris, Didier).

—— (1978), *Répertoire des dictionnaires scientifiques monolingues et multilingues 1950–1975* (Paris, CNRS).

Radtke, E. (1994), *Gesprochenes Französische und Sprachgeschichte. Zur Rekonstruktion der Gesprächskonstitution in Dialogen französischer Sprachlehrbücher des 17. Jahrhunderts unter besonderer Berücksichtigung der italienischen Adaptionen* (Tübingen: Niemeyer) (Beiheft 255, *Zeitschrift für romanische Philologie*).

Raible, W. (ed.) (1989), *Romanistik, Sprachtypologie und Universalienforschung* (Tübingen, Narr).

Ramat-Giacolone, A., Carruba, O., and Bernini, G. (eds.) (1987), *Papers from the Seventh International Conference on Historical Linguistics* (Amsterdam, Benjamins).

Ramsden, H. (1963), *Weak Pronoun Position in Early Romance Languages* (Manchester, University Press).

Rapport général sur les modalités d'une simplification éventuelles de l'orthographe française, élaboré par la Commission ministérielle d'études orthographiques, sous la présidence de M. A. Beslais (1965) (Paris, Didier).

Reenen, P. van (1985), 'La Fiabilité des données linguistiques (à propos de la formation des voyelles nasales en ancien français)', in Moll (1985), 37–51.

—— (1987), 'La Formation des voyelles nasales d'après le témoignage des assonances', in B. Kampers-Manhe and C. Vet (eds.) (1987), *Études de linguistique française offertes à Robert de Dardel par ses amis et collègues* (Amsterdam, Rodopi), 127–41.

—— (1988*a*), 'An/en en ancien français: distribution (géo)graphiques', in R. Landheer (ed.) (1988), *Aspects de linguistique françaises. Hommage à Q. I. M. Mok* (Amsterdam, Rodopi), 141–60.

—— (1988*b*), 'Les Variations des graphies *o/ou* et *an/en* en ancien français', in van Reenen and van Reenen-Stein (1988), 163–76.

—— (1989), 'Isoglosses and Gradual Differences across Dialects in Medieval French', in Schouten and van Reenen (1989), 135–54.

—— (1992), 'Contractions of Preposition and Plural Article without *s* (e.g. *a + les* to *au*) in Old French: A Completely Overlooked Problem of Paradigm Formation with Implications for the Theory of Language Change', *Vrije Universiteit Working Papers in Linguistics*, 40.

—— and Reenen-Stein, K. van (eds.) (1988), *Distribution Spatiales et temporelles, constellations des manuscrits: Études de variation linguistique offertes a Anthonij Dees* (Amsterdam, Benjamins).

—— and Schøsler, L. (1986), 'Le Système des cas et sa disparition en ancien français', *Actes XVIIe Cong.* (1984–6), 4. 79–114.

—— (1988), 'Formation and Evolution of the Feminine and Masculine Nominative Singular Nouns in Old French *la maison(s)* and *li charbons*', in Fisiak (1988), 506–45.

—— (1990), 'Le Problème de la prolifération des explications', *Travaux de Linguistique et de Philologie de Strasbourg*, 28: 221–38.

—— (1992), 'Ancien et moyen français: SI thématique: analyse exhaustive d'une série de textes', *Vox Romanica*, 51: 101–27.

—— (1995), 'The Thematic Structure of the Main Clause in Old French: OR versus SI', in H. Andersen (1995), 401–20.

Regula, M. (1955–66), *Historische Grammatik des französischen*, 3 vols. (Heidelberg, Winter).

Reid, T. B. W. (1955), 'On the Analysis of the Tense System of French', *Revue de linguistique romane*, 19: 23–38.

—— (1970), 'Verbal Aspect in Modern French', in T. G. S. Combe and

P. Rickard (eds.) (1970), *The French Language: Studies Presented to Lewis Charles Harmer* (London, Harrap), 146–71.

Reighard, J. (1986), 'La Vélarisation de l'r en français et en portugais', in *Actes XVIIᵉ Cong.* (1984–6), 2. 313–23.

Renchon, H. (1967), *Études de syntaxe descriptive.* Vol. 1: *La Syntaxe de l'interrogation* (Brussels, Académie Royale).

Renfrew, C. (1987), *Archaeology and Language: The Puzzle of Indo-European Origins* (Cambridge, CUP).

Renzi, L. (1979), 'Per la storia dell' articolo romanza', in *Atti. XIV Cong.*, 3. 251–84.

—— (1981), *La politica linguistica della Rivoluzione francese* (Naples, Liguori).

Rey, A. (1973–6), *Théories du signe et du sens* (Paris, Klincksieck).

—— (1982), *Encyclopédies et dictionnaires* (Paris, PUF) (*Que sais-je?*).

Rey-Debove, J. (1971), *Étude linguistique et sémiotique des dictionnaires français contemporains* (The Hague, Mouton).

Richter, E. (1903), *Zur Entwicklung der romanischen Wortstellung aus der lateinischen* (Halle, Niemeyer).

Rickard, P. (1959), 'The Rivalry of *m(a)*, *t(a)*, *s(a)*, and *mon, ton, son*, before Feminine Nouns in Old and Middle French', *Archivum Linguisticum*, 11: 21– 47, 115–47.

—— (1962), 'The Word Order Object-Verb-Subject in Medieval French', *Transactions of the Philological Society* (1962), 1–39.

—— (1968), *La Langue française au seizième siècle* (Cambridge, CUP).

—— (1974, 1989²) *A History of the French Language* (London, Hutchinson).

—— (1976), *Chréstomathie de la langue française au quinzième siècle* (Cambridge, CUP).

—— (1981), *The Embarrassments of Irregularity: The French Language in the Eighteenth Century* (Cambridge, CUP).

—— (1992), *The French Language in the Seventeenth Century. Contemporary opinion in France* (Cambridge, Brewer).

—— (1993), 'From Villehardouin to Du Cange *via* Vigenère', *Zeitschrift für Französische Sprache und Literatur*, 103: 113–43.

Ricœur, P. (1980), *The Contribution of French Historiography to the Theory of History* (Oxford, Clarendon Press).

Rigault, A. (1971*a*), 'Les Marques du genre', in Rigault (1971*b*), 79–92.

—— (ed.) (1971*b*), *La Grammaire du français parlé* (Paris, Hachette).

Ringenson, K. (1922), *Étude sur la palatalisation de k devant une voyelle en français* (Paris, Champion).

Rivero, M. L. (1986), 'Parameters in the Typology of Clitics in Romance', *Language*, 62: 774–807.

Rizzi, L. (1984), 'On the Status of Subject Clitics in Romance', in Jaeggli and Silva-Corvalán (1984), 391–419.

—— (1990), 'Speculation on Verb Second', in J. Mascarò and M. Nespor (eds.), *Grammar in Progress: Glow Essays for Henk van Riemsdijk*, (Dordrecht, Foris), 375–86.

—— and Roberts, I. (1989), 'Complex Inversion in French', *Probus*, 1: 1–30.

Roberts, I. (1993), *Verbs and Diachronic Syntax. A Comparative History of English and French* (Dordrecht, Kluwer).

—— (1994), 'Two Types of Head Movement in Romance', in Lightfoot and Hornstein (1994), 207–42.

—— (1996), *Comparative Syntax* (London, Arnold).

Robillard, D. de, and Beniamino, M. (eds.) (1993), *Le Français dans l'espace francophone: description linguistique et sociolinguistique de la francophonie*, vol. 1 (Paris, Champion).

Roche, D. (1981), *Le Peuple de Paris. Essai sur la culture populaire au XVIIIe siècle* (Paris, Aubier Montaigne).

Roche, G. (1990), 'Étymologie', in Holtus *et al.* (1988–), vol. 5.1: 507–17.

Rochet, B. (1976), *The Formation and Evolution of French Nasal Vowels* (Tübingen, Niemeyer).

—— (1982), 'The Mid-Vowels in Bordeaux French', *Orbis*, 29: 76–104.

Romaine, S. (1982), *Socio-Historical Linguistics: Its Status and Methodology* (Cambridge, CUP).

Ronat, M. (1977), 'Une contrainte sur l'effacement du nom', in M. Ronat (ed.) (1977), *Langue. Théorie générative étendue* (Paris, Hermann), 153–69.

Rondeau, G., Bibeau, G., Gagné, G., and Taggart, G. (eds.) (1979), *Vingt-cinq ans de linguistique au Canada: Hommage à Jean-Paul Vinay* (Montreal, CEC).

Rorty, R. (1980), *Philosophy and the Mirror of Nature* (Oxford, Blackwell).

—— (1989), *Contingency, Irony and Solidarity* (Cambridge, CUP).

Rosset, T. (1911), *Les Origines de la prononciation moderne étudiées au XVIe siècle, d'après les remarques des grammairiens et les textes en patois de la banlieue parisienne* (Paris, Armand Colin).

Rossillon, P. (ed.) (1995), *Atlas de la langue française: histoire, géographie, statistiques* (Paris, Bordas).

Rothenberg, M. (1979), 'Les Propositions relatives prédicatives et attributives: problème de linguistique française', *Bulletin de la Société Linguistique de Paris*, 74: 351–83.

Rothwell, W. (1993), 'From Latin to Anglo-French and Middle English: The Role of the Multilingual Gloss', *Modern Language Review*, 88: 581–99.

Rousselot, P., and Laclotte, F. (1899–1902) [1927³], *Précis de prononciation français* (Paris, Welter/Didier).

Rowlett, P. (1993), 'On the Syntactic Representation of Negative Sentence Adverbials', *Journal of French Language Studies*, 3: 36–69.

Roy, G.-R. (1976), *Contribution à l'analyse du syntagme verbal: étude morphosyntaxique et statistique des coverbes* (Quebec, Presses Universitaires Laval/Paris, Klincksieck).

Rudes, B. A. (1980*a*), 'On the Nature of Verbal Suppletion', *Linguistics*, 18: 655–76.

Ruwet, N. (1990), '*En* et *y*: deux clitiques pronominaux antilogophoriques', *Langages*, 97: 51–81.

Safir, K. (1986), 'Subject Clitics and the Nominative Drop Parameter', in Borer (1986), 333–65.

Saint-Gérand, J.-Ph. (ed.), (1993), *Mutations et sclérose de la langue française, 1789–1848* (Stuttgart, Steiner).

Salmon, G.-L. (ed.) (1991), *Le Français en Alsace* (Paris, Champion-Slatkine).

Sampson, R. (1980), 'On the History of Final Vowels from Latin to Old French', *Zeitschrift für romanische Philologie*, 96: 23–48.

—— (ed.) (1993), *Authority and the French Language: Papers from a Conference at the University of Bristol* (Münster, Nodus).

Sancier-Château, A. (1993), *Introduction à la langue française du XVIIᵉ siècle* (Paris, Nathan).

Sanders, C. (1993*a*), 'Socio-Situational Variation', in Sanders (1993*b*), 27–53.

—— (ed.) (1993*b*), *French Today. Language in its Social Context* (Cambridge, CUP).

Sankoff, D. (ed.) (1986), *Diversity and Diachrony* (Amsterdam, Benjamins).

Sankoff, G. (1980), *The Social Life of Language* (Philadelphia, University of Pennsylvania Press).

—— and Vincent D., (1977), 'L'Emploi productif du **ne** dans le français parlé à Montréal', *Le Français Moderne*, 43: 243–56.

Sapir, E. (1921), *Language* (New York, Harcourt, Brace & Co).

Sauvageot, A. (1964), *Portrait du vocabulaire français* (Paris, Larousse).

Scaglione, A. (ed.) (1984), *The Emergence of national languages* (Ravenna, Longo).

Schane, S. (1968), *French Phonology and Morphology* (Cambridge, Mass., MIT Press).

—— (1974), 'There is No French Truncation Rule', in Campbell *et al.* (1974), 89–99.

—— (1978), 'Deletion vs. Epenthesis: A Pseudocontroversy', *Studies in French Linguistics*, 1: 71–8.

Schein, B., and Steriade, D. (1986), 'On Geminates', *Linguistic Inquiry*, 17: 691–744.

Schlickum, J. (1882), *Die Wortstellung in der altfranzösischen Dichtung 'Aucassin und Nicolete'* (= *Französische Studien* 3.3) (Heilbronn, Henninger).

Schlieben-Lange, B. (1976), 'L'Origine des langues romanes—un cas de créolisation', in J. Meisel (ed.), *Langues en contact: Pidgin—Creoles* (Tübingen, Narr), 267–85.

Schmitt, C. (1986), 'Der französiche Substandard', in G. Holtus and E. Radtke (eds.) (1986), *Sprachlicher Substandard* (Tübingen, Niemeyer), 125–86.

—— (1987), 'Die Ausbildung des Artikels in der Romania', in Dahmen *et al.* (1987), 94–125.

Schmitt, R. (1972), 'Bibliographie de lexicologie française', *Revue des langues romanes*, 80: 421–5.

Schogt, Henri G. (1964), 'L'Aspect verbal en français et l'élimination du passé simple', *Word*, 20: 1–17.

—— (1968a), *Le Système verbal du français contemporain* (The Hague, Mouton).

—— (1968), 'Les Auxiliaires in français', *La Linguistique* (1968) 2: 5–19.

Schöne, M. (1951), *La Vie et mort des mots* (Paris, PUF) (*Que sais-je?*).

Schøsler, L. (1984), *La déclinaison bicasuelle de l'ancien français: Son rôle dans la syntaxe de la phrase, les causes de sa disparition* (Odense, University Press).

Schouten, M. E. H., and van Reenen, P. Th. (eds.) (1989), *New Methods in Dialectology: Proceedings of a Workshop Held at the Free University, Amsterdam, December 7–10, 1987* (Dordrecht, Foris).

Schuchardt, H. (1885), *Ueber die Lautgesetze. Gegen die Junggrammatiker* (Berlin, Oppenheim).

Schulze, A. (1884), 'Die Wortstellung im altfranzösischen direkten Frage-satz', *Archiv für das Studium der neueren Sprachen*, 7: 185–212, 303–56.

—— (1888), *Der altfranzösische direkte Fragesatz. Ein Beitrage zur Syntax des Französischen* (Leipzig, Hirzel).

Schürr, F. (1970), *La Diptongaison romane* (Tübingen, Narr).

Schwarze, C. (1974), 'Les Constructions du type "Je le vois qui arrive"', in C. Rohrer and N. Ruwet (eds.) (1974), *Actes du colloque franco-allemand de grammaire transformationnelle* (Tübingen, Narr), 18–30.

Schwegler, A. (1983), 'Predicate Negation and Word-Order Change: A Problem of Multiple Causation', *Lingua*, 61: 297–334.

—— (1988), 'Word-Order Changes in Predicate Negation Strategies in Romance Languages', *Diachronica*, 5: 21–58.

—— (1990), *Analyticity and Syntheticity: A Diachronic Perspective with Special Reference to Romance languages* (Berlin and New York, Mouton de Gruyter).

Scott, C. (1986), *A Question of Syllables. Essays in Nineteenth Century French Verse* (Cambridge, CUP).

Séguin, Hubert (1979), 'Rapports de variabilité grammaticale entre les formes phoniques et graphiques des adjectifs français', in Rondeau *et al.* (1979), 235–55.

Séguin, J.-P. (1972), *La Langue française au dix-huitième siècle* (Paris, Bordas).

Seklaoui, D. R. (1989), *Change and Compensation: Parallel Weakening of /s/ in Italian, French and Spanish* (New York, Lang).

Selig, M. (1989), 'Die Entwicklung des Determinantensystems im Spätlateinisch', in Raible (1989), 99–130.

Selkirk, E. (1982), 'The Syllable', in van der Hulst and Smith (1982), 337–83.

Sellers, S. (1991), *Language and Sexual Difference: Feminist Writing in France* (London, Macmillan).

Sesto, Steven L. del, and Gibson, J. L. (eds.) (1975), *The Culture of Acadiana: Tradition and Change in South Louisiana* (Lafayette, La., University of Southwestern Louisiana Press).

Seuren, P. A. M. (1976), 'Clitic Pronoun Clusters', *Italian Linguistics*, 2: 7–33.

Shapiro, M. (1991), *The Sense of Change: Language as History* (Bloomington, Ind., Indiana University Press).

Siccardo, F. (1984), '*Nationalisme*': *Contributo linguistico, contributo storico-letterario* (Genoa, Ecig).

Skårup, P. (1975), *Les Premières Zones de la proposition en ancien français* (Copenhagen, Akademisk Forlag).

Skousen, R. J. (1992), *Analogy and Structure* (Dordrecht, Kluwer).

Slobin, D. I. (1977), 'Language Change in Childhood and History', in J. Macnamara (ed.) (1977), *Language Learning and Thought* (New York, Academic Press), 183–214.

Smith, J. C. (1993), 'The Agreement between Past Participle Conjugated with *avoir* and a Preceding Direct Object: A Brief History of Prescriptive Attitudes', in Sampson (1993), 87–125.

—— (1995), 'Perceptual Strategies and the Disappearance of Agreement between Past Participle and Direct Object in Romance', in J. C. Smith and M. D. Maiden (eds.) (1995), *Linguistic theory and the Romance Languages* (Amsterdam, Benjamins), 161–80.

Smith, O. (1984), *The Politics of Language 1791–1819* (Oxford, Clarendon Press).

Sneyders de Vogel, K. (1927²) *Syntaxe historique du français* (Groningen, Wolters).

Snyder, E., and Valdman, A. (eds.) (1976), *Identité culturelle et francophonie dans les Amériques* (Quebec, Presses de l'Université Laval).

Sommerstein, A. H. (1972), 'On the So-Called Definite Article in English', *Linguistic Inquiry*, 3: 197–209.

Spence, N. C. W. (1961), 'Linguistic Fields, Conceptual Systems and the Weltbild', *Transactions of the Philological Society* (1961), 87–106.

—— (1965), 'La Survivance en français moderne des formes du nominatif latin', *Actes du Xe Congrès International de Linguistique et de Philologie Romanes, Paris*, 231–43.

—— (1966), 'Existait-il en ancien français une opposition actuel/virtuel?', *Revue de Linguistique Romane*, 30: 183–97.

—— (1971), 'La Survivance des formes du nominatif latin en français. Fréquence ou analogie?', *Revue Romane*, 6: 74–84.

—— (1980), 'The Gender of French Compounds', *Zeitschrift für romanische Philologie*, 96: 68–91.

—— (1982), 'Another Look at the "loi des trois consonnes"', *French Studies*, 36: 1–11.

—— (1983*a*), 'Partitives and Mass-Nouns in French', *Romanische Forschungen*, 95: 1–22.

—— (1983*b*), 'Some Reflections on Gender in French', *Zeitschrift für romanische Philologie*, 99: 16–28.

—— (1988), 'Loi de position ou durée vocalique?', *Revue Québécoise de Linguistique* 17: 223–35.

—— (1996), *The Structure(s) of French* (London, Runnymede).

Spillebout, G. (1985), *Grammaire de la langue française du XVIIe siècle* (Paris, Picard).

Spore, P. (1972), *La Diptongaison romane* (Odense, University Press).

Staes, J. (1979–83), 'Lettres de soldats béarnais de la Révolution et du Premier Empire', *Revue de Pau et du Béarn*, 7: 173–189; 8: 151–65; 9: 135, 159; 10: 185, 199; 11: 153–66.

Stéfanini, J. (1983), 'Approches historiques de la langue parlée', *Recherches sur le français parlé*, 5: 1–21.

Stefenelli, A. (1967), *Der Synonymenreichtum in der altfranzösischen Dichtersprache* (Vienna, Österreichische Akademie de Wissenschaften).

—— (1981), *Geschichte des französischen Kernwortschatzes* (Berlin, Schmidt).

—— (1992), *Das Schicksal des lateinischen Wortschatzes in den romanischen Sprachen* (Passauer, Schriften zu Sprache und Literatur).

Steinmeyer, G. (1979), *Historische Aspekte des français avancé* (Geneva, Droz).

Sten, H. (1952), *Les Temps du verbe fini (indicatif) en français moderne* (Copenhagen, Munksgaard).

Stimm, H. (ed.) (1980), *Zur Geschichte des gesprochenen Französisch und zur Sprachlenkung im Gegenwartfranzösichen* (Wiesbaden, Steiner) (Beiheft 6, *Zeitschrift für französiche Sprache und Literatur*).

Stock, B. (1983), *The Implication of Literacy: Written Language and Models of Interpretation in the 11th and the 12th Centuries* (Princeton, University Press).

Straka, G. (1952*a*), 'La Prononciation parisienne, ses divers aspects et ses traits généraux', *Bulletin de la Faculté des lettres de Strasbourg*, 30: 212–25, 239–53.

Straka, G. (1952*b*), 'Quelques observations phonétiques sur le langage des femmes', *Orbis*, 1: 335–57.

—— (1953), 'Observations sur la chronologie et les dates de quelques modifications phonétiques en roman et en français prélittéraire', *Revue des langues romanes*, 71: 247–307.

—— (1955), 'Remarques sur les voyelles nasales, leur origine et leur évolution en français', *Revue de Linguistique Romane*, 19: 245–74.

—— (1959), 'Durée et timbre vocalique, observations de phonétique générale, appliquée à la phonétique historique des langues romanes', *Zeitschrift für Phonetik*, 12: 276–300 (reprinted in Straka 1979*b*: 141–50).

—— (1964), 'L'Évolution phonétique du latin au français sous l'effet de l'énergie et de la faiblesse articulatoires', *Travaux de Linguistique et de Littérature de Strasbourg*, 2: 17–98.

—— (1965*a*), 'Contribution à l'histoire de la consonne *r* en français', *Neophilologische Mitteilungen*, 66: 572–606 (reprinted in Straka 1979*b*: 465–500).

—— (1965*b*), 'Naissance et disparition des consonnes palatales dans l'évolution du latin au français', *Travaux de Linguistique et de Littérature de Strasbourg*, 3: 117–67 (reprinted in Straka 1979*b*: 295–345).

—— (ed.) (1972), *Les Dialectes de France au moyen âge et aujourd'hui* (Paris, Klincksieck), 205–33.

—— (1979*a*), 'Le Décès d'un mot: afr. et mfr. *moillier*', in Höfler *et al.* (1979), 535–51.

—— (1979*b*), *Les Sons et les mots* (Paris, Klincksieck).

—— (1981), 'Sur la formation de la prononciation française d'aujourd'hui', *Travaux de Linguistique et de Littérature de Strasbourg*, 19: 161–248.

—— (1985), 'Les Rimes classiques et la prononciation de l'époque', *Travaux de Linguistique et de Littérature de Strasbourg*, 23: 61–138.

—— (1990), 'Phonétique et phonématique', in Holtus *et al.* (1988–), 5/1: 1–33.

—— and Gardette, P. (eds.) (1973), *Les Dialectes romans de France à la lumière des Atlas régionaux* (Paris, CNRS).

Sturm, J. (1981), *Morphosyntaktische Untersuchungen zur Phrase **négative** im gesprochenen Französisch. Die Negation mit und ohne NE* (Frankfurt/ M, Lang).

Suchier, Walther (1963[2]), *Französische Verslehre auf historischer Grundlage* (Tübingen, Niemeyer).

Suñer, M. (ed.) (1978), *Contemporary Studies in Romance linguistics* (Washington, Georgetown University Press).

Sweetser, E. (1990), *From Etymology to Pragmatics: Metaphorical and Cultural Aspects of Semantic Structure* (Cambridge, CUP).

Swiggers, P. (1985), 'La Linguistique historique devant la variation: le cas de Meillet', *Recherches sur le français parlé*, 7: 61–74.

—— (ed.) (1984), *Grammaire et méthode au XVIIe siècle* (Leuven, Peeters).

—— and Hoecke, W. van (eds.) (1989), *La Langue française au XVIe siècle: usage, enseignement et approches descriptives* (Louvain, UP/Paris, Peeters).

Tabouret-Keller, A. (ed.) (1981), *Regional Languages in France* (*International Journal of the Sociology of Language* 29).

Tamba(-Mecz), I. (ed.) (1987), *Études de lexicologie, lexicographie et stylistique offertes en hommage à Georges Matoré* (Paris, Université de Paris-Sorbonne).

—— (1988), *La Sémantique* (Paris, PUF) (*Que sais-je?*)

Taverdet, G., and Straka, G. (eds.) (1977), *Les Français Régionaux* (Paris, Klincksieck).

Tellier, C., and Valois, D. (1996), '*DE*-AP Nominals and Variable Binding', in Parodi *et al.* (1996), 397–408.

Tentchoff, D. (1975), 'Cajun French and French Creole: Their Speakers and the Questions of Identities', in del Sesto and Gibson (1975), 87–109.

Thibault, P. (ed.) (1980), *Le Français parlé: études sociolinguistiques* (Edmonton, Linguistic Research Inc).

Thiele, J. (1987), *La Formation des mots en français moderne* (Montreal, Presses Universitaires) (1985 *Wortbildung der französischen Gegenwartssprache* Leipzig, VEB).

Thomas, G. (1991), *Linguistic Purism* (London, Longman).

Thomason, S. G. (1976), 'Analogical Change as Grammar Complication', in Christie (1976), 401–9.

—— and Kaufman, T. (1988), *Language Contact: Creolization and Genetic Linguistics* (Berkeley, University of California Press).

Thurneysen, R. (1892), 'Die Stellung des Verbums im Altfranzösischen', *Zeitschrift für romanische Philologie*, 16: 289–371.

Thurot, Charles (1881–3), *De la prononciation française depuis le commencement du XVIe siècle, d'après le témoignage des grammairiens* (Paris, Imprimerie Nationale).

Tinker, E. L. (1932), 'Louisiana Gombo', *Yale Review*, 21: 566–79.

—— (1935), 'Gombo, the Creole of Louisiana', *Proceedings of the American Antiquarian Society*, 45: 101–42.

Togeby, K. (1964), 'Les Désinences de l'imparfait (et du parfait) dans les langues romanes', *Studia Neophilologica*, 36: 3–8.

—— (1968), '*Suus* & *illorum* dans les langues romanes', *Revue romane*, 3: 66–71.

—— (1974), *Précis historique de grammaire française* (Copenhagen, Akademisk Forlag).

Tousignant, C. (1987), *La Variation sociolinguistique. Modèle québécois et méthode d'analyse* (Quebec, Presses Universitaires).

Trager, G. L. (1932), *The use of Latin demonstratives (especially* ILLE *and* IPSE*) up to 600 as the Source of the Romance Article* (New York, Institute of French Studies).

Tranel, B. (1981), *Concreteness in Generative Phonology: Evidence from French* (Berkeley, University of California Press).

—— (1985), 'On Closed Syllable Adjustment in French', in King and Maley (1985), 377–405.

—— (1987), *The Sounds of French* (Cambridge, CUP).

—— (1990), 'On Suppletion and French Liaison', *Probus*, 2: 169–208.

—— (1995), 'Current Issues in French Phonology: Liaison and Position Theories', in Goldsmith (1995), 798–816.

—— (1996), 'Exceptionality in Optimality Theory and Final Consonants in French', in Zagona (1996), 275–92.

Trask, R. L. (1993), *A Dictionary of Grammatical Terms in Linguistics* (London, Routledge).

—— (1995), *A Dictionary of Phonetics and Phonology* (London, Routledge).

—— (1996), *Historical Linguistics* (London, Arnold).

Traugott, E. C. (1965), 'Diachronic Syntax and Generative Grammar', *Language*, 41: 402–15.

—— (1969), 'Towards a Grammar of Syntactic Change, *Lingua*, 23: 1–27.

—— and Heine, B. (eds.) (1991), *Approaches to Grammaticalization*, 2 vols. (Amsterdam, Benjamins).

—— Labrum, R., and Shepherd, S. (1980), *Papers from the Fourth International Conference on Historical Linguistics, Stanford, March 26–30, 1979* (Amsterdam, Benjamins).

—— Meulen, A. ter, Reilly, J. S., and Ferguson, Charles A. (1986) *On Conditionals* (Cambridge, CUP).

—— and Smith, H. (1993), 'Arguments from Language Change', *Journal of Linguistics*, 29: 431–47.

Trudeau, D. (1983), 'L'Ordonnance de Villers-Cotterêts: histoire ou interprétation?', *Bibliothèque d'Humanisme et Renaissance* 45: 461–72.

—— (1992), *Les Inventeurs du bon usage (1529–1647)* (Paris, Minuit).

Tuaillon, G. (1972), 'Aspects géographiques de la palatalisation *u* > *ü*, en gallo-roman et notamment en franco-provençal', in Straka (1972), 205–33.

Tucker, G. R., Lambert, W. E., and Rigault, A. A. (1977), *The French Speaker's Skill with Grammatical Gender: An Example of Rule-Governed Behaviour* (The Hague, Mouton).

Tuțescu, M. (1975), *Précis de sémantique française* (Paris, Klincksieck).

Ullmann, S. (1952), *Précis de sémantique française* (Berne, Franck).

—— (1957) [1963[2]] *Principles of Semantics* (Oxford, Blackwell).

Ultan, R. (1978), 'Some General Characteristics of Interrogative Systems', in Greenberg *et al.* (1978), 211–48.

Uriagereka, J. (1995), 'Aspects of the Syntax of Clitic Placement in Western Romance', *Linguistic Inquiry*, 26: 79–123.

Väänänen, V. (1981), *Recherches et récréations latino-romanes* (Naples, Bibliopolis).

Valdman, A. (ed.) (1969), *Le Français en France et hors de France* (Paris, Champion).

—— (ed.) (1972), *Papers in Linguistics and Phonetics to the Memory of Pierre Delattre* (The Hague, Mouton).

—— (1974), 'Le Parler vernaculaire des isolats français en Amérique du Nord', *Louisiana Review* 3: 43–54.

—— (1978a), 'The "loi de position" and the Direction of Phonological Change in the French Mid-Vowel System', in Suñer (1978), 316–29.

—— (1978b), *Le Créole: Structure, statut et origine* (Paris, Champion).

—— (1979), *Le Français hors de France* (Paris, Champion).

—— (1982), 'Français standard et français populaire: sociolectes ou fictions?', *French Review*, 56: 218–27.

—— (1992), 'On the Socio-Historical Content in the Development of Louisiana and St-Domingue Creoles', *Journal of French Language Studies*, 2: 99–119.

Valli, A. (1983), 'Un exemple d'approche du problème des variantes syntaxiques en linguistique diachronique', *Recherches sur le français parlé*, 5: 125–46.

—— (1984), 'A propos de changements dans le système du relatif: état de la question en moyen français', *Recherches sur le français parlé*, 6: 119–36.

—— (1985), 'Changements de norme. Décalage grammaticaux et représentations du français parlé: l'exemple du *Télémaque Travesti* de Marivaux', *Recherches sur le français parlé*, 6: 7–19.

—— (1992), 'Transcription et grammaire. La distribution de que "sujet" dans deux versions manuscrits d'une œuvre du XVe siècle, *Pierre de Provence et la belle Maguelonne*', *Recherches sur le français parlé*, 11: 87–105.

Vance, B. S. (1988b), 'L'Évolution de pro-drop en français médiéval', *Revue québécoise de linguistique théorique et appliquée*, 7: 85–109.

—— (1989), *Null Subjects and Syntactic Change in Medieval French* (Ann Arbor, University Microfilms).

—— (1996), 'Null Subjects in Middle French Discourse', in Parodi *et al.* (1996), 457–56.

Vanelli, L., Renzi, L., and Benincà, P. (1985), 'Typologie des pronoms sujets dans les langues romanes', *Actes XVIIe Cong.* (1984–6), 3. 164–76.

Vennemann, T. (1974), 'Topics, Subjects and Word Order: From SXV to SVX via TVX', in H. Andersen and Jones (1974), 339–76.

Verkuyl, H. J. (1993), *A Theory of Aspectuality: The Interaction between Temporal and Atemporal Structure* (Cambridge, CUP).

Vermes, G. (ed.) (1988), *Vingt-cinq communautés linguistiques de la France* (Paris, L'Harmattan).

Vermes, G. and Boutet, J. (eds.) (1987), *France, pays multilingue* (Paris, L'Harmattan).

Versteegh, K. (1991), 'The Substratum Debate in Creole Linguistics', *Diachronica*, 8: 59–80.

Vet, C. (ed.) (1985), 'La Pragmatique des temps verbaux' (*Langue française*, 67).

Vincent, N. (1974), 'Analogy Reconsidered', in H. Anderson and Jones (1974), 427–45.

—— (1982), 'The Development of the Auxiliaires HABERE and ESSE in Romance', in Vincent and Harris (1982), 71–96.

—— and Harris, M. B. (eds.) (1982), *Studies in the Romance Verb* (London, Croome Helm).

—— (1995), 'Exaptation and Grammaticalization', in H. Andersen (1995), 433–45.

Vliet, Edward R. van (1983), 'The Disappearance of the French passé simple: A Morphological and Sociolinguistic Study', *Word*, 34: 89–113.

Wagner, R.-L. (1939), *Les Phrases hypothétiques commençant par 'si' dans la langue française des origines à la fin du XVIe siècle* (Paris, Droz).

—— (1955^2*a*), *Introduction à la linguistique française* (Geneva/Lille, Droz/ Giard).

—— (1955*b*), *Supplément bibliographique à l'introduction à la linguistique française (1947–1953)* (Geneva, Droz/Lille, Giard).

—— (1967–70), *Les Vocabulaires français* (Paris/Brussels, Didier).

Wahlgren, E. G. (1920), *Étude sur les actions analogiques réciproques du parfait et du participe passé dans les langues romanes* (Uppsala, Almqvist & Wiksell).

Walker, D. C. (1981), *An Introduction to Old French Morphophonology* (Paris, Didier).

—— (1984), *The Pronunciation of Canadian French* (Ottawa, University Press).

—— (1995), 'Patterns of Analogy in the Canadian French Verb-System', *Journal of French Language Studies*, 5: 85–107.

Wall, K. (1980), *L'Inversion dans la subordonnée en français contemporain* (Uppsala, Almqvist & Wiksell).

Walsh, T. (ed.) (1989), *Georgetown University Round Table on Languages and Linguistics 1988* (Washington: Georgetown University Press).

Walter, H. (1976), *La Dynamique des phonèmes dans le lexique français contemporain* (Paris, France-Expansion).

—— (ed.) (1977), *Phonologie et société* (Paris, Didier).

—— (1982), *Enquêtes phonologiques et variétés régionales du français* (Paris, PUF).

—— (1988), *Le Français dans tous les sens* (Paris, Laffont) (translation 1994 *French Inside Out* by Peter Fawcett (London and New York, Routledge).

—— (1989*a*), *Les Mots sans-culottes* (Paris, Laffont).

—— (1989*b*), 'Prononciation et phonologie du français à la fin du XVIIe siècle d'après le corpus de Gile Vaudelin', in Baddeley (1989*b*), 70–3.

Wang, W. S.-Y. (1969), 'Competing Sound Changes as a Cause of Residue', *Language*, 45: 9–25.

Wanner, D. (1974), 'The Evolution of Romance Clitic Order', in Campbell *et al.* (1974), 158–77.

—— (1986), 'Protohistoire du placement des clitiques en roman', *Actes XVIIe Cong.* (1984–6), 2. 389–406.

—— (1987), *The Development of Romance Clitic Pronouns: From Latin to Old Romance* (Berlin, Mouton de Gruyter).

—— (1993), 'Multiple Clitic Linearization Principles', in Ashby *et al.* (1993), 281–302.

—— and Kibbee, D. A. (eds.) (1991), *New Analyses in Romance Linguistics* (Amsterdam, Benjamins).

Warnant, L. (1980), 'La Détermination des pronoms', in M. Dominicy and M. Wilmet (eds.) (1980), *Linguistique romane et linguistique française. Hommage Jacques Pohl* (Brussels, Université Libre de Bruxelles), 231–4.

Wartburg, W. von (1941), 'Les Pronoms sujets en français', *Revista Filología Española*, 25: 465–77.

—— (1970¹⁰) [1934], *Évolution et structure de la langue français* (Berne, Francke).

Waswo, R. (1987), *Language and Meaning in the Renaissance* (Princeton, University Press).

Watbled, J. P. (1991), 'Les Processus de sandhi externe en français de Marseille', *Journal of French Language Studies*, 1: 71–91.

Waugh, L. R. (1976), 'A Semantic Analysis of the French Tense System', *Orbis*, 24: 436–85.

—— (1977), *A Semantic Analysis of Word Order: Position of the Adjective in French* (Leiden, Brill).

—— (1986), 'Marking Time with the *passé composé*: Toward a Theory of the Perfect', *Lingvisticae Investigationes*, 11: 1–47.

—— and Burston, M. M. (1986), 'Aspect and Discourse Function: The French Simple Past in Newspaper Usage', *Language*, 62: 846–77.

Webelhuth, G. (ed.) (1995), *Government and Binding Theory and the Minimalist Program: Principles and Parameters in Syntactic Theory* (Oxford, Blackwell).

Weber, E. (1977), *Peasants in Frenchmen: The Modernization of Rural France, 1870–1914* (London, Chatto & Windus).

Weinrich, H. (1964), *Tempus: Besprochene und erzahlte Welt* (Stuttgart, Kohlhammer) (French trans. 1973 *Le temps* Paris, Seuil).

Weinreich, U., Labov, W., and Herzog, M. I. (1968), 'Empirical Foundations for a Theory of Language Change', in Lehmann and Malkiel (1968), 98–188.

Wenk, B. J. (1983), 'Effets de rhythme dans le français parlé', *Recherches sur le français parlé*, 5: 147–61.

—— (1987), 'Just in Time: On Speech Rhythms in Music', *Linguistics*, 25: 969–81.

—— and Wioland, F. (1982), 'Is French Really Syllable-Timed?', *Journal of Phonetics*, 20: 193–216.

Wetzels, L., and Sezer, E. (eds.) (1986), *Studies in Compensatory Lengthening* (Dordrecht, Foris).

Wexler, P. J. (1964), 'On the Grammetrics of the Classical Alexandrine', *Cahiers de lexicologie*, 4: 61–72.

—— (1966), 'Distich and Sentence in Corneille and Racine', in R. Fowler (ed.) (1966), *Essays on Style and Language* (London, Routledge & Kegan Paul), 100–20.

Wheeler, M. W. (1980), 'Analogy and Inflectional Affix Replacement', in Traugott *et al.* (1980), 275–83.

—— (1985), 'Sincretismo entre categorías modales y cambio desinencial en el verbo románico', in *Actes XVIIe Cong.* (1984–6), 2. 451–60.

—— (1993), 'On the Hierarchy of Naturalness Principles in Inflectional Morphology', *Journal of Linguistics*, 29: 95–111.

—— (1994), 'Politeness, Sociolinguistic Theory and Language Change', *Folia Linguistica Historica*, 17: 149–74.

Wilkinson, H. E. (1973–5), 'The Strong Perfects in the Romance Languages', *Aoyama Gakuin Univ. Ronshu*, 14: 157–94; 15: 23–44; 16: 15–31.

—— (1978–83), 'Palatal vs. Velar in the Stem of the Romance Perfect', *Aoyama Gakuin Univ. Ronshu*, 19: 19–35; 20: 19–35; 21: 41–62; 22: 67–83; 23: 115–36; 24: 177–99.

—— (1980), 'Evidence in English for the Occurrence of [š] in Old French', *Aoyama Keiei Ronshu*, 15: 520–36.

Williams, E. (1994), 'A Reinterpretation of Evidence for Verb Movement in French', in Lightfoot and Hornstein (1994), 189–206.

Wilmet, M. (1978), 'Sur certains emplois de *que* en moyen français', in R. Martin (1978), 83–111.

—— (ed.) (1980), *Sémantique lexicale et sémantique grammaticale en moyen français* (Brussels, Centrum voor Taal-en Literatuurwetenschap).

—— (1981), 'La Place de l'épithète qualificative en français contemporain', *Revue de linguistique romane* 45: 17–73.

—— (1986), *La Détermination nominale* (Paris, PUF).

Wind, J. M. de (1994), 'Against V-to-C in French Complex Inversion', in Mazzola (1994), 271–84.

Winters, M. E. (1987), 'Innovations in French Negation: A Cognitive Grammar Account', *Diachronica*, 4: 27–54.

Wise, H. (1997) *The Vocabulary of Modern French. Origins, Structure and Function* (London, Routledge).

Wittmann, H. (1973), 'Le Joual, c'est-tu un créole?', *La Linguistique*, 9: 83–93.

Woledge, B. (1973), 'Noun Declension in Twelfth Century French', *Transactions of the Philological Society* (1973), 75–97.

—— Erk, H. M., Grant, P. B., and Macdougall, I. A. (1967, 1969), 'La Déclinaison des substantifs dans la Chanson de Roland', *Romania*, 88: 145–74; 90: 174–201.

Wolf, L. (1983), 'La Normalisation du langage en France: de Malherbe à Grevisse', in Bédard and Maurais (1983), 105–37.

Wolf, N. (1990), *Le Peuple dans le roman français de Zola à Céline* (Paris, PUF).

Wolff, P. (1982^2) *Les Origines linguistiques de l'Europe occidentale* (Toulouse, Université Toulouse-le Mirail) (trans. 1971 *Western Languages. AD. 100–1500*, London, Weidenfeld and Nicolson).

Wooldridge, T. R. (1979), *Les Débuts de la lexicographie: Estienne, Nicot et le 'Thresor de la langue françoise' (1606)* (Toronto, University Press).

Wright, R. (1982), *Late Latin and Early Romance in Spain and Carolingian France* (Liverpool, Cairns).

—— (ed.) (1991), *Late Latin and the Romance Languages in the Early Middle Ages* (London and New York, Routledge).

Wunderli, P. (1970), *Die Teilaktualisierung des Verbalgeschehens (subjonctif) im Mittelfranzösischen* (Tübingen, Niemeyer).

—— (1978), 'Les Structures du possessif en moyen français', in R. Martin (1978), 111–52.

—— (1982), 'Funktionen und Leistungen von *y* im Mittelfranzösischen', in Q. I. M. Mok *et al.* (eds.) (1982), *Mélanges de linguistique, de littérature et de philologie médiévale, offerts à J. R. Smeets* (Leiden, [s.n.]), 337–72.

—— (1987), 'Die Funktion von *en* im Mittelfranzösischen: Syntax, Semantik und Pragmatik', in Dahmen *et al.* (1987), 197–244.

—— (1989), *Französische Lexicologie. Einführung in die Theorie und Geschichte des französischen Wortschatzes* (Tübingen, Niemeyer).

—— (1990), 'Lexicologie und Semantik', in Holtus *et al.* (1988–), 5/1: 94–112.

Wurzel, W. (1989), *Inflectional Morphology and Naturalness* (Dordrecht, Kluwer).

Yaguello, M. (1978*a*), *Les Mots et les femmes* (Paris, Payot).

—— (1978*b*), *Le Sexe des mots* (Paris, Belfond).

—— (ed.) (1994), *Subjecthood and Subjectivity: The Status of the Subject in Linguistic Theory* (Paris, Ophrys).

Zagona, K. (ed.) (1996), *Grammatical Theory and Romance Languages: Selected Papers from the 25th Linguistic Symposium on Romance Languages (LSRL XXV), Seattle, 2–4 March 1995* (Amsterdam, Benjamins).

Zink, G. (1986), *Phonétique historique du français* (Paris, PUF).

Zink, G. (1987), *L'Ancien Français (XIe–XIIIe siècle)* (Paris, PUF) (*Que sais-je?*).

—— (1989), *Morphologie du français médiéval* (Paris, PUF).

—— (1990), *Le Moyen français (XIVe et XVe siècles)* (Paris, PUF) (*Que sais-je?*).

Zubizaretta, M. L., and Vergnaud, J.-R. (1992), 'The Definite Determiners and the Inalienable Constructions in French and English', *Linguistic Inquiry*, 23: 595–652.

Zwanenburg, W. (1965), *Recherches sur la prosodie de la phrase française* (Leiden, University Press).

—— (1978), 'L'Ordre des mots en français médiéval', in R. Martin (1978), 153–71.

Zwicky, A. M. (1976), *On Clitics* (Bloomington, Ind., Indiana University Linguistics Club).

—— (1985), 'Clitics and Particles', *Language*, 61: 283–305.

Name Index

Abel, F. 215
Achard, P. 100
Acton, H. B. 100
Adam, Mystère d' (*c*.1170) 365, 367
Adams, J. N. 417
Adams, M. 417
Aebischer, P. 100
Ager, D. 100
Ahlqvist, A. 142
Aitchison, J. 142, 183, 214
Alcuin of York (*c*. 730–*c*.804) 17
Alexis, Saint (*Vie de, c*.1040) 17, 173, 197, 204, 210, 323, 332, 392, 413
Aliscans (late 12th–early 13th c.) 214
Allen, W. S. 292
Allieres, J. 8, 56
Amis et Amile (12th c.) 414
Andersen, B. 48, 293
Andersen, H. 115, 116, 142, 292
Anderson, J. M. 142
Anderson, R. D. 99
Anderson, S. R. 284, 293, 343
Andrieux, N. 343
Antoine, G. 2–3, 56
Anttila, R. 142, 343
Arc, Jeanne d', (Saint Joan of Arc: *c*.1412–31) 16, 89, 196
Ardener, E. 142
Arends, J. 56, 142
Ariel, M. 215
Aristotle 42–3
Armstrong, N. 387
Ashby, W. J. 293, 343, 417–18,
Aski, J. M. 343
Aspremont, Chanson de (late 12th c.-early 13th c.) 414
Asselin, C. 100
Asterix (cartoon character) 14–15
Atkinson, J. C. 417
Aucassin et Nicolete (13th c.) 205, 368, 374, 414
Auger, J. 417
Austen, Jane (1775–1817) 79
Ayres-Bennett, W. 3, 7–8, 44, 56, 78, 100, 206, 417
Azra, J.- L. 293

Bache, C. 215
Baciu, I. 418
Baddeley, S. 56, 100, 292
Bal, W. 8
Baldinger, K. 183, 214
Balibar, R. 48, 56, 60, 99
Ball, R. 100
Balzac, Honoré de (1799–1850) 67, 79, 366
Barbaud, P. 100
Barbusse, Henri (1874–1935) 69
Barnes, B. 417
Barthes, Roland 45
Bartning, I. 417
Barton, D. 99
Bartsch, K. 246, 270
Bartsch, R. 34, 56, 246, 270
Basbøll, H. 293
Batany, J. 56
Batchelor, R. E. 184
Battye, A. 56, 215, 417
Bauche, H. 41, 71, 100
Bauer, B. L. M. 417
Baum, R. 56
Baumgartner, E. 343
Baylon, C. 100
Beauchemin, N 100
Beaulieux, C. 50, 56
Beaune, C. 14, 55
Beauzée, Nicolas (1717–89) 178
Bédard, E. 56
Bélise (character in Moliere's *Les Femmes Savantes*) 238
Belletti, A. 416
Bembo, Pietro (1470–1547) 49
Beniak, E. 100
Beniamino, M. 100
Benincà, P. 100, 418
Benoist, J. 101
Benveniste, E. 215, 343
Berchem, T. 343
Béroul (*Tristan*, late 12th c.) 354
Berschin, H. 8
Bernadette, Saint (1844–1879) 89
Bernardin de Saint-Pierre, Jacques-Henri (1737–1814) 33

Bernini, G. 417
Bèze, Théodore de (1519–1605) 54
Bichakijian , B. H. 293, 417
Bickerton, D. 128, 142
Bierbach, C. 100
Binnick, R. I. 215
Bisson, T. N. 18
Blake, B. 343
Blanc, M. 100
Blanche-Benveniste, C. 56, 100, 343, 416–17
Blinkenberg, A. 417–18
Bloch, Marc (historian: 1886–1944) 6, 18
Bloomfield, L. 192
Boinvilliers (Desjardins), Jean Étienne (1764–1830) 374
Bollée, A. 56
Boltanski, J. 142
Bonin, M. 343
Booij, G. 343
Borer, H. 418
Bossuet, Jacques Bénigne (1627–1704) 366
Bostock, W. W. 100
Bouhours, Dominique (1628–1702) 43–4
Bourdieu, P. 45, 58, 91, 99, 100
Bouscayrol, R. 205
Boutet, J. 100
Bovelles, Charles de (*floreat* 1533) 38
Boysen, G. 56
Branca(-Rosoff), S. 56, 100, 209
Brasseux, C. A. 101
Braudel, F. 7, 14, 55
Bréal, Michel-Jules-Alfred (1832–1915) 188–9, 192, 215
Breivik, L. E. 142
Bremen, K. von. 417
Brontës (Anne, Charlotte, Emily: *floreant* 1840s) 79
Broussard, J. F. 101
Brown, B. 418
Brown, R. 100
Brown, R. A. 101
Brucker, C. 183
Brun, A. 100
Bruneau, Charles 2
Brunet, E. 155, 178, 182–3
Brunot, Ferdinand (1860–1938) 1, 2, 6, 8, 56, 83, 183
Buben, V. 293
Bueil, Jean de (died *c.*1478) 388
Burger, A. 292
Burger, M. 292
Buridant, C. 184, 353, 417
Burke, P. 55, 58, 99
Burston *see* Monville-Burston
Bussche, H. van der 293
Bybee, J. 215, 343
Byers, B. A. 101
Bynon, T. 142

Caesar, Julius (101–44 B.C.) 356
Calabrese, A. 292
Calvet, L.-J. 100
Calvin, Jean (1509–64) 27, 38, 43, 87, 99
Campbell, L. 417
Capet, Hugues (king of France: 941–96) 15
Caput, J. P. 7, 8
Carayol, M. 56
Carruthers, J. 206
Cartier, Jacques (1491–1557) 92
Carton, F. 292
Castiglione, Baldassare (1478–1529) 49
Catach, N. 56
Catherine of Alexandria, Saint (died *c.*310) 89
Cator, G. 56
Cave, T. 56
Cayrou, G. 183
Cedergren, H. 100
Céline, Louis-Ferdinand (1894–1961) 69
Cellard, J. 100
Cent Nouvelles Nouvelles (15th c.) 397
Cerquiglini, B. 8, 56, 140
Certeau, M. de 100
Champagne, M. 343
Chapsal, Charles-Pierre (*floreat* from 1823) 44
Charlemagne (Holy Roman Emperor: 742–814) 15, 17, 134
Charles le Chauve (Frankish king: 823–77) 15
Chastelaine de Vergi (*c.*1288) 365, 413
Châtelain de Coucy (end 12th c.) 401
Chaudenson, R. 56, 142
Chaunu, P. 14, 55
Chaurand, J. 8, 100, 183, 292
Chen, M. 125, 142, 292
Chene, B. 284, 293
Cheneau, V. 293
Chervel, A. 56, 99
Chevalier, J. C. 99
Chiflet, Laurent (*floreat* 1659) 237, 241
Chomsky, Noam 111, 113–4, 115, 127, 142
Chrétien de Troyes (*floreat* late 12th c.) 135, 259, 334, 402, 414
Christie, W. 142
Chung, S. 215
Cibois, P. 56
Cinque, G. 417
Citton, Y. 56
Clari, Robert de (13th c.) 392, 408
Clark, E.V. 183
Clark, R. 142
Clements, G. N. 292–3
Clifford, P. 417
Cohen, Marcel S. R. 8, 100, 215, 301
Collignon, L. 183
Commynes, Phillipe de (*c.*1446– *c.*1511) 360, 374, 379
Comrie, B. 215
Condorcet, Antoine-Nicholas de (1743–94) 61
Conein, B. 184

Connors, K. 215
Conrad, G, R. 101
Conwell, M. 101
Cook, V. 113
Cooper, R. L. 56, 100
Corbeil, J.-C. 100
Corbett, G. G. 343
Corbett, N. L. 100, 343
Corblin, F. 183, 215
Corfield. P. J. 55, 99
Coseriu, E. 13, 142, 184, 215
Couronnement de Louis (*c.* 1130) 202
Courtois d'Arras (late 12th-early 13th c.) 358
Couté, B. 343
Coveney, A. 417
Crabb, D. M. 417
Craddock, J. R. 183
Cruse, D. A. 172, 214
Curat, H. 215
Currie, M. 215

Dagenais, L. 293
Dahl, O. 215
Dahmen, W. 100
Dahrendorf, R. 70–2, 100
Dalphinis, M. 56
Dangeau, l'abbé (*floreat* 1694) 237, 239, 241
D'Ans, A. M. 56
Dann, O. 48, 100
Dardel, R. de 343, 357, 417
Darmesteter, A. 183
Dauses, A. 215, 343
Dauzat, A. 56, 292
David, J. 215
Davis, G. W. 142
Davis, S. 343
Dees, A. 100, 343, 417
Degraff, M. 417
Deimier, Pierre de (1570–1618) 176
Delais, E. 292
Delasalle, S. 99
Delattre, P. 290, 292–3
Dell, F. 292
Deloffre, F. 65
Delomier, D. 417
Demaizières, C. 38
Dembowski, P. F. 198
Deniau, X. 100
Densusianu, O. 292
Desaulniers, G. 293
Desgrouais (? L'abbé Jacques Destrées 1703–1766) 172
Désirat, C. 56
Desmet, P. 124
Desportes, Philippe (1546–1606) 365
Deulofeu, J. 417
Deyck, R. van 292
Diderot, Denis (1713–84) 175
Dietrich, W. 215

Dill, W. 417
Dinwiddy, J. R. 48, 100
Ditchy, J. K. 101
Dolet, Etienne (1509–46) 42
Domergue, François-Urbain (1744–1810) 278
Dorian, N. C. 26
Dressler, W. U. 343
Drijkoningen, F. 215, 383
Droixhe, D. 3
Du Bellay, Joachim (1522–60) 48–9
Dubois, C. 183
Dubois, C. G. 15, 99
Dubois, J. 183, 381
Ducrot, O. 215
Dufresne, M. 417
Dumas, D. 100
Dumonceaux, P. 56, 184
Dupuis, F. 417
Dupuis, Sophie (*floreat* 1836) 249
Durand, M. 343
Durand, J. 100, 292
Durkheim, Émile (1858–1917) 71, 109, 191
Duruy, Victor (1811–94) 61–2, 87
Dutilleul, T. 3

Eckert, G. 16, 55, 417
Eckert, P. 292
Edmont, E. 100
Eliot, George (Mary Ann Evans: 1819–80) 79
Elliot, W. N. 418
Ellrich, B. 100
Eloy, J.-M. 100
Elwert, W. T. 292
Emonds, J. 418
Énéas (*c.*1160) 204
Engels, D. M. 215
Erasmus, Desiderius (*c.*1466–1536) 27, 54, 231
Ernst, G. 66, 100
Esnault, Gaston 192
Estienne, Henri (*d.*1520) 204
Estienne, Robert (1503–59) 42
Eulalia, Cantilena of (? *c.*880) 196, 204, 321, 370
Ewert, A. 8

Faarlund, J. T. 417
Fauquenoy-St. Jacques, M. 100
Félibrige (1854) 91
Féraud, Jean-François, L'abbé (1725–1807) 183
Ferry, Jules (1852–1893) 61, 62
Feuillée, Jeu de la (by Adam de la Halle, 13th c.) 358, 364
Finke, A. 417
Fiorelli, P. 100
Fisiak, J. 99, 100, 142, 183, 215, 343, 417
Flaubert, Gustave (1821–80) 79, 343
Fleischman, S. 120, 198, 215, 343, 417
Flydal, L. 215

Fodor, I. 56
Forel, C. 100
Førsgren, M. 417
Fortier, A. 96,101
Fouché, P. 100, 259, 292
Foulet, L. 388, 417–18
Fox, A. 4
Francard, M. 100
François, A. 8, 56
François, D. 100
François I (king of France: 1494–1547) 47, 83–4
Franzén, T. 417
Fraser, Nancy 195
Fredegar (*floreat c.* 660) 320
Frei, Henri 69,100
Frey, M. 100, 183
Froissart, Jean (*c.*1337– *c.*1410) 214
Fuchs, C. 215
Fumaroli, M. 56
Furet, F. 60, 99
Furetière, Antoine (1619–88) 171

Gaatone, D. 417–18
Gadet, F. 56, 73, 100
Gaitet, P. 69, 100
Galet, Y. 418
Galmiche, M. 215
Gamillscheg, E. 292, 417
Garde, P. 292
Gardette, P. 100
Gardin, B. 100
Garey, H. 215
Gautier d'Arras (12th c.) 259
Gebhardt, K. 183
Geisler, H. 417
Gellner, E. 48
Gerritsen, M. 142, 417
Gertner, M. H. 343
Gervais, M.- M. 79, 100
Gibson, J. L. 101
Gide, André (1869–1951) 353
Gildea, R. 6
Gilliéron, J. (1854–1926) 100
Gilman, A. 100
Girard, L'abbé Gabriel (1677–1748) 175, 278
Giraudoux, Jean (1882–1944) 165
Glatigny, M. 183–4
Goethe, Johann Wolfgang (1749–1832) 294
Goldsmith, J. A. 292
Goncourt, Edmond (1822–96) 201
Goody, E. N. 417
Goosse, A. 100
Gordon, D. C. 48, 56
Gougenheim, G. 56, 100, 184, 215
Gouges, Olympe de (*floreat* 1791) 78
Goyens, M. 343, 346
Grad, A. 417
Graff, H. J. 99

Grammont, M. 267, 292
Grandgent, C. H. 55
Green, J. N. 8, 56, 99–100, 183, 293
Greenberg, J. H. 215, 343, 350, 381, 417
Grégoire, L'abbé Henri (1750–1851) 85–6
Greimas, A.- J. 214
Grevisse, M. 11, 90
Grillo, R. D. 56
Grimarest, Jean Léonor le Gallois (1659– *c.*1715) 226
Grimm, Jacob (1785–1863) 107, 219
Griolet, P. 97, 101
Grisay, A. 174
Gruenais, M.- P. 56
Guenthner, F. J. 215
Guernes de Pont-Sainte-Maxence (late 12th c.) 211
Guéron, J. 382
Gueunier, N. 56, 61, 91, 100
Guilbert, L. 100, 183
Guilhaumou, J. 48, 100, 184
Guillaume, Gustave (1883–1960) 118, 215, 383
Guillaume le Vinier (*died* before 1245) 395
Guinet, L. 99, 183
Guiot de Provins (12th–13th c.) 334
Guiraud, P. 100, 183, 292, 417
Guizot, François (1787–1874) 55, 61–2, 175
Gumperz, J. J. 110

Haadsma, R. A. 417
Haarhoff, A. 417
Haase, A. 417
Haegeman, L. 417
Hagège, C. 56, 343, 417
Haiman, J. 24, 417
Hajek, J. 292
Halbwachs, M. 7
Hall, G. M. 101
Hall, R. A. Jr. 19
Hannahs, S. J. 292
Harmer, L. 416
Harré, C. E. 215
Harris, A. C. 215, 417
Harris, M. B. 8, 215, 381, 417
Harrison, J. A. 101
Haudricourt, A. 292
Haussmann, F. J. 183
Hawkins, J. A. 215, 417
Hawkins, R. 100
Hayes, B. 293
Hazaël-Massieux, G. 56, 101
Hazaël-Massieux, M.-C. 56
Heidegger, Martin (1889–1976) 183
Heine, B. 343
Heinimann, S. 215, 383
Heinz, S. 215
Helgorsky, F. 142
Henri II (king of France: 1519–59) 42

Henry IV (king of France: 1553–1610) 14, 27, 66
Herder, Johann Gottfried (1744–1803) 48
Herman, J. 55, 417
Héroard, Jean (doctor to Louis XIII as Dauphin, 1605–10) 66, 208–9
Herschensohn, J. 418
Herslund, M. 292, 343, 417
Highfield, A. R. 101
Hilty, G. 56, 292
Hindret, J. (*floreat* 1687) 270
Hintze, M.-A. 56, 292
Hirschbühler, P. 417
Hitler, Adolf 88
Hobsbawn, E. J. 48
Hock, H. H. 142, 293
Hoecke, W. van 56, 124, 343, 346
Hoenigswald, H. M. 4, 124, 142
Hollerbach, W. 416
Holm, J. 142
Holtus, G. 8, 183
Hooper, J. B. *see also* Bybee, J. 292
Hope, T. E. 183
Hopper, P. J. 142, 343
Hordé, T. 56
Hornstein, N. 215, 417
Houdebine, A.-M. 100
Høybye, P. 418
Huchon, M. 56
Hudson, R. 383
Hugo, Victor (1802–85) 71
Huguet, E. 183, 215
Humboldt, W. von 106, 110, 193
Humphreys , H. L. 417
Huot, H. 388
Hyman, L. M. 293
Hymes, Dell 34

Ibrahim, M. H. 343
Iliescu, M. 343
Ille et Galeron (by Gautier d'Arras, 12th c.) 406
Imbs, P. 183, 215
Iordan, I. 8
Iordanskaja, L. 418
Irigaray, L. 100
Iverson, C. K. 142

Jacob, D. 417
Jacobs, H. 219, 418
Jaeggli, O.114
Jahr, E. H. 142
James, E. 99
Jeanjean, C. 100
Jeffers, R. J. 142
Jensen, F. 215
Jernudd, B. 40, 48, 56
Johnson, M. 189, 214
Joinville, Jean de (1224–1317) 214, 306

Jokinen, U. 417
Joly, A. 142
Jones, C. 142
Jones, M. A. 416
Jones, M. C. 88
Joris, A. 99
Joseph, B. D. 417
Joseph, J. E. 56, 142
Journet, R. 183
Juilland, A. 101, 292
Junker, J. 417
Justinian I (Byzantine emperor: 483–565) 320

Kaiser, E. 417
Karmiloff-Smith, A. 215, 390
Kaufman, T. 99
Kayne, R. S. 215, 417–18
Keller, M. 56
Keller, R. 122
Keller, R. E. 99
Kenstowicz, M. 292
Kesselring, W. 56
Keyes, John Maynard (economist: 1883–1946) 122
Keys, A. C. 343
Keyser, S. J. 293
Kibbee, D. A. 19, 41, 56
Kiefer, F. 329–30, 343
King, R. D. 116, 142, 292
Kiparsky, P. 292, 343
Klaus, G. 183
Klausenburger, J. 292–3, 343
Klavans, J. 418
Kleiber, G. 215, 340, 382, 343, 382
Klein, H. G. 215
Klein, J. R. 184
Klöden, H. 183
Klum, A. 215
Knecht, P. 56
Koerner, E. F. K. 142, 292
Kok, A. de 418
Kontzi, R. 99
Koopman, W. 142
Korzen, H. 417
Koschwitz, E. 99, 292
Krámský, J. 215
Kreigel, S. 56
Kroch, A. S. 142
Kukenheim, L. 8
Kuryłowicz, J. 135, 343

Labelle, M. 215, 418
Laberge, S. 100
Labov, W. 72, 100, 142, 292
La Chaussée, F. de 292, 343
Laclotte, F. 292
Laenzlinger, C. 418
La Bruyère, Jean de (1645–96) 381, 409

La Fayette, Marie-Madeleine, Comtesse de (1634–93) 78
La Fontaine, Jean de (1621–95) 207, 213, 375
Lakoff, G. 189, 214
Lambert, P.-Y. 242
Lambert, W. 100
Lambrecht, K. 417
Lancelot (early 13th c.) 214
Lane, G. S. 101
Langenbacher, J. 100
Lanly, A. 343
Lanoue, Odet (*floreat* 1596) 237
Laparra, M. 56
Laporte, D. 48, 56, 99
Larochette, J. 215, 383
Lass, R. 107, 126, 139, 142
Latin, D. 100
Laubscher, G. G. 343
Le Bel, E. 343
Le Bidois, G. and R. 416–17
Le Bras, H. 14, 55
Leconte, J. 56
Leconte de Lisle, Charles-Marie René (1818–94) 249
Lefebvre, A. 82
Lefebvre, C. 418
Lefebvre, G. R. 101
Le Flem, D. C. 418
Le Goff, J. 6, 18
Le Goffic, P. 215
Le Hir, Y. 292
Lehiste, I. 142
Lehmann, W. P. 142
Leischner, S. 417
Lemieux, M. 100
Léon, A. 99
Léonard, A. M. 215
Leonard, C. S. Jr. 292–3
Lepschy, G. 382
Lerch, E. 418
Lesaint, M. A. (*floreat* 1870–90) 249, 292
Létoublon, F. 215
Levinson, S. 110
Levitt, J. 418
Levy, R. 183
Lewinsky, B. 417
Li, C. N. 142, 417
Lightfoot, D. 114, 142, 417
Lindhorst, P. 417
Littré, Émile (1801–81) 249, 311
Livre de la Conqueste (?13th c.-14th c.) 403
Llomond, François (*floreat* 1780) 44
Lloyd, P. M. 17, 55, 183
Lodge, R. A. 3, 7, 8, 36, 56, 73, 100
Longfellow, Henry Wadsworth (1807–1882) 95
Lönne, K.-E. 55
Lote, G. 292
Louis (I) le Pieux (king of France: 778–840) 17

Louis XIII (king of France: 1610–43) 66, 208
Louis XIV (king of France: 1643–1715) 14, 19, 38, 44, 46–7, 87
Louis XV (king of France: 1715–74) 393
Louis XVI (king of France: 1774–92) 85
Louis-Philippe (king of France: 1830–1848) 55
Lozachmeur, J.-C. 293
Lucy, J. A. 110
Ludwig, R. 56, 215
Lusignan, S. 56
Luther, Martin (1483–1546) 27, 61, 87
Lutzeier, P. R. 184
Lyche, C. 292
Lyons, C. 343, 418
Lyons, J. 214

Machiavelli, Niccolò di (1469–1527) 49
McDonald, R. A. 101
MacKenzie, F. 183
McKitterick, R. 99
McLaughlin, A. 100
McMahon, A. 142
Maeda, S. 292
Maher, J. 101,
Maher, J. P. 142
Malachowski, A. 183, 195
Malherbe, François de (1555–1628) 27, 39, 43, 202, 365, 393
Malkiel, Y. 3, 121, 142, 183, 343
Mallarmé, Stéphane (1842–98) 357
Mańczak, W. 343
Manessy, G. 56, 142
Mangold, M. 417
Maniet, A. 99
Manzelli, G. 343
Marcellesi, J.-B. 56, 100
Marchello-Nizia, C. 3, 8, 56, 125, 215, 229, 341, 343, 417
Markey, T. L. 343
Marle, J. van 142, 343
Marot, Jean (*died* 1526) 43, 365, 415
Marouzeau, J. 361
Marshall, M. M. 101
Martin, P. 292
Martin, R. 2, 8, 56, 215, 417
Martineau, F. 417
Martinet, A. 56, 108, 208, 276, 292–3, 326
Martinon, P. 292–3
Marx, G. 417
Marx, Karl (1818–83) 71–2, 110
Marxgut, W. 184
Mary, The Holy Virgin 89
Marzys, Z. 56
Massicotte, F. 417
Matoré, G. 56, 144, 181, 183–4
Matte, E. J. 292
Matthews, P. H. 343, 416
Maupas, Charles (*floreat* 1618–30) 200, 393
Maupassant, Guy de (1850–93) 88

Maurais, J. 56
Maurel, J. P. 215, 382
Médici, Cathérine de (Queen, Queen-Mother and Regent of France: 1519–89) 42–3, 49
Meigret, Louis (*floreat* 1530–50) 38, 42–3, 372
Meillet, Antoine (1866–1936) 135, 142
Meisenburg, T. 56
Melander, J. 418
Mel'čuk, I. A. 343
Ménage, Gilles (1613–92) 249
Ménard, P. 417
Messner, D. 155, 166, 183
Meung, Jehan de (*died c.*1305) 209, 373
Meyer-Lübke, W. (1861–1936) 292, 418
Michelet, Jules (1798–1874) 6
Millet, A. 292
Milner, J.-C. 417
Milroy, J. 5, 56, 73, 100
Milroy, L. 56, 73, 100
Miracles (. . . . de Notre-Dame par personnages: 14th c.) 210, 403
Mitterand, H. 183
Möhren, F. 417
Moignet, G. 56, 200, 215, 323, 417–18
Mok, Q. I. M. 343
Molendijk, A. 215
Molière (Jean-Baptiste Pocquelin: 1622–73) 65, 43, 76, 127, 238, 268, 289, 371, 374, 409
Monnier, D. 100
Montaigne, Michel Eyquem de (1533–92) 355
Montreuil, J.-P. Y. 280, 287, 292–3
Monglat, Madame de (governess to Louis XIII) 209
Monville-Burston, M. 215
Moravcsik, E. A. 418
Moreau, M.-L. 417
Morgan, R. Jr. 56, 101
Morin, J.-Y. 418
Morin Y.-C. 100, 292–3, 343, 418
Moritz, L. 418
Mort (le roi) Artu (1225–30) 373, 397, 399
Mougeon, R. 100
Mourin, L. 343
Muller, Ch. 183
Muller, Cl. 417
Müller, B. 56
Mussafia, A. (1835–1905) 395, 397
Musset, Alfred de (1810–57) 398
Musset, L. 99

Napoleon (Bonaparte) I (Emperor of the French: 1804–1815) 74, 95
Napoleon (Bonaparte) III (Emperor of the French: 1852–70) 62, 87
Napoli, D. J. N. 343, 418
Narbonnais, Les (12th-13th c.) 402
Nelson, J. L. 99
Neumann. I. 101
Neumann, S.-G. 56

Newson, M. 113
Niederehe, H.-J. 100
Nisard, C. 100
Nithard (9th c.) 17
Noël, François-Joseph-Michel (*floreat* from 1823) 44
Nora, P. 6, 18
Novare, Philippe de (*c.*1195–*c.*1264, *Mémoires c.*1252) 353
Nyrop, K. (1858–1931) 3, 8

Obenhauer, H.-G. 417
Occam, William of (*c.*1280–1349) 138
Offord, M. H. 100, 184, 417
Ong, W. J. (S. J.) 99
Oudin, Antoine (*floreat* 1632–56) 270
Ouellet, M. 293
Outram, D. 78
Ouzof, J. 60, 99

Padley, G. A. 215, 383
Pagliuca, W. 343
Palm, L. 343
Palmer, F. R. 215
Palsgrave, John (*floreat* 1530) 226, 237, 241, 251, 258, 270, 372
Panhuis, D. G. J. 417
Pasques, L. 100, 292
Pasquier, Étienne (1529–1615) 16, 55
Passy, Paul (1859–1940) 249, 292
Pathelin, La Farce de maistre Pierre (1464) 210
Paul, H. (1846–1921) 123, 142
Pearce, E. 418
Peirce, Charles S. (1813–1914) 116
Peletier, Jacques (1517–82) 54, 241, 325
Pensado, C. 343
Pensom, R. 292
Péronnet, L. 100
Pétain, Maréchal Henri-Philippe (1856–1951) 62
Peyre, H. 83, 100
Pfister, M. 56, 183
Phillips, H. 101
Piatt, H. 417
Picabia, L. 215, 418
Picard, M. 417
Picoche, J. 8, 184, 214, 343
Picone, M. D. 183
Pinchon, J. 343, 418
Pinkster, H. 215, 382
Planhol, X. de 14, 55
Plank, F. 343
Plénat, M. 273, 293
Pohl, J. 100
Pohoryles, B. M. 343
Poliakov, L. 15
Pollack, W. 215
Pollock, J.-Y. 417–18

Polomé, E. C. 4
Pont-Saint-Maxence, Guernes de (*floreat* late
    12th c.) 211
Pooley, T. 100, 293
Pope, M. K. 3, 8, 292, 343
Poplack, S. 183, 387
Porter, R. 55
Posner, R. 2, 3, 8, 55, 56, 99, 101, 108, 124,
    140, 142, 183, 215, 292–3, 327, 343, 417–18
Postal, P. 215, 383
Poston, L. 183
Poyet, Guillaume (Chancellor of France:
    1473–1548) 84
Prebensen, H. 417
Price, G. 8, 343, 417
Priestley, L. 417
Pulgram, E. 292
Purschinsky, J. 292

Quatre Livres des Rois (12th c.) 365, 371, 392,
    395, 408–9, 414
Quéffelec, A. 417
Quemada, B. 183
Queneau, Raymond (1903–1976) 69
Queste (del Saint Graal, early 13th c.) 210,
    374, 397, 399, 402, 408, 413

Rabelais, François (*c.*1494–*c.*1553) 41, 213
Racine, Jean (1639–99) 208, 416
Radtke, E. 56
Ramat, P. 142, 215
Ramsden, H. 418
Ramus (de la Ramée) Petrus (Pierre) (1515–
    72) 37–8, 42, 83
Rebuffe, P. 83
Reenen, P. van 5, 100, 142, 292, 343, 417
Reenen-Stein, K. van 100
Regula, M. 8
Reid, T. B. W. 215
Reighard, J. 293
Renchon, H. 417
Renfrew, C. 421
Renzi, L. 100, 418
Rey, A. 183, 214
Rey-Debove, J. 183
Richelieu, Armand du Plessis, Cardinal de
    (1585–1642) 14, 92, 171
Richter, E. 417
Rickard, P. 7, 8, 56, 343, 346, 417
Ricœur, P. 6
Rigault, A. 343
Ringenson, K. 292
Rivarol, Antoine de (1733–1801) 354
Rivero, M. L. 418
Rizzi, L. 416–17
Robert de Clari (early 13th c.) 392, 408
Robert, Charles (Frédéric) (1827–?1880) 86
Roberts, I. 349, 416–17
Robillard, D. de 56, 101

Robinson, Joan (economist: 1903–83) 122
Roche, D. 99
Roche, G. 183
Rochet, B. 292
Roland, Chanson de (early 12th c.) 76, 207,
    241, 358, 364, 371, 379, 395, 408, 413
Roland, Marie-Jeanne Philipon, Madame
    (1754–93) 79
Romaine, S. 63, 100
Roman de Troie (by Benoît de Saint-Maure
    *c.*1160) 398
Ronat, M. 386
Ronsard, Pierre de (1524–85) 38, 283
Rorty, R. 183, 194–5
Rosset, T. 56, 292
Rossillon, P. ix, 55
Rostand, Edmond (1868–1918) 416
Rothenberg, M. 417
Rothwell, W. 6
Roubaud, Pierre (*floreat* 1785) 171, 177
Rousseau, Jean-Jacques (1712–78) 48
Rousselot, l'abbé Pierre (1846–1924) 249
Rowlett, P. 417
Roy, G.-R. 215
Rudes, B. A. 343
Ruwet, N. 418

Safir, K. 114, 417
Sainliens (Hollyband), Claude de (*floreat*
    1580) 365
Saint-Gérand, J.-Ph. 56
Salmon, G.-L. 100
Sampson, R. 40, 56, 293
San Antonio (popular novelist) 70
Sancier-Château, A. 56
Sand, George (Lucile-Aurore Dupin, Baronne
    Dudevant: 1804–76) 68, 79, 208
Sanders, C. 100
Sankoff, D. 72, 100, 183, 417
Sankoff, G. 100
Sapir, E. (1884–1939) 110, 121, 142, 193
Saussure, Ferdinand de (1857–1913) 3, 108–9,
    113, 115, 118, 145, 193, 383
Sauvageot, A. 183
Scaglione, A. 56
Schane, S. A. 233, 266, 292–3, 343
Schlegel, August Wilhelm von (1767–1845)
    294–5
Schlickum, J. 417
Schlieben-Lange, B. 30, 142
Schmitt, C. 100, 418
Schmitt, R. 184
Schogt, H. G. 215
Schöne, M. 183
Schøsler, L. 142, 343, 417
Schouten, M. E. H. 100
Schuchardt, H. (1842–1927) 128, 255
Schulze, A. 417
Schürr, F. 292

Schwarze, C. 417
Schwegler, A. 24, 30, 120, 417
Scott, C. 292
Séguin, H. 56, 343
Séguin, J.-P. 56
Seklaoui, D. R. 293
Selig, M. 215
Selkirk, E. 292
Sellers, S. 79, 100
Sesto, S. L. del 101
Seuren, P. A. M. 418
Sévigné, Marie de Rabutin-Chantal, Marquise de (1626–96) 78, 213, 409
Sezer, E. 293
Shapiro, M. 40, 48, 56, 142
Siccardo, F. 48, 100
Simon, Jules (1814–1896) 61
Skårup, P. 56, 417
Skousen, R. J. 343
Slobin, D. I. 142
Smith, Adam (economist: 1723–90) 122
Smith, H. 142
Smith, J. C. 418
Smith, O. 48
Sneyders de Vogel, K. 417
Snyder, E. 100
Sommerstein, A. H. 215, 383
Sorel, Julien (character in Stendhal's *Le Rouge et le Noir*) 62
Spence, N. C. W. 56, 183, 215, 293, 343
Speroni, Sperone (1500–88) 49
Spillebout, G. 56
Spore, P. 292
Staël, Anne-Louise-Germaine Necker, Madame de (1766–1817) 79
Staes, J. 100
Stalin, Joseph (1879–1953) 72
Stéfanini, J. 100
Stefenelli, A. 155, 173, 183–4
Stein, D. 142, 417
Steinmeyer, G. 100
Sten, H. 215
Stendhal (Henri Beyle: 1783–1842) 62, 79, 416
Stern, Gustaf 192
Stimm, H. 100
Stock, B. 99
Straka, G. 100, 174, 183, 230, 290, 292–3
Sturm, J. 417
Suchier, W. 292
Sun King, *see* Louis XIV
Sweetser, E. 214
Swiggers, P. 56, 100
Sylvius (Dubois), Jacques (1464–1555) 38, 41

Tabouret-Keller, A. 100
Tabourot, Étienne (1549–90) 100, 278
Tamba (Mecz), I. 184, 214
Taverdet, G. 100
Taylor, T. 56

Tellier, C. 392
Tentchoff, D. 101
Thibault, P. 100
Thiele, J. 183
Thomas, G. 40, 48, 56
Thomason, S. G. 99, 343
Thurneysen, R. 417
Thurot, C. 292
Timberlake, A. 215
Tinker E. L. 101
Tobler, A. (1835–1910) 395, 397
Todd, E. 14, 55
Togeby, K. 8, 343
Tory, Geoffroy (*c.*1480–*c.*1533) 38, 52, 83
Tousignant, C. 100
Trager, G. L. 215
Tranel, B. 233, 265–6, 273, 292–3, 326, 343
Trask, R. L. 142, 292, 416
Traugott, E. C. 142, 215, 343, 416–7
Trudeau, D. 43, 100
Tuaillon, G. 292
Tucker, G. R. 100, 326, 343
Tuţescu, M. 214

Ullmann, S. 192, 214–15
Ultan, R. 417
Urfé, Honoré d' (1567–1625) 15
Uriagereka, J. 418

Väänänen, V. 55
Vair Palefroi (*c.*1270) 414
Valdman, A. 56, 74, 93, 100–1, 280, 293
Valéry, Paul-Ambroise (1871–1945) 13
Valli, A. 67, 100, 380
Valois (French dynasty) 16
Valois, D. 392, 418
Vance, B. S. 417
Vanelli, L. 417
Vaugelas, Claude Favre de (1585–1650) 43–4, 66, 78, 175, 207, 302, 304, 312, 375, 397, 405, 410, 415
Vennemann, T. 142, 417
Vergnaud, J.-R. 215, 383
Vermes, G. 100
Versteegh, K. 142
Vet, C. 215
Villehardouin, Geoffroy de (*c.*1162–*c.*1212), 407, 409
Villon, François (1431–?) 19, 334
Vincent, D. 417
Vincent, N. 8, 343
Vliet, E. R. van 215
Voltaire (François-Marie Arouet: 1694–1778) 53

Wackernagel, J. (1853–1913) 359, 395
Wagner, R.-L. 8, 183
Wahlgren, E. G. 343
Walker, D. C. 100, 343, 387

Wall, K. 417
Walter, H. 8, 100, 292
Wang, W. S.-Y. 124, 292
Wanner, D. 418
Warnant, L. 215, 387
Wartburg, W. von 8, 379, 417
Waswo, R. 56
Watbled, J. P. 293
Waugh, L. R. 215, 417
Webelhuth, G. 115
Weber, E. 100
Weiner, L. F. 4
Weinreich, Max 16
Weinreich, U. 142
Weinrich, H. 215
Wenk, B. J. 292
Wetzels, L. 219, 293
Wexler, P. J. 292
Wheeler, M. W. 100, 343
Whorf, Benjamin Lee (1897–1941) 110, 193
Wilkinson, H. E. 243, 292, 343
Williams, E. 417
Wilmet, M. 56, 214–15, 417
Wind, J. M. de 417

Winter, W. 4
Winters, M. E. 417
Wioland, F. 292
Wise, H. 183
Witte, J. J. de 192
Wittmann, H. 94, 100
Woledge, B. 343
Wolf, L. 56, 100
Wolf, N. 100
Wolfe, General James (1726–59) 92
Wolff, P. 55
Wooldridge, T. R. 183
Wright, R. 55
Wunderli, P. 183, 215, 343, 418
Wurzel, W. 343
Wyss, A. 56

Yaguello, M. 100

Zink, G. 56, 292
Zola, Émile (1840–1902) 68
Zubizaretta, M. L. 215, 383
Zwanenburg, W. 292, 417
Zwicky, A. M. 394, 418

Subject Index

abduction 117, 132
ablative 135
Académie Française 8, 40, 49, 51–2, 155, 168, 171, 311, 374, 410
Accademia della Crusca 4, 9, 171
accent, accentuation 22, 64, 93, 225–7, 229–30, 252, 260–1, 268, 274, 306, 359, 362, 376
  circumflex 52, 283, 291, 318
  oxytonic 225–6
  paroxytonic 225–6
  pitch 22, 226, 229
accent 'd'insistance 226, 267
accommodation 63, 82, 99, 116–17, 122, 127
acquisition 13, 112–13, 133, 136–7
accusative 331, 332, 336, 380, 387, 397, 405, 409
  and infinitive 23, 201, 401
acrolect 129
acronym 166
active 416
adaptive 4, 109, 116, 420
adjective, adjectival 44–5, 13, 166, 206, 239–40, 265, 327–30, 334, 338–9, 342, 350, 352, 360–3, 382–3, 388, 392–4, 397, 410–13, 416–17
  attributive 361
  determining (or 'emphatic') 361
  placement 360–3
adnominal 342, 384
adverb, adverbials 76, 352–3, 360, 369–70, 373, 375–6, 401, 407, 412
affix, affixation 145, 167, 169–70, 298, 300, 323, 395, 400, 410
affricate *see* consonant
agglutination, agglutinative 294
agreement 45, 71, 76, 94, 138, 209, 325, 347, 356, 375, 379, 384, 389–90, 395, 401, 410–416, 418
Albigensian Crusade 15, 88
allomorphy, allomorph 295, 313–16, 322
allophone, allophonic 22, 124, 136, 245–6, 257, 261–2, 276, 295, 309, 337
alsacien 87–8
a-morphous 295
analogy 106, 108, 112, 121, 125, 135, 221,

296–7, 300–3, 305–6, 310, 312, 316–18, 322, 325, 333, 335, 337, 339, 343, 387, 403
analysis, analytic 24, 30, 120, 294–5, 299, 302, 320, 347
anaphoric 212–13, 381–2, 385, 387, 394–5, 405–6
ancien régime 14, 47, 60, 79, 83, 85
animate 332, 406–7, 411
anterior 206, 323
anti-topic 354, 365, 413
apocope 228, 267
apodosis 202
apophony 227, 262, 275, 306–12
apparent time 80
approximant *see* glide; jod
archaism, archaizing 39, 75, 82, 335, 346, 372, 402
archiphoneme 274
areal 250
argot 74–5
argument 333, 378, 382–3, 395–6, 406, 410
article 21, 23, 212, 299, 342, 348, 381, 386–91, 393, 399, 418
  definite 31, 186, 198, 211–14, 267, 299, 326–7, 331, 334, 339–40, 342, 381–91, 394
  indefinite 327, 382, 385, 393
  partitive 213, 390–3, 408
  possessive 339
  zero 214
articulation 132, 218, 221, 228–9, 236, 242, 245, 258, 260, 269, 278, 284, 287–8, 290
aspect 30, 110, 198–200, 203, 228
  habitual 28, 30, 199
  imperfective 199–200
  perfective 199
  progressive 25, 30, 199, 201
  punctual 199, 201, 204, 206–7
aspirate *see* consonant
aspiration 227
assibilation 244, 247, 248
assimilation 77, 86, 106, 132, 217, 219–20, 226, 228, 230, 239, 242, 244–5, 248, 250–1, 257, 298, 344
assonance 236, 241, 256, 278, 281, 286
attrition 4, 115, 121, 137, 237, 380, 390, 410

autosegmental *see* multidimensional phonology
auxiliary *see* verb

back formation (*dérivation régressive*) 166, 170
Bartsch's Law 246, 270
base-generation 352
basic lexicon *see* vocabulary
basilect 129
béké 33
bilingualism 18, 83–4, 105
  assymetrical 99
bimoraic *see* diphthong; vowel
bioprogramme 128
bleaching 207, 299, 384
bleeding 223–4
bon usage 66, 416
borrowing, loanwords 26, 39–40, 93, 143, 155–6, 158, 160, 163–5, 183, 193, 221, 223, 243, 245–6, 250–1, 257, 262, 273, 275, 277–9, 281–2, 285, 325, 345
bounded 383
bound-form 136, 145, 295, 298
breaking 245, 270
breath-group *see* rhythmic group
burlesque, le genre 67

Cahiers de Doléances 67
caesura 271
cajun 92–9, 306, 380
Canadian 92–4, 101, 139, 234, 248, 258, 273, 276, 279, 284, 287, 290, 387, 389
case *see also* dative, genitive 25, 72, 119, 138, 198, 211, 228, 331–5, 342–3, 347, 350, 378, 380, 382–3, 391, 395, 406, 410
  oblique 331, 378
  Old French nominal 332–5
category 294, 339, 381–3, 388, 414
  change 26, 166, 338, 375, 381
causative *see* factitive
cedilla 52
Celtic 57, 64, 86, 163, 250–2, 258, 357, 359, 420
chain-shift 108, 219–20
  push-chain 219, 245, 252
  drag-chain 219, 252
chronology 223–5
clause union 401
clefting 25, 348, 354–5, 378
clitic, cliticization 23, 30, 76, 121, 135, 227, 265, 299, 304–5, 332, 338–9, 348, 352–3, 355, 370, 372, 374–7, 381, 383–4, 387–90, 392, 394–9, 404–8, 410, 415
  adverbial 76, 372, 396, 401, 404–10, 418
  array, cluster 76, 296, 372, 404–5, 407–10, 418
  climbing 388, 400–4, 418
  doubling, copying 355, 377–8, 389, 395

enclitic 227, 268, 368, 388, 392, 394–5, 398, 400, 403, 406
object 331, 374, 387, 394–400, 415, 418
proclitic 25, 227, 378, 389, 394, 397–8, 400–1, 405–6, 414
simple 394
special 394
subject, person markers 135, 307, 331, 348, 352, 374, 376, 387
closed syllable adjustment 240, 274, 300, 311
coarticulation 226, 228
coda 221, 227–8, 230–1, 234–5, 237, 239–43, 252, 264–5, 272–3, 283–6, 311–13
code-switching 18, 129
codification 36, 38, 40–6, 83, 406
coding 24, 348–9
cognate, cognate forms 120, 167
collective 385
Collège des lecteurs royaux, Collège de France 37, 43
colonial levelling 93
communicative competence 109
comparative 374
comparative philology 4, 118, 145, 217, 421
concord *see* agreement
compensatory lengthening *see also* vowel, long 22, 24, 126, 132, 235, 240, 264, 273, 280–1, 284, 286, 318
competence 64, 111
complement, complementation 211, 348, 372, 388, 401, 404
complementizer 76, 209, 211, 380–1, 388, 401
compound tenses 76, 135, 199, 203–5, 319, 347, 354, 366, 403, 411, 416
compounding, *composition* 149, 167, 170, 408
conditional 6, 202, 211, 317, 319–24, 343
conjugation 22, 41, 175, 203, 268, 271, 294, 302–3, 316
conjoined, conjunction 31, 209, 294, 300, 302–3, 316–7, 320, 322, 324–5, 348, 395
consonant 77, 219, 221, 231–2, 234, 236–7, 241–2, 253, 263–6, 271–3, 280, 304, 314, 318, 324, 327, 328–30, 335, 415
  affricate 22, 25, 243–5, 247
  aspirate 273
  back 244–5, 289
  cluster 77, 227, 249, 261–2, 267–8, 272, 291, 303
  dental 138, 220, 244, 247–8, 289
  devoicing 22, 220, 227, 229, 271–2, 288, 303, 327, 330
  dorsal 288
  double, geminate 150, 223–4, 237, 288–9, 309
  flapped 288
  fricative 22, 220, 242, 244, 288–9
  fronting 244
  labial 243, 245, 251
  labiovelar 244–6

lateral 249–50
 loss 272, 283, 289
 medial 264–5, 285
 nasal 22, 132, 230–3, 235, 237, 239, 241, 264, 284, 298
 obstruent 220, 223–4, 244, 272
 palatal, palatalization 24, 93, 244–8
 palatal-alveolar, palatoalveolar 22, 243–5, 247, 302
 plosive 220, 244–5
 sibilant 22, 244, 248, 264–5, 314, 318, 322
 syllable-final 235, 289
 trilled 288–9
 truncation 119, 226, 238, 287
 velar 22, 220, 243–5, 238, 287
 voiced 234, 314
 voiceless 220, 224, 246, 271–2, 285, 288, 291
 word-final 22, 119, 154, 174, 220, 224, 227–30, 253, 257, 262–3, 265–6, 268, 272, 280, 289, 291, 313, 330, 333–4
 word-initial 221, 230, 263
conspiracy 121
constituent 354–5
constituent ordering 31
contact, language 57, 99, 112, 131, 143, 146, 219, 421–2
continuant 244, 283, 314, 321, 322
continuum 16, 21, 129
contrastive 361
control 410
convergence 123
copula 30
coronal, coronalization 245, 248
corpus planning 40
Council of Tours (813) 17
coupe lyrique, épique 271
covert prestige 78
creole, creolization 14, 20, 24, 28–33, 56, 63, 67, 94–9, 119, 123, 127–31, 146, 198, 208, 211, 214, 234, 252, 280, 290, 295, 304, 326, 331, 333, 370, 380, 384, 390, 420, 424
Crusades 35
cursus *see also* rhythmic group 227, 229
cycle, cyclicity 120, 295, 299, 320
Cyrillic 269

dative 332, 341, 380, 387, 399, 405–6, 407
 ethic, of interest 396, 404
decreolization 97–8, 130
death, language 4, 81, 90, 105, 108, 119, 122
declension 294, 327, 390
deduction 117, 420
definiteness 212, 215, 347, 381, 389
deictic, demonstratives 23, 212, 327, 339–43, 356, 381–5, 389, 392
 distal 212, 340–2
 proximal 212, 340–1
delinking 251
demotion 404

denasalization 232–41, 298
deontic *see* modality
derivation (word-formation), derivatives 29, 39–40, 147, 154, 158, 165–70, 183, 273, 275, 294, 323, 328
determiner 23, 25, 113, 196, 198, 213, 265, 297, 299, 326, 334–56, 338–9, 341–2, 361, 375, 381–6, 389–90, 393
 partitive 385, 390–400
Determiner Phrase (DP) 383
devoicing *see* consonant
diachronic 3, 108, 186, 188, 218, 279, 296, 300, 314, 344
diacritic 52, 267, 283, 285
dialects 5, 16, 29, 33, 35, 50, 62, 65, 71, 73–4, 80–2, 89–91, 93–5, 97, 129, 142, 156, 207, 235, 250, 252–3, 255, 270, 278, 285–6, 289, 332, 372, 396, 409, 419–20
dictionaries, lexicography 144–5, 163, 171–2, 177, 182–3
differentiation 5, 39, 58, 86, 97, 123, 250, 252, 257–8, 260, 267, 269, 279, 281, 288, 300, 302–3, 310, 340, 348–9, 371, 383, 390
diglossia 18, 48, 58, 134, 163
diffusion *see* lexical diffusion
diphthong 24–6, 231–2, 235, 240, 245–7, 251–62, 270, 278, 281, 284, 286, 311–12
 falling 242, 253, 255, 269, 287
 heavy (bimoraic) 255–6, 284, 286
 light 255–6
 lengthening 287
 levelling 22, 240, 258, 261, 280
 nasal 231, 235
 rising 254–5
diphthongization 22, 72, 93, 225–7, 246, 253–5, 257–8, 260, 262, 306, 310–12, 335
 metaphonic *see* metaphony
direct order 350, 358
disagreement 326–7, 337
discours 383
discourse 344
dislocation, topicalization 25, 76, 213, 227, 347–8, 351, 354–5, 357–8, 368, 377–8, 399, 413–4
 left 354, 364, 377, 389, 396–7, 413
 right 354–5, 360, 364, 389, 396, 399, 408
dissimilation 124, 244–5, 300
DOM 28, 93–4, 129
doublets 160, 272–3
drift 70, 116, 120, 295

e caduc, e muet see mute *e*
echo-question 367
e instable, see mute *e*
elaboration 36, 39–40
elision 22, 94, 226, 245, 263, 266–9, 271, 273, 327, 372, 377, 380, 387, 389, 414
ellipsis 191
empty nucleus 265

enchaînement 263, 271
endogenous linguistic change 72
enclisis *see* clitic
energeia 106
Enlightenment 21, 85
epenthesis 233, 267–70, 286, 314
ergon 106
etymon, etymology 144, 147–51, 183, 221, 236, 265–6, 272, 277, 299–300, 310, 323, 332, 335, 337, 340–1, 372, 381, 387, 390
euphemism 190
exaptation 139, 140, 299, 423
exogenous change 72
experiencer 203
expletive 372–3, 378, 382–3, 395–6
extension 345
external history 3, 6
extrametrical 257, 266, 335

factitives 402, 404
feeding 118, 223–4, 233, 265
feminine *e see* mute *e*
féminisation 79, 326
fission 243, 251, 253, 255
flexion, inflection 23, 25–6, 29, 94, 114–15, 120–1, 125, 139, 200, 203, 228, 264, 265, 268, 271, 294–5, 297–8, 304, 306, 320, 323, 329, 331, 334–5, 348, 350, 355, 368, 377, 379–80, 384, 390, 399, 410
floating 264–6, 270–1
focalization 227, 277, 355
focus 389
folk etymology 191
forclusif 370, 372–3, 375–6
form-class *see* category
fortition *see* hardening
français avancé 21, 69, 72
français familier 74
français fondamental 46, 163
français populaire 21, 28, 58–9, 67–9, 72–4, 100, 121, 234, 271
francien 15, 353
francité 12
Francophonie 48, 91
Franks 14, 35, 88, 130
franglais 48, 121
free-form 136, 143, 145, 196, 295
Frondes 19, 65
fronting 251–2, 281, 358, 414–15
function, functional 22, 198, 299, 375
functionalism, functionalists 108, 115, 276
functional load 200, 220, 276–7
fusion 242–3, 255, 257, 302, 387
future 30, 198–200, 207–8, 211, 303, 305, 313–14, 319–24, 343
    GO-future 23, 207
    synthetic 23, 120, 299, 319, 321
future participle 206
future stem 302

future-in-the-past *see* conditional

gaumais 91
geminate *see* consonant
gender 29, 30, 71, 94, 119, 138, 166, 211, 213, 228, 239–40, 266–7, 269, 271–2, 278, 297–8, 316, 325–8, 336, 341, 343, 382, 387, 395, 397, 410, 412, 415
generalization 162, 198, 306, 310, 318, 333, 345, 376
generative phonology xix, 218–19, 233, 295, 330
generativist 116, 218–9, 267, 274, 295–6, 301, 328, 344, 352, 375, 379, 381, 402
generative syntax 344, 383
generic 213, 394
genitive 198, 332–3, 385, 391
gerund(ive) 206–7, 402
glide *see also* jod 242–4, 246, 252, 254, 256, 258, 285–6, 287
glottopolitique 33
grammaticalization 129, 135–6, 200, 207–8, 211, 228, 298–300, 322, 343, 349, 352, 354, 356, 358, 375, 395
grammatical meaning 198–215, 347
graphy *see* spelling
Grimm's Law 107, 219
gumbo 33, 95–9

habitual *see* aspect
hardening, fortition 77, 235, 248, 256, 258, 302, 314, 321–2
h aspiré 22, 24, 93, 262, 273
head 113–14, 227, 350, 375
hiatus 240, 252, 283–4, 286
High Language 48, 58
homonyms, homonymy 52, 154, 174, 187, 247, 258, 387–8, 415
homophony 252, 280, 415
host 377, 394
Huguenot 49, 87
Humanism 49, 50, 84, 182
Hundred Years War 41, 424
hypercorrect, hypercorrection 71, 211, 263, 291, 334, 344, 345, 416
hypotaxis 25, 348

iconic, iconicity 24, 137, 296, 313, 348, 354
idiolect 1, 2, 64, 111
imperative 209, 268, 324, 351, 359, 379, 398, 405, 410
imperfect 22, 198–9, 200–4, 215, 277, 303–4, 306, 313, 316–17, 323–4, 343
imperfective *see* aspect
impersonal 76, 359, 378–9, 413
inalienable possession 382
inchoative 300, 309
incorporation 384
indefinite 360 *see also* article

indicative 139, 199–200, 209–10, 254, 302–3, 306, 314, 316–17, 320, 322, 324
induction 117
infinitive 23, 30, 76, 166, 168, 201, 207–8, 300, 309–10, 313, 320–3, 353, 375, 388, 399–404, 408
  personal 323
infix 368
inflection, inflexional *see* flexion
inherent pronominal 396
innate grammar *see* Universal Grammar
innovation 28, 71, 75, 109, 116, 126, 131, 133, 135, 195, 284, 294, 319–20, 420
insecurity, linguistic 12, 91
interlect 63
internal history 3
interrogation, interrogative 23, 25, 26, 72, 75–6, 210, 268, 335, 348, 350, 358, 363–9, 375, 380–1, 417
  negative 210
  polar 323, 364, 368, 398
  WH- 366, 368
intervocalic 219–20, 224, 249, 289, 291, 317
intonation, 355–6, 364
intransitive *see* verb
inversion 23, 25, 26, 75–6, 334, 350, 359, 362, 364–8, 378
  complex 25, 364–6
  simple 364
  stylistic 359, 366, 368
invisible hand 121–2
irregularity 146, 154, 175, 296, 305, 312, 317, 319
isolating languages 294
iterative, iterativity 199

Jansenist 49–50
jargon 63
Jesuit 32, 49, 61
jod, jodization 22, 243–4, 246, 248, 253, 257, 286, 302, 324

koine, koineization 34, 37, 63, 81–4, 93, 420–1

langaige maternel françois 83
language planning 33–4
langue 13, 108–9, 383, 422
lateral *see* consonant
Latinism 26, 120, 156, 160–3, 311
laxing 232, 242, 279
legitimate language *see* standard
lenition 219–20, 224
levelling *see also* diphthong 246–7, 272, 282, 286–7, 297
lexical diffusion 124, 222
lexical or semantic field 144, 172–81, 184
lexical inflation 155–6, 192
lexical loss 132–5, 138, 152–5, 183
lexical semantics *see* semantics

lexical statistics 144, 183
lexicalization 136, 157, 165, 167–70, 186, 193, 198, 219, 234, 237, 267–9, 273, 298, 312, 326, 333, 337
lexicologie 144, 181–4
lexicon *see also* vocabulary 5, 20–1, 24, 26, 28–31, 39, 57, 65, 71, 82, 107, 109–10, 113, 124–5, 127–30, 133, 135, 136–8, 141, 143–86, 191–3, 195, 197–8, 203, 211, 219, 222, 225, 227, 233, 262–3, 267, 273, 282, 295–6, 298, 301, 310–11, 322, 328, 330–1, 334–5, 337, 340, 345, 347–9, 352, 355, 357, 362, 364–6, 369, 377–8, 382–4, 389, 393, 395, 403–4, 410, 413, 414
lexicography *see* dictionaries
lexico-phonetic 113
lexico-semantics 137, 216
liaison 22, 24, 77, 226, 228, 232, 240, 262–6, 273, 304, 333, 386
lingua gallica 15
lingua franca 35, 127
linking *see* sandhi
literacy 50–1, 53, 58, 60–1, 67, 99, 133, 141, 222, 290, 335, 344
levelling 24, 252, 303, 310
l mouillé 249–50
loanword *see* borrowing
locative 340–2, 381, 407
locus 199, 201
loi de position 77, 242, *275*, 273–82, 287, 311
loi Falloux 61
loi de répartition 192
loi des trois consonnes 267
Low Language 48, 58
lowering 232–3, 235–6, 237–42, 276, 278, 280–1, 289, 291

marché linguistique 72
marked 114
markers, marking 29, 30–1, 52, 76, 121, 135, 198–9, 203, 227–8, 233, 247, 264, 272–3, 285, 296–9, 303–4, 306, 314, 316–7, 322–3, 324, 326–7, 334, 336, 347, 365, 369, 380–2, 384–5, 389, 395, 410
  case 198, 228 331, 333–4, 341, 355–6, 381, 383, 390–1, 406
  concord 373
  future *r* 322–3, 324
  gender 211, 213, 228, 238, 269, 271, 325–32, 381, 383, 397
  number 211, 213
  person 26, 135, 138, 228, 297, 303–4, 314, 343, 348, 355, 378, 380
  tense, aspect, mood (TAM) 30, 129, 186, 198, 207–8, 215, 297, 314, 370
maroon 32
masculine 166, 239–40, 298, 325, 327–8, 331–2, 334, 337, 340–1, 387
mazarinade 53, 65

melody, melodic tier xix, 218, 255
merger 247, 289
mesolect 129
meta-rules 119
metalanguage, metalinguistic 40, 236, 239
metaphony, metaphonic raising, *umlaut*, 255, 318, 335, 340
metaphor 187, 189, 192–3, 299
metonymy 188
metre, metrics 173, 228, 268, 271, 282–3, 286, 372
metrical foot 276, 311
middle 396
minimal pair 233
minimalism 219
Minimalist Programme 115
mise en relief 26, 227, 356
mixing, language 129
modal *see* verb
modality 110, 199–201, 203, 211, 379
  deontic 199
  epistemic 199
mode 199, 284, 290
mode croissant, décroissant 228, 237
mode tendu 290
modulation 199
monolingual 92, 129
monophthong 24, 252, 254–5, 257, 261, 269–70, 286
mood 199–200, 208–9, 303, 347
mora, moraic xix, 218, 230–1, 244, 251, 254, 256, 264, 279, 280, 284
morph *see* allomorph
morpheme 110, 136, 165, 295, 328
morphologization 136, 232, 241, 262, 297–8, 343, 412
morphology *see also* flexion; derivation 21, 24–5, 28, 41, 65, 72, 93, 107, 110, 113–5, 124, 128, 134, 136–7, 154, 180, 195, 198, 199, 203, 205–6, 208, 211, 227–8, 232–3, 238, 241, 247, 262, 264, 272–3, 274, 294–350, 356, 369, 379, 381–2, 384, 390, 391, 400, 410, 415, 421
morpho(pho)nology, mor(pho)phonological rules 51, 260, 295, 328, 331, 337–9, 348, 383, 390, 394
morphosyntax, morphosyntactic change 110, 115, 133, 141, 228, 296, 299, 339, 344–5
morphologization 136, 232, 241, 287, 297–8, 412
mot juste 39
mot témoin 181
mot clé 181–2
movement 113, 352, 354–5, 388
multidimensional , non-linear phonology xix, 218, 264, 284
mute *e* 22, 25, 77, 225–7, 238–9, 255–6, 263, 266–73, 278–9, 297–9, 301, 303–4, 311, 328, 335, 343, 398, 413

nasalization, nasality, nasal vowels 22, 25–6, 77, 93, 119, 132, 136, 138, 218, 225, 227, 230–42, 248, 254, 270, 286, 297–8, 335
nativization 29, 127
natural 217, 219, 296
ne explétif, ne redondant, ne abusif 373
ne discordantiel 375
negation, negative, negator 23, 25–6, 31, 38, 42, 72, 135, 191, 210, 348, 369–76, 385, 392, 398, 417
  concord 370, 373
  polarity 370–1, 375
Neogrammarians 107, 118, 123, 221–3, 237, 279, 296–7
neologism 26, 39–40, 144, 155–6, 163, 169, 172, 181
networks 73
neuter 76, 325, 397, 409
neutralization 270, 274, 278
nexus 227, 229, 266
nominalization 25, 166, 200
nominative 254, 322, 333–4, 336, 340, 380, 388
non-pro-drop *see* pro-drop
non-standard 69, 74–5, 78, 81, 90, 93, 221, 369, 374, 376, 380, 387, 390, 396–8, 405, 423, 411, 420
norm 6, 34, 65, 78, 107, 109, 111, 116, 122, 288, 361, 419–20
normative 210, 349, 386, 393
normativization 40–5
normalization 39–40
noun 26, 30, 45, 113, 135, 138, 166, 168, 191, 196, 211, 213, 265–6, 332, 333–4, 339, 350, 352, 360–3, 382–4, 386, 389, 391, 393–5, 410–11, 414
  abstract, 382, 385
  gender 25, 29, 94, 166, 325
  noncount 214, 392–3
  verbal 165, 168, 312
nouniness 213, 403
Noun Phrase (NP) 31, 76, 113, 203, 212–4, 332–3, 351, 354–5, 357, 361, 366, 377–8, 381–4, 389– 90, 392–3, 403, 407–8, 413 416
  heavy 359
nucleus 231, 235, 252, 255–6, 260–1, 265, 284, 287
null subject language (NSL) *see* pro-drop
number 25, 213, 335, 382, 410, 415
numeral 385, 408

object 76, 113, 128, 331, 334, 350–1, 357, 389, 395, 404–5, 411–15
objective conjugation 395
obligative 320, 336
oblique *see* case
obstruent *see* consonant
Occitan 14, 35, 64, 81, 91, 105, 231, 250–1, 270, 288, 321, 420

off-glide 253, 303
on-glide 340
onomasiology 144, 173
onomatopœia 151
onset 227–8, 231–2, 246, 252–3, 256, 263–4, 286
optative 209
operator *see* head
Optimality Theory 219, 265–6
orthoepic 231–2
orthography *see* spelling
ouiste 278
OVS *see* word order
oxytonic *see* accent

palatal, palatalization 22, 77, 119, 138, 227, 242–52, 254, 256, 262, 302–3, 313, 324
palatoalveolar *see* consonant
paradigm, paradigmatic 154, 219, 262, 295, 303, 306, 309–10, 312, 317, 322–3, 342, 387, 389, 410
para-language 128
paragogic 272
parameter setting *see* Principles and Parameters
parataxis 348
parole 108–9. 141, 344
paroxytonic *see* accent
Partage de Verdun 15
particle 31, 42, 121, 191, 342, 358, 364, 366, 368–9, 395
participle *see also* past participle, present participle 354, 362, 413
partitive *see* article
part-of-speech *see* category
passive 23, 113, 200, 204, 206–7, 347, 396, 411–13, 416
past *see also* imperfect 22, 199–201, 205–6, 208, 215, 303
  compound *(passé composé) see also* perfect 25, 76, 135, 203–16, 411–12
  passé surcomposé 206
  simple *(passé simple)* 22, 41, 198, 204–6, 277, 303, 305, 314, 317–20, 324–5, 343
past participle 42–3, 71, 203, 205–6, 319, 362, 411–15, 418
past participle agreement 42–3, 410–16
patois 29, 63, 66, 81, 89
perception *see* verb
perfect 199, 318, 320, 411
  future 23
perfective *see* aspect
performance 13, 112, 141, 422
periodization 16, 135
periphrasis, periphrastic 23, 25, 120, 200, 206–7, 208, 215, 268, 317, 320, 324, 267
person 23, 138, 212, 228, 331, 340, 348, 356, 377, 380, 405, 410

first 268, 302–3, 313, 318, 322, 324–5, 332, 368, 389, 397
plural 302–3, 313, 318, 322, 325, 337, 397
second 139, 302–3, 305–6, 322, 324–5, 332, 389, 397, 405
singular 268, 303–4, 306, 310, 313, 323, 332, 335, 368
third 299, 305–6, 314, 317, 323, 337, 340–1, 378, 381, 384, 387, 389–90, 399, 405, 415
personal pronoun subject 38, 42, 304
phatic speech 106
philologie sociologique 2
philology *see also* comparative philology 4, 7, 145, 221, 236, 296, 318, 348, 395, 421
phoneme xix, 25, 50, 64, 119, 124, 132, 136, 138, 216, 219, 295
phonemic split 136
phonetic distortion 216
phonetics 50, 64, 70, 106–7, 113, 116, 199–20, 123–4, 137–8, 141, 145, 192, 217–20, 226, 228, 230, 235, 237, 241, 244–5, 249, 252, 255–6, 258, 267–9, 273, 276, 278–9, 280, 283, 285, 287, 289–90, 306–7, 371, 374, 376, 398, 412
phonology, phonological system 21–3, 25, 28, 64, 107–8, 110, 113, 118–19, 124, 131, 133, 138, 141, 146–52, 154, 158, 185, 195, 197, 203, 211, 216–93, 295–8, 300, 313, 318, 320, 322, 326–30, 335, 337–8, 346–7, 349, 376–7, 379, 383–4, 387–8, 399, 404, 415, 421
phonologization 136, 219, 232, 234, 237–8, 244–5, 273'
phonotactic 25
Picard 38, 41, 42, 82–3, 250, 253, 270, 272, 286, 331, 336, 420–2
pidgin, pidginization 28–9, 35, 127–8, 130, 196
pitch *see* accent
plosive *see* consonant
pluperfect 199–200, 323–4
plural, plurality 139, 211, 264, 304–6, 313, 332–7, 340–1, 380, 387–8, 393, 396
polar (yes/no) questions *see* interrogative
polarity *see* negation
polynomic 37, 91
polysemy 174, 187–8
popular French *see français populaire*
Port Royal (*Grammaire générale et raisonée,* anon. 1660 [by Claude Lancelot and Antoine Arnauld]—known as *Grammaire du Port Royal,*) 44, 50, 200–1, 270, 325
possessive 23, 326, 335–9, 342–3, 361, 382, 385, 389–90, 409
potential 209
PP *see* prepositional phrase
pragmatic 212, 344, 350, 354
Prague School 108
predicative (*attribut*) 339, 362, 380, 411

prefix, prefixing 167, 170, 228, 231, 353, 364, 370, 389, 401, 410
prepausal 240, 271, 285
preposition 31, 128, 167, 333, 341, 350, 387–8, 391, 399, 401, 403, 408
prepositional phrase (PP) 332, 407–8
prescriptive grammar *see* normative
present 25, 199–200, 204, 208, 254, 300, 302–3, 306, 314, 322
present participle 206–7, 236, 305
present perfect *see* compound tenses
presentative 354, 356, 359–60, 410
preterite (punctual past) *see* past, simple
Principle of Economy 115
Principle of Least Effort 220
Principles-and-Parameters 113–5, 127, 130, 296, 345, 349, 352, 377, 379
pro-adjective 397
pro-drop 23, 114, 138, 304, 352, 377–80, 417
proclitic *see* clitic
productive 167, 232, 316
progressive *see* aspect
promotion *see* clitic climbing
pronominal 25, 136, 203, 214, 294, 297, 325–42, 351, 358, 382, 385, 393, 400, 408, 411
pronominal verb ('reflexive') 395–6
pronoun 94, 139, 299, 332, 335, 338–42, 353, 355, 376–8, 380–2, 385, 387–8, 390, 396–7, 399, 403, 405, 407, 414
  atonic 377, 398–9, 414
  clitic, conjunctive, weak *see* clitic
  copying *see* clitic, doubling
  disjunctive, free-standing, strong 25, 30, 31–2, 331–2, 338–9, 378, 383, 389, 394, 398–9
  distal 212
  expletive 396
  object 25, 76, 268, 352, 357, 379, 387, 389, 399, 403, 308, 414–15
  personal 23, 30, 38, 42, 299, 331, 340, 342, 378
  reflexive 30, 136
  subject 23, 191, 304, 335, 355, 358–60, 364, 367, 369, 375, 377, 379, 387, 389, 399
  tonic 76, 380, 387, 399, 403
pronoun copying *see* clitic, doubling
pro-NP 416
pronunciation 28, 42, 50–1, 53, 54, 64, 77–9, 82, 94, 99, 112, 116, 123–4, 133, 135, 136, 171, 174, 216, 218, 226–7, 231–2, 236, 238–9, 245, 249–50, 251, 253–4, 258, 262–3, 267–70, 277–80, 287–8, 290–1, 310–11, 325, 327, 342
pro-PP 332, 405, 407, 416
prosodic 377–8
protasis 203
Protestant *see also* Huguenot 14, 42–3, 49, 53, 60–1, 85
proto-language 224
Proto-Romance 4, 17, 217, 357

prototype, prototypical 187–8
proximal forms 340–2
pseudo-adjective 363
pseudo-clefting 354
pseudo-partitive 391
pseudo-relative 390, 402
psycho-systématique 118
punctual *see* aspect, past
punctuation 369
purism, purist 37, 40, 45, 48, 133, 156, 168, 419

quantifier 385, 391, 416
questione della lingua 27

raising *see* vowel; verb-raising
realization 122, 238, 262, 266–7, 269, 284, 290, 329, 344
reanalysis 112, 338, 345, 368, 379, 416
reciprocal 30
reflex 6, 312, 316, 335–6, 340, 376
reflexive 30, 76, 136, 348, 396, 398, 403, 405, 411
Reformation 72, 424
register 65, 267
regularist 221–2
regularity 216, 250, 296, 298–9, 296, 298, 300, 318, 335, 398, 403
regularization 318
relative 210, 335, 355, 380–1
  predicative, attributive 380, 402
relativization 348
relexification 127
Renaissance 18, 49–50, 53, 55, 72, 152, 156, 169, 182, 363, 416, 424
resyllabification 272
Revolution, French (1789) 8, 14, 20, 27, 32, 35, 38–9, 44, 46–7, 50, 59–60, 71, 74, 78–9, 83, 85, 95, 100, 128, 176, 206, 249, 288, 290, 306
r grasseyé see uvular *r*
rhetoric 109, 188
rhythm 12, 255, 228–9, 282, 353, 398
rhythmic group 25, 54, 225–7, 229–30, 261–3, 267–8, 362, 375, 379, 384, 398–9
rime chartraine 287
rime féminine 271
roman 18
root 300, 303–8, 310, 312–15, 322, 324
rule inversion 297–8

sabir 35, 127
sandhi 226, 230, 263
Sapir-Whorf hypothesis 100
saturation 383
schwa *see* mute *e*
selection 36–9
semantics 6, 107, 110, 148–52, 154, 167, 171–3, 178–9, 183, 185–214, 215, 221, 299, 325, 330, 345, 347, 358, 361, 364, 366, 370, 372, 381–5, 391, 402–3, 412

semantic change 21, 151, 183, 185–214
semantic field 110, 193–4
semantic laws 192
lexical semantics 6, 172, 186–7, 190–193, 215
semantic primes 187–193
utterance semantics 195–8
semantico-syntax 198–214
seme 187–8
semi-auxiliary *see* verb
semiotic *see also* sign-system 108
sentence 344
sentence roles 347
servitude grammaticale 209
sex 66
sexe fictif 325
shift, language 6, 57, 63–4, 71–3, 75, 81, 91, 105, 112, 122–3, 125, 132–3, 135, 148, 181, 188, 190, 193–5, 217–19, 251, 390, 419, 421, 423
sibilant *see* consonant
signifiant, signifié 383
sign-system 111
simplex words 167
simplification 24, 31, 64, 77–8, 94, 122, 131, 217, 224, 242, 247, 249–50, 261, 269, 281, 295, 314, 410
singular 254, 302, 305–6, 313, 326, 333–4, 337–8, 341, 380, 393
skeletal tier xix, 218, 264
slaves, slavery, slave trade 28–9, 32–3, 92, 95–8, 419–20
small clause 404, 412
sociolinguistics 7, 20, 63, 72–3, 97, 100, 132, 141, 195, 217, 281
historical 63
Sorbonne 37, 42
sound-change 123, 125, 150, 216–90, 297, 301, 306, 331, 339
sound-laws 123, 125, 150. 221–2, 279, 335
sound-substitution *see* sporadic change
sound-system 31
speciation 4
specifier 23, 375
spelling 41–3, 50–5, 64, 133–4, 216, 223, 231, 235–7, 239–41, 244, 249, 257, 263–4, 266–75, 279–80, 285, 287, 290–2, 304, 309, 318, 331, 334, 361
spelling pronunciation 71, 119, 154, 228, 231, 264, 272, 283, 285, 289, 290–1
spirantization 219–20
spontaneous sound-change 250, 253
sporadic change 221–2
standardization 20, 26, 33–48, 50, 56, 75, 81, 141, 210, 222, 287, 311, 331, 346, 349, 363, 408, 420
standard language 7, 11–12, 31, 33–6, 39, 46–8, 50, 52, 69, 73–5, 78, 80, 82–3, 89–91, 93, 96, 134, 145, 169, 171–2, 174, 203,

209, 227, 230–2, 235, 237, 239, 250, 256, 280, 284, 286–7, 288–9, 298, 302, 305, 318, 342, 349, 364, 372, 376, 379, 390, 398, 400, 403, 405–6, 410– 12, 416
stative 203
status planning *see* normalization
stem 22, 200, 300, 302, 307, 309–10, 318, 321–3, 380
Strasburg Oaths (842) 3, 15, 17, 140, 269, 313, 321, 335, 370, 407
strength, strengthening *see also* hardening 220, 288, 317, 338
stress 221, 224–6, 228–30, 237, 260–1, 268–270, 282–4, 302, 305–7, 322–3, 331–2, 335, 350, 356, 358, 362, 367, 369, 374–9, 383, 394–5, 397, 399, 405, 408, 410
stress-timed 226
structuralism 219, 267, 276, 295, 381
style 28, 58, 67, 78–9, 114, 209, 262, 353, 356, 359, 363, 366–7
stylistic inversion *see* inversion
stylistics 58, 78–9, 114, 187–8, 195, 198, 201, 205, 311, 349–50, 353, 362, 365, 374,
sub-categorization 334
subject 23, 38, 42, 76, 114, 136, 203–4, 333–4, 350–2. 359–60, 364–6, 368, 377–80, 394–5, 397, 404–5, 410–11
logical 359
subject-object-verb (SOV) *see* word-order
subject-verb-object (SVO) *see* word-order
subjunctive 23, 76, 126, 139, 199, 201, 205, 208–11, 215, 301–3, 320, 324–5, 343, 345, 373
future 303
imperfect 126, 202, 323–4
past 303, 323
present 303, 306, 313, 324–5
subordination, subordinate clauses 202–3, 209–11, 348, 357, 373, 377–9, 383, 401
subordinate, subordinated language 99, 122
substratum 57, 64, 230, 250
substratomane 128
substantivized 388, 399
suffix, suffixation 136, 167–8, 170, 200, 228, 245, 352, 362, 384
suicide, language 91, 105
superstratum 230
Suisse Romande 89
suppletion, suppletive 219, 234, 300–2, 312, 318–19, 322, 324, 329–30, 394
surface filter 406
surface structures 122
SVX ordering *see* word-order
syllabic contraction 283, 285
syllable *see also* closed syllable adjustment 204, 225–6, 228, 231, 235, 238, 240, 243, 246, 257, 263–4, 266, 283, 268–71, 276, 283, 303–4, 323, 326, 362, 413
atonic 228, 311

syllable (*cont.*)
  blocked, checked, closed 151, 224, 230, 240,
    242, 251, 253–4, 255, 261, 274–80, 309–11
  free, open 224, 231–2, 238, 240, 246, 25,
    254–5, 257–9, 259, 261, 267, 270, 272,
    274–5, 280, 306, 311, 335
  tonic 228, 246, 251, 254–5, 257–9, 274–5,
    278–80, 285, 311
  weight 23, 225, 282, 285
syllable-timed 226
syncope 251, 254, 267, 309
synchronic 108, 167, 182, 187–8, 189, 218, 220,
  223, 225, 261, 265–6, 273–4, 279–80
syncretism 208
synecdoche 188
synonym, synonymy 39, 144–5, 153, 172–81,
  184, 192–3, 204
syntactic change 114–15, 195, 214, 344–416
syntacticization 136
syntagma, syntagmatic 136, 154, 211, 219
syntax 21, 24–5, 28, 41, 65, 71, 75–7, 93, 107,
  110–11, 113–15, 124–5, 136, 165, 179,
  187, 195, 198, 212, 214, 225, 228, 294,
  344–416
synthesis, synthetic 30, 120, 294, 299, 302, 317,
  320, 324, 347
systematic phonemic 295, 310

TAM (tense, aspect, mood) 110, 129, 186, 198,
  207–8, 215, 297
template 125, 302, 310–11
tense 25, 110, 196, 200–2, 204–8, 226–8, 239,
  274, 279, 284, 305, 314, 324, 347, 375
Tense projection 375
tense sequence 208
Terror, Reign of 59, 85, 258
theme 203
timbre 274, 276–7, 282, 287
time frame 198, 200–1
tmesis 321
Tobler-Mussafia law 395, 397
tokens 155
tone, tonal 22
tonic *see* accent
topic 136, 389
topicalization *see* dislocation
toponym 149
tough movement 388
trace 386
trailer-timing 228
transitive *see* verb
transparency 137, 296
trilled *see* consonant
triphthong 286
tropes 188
troubadour 15
truncation 25, 119, 226, 235, 238, 240–1, 266,
  287, 304, 327, 395
TV(X) ordering *see* word order

type *see* typology
types 155
typology 115, 129–30, 213, 295, 321, 346–7,
  352, 360, 420, 424

umlaut see metaphony
unaccusative 203, 411
underlying representation 232–3, 238, 264, 298
underspecification 219, 270
uniformitarian 140
Universal Grammar 113, 128, 132, 296, 345
universals 112, 122, 237, 273, 375
unmarked 131, 325, 327–8, 330, 353–4
utterance 195, 344
uvular *r* 22, 277, 288–90

variation 13, 20, 26, 38, 41, 46, 51, 59, 63, 65,
  67–8, 108, 117, 124, 132, 135, 139, 141, 171,
  217, 222, 226, 230, 232, 239, 257–8, 273,
  283, 287, 311, 329, 349, 363, 410, 413, 419
  geographical 21, 33, 37–8, 51, 65–6, 80, 100,
    141, 239, 271, 273, 282
  socio-economic 38, 51, 62–3, 66, 72, 239,
    271
variationist 73
velar, velarization *see also* consonant 138, 220,
  281, 283, 285, 288
verb 30–1, 42, 94, 113, 139, 165–6, 168, 198,
  204, 206, 209, 210–11, 262, 265, 268, 271,
  297, 300–4, 306–12, 314–17, 324, 333–4,
  343, 348, 350, 352–3, 355, 357–8, 360,
  362, 364–5, 368–70, 373, 375, 377–9, 380,
  383–4, 389–90, 393–406, 410–11, 413–14,
  416
  auxiliary 94, 121, 135, 203–4, 206–7, 317,
    350, 352, 354, 368, 403, 411–14
  defective 301
  impersonal 378, 413
  intransitive 203, 351, 357, 359–60
  irregular 300–1, 304, 311, 314
  modal 211, 317, 402–3
  perception 402, 404
  regular 22
  semi-auxiliary 206–8
  transitive 203
verb phrase (VP) 25, 353, 368, 370, 400
verb-first(V1) ordering *see* word order
verb-raising 115
Verb-second (V2) *see* word order
verb-subject ordering *see* word order
verlan 271, 277
versification 228–9, 268, 271–2, 282, 413
Villers-Cotterêts, Edict of (1539) 8, 37, 60, 83–
  4, 100
vocabulary *see also* lexicon 39–41, 70–1, 75,
  79, 112, 146, 154, 182, 195, 197
  basic 26, 146, 152, 155, 166, 190
  dialectal 143
  technical 143

vocalization 251–7, 264, 284–6, 313, 318, 342
voice, voicing 219–20, 224, 229, 246, 283
volition, volitive 209, 211
vowel 72, 77, 119, 218, 224, 231, 234, 241, 243,
    252, 254–5, 257, 261–2, 264, 271, 276–8,
    290–1, 306, 309–10, 312, 318, 326, 329–
    30, 339–4, 377, 380, 386
    accented, tonic, stressed 93, 226–7, 238, 246,
      253, 255, 258, 270, 272, 279–82, 284–6.
    atonic, unaccented, unstressed 93, 219, 225–
      8, 237, 257, 260, 267–70, 272, 279–80,
      306, 311, 335
    back 227, 247, 252, 257, 281
    bimoraic 284
    blocked 270, 285
    central 250, 252, 257, 267, 278
    double 240
    final 268–70, 280, 278, 311, 329
    fronting, front 224–7, 248, 250, 252, 281,
      307
    height, high 235–9, 242, 245, 250, 252, 255,
      279
    lax 274, 276
    long, length 22, 52, 126, 131, 220, 224–5,
      230, 240, 257–8, 271–2, 276, 279–88, 412,
      415
    loss 225, 227, 329
    low 235–7, 276, 279, 283, 286
    mid 221, 254
    nasal *see* nasalization
    nuclear 122, 230, 235, 237, 264, 284, 286
    oral 119, 232–3, 235, 239–41, 297–8
    protonic 269–70, 273, 285
    raising 251–2, 281
    short 53, 223, 243, 254, 282, 291
    reduction 77, 131, 219, 227, 235
    rounded 235, 242, 250, 267, 270, 282

weakening 220, 225, 228
word-initial 262–3
word-final 52, 226, 228, 233, 257, 278–9
vowel height hierarchy 236
vulgarism 71
Vulgar Latin *see* Proto-Romance

Wackernagel's Law, 359, 395
Wars of Religion 19
wave-model 118, 125
weakening 220, 331, 356, 374–5, 379–81
womens' language 66, 78, 100
WH- (or QU-) questions: 366–7
WH- in situ 367
word order 76, 129, 138, 212, 321, 334–5, 348–
    60, 377, 390, 404, 417
    fixed 25, 136, 138, 348
    Object-Subject-Verb (OSV) 351
    Object-Verb (OV) 350–2
    Object-Verb-Subject (OVS), 351, 357
    pragmatic 136
    Subject-Object-Verb (SOV) 23, 346, 351,
      356–7, 360, 394
    Subject-Verb-Object (SVO or SVX) 25, 31,
      136, 254, 272, 346–7, 254, 272, 350–1,
      354, 356–7, 360, 377, 379
    TVO(X) ordering 352, 357, 379
    verb-first (V1) 357, 359, 365, 367
    verb-last 356
    Verb-Object (VO) 350–1, 412
    verb-second (V2) 23, 358, 365–7, 378, 406
word-accent 54, 300, 356, 390
Word-and-Paradigm (WP) 295
word-stress 26, 379
word-web 193

zero person marker 378